The Theophrastan 'Character'

The Theophrastan 'Character'

The history of a literary genre

J. W. SMEED

OXFORD · NEW YORK
CLARENDON PRESS · 1985

Oxford University Press, Walton Street, Oxford OX2 6DP
London New York Toronto
Delhi Bombay Calcutta Madras Karachi
Kuala Lumpur Singapore Hong Kong Tokyo
Nairobi Dar es Salaam Cape Town
Melbourne Auckland
and associated companies in
Beirut Berlin Ibadan Mexico City Nicosia

Oxford is a trade mark of Oxford University Press

Published in the United States
by Oxford University Press, New York

British Library Cataloguing in Publication Data
Smeed, J. W.
The Theophrastan 'character': the history of a literary genre.
1. Literature—History and criticism
2. Characters and characteristics in literature
I. Title
809'.93352 PN56.4
ISBN 0–19–815805–X

Library of Congress Cataloging in Publication Data
Smeed, J. W. (John William)
The Theophrastan 'character'.
Bibliography: p.
Includes index.
1. Characters and characteristics in literature.
I. Title
PN56.4.S64 1985 809'.927 84-25579
ISBN 0–19–815805–X

Set by DMB (Typesetting), Oxford
Printed in Great Britain at
the University Press, Oxford
by David Stanford,
Printer to the University

Preface

The history of the Theophrastan 'character' stretches from 319 BC up to the present day. Some aspects have attracted a good deal of critical attention: Theophrastus himself, a handful of seventeenth-century English character-books, La Bruyère, the *Spectator* and a few of its imitators. But no one, to my knowledge, has tried to draw the strands together in order to show the continuity, the unity within the diversity. Some periods—the latter part of the eighteenth century, the nineteenth and twentieth centuries in England—have been virtually ignored. Nor has anything been done, other than in a very piecemeal way, to answer such questions as how the 'character' provides evidence of changing social attitudes or how it relates to the play and the novel.

It seemed to me worth while to attempt this exercise, even if it has necessarily meant that some aspects have only been touched on: the complex links between 'character' and essay in England and *caractère* and *portrait* in France, the relationship of the 'character' to French novels and plays, its influence on poetry and the sermon, the 'character' in America, and so on. Had I pursued all topics in detail, the book would have become far too long; had I saved space by ignoring the less familiar corners of character-writing, I would not have achieved my purpose of drawing attention to many pieces that seem to me undeservedly forgotten. But perhaps the hints contained in this book may encourage others to explore and speculate further. In the same way, I felt that it was necessary to say something about the implications of the very conscious pursuit of wit by the English character-writers of the seventeenth century, without going into the broader question of the rival claims of the 'plain' and the 'witty' manner. More detailed discussions of this complex topic are referred to in the Bibliography (see especially under Adolph, Martens, and Williamson). So many authors, major and minor, are mentioned in passing, that it was not possible to give even brief accounts of their more general literary activities, lives, and personalities without interrupting the flow of the argument. Biographical details are given only where these seem to bear directly on the question of character-writing.

I have confined my attention to the written word in this study, since it seems to me doubtful whether anything resembling a 'character' other than in very superficial ways can be achieved in the visual arts or in music. (Composers often gave their pieces titles which imply an attempt to characterize human types, but in the end it is the emotion or mood which is conjured up, not the person who displays or experiences it.)

I have followed original spelling and punctuation except with regard to i/j and u/v; 'serueth' for 'serveth', etc. would today be merely confusing for most readers. The author's usage regarding capital letters has always been strictly adhered to, since, even where it seems arbitrary at first sight, it was often a means of indicating stress. 'Character' (in inverted commas) always refers to the literary genre; types forming the subject of 'characters' are capitalized (the Snob, the Proud Man, etc.). Quotations from foreign languages are given in English translation, except where the original is necessary for the making of a stylistic point or where the meaning is self-evident from the context. In all other cases, the original passages are given in Appendix 2. The Bibliography has been subdivided for the sake of clarity and rigorously excludes anything which does not bear directly on the 'character': for instance, treatments of eighteenth-century periodicals which ignore or make only passing reference to the character-sketches contained in them and studies of novelists which treat characterization without mentioning the possible influence of the Theophrastan 'character' (e.g. Cynthia Griffin Wolff's perceptive study, *Samuel Richardson and the eighteenth-century Puritan Character*, 1972).

I would like here to express my gratitude to those colleagues, in Durham and elsewhere, who read the whole or parts of the typescript and made many helpful suggestions. I would particularly like to mention Professors W. P. Bridgwater and T. W. Craik, Mr David Crane, Dr Richard Maber, and Professor W. E. Yates. I am also much indebted to the following institutions for grants made at various times between 1975 and 1981: The Research Fund Committee of the University of Durham, the Austrian Institute, the German Academic Exchange Service, and the Pro Helvetia Foundation. Without this assistance, it would have been impossible for me to gather the material for this study.

Contents

1. From Theophrastus to Seventeenth-Century England
    (i) The Beginnings 1
    (ii) Hall, Overbury, Earle 19
    (iii) The Rest of the Seventeenth Century 35
2. The 'Character' in France 47
3. The Eighteenth Century in England 64
4. Germany and Switzerland 82
5. Character-Writing in Vienna: the *Wiener Skizzen* 101
6. The Nineteenth and Twentieth Centuries
    (i) The Nineteenth Century 114
    (ii) The Twentieth Century 124
7. The 'Character' and Society
    (i) The Good Man, the Country Gentleman, the Merchant, and the Professions 132
    (ii) Old Men, Drunkards, and Others 150
    (iii) The Poorer Classes 169
8. Two Points Regarding Style
    (i) The Witty Manner 179
    (ii) Must the 'Characters' of Ideal Types be Dull? 190
9. The 'Character' and the Play 199
10. The 'Character' and the Novel
    (i) England 225
    (ii) Germany 246
11. Conclusion 263

Appendix 1. Physiognomy and the 'Character' 292

Appendix 2. Original Versions of Passages Quoted in Translation 295

Notes 311

Bibliography 339

Index of Types Treated in the Form of 'Characters' 383

General Index 387

1

From Theophrastus to Seventeenth-Century England

(i) The Beginnings

Although there is something that goes against the grain for a modern man in the notion of 'human types', we still find it useful as we confront the complexity of humankind, and it is a fact that men have been given to type-casting their fellows since the days of classical antiquity. We find the notion at the core of a remarkably popular and enduring *petit genre*, the 'character':

A coward

Is the man that is commonly most fierce against the coward, and labouring to take off this suspicion from himself; for the opinion of valour is a good protection to those that dare not use it. No man is valianter than he is in civil company, and where he thinks no danger may come on it, and is the readiest man to fall upon a drawer and those that must not strike again: wonderful exceptious and choleric where he sees men are loth to give him occasion, and you cannot pacify him better than by quarrelling with him. The hotter you grow, the more temperate man is he; he protests he always honoured you, and the more you rail upon him, the more he honours you, and you threaten him at last into a very honest quiet man. The sight of a sword wounds him more sensibly than the stroke, for before that come he is dead already. Every man is his master that dare beat him, and every man dares that knows him. And he that dare do this is the only man can do much with him; for his friend he cares not for, as a man that carries no such terror as his enemy which for this cause only is more potent with him of the two: and men fall out with him of purpose to get courtesies from him, and be bribed again to a reconcilement. A man in whom no secret can be bound up, for the apprehension of each danger loosens him, and makes him bewray both the room and it. He is a christian merely for fear of hell-fire; and if any religion could fright him more, would be of that. (John Earle, *Microcosmography*, 1628)

Anyone interested in the literature of England, France, or Germany in the seventeenth and eighteenth centuries is likely to come across character-sketches similar to the one just quoted—of the Miser, the Envious Man, the Dandy, the Jealous Husband, the Lawyer, and so on. They may be found gathered together in collections (a volume containing anything from eight to eighty 'characters'), singly in pamphlet form, or scattered in the periodicals of the day. They are usually in prose, vary in length from a paragraph to about eight pages, and often begin with some such conventional formula as 'A Hypocrite is the sort of man who . . .'. The subject may be described through carefully chosen behavioural details, or by a list of abstract characteristics, or metaphorically, or by a combination of all three methods. The 'character' obviously involves a typological approach to human personality: the subject, although presented to us as an individual person, must also stand for a social, moral, or psychological category. Thus 'characters' are not concerned with complex, many-sided personalities: they are always selective and exaggerated to a greater or lesser degree. (Earle's Coward is all coward and a coward all the time.) However it has usually been felt that the 'character' should not stray *too* far in the direction of eccentricity and extravagance. It should illustrate what happens when a particular quality is carried to an extreme, without making us disbelieve in the human being depicted. In fact, most character-writers seem to have realized and surmounted the problems involved in combining the individual and the generic, so that the reader seldom has difficulty in recognizing all drunkards within the individual Drunkard, all quacks within the individual Quack.

As far as formal presentation is concerned, nearly all authors of 'characters' choose their representative figure and stick to 'he' or 'she' throughout. The tacit feeling seems to be that to veer between different forms ('he' and 'they'; 'he' and 'she') would stress the generic at the cost of the individual. For the same reason, the portrayal of character is seldom cut across by a more general discussion of qualities unattached to a particular person. (Where this happens, it is usually because the author is carried away by moralizing or polemical zeal.) These and other formal criteria will be discussed in detail later (see chapter 11). They are anything but cast-iron; although attempts have been made from time to time to define the 'character', it has meant different things to different ages and in different countries. Hence it may be as well to let a more detailed definition emerge gradually. 'Characters' were written in their thousands and nearly all go back, directly or indirectly, to one remarkable short work, the χαρακτῆρες (*Characters*) of Theophrastus.

Theophrastus, who was a pupil of Aristotle, lived from about 371 to 287 BC. In or around 319 BC he produced his *Characters*: thirty short prose sketches of imaginary but typical individuals (the Coward, the Boor, the Chatterer, and so on). These 'characters' are all of bad or foolish types, but a preface, once thought to be by Theophrastus himself but now generally regarded as spurious, talks of comparing good men with bad and of describing the habits of both. This could suggest that the unknown writer of the preface had a combination of good and bad 'characters' before him. Only the latter have survived however.

No one knows exactly how or for what purpose the *Characters* were written. It was once thought that they could have been part of a lost work on ethics,[1] illustrations of the various qualities under discussion. (It would, for instance, be easy to show how Theophrastus's Coward exemplifies and 'dramatizes' what Aristotle has to say in more abstract terms on the subject of fear in the *Nicomachean Ethics* and elsewhere.) Other critics[2] have tended to see the *Characters* as divorced from any extraneous purpose and as existing purely for their own sake, perhaps even written by Theophrastus as relief from his more serious work as a philosopher and botanist. Or it has been suggested[3] that they might have been composed as examples of a technique of character-portrayal which was traditionally part of rhetorical teaching. More recently, R. G. Ussher and Philip Vellacott have come down in favour of the view that the *Characters* were written as an illustrative appendix to a treatise on comedy.[4] It is unlikely that these uncertainties will ever be resolved. They are tantalizing to the general reader and the classical scholar alike but, as far as Theophrastus's influence is concerned, they are of little account; we know what later generations saw in him and learned from him. To give a brief sketch of this will be the purpose of the first part of this book.

The 'characters' are written in a straightforward style, 'as though the stark phrases were deliberately chosen to lay bare the failings of mankind'.[5] The interest is in the matter, not the manner. Each 'character' begins with an abstract definition of a quality (although it has more than once been questioned whether Theophrastus himself wrote these opening definitions), but immediately proceeds to the description of a typical man who exhibits that quality:

> Lack of trust is the assumption that everyone is cheating you. The distrustful man is the sort who, after sending a slave to buy provisions, sends another whose job is to find out how much he paid for them. He carries his money himself, and sits down twice in a quarter of a mile to count how much he has, etc. (No. 18)

The chosen figures are set against a background of Athenian daily life and are characterized by a succession of typical actions, ways of speech, and (less frequently) physical details. As an example of a 'character' shown through his actions, here is part of the Miser:

> If a servant breaks a jug or a dish, he stops the price of it out of his allowance. If his wife has dropped a threepenny-bit, he is the sort of person to start moving the furniture, shifting couches and cupboards, rummaging among the rugs. If he has anything to sell, he will only let it go at a price which means a bad bargain for the buyer. He would never let you eat a fig out of his garden, or walk through his land, or pick up one of his windfall olives or dates. (No. 10)

And, for a 'character' which depends on what a man says rather than on what he does, the Bore:

> The chatterer is the sort of man who sits down beside someone he doesn't know and begins by delivering a panegyric on his own wife; continues with an account of his dream of the night before; then describes in detail what he had for supper. Next, getting into his stride, he remarks how far inferior men of the present day are to the ancients; how reasonable wheat is now in the shops; how full of foreigners Athens is getting. He observes that since the Dionysia it has been good sailing weather; and that if only Zeus would send more rain it would be better for the farmers. Then he tells you what part of his land he will put down to crops next year; and how difficult it is to live . . . (No. 3)

Generally speaking, a 'character' by Theophrastus will consist of a dozen or more typical actions or sayings. The inner man emerges from this description of externals; there is no abstract analysis. Some later character-writers were to ignore Theophrastus's example in this respect, usually paying for it in terms of lost vividness and immediacy. Although many of his imitators in the seventeenth and eighteenth centuries—including the first and one of the most important, Joseph Hall—were to combine delineation of character with a didactic aim, or subordinate description to moralizing, there is little trace of this in Theophrastus himself: he is a reporter, a deadpan observer of human affairs.

It is not difficult to see the reasons for his popularity and influence. To begin with, there is the intrinsic merit of the *Characters* as vivid and exact miniatures. Theophrastus's manner of proceeding seems simple at first sight, but as one comes to know these short pieces better, one sees that each detail chosen, each habit of speech recorded, each episode related is telling and appropriate, one more significant piece in the design. The art is of the kind that conceals art (and the plain writing conceals it still further). Writer after writer has paid tribute to Theophrastus and acknowledged him as master. Furthermore, he is not an author who demands antiquarian or scholarly knowledge; he deals unassumingly with perennial human types. His account of the Bore makes this clear: only a couple of minor details place the figure in classical Athens—for the rest, he is timeless. The Superstitious Man has in the main somewhat different obsessions from those of his English counterpart in the seventeenth century, but they are none the less brothers. (Theophrastus's Superstitious Man is afraid of owls and weasels, Hall's of ravens and hares. The Greek is obsessed with days of the month involving the figures four or seven, the Englishman with certain Saints' Days. The one has superstitious fears connected with epileptics and women in childbirth, the other sees ghosts and 'bugs' everywhere. Theophrastus represents his subject as running to the expounder of omens about every triviality; Hall depicts his Superstitious Man as guided by 'old wives and stars'.) Such variations within a mode of behaviour which persists in its basic essentials through the centuries must fascinate anyone interested in observing and recording details of human personality. Finally, the *Characters* suggested an adaptable form and a set of basic techniques, according to which human types of any century or country could be depicted. The book seemed to offer an invitation to later writers to borrow the method and use it to describe their own contemporaries. I cannot think of a smaller book with a greater influence.

Critics have often sought forerunners of the *Characters* in the works of Theophrastus's master, Aristotle. Aristotle certainly uses set descriptions of human types to illustrate ethical points from time to time. The picture of the Magnificent Man (*Nicomachean Ethics*, iv. 2) is the most famous and oft-cited example, but there are others. However, a basic difference of attitude and intention is immediately apparent: Aristotle uses his character-sketches primarily to illustrate a philosophical or moral point. The description of a man or the definition of an abstract moral characteristic will suit his argument equally well and he often alternates between the two quite rapidly. We see him patiently working towards the ethical conclusion he wishes to draw and using the occasional delineation of character as a means to this end. Thus the character-sketch is, for all its eloquence, almost a luxury for him. It may be that the master gave the pupil a hint of what might be done, but Theophrastus seems to have been the first to have hit on the idea of taking various moral and social qualities, examining them as manifested in imaginary but typical individuals, and presenting these descriptions in a complete and self-contained form.[6]

It was Joseph Hall's *Characters of Virtues and Vices* of 1608 that created the vogue, almost the craze, for character-writing that lasted throughout the seventeenth century in England. But this could not have happened if the moment had not been propitious and the ground prepared. A glance at the various ways in which human types were portrayed in the literature of the late sixteenth century shows many traditional means of character-delineation coming together. Some of these techniques are essentially medieval in origin, others go back to classical antiquity. What follows is necessarily a very brief account, since it is obviously impossible to carry out a detailed examination of all these strands in a book primarily devoted to the Theophrastan 'character'. First, a word on the rhetorical tradition.

R. R. Bolgar[7] believes that surviving treatises on rhetoric are no more than the 'debris' of a much older science. Be that as it may, the tradition can certainly be easily traced from Aristotle by way of later Greek rhetoricians to Rome, thence to the Middle Ages and the Renaissance and, through the influence of Western educational methods, well into the eighteenth century. Now rhetoric is commonly thought of as the art of persuasion through well-chosen and well-arranged speech. But rhetorical treatises had also, from very early times, contained examples of how to depict human types, concentrating less on style than on the selection and arrangement of material. Aristotle, in his *Rhetoric* (ii. 12–17), gives brief descriptions of a few basic types (the young, the old, the rich) to show a student how to generalize about human nature. These are not yet 'characters' in the Theophrastan sense: Aristotle is concerned mainly with inner characteristics and does not individualize, preferring to talk of a class of people, of 'them' rather than of 'him'. But, quite soon, practical demonstrations of character-depiction, often at least as long as a 'character' by Theophrastus, were to form part of treatises on rhetoric.

An early example of what is to all intents and purposes the 'character' of a Drunkard can be found in the *De figuris sententiarum* of Rutilius Lupus, a translation of a lost work by a Greek rhetorician of the first century BC. The drunkard is shown waking with difficulty from the previous day's debauchery, supported and pampered by his servants as if he were an invalid, but soon joining his friends and competing with them to down the most liquor. Finally he is left alone to collapse once again into a drunken sleep. More than one writer has pointed out the link between such sketches in the works of the rhetoricians and Theophrastus's *Characters*.[8] Rutilius uses the label 'charakterismos'; it may be said in passing that the terminology was to become very confused—'descriptio', 'notatio', and 'ethopoeia' are all to be encountered in later writers as labels for such character-descriptions. By the time of Quintilian, the composition of character-sketches is firmly regarded as part of education, and it is clear that the depiction of types (Quintilian mentions rustics, misers, cowards, and superstitious persons) has a moral function.[9] Overt moralizing had been almost entirely absent from Theophrastus's *Characters*, but it certainly figures in Rutilius, who prefaces his account of the Drunkard: 'What hope remains for him who spends all his life in a single, despicable habit?'[10]

Perhaps the most 'Theophrastan' example of character-writing surviving from classical rhetoric occurs in the *Rhetorica ad Herennium* of about 80 BC. This work, long thought to be by Cicero, has been termed 'one of the most influential books on speaking and writing ever produced in the Western world'.[11] The author at one point praises the art of delineating character (he uses the term 'notatio') and gives a long exemplary description of a man who wishes to appear richer than he actually is. Like Theophrastus before him, the anonymous author provides a list of typical actions: this would-be rich man pretends to more servants and showy possessions than he really has, issues bogus orders regarding the counting of money, plays the part of a man of property, and so on. Not only is the general method similar to that of Theophrastus;

there are actual parallels to Theophrastus's 'characters' of 'Petty Ambition' and 'The Boaster'.

The rhetoricians therefore regarded character-description as part of their art and provided examples of how it might be done. In fact, an almost symbiotic relationship may be seen between these character-sketches and the Theophrastan 'character' proper: Theophrastus's pieces are found in manuscripts together with the works of the rhetoricians, while Casaubon, in the Prolegomena to his edition of Theophrastus (1592), relates the 'character' to the rhetorical tradition, referring to Seneca, Cicero, and Rutilius Lupus.[12] There can be little doubt that the description of types in medieval literature derives in large part from this tradition. Many treatises on rhetoric—usually more or less direct adaptations of classical works—appeared in England throughout the sixteenth century and in some of these the exemplary character-sketch figures. Here is Thomas Wilson's picture of the Covetous Man from his *Arte of Rhetorique*, first published in 1553:

> There is no such pinch peney on live as this good fellowe is. He will not lose the paring of his nailes. His haire is never rounded for sparing of money, one paire of shone serveth him a twelve moneth, he is shod with nailes like a Horse. He hath bene knowne by his coate this thirtie Winter. He spend once a groate at good ale, being forced through companie, and taken short at his worde, whereupon he hath taken such conceipt since that time, that it hath almost cost him his life.[13]

G. S. Gordon (p. 66) rightly points out that this is an example of truly Theophrastan writing half a century before Theophrastus was explicitly taken up as a model. The detailed instances of miserliness are all different from those in Theophrastus's Miser, but the method is identical. Henry Peacham's *Garden of Eloquence* (1593) contains, if not quite a 'character' of an Old Man, at least the basis for one: he may be described, says Peacham,

> in this manner, with crooked limmes; and trembling jointes, his head white, his eies hollow, his sight dimme, his hearing thicke, his handes shaking, his legges bowing, his colour pale, his skin wrinkled, weake of memory, childish, yet covetous, suspicious, testy, greedy of newes, credulous, misliking of the present world, and praising the former times. (p. 135)

In fact, more than one early seventeenth-century 'character' of the Old Man reads like a free expansion of that little sketch, with a measure of 'wit'.

It could be objected that the examples of character-writing to be found in the books on rhetoric are too few to be of much importance. But this would ignore the central part played in the educational system by rhetoric.[14] Treatises, such as those mentioned above, were used as the basis for instruction in schools. The various tropes and figures were first memorized, then hunted down and identified in the classical authors under scrutiny. Since, as we have seen, some of the treatises and manuals included sections on character-drawing with model examples of how to represent various human types, the educated man of the sixteenth century would have been familiar with such pen-portraits from his youth. Indeed, Bolgar records that, at Eton and Westminster, pupils were encouraged to practise all the traditional rhetorical exercises, including the portrayal of character (p. 364). There can be no doubt that the development of character-portrayal in England up to 1608 owed a good deal to the study and practice of rhetoric. The ways in which this influence combined with other strands in English literary and homiletic traditions will be discussed presently.[15]

But first we must consider briefly another important offshoot of rhetorical studies. As well as composing exercises in the approved styles, schoolboys and students were encouraged to keep 'commonplace books', in which metaphors, similes, apt phrases, and so on were jotted down for future use. Schoolmasters and others published commonplace books as examples. The earliest compilations of this kind to appear in English in the sixteenth century (those of Nicolas Udall in 1542 and Richard Taverner five years later) are largely sententious in manner and plain in style. However later collections[16] give increasing space to figures of speech and fanciful analogies from all branches of knowledge. The entries are no longer arranged under authors, as in Udall, but under subject headings: human types or professions, virtues, vices. Attributions are often omitted; no doubt this helped to create the impression of a common storehouse of material. Side by side with the conventional and expected similes (a lawyer is like a vulture, a good prince like the sun), we encounter more far-fetched parallels, many from natural history. The natural history is that of the bestiaries and fables, of course: 'Like as a Camelion hath all colours save white, so hath a flatterer all poynts save honestie.'[17] That chameleon (variously spelt and once even transmogrified into a camel!) will figure in most of the commonplace books, usually making the same point.

The influence of the commonplace books did not stop with formal education: Don Cameron Allen[18] has said that 'almost everyone with any claim to learning' at the end of the sixteenth century would have owned or compiled a commonplace book. Such books did not contain sustained and unified descriptions, but were made up of scattered entries in no particular order. Thus the Hypocrite, according to Meres, is like a chameleon, a toad, a fox, a spider, even a swan (white feathers, black flesh). He is a gilded pill, a whited sepulchre, a stage player, a plant that shows green but bears no fruit, etc., etc. As we will see, an elaborate and 'witty' style quickly came to be regarded as a *sine qua non* among the character-writers of the early seventeenth century. One can find various quite specific cases where the author of a particular 'character' drew on the commonplace books: an example would be Samuel Person in his *Anatomical Lecture of Man*, 1664 (see below, p. 39). But their real importance is more general. Most character-writers (although there are a few dishonourable exceptions, flagrant plagiarists) were men of quick wit, who would have scorned slavish transcription. Much in the commonplace books must have seemed pedantic and laboured to them: they would have seen there not so much something to draw on as something to outdo. But, encouraged to view character-writing as 'wits descant upon any plaine song' (see below, p. 25), they would certainly have found hints in the commonplace books of how to set about their business of composing elaborate variations on basic human themes.

At this point, a word must be said about Roman verse-satire and character-epigrams. There are several famous and much-imitated pen portraits in the satires of Horace: the Usurer (i. 2), the Miser (ii. 2), and—most celebrated of all—the Bore who accosts the poet while he is out walking (i. 9). To ask whether these are portraits of actual contemporaries of Horace or imaginary types has little point as far as our topic is concerned for, even where the portrait is based on a real person, it can be generalized to the point where it approaches a typified 'character'. This is clear in Martial's epigram on Cotilus, the Dandy:

Cotilus, you are a 'pretty fellow': many call you so, Cotilus; I hear them. But, tell me, what is a pretty fellow? 'A pretty fellow is one who arranges neatly his curled locks, who continually smells of balsam, continually of cinnamon; who hums catches from the Nile and Gades; who waves his depilated arms in time to varied measures; who all the day lolls amid the women's chairs, and is ever whispering in some ear; who reads billets sent from one quarter or another, and writes them; who shrinks from contact with the cloak on his neighbour's elbow; who knows who is the lover of whom; who hurries from one party to another; who has at his fingers' ends the long pedigree of Hirpinus'. (iii. 63, trans. W. C. A. Ker, Loeb Classics)

Here the description quickly moves from the individual to the type; Martial abandons Cotilus after one sentence in order to tell us what 'a pretty fellow' is. And certainly, when we turn to imitations in later ages, it is the delineation of types (*the* Bore, *the* Dandy) which is taken up. There are many imitations of Roman satires and epigrams towards the end of the sixteenth century in England. Martial, Horace, and, occasionally, Juvenal are the authors favoured. Everard Guilpin's *Skialethia* (1598) is the most interesting collection of epigrams and satires for anyone concerned with the development of character-writing. Here is the Antiquary:

> The Antiquary would perswade us to[o]:
> He shewes a peece of blacke-jack for the shooe,
> Which old *Aegeus* bequeathed his valiant sonne:
> A peece of pollisht mother of pearle's the spoone
> *Cupid* eate pappe with; and he hath a dagger
> Made of the sword wherwith great *Charles* did swagger. (c5^{r})

The time is ripe for the direct Theophrastan approach: here the observation and enumeration of details seems to be forced into a rather restricting mould. Guilpin, of course, was an author of decidedly minor talent; yet the cumulative method of listing typical actions does seem to demand the freer prose form of the Theophrastan 'character' (in which, one may add, even minor talents, given a keen eye and a measure of wit, could produce telling and entertaining results). The fashion for 'characters' in the style of Horace or Martial continued after the establishment in 1608 of the Theophrastan 'character' in England and gradually merged with it, for example in Henry Hutton's *Follie's Anatomy* of 1619. To turn to more positive pictures of human nature in classical times, the ideal of the man who practises virtue in rural retirement and is indifferent to public applause (Horace, *Epistles*, i. 16) was also to influence English character-writing. As will be seen in a later chapter, many 'characters' of the Happy Man or the Wise Man are little more than updated and Christianized versions of this Horatian ideal.[19]

No account of the forerunners of the 'character' can ignore the allegorical personification of moral qualities which played such a large part in satirical and didactic literature from the Middle Ages on. Since this huge subject cannot possibly be discussed in detail here, I propose to confine myself to a few examples which most people would, I hope, accept as representative. In *Piers Plowman* (Passus 5), the Seven Deadly Sins confess to Repentance. Now in some cases the personification of the Sin hardly strikes us as an individual figure and was probably not conceived as such by the author. With Coveytise (Avarice), for instance, the conceit that this is one person wears very thin as Avarice describes all the trades and professions that he has practised. What we have is not an avaricious man but a study of avarice in all men.[20] Conversely, Langland's depiction of Envy is much more individualized, far more like the description of a person consumed and dominated by envy. Envy's account of himself is quite compatible with the behaviour of a single envious person: he slanders his neighbours, causes strife through evil talk, gloats over men's losses and laments their gains. Skelton's personification of Riot in *The Bouge of Court* is again the presentation of a violent, lewd, and disorderly *individual*, a sort of early sixteenth-century roaring boy, with his boasting and oaths, his ribaldry and gambling.[21] But if we turn to Marcellus Palingenius's *Zodiacus Vitae*, that encyclopaedic and moralizing poem of the 1530s, we find a type of allegorical description which is concerned with sins and their power over men, not with typical sinners. Avarice, for instance, is a fury with a hundred heads, bred in Hell: 'Her greedy jawes with bloud of men, coulde never have their fill',[22] while Gluttony is represented as a god, worshipped by the great mass of mankind. The author is therefore not concerned with showing *a man* consumed by avarice or gluttony, or even a composite picture of many avaricious or gluttonous men, but rather with the personification of a quality that preys upon humankind. The nearest thing to a 'character' in this work is in the treatment of Covetousness, where there is a short description of a Covetous Man—but even here the author quickly abandons description in order to moralize (ed. cit., p. 177).

Thomas Nashe's *Pierce Pennilesse*, although first published in the same year (1592) as Casaubon's edition of Theophrastus, harks back to the medieval scheme of the Seven Deadly Sins. Nashe combines observations, reflections, and anecdotes with brief descriptions of typical imaginary sinners and references to actual historical persons. In the case of Pride and Sloth, we find passages which are short 'characters' in all but name. Here is part of the proud, malcontent upstart:

Hee will bee humorous, forsoth, and have a broode of fashions by himselfe. Sometimes . . . he will be an *Inamorato Poeta*, & sonnet a whole quire of paper in praise of Lady *Swin-snout*, his yeolow fac'd Mistres. . . . Al *Italionato* is his talke, & his spade peake [a type of beard] is as sharpe as if he had been a Pioner before the walls of *Roan* [Rouen]. Hee wil despise the barbarisme of his own Countrey, & tel a whole Legend of lyes of his travailes unto *Constantinople*.[23]

And here is the proud merchant's wife:

In an other corner, Mistris Minx, a Marchants wife, that wil eate no Cherries, forsooth, but when they are at twenty shillings a pound . . . she is so finicall in her speech, as though she spake nothing but what shee had first sewd over in her Samplers . . . (ed. cit., p. 173).

The anticipation of, and close affinity with, witty seventeenth-century character-writing is clear if we compare this with Saltonstall's Townsman in Oxford, dating from 1631, whose words have 'such a punctuall stiffe pronunciation, as though they were starcht into his mouth, and durst not come out faster for feare of ruffling'.[24] Contrast Marlowe's treatment of Pride:

I am Pride, I disdaine to have any parents, I am like to Ovids flea, I can creepe into every corner of a wench, Sometimes, like a periwig, I sit upon her brow, or like a fan of feathers, I kisse her lips . . . (*Dr Faustus*, A-text, ed. Greg, OUP, 1950, pp. 204 and 206)

We can see a similar contrast in the treatments of Sloth: Marlowe is concerned with the quality ('I am sloath, I was begotten on a sunny banke, where I have laine ever since . . .'), but Nashe begins with the quality and immediately passes to a typical individual illustration: 'If I were to paint Sloth . . . I would draw it like a Stationer that I knowe . . .' There follows that delectable motif of the little finger, exactly the kind of telling, concrete detail that the best and shrewdest character-writers were to seize on:

. . . if a man come to his stall and aske him for a booke, [he] never stirs his head, but stands stone still, and speakes not a word: onely with his little finger points backwards to his boy, who must be his interpreter, and so all the day, gaping like a dumbe image, he sits without motion . . . (p. 209)

So in Nashe we see the allegorical presentation of qualities yielding to a more individualized and concrete approach. Previously, the details too often seemed to have been dictated by the moral intentions of the author and to have no point—indeed, often no existence—beyond these intentions. For instance, Langland's Wratthe (Anger), during his period as cook, prepares *stews of gossip* (v. 158). Nashe's details, however, have a firm basis in empirical reality (cherries at out-of-season prices). To the modern reader, at least, *Pierce Pennilesse* seems to show a newer, more exact and realistic technique of characterization existing not too happily within an older allegorical framework. The work appears to be on the threshold between the 'allegorical' and the 'Theophrastan' methods of description.[25]

As to whether the Prologue to Chaucer's *Canterbury Tales* can be regarded as a precursor of the character-book, opinions differ. Morley and Ussher would say 'yes'; Boyce has strong reservations.[26] Certainly the idea of any direct Theophrastan influence has been largely abandoned; some writers see the influence of rhetorical 'descriptio' at work, others see Chaucer's figures as vitalized and more realistic descendants of those in medieval allegory, while Morley prefers the view that Chaucer drew on nature and his own wit.[27] Although all twentieth-century Chaucer scholars would regard that last judgement as over-simplified, J. M. Manley opposes what he regards as the exaggerated attention paid to literary and scientific sources and believes that Chaucer took much of his material from the observation of life around him (*Some New Light on Chaucer*, 1926). However that may be, critics have continued to document Chaucer's indebtedness to contemporary theories of physiognomy and the humours, to the literature of the 'Estates' (see below), and to much else. The arguments about his exact sources, and precisely how the individual and the generic are combined in his character-sketches, have no end. Each and every motif in the Prologue has been the subject of conjecture, while possible originals have been put forward for virtually every phrase. This in turn has fuelled the debate about the combination of literary models and direct observation in these character-descriptions.

Although I am not qualified to join in this highly specialized dispute, I do not think that any dispassionate observer could argue a similarity of intention between Theophrastus and Chaucer. Every detail in the Greek writer is calculated to add to the impression of a typical Coward, Bore, Miser, or whatever; there are no quirkish luxuries. There are certainly typified pictures in Chaucer, of the Knight, the Monk, and the Parson, while the Clerk of Oxenford has his parallel in many a later portrayal of the young scholar, too unworldly ever to gain preferment in the Church. But, as Boyce has pointed out (p. 61), many of Chaucer's details do not strengthen the impression that we are dealing with a general category of human beings; indeed, some actually seem to point away from the representative towards the particular. The Prioress is an example. Theophrastus, had the type been known in classical Athens, would no doubt have mentioned her fastidious manners and her soft-heartedness. But what of her French, spoken 'after the schole of Stratford atte Bowe'? Chaucer obviously had no fixed theory or method; he would delineate types, but sometimes—apparently out of love of incongruous detail—would throw in a little touch which makes the figure more vivid but much less typical. Boyce mentions the sore on the Cook's shin; another example would be the wart on the Miller's nose. No character-writer would give those details in the course of pieces meant to describe *any* Cook or *any* Miller; they are clearly different in their effect from the gouty foot and the bulbous red nose which (properly) figure in 'characters' of the Drunkard.

For our purpose it is perhaps better to regard the Prologue as an isolated masterpiece. One thing is certain: as far as the history of the Theophrastan 'character' proper is concerned, Chaucer lives on only in pastiche and parody, from the *Tincker of Turvey* (1630) to nineteenth- and twentieth-century examples (see below, chapter 6).[28]

From the Middle Ages to the sixteenth century, we find numerous attempts to devise a general framework within which men could be categorized and described. The most important are those concerned with the 'Estates' and the various satirical compilations of the 'Ship of Fools' type. Works belonging to the literature of the Estates describe the various classes in society, usually beginning with the Pope and the ecclesiastical orders, then proceeding to secular groups.[29] The earliest examples are Latin poems dating from the Middle Ages, but they were quickly imitated in the vernacular, especially in England and Germany. In most cases the author laments the shortcomings of each class in turn, sometimes adding an exhortation to the various classes to improve their way of life and be content in their station.

Of the 'fool-satires', Sebastian Brant's *Narrenschiff* (*Ship of Fools*) of 1494 is the most famous. It enjoyed astonishing popularity in its day, Brant being compared to Homer, Dante, and Petrarch. Through translations by Alexander Barclay (1509) and others, the work became well known in England. It contains over a hundred short chapters in verse, each accompanied by a woodcut. It should be said that 'Narr' has a very wide meaning for Brant, extending from fairly harmless types of folly (pedantry, the mania for dancing, and so on) through the whole gamut of sins up to blasphemy, rebellion against God, and contempt for Holy Writ.

The influence of the literature of Estates and of the fool-satires does not lie in the examples they offer of individual character-portrayal, for the strong tendency is to describe classes collectively, as classes. Their importance lies elsewhere: they offer suggestions of broad and flexible schemes into which all types of men can be fitted, according to either their rank in society or the type of folly or vice—or, by contrast, virtue—that they exhibit. In Barnaby Rich's *Faultes, Faults, And nothing else but Faultes* (1606), we can see that the old notion of the company of fools can lead to something very like a series of short 'characters', provided that the author's main intention is not the general castigation of human imperfections, but individualized pictures of the different types of fool. Rich's preamble might lead us to expect something like the old ship's company (Brant), or realm (Erasmus), or guild (Thomas Murner) of fools: 'But will you see how I am pestered with a finicall companie that comes in now all together . . . birdes of a wing, and it is fittest for them to flie together . . .'; but the fools are much more sharply drawn as individuals than in the older satires:

> Here comes now the *Malecontent*, a singular fellow, and very formall in all his demeanours, one that can reproove the world but with a word, the follies of the people with a shrug, and sparing of his speach, giveth his answer with signs and dumb shews, pasing his steps with sad and soure countenance, as if hee would have it saide; Lo, yonder goes the melancholy Gentleman, see there Vertue and Wisedome despised . . .[30]

However, we find little trace of the old fool-literature once the 'classic' Theophrastan mode becomes established in England.

By contrast, the literature of Estates continues in England up to the beginnings of character-writing proper and somewhat beyond. A glance at the writings of Samuel Rowlands and Thomas Dekker suggests a reason. In works like Rowlands's *The Letting of*

Humour's Blood (1600) and *Looke to it* (1607), or Dekker's *The Double PP* (1606) and his *Belman of London* (1608), we find a keen interest in character-portrayal, coinciding with something like a quest for a suitable formal vehicle. The links are sometimes with Roman satire, sometimes with the now declining allegorical tradition, sometimes with the popular rogue-literature of the day. One might legitimately feel that the types portrayed by Rowlands, Dekker, and others in the decade and a half leading up to 1608 were wandering abroad, seeking a home. Now the arrangement of mankind according to Estates would appear to be made to order: could not all types, ecclesiastical and secular, high and low, be brought in this way between the covers of a single book?

And so it comes as no surprise to find Nicholas Breton, in *The Good and the Badde* (1616), accommodating his 'characters' of virtues and vices within the general plan of an Estates book. He begins with the worthy and the unworthy king and passes by way of the royal family and the nobility to the professions. (The trades do not interest him; the latter part of his book is largely concerned with moral types.)[31] A few authors were to follow Breton's example (see below, p. 44). However, such assimilation of character-writing into the framework of Estates literature was not often tried, although Edward Ward's *Wooden World* of 1707 is something like a book of Estates on board ship, with the captain as king, officers as the nobility, the Church and secular professions represented by the sea-chaplain and the ship's surgeon, and so on through the trades to the common seaman, who occupies the place previously taken by the peasant or the day-labourer. But this work is an isolated curiosity as far as character-writing in England is concerned.

Why did the formal model offered by the literature of Estates not have more influence? The answer is probably that the origins of this literary genre go back to a period in which a passion for cataloguing and classifying was combined with the strongly held notion of a divinely ordained social hierarchy.[32] Types were portrayed primarily in order to make moral and metaphysical points about God's ordinances, the necessity to put aside wordly things, the fearful ubiquity of death, and so on. But in the early seventeenth century, when the Theophrastan 'character' was resuscitated, the prime motive was—or rapidly became—the delineation of human types for its own sake. And here no formal framework seemed necessary: Theophrastus had apparently worked from no plan; the order of his 'characters' could be changed without seriously affecting the work. Writers began to allow 'character' to follow on 'character' simply in the order in which they came to mind. The various types are seen, says Boyce, 'not as necessary, numbered bricks in a venerable social arch but merely as picturesque and interesting parts of the giddy social scene' (*Character to 1642*, p. 160). What would the medieval mind have made of this sequence from John Stephens's *Essayes and Characters* of 1615, for instance: a Contented Man, a good Emperor, a worthy Poet, an honest Lawyer, a Detractor, an Humorist, a Gull? Where a plan *is* evident in seventeenth-century character-books, it seldom has the medieval schematic quality of Estates literature.

The foregoing pages have briefly described the main influences which prepared the ground for Hall's essay in the Theophrastan manner and have suggested how old forms were taken up afresh and revitalized, how various strands could combine and coexist in one author, sometimes in one work. Two writers—Thomas Lodge and Francis Thynne—appear to stand on the threshold of Hall's revival of the classical 'character'.

Boyce sees Lodge's *Wit's Miserie* (1596) as a case where the allegorical literature of virtues and vices has gone as far as it can in the direction of the Theophrastan 'character' proper before there was any direct influence from the classical model.[33] *Wit's Miserie* is a moral satire with a fanciful allegorical wrapping, in which the vices are personified as the progeny of the Princes of Hell. One sees a decidedly old-fashioned method of allegorical portrayal rubbing shoulders with a more sharply individualized approach. Here is Lodge's Novel-Monger:

> . . . Sometimes he is a cooke, inventing new sauces and banquets, sometimes devising strange confections to besot an idolater of his bellie, sometimes for an ireful man he deviseth strange revenges, sometimes for a fearfull, strong towers to keepe him in . . .

This is no more the picture of one man than Langland's or Palingenius's Avarice had been. On the other hand, Contempt is envisaged as an individual and described through characteristic gestures, actions, and words:

> Behold next I see CONTEMPT marching forth, giving mee the Fico with his thombe in his mouthe, for concealing him so long from your eie sight. . . . This is he dare breake statutes, blab the lip at superiours, Mocke

Preachers, beat Constables, and resist Writs. . . . If a poore man salute him, hee lookes as if he scorned him. . . . The wisest man is a foole in his tongue, and there is no Philosophie (saith he) but in my Method and carriage: he never speaks but hee first wags his head twise or thrise like a wanton mare over her bit . . .[34]

This seems very near to the Theophrastan method: one could in fact replace 'Contempt' by 'the Contemptuous Man'.

A similar juxtaposition of old and new can be seen in Francis Thynne's *Emblemes and Epigrammes* (1600). The twenty-four-line poem on Flatterers begins with Flattery's parentage and nurture: 'There is a kinde of men, whome hell hath bredd, Deceit hath nourc'd, and doble speech hath fedd'. Next the flatterer in his inconstancy is likened to the 'fishe *Polipus*' which can 'turn his cullor to everie kinde of Hue'. Finally, since he preys on those whom he flatters, he is said to be worse than carrion crows which feed only on the dead. The beginning of this poem is clearly related to the old type of allegorical genealogy, while the parallels from the animal kingdom are simply filched from one or other of the commonplace books. Envy too is an old-fashioned exercise in personification, an allegorical anatomy, 'with brests defylld with gall, and hart of flaminge Ire, whose nayles are harpies clawes, and bodie leane and spare'. By contrast, Thynne's 'goddly mann' is a true verse-character, the ideal being firmly embodied in one person:

He is a godlie mann, that doth with tongue and minde
and sincere hart, the heavenlie god
  adore in his true kinde,
That liberall is to pore, that Justice doth maintaine,
And beinge chosen for a Judge
  takes noe reward for gayne . . .[35]

(ii) **Hall, Overbury, Earle**

When Joseph Hall—later to become Bishop of Exeter, then of Norwich—published his *Characters of Virtues and Vices* in 1608, the earlier, 'non-Theophrastan' forms of character-portrayal which we have been discussing did not, of course, vanish overnight. Some, such as the type of presentation associated with the fool-satires, dropped out of favour but the others tended to merge with the 'character' and coexist with it. Reading a 'character' from, say, the 1620s, one will often find, for instance, a motif that could go back to a late sixteenth-century imitation of Roman satire, or one that could have been prompted by the commonplace books or by memories of some allegorical work or book of Estates. Boyce, with proper caution, speaks of the 'involved and uncertain genealogy of the Jacobean Character' (op. cit., p. 74). By now the tributaries have joined the main stream. To have traced, however briefly, the predecessors of the Theophrastan 'character' shows that its revival in the early years of the seventeenth century was one more manifestation of a perennial fascination with human types and the unceasing quest to find appropriate forms in which to portray these. The durability and the capacity for adaptation of the English Theophrastan mode will be the subject of the following pages.

The *Characters of Virtues and Vices* consists of two books, one containing nine 'Virtues' (eleven in later editions), the other fifteen 'Vices'.[1] The Proem to Book 1 makes it clear that Hall's model was Theophrastus although, of course, the Greek author offered no models for virtuous types; for these Hall, where he did not depend on his own reflections regarding religion and morality, will have drawn on the homiletic tradition.

Hall's Dedication to Edward, Lord Denny, sees 'charactery' in classical antiquity as the practical side of moral philosophy and the Proem to Book 1 describes Theophrastus as 'that ancient Master of Morality'.[2] In view of the *lack* of moralizing in Theophrastus, this may seem strange, but the spurious Preface (which Hall, like all men of his age, accounted genuine) had described the 'characters' as object lessons, through the study of which men might improve themselves. Another factor enters in here: Hall's Theophrastus was not quite our Theophrastus. In modern editions a 'character' by Theophrastus simply stops after the last behavioural detail: 'He sings in the public bath; and he drives hobnails into his shoes' (The Boor). At some stage in their transmission, the 'characters' must have been felt to finish too abruptly, for an unknown emendator added short summings-up to eight of them. These additions survive in the manuscripts, were for centuries accepted as authentic, and appear in all early editions and translations. Therefore, when Hall read that the man who dissimulates is worse than a venomous snake (No. 1) or that newsmongers are pitiable, a plague to themselves and others (No. 8), he would not have known that these remarks were additions by another hand but would have seen in them a confirmation of the moral intentions proclaimed in the (equally spurious) Preface.

Hall's ideal of character and conduct[3] has clear affinities with the classical notion of the Happy Man; it is a Horatian ideal on to which—as so often in the seventeenth and eighteenth centuries—Christian elements have been grafted. But there is little of ascetic or Stoic retirement about Hall's picture: some form of participation in wordly affairs is implied, as might be expected from an author who was Fellow of a Cambridge college, held two livings before becoming first Dean, then Bishop, travelled to Brussels, Paris, Scotland, and elsewhere, and took an active part in various ecclesiastical controversies of the day. As for Hall's Wise Man, it is not possible to tell exactly what sort of activity the author envisages him as undertaking; whether this is simply a result of the rather abstract style or whether Hall deliberately avoids details in order to stress general moral characteristics is not altogether clear.

The 'vicious' exhibit, as Müller-Schwefe[4] points out, two features in common: a gulf between appearance and reality and a fatal lack of that true self-knowledge which Hall seems to view as an indispensable moral quality (the 'characters' of both the Wise Man and the Happy Man stress the necessity of self-knowledge in the very first sentence). The way in which sin merges with vice is very clear if we compare Hall's Superstitious Man (ii. 3) with that of Theophrastus (No. 16). Hall begins with a theological view of superstition ('godless religion, devout impiety') and only then passes to a catalogue of acts and obsessions similar to those which had made up the corresponding 'character' in Theophrastus (see above, p. 5).

Most commentators have pointed out that Hall deals much more with abstract, inner values and is less inclined to let actions and gestures speak for themselves than Theophrastus had been. This tendency is most marked in the 'Virtues', but is by no means absent from the 'Vices'. Of the Unconstant:

> His proceedings are ever heady and peremptory: for he hath not the patience to consult with reason. . . No man is so hot in the pursuit of what he liketh; no man sooner weary. He is fiery in his passions, which yet are not more violent than momentary. (ii. 6)

I do not wish to play off one method against the other and imply that abstract formulations are necessarily inferior to descriptions of gestures and actions; each method has its function within character-writing. In fact, the two coexist quite happily in many authors. Yet it seems self-evident that accounts of actions, gestures, speech, and appearance are best when they are most exact and most clearly particularized. There is sometimes a difference of degree here between Hall and Theophrastus. Hall writes of the Flatterer: 'He hangs upon the lips which he admireth, as if they could let fall nothing but oracles . . .' (ii. 7). The corresponding motif from Theophrastus is:

> Then he will tell the company to keep silent while the great man is speaking. . . . When his patron makes a feeble joke he laughs, stuffing his cloak into his mouth as if he couldn't contain his merriment. (No. 2)

Certainly as far as the 'Vices' are concerned, Hall is not merely at his most Theophrastan but at his best when he is most precise and particular. His Vain-Glorious Man 'picks his teeth, when his stomach is empty; and calls for pheasants, at a common inn' (ii. 10), while the Covetous, 'When he returns from his field . . . asks, not without much rage, what became of the loose crust in his cupboard, and who hath rioted amongst his leeks' (ii. 9).

Hall's sentences are balanced, regular, often depending on antithesis. This balance (not only within the sentence, but also between sentences) can only be fully appreciated through an extended quotation.

> [The Truly-Noble Man] stands not upon what he borrowed of his ancestors; but thinks he must work out his own honour: and, if he cannot reach the virtue of them that gave him outward glory by inheritance, he is more abashed of his impotency, than transported with a great name. Greatness doth not make him scornful and imperious, but rather like the fixed stars; the higher he is, the less he desires to seem: neither cares he so much for pomp and frothy ostentation, as for the solid truth of nobleness. Courtesy and sweet affability can be no more severed from him, than life from his soul: not out of a base and servile popularity, and desire of ambitious insinuation; but of a native gentleness of disposition, and true value of himself. (i. 8)

One could easily guess that Hall had studied rhetoric (indeed, he had lectured on it in Cambridge):

> . . . is [the Faithful Man] threatened banishment? there he sees the dear Evangelist in Patmos: cutting in pieces? he sees Isaiah under the saw: drowning? he sees Jonas diving into the living gulf: burning? he sees the three children in the hot walk of the furnace . . . etc. (i. 3)

Figures of speech are used sparingly, except for an occasional flourish at the end of a 'character':

[The Humble Man] is a lowly valley, sweetly planted and well watered: the proud man's earth, whereon he trampleth; but secretly full of wealthy mines, more worth than he that walks over them: a rich stone, set in lead: and, lastly, a true Temple of God, built with a low roof. (i. 4)

When one encounters a simile or metaphor in the body of a 'character', it is seldom very striking. Hall is out to communicate and persuade, not to dazzle. The occasional unexpected metaphor is the more telling because it is unexpected: the Good Magistrate is 'the guard of good laws; the refuge of innocency; the *comet of the guilty* . . .' (i. 9: my italics).

The traditional figures of rhetoric are present in Hall, but they are never mere embellishment: they carry the argument along in a way that is both concentrated and thought-provoking, as in this example of oxymoron from the Good Magistrate: 'the good, fear him lovingly; the middle sort, love him fearfully . . .'. Or here is a fine condensed use of 'enumeratio' employed to work up to a climax: 'The Penitent accuseth, arraigneth, sentenceth, punisheth himself unpartially . . .' (i. 10). Isocolon too is used to achieve the most extreme concision: 'Appetite is his lord; and reason, his servant; and religion his drudge' (ii. 4). Hall's metaphors seldom merely repeat tuppence-coloured what has already been said penny-plain. They too develop the argument in a concentrated form: the Happy Man 'can cross his will without a mutiny, and so please it that he makes it not a wanton . . .' (i. 11).

It has been worth making these points about Hall's use of language in a little detail because, stylistically, he stands half-way between Theophrastus and the host of character-writers who operated in England from 1610 onwards through the century. Theophrastus seems to have been content to let his chosen examples make their effect without benefit of stylishness. Hall, as we have seen, uses all manner of stylistic devices, including the greater part of the rhetorician's armoury. The beginnings of a 'witty' manner of character-writing are here, pre-eminently in the clusters of images which may close a 'character' (as in the ending of the Humble Man, above). But a 'character' can open with a witty formulation too: 'Presumption is nothing but hope out of his wits; a high house, upon weak pillars . . .' (ii. 11). This is obviously quite different from the workaday, abstract definitions which are the starting-point in Theophrastus: 'Avarice is the craving for sordid gain' (No. 30).

Hall, then, must have suggested to his contemporaries the possibility of combining the material of the 'character' as found in Theophrastus with a much more conscious regard for style and, specifically, for a witty style. This point is often overlooked, especially when Hall is compared with his successors and imitators rather than with his model. As we have seen, the stylistic ingenuity is held in check by Hall's sense of purpose. Many of his successors were to become slaves of the witty manner, but Hall cannot be blamed for this. As far as the near-exact balance between good and bad 'characters' is concerned, few of his imitators were to follow him, most of them preferring a loose succession of types, with the good in a minority. Nor was Hall's insistence on the moral purpose of 'charactery' to have much influence outside moral treatises and sermons: in most of the character-books proper, the desire to entertain soon gained the upper hand.

After Hall, the writing of 'characters' became highly popular. Between 1608 and 1700 over a score of character-books were published, some containing only a handful of 'characters', some seventy or eighty. During the same period, great numbers of individual 'characters', usually polemic, were brought out as broadsheets or as pamphlets; there were also scores of cases where one or more 'characters' were incorporated into larger works, such as treatises, or coexisted with other genres within one book.[5] In addition, 'characters' figured in sermons, plays, and novels. Of the larger collections, those of Sir Thomas Overbury and John Earle deserve particular attention here, both because of their intrinsic qualities and because of their importance as far as later developments are concerned.

Overbury's *Characters* were first published posthumously in 1614 and there were many editions up to 1664. The first edition contains twenty-one 'characters'; this number had swollen to seventy-three by the following year and to eighty-two by 1622. Of the 'characters' in the first printing, about half are probably by Overbury himself and the rest by 'other learned Gentlemen his friends' (title-page). Thirty-two 'characters' in the 1615 edition are often attributed to Webster, six concerning prison life which were added in 1616 are thought to be by Dekker, and the Dunce in the 1622 edition is certainly by John Donne. Many 'characters' are, and are likely to remain, unattributed.

The Overbury *Characters* (as they are always called for the sake of convenience) differ from those of Theophrastus and Hall in two main ways: in the range of human types chosen and in the stress placed on writing in a 'witty' manner. Where thematic range is concerned, if we look even at the relatively few 'characters' in the first edition, we already find something new. As well as the expected types (the Good Woman, the Wise Man, the Flatterer), we find a Courtier, an Amorist (i.e. a lovesick man), a Serving-Man, the Host of an inn, and an Ostler. A glance at the complete collection shows that the moral types are actually in a minority (about one third) and that social types and members of various trades and professions predominate. There seems to be a desire to cover early seventeenth-century English society (mainly but not exclusively that of London) in all its complexity. The 'character' can by now embrace national types (the Welshman, the Dutchman residing in England) and even places (a Prison).

Although there are occasional contrasting pairs of 'characters' (a virtuous Widow, an ordinary Widow) and one short cluster of 'characters' all relating to prison life, there is on the whole no logical sequence in Overbury, no discernible reason for putting the Sexton between the French Cook and the Jesuit, or the Watchman between the Usurer and the Judge.

The question of style in the Overbury *Characters* is not a simple one, if only because there were so many fingers in the pie. The witty writing has come in for a good deal of censure from modern critics on the grounds that it is overdone, that it subordinates matter to manner, and that it does not contribute towards—or positively gets in the way of—a knowledge of the types described.[6] One might add, quite simply, that it sometimes makes a 'character' very difficult to understand!

The short piece 'What a Character is' first appeared in the last of the three 1616 editions. The author states that a 'character' is short and memorable, that it concentrates on one ruling quality, that it says much within a little span, and that it is 'wits descant on any plaine song'.[7] If taken at its face value, that last phrase would suggest that a 'character' consists of ingenious variations on a fundamentally simple theme, that it is a literary equivalent to, shall we say, the brilliant keyboard and instrumental pieces based on the 'In Nomine' that were so popular in those days, or the virtuoso sets of divisions on popular songs. But we cannot and should not expect a bulky collection of 'characters' by different hands, a collection which gradually grew up over the course of some years, to be reducible to one formula, however seductive.

It may be profitable to begin by looking at the group of 'characters' tentatively attributed to Overbury himself (Nos. 1–11: from the Good Woman to the Wise Man). There are certainly grounds for thinking that they are all by the same hand. They contain occasional faintly old-fashioned elements: an allegorical touch—

Dishonesty never comes neerer than [the Good Woman's] eares, and then wonder stops it out, and saves vertue the labour (ed. cit., p. 47)

—or borrowings from the commonplace books, much in the manner of the satirists and moralists of the closing years of the sixteenth century:

[*A Flatterer*] *is the shadow of a foole*. . . . His carriage is ever of the colour of his patient; and for his sake hee will halt or weare a wrie necke. (p. 54)

The wit is, on the whole, restrained: direct and unembellished statements relieve the density of the figurative language. Where rhetorical devices are used, these are elegant, unforced, and easily understandable: the Courtier 'puts more confidence in his words than meaning, and more in his pronunciation than his words' p. 53). The wit is usually germane to the argument and helps to carry it along: of the Glory-hunter, for instance, 'his behaviour is another thing from himselfe, and is glewed, and but set on' (p. 55), while of the Affectate Traveller: 'His attire speakes *French* or *Italian*, and his *gate* cries, *Behold me*' (p. 58). This first group of 'characters' is full of telling details of behaviour. The Glory-hunter 'confesseth vices that he is guiltlesse of, if they be in fashion' and 'defends his wardrobe, diet, and all customes, with entituling their beginnings from princes, great souldiers, and strange nations' (pp. 55 f.). Such motifs are combined with abstract description of inner states, reminiscent of Hall. The Glory-hunter 'is ignorant of nothing, no not of those things, where ignorance is the lesser shame' (p. 55). The same 'character' has a moral summing-up which, with its stress on the need for self-knowledge, is very like Hall: 'In a word, to make sure of admiration, he will not let himselfe understand himselfe, but hopes fame and opinion will be the readers of his riddles' (p. 56). The Affectate Traveller (pp. 58 f.) may perhaps stand as a typical example of the 'characters' supposedly by Overbury. Its substance is that of a 'character' by Theophrastus, but a discreetly moralizing ending (again somewhat reminiscent of Hall) and a seasoning of wit have been added. Of the first eleven 'characters' in the collection, only the Dissembler carries the witty manner to a point where it becomes convoluted and difficult.

Now we must turn to the remaining 'characters' in the first edition, those presumed to be by Overbury's 'learned friends'. The Country Gentleman begins with a metaphor somewhat more crowded and mannered than most of the stylistic figures encountered so far: he is 'a thing, out of whose corruption the generation of a justice of peace is produced' (p. 64). But the method in the rest of this 'character' is still fundamentally that of Theophrastus:

> His travell is seldome farther then the next market towne, and his inquisition is about the price of corne: when he travelleth, he will goe ten mile out of the way to a cousins house of his to save charges; and rewards the servants by taking them by the hand when hee departs. Nothing under a *sub poena* can draw him to *London*. . . . (p. 64)

The Elder Brother is 'Theophrastan' in this sense too (see pp. 67 f.), but in the Fine Gentleman, the actions are increasingly expressed through similes and metaphors: 'He unlockes maiden-heads with his language. . . . His discourse makes not his behaviour, but hee buyes it at Court. . . . He is somewhat like the *Salamander*, and lives in the flame of love' (pp. 65 f.).

The 'characters' of the Welshman and the Pedant are not merely 'wit's descant'; the wit seems to have been manufactured in the study. The Welshman 'hath the abilities of the mind in *potentia*, and *actu* nothing but boldnesse'; the Pedant 'is a *heteroclite*, for hee wants the plurall number, having onely the single quality of words' (pp. 68 and 69). As for the Host, the opening conceit, as Boyce points out (p. 143), is merely the wit of the conundrum: the Host is 'the kernell of a signe: or the sign is the shell, and *mine host* is the snaile' (p. 71: there are similar touches in the following 'character', that of an Ostler).

Therefore in the twenty-one 'characters' of the first edition we see a movement towards the conscious practice of wit as a major element in character-writing, but little as yet to justify such phrases as 'the ubiquitous exaggeration of wit and fancy' (Boyce, p. 143). Only in the cases of the Host and the Ostler and in Overbury's Dissembler is the matter swallowed up in conceits.

What of the additions made to this nucleus over the following years? As we have seen, several different authors, known and unknown, were involved, so that we can hardly expect to find one single, unambiguous stylistic trend. Most of the idealized 'characters' are quite straightforwardly written. The Good Wife still shows the balanced, slightly abstract style that we associate with Hall: [She is] one that to her husband is more then a friend, lesse than trouble. . . . Her pride is but to be cleanly, and her thrift not to be prodigall' (pp. 72 f.). The occasional metaphors in this 'character' are, where not totally conventional (a staff to her husband, etc.), mainly drawn from horticulture and suggest the influence of the commonplace books, either directly or by way of Euphuistic language:

> *A Good Wife* is . . . a scien incorporate with the stocke, bringing sweet fruit. . . . She frames her nature unto [her husband's] howsoever: the *hiacinth* followes not the *sun* more willingly. Stubbornnesse and obstinacy are hearbs that grow not in her garden. (pp. 72 f.)

These two elements combine with straightforward behavioural details in the manner of Theophrastus, to produce a pleasing and easily readable whole: 'She leaves tattling to the gossips of the town, and is more seene then heard' (p. 73). Another successful ideal 'character' in similar style is that of the Reverend Judge (pp. 136 f.).

Some of the later Overburian 'characters' follow the method of Theophrastus himself fairly closely, listing appearance, habits, and characteristic turns of phrase. Wit is used sparingly. The Inns of Court Man is a good example (ed. cit., pp. 103 f.), as are the 1616 'characters' of the Covetous Man and the Proud Man, probably both by the same writer. (The second of these contains direct borrowings from Theophrastus.) Many of the 'characters' attributed to Webster are fairly restrained in manner, combining direct authorial comment with illustrative detail and making wit serve an expository purpose. The Milkmaid, one of the pieces by Webster, is in a slightly different category and consists of Arcadian romanticism joined not too happily with homelier touches:

> The golden eares of corne fall and kisse her feet when shee reapes them, as if they wisht to be bound and led prisoners by the same hand that fell'd them. . . . She bestowes her yeares wages at next faire. . . . The *garden* and *bee-hive* are all her *physick* and *chyrurgery*, and she lives the longer for't. (pp. 118 f.)

However, many 'characters' are merely collections of conceits. The unknown author of the Sailor shows off his knowledge of nautical terms not to paint a picture of life at sea, but solely to set the reader word-puzzles; the 'character' has become a game.[8] Concrete details serve as emblems: '[The Saylor's] keele is the embleme of his conscience, till it be split he never repents . . .' (p. 76). Most 'characters' of working-class types are all conceit, pun, and metaphor. The 'character' of the Horse-courser is a string of witty variations on the theme of passing off decrepit old nags as good horses. This is not even 'wit's descant'; it is five-finger exercises. Similarly, the 'character' of the French Cook elaborates with unconscious irony the single notion that he makes a little go a long way by means of fancy sauces and dressings. The 'characters' of the Whore and Maquerela (Bawd) are likewise built up almost wholly out of conceits. Even the group of 'prison characters' of 1616 are in a highly elaborate witty style.

In the more restrained and diversified 'characters' too, it is easy to find empty puns:

> Good deeds [the Usurer] loves none, but seal'd and delivered: nor doth he wish any thing to thrive in the country, but bee-hives; for they make him wax rich. . . . He seems to be the sonne of a jaylor, for all his estate is in most heavy and cruell bonds (p. 133)

or figures of speech put in, not because they add anything, but because they are by now *de rigueur*:

> [The Melancholy Man] thinkes businesse, but never does any: he is all contemplation, no action. He hewes and fashions his thoughts, as if he meant them to some purpose; but they prove unprofitable, as a peece of wrought timber to no use. (p. 74)

There is therefore no one style in the Overbury *Characters*; they are not all art and no matter. But, as we have seen, witty devices tended to predominate as the collection grew. This circumstance, with the fact that 'What a Character is' closes, and apparently reaches its climax, with the phrase about 'wit's descant', must have helped to give the impression that ingenious writing was now of central importance. At all events, the history of the 'character' in seventeenth-century England shows that most later writers learnt the lesson only too well and seem to have taken the most mannered aspects of the Overburian *Characters* as their models. John Earle, however, is an exception.

Earle's *Microcosmography* was first published in 1628 and contained sixty-five 'characters'. By the sixth edition of 1633 the number had increased to seventy-eight. Earle, later to become Bishop of Worcester under Charles II, wrote these 'characters' while a Fellow of Merton College and, if we are to believe his first publisher, intended them originally for his private recreation and for the amusement of friends. Once published, the *Microcosmography* immediately became popular and has remained so; most students of character-writing, myself included, would prize Earle's work above all other English character-books. Earle borrows occasionally from Theophrastus (whom he, as a scholar, may well have read in the original) and from English writers, especially Overbury. He certainly learnt basic lessons regarding method and approach from his predecessors. He drew from Theophrastus the technique of constructing a 'character' by listing telling features and actions; from Hall some habits of style, especially in those 'characters' with the highest degree of moral earnestness; and from Overbury an expanded range of possible subjects and the witty manner. But for all that, Earle remains his own man and the *Microcosmography* is a fresh and original work.

Earle begins with the 'character' of a child but follows no particular sequence thereafter—the 'characters' could be shuffled without at all affecting the point or force of the book. Of the seventy-eight pieces in the complete collection, nearly half are concerned with moral or social types and a slightly smaller number with trades and professions. A handful of figures are taken from the university world that Earle knew best at this early stage in his career (types of Student, the College Butler, and so on), there are three 'characters' concerning the Ages of Man, and four of places. Only half a dozen or so out of this total of nearly fourscore are 'characters' of ideal types.

The Contemplative Man (No. 33) shows us a meditative observer of the world rather than an active participant in its affairs, a classical ideal of contented retirement into which Christian elements have been incorporated. For all its beauty, this 'character' is something of a young man's literary exercise. The Stayed Man (No. 54)—the man of steady purpose, who promises no more than he is sure of—is much less of a spectator. He is 'active in the world without disquiet, and careful without misery; yet neither ingulpht in his pleasures, nor a seeker of business, but has his hour for both'.[9] A knowledge of Earle's subsequent life, with his active espousal—at some personal cost—of the Royalist cause, suggests that this is nearer to his true ideal than the Contemplative Man who 'looks upon man from a high tower' (p. 49). For the rest, we must deduce Earle's positive values from the bad 'characters', as when he says of the Hypocrite that she is 'so taken up with faith she has no room for charity, and understands no good works but what are wrought on the sampler' (pp. 50 f.).

The prevailing tone in the *Microcosmography* is neither as austere as in most of Hall's 'characters' nor as extravagantly witty as with many of the Overbury collection. Often Earle's wit is tinged with sadness, as in his elegy on the passing of innocence (A Child), or in his wry picture of the Poor Man, 'whom men fall out with before-hand to prevent friendship, and his friends too to prevent engagements, or if they own him 'tis in private and a by-room, and on condition not to know them before company' (p. 106: see too the endings to Nos. 9 and 26).

The temper of the writing seems at all times exactly to reflect the subject-matter. Fairly harmless follies or pretensions are treated with good humour. Thus the Young Raw Preacher 'is a bird not yet fledged, that hath hopped out of his nest to be chirping on a hedge, and will be straggling abroad at what peril soever'. He makes one sermon last a year and 'takes on against the pope without mercy' (pp. 6 and 7: see also the Plodding Student, No. 40). In passing it may be said that much of the wit in seventeenth-century character-writing was harsh or disagreeably patronizing. Even when Earle obviously dislikes his subject, there is none of that hysteria which disfigures some later works. One may contrast the conclusion of his Meer Dull Physician:

> he is a sucking consumption, and very brother to the worms, for they are both ingendered out of man's corruption (p. 11)

with the Quack Doctor in an anonymous pamphlet of 1676:

> [he is] one of the Epidemical Diseases of this Age, a Younger Brother to the *Pox*, and the *Scurvy*, but more destructive than either. . . . To trace his pedigree, is to rake a Dunghill . . . (p. 1)

One revealing remark comes at the close of the 'character' of the Insolent Man: 'They are men whose preferment does us a great deal of wrong, and when they are down, we may laugh at them without breach of good-nature.'[10] Urbanity and good humour must be preserved—and most vices bring their own retribution anyway. (See the endings of Nos. 14, 18, 19, and 69.)

A more severe moralizing tone may be perceived in the 'characters' of the Lascivious Man and the Profane Man (Nos. 69 and 72). Of the first, Earle writes: 'There is a great deal of malignity in this vice, for it loves still to spoil the best things, and a virgin sometimes rather than beauty, because the undoing here is greater' (p. 97); and of the Profane Man: 'His words are but so many vomitings cast up to the loathsomeness of the hearers' (p. 101). 'Vomiting', 'loathsome', 'malign': such words are the stock-in-trade of later character-writers, but are very rare in Earle. However, the Lascivious Man hurts innocence and the Profane Man threatens the very world-order by denying God and mocking virtue. Strong tones are reserved by Earle for such cases, where his less discriminating successors will rant and thunder without ceasing.

Earle's title-page describes the contents of his books as 'essays and characters'. Boyce sees the occasional inclination to meditate rather than to describe as the one serious threat to character-writing in the *Microcosmography* (p. 252). There is some substance in this, as may be seen from the extracts given above from the Insolent Man and the Lascivious Man. Earle's 'character' of A Child is less a 'character' in the normal sense than reflections on innocence; the child is an emblem:

> . . . a man in a small letter, yet the best copy of Adam before he tasted of Eve or the apple. . . . His soul is yet a white paper unscribbled with observations of the world. . . . The elder he grows, he is a stair lower from God . . . (pp. 5 f.)

But Earle's usual method is that of Theophrastus: the types are revealed in a succession of characteristic actions, phrases, and details of appearance. The turn of speech that epitomizes a type is unerringly picked on. The Flatterer 'is one never chides you but for your vertues, as, *you are too good, too honest, too religious*, when his chiding may seem but the earnester commendation' (p. 93). Actions are recorded with as much precision as words. The Pretender to Learning 'is oftner in his study than at his book, and you cannot pleasure him better than to deprehend [discover] him: yet he hears you not till the third knock, and then comes out very angry as interrupted' (p. 65). Several of the 'characters', consisting entirely of such details virtually unembellished by witty figures or rhetorical devices, must be as near to Theophrastus as any seventeenth-century English writer ever came:

[The Antiquary is] a great admirer of the rust of old monuments, and reads only those characters, where time hath eaten out the letters. . . . His estate consists much in shekels, and Roman coins. . . . Printed books he contemns, as a novelty of this latter age, but a manuscript he pores on everlastingly, especially if the cover be all motheaten, and the dust make a parenthesis between every syllable. He would give all the books in his study . . . for . . . six lines of Tully in his own hand. . . . He never looks upon himself till he is grey-haired, and then he is pleased with his own antiquity. (pp. 14 f.).

Many 'characters', as might be expected from a collection dating from the 1620s, add a measure of witty elaboration. We have already seen the Young Raw Preacher likened to a fledgeling:

His backwardness in the university hath set him thus forward; for had he not truanted there, he had not been so hasty a divine. . . . The pace of his sermon is a full career, and he runs wildly over hill and dale, till the clock stop him. . . . He has more tricks with a sermon, than a taylor with an old cloak, to turn it, and piece it, and at last quite disguise it . . . (pp. 6 f.)

Earle's wit is ingenious, but hardly ever forced:

A self conceited man is one that knows himself so well, that he does not know himself. Two *excellent well-dones* have undone him. . . . He is now become his own book, which he pores on continually, yet like a truant reader skips over the harsh places. . . . In the speculation of his own good parts, his eyes, like a drunkard's, see all double . . . (p. 19)

Similes are exact: the Bold Forward Man displays his good parts 'like some needy flaunting goldsmith, nothing in the inner room, but all on the cupboard' (p. 63). It would be difficult to find anyone among the English character-writers who habitually says as much in so few words. Of the Hypocrite: 'her purity consists much in her linnen' (p. 50); while A Plain Country Fellow 'Is one that manures his ground well, but lets himself lie fallow and untilled. He has reason enough to do his business, and not enough to be idle or melancholy' (p. 34). Here the implications—regarding work, self-fulfilment, the source of idleness and melancholy—go far beyond the immediate subject-matter of the particular type under discussion. But it is not a question of 'essay-writing' as opposed to 'character-writing'. Earle does not digress or reflect in the way that would pose a threat to the genre: he throws out laconic hints within the framework of his 'character' and forces the reader to reflect.

Many 'characters' of Earle's day end with a little flourish of metaphors.[11] Nicholas Breton is particularly given to this practice, which can easily become somewhat mechanical. His Drunkard concludes: 'In sum, he is a tub of swill, a spirit of sleep, a picture of a beast, and a monster of a man' (from *The Good and the Badde*, 1616). (The arrangement of the metaphors in groups of four is a mannerism of Breton's: see below, chapter 8(i).)

Earle's final cadences are much less of a pattern and can vary between the extreme terseness of the ending to the Carrier ('But let him pass'—p. 26) to the long and elaborate close to A Tavern:

> To give you the total reckoning of it; it is the busy man's recreation, the idle man's business, the melancholy man's sanctuary, the stranger's welcome, the inn's-a-court man's entertainment, the scholar's kindness, and the citizen's courtesy. It is the study of sparkling wits, and a cup of canary their book, whence we leave them. (p. 23)

To say what the tavern is to different people is to add new material to the 'character'; the long list of terms is justified by the pun on 'reckoning'. Often Earle will end his 'character' with a devastating summing-up of the moral, human, or social essence of his subject. Of the Hypocrite: 'She is an everlasting argument; but I am weary of her' (p. 52). Or, as a culmination of all the pretensions and posturings of the Affected Man: 'the best use of such men is, they are good parts in a play' (p. 101). A piece sometimes closes with a metaphor taken from the character's activity or profession. The effect is witty, but there can be underlying seriousness: 'when the time, or term of [the Attorney's] life is going out, for dooms-day he is secure; for he hopes he has a trick to reverse judgement' (p. 55: see too the endings of Nos. 17 and 18).

It will have become clear that Earle's endings can vary from the most light-hearted puns on a calling or trade to profoundly serious judgements. The close of the Insolent Man, with its judicious moral recapitulation and its implications not only for the Insolent Man himself but for the reader, has already been quoted. The ending of the Meer Empty Wit is none the less serious for its play on 'laugh' and 'jest': 'Briefly they are such whose life is but to laugh and be laughed at; and only wits in jest and fools in earnest' (p. 80).

For Earle, there are as many different ways of ending a 'character' as there are types to make 'characters' from; both the degree of levity or moral seriousness and the choice of words and metaphors exactly fit the type in every case. No other single aspect shows more clearly his originality and independence, his ability to match the style to the subject and his unwillingness to use hackneyed formulas.

Only in one category does Earle descend to empty conceits, in his 'working-class characters': the Shop-Keeper, the Trumpeter, the Cook, the (itinerant) Fiddler, and so on. The Trumpeter is 'the elephant with the great trunk, for he eats nothing but what comes through this way' (p. 56); the Cook is cunning in architecture, 'for he builds strange fabrics in paste, towers and castles, which are offered to the assault of valiant teeth' (p. 62). But this approach to character-writing, as soon as it touches on the humbler orders of society, is a general one. (See below, chapter 7(iii).)

(iii) The Rest of the Seventeenth Century

We have looked at three of the most widely read and influential character-books of seventeenth-century England. Not every writer can be discussed in such detail as Hall, Overbury, or Earle. In the following pages, I shall try to give a general picture of the development of character-writing during the rest of the century, touching on the rapidly expanding range of types (arguably reaching a point where the original notion of the 'character' is imperilled), the main stylistic features, the appearance of 'characters' in treatises, sermons, and pamphlets, the balance between virtues and vices, and the gradual ascendancy of moralizing and polemical 'characters' after a period in which a near-disinterested play of wit had seemed to predominate.

Despite the fact that there were various editions of Theophrastus in the early seventeenth century and, in addition to these, John Healey's racy English translation first published in 1616, the direct influence of Theophrastus on the English character-writers is probably not very great.[1] Once the notion of character-writing in the Theophrastan manner had been introduced into English letters by Hall and once the Overbury collection had shown how the range of types could be expanded to include specifically English social and professional figures, Greek influence acts indirectly, and the

English Theophrastan 'character' (if one may be permitted such a cumbersome phrase) takes on a life of its own and begins to go its own way.

It is worth repeating that we are dealing here with a huge mass of material: if we take into account the character-books, the scattered 'characters' incorporated into larger works, and the single ones published as pamphlets, the total runs into four figures. There are many indications that character-writing quickly became a vogue. William Fennor, finding himself imprisoned for debt, recounts his experiences from his arrest onwards. Presently he pauses, to give the formal 'character' of a Prison:

> . . . in the midst of melancholy [I] writ this character of a prison:
>
> It is a fabric built of the same stuff the keepers of it are made of, stone and iron. . . . It is a book where an honest man may learn and read a lesson of bettering himself, and where a bad man may study to be ten times worse. It is a costive creature, that surfeits almost all the year long, yet very seldom doth purge itself. . . . When *Epimetheus* opened *Pandora's* box there did not more mischiefs and maladies fly out of it into the world than there is in this cursed place. . . . It is a bankrupt's banquetting-house . . . a prodigal's purgatory and a sickness that many young gentlemen and citizens' sons and heirs are incident to be troubled with. . . . It is a dicing-house where much cheating is used . . .
>
> This being finished, I viewed it over . . .[2]

The newly arrived prisoner sits down to write his impressions of the place and chooses the 'character' as the appropriate form for this purpose. He does not say, 'The prison in which I find myself is . . .', or 'Prisons are . . .', but '*A* prison is . . .'. Indeed, the 'character' seems to have been one of the commonest forms of literary exercise in the seventeenth century. When, in 1665, Ralph Johnson came to write his *Scholar's Guide*, he clearly felt that character-writing was a necessary accomplishment for an educated person:

> *A Character*
>
> A Character is a witty and facetious description of the nature and qualities of some person, or sort of people.
>
> RULES *for making it*
>
> 1. Chuse a Subject, *viz.* such a sort of men as will admit a variety of observation, such be, drunkards, usurers, lyars, taylors, excise-men, travellers, pedlars, merchants, tapsters, lawyers, an upstart gentleman, a young Justice, a Constable, an Alderman, and the like.

2. Express their natures, qualities, conditions, practices, tools, desires, aims or ends, by witty Allegories, or Allusions, to things or terms in nature, or art, of like nature and resemblance, still striving for wit and pleasantness, together with tart nipping jerks about their vices or miscarriages.

3. Conclude with some witty and neat passage, leaving them to the effect of their follies or studies. (p. 15)

One inevitable consequence of the craze for writing 'characters' was that there was a good deal of imitation and plagiarism and many of the recurrent figures came to be treated in a stereotyped way. Overbury, Hall, Breton, and Earle are ransacked for motifs. Sometimes, even, whole 'characters' are taken over without acknowledgement.[3] When we examine the collection *Twelve Ingenious Characters* of 1686, we find that the ingenuity consists to a large degree of wholesale literary embezzlement, for two of the twelve are stolen from Overbury, two from Earle, and one from Flecknoe.

It is instructive to take one of the most frequently treated figures, the Drunkard. In *Wit's Cabinet* (*c.* 1700) we find the following short 'character':

. . . a *Drunkard* is the Annoyance of *Modesty*, the Trouble of *Civility*, the Spoil of *Wealth*, the Destruction of *Reason*, the Brewer's *Agent*, the Alehouse's *Benefactor*, the Beggar's *Companion*, the Constable's *Trouble*, his Wife's *Woe*, his Childrens *Sorrow*, his Neighbours *Scoff*, his own *Shame*, a Walking *Swill-tub*, a *Picture of a Beast*, and a *Monster of a Man*. (p. 141)

Before we admire the anonymous author's eloquence, we should turn to the *Looking-Glasse for a Drunkard*, a broadsheet of 1652, which contains exactly the same passage, as does Thomas Young's long moralizing pamphlet of 1617, *Englands Bane*. And Young got it from Breton's *The Good and the Badde* (1616). Even when writers manage the 'character' of a Drunkard without plagiarizing Breton, they seem—with few exceptions—to restrict themselves to variations on a small group of time-worn themes: the Drunkard as a beast in human guise, his filthiness and blabbing of secrets, his improvidence, and so on. Other out-and-out stereotypes, where most writers appear unable to leave the beaten track, are the numerous 'characters' of the Whore, the Dandy, the Society Beauty, and the Swindling Lawyer. This question of plagiarism and imitation will be important when we come to consider the extent to which the 'character' can be taken as reliable evidence of the society of past centuries (see below, chapter 7). But it may perhaps be said in passing that originality did not appear to a seventeenth-century writer as a prime and absolute virtue, nor copying necessarily as an evil. It must be recalled that the educational system still encouraged the study and imitation of the best available models.

As the fashion for writing 'characters' gained ground, there was a huge increase in the number of types written about. Theophrastus had been confronted with a fairly unified society and in any case had been interested only in male free citizens. Hall's concern had been with moral types. But, as we have seen, the Overbury collection had expanded the thematic possibilities very considerably. Thereafter, we are likely to find 'characters' of almost every type imaginable: the Witch, the Executioner, the Rope-Maker, the Tobacconist (i.e. compulsive smoker), the Alderman's Daughter, the Chimerical Poet, the Petty French Lutanist, the Translator, the Mendicant Irish Priest, the Sharking Committee Man. As the character-books multiply, there seems to be a conscious quest for types not yet treated. The world is mainly that of London, with occasional day-trips to Oxford and Cambridge, but Saltonstall (1631) has a sizeable minority of very interesting rural types and in the following year Lupton strikes an almost exact balance in his collection *London and the Country*.

Character-writing was not confined to the depiction of human beings. Most character-books from Overbury onwards include one or more 'characters' of places. The commonest are of Prisons, Taverns, and, later, Coffee Houses. Lupton actually devotes two-thirds of *London and the Country* to 'characters' of places. One even finds occasional 'characters' of animals. Flecknoe (1658) has 'a Ladies little Dogg', but the greatest oddity in this respect is the collection *A Strange Metamorphosis of Man, transformed into a Wildernesse. Deciphered in Characters* (1634). The Preface suggests an allegorical purpose: man is lost in the wilderness and transformed into the shape of various beasts; therefore the author has delivered his character 'in those borrowed shapes, not to put him to the blush'. And so we encounter 'characters' of a Bat, a Goat, a Squirrel, and the like.

Since we have covered only part of the long history of the 'character', I do not wish to enter prematurely into a detailed discussion of 'what a character is'. Nevertheless, a question poses itself at this stage. Bearing in mind the origins of the 'character' and the exclusive concern of both Theophrastus and Hall with human beings, some readers may feel that many of the seventeenth-century examples have moved so far from the original notion as to require a different label. Can one really have 'characters' of Smithfield and St. Paul's (Lupton)? Or of a Gnat, a Snail, and a Crab (*A Strange Metamorphosis*)? Or of a Law-term (Saltonstall) and a Newspaper (John Cleveland)? Yet all these authors expressly labelled their pieces 'characters', so that it seems presumptuous for today's reader to claim to know better on the basis of historical or formal criteria which would simply not have occurred to a seventeenth-century writer.

In the human realm, the seventeenth century saw the growing popularity of national 'characters'. Here too the Overbury collection pointed the way, including a Welshman, a Dutchman residing in England, a Button-maker in Amsterdam, a French Cook. Most later examples either figure in political pamphlets or form part of travel-journals. The commonest types encountered are the Dutchman and the Frenchman, both invariably objects of scorn.

The Overbury collection had established wit as one of the main ingredients of character-writing. Later authors were quick to take the hint. Indeed, by 1631, we find Richard Brathwaite complaining that character-writing has been spoilt by exaggerated wit ('squibbs or crackers')[4] and should return to greater simplicity. Yet Ralph Johnson, over thirty years later, still regards wit as essential (see above, p. 36). Minor writers simply pile conceit on conceit in the manner of the commonplace books. According to Samuel Person, the Covetous Man is

> . . . an Idolater, for he worships Images. . . . He wishes with *Midas*, all were turned into Gold . . . This greedy man would (with *Augustus Caesar*) make all men Tributaries to him . . . The Crosses on his coyne, are those upon which his mind is Crucified. . . . [He is] a good Chymist, for out of his labours he extracts gold. A Covetous man is a *Griffen*, for he doth build his nest of Gold.[5]

(The gryphon often stood for the type of man who hoards wealth without enjoying it: cf. Meres, 297ʳ.) It will be noticed that Person has done little more than put the one thought in half a dozen different wrappings.

Samuel Butler, who wrote more 'characters' than any other author (nearly two hundred), often succumbs to the temptation of saying the same thing over and over again by means of obscure allusions and witty analogies. Wit easily became a tyrannical master rather than a servant.[6] Even as good a writer as Saltonstall sometimes offends. His 'character' of a 'poore Village' is serious, realistic, and compassionate. Yet at one point he obviously feels that it is time to work in a classical allusion, however inappropriate in the context: 'all the Roomes are hung round with the worke of Arachne, that is, with dusty cobwebs'.[7]

Francis Lenton's *Characterismi* of 1631 is probably the most interesting English character-book to appear after Earle. Lenton does not always avoid the stylistic faults just discussed: for instance, his Drunkard consists of the mere spinning out of conceits, while his Widow is little more than witty embroidery on the single notion that the lady is anxious to find a second husband. But for the most part *Characterismi* is a good example of the English Theophrastan manner, with each picture made up of telling individual touches. The affinity with (as opposed to the imitation of) Earle is clear from Lenton's 'double benefic't Parson', who

> hath two Pulpits and one Sermon, which he preacheth at both his Parishes at his primer induction, and then a couple of silly Curates read out the rest of his Incumbency for the twentieth part of his Parsonages. Hee is one who hath the cure of others soules, and yet . . . cares not for his owne; and . . . is clad with the fleece, without feeding the flocke.[8]

This is clearly Earle's Young Raw Preacher, grown older and more worldly-wise. As Theophrastus incidentally gives us a picture of Athenian life, so Lenton—in his better pieces, at least—is full of little realistic details. The Young Schoolmaster

> broadly adventures into the broad world . . . where in some small Village hee first exerciseth the Art of a Pedagogue, for instruction of infants. Two pence a week, by the Rurals, is proferred him at his first entrance, for the literature of little Primmer Boyes, and foure pence a weeke for Accidences, besides his Sundayes dinner, by turne, together with the plaine gifts of some of their plainer mothers; by the which, hee atchieveth to the annual pension of ten pound *Sterling*. (No. 16)

When Lenton allows himself an abstract formulation, it is usually terse and to the point. Of the same Schoolmaster: 'Hee is one commonly of more desert than respect . . .'. Or the Parasite: 'He cannot be truely generous, for he is a slave to other mens humours . . .' (No. 5).

Lenton's realism extends to his working-class 'characters'. Here is part of the 'Carle, or Farmer Tenant':

> Sorrow, the sweat of his face, and a barren field, are his wrackt rents and revenues, and a griping Landlord his intollerable griefe. . . . He is the soyle on which all Citizens and Idle folke feede, the very drudge and doghorse of the world, one that dares not eate the fruit of his labour lest his rent should fall short . . . (No. 14)

Such compassionate realism in the service of radical social indignation is never sustained throughout an entire 'character', but to encounter it at all is rare in character-writing of this period.

Another writer who deserves to be singled out from the throng is William Sprigge, whose *Philosophicall Essayes* (1657) contains five 'characters'. That of a Covetous Man, to be sure, is not much more than a string of conceits from mythology, history, the Bible, the natural sciences, and so on, but elsewhere Sprigge reveals himself as an individual contributor to the genre, restraining his ingenuity and harnessing it to serious purposes. His 'Foole or Naturall' is worth quoting in full for its sad wit, its total absence of any heartless mockery, and its curious combination of the metaphysical and the strictly practical:

> A Foole is an animal, the Organs and Pipes of whose body, like a sorry instrument, being miserably out of tune, his soul cannot play those sweet notes, and lofty straines of reason, that in better tun'd bodyes she useth to do and therefore he is sayd to have reason only in the seed or root, which shoots not forth, till death hath broken up the rough clods of his body; and his soul be tranplanted to a soyle govern'd by better influences, than any earth receives. Or in brief, he is one whom nature never suffer'd to take his discretion into his own hands, and therefore the law trusts not with the management of his own estate. (p. 43)

At the same time as most seventeenth-century character-writers enthusiastically strove to dazzle and entertain, some followed in the steps of Hall and used the 'character' for the purpose of practical moralizing. It was quickly realized that the 'character' could be used to illustrate a tract. As we have seen, Thomas Young, in his long pamphlet on the evils of drink (*Englands Bane*, 1617), simply steals his Drunkard from Breton, perhaps thinking that this highly concentrated miniature would best sum up his forty pages of moralizing. A similar use of a 'character' to conclude an ethical treatise and epitomize its burden can be found in John Ford's

Line of Life (1620), which ends with the 'character' of a Good Man. (Unlike Young, Ford writes the 'character' himself.) Another early seventeenth-century writer to use 'characters' in this way was Thomas Tuke, rector of Saint Giles in the Fields. In *The Christian's Looking-Glasse* (1615), he gives the 'character' of a Proud Man as part of his denunciation of pride. This is true character-writing, not unlike Hall's in style, with its mixture of abstract formulations and concrete examples and its restrained use of rhetoric:

> . . . the proud person envies the good of another, as if he deemed himselfe either onely worthy, or else the greatnesse of others to hinder his. . . . [He] useth his equals as inferiors, his inferiors as servants, his servants as beasts: he thunders, lightens, crackes, threatens. . . . If hee give backe, it is but to fetch a better leap: if he stoope a little, it is but to vant and climbe the higher. . . . And when he is climbed up, he plucks up the ladder after him, if he can, that no man shall come up after, or but such as he pleaseth. (pp. 114 f.)

In addition to such illustrative 'characters' which crop up in treatises on morality, education, manners, and so forth, we find many 'characters' in seventeenth-century sermons.

Personifications of the virtues and vices and pictures of types such as slothful and worldly clergymen occur in sermons from the Middle Ages on,[9] but the first true 'characters' to figure in sermons are those by Thomas Adams. His sermon *The White Devil, or the Hypocrite uncased* (1614) combines a discussion of hypocrisy as a quality with passages of character-writing. The stress is almost entirely on the Hypocrite's inner, spiritual condition, with few of the behavioural details that we find in Hall, but it is nevertheless clear that the impulse comes from the *Characters of Virtues and Vices*:

> An Hypocrite is a kind of honest Atheist: for his owne *Good* is his *God*: his heaven is upon earth, & that not the *Peace of his Conscience*, or *that kingdome of heaven, which may be in a soule living on earth*, but the secure peace of a worldly estate: he stands in awe of no judge, but mans eie. . . . [He] dares not trust God with a pennie, except before a whole congregation of witnesses, lest perhaps, God should denie the receipt. (p. 31)

One may compare Hall on the same type:

> When he should give, he looks about him, and says, 'Who sees me?' No alms, no prayers fall from him, without a witness; belike, lest God should deny, that he hath received them . . . (p. 105)

Adams's *Mystical Bedlam* (1615) is a cycle of sermons on various forms of 'madness' (i.e. sin and folly): the Busybody, the Epicure, the Proud Man, the Lustful, the Hypocrite, the Usurer, nineteen types in all. It is not unmixed character-writing—general reflections and passages of individualized description alternate—but it must be the most ambitious and elaborate attempt to adapt the structure and methods of a moral character-book to the needs of the pulpit:

> The DRUNKARD will, sure, wrangle with me that his name comes so late in this catalogue, that deserved to be in the front or vanguard of madmen. *Demens ebrietas* is an attribute given him by a heathen. It is a voluntary madness, and makes a man so like a beast, that whereas a beast hath no reason, he hath the use of no reason; and, the power or faculty of reason suspended, gives way to madness. Nay, he is in some respect worse than a beast; for few beasts will drink more than they need, whereas mad drunkards drink when they have no need, till they have need again. . . . To prove himself a madman, he dares quarrel with every man; nay, with posts and walls, imagining them to be men.[10]

One obviously needs to exercise caution when talking of 'characters' within sermons. Often enough, when a man preaches on a virtue or vice, he veers between abstract discussion of the quality and description of a man who exhibits it. But Adams's case is clearly different: he seems to have started out with the notion of a community of madmen, a series of types akin to Hall's Vices, and to have built upon that foundation, characterizing each in turn.

In his sermon *The Unmasking of the Hypocrite* (1616), John Rawlinson takes the hypocritical kiss of Judas as his starting-point. He goes on to describe various types of hypocrites in contemporary society:

> The PATRON, he under a charitable praetense of praeferring a poore Scholar that hath most neede, will choose one whose *braine* is as empty as his *purse*; who will rather *bite at a crust*, than *sterve for lack of bread*; that so he may turne Judas his *Quid dabis*? what will you give me? into *Dabis quid*: you shall give me the very quiddity and substance of your living. His gift is (as *Sophocles* speaks) . . . a giftles gift, making . . . an unfortunate Clergy: like the *poysoned shirt* which *Deianira* gave to *Hercules*; of which one wittily said, that . . . when shee should have cloathed him with a *shirt*, she cloathed him with a *winding-sheete*. (p. 31 f.)

The sermon was preached at Oxford, where we may hope that Rawlinson's erudite hearers appreciated the classical allusions and learned conceits, and is quite indistinguishable from the more mannered type of witty 'character' then coming into fashion.[11] So the two trends in seventeenth-century character-writing (the free play of wit and the 'character' with a didactic purpose) are not always in opposition. In general, however, it is true to say that authors with a serious purpose tend to write in a comparatively plain style (this point is discussed further in chapter 8).

As I have already said, few English character-books have any general plan. Breton's *The Good and the Badde* combines the old framework of the Estates with the notion of a moral microcosm, as does Thomas Fuller's *The Holy State, and the Profane State* (1642), the situation here being complicated by the fact that some of the 'characters' are followed by illustrative portraits of actual persons. Two collections which appear to promise a moral or social conspectus are Humphrey Browne's *A Map of the Microcosme, or, A Morall Description of Man* (1642) and Samuel Person's *An Anatomical Lecture of Man. Or a Map of the Little World . . .* (1664), but there is no particular plan in the ordering of their 'characters' and one is forced to suspect that the high-sounding titles are mere window-dressing. *The Times Anatomiz'd* by Thomas Ford (1647) is, as far as I know, unique in that it offers something like a microcosm in a strictly contemporary sense, containing 'A Good King', 'Rebellion', 'An honest Subject', 'An hypocriticall Convert of the times', 'A Souldier of fortune', and so on. The rest of the seventeenth-century character-books consist of an arbitrary succession of types. The authors seem to have conceived each 'character' as a self-contained and independent entity. And why not?

Satirical depictions of bad types continue to outweigh the ideal 'characters'. Only Breton and Fuller follow Hall in aiming at a balance between good and bad, while Dudley, Lord North, who wrote a group of ten 'characters', all idealized, is unique. Books containing a handful of good 'characters' and a score of bad are more typical, while the largest collection by any single hand (that of Samuel Butler) contains no good 'characters' at all. Where ideal 'characters' do occur, they sometimes relate to particular Estates or professions (the just Ruler, the good Magistrate, and so on). There are several of the Good Wife, written firmly from the point of view of masculine convenience and satisfaction, and many of the Good or Wise Man. These continue to be either Christianized versions of the Stoic ideal or an Anglicized form of Horace's country gentleman living in contented retirement. Occasionally we encounter propagandizing pictures of the patriotic and public-spirited member of the Church of England, as in Francis Wortley's true English Protestant,[12] or the anonymous 'characters' of an *Englishman* (1680) and a *True English Protestant Souldier* (1689). There are also two laudatory 'characters' of the Puritan,[13] as counterblasts to the scorn poured on that sect by its enemies. (Hostile 'characters' of the Puritan are not uncommon.)

From the 1640s onwards, increasing numbers of 'characters' were published separately, either as single sheets or as pamphlets, usually of between two and eight pages. The subjects were mostly political (the Royalist, the Parliamentarian, the Agitator, the political Time-server) or religious (the Jesuit, the Protestant, the Puritan, the Vicar of Bray type), although there were a fair number devoted to the professions and a miscellaneous group including the Drunkard, the Gallant, and the Town-Miss (i.e. Whore). Many, especially those relating to the Civil War and the religious controversies of the mid-century, are today of more interest to the historian than to the student of literature. It is significant that Boyce, in his book on them,[14] devotes nearly half his space to 'the Character and Contemporary History'.

In the last thirty years of the century, such polemical 'characters' in broadsheet or pamphlet-form came to predominate over the older type of character-book. The object was usually to 'lash with Satyrical Invectives', a phrase taken from the *Character of a Jesuit* (1681):

> He'l Sacrifice Virginity to the rising Ghost of his own Lust, and will drown the Widow in the Tears of her Orphan: He'l Murther with Zeal and Devotion, and be villanous with Authority and License. . . . He'l corrupt the thoughts of the strictest Matron, and perswade her, that the abuse of her Husbands Bed is Meritorious . . . (p. 2)

The witty manner often runs mad. The Quaker is 'a *Vessel of Phanaticisme* . . . a *Common-Shore* of Heresie . . . the *fag-end* of Reformation . . . this troublesome *Insect* . . . a *Puppet of Religion* contrived to amuse the *Rabble*'; he is like a hedgehog or an inhospitable coast.[15]

Where the 'character' is not wholly given over to invective, it tends to be a summary of the real or alleged views and doctrines of the subject, often very loose and digressive in its form. It would seem that the vein of character-writing, as developed throughout the seventeenth century, is by now worked out. When we find a rare example of a character-book cast in the old form, the point is merely confirmed. In 1700, that incorrigible scribbler Ned Ward published *The Reformer. Exposing the Vices of the Age in several CHARACTERS.* It is not that Ward has committed wholesale plagiarism (although thefts from Hall and others are easily detected); rather that the whole collection reads like a stale imitation of earlier works. There is nothing in the whole book that gives any impression of freshness, nothing that has not been said before, and said better. It is clear that some sort of new impetus was needed if the 'character' was to be revitalized; that impetus came from France.

2

The 'Character' in France

> What an admirable book is La Bruyère's! Inimitable 'characters', which one nevertheless strives to imitate! (P. J. Brillon)[1]

In France, one work of unquestioned genius stands out: *Les Caractères de Théophraste traduits du grec avec les Caractères ou les Mœurs de ce Siècle* by La Bruyère, first published in 1688. Not only is this a great work by any standards, its influence completely dominated French character-writing. But La Bruyère was not without predecessors. As early as 1610, Hall's *Characters* had appeared in a translation by J. L. de Tourval.[2] Urbain Chevreau (1613–1701) was also fascinated by Hall, whom he translated in *L'Escole du Sage* (1646) and to whom he returned throughout his life, paraphrasing in prose and verse and producing his own imitations. Hall's were not the only English 'characters' to appear in French versions: sixty-one years after Tourval, James Dynocke, an English Catholic living in France, published *Le Vice ridicule et la vertu loüée*, a collection of 'characters' mostly taken from Earle and Overbury. Now although the *Microcosmography* and the Overbury collection, with their constant references to English life and institutions, would not transplant very readily, one might expect Hall's work, which lays much more emphasis on general moral qualities, to have had some influence in France. But this does not seem to be the case. Although some critics see Hall, through the mediation of Chevreau, as an important influence on La Bruyère, I find it difficult to agree in view of the paucity of solid evidence.[3] The main sources of character-writing in France must be looked for elsewhere.

In discussions of La Bruyère's predecessors, various treatises on psychology and morality are sometimes mentioned. Eustache Du Refugé's *Traicté de la Cour* (1615)—a formal psychological treatise combined with a practical manual of conduct—certainly contains, by way of illustration, a few set descriptions which resemble 'characters', although they are much more abstract in style than

Theophrastus or even Hall.[4] Du Refugé's almost complete lack of concrete detail suggests that he was either unacquainted with, or unimpressed by, Theophrastus and the examples of character-portrayal (often full of concrete particulars) in the books on rhetoric.[5] The direct influence of Aristotle would seem more likely.

The only explicit acknowledgement of Theophrastus's influence in this period occurs, as far as I know, in the *Peintures Morales* of Pierre le Moyne. The author, a Jesuit who lived from 1602 to 1671, published the *Peintures* in two parts in 1640 and 1643.[6] It is a treatise on morality and the passions, illustrated both by figures and anecdotes from history and legend and by 'characters', which le Moyne defines as 'pen-paintings in which the nature of each passion is expressed by the distinguishing marks peculiar to it', here singling out Theophrastus as his model. The most celebrated 'character' in the *Peintures Morales*, 'Le Sauvage. Caractere Moral' (i. 620 ff.)—that is, the rude and uncivilized Misanthrope and Puritan—was widely held at the time to be an attack on the Jansenists. 'Le Sauvage' is certainly a 'character' in that it is a picture of an imaginary representative of a category of men, a figure whose every characteristic adds to this impression. But it lacks the terseness of the best 'characters'; for instance, le Moyne takes fourteen lines to tell us that the Savage is untouched by the charms of music. In addition, the author's incontinent dislike of his subject seems to have driven him to adopt an almost pathologically hostile tone. Where English writers would sometimes liken the Drunkard to a beast or the Whore to a pestilence, le Moyne develops his metaphor of the savage as if it were literal truth: 'He does not wait until the fire has prepared his meats; he takes them quite raw and sometimes still bloody and living' (p. 622).

These isolated examples from the early and mid seventeenth century cannot have given La Bruyère more than a nudge in the general direction of character-writing. Paradoxically, the most important native influence on him was the sudden popularity of a different, although related, *petit genre*, the so-called 'portrait'. This was the term applied in seventeenth-century France to the more or less camouflaged description of an actual person. The fashion seems to have been started by the *romans à clef* of Honoré d'Urfé (*L'Astrée*, 1607–27) and Madeleine de Scudéry (*Le Grand Cyrus*, 1648–53; *Clélie*, 1654–61), which contain thinly veiled and often sycophantic depictions of figures from contemporary society. The popularity enjoyed by such works is not difficult to understand: the subject felt himself or herself flattered and the readers were caught up in a delectable guessing game. The search for 'keys' became part of this game; both the characters and the events in the novels were scrutinized in an attempt to find real-life sources.[7]

In the 1650s and 1660s, the vogue spread to the fashionable *salons*: Mlle de Montpensier composed portraits herself and encouraged her friends to do likewise. In 1659, a large collection of portraits by over two dozen different hands was compiled and published by Mlle de Montpensier's secretary, Regnauld de Segrais, under the title *La Galerie des Portraits.*[8] The portraits comprising this 'gallery' are fairly short and the great majority are in prose. In most cases the author and subject are identified and there is a sizeable minority (about three dozen) of self-portraits, the most famous being that by La Rochefoucauld. In the comparatively few cases where the subject is not named, but is either given a Greek or Roman alias or an initial, the task of guessing or speculating must have added to the appeal, as in the *roman à clef.*[9] No doubt a severe social historian would see the composition of these pieces as the idle and self-indulgent pastime of a class with too much leisure, but, even if some of them carry flattery to absurd lengths,[10] they indubitably show a genuine and lively psychological curiosity.

By now, the portrait was part of the fashionable way of life. When, in *Les Précieuses ridicules*, Magdelon admits her weakness for the portrait, 'Je vous avoue que je suis furieusement pour les portraits; je ne vois rien de si galant que cela', she is only echoing Mlle de Montpensier: 'je trouvai cette manière d'écrire fort galante'.[11] The *Galerie des Portraits* was much imitated; works with titles such as *Les Pourctraits de la Cour* (1667) were common and the genre spread to sermons, histories, memoirs, funeral orations, and other forms of writing. If the sycophantic vein has been stressed in this brief account, it should be remembered that there were hostile portraits as well. Two of the most invigorating examples are the portrait of La Rochefoucauld by Cardinal de Retz and La Rochefoucauld's retaliation.[12] Nor, if Molière's *Misanthrope* (ii. 4) is to be believed, were the portraits bandied about extempore in the *salons* always flattering.[13]

So, when La Bruyère conceived the idea of recording the 'customs of the century' in character-form, he had two distinct models before him: the imaginary representative of a category of men (the Theophrastan 'character') and the more sharply individualized portrait of an actual person, nearly always a well-known contemporary of the writer and often his or her social intimate. La Bruyère is undoubtedly influenced by both types of writing. The practice of giving his subjects classical names (Gnatho, Clito, Timon, etc.) derives from the portrait, of course; neither Theophrastus nor any other character-writer to date had been in the habit of naming his 'characters'. In La Bruyère's case, I take the device to be an ironic play on the craze for portraits, as if he were saying, 'Look around and you will find someone who fits this description.' It must have encouraged contemporary readers to hunt for keys, even where such a quest was inappropriate.

As far as the form of his book is concerned, La Bruyère is interested neither in an unbroken succession of self-contained 'characters', as favoured by Theophrastus and most seventeenth-century English writers, nor in any kind of formal and systematic treatise in which the 'characters' provide no more than occasional light relief. Instead, he chooses to devote a series of chapters to various qualities, types of people, and aspects of society (Of Personal Merit, Of Great Nobles, Of Fashion, etc.), each chapter consisting of an informal sequence of aphorisms, longer passages of reflection, and 'characters' of varying length. His book thus combines three main traditions of writing: the 'character', the portrait, and the type of reflective prose of which the most famous examples in France are Pascal's *Pensées* and La Rochefoucauld's *Maximes*. Debts to Montaigne's *Essais* have also been noted.

La Bruyère's book, when first published in 1688, contained 420 items, of which only a small number were 'characters'. The author expanded his work in subsequent editions, until the eighth (1694) had grown almost threefold.[14] By now there was a balance between maxims, longer reflections, and 'characters'. La Bruyère prefaces his work with a translation of Theophrastus,[15] clearly suggesting the intention of offering a contemporary equivalent to Theophrastus's picture of men and manners in fourth-century Athens.

Although keys were in circulation as early as the 1690s, there seems no reason to doubt La Bruyère's disclaimer that he did not always paint this or that individual from nature, but took one trait from one person and one from another in order to make up a composite figure which would possess verisimilitude.[16] The book contains descriptions ranging from fairly straightforward 'portraits'

(Aemile = Condé, Cydias = Fontenelle) to cases where the urge to depict real persons has yielded to a desire to give a representative figure. Often the degree of individualization would give us a clue even if there were no keys extant. Thus the account of Aemile contains too much biographical detail to be anything but a 'portrait', while that of Theodas (Santeul) is too quirkish ever to qualify as a type-cast 'character'.[17] Similarly, the personality of Strato (the Duke of Lauzun) is, La Bruyère tells us, a near-insoluble enigma (viii. 96). That is, Strato is sure to be a 'portrait'; he is too ambiguous and mysterious (*équivoque, mêlé, enveloppé*) ever to pass as a 'character', which must clearly reveal itself as standing for a whole class of people. The only improbabilities admissible in the 'character' are those of caricature and exaggeration.

Other, perhaps more interesting, examples seem to lie on the borderline between 'portrait' and 'character'. Is the account of Mopsus the 'character' of a thrusting social climber or—as the keys have it—a 'portrait' of the Abbé St. Pierre?

> I know *Mopsus* from a visit he paid me, without knowing me; he beseeches people with whom he is quite unacquainted to take him to others who are not acquainted with him; he writes to ladies whom he knows only by sight. He insinuates himself into a circle of respectable people who do not know what sort of a person he is and there, without waiting to be asked or being aware that he is interrupting, he talks frequently and ridiculously. Another time he will come into an assembly and sit down at random, heedless of others and of himself. He is removed from a seat intended for a minister and sits down in the Duke's place. He is the one at whom everyone laughs and who alone remains grave and unsmiling. If you drive a dog from the King's chair, it will clamber up into the preacher's pulpit . . . (ii. 38)

Let us believe the keys and assume that there is a real person hidden behind that description; nevertheless, it is a typified account which makes us aware of a perennial human quality manifested in a particular social and historical context. That is, it has the impact of a 'character'. Stegmann is surely right when he talks of La Bruyère's double purpose: to present us with an actual person but also to develop a 'typology' which transcends individual personalities.[18]

His Theophilus, an ambitious clerical intriguer, whom the keys identify as the Bishop of Autun, also illustrates this point. The author's uncertainty about his subject's exact motives suggests the 'portrait'—'Is it zeal in him on behalf of his neighbour? is it habit? is it an inflated opinion of himself?' (ix. 15)—but the terms in which Theophilus's overweening ambition is described are generalized in a way that expands the implications of the passage: 'death alone, in depriving him of life, will deprive him of this thirst to dominate and control men's minds. . . . He listens, he keeps a watchful eye on everything that could serve to nourish his intriguing spirit' (ibid.).

To give a 'character' a classical setting, as La Bruyère sometimes does, also serves to emphasize the perennial within the particular. Irene (xi. 35) may indeed be a portrait of—or may originally have been suggested by—Mlle de Montespan, but can also stand for any hypochondriac. La Bruyère's chosen setting helps to make this clear, implying that there have been hypochondriacs ever since there have been idle, self-obsessed folk and doctors for them to consult:

> Irene betakes herself at great expense to Epidaurus, sees Aesculapius in his temple and consults him about all her ailments. . . . She asks him why she is putting on weight and what is the remedy? The oracle replies that she should get up before midday and sometimes use her legs for walking. She declares that wine is harmful to her; the oracle tells her to drink water . . .

In other cases, La Bruyère makes it clear through simple multiplication that his subject stands for a class of men: 'The world is full of such as Euthyphron', 'One could go on talking about people like Pamphile for ever' (v. 24; ix. 50). All the evidence suggests that he wished to combine the particular and the generally valid; most readers would surely agree that he succeeded triumphantly, perhaps uniquely.

The influence of the *portrait* helps to account for an important difference between La Bruyère and his predecessors. Until now there had been a sort of formality in the presentation of a 'character'; the reader was aware that it was a set-piece:

> The boor is the sort of man who . . . (Theophrastus)
> A Good Wife is a world of wealth . . . (Breton)
> A Flatterer is the picture of a friend . . . (Earle)

But La Bruyère will address the reader casually, as if sharing impressions of a common acquaintance: 'I name Europyle, and you say . . .' (xii. 20). Or he will apostrophize the subject of the 'character': 'I come to your door, Clitiphon . . .' (vi. 12). This has the effect of making the 'characters' appear less like fictitious figures than descriptions of typical but real persons from a social background shared by author and reader. (The 'character' of

Menalcas is an exception, but it is significant that La Bruyère felt the need to tell the reader so quite explicitly.)

With an author who prints Theophrastus's 'characters' together with his own—and, moreover, gives the two ingredients equal prominence on the title-page—one will expect to find some kind of influence. But if the author is La Bruyère, it will certainly not be mere borrowing of motifs. It seems to have been Theophrastus's habit of laconically building up a 'character' out of details of appearance and behaviour laid end to end that attracted La Bruyère. Examples of this method can be found in the 'characters' of Irene and, except for the scornful analogy with the dog who clambers into a great man's chair, of Mopsus. The technique has one notable advantage for anyone who believes that reading ought to be an attentive and even creative activity: it invites the reader to work out for himself the significance of each external detail and the motives behind each action. It also packs much into a little space.

But, at the same time, La Bruyère seems to have realized that this method had an inbuilt limitation. The author needs to step in from time to time with a comment if he is to make clear what is in his subject's mind:

Menippus . . . naively believes that he has as much [intelligence] as anyone can have . . . (ii. 40)

Pamphilus . . . would like to be great and thinks himself great; but he is only a copy of a great man. (ix. 50)

Quite apart from such necessary intrusions, La Bruyère, whose inclination to moralize has been remarked on often enough, likes to pass explicit judgement on his 'characters':

Narcissus gets up in the morning in order to go to bed at night . . . (vii. 12)

All his plans, all his maxims, all the subtleties of his policy are directed towards a single end, which is not to be taken in, while taking in other people. (x. 12)

In short, La Bruyère is not fixed in his methods. He moves freely and without apparent preference between the plain recording of behaviour and comment upon it. There is a similarly open-minded approach in Vauvenargues' *Essai sur quelques Caractères* (see below).

One of the things that makes La Bruyère supreme among French character-writers—perhaps among all character-writers since Earle

—is his style. His opening chapter ('Of Books') contains three important statements on the craft of writing, deceptively simple but exacting in their implications. There is, says La Bruyère, only one absolutely right way of expressing any given thought. The author must not be satisfied until he has found this way, which will often turn out to be the simplest and the most natural. Perfect clarity can be achieved only if the writer puts himself in the place of an imaginary reader and examines his own work as if it were the work of another. But merely to write aptly and clearly is not enough: a writer must have something worth saying (*des pensées nobles, vives, solides et qui renferment un très beau sens*).[19]

The icy precision of La Bruyère's style often reminds one of La Rochefoucauld; indeed, it would be surprising if an aphorist in the 1680s were to remain unaffected by the *Maximes*:

La Bruyère	*La Rochefoucauld*
Les amours meurent par le dégoût, et l'oubli les enterre.	Il n'y a guère de gens qui ne soient honteux de s'être aimés, quand ils ne s'aiment plus.
L'on me dit tant de mal de cet homme, et j'y en vois si peu, que je commence à soupçonner qu'il n'ait un mérite importun qui éteigne celui des autres.[20]	Le mal que nous faisons ne nous attire pas tant de persécution et de haine que nos bonnes qualités.

As is implicit in La Bruyère's statements of his stylistic ideal, rhetoric is used sparingly and figures of speech are fairly conventional and severely functional,[21] an effective but minor weapon in his stylistic armoury. Behind the character-writers of seventeenth-century England lies a rhetorical tradition which demonstrates all the ways in which a simple idea can be made telling through ornate expressive devices; behind La Bruyère stands the art of the aphorism, which discards all superfluous detail and counts every word. To read La Bruyère is to go through the gamut of tones and emotions, from calm analysis to passionate indignation, from the lightest irony to broad humour. As many of his admirers have said, his book is to be taken a little at a time; the reading demands attention and devotion, as surely as the writing of it did.

La Bruyère's view of man, although it stops well short of La Rochefoucauld's cynicism, is disillusioned. Greed, enslavement to the passions, ambition, envy, hypocrisy, snobbery, sycophancy—these are his constant themes. Men of intelligence and good faith are rare. Life is short, full of suffering, and overshadowed by thoughts of death. At times, La Bruyère expresses himself with the deepest gloom: 'If life is wretched, it is hard to bear; if it is happy, it is horrible to lose it. It amounts to the same thing' (xi. 33).

The only appropriate response is Stoic resignation and self-sufficiency: a Christianized Stoicism, of course.[22] La Bruyère seems to have regarded virtue as inseparable from religious faith and was unreasoning and bigoted in his attitude towards the Freethinkers. It has often been pointed out that he lacks his usual sensitivity and subtlety as soon as he leaves psychological and social comment and ventures into the realms of religion and metaphysics. But the exact degree of sophistication with which his religious ideas are expressed is less important than the way in which these ideas relate to his work as a whole. It seems at first incongruous to read in a work on 'the Customs of this Century', 'The whole of time is but an instant compared with the permanency of God, who is eternal; the whole of space is a mere dot, an insubstantial atom, compared with His immensity' (xvi. 47); yet such comments hint at a general plan behind the work. The metaphysical ground-bass gives greater meaning to La Bruyère's strictures on the vices and follies of his contemporaries, their pursuit of toys and vanities. This is clear at the end of the chapter on Fashion ('De la Mode'), with its condemnation not only of fashion in dress, but of the mania for collecting, the passion for handsome houses and rare belongings, the affectation of piety, and many other 'frivolities:

> Days, months, years sink down and are lost, never to return, in the abyss of time; time itself will be destroyed; it is but a point in the vastness of eternity and will be obliterated. There are some slight and frivolous circumstances of temporal existence which are not lasting and which I call fashions: greatness, favour, riches, power, authority, independence, pleasure, delights, luxuries. What will become of these fashions when time itself has disappeared? Virtue alone, so much out of fashion, transcends time. (xiii. 31)

Therefore I believe that the frequent criticisms of La Bruyère's work on the grounds of its formal untidiness[23] are unfair. It is arguably a unity, not only in the sense that it is stylistically all of a piece and that *pensées* and *caractères* combine to reflect the author's sombre views on life, but also by virtue of the fact that temporal and eternal, timeless virtues and the fleeting pursuit of vanities, are shown to be the opposite but related poles of human existence.

In 1701, the anonymous author of an article entitled 'Sentimens critiques sur les Caracteres de Mr. de la Bruyère'[24] claimed to have come across more than thirty imitations of that work and concluded that the Republic of Letters was inundated with 'characters'. This process of imitation continued throughout the century, up to Mme de Genlis' *Le Petit La Bruyère* of 1799. Most of these works offer the reader that informal mixture of reflections and 'characters' already noted in La Bruyère,[25] although few of the authors achieve anything like the unity of their model or the concrete precision of character-writing to be found in it. Often the 'character' is subordinated to the *maxime*, merely adding a little seasoning to a succession of more or less abstract thoughts.[26] The writers who come closest to La Bruyère, as far as general layout and proportions are concerned, are J. P. de Varennes (*Les Hommes*, 1712) and Sénac de Meilhans (*Considérations sur l'Esprit et les Mœurs*, 1787).

We have seen that portrait and 'character' often merge in La Bruyère. In one of his imitators, they are kept quite distinct from each other and perform different, although complementary, functions. The work in question is P. J. Brillon's *Portraits serieux, galands et critiques* of 1696. Here the 'portraits critiques' are 'characters' of vices and the 'portraits serieux et galands' for the most part idealized pictures of actual people.[27] The 'portraits critiques' are forty-six in number, twenty-four men and twenty-two women. Most are given the sort of names encountered in La Bruyère's *Caractères*, although a few are merely described as types ('Portrait d'une femme avare, d'une Coquette', and so on). The writing is terse and businesslike, although not marked by much concrete detail. Even in the case of the Fop (*Le Fat*), the author is more interested in the essence than the appearance: 'Let us leave the externals in order to move on to an examination of Myrille's inner being . . .' (p. 180). This is very different from the English 'characters' of the Dandy, or, indeed, from La Bruyère's Iphis (xiii. 14).

Brillon's *Portraits* show, as well as any single work could, one basic difference between French and English styles of character-writing. In France, the desire for constraint and decorum rules out any except the most muted and unobtrusive witty or rhetorical devices and embellishments, while the same regard for decorum, combined with a growing desire to analyse the inner self, encourages the author to limit the amount of physical detail provided.

The only exception in this work is Brillon's 'character' of an Old Man ('Portrait d'un Vieillard fâcheux'), which contains details of physical decay which seem to go well beyond those limits of propriety normally observed in seventeenth- and eighteenth-century French character-writing. The only reason which I can think of to explain this—unless Brillon had personally been annoyed by just such a *vieillard fâcheux*—is that he feels secure in following a long tradition of vilifying the old which goes back to classical times and carries seals of approval from Aristotle and Horace. (See below, chapter 7(ii).)

Where Brillon covers a wide range of types, some of the minor character-books show a high degree of specialization. For instance, Claude Boyer's *Caractères des Prédicateurs* (1695) is a commentary in verse on the art of preaching, illustrated by short 'characters', while Mme de Genlis' *Le Petit La Bruyère* is written entirely for and about the young, a part of her general concern for education. The anonymous *Caractères du faux et du veritable Amour* of 1716 is restricted to various aspects of the battle between the sexes as fought out in French *salon* society. Again, the style is somewhat abstract and the intention seems more didactic than in the majority of character-writers to date.[28]

The best of the works inspired by La Bruyère is, by general consent, the *Essai sur quelques Caractères* by Luc de Clapiers, Marquis de Vauvenargues (1715–47). It consists of sixty prose 'characters', was probably written in 1746, and was published posthumously.[29] In his Preface, Vauvenargues acknowledges La Bruyère and Theophrastus as his masters, but in terms which should put us on our guard against merely seeking parallels and borrowings. Both writers have imperfections, says Vauvenargues: La Bruyère can be too polished, Theophrastus abrupt and lacking in variety.

Both, however, strive to imitate nature and to portray the customs of their respective centuries.

One obvious similarity to Theophrastus is a formal one, in that Vauvenargues' book is a simple succession of 'characters' without any linking passages of reflection. This, as we have seen, was unusual in French character-writing, although common enough in England throughout the seventeenth century. As far as the manner of writing is concerned, the links are clearest whenever Vauvenargues builds up his 'character' by relating typical words, actions, and anecdotes without explicitly commenting on motives. The account of Thersite, a cowardly and sycophantic army officer, consists of such a series of characteristic actions, laconically described. The following juxtaposition clearly shows the similarity of approach:

Vauvenargues	*Theophrastus*
If he is in the presence of Duke Eugene when the latter is taking off his boots, Thersite goes as if to hand him his shoes; but as he notices that there are many people present besides himself, he lets a valet take the shoes and blushes as he rises.[30]	Then he will tell the company to keep silent while the great man is speaking. . . . In the theatre, he will take the cushions from the slave, and himself arrange them on his patron's seat.

The close of the Sluggish Man (*l'Homme pesant*) is likewise truly Theophrastan without being in any way an imitation: 'When he returns home, he is told that the man [with whom he had made a business appointment] waited a long time for him and finally went away. He replies that there is no great harm done and orders supper' (p. 183).

What Vauvenargues learnt from La Bruyère was the power of precise psychological diagnosis and analysis to augment the straightforward Theophrastan revelation of character through word and deed. Here is Varus, the Liberal Man:

If he has money to give to a man who is . . . poor and of humble station, Varus' sole fear is of making a present to this poor wretch in a manner that would make him aware of his condition. He embraces him, he presses his hands, he excuses in some degree his own benefaction . . . (pp. 184 f.)

An unexpected feature of the *Essai* is the number of pieces which have an unmistakably personal reference. These pieces are not self-portraits in the seventeenth-century manner, but true 'characters' into which Vauvenargues has introduced elements from his own life, suitably camouflaged. 'Clazomène or Unhappy Virtue' (pp. 147 f.) is the most striking example, the picture of a man who 'has experienced all human miseries'. Poor health, poverty, and undeserved snubs have prevented him from realizing his ambitions. In addition to these unmerited ills, he has brought further misfortunes on himself through imprudence (*il a souffert le mal qu'il ne méritait pas, et celui que son imprudence lui a attiré*). Although no reader acquainted with Vauvenargues' short and unhappy life will fail to see parallels here,[31] he has expressed himself in sufficiently general terms to maintain the 'character'. Other pieces which contain subjective elements are the descriptions of Phérécide, Cyrus, and Cléon.[32]

It may be that this strong introspective element in Vauvenargues' character-writing has something to do with the comparatively lonely life into which ill health forced him in his last years (the years in which the 'characters' appear to have been written); by contrast, most French character-books give the impression that the author passed his days in a social whirl. Certainly, Vauvenargues' understandable obsession with his own misfortunes and lost opportunities helps to account for the Stoic element in the *Essai*. The Good or Wise Man, possessed of Stoic calm, had, of course been a common feature of character-books from the early seventeenth century onwards; indeed, he was in danger of becoming a stereotype. Saltonstall writes of the Happy Man: 'Fortune may aflict him, and change his estate, yet he is always the same.' Vauvenargues' depiction of Clazomène seems more deeply felt, because rooted in personal experience. Fortune has indeed, since childhood, afflicted Clazomène/Vauvenargues. The conclusion is less triumphant than Saltonstall's conventional formulation, but more convincing: 'Nevertheless, one should not think that Clazomène would have wished to exchange his misery for the prosperity of weak men. Fortune may render the wisdom of brave men bootless, but it cannot make their courage flinch' (p. 148).

In one of his 'characters', Vauvenargues speaks of 'that mixture of weakness and strength, of grandeur and pettiness, so natural to men' (p. 165). Now we normally expect any given 'character' to exhibit one quality or the other. But a single 'character' by Vauvenargues does, in fact, often show a combination of positive and negative traits. Thus Thyeste is good but naïve and Titus is governed by an impatient disposition which is both good (because it ensures a full and active life) and bad (because projects are left half-finished).[33] Although unusual, this attitude towards character-writing seems perfectly admissible. For, while one can hardly imagine a satisfactory 'character' which was a commingling of several disparate and unrelated traits, a figure whose two ruling characteristics are interrelated or whose dominant humour manifests itself simultaneously for good and ill is surely a fit subject. 'Varus or Liberality' is perhaps the most absorbing example in the *Essai*. The piece begins: 'Varus hates useless display and purposeless abundance; he dresses simply and he goes on foot; he likes order in his affairs and retreats to the countryside in order to live more cheaply' (p. 184). This is not because he is miserly, but because he needs his money for better things; he is a philanthropist (*tendre pour les malheureux . . . bienfaisant envers tous ceux qui souffrent*—ibid.). The author goes on to show how Varus is at pains to relieve hardship without giving offence, but also how he detects and outmanœuvres a sponger (pp. 185 f.). Therefore this is not the expected 'Character of a Generous Man', monochrome and unproblematic, but a demonstration of how true generosity demands tact, discrimination, and a certain wily resourcefulness.

By contrast, Vauvenargues is at his weakest in his depiction of characters such as Phalante and Lipse, whose wickedness is unmixed and unmotivated. Phalante is driven on by an apparently disinterested iniquity: 'He knows neither love, nor fear, nor good faith, nor compassion; he scorns honour as much as virtue . . . crime in itself pleases him; he is an aimless villain' (p. 162). Lipse, the 'Man without Principles', is similar (*capable d'exécuter, sans intérêt et sans malice, les plus grands crimes*—p. 164). Where real wickedness had figured previously in character-writing, there had always been an attempt at motivation, usually by reference to greed, ambition, or irreligiosity. However, Vauvenargues' curious inability to come to terms with evil is an isolated flaw in his book; the *Essai sur quelques Caractères* is a worthy successor—perhaps the only worthy successor in France—to La Bruyère's work.[34]

The most obvious difference between character-writing in France and in England (at least, until the early eighteenth century) is a formal one. English writers in the seventeenth century were largely content to take up Theophrastus's practice of laying a number of 'characters' end to end without connecting links or commentary; the 'characters' *were* the book. La Bruyère, however, saw 'characters' as only part of a sequence of descriptions, aphorisms, and reflections. His successors, with the exception of Vauvenargues, adopted this pattern, the proportion of 'characters' to *pensées* varying considerably from work to work.[35]

Another difference between France and England is that—for historical reasons—the boundary between portrait and 'character' was vaguer in France. The portrait was normally employed in England by historians and polemicists for the unambiguous and clearly identified depiction of a famous person.[36] It is true that terminological distinctions were rarely made ('character' serving as label for both types of description), true also that one can find borderline cases where the apparent 'character' is the camouflaged portrait of a contemporary (see below, chapter 11). But, in general, the distinction between describing a real person and creating the imaginary representative of a type was perfectly obvious. The two genres arose independently of each other and had different traditions behind them.[37] Even Fuller, who combines both types in the one volume (*The Holy State*, 1642), distinguishes clearly between them.

In France, on the other hand, the vogue of the portrait merged into character-writing in the Theophrastan sense. The main ways in which the French 'character' came to resemble the portrait were in its comparatively high degree of individualization and in its tendency to analyse inner states and characteristics. The authors of portraits intended their models to be recognized. If the subject was hidden behind a pseudonym, the qualities and features singled out must make identification possible; if he or she was named, readers would check the description against the actuality. In either case, the complex of features which made up that particular individual had to be present in their essentials, if the portrait was not to fall flat. By contrast, the writer of 'characters' had to build up his picture out of details which could apply to a whole class of people, and avoid motifs which might draw the reader away from contemplation of the type. La Bruyère and his followers had both Theophrastus's 'characters' and the fashionable portrait before them, so that it is not surprising if they veer between the two methods; it has been shown how La Bruyère worked on the borderline between 'character' and portrait and how Vauvenargues combined 'character' and self-portrait. French character-writers had various aims: to entertain, to instruct, to attack vice and folly, to record impressions as objectively as possible, and so on. But their intentions certainly did not include the cultivation of a pure literary genre, whether 'character' or portrait.

The question of external detail as opposed to analysis of inner states seems also to be bound up with the provenance of French character-writing. The portrait, after a brief physical description or tribute to the subject's beauty, had naturally enough concentrated on psychological analysis. The view that the dissection of human passions and motives was one of the subtlest tasks that a writer could undertake must also have been greatly encouraged by the collections of aphorisms and *pensées*. When French writers, for all their admiration of Theophrastus, tend to see him as a little lacking in refinement,[38] one reason will certainly have been his lack of interest in psychological analysis, his apparent determination to make concrete details speak for themselves. I am not, of course, arguing that the best French character-writing lacks concreteness, merely that a 'character' built up almost entirely of physical details and actions without authorial comment is much rarer in France than in England.

But the most far-reaching difference between the two countries concerns the range of the 'characters'. La Bruyère spreads his net wide; he gives us peasants and the bourgeoisie, rich and poor, the snob and the *parvenu*, the great noble and the mob of social climbers and parasites who beset him, together with a host of what, in the broadest sense, could be called 'moral characters': the Heartless Man, the Proud Man, the Optimist, the Pessimist, the Epicure, the Coward, the Hypocrite, and so on. But no one can read a representative selection of French character-books without noticing certain serious limitations. Although the English authors certainly concentrate on London, they record types from country life, the universities, even life at sea; French character-writing, however, hardly leaves Paris at all. La Bruyère's peasants (xi. 128) barely seem to belong to the same race as townspeople, while Brillon (*Le Theophraste Moderne*) devotes only one of twenty-six chapters—seventeen pages out of over five hundred—to the provinces. It is impossible to imagine a French equivalent to Lupton's *London and the Country* (1632).

The social spread is no less limited than the geographical. Apart from La Bruyère's sun-scorched peasants, the working classes are virtually absent from French character-writing. There are no depictions of tradespeople or craftsmen. The bourgeoisie is, on the whole, treated scornfully[39] and much less heed is paid to the professions than in the English character-books. French character-writing is, to an unbalanced and almost unhealthy extent, about an élite, a fashionable and leisured society, in which people reveal their moral and social virtues or failings as they converse, flirt, show off, jockey for position, and so on. We must assume that work gets done somehow, but there seems to be little awareness that a man's work could be a major part of his being or could help to define his place in society and his relationship to his fellows. French character-writing is often shrewd, witty, and elegant—but one occasionally longs for the greater social spread and the more realistic appraisal of work found among the English writers.

3

The Eighteenth Century in England

In the early years of the eighteenth century, the older type of character-writing was not wholly forgotten. There were occasional reprints of seventeenth-century character-books and cases of plagiarism from them.[1] The publication of satirical 'characters' in pamphlet form also continued. While their authors did not descend to simple copying, they still relied very heavily on the stylistic devices of late seventeenth-century polemical character-writing.[2] A few character-books of the old sort continued to appear in the early years of the new century. Thomas Brown's *Legacy for the Ladies* (1705) is such a book and Ned Ward contributed more than one.[3]

But from the second decade onwards, a somewhat different attitude towards character-writing was to manifest itself. The new impetus came from La Bruyère. One early attempt to adapt him to English tastes and interests came with the publication, in 1702, of *The English Theophrastus: or, the Manners of the Age*. In his Preface, the author, Abel Boyer, states that he has compiled his book out of La Bruyère, together with La Rochefoucauld and St. Evremond. However the resultant work is not quite the mixture of *pensées* and *caractères* in translation that one might have expected. Realizing that La Bruyère's 'characters' are 'so calculated for the *Meridian* of *Paris*, that they look very dull and faint when view'd here in London' (A5^{r}), the author has added a number taken over from English sources.[4] The book might thus be expected to have prepared the way for a succession of works resembling La Bruyère in form while taking their material from English life and conditions. But no such works appeared. Instead, La Bruyère's influence is to be found in the periodicals of eighteenth-century England, beginning with the publication of the *Tatler* in 1709 and the *Spectator* in 1711. As is well known, these papers became very popular and were widely imitated throughout the century. Many famous writers were contributors, including Addison, Steele, Swift, Pope,

Gay, Johnson, Goldsmith, and Chesterfield. The *Spectator*, in particular, was regarded with reverence. These coffee-house journals included essays on social, moral, philosophical, and cultural topics, satires, visions, stories, reports of actual occurrences, 'letters to the editor', and, of course, 'characters'.

Admiring references to La Bruyère were common. Budgell paid a graceful tribute to him by including part of the famous 'character' of Menalcas in a paper on absent-mindedness.[5] But not all writers shared Budgell's admiration for that particular example. According to Joseph Warton, writing in the *Adventurer*, La Bruyère's figures are drawn

> with spirit and propriety, without a total departure from nature and resemblance, as sometimes is the case in pretended pictures of life. In a few instances only has he failed, by over-charging his portraits with many ridiculous features that cannot exist together in one subject: as in the character of Menalcas the absent man. . . . [La Bruyère] appears to be a warm admirer of virtue, and a steady promoter of her interest: he was neither ashamed of Christianity, nor afraid to defend it . . . he disdained to sacrifice truth to levity and licentiousness.[6]

The dislike of anything which could be labelled improper, caricatured, or 'unnatural' is clear from this extract, as is the readiness to subordinate character-writing to moral aims.

Theophrastus was translated into English more than once between the 1690s and the 1720s and, in addition, was brought to the attention of English readers through La Bruyère. Theophrastus commanded respect as the inventor of the 'character', as the original Master, but it was La Bruyère who was the more admired and it was emphatically La Bruyère who was taken as a model.[7] What did English writers derive from him? It is worth recalling that each chapter of *Les Caractères ou les Mœurs de ce Siècle* contains a wide variety of loosely related items: brief maxims and aphorisms, longer passages of social, political, historical, or philosophical reflection, short anecdotes, and 'characters'. Such a diffuse and leisurely sequence was obviously of little use to essayists operating within rigid limitations of space, but they were quick to see that La Bruyère's employment of one or more 'characters' to illustrate an abstract theme in a concrete way could be adapted and modified to suit the demands of journalism. Where La Bruyère devotes a chapter to such general topics as 'Women' or 'Worldly Goods', his

English followers devote a paper to the Flirt or the Parvenu. In the *Tatler*, the *Spectator*, and all their imitators, we find essay after essay in which musings on a particular theme are followed by one or more 'characters'. Whether the general reflections owe more to the longer passages of speculation or philosophizing in La Bruyère or to the century-old tradition of essay-writing in England is impossible to determine, but the way in which essay and 'character' are combined was certainly suggested by the French author.[8]

There was a more general way in which La Bruyère must have influenced or encouraged English writers: by the end of the seventeenth century, as we have seen, the 'character' had reached something of a dead end in England. La Bruyère demonstrated how it could reflect the 'customs of a century' in a less restricted way than in the polemical pamphlets and broadsheets, how it could show the contemporary forms taken by perennial human qualities and attitudes rather than merely reflecting the sectarian quarrels of a particular decade. Moreover, the unfussy elegance of his style would have enhanced his appeal to a generation of writers reacting against 'false wit' and 'thick sown' metaphors. Henry Gally, in 1725, condemns the seventeenth-century witty manner as going against the true nature of character-writing, and comments on the Overbury collection:

> . . . nothing can possibly be more contrary to the Nature of *Characteristic-Writings*, than the corrupted Taste which prevail'd in the Age. A continued Affectation of far-fetch'd and quaint Simile's, which runs thro' almost all these Characters, makes 'em appear like so many Pieces of mere Grotesque . . .[9]

As an example of the most straightforward type of paper which uses a single 'character' to illustrate the central point, we may take Addison's celebrated portrayal of a gloomy Puritan (*Spectator*, No. 494). Addison begins with reflections on the misguided identification of religiosity with gloom and proceeds to the 'character' of Sombrius:

> About an Age ago it was the Fashion in *England*, for every one that would be thought religious, to throw as much Sanctity as possible into his Face, and in particular to abstain from all Appearances of Mirth and Pleasantry, which were looked upon as the Marks of a Carnal Mind. The Saint was of a sorrowfull Countenance, and generally eaten up with Spleen and Melancholly. . . .

Sombrius is one of these Sons of Sorrow. He thinks himself obliged in Duty to be sad and disconsolate. He looks on a sudden Fit of Laughter, as a Breach of his Baptismal Vow. An innocent Jest startles him like Blasphemy. Tell him of one who is advanced to a Title of Honour, he lifts up his Hands and Eyes; describe a Publick Ceremony, he shakes his Head; show him a gay Equipage, he blesses himself. All the little Ornaments of Life are Pomps and Vanities. Mirth is wanton, and Wit prophane. He is scandalized at Youth for being lively, and at Childhood for being playful. He sits at a Christening, or a Marriage-Feast, as at a Funeral; sighs at the Conclusion of a merry Story; and grows devout when the Rest of the Company grow pleasant. After all, *Sombrius* is a religious Man, and would have behaved himself very properly, had he lived when Christianity was under a general Persecution.

The point illustrated by Sombrius is then summed up and reinforced by some concluding reflections:

In a word, the true Spirit of Religion cheers, as well as composes, the Soul: it banishes indeed all Levity of Behaviour, all vicious and dissolute Mirth, but in exchange fills the Mind with a perpetual Serenity, uninterrupted Chearfulness, and an habitual Inclination to please others, as well as to be pleased in it self.[10]

The 'character' is the relish in the sandwich, the entertainment between two slices of instruction.

Not all papers show such an exact balance, but provided that the relationship between the two parts is a truly complementary one—provided, that is, that the 'character' gives a lively illustration of a point already formulated in more abstract terms—the exact proportions do not greatly matter. The effect is less than satisfactory if the 'character' becomes submerged beneath reflection or entangled with it. An example of this occurs in the *Spectator* (No. 151), where Steele seems uncertain whether he is simply animadverting on hedonism or giving the 'character' of a Man of Pleasure. At one juncture, he seems to realize this: 'But to return more directly to my Man of Wit and Pleasure . . .'.

Where 'character' and reflection are well combined, the reader seems to get the best of two worlds. An essay may present a wide-ranging argument but can easily become bloodless; the 'character' is naturally more vivid. With the best intentions in the world, the reader can tire of moralizing sentiments (and it must be remembered that these periodicals were not intended for divines and philosophers). The point can best be illustrated by Dr

Johnson's ventures into this type of writing. He clearly enjoyed musing on grave moral topics yet, aware of the role of such periodical literature and perhaps with the lighter touch of the *Tatler* and *Spectator* in his mind, used the 'character' to develop and illustrate his moral argument in an entertaining way. A marked stylistic contrast can sometimes be observed between the opening reflections and the 'character'. From the *Rambler*:

> Peevishness, when it has been so far indulged, as to outrun the motions of the will, and discover itself without premeditation, is a species of depravity in the highest degree disgusting and offensive, because no rectitude of intention nor softness of address can ensure a moment's exemption from affront and indignity. . . . [Peevishness] is frequently one of the attendants on the prosperous, and is employed by insolence in exacting homage, or by tyranny in harrassing subjection. It is the offspring of idleness or pride; of idleness anxious for trifles; or pride unwilling to endure the least obstruction of her wishes. . . .
>
> If Tetrica takes the air, she is offended with the heat or cold, the glare of the sun, or the gloom of the clouds; if she makes a visit, the room in which she is to be received, is too light, or too dark, or furnished with something which she cannot see without aversion. Her tea is never of the right sort; the figures on the *China* give her disgust. Where there are children, she hates the gabble of brats; where there are none, she cannot bear a place without some cheerfulness and rattle . . .[11]

The commonest form in which 'characters' are encountered in the eighteenth-century periodicals is in contrasting pairs. The attractions of such a device are evident. A virtue and its corresponding vice can be opposed to each other, as when Addison illustrates his remarks on the fatal attractiveness of the showy and superficial with two 'characters', one of a woman who is content with a modest and retiring existence, the other of a fashionable lady of the town who spends her life 'in a perpetual Motion of Body, and Restlessness of Thought' (*Spectator*, No. 15). Or an author may represent two extremes in a pair of 'characters', in order to point to the golden mean, as when Lovibond sets off the 'character' of a slattern against that of an excessively scrupulous woman.[12]

There is more searching use of a contrasting pair of 'characters' in one of Steele's contributions to the *Spectator* (No. 75). He begins by musing on the many false notions of what constitutes a true gentleman and then gives two short 'characters':

> *Vocifer* passes for a Fine Gentleman. He is Loud, Haughty, Gentle, Soft, Lewd, and Obsequious by turns, just as a little Understanding and great Impudence prompt him at the present Moment. He passes among the Silly Part of our Women for a Man of Wit, because he is generally in Doubt. He Contradicts with a Shrug, and confutes with a certain Sufficiency, in professing such or such a Thing is above his Capacity. What makes his Character the pleasanter is, that he is a professed Deluder of Women; and because the empty Coxcomb has no regard to any thing that is of it self Sacred and Inviolable, I have heard an unmarried Lady of Fortune say, it is Pity so fine a Gentleman as *Vocifer* is so great an Atheist. . . .
>
> I hardly have observed any one fill his several Duties of Life better than *Ignotus*. . . . A firm and unshaken Expectation of another Life, makes him become this; Humanity and good Nature, fortified by the Sense of Virtue, has the same Effect upon him, as the Neglect of all Goodness has upon many others. . . .

These 'characters' do not merely illustrate the preceding argument but continue it and expand its scope, enabling Steele to conclude his paper with the general contention that true gentility is always combined with religion and morality.

The use of several short 'characters' in a single essay is somewhat less common. The dangers of such a device are clear from the hundred and forty-fourth issue of the *Spectator*, in which Steele follows up some general observations on beauty with seven 'characters', each displaying a different aspect of feminine beauty. These illustrations are of necessity so brief as to be cursory. Dr Johnson's club of 'Virtuosi'—that is, pseudo-scientific collectors of antiques and curiosities—is more successful, since each 'character' illustrates one manifestation of this ruling passion, so that the whole comes to constitute the sum of all that the bluff common sense of the eighteenth century found ridiculous in the Virtuoso (*Rambler*, No. 177). Thus, one collects only blackletter books, another copper coins, another original editions of old ballads. (For a discussion of the hostility towards Virtuosi and Antiquaries, see below, chapter 7(ii).)

Many writers use the convenient fiction of a club or society to justify a group of 'characters'. The most celebrated instance is the club of men who form the editorial committee of the *Spectator*. Of course, these descriptions are much more than short 'characters'. Normally, the person forming the subject of a 'character' is described and, once described, is finished with. However the men portrayed by Steele in the second number of the *Spectator* will continue to play a part in subsequent issues; these character-sketches have a function similar to that of a novelist's description of a figure on his first appearance within the novel. (This is particularly noticeable in the cases of Sir Roger and Will Honeycomb.) Other writers occasionally use the fiction of a visit to the Pump Room in a spa as excuse for a series of 'characters'.[13]

'Characters' had hitherto nearly always been presented in the third person, but in the eighteenth century we find many written in the first person. A common device is the fictitious 'letter to the editor'—from a Hypochondriac (*Spectator*, No. 25), a Blood (*Adventurer*, No. 98), a Virtuoso (*Rambler*, No. 82), and so on. A natural extension of this is to allow the fictitious person to depict himself through his diary, as in this extract from Johnson's lazy Don (*Idler*, No. 33):

Monday, Eleven. Went down into my cellar. *Mem*. My *Mountain* will be fit to drink in a month's time. *N.B.* To remove the five-year-old port into the new bin on the left hand.

Ditto, Twelve. Mended a pen. Looked at my weather-glass again. Quicksilver very low. Shaved. Barber's hand shakes.

Ditto, One. Dined alone in my room on a soal. *N.B.* The shrimp-sauce not so good as Mr. *H.* of *Peterhouse* and I used to eat in *London* last winter, at the *Mitre* in *Fleet-street*. Sat down to a pint of *Madeira*. Mr. *H.* surprised me over it. We finished two bottles of port together, and were very cheerful. *Mem.* To dine with Mr. *H.* at *Peterhouse* next *Wednesday*. One of the dishes a leg of pork and peas, by my desire.

Ditto, Six. Newspaper in the common room.

Ditto, Seven. Returned to my room. Made a tiff of warm punch, and to bed before nine; did not fall asleep till ten, a young fellow-commoner being very noisy over my head.

Tuesday, Nine. Rose squeamish.[14]

The periodicals always sought to combine entertainment with instruction. Often, as we have seen, the 'character' is used to provide light relief after a page or so of earnest moralizing. It is also noteworthy that a serious lesson will often be extracted from an apparently quite light-hearted 'character'. An example is Will Wimble, the obliging Man, who

furnishes the whole Country with Angle-Rods. . . . He carries a Tulip-Root in his Pocket from one [Gentleman] to another, or exchanges a Puppy between a couple of Friends that live perhaps in the opposite Sides of the County. *Will.* is a particular Favourite of all the young Heirs, whom he frequently obliges with a Net that he has weaved . . . (*Spectator*, No. 108)

On hearing of him, Mr Spectator exhibits all the innocent delight of a collector who has just come across a curiosity: 'Odd and uncommon Characters are the Game that I look for, and most delight in.' All harmless enough; yet, before long, Addison is musing priggishly on the waste of talent, the dedication of so much good will and industry to trifles: 'The same Temper of Mind and Application to Affairs might have recommended him to the publick Esteem, and have raised his Fortune in another Station of Life.' Will should have served his country instead of making fishing-rods. Somewhat similar is Dr Johnson's 'character' of the country lady whose energies are exclusively devoted to cooking, preserving, and bottling. Soon he is reflecting gloomily: 'Such are the tasks . . . in which that time is passing away which never shall return' (*Rambler*, No. 51). What has preceded—the drying of flowers and the making of cheesecake—will hardly have prepared the reader for that austere meditation.

The types most often depicted give us some idea of the main preoccupations of these writers. The commonest ideal figures encountered are the Merchant, the Country Squire, the just Magistrate, the Philanthropist, and the pious Clergyman (the main recurring female types are discussed below). Although there are a number of harmless eccentrics (for example, the inveterate Bargain-hunter), the prevailing attitude is, as we have seen, a serious one and concentrates very much on man in society. 'Characters' of virtues and vices in the seventeenth-century sense are extremely rare; for instance, we no longer encounter the Proud Man, rather the Snob, the Parvenu, or the insolent Country Squire. With Hall's 'characters' of vices, it had often been impossible to determine the exact social rank or setting; it was the moral quality that chiefly interested him, in whatever guise or station it might appear. One could even say, with no more than slight exaggeration, that moral 'characters' and precisely defined social 'characters' formed two independent categories in the seventeenth century. But now the virtues and vices are exemplified in clearly defined social types and are so depicted as to demonstrate their importance, for good or ill, within their particular social sphere. Even when Addison describes the Envious Man (*Spectator*, No. 19), it is wholly from a social and psychological point of view—the fault of envy divorced from the notion of sin. There is a very marked contrast to Hall's 'character' of the Envious Man, with its repeated insistence on ingratitude towards God. This movement away from the purely moral—let alone the theological—towards the social brings us to a central question regarding the 'characters' in the eighteenth-century periodicals.

Dr Johnson writing on Addison in *The Lives of the English Poets*, sees the *Tatler* and *Spectator* as primarily concerned with social education and refinement:

> to teach the minuter decencies and inferior duties, to regulate the practice of daily conversation, to correct those depravities which are rather ridiculous than criminal . . . to shew when to speak, or to be silent; how to refuse, or how to comply. We had many books to teach us our more important duties . . . but an *Arbiter elegantiarum*, a judge of propriety, was yet wanting . . .[15]

This might, at first view, seem a restricted notion, but there is no doubt that many 'characters' point out what it is that society finds pleasing or displeasing about a certain type, and stop there. Steele's picture of a Gentleman (*Tatler*, No. 21) concentrates on good breeding, the art of not giving offence, the faculty of judgement that enables a man to be agreeable in any company, and so on (see also *Tatler*, No. 45). It is as if the author were deliberately excluding wider moral considerations (which could, after all, quite properly figure in the definition of a Gentleman). Addison's reaction to the bluff Country Squire, who thinks he is frank when he is merely uncouth, again seems to bear out Johnson's point: 'This fellow's behaviour made me reflect on the usefulness of complaisance, to make all conversation agreeable. This, though in itself it be scarce reckoned in the number of moral virtues, is that which gives a lustre to every talent a man can be possest of' (*Guardian*, No. 162).

However, one should not regard the eighteenth-century journals merely as guides to 'propriety'. The ideal most often implied by the *Tatler*, the *Spectator*, and the rest goes beyond the examples just mentioned and views religion, practical morality, reason, sociability, and refinement of manners as a connected whole. We have already encountered a 'character' by Steele in which the fulfilment of social obligations is explicitly linked with virtue and religion (see above, p. 69). Even when the stress is almost exclusively on practical matters, a basis of solid moral worth is often presupposed. Steele portrays Sir Harry Lizard as punctilious in the payment of debts, as a good employer, and as complete master of all matters necessary to the running of an estate (*Guardian*, No. 6). Although there is little talk of virtue, it is clear that Sir Harry is a good man, not only a successful and practical one. His efficient and meticulous estate-management *is* his virtue. Similarly, the ideal woman always combines practical philanthropy and the orderly running of her home with virtue and religion (see below, p. 74).

The hope is that a man's obligations to himself, to society, and to God will coincide. However, when the enjoyment of society's approval is plainly incompatible with moral rectitude, it is 'public applause' that must be sacrificed (*Spectator*, No. 122). Steele's 'character' of a Pleasant Fellow (*Spectator*, No. 462) shows how easily people can be taken in by airs and graces divorced from morality: 'A very pleasant Fellow shall turn your good Name to a Jest, make your Character contemptible, debauch your Wife or Daughter, and yet be receiv'd by the rest of the World with Welcome where-ever he appears.' A similar gulf between a socially accepted mode of conduct and true morality inspired Chesterfield's portrayal of the Man of Honour, who can seduce women and bilk tradesmen, but may not cheat at cards (*The World*, 1753, No. 49). Such examinations, scattered and piecemeal though they may be, of the relationship between what is sanctioned by opinion and what is truly moral show that these writers sometimes go deeper than the passage quoted from Dr Johnson's essay on Addison might imply.

However, the morality expressed in these papers is anything but severe. A moderate hedonism is seen as lawful and desirable, provided that it enjoys the approval of philosophy and religion (*Spectator*, No. 224). The resigned or despairing flight from the world that is writ large in many seventeenth-century 'characters' of the Wise Man is foreign to the eighteenth-century temperament, at least as manifested in its periodical literature. With the one reservation just made, the social hierarchy and the status quo are accepted, and the main concern is to show how faults and vices, if uncorrected, can disturb the rightful order of things.

Contentment with one's station in life is a constant theme. The merchant or tradesman who neglects his business in order to ape the life of fashion is a common object of scorn. (The merchant who, by industry and thrift, makes his fortune, buys an estate, and manages it skilfully is another matter: see chapter 7.) There are frequent strictures on the improper use of patronage or power[16] and on the wasteful effects of idleness and pretentiousness. One's immediate concerns—as landowner, merchant, shopkeeper, or whatever— were what mattered; to forget these out of a passion for world politics was always seen as absurd. Thus Addison's Political Upholsterer 'had a wife and several children; but was much more inquisitive to know what passed in Poland than in his own family' (*Tatler*, No. 155). Mrs Jellyby has many eighteenth-century predecessors.[17]

It may be added that an assumption of broad agreement on moral and social values must have encouraged character-writing, which thrives on a consensus of opinion.[18] The coffee-house periodicals are chiefly addressed to, and concerned with, the comfortably-off middle classes, and to a lesser extent with the country gentry and minor aristocracy. Although the impression is of a masculine world, there are many 'characters' of women.

The Flirt or 'Jilt' is a common subject and is always treated with great harshness. Steele writes of 'a sect among women of all others the most mischievous, and makes the greatest havoc and disorder in society', 'dangerous Animals' (*Tatler*, No. 126 and *Spectator*, No. 187). It is instructive to contrast these judgements with his treatment—which is almost a vindication—of the Rake:

> A Rake is a man always to be pitied; and, if he lives, is one day certainly reclaimed; for his faults proceed not from choice or inclination, but from strong passions and appetites, which are in youth too violent for the curb of reason, good sense, good manners, and good nature . . . (*Tatler*, No. 27)

Another favourite target is the idle Society Lady, who divides her time between the dressing-table, the playhouse, the fashionable salon, the ballroom, and the card-table, whose greatest concerns are what dress to wear or whether Mr Froth deliberately squeezed her hand at the opera (*Spectator*, No. 323 and *Rambler*, No. 191).

If the Coquette was censured, so was the Prude (*Tatler*, No. 126). Scorn was poured on empty-headed beauties, but the Bluestocking did not escape either. Women had to walk a tightrope if they were to please. They must possess beauty, but not flaunt or exploit it; they must be accomplished, but not in any showy way and certainly not in fields where they might appear to pose a threat to men.[19] They must be guided by religion, but again without ostentation.[20] It is small wonder that the pictures of the Ideal Woman which we find scattered about these periodicals are rather colourless. She is gifted, but prefers to concentrate her energies on running her home and estate with 'exact economy' (*Tatler*, No. 42). The gentle Fidelia (*Spectator*, No. 449) plays the lute and the spinet to perfection, but never shows off in company, confining herself to diverting her old father as he sits in his easy-chair.[21] It is unusual to find an author who genuinely prizes learning in women and wishes to encourage it, as does Charles Povey, whose 'character' of a Virtuous Woman includes praise of her translations from the French and Latin and of her own literary compositions. The piece actually has more to say of her accomplishments than of her virtue.[22]

I have mentioned the movement in the eighteenth century towards a more restrained and sober manner of character-writing. That it is in part attributable to the authors' didactic intentions is clear enough from the last issue of the *Rambler* (No. 208), where Johnson says that he has aimed at truth to life and has avoided caricature, because violent exaggeration would make it impossible for the reader to recognize a living type. In that case, we would not be reformed, but merely amused.

It must be stressed, however, that the moralizing intentions seldom come to dominate to a degree that would threaten the 'character' as a work of art. That a light touch is perfectly compatible with seriousness is demonstrated by Addison's picture of Sombrius and Johnson's of Tetrica (see above, pp. 67 and 68). Nevertheless, some sort of didactic aim lies behind virtually all the character-writing in the eighteenth-century periodicals. There is hardly any of that apparently pure and disinterested play of wit that provoked many of the seventeenth-century 'characters'. Given this, it is not surprising that the dividing line between 'characters' in the periodical essays and those in treatises and sermons is no longer a clear one.[23] Illustrative 'characters' are much commoner in eighteenth-century sermons than in those of the seventeenth, doubtless because the 'character' was by now so firmly associated with a desire to improve the reader.

Swift's sermon 'On Brotherly Love', dating from 1717, may serve as a starting-point, for it provides an exact parallel to the use of pairs of 'characters' in the coffee-house periodicals. The sermon is chiefly devoted to the *lack* of brotherly love in Swift's day, and, in the course of it, he speaks of squabbles between religious factions and the misuse of the word 'moderation': 'Therefore, to set you right in this matter, I will lay before you the character of a truly moderate man; and then I will give you the description of such a one as falsely pretendeth to that title.'[24] There follow the 'characters' of a truly moderate man and of one termed 'moderate' in the new, false meaning of that word: one to whom religion is a matter of indifference. The 'characters' are a stage in Swift's argument, just as a contrasting pair might illustrate the point of an essay in the *Spectator*.[25]

'Characters' in sermons, being chiefly concerned with states of soul, tend towards the abstract. The concrete details of behaviour which vivify so much English character-writing seem at best inessential to the preacher. Indeed, where such details help to define a man's profession, rank, or position in society, they might even be undesirable in a sermon concerned with man's position in relation to his God rather than his fellow-men. The three 'characters' in John Tillotson's sermon on 'Knowledge and Practice necessary in Religion' illustrate this point. Tillotson wishes to show three ways in which religious knowledge and religious practice can diverge. His examples are the speculative, the formal, and the hypocritical types of Christian. The last is described as one who masters and understands his religion in order to 'counterfeit it handsomely', who 'puts on the garb of it' for advantage (i. 417). This is precisely the point at which the character-writer would pause to show us the Hypocrite giving alms ostentatiously, spoiling others' pleasures by frowning on worldly 'frivolities', impressing his hearers with quotations from the Scriptures, and so on. But Tillotson has said enough to make his point and hurries on to his application. The 'character' has become abstract and functional.[26] When, rarely, exact and concrete touches are included, the effect is refreshing. Thus Robert South's Puritan curries favour among 'thriving seditious tradesmen, and groaning, ignorant, but rich widows', while his Hypocrite 'steps forth with a *Friday*-look and a *Lenten* face'.[27]

The most famous examples of 'characters' used to illustrate a moral treatise occur in the works of William Law. In his *Practical Treatise upon Christian Perfection* (1726), he gives a number of short 'characters' in support of his general point that even apparently trivial vanities can make a man dead to religion (chapter 9). Here the 'characters' enliven Law's abstract argument; in spirit and method, he is nearer to South than to Tillotson:

'Tis acknowledged by all, that a Life of *Intemperance* and *Debauchery* makes us dead and senseless of Religion, and incapable of receiving its Truths: But then it is not enough considered, that the *Vanity* of the Mind and Understanding busied in *Trifles*, an *impertinent Course* of Life, will as certainly produce the *same Effect*. . . .

[The *Virtuoso's*] Soul is extended to all the *Curiosities* in the World, and thinks all Time to be lost, that is not spent in the Search of *Shells*, *Urns*, *Inscriptions*, and *broken Pieces* of *Pavements*. . . .

[Patronus] never comes to the *Sacrament*, but will go forty Miles to see a *fine Altar-piece*. He goes to Church when there is a *new Tune* to be heard, but never had any more serious Thoughts about *Salvation*, than about *Flying*.[28]

The link with periodical character-writing is unmistakable. The general reflections lead straight into a series of 'characters', each of which illustrates one aspect of Law's theme. They are given formalized, classical or pseudo-classical names as in La Bruyère and his English admirers. The concrete presentation of character coming immediately after an austerely generalized and abstract formulation anticipates with odd precision Dr Johnson's practice in the *Rambler* and the *Idler*.

In Law's *Serious Call to a Devout and Holy Life* (1728) we find about two dozen 'characters' of varying length, again all named, after the manner of La Bruyère. Many of these became sufficiently famous to be published singly or in collections independently of their original context. Calidus, the Man of Business, who 'would say grace if he had time' and always prays in stormy weather because he has a cargo at sea (chapter 4) is justly celebrated, as is Flatus, the changeable and vain Dilettante (chapter 12). Flatus turns from dandyism, gaming, and the fashionable life first to hunting, then to being a patron of architecture, thence ('for one whole year') to study and finally to the simple life and jogging: 'But here a new project comes in to his relief. He is now living upon *herbs*, and running about the country, to get himself into as *good wind* as any *running-footman* in the kingdom.'[29] The zest and humour of such descriptions may surprise us when we recall the title and purpose of the work,[30] and in fact Law feels it necessary to explain and justify his practice: 'I have been thus circumstantial, in so many foolish particulars of this kind of life, because I hope, that every particular folly that you see here, will naturally turn itself into an argument, for the wisdom and happiness of a religious life.'[31]

Where any of the contemporary essayists would have been proud of such 'foolish particulars', Law distrusts his own ebullience and is suspicious of anything that might look like mere entertainment.

The great majority of seventeenth-century 'characters' had been written in prose. There were exceptions—such as stereotyped pictures of the Happy Man—and there were even one or two character-books composed entirely in verse, such as Thomas Jordan's *Pictures of Passions, Fancies, & Affectations* of 1641. But it would certainly appear that most writers felt prose to be the more appropriate vehicle. In Jeremiah Wells's *Poems upon divers Occasions* (1667), the sole prose piece is also the only 'character', while *Floskulum Poeticum* by P. K. (1684) has a group of prose 'characters' appended to a book of verse. From the turn of the century onwards, however, verse-characters came to take on more importance. At first they tended to be very pedestrian;[32] it was Pope who took up the form, refined it, and turned it into something elegant and expressive.[33]

Pope is clearly indebted to Roman verse-satire and its many imitations in England, but also in a less direct and obvious way to La Bruyère and the 'characters' in the early eighteenth-century periodicals. The link with Horace is unmistakable in the *Epistle to Dr Arbuthnot* of 1735.[34] At the same time, it is plausible that Pope wished to show that 'characters' could be worked into a sustained poetic argument, that a verse equivalent to the use of illustrative 'characters' in the periodical essays was possible. So, for example, the *Dunciad* contains two brief depictions of Virtuosi, the *Essay on Criticism* sketches of the good and bad Critic, and the *Epistle to Sir William Temple, Lord Cobham* a few short 'characters' to illustrate the notion of the 'ruling passion'. Perhaps Pope also wished to show by how much he could outstrip his predecessors in the composition of verse-characters; certainly only Dryden approaches him, although the thinly veiled portraits in *Absalom and Achitophel* are a different proposition from anything that we find in Pope.

That Pope was drawn to character-writing is not surprising.

> Search, then, the RULING PASSION: There, alone,
> The Wild are constant, and the Cunning known;
> The Fool consistent, and the False sincere;
> Priests, Princes, Women, no dissemblers here.
> This clue once found, unravels all the rest.[35]

However, in talking of his 'characters' we must make one reservation. Pope further weakens the traditional distinction between the imaginary 'character' and the 'portrait' of an actual person, already somewhat blurred in La Bruyère. The lines on the Fop in the *Epistle to Dr Arbuthnot* (1735) read like a true Theophrastan 'character'. They begin with a kind of definition:

> That fop, whose pride affects a patron's name,
> Yet absent, wounds an author's honest fame (lines 291 f.)

and continue with a series of relative clauses listing the subject's misdeeds. The organization is not dissimilar to that of Theophrastus's own 'characters', where the type is first defined, then characterized in a string of sentences, each of which records a typical detail of behaviour. Even if the concluding 'Let Sporus tremble' (1.305) is usually interpreted as a reference to Pope's enemy John, Lord Hervey, the effect of the passage will have been to suggest a type. This impression is strengthened by Pope's general application: his lines apply to 'all such babbling blockheads', of whom Sporus is only the chosen representative. Pope's verse-characters clearly show how the sketch of an actual individual can be generalized to the point where it virtually becomes a 'character'. The Advertisement to the first edition of the *Moral Essays* carries the usual disclaimer that none of the women there described was based on an actual person.[36] This may be true of some figures in the poem, but certainly does not apply to Pope's incomparable picture of the Heartless Beauty, Chloe, who is by general agreement identified with Henrietta, Countess of Suffolk. Yet even if we recognize that this is, theoretically and technically, a 'portrait' in the French sense of the word, the passage works on us like a 'character':

> 'Yet Chloe sure was formed without a spot'—
> Nature in her then erred not, but forgot.
> 'With every pleasing, every prudent part,
> Say, what can Chloe want?'—She wants a heart.
> She speaks, behaves, and acts, just as she ought,
> But never, never reached one generous thought.
> Virtue she finds too painful an endeavour,
> Content to dwell in decencies for ever.
> So very reasonable, so unmoved,
> As never yet to love, or to be loved.

She, while her lover pants upon her breast,
Can mark the figures on an Indian chest;
And when she sees her friend in deep despair,
Observes how much a chintz exceeds mohair!
Forbid it Heaven, a favour or a debt
She e'er should cancel—but she may forget.
Safe is your secret still in Chloe's ear;
But none of Chloe's shall you ever hear.
Of all her dears she never slandered one,
But cares not if a thousand are undone.
Would Chloe know if you're alive or dead?
She bids her footman put it in her head.
Chloe is prudent—would you too, be wise?
Then never break your heart when Chloe dies.[37]

Why is this? Partly because Pope—with what degree of conscious intention it is impossible to determine—has followed orthodox Theophrastan methods in first defining his type ('she wants a heart') and then listing typical actions and manifestations of that ruling characteristic. The exact observations in lines 11–14 correspond to the carefully chosen details in the best prose 'characters'. Furthermore, Pope includes Chloe in a poem on women in general and seeks to show what is typical in her; we do not feel that we have simply read of one heartless woman of his acquaintance, but of a representative of all callous beauties. The formalism of the verse, with its measure and discipline, its ordered and elegant progressions, contributes too.

An occasional bold spirit might venture on a 'character' in tetrameters,[38] but the subsequent history of the verse-character in the eighteenth century is to a very large extent the history of Pope's influence. Richard Savage's poem 'The Gentleman' (*c.*1726) shows how Pope's eulogistic vein could be emulated, but it was understandably the satirical side of his genius that was the greater spur. Vain Beaux and Fashionable Ladies (all with names such as Clarinda, Daphne, or Lavinia) strut across the pages of his imitators. In addition to such satirical 'characters' in the style of Pope, we find a number of verse-characters of Country Gentlemen, pieces praising an existence of rural retreat. Several appeared in the *Gentleman's Magazine*.[39] They are usually written in the first person and evoke a simple life: plain food and dress, unpretentious social pleasures, the contemplation of nature and, through nature, of God. This Christianized version of a Horatian ideal is always set off against the restless life of the town, with its frenetic pursuit of fashion, its playhouses, and its 'high-seasoned *ragouts*'.

Although 'characters' continued to appear in journals up to the end of the eighteenth century, they became less common and less important as a means of illustrating the message of a paper.[40] The reasons for this decline will be discussed in detail in chapter 11. In brief, from the beginning of the nineteenth century onwards, the 'character' moved increasingly into the realm of light entertainment. Before we trace this process, however, we must give some account of the 'character' in German-speaking countries.

4
Germany and Switzerland

Germany was slow to recover culturally from the Thirty Years' War. During the second half of the seventeenth century and for much of the eighteenth, writers tried to make up for lost time to a large extent through the imitation of foreign models. But the generally derivative state of German literature would not in itself account for the wholesale imitation of the *Tatler* and the *Spectator* throughout the eighteenth century. The specific reason was that these papers showed a way of providing the rising middle classes in Germany with material which would be entertaining but—unlike the sensational popular novels of the day—socially and morally 'respectable' and instructive. The German equivalents of the English coffee-house papers were, and still are, called 'moral weeklies' (*moralische Wochenschriften*), for reasons which will presently become obvious. In his authoritative study of these papers (*Die Botschaft der Tugend*, 1968), Wolfgang Martens lists about 150 titles. 'Another moral weekly!' cries the editor of *Der Neue Eidsgenosse* (1750). 'There will soon be so many that we will be able to build mountains out of them or use them to dam the Rhine!'

Switzerland in fact showed the way with *Die Discourse der Mahlern*, published in Zurich from 1721 to 1723 by J. J. Bodmer and J. J. Breitinger. The Germans were quick to follow suit, and the German and Swiss weeklies of the eighteenth century have so much in common—in character-writing as in most other things—that they are treated together in this chapter. However, the many periodicals published in Zurich, Berne, and Basle between the early 1720s and the end of the 1750s have a political flavour of their own.

The first thing that strikes the reader is the intense national pride. An article in *Der Eidsgenoß* (1749) glorifies the Swiss homeland, whose very landscape testifies dramatically to God's might. Who can doubt that His eye rests with particular favour on Switzerland and that her freedom was achieved by virtue of His protection and well-wishing? The founding of the first Swiss confederation is likened to liberation from the yoke of the Pharaohs.[1] The Swiss moral weeklies always combine love of country with love of political freedom:

No one needs to work in order to support courtly show or provide money to pay a royal bodyguard. We need have no fear of death proceeding from a king's wrath, there are no flatterers with their golden chains to lay iron chains on the common people. Every man . . . remains master of his possessions. (*Der Teutsche Bernerische Spectateur*, 1734, No. 2).

Great stress is placed on independence of spirit, simple piety, and traditional regard for republican ideals. Many writers see these values under threat, from too much concern for material possessions, from pretentiousness and ostentation, or from the copying of foreign customs and fashions. This means that many subjects (such as dandyism, living above one's station, the corruption of the German language through French influences) which have moral and social significance for German writers take on political overtones for the Swiss.

The early *moralische Wochenschriften* flourished equally in North Germany (especially Hamburg, with its strong English links) and in Switzerland. Since they were closely associated with Protestantism and the spirit of the Enlightenment, they hardly appeared in Catholic Southern Germany, and in Austria only from the 1760s onwards, as part of a general attempt to import the literary culture of the German Enlightenment into that country. There is no doubt whatever that England provided the main impetus and model for the German and Swiss moral weeklies. As early as 1713, the composer Johann Mattheson began to publish extracts from the *Tatler* and the *Spectator* in translation (*Der Vernünfftler*, Hamburg, 1713–14). Although it was not until 1739 that a complete German translation of the *Spectator* began to appear,[2] the influence of that journal was strong in German-speaking countries long before. Bodmer and Breitinger dedicate *Die Discourse der Mahlern* to the 'exalted Spectator' (*erlauchter Zuschauer*) and readily admit their indebtedness, praising the 'delightful manner' (*ergetzende Manir*) of their model and the combination of entertainment and instruction to be found in it.[3] Another clear indication is the way in which the title was borrowed and adapted: *Der Teutsche Bernerische Spectateur* (1734), *Die Deutsche Zuschauerin* (1748), *Der Leipziger Zuschauer* (1751), *Die Niederrheinische Zuschauerin* (1770), *Der*

Casselsche Zuschauer (1772). Tribute is commonly paid to Addison although more than one editor singles out Steele.[4] *Der Neue Eidsgenosse* and *Der Casselsche Zuschauer* mention both authors.

It is interesting to see how the editor of one of the Swiss papers defines the moral weekly. Since he does not single out the specifically Swiss republican element, presumably taking this for granted under the general heading of 'instruct', his definition applies to the German papers too. He gives six conditions:

1. It should fully deserve the name 'moral'.
2. Although it should not treat its themes superficially, it should aim at a light touch; it is not written for philosophers.
3. It should possess novelty and not serve its readers 'warmed-up cabbage'.
4. It should be written in a 'strong and manly' style; imagination and wit should be disciplined by understanding.
5. It should both entertain and instruct.
6. It should explore all the byways of moral conduct and apply general ethical principles to specific cases.

(*Der Neue Eidsgenosse*, Preface)

All the chief ingredients of the English coffee-house papers reappear in the *moralische Wochenschriften*: essays, 'characters', articles of general interest, fables, poems, visions, 'letters to the editor', short stories and so on. The 'editor' often characterizes himself in the first issue, usually as observer and would-be improver of mankind, sometimes going on to describe an editorial club or panel of contributors in the manner of the Spectator Club. The English and German[5] periodicals have certain fundamental values in common, such as reasonableness, virtue, moderation, and philanthropic activity within a context of solid but unassuming prosperity.[6] Man is viewed as a social being and his actions and qualities are assessed accordingly. Pretence, ostentation, superstition, and bigotry are frowned on. But inevitably, given the different social, political, and cultural conditions, there are differences of stress. In the *moralische Wochenschriften*, religious attitudes, where not Pietistic, tend to be much more directly and obviously linked to the rationalistic views that ran strong in Western Europe at the time than is the case in the English papers, where a middle-of-the-road, Church of England Christianity usually seems to be taken for granted. As for politics, the notion hardly figures in the moral weeklies before about 1770, except in the parochial sense of city affairs. Switzerland is an exception, of course: *Der Helvetische Patriot* (1755–6) gives the 'characters' of a calculating, vote-catching Politician (*Der Politikus*) and of a true Republican,[7] types which would have been unthinkable in the German papers. In Germany, where an apparently national element does appear, it is not political nationalism but praise of a traditional 'old German' way of life, often seen as under threat because of courtly obeisance to foreign fashions and models (see *Der alte Deutsche*, 1730, *passim*). These German papers are more obstinately middle-class in subject-matter and tone than the *Tatler* and *Spectator*.[8] The rising mercantile bourgeoisie was extremely aware of its economic, social, and cultural responsibilities, feeling strongly that the courts—frivolous, amoral, showy, given to aping the French and the Italians—were failing in this respect. The merchant should stick to his class; there is nothing but scorn for him when he tries to imitate the nobility. This is in marked contrast to the English attitude that a prosperous merchant might buy himself an estate and do something useful with it, even teaching the landed aristocracy something in the process.

Another major difference concerns style. Few would deny that the English papers, in the half century that separates the *Tatler* from Johnson's *Idler* and Goldsmith's *Citizen of the World*, maintained an unprecedented standard of journalistic prose. But the Germans had no Addison, no Steele, no Johnson—indeed, nobody of surpassing stature as a prose stylist until Lessing in the 1760s. When the moral weeklies first began to appear in the 1720s, the state of the German language was comparatively primitive: hardly surprising if one recalls that German aristocrats preferred to talk French and that most scholars still favoured Latin for lecturing and serious writing. The moral weeklies were a major educative force in eighteenth-century Germany, and some of them certainly attain a vigorous and confident prose style.[9] But anyone who opens one at random, expecting to find a German equivalent to Addison's English, is bound to be disappointed.

It has seemed worthwhile to say something in general terms about these German periodicals, since they are little known, except to specialists in the field. But our main concern is, of course, with the character-writing. Praise of Theophrastus and La Bruyère or extracts from their writings are not uncommon,[10] but can be misleading, for, although a writer in *Das Reich der Natur und der*

Sitten (1757–62) commends Theophrastus for delineating character through actions (No. 96), most Germans tended towards a moralizing and often abstract style, quite foreign to the Greek.[11] Similarly, although it is true that more than one early journal borrows its terminology from the French (*der Caractere*, *der caractère*), one cannot see very much trace of La Bruyère's direct influence on the actual character-writing.[12] The immediate and obvious models for this, as for most other features of the *moralische Wochenschriften*, are to be found in the English papers.[13] To begin with, there are close formal similarities.

The straightforward passage from general reflections to illustrative 'character', meat and drink to the English essayists, became common procedure among their German imitators:

> For most people, friendship is nothing but a mere way of passing the time. They use it to try to keep at bay the discontent which comes from loneliness. And a constant change of friends protects them against the aversion which a lasting friendship would arouse in them.
>
> Such a friend is Hermippus . . .[14]

Perhaps even more common than such single illustrative 'characters' is the contrasting pair, also a favourite device among the English writers. The contrast may simply be between an ideal and a foolish or sinful aberration (*Der Patriot*, No. 31), or it may be between two equally undesirable extremes, as when Gottsched paints the pictures of a facile Optimist and a neurotically timorous Pessimist, in order to extract a (thoroughly Aristotelian) moral concerning the proper degrees and functions of hope and fear (*Der Biedermann*, 1727–9, No. 74).[15] The hint that a larger group of 'characters' could be used to illustrate several facets of the essayist's theme was also taken up. Several of the Swiss papers (*Bernisches Freytags-Blätlein*, 1722–4; *Der Teutsche Bernerische Spectateur*, 1734; *Der Brachmann*, 1740) favour anything up to ten 'characters' in a single issue. The danger is, of course, that these may become cursory, little more than labels. A better method is adopted in the thirteenth issue of *Der Patriot*, where three slightly more extended 'characters' (of an ambitious Minister of State, a high-living Nobleman, and a rich Malcontent) are made to illustrate that favourite homespun moral of eighteenth-century bourgeois literature: that fame and riches fan discontent.[16] Other methods of presentation clearly derived from the English periodicals are the 'letter to the editor' (in which, for instance, an aggrieved wife describes her jealous husband), the 'character' in the form of an unconsciously revealing self-portrait, or the account of a typical day in the subject's life.[17] In addition to such formal parallels, there are a few cases of near-paraphrase. The 'character' of Herr von Niemandsfreund, a Peevish Man (*Der Patriot*, No. 75) unmistakably echoes Addison's Sombrius:

Der Patriot	*Spectator*, No. 494
All luxuries are follies to him. He laughs at so-called courteous behaviour. All forms of elegance and politeness are foolish antics in his eyes.	All the little Ornaments of Life are Pomps and Vanities. . . . Describe a Publick Ceremony, he shakes his Head; show him a gay Equipage, he blesses himself.

The 'character' of Sombrius seems to have fascinated more than one writer in the moral weeklies, suggesting a model for attacks on the sort of Pietist who embarrassed others by his fanatical observance of outward forms and his dislike of innocent mirth.[18]

However, such direct imitation is not very common; what the German writers sought (and found) in the English coffee-house papers was above all a model which would help them to depict German manners and morals. Certainly there are a very great number of 'characters' in the *moralische Wochenschriften*; O. A. Müller goes so far as to speak of an epidemic.[19]

The stylistic ideal was one of clarity, naturalness, and correct German, free alike from dialect and Baroque rhetoric. Here there is a parallel to the reaction, by Addison, Budgell, and others, against the flamboyant wit of the previous century. The Germans, however, were more urgent in their censure, since fustian and elaborately flowery language lived on in their tongue well into the eighteenth century, in both sacred and secular poetry, in feeble survivals of the Baroque novel of adventure, and on the popular stage. To 'purify' the language became a central concern. Foreign influences, especially French ones, were widely attacked. The virtual equation of a Gallicized German with moral turpitude can strike the modern reader as amusing. However, the resentment ran deep. To pepper your language with French words and expressions signified not only a contempt for your mother tongue, but also for your native culture.[20] In practice, the desire to avoid 'impurities' and verbal extravagance at all costs often led to a somewhat flat and colourless style:

[Ohnsorge] suchet einen Theil der Stoischen Glückseeligkeit zu erlangen. Er verbannt alle Leidenschafften von sich, durch welche er in einige Empfindung könte gesetzet werden. Doch er hat eine falsche Absicht. Deßwegen wendet er unrechte Mittel an. Das gründliche in der Erkänntniß von Dingen fehlet ihm. (*Die mühsame Bemerckerin*, 1737, No. 18).

('Ohnsorge tries to achieve a degree of stoical cheerfulness. He bans all passions which might arouse some feeling in him. But his intention is false. And for that reason he uses false means. He does not see into things thoroughly.' The only foreign word in this passage is the unavoidable *stoisch.*) It may be noted that the 'character' of Ohnsorge comes from a periodical which explicitly states that language is functional and that clarity is its prime aim (see No. 11). When, infrequently, an imaginative simile occurs in one of the moral weeklies, it positively jumps out from its context:

Herr Faulthier is constantly asking 'what was that?', because he never troubles himself to pay attention in the slightest. Words seem to impress themselves on his soul even less than a passing bird impresses itself on a mirror. There are lethargic souls, but Herr Faulthier is totally inactive. (*Das Reich der Natur und der Sitten*, No. 13)

We have already noted a certain abstract quality in German character-writing. One might expect ideal types to be described in such a way, but the writers in the moral weeklies often seem unable to escape from abstraction even in their satirical and hostile 'characters':

Critias is entirely dedicated to the betterment of his understanding. He devotes all his care to this duty. He takes pains to sharpen his intellect daily. But these concerns make him forget domestic matters. He is always thinking of truth and not of his wife and children. He rejoices when he has come to a more exact understanding of a truth, but the tears of his wife, who sees the disorder in his business affairs, do not worry him. His affairs sink from day to day into yet greater disorder.[21]

Thematically, this 'character' has clear links with Addison's 'Political Upholsterer', but the stylistic contrast could hardly be greater:

He had a wife and several children; but was much more inquisitive to know what passed in Poland than in his own family, and was in greater pain and anxiety of mind for King Augustus's welfare than that of his nearest relations. . . .I . . . asked him whether he had yet married his eldest daughter? He told me, No. 'But pray,' says he, 'tell me sincerely, what are your thoughts of the King of Sweden?' (*Tatler*, No. 155)

It is noticeable how a 'character' will come to life as soon as the writer abandons abstraction for concrete particulars. This can be seen in the following extract from the 'character' of a Superstitious Man, although the details themselves are conventional enough:

> The Superstitious Man serves a God to whom he ascribes human failings. . . . In order to appease this severe Divinity and fend off imaginary and non-existent ills, he suffers severe and present ills. . . . A dream, a false step over his threshold, a hare running across his path before the gate, a crow—these are sufficient to move him to postpone a journey which his own advantage and his most reasonable friends commend to him. He falls sick with fear if he sees an owl on his roof . . . (*Das Reich der Natur und der Sitten*, No. 273)

Unless a writer is extraordinarily acute, original, or eloquent, an abstract manner is always likely to be detrimental to character-writing. But in the eighteenth-century journals, the problem is compounded; here the 'character' needs to be written in a concrete and highly particularized way if it is to stand out from the more general reflections which usually introduce it.

Not surprisingly, since we are dealing with self-styled 'moral weeklies', the didactic element is virtually ubiquitous.[22] The religious ideal is that of a 'reasonable' and 'natural' Christianity which relies on the proper interpretation of God's creation through the use of reason and plays down the importance of dogma and revelation. 'Theological' virtues such as asceticism and ceremonial observance are rejected in favour of 'practical' ones like usefulness in society and philanthropy. A moderate and socially acceptable hedonism is approved. This last point is well illustrated by a pair of 'characters' in *Der Patriot*, the first of which stresses the Idler's fundamental selfishness and social uselessness:

> [Argus] eats, drinks, sleeps and gets up again; every day he puts on clean linen, plays at ombre and goes to the opera. But how does all that profit the community? How does it help the poor? What do widows and orphans get out of it? (No. 54)

The writer then turns to the Miser, but not, however, to chide him for neglecting widows and orphans:

> Chrysophilo eats poorly, lives poorly, dresses poorly and is poorly waited on. I do not know who will be his heir, for he has no children, no brothers or sisters, no other relatives. For whose sake does he cut himself short of everything which propriety and necessity demand? (ibid.)

This cannot mean that he is actually starving or that his clothing is ragged to the point of indecency (the fourfold repeated word in the original is *schlecht*, by no means the strongest term available to the writer). The suggestion is clearly that Chrysophilo has a duty to himself and to others to preserve a reasonable degree of comfort and solid affluence. Excessive self-denial has, at best, no point. (A similar point is made in *Der Neue Eidsgenosse*, No. 11.) One writer goes further and argues that the pursuit of happiness—provided that it is compatible with religion, morality and social duty—is not only permissible, but is part of God's plan for mankind (*Der Kundschafter*, 1743–4, No. 10).

Often in the German 'characters' the choice of particulars seems to have been dictated by the author's moralizing intentions rather than by his desire to analyse social behaviour, psychological traits, or professional characteristics—as, for instance, in *Der Patriot*, No. 9.[23] That same periodical will often follow up a 'character' with a set of rules defining an ideal mode of conduct, as if the author could not trust his readers to extract the necessary conclusions for themselves.[24] A similar loss of nerve on the part of the author can be seen in the 'character' of a rich Malcontent in *Mannigfaltigkeiten* (1769–73, No. 4). The style bristles with disapproving adjectives: 'Disgusting flatterers and over-exuberant enthusiasts make up the greater part of the company. Their entertainments begin with empty talk . . . tasteless fancies of a dizzy wit . . .'. Later the writer even falls back on old-fashioned allegorical personifications: 'The gregarious Lautus is accompanied by sportive Frivolity and brainless Mockery or Slander; Artfulness leads the company . . .'.

It is therefore no coincidence that the term *moralischer Charakter* became widespread in the eighteenth century. Moralizing reflections and 'characters' were simply two different means to the same end. The zest and the desire to entertain that were clearly important for the English character-writers play a subordinate role in the moral weeklies, or rather such qualities need to be justified by a more serious intention. Sperantius (*Der Biedermann*, No. 74) is confident of winning vast sums in the lottery, of unearthing buried treasure in his cellar, even of finding the philosophers' stone. But these details are presently shown as trivial manifestations of a false optimism which has a much graver aspect: 'What I have to complain about most concerning this otherwise blissful fool is that he believes he can achieve not only earthly fortune but also heavenly bliss through mere hoping, that it is enough if he professes his faith in the Church as source of salvation.' In the same year, 1728, William Law felt it necessary to apologize for the 'foolish particulars' in the 'characters' incorporated into the *Serious Call* and to justify himself by reference to his exalted motives. The writer in *Der Biedermann* is not so explicit, but his attitude is the same. 'Characters' are there to sugar the moral pill.[25]

I have invoked Law's *Serious Call*; in fact, the dividing-line between the 'characters' in the German weeklies and those in moral treatises was not very distinct. Many an essay in the weeklies strongly resembles a short sermon, with the main points illustrated by short 'characters'. The link is further underlined by the way in which the essayists round off their 'characters' with an explicit moral application or warning:

> If only he would do/be otherwise . . .
> If all people were like him . . .
> Unhappy man, I said to myself . . .

Addison, Steele, and Johnson did not conceal similar hopes and fears from the reader, but seldom adopted such a sermonizing tone.

As examples of German moral treatises, I will take works by J. M. von Loen and C. F. Gellert. The first section of Loen's *Moralische Schildereyen*[26] contains a number of 'characters'. (It may be noted that *Abbildung*, *Porträt*, *Gemälde*, *Schilderung*, together with its less common variant *Schilderei*, all served from time to time as synonyms for *Charakter*.) In his Preface, the author pays tribute to Theophrastus and La Bruyère; he could have added that he is also indebted to the German moral weeklies (indeed, he once planned to edit one himself)[27] and to the *Spectator*. The formal ways in which 'characters' relate to abstract reflections could have been suggested by either the *Spectator* or, say, by *Der Biedermann* or *Der Patriot* (although not by La Bruyère). The description of Gellia, a Hypocrite, clearly recalls Addison's Sombrius, in content as well as style: 'If [her husband] went out, he was too worldly; if he stayed at home, he disturbed her in her devotions. If he invited friends round, they were worldlings, whose whole conversation was sinful.' (pp. 124 f.)

Loen is at his least interesting when he attempts to describe an impossible paragon ('Abbildung eines vollkommenen Mannes',

p. 12 ff.). Elsewhere, however, he senses exactly how far a writer can go in showing a balance between favourable and (at least superficially) unfavourable attributes without endangering the genre, an instinct which he shares with Vauvenargues. Erast is a Wise Man, an erudite yet modest scholar, generous in sharing his findings. Yet, at first sight, he is unprepossessing:

> He is not tall and his limbs have none of the suppleness which one admires in a skilful dancer. His whole being is stiff and his manners have something forced about them whenever he tries to be agreeable. He has black, deep-set little eyes. His face is thin and his complexion a yellowish brown. . . . When he laughs, he appears somewhat stupid; even his friendliness has nothing pleasing about it . . . (p. 28)

This is certainly more realistic than the convention commonly observed in character-writing that the truly Wise Man always has a noble and sagacious air, while the Pedant looks ridiculous. A similar point—but in reverse—is made in the section on drunkenness, where Professor Altwitz is first described as appearing almost desiccated in his learned sobriety, but degenerates into riotous swinishness as the wine circulates (pp. 70–3).

Gellert's moral treatise in the form of twenty-six lectures (*Moralische Vorlesungen*) contains numerous short illustrative 'characters' and has, as an appendix, a series of more extended *Moralische Charaktere*.[28] Since Gellert, who lived from 1715 to 1769, was one of the most popular writers of his day as well as an influential Professor of Philosophy at Leipzig, his contribution to this form of didactic literature deserves some consideration. His moral position is typical of the tolerant and rationalistically inclined Christianity of the German Enlightenment. His work implies a comfortable state of affairs, in which a judicious pursuit of pleasure, success in one's business or profession, the approbation both of one's fellow-men and of God, material well-being, and peace of mind reinforce each other. Neither the traditional dichotomy of bodily and spiritual welfare nor the more specific fear that to flourish in the world might endanger a man's moral probity troubles the picture.

Gellert is quite explicit about how the 'characters' fit into the plan of his work; they are to show the practical application (*Anwendung*) of his general argument.[29] He will constantly interrupt a 'character', asking the reader to muse on the moral implications of some deed or attitude:

Damon cares for nothing but how he can satisfy his wishes and passions. He loves nothing but what pleases his senses. . . . Does your heart approve of these actions and inclinations? . . . Damon carries his sensuality to a pitch where it weakens his health and causes him intolerable pains. Does he not seem even more contemptible to you? (vi. 35 f.)

In the next 'character', we see the author adding brush-stroke after brush-stroke, pausing after each to examine the effect; the 'character' has become an agglomeration of isolated traits, each dictated by a didactic motive:

Now think of a person of contrasting character. *Semnon* enjoys sensual pleasures with a degree of moderation, so that he keeps his health. We approve of him more than of Damon. . . . He spends his wealth on finery and comfort, because it gives his friends pleasure and they are grateful. Semnon pleases us more. . . . He develops his taste and his perceptions to a point where he gives pleasure to others; this is his intention too. Our approval grows still stronger. (vi. 38 f.)

We may appreciate the value and significance of each feature, but, as a result of the constant interruptions, it is doubtful whether we end up with a mental picture of Semnon quite in the way that we have a picture of Sombrius, or Earle's Antiquary, or Theophrastus's Miser. It is significant that Gellert praises both La Bruyère and the *Spectator* primarily for the moral lessons which they inculcate.[30]

Of the works just discussed, the *Moralische Schildereyen* is psychologically the more acute and is written with the surer touch, so that it comes as no surprise to find that Loen was widely imitated between the 1750s and the 1780s.[31] The indebtedness is often openly proclaimed in the titles (*Moralische Briefe*, *Historischmoralische Schilderungen*), but the tendency to sermonize is much stronger; one author, G. C. E. Westphal, sees himself as a doctor and his readers as patients.[32] Except for this comparatively late work by Westphal, these books are written in a nagging and jogtrot style and lack the precision and urbanity of their model. But they have a certain interest, in that they show how the didactic trend, already strong in the periodicals of the 1720s, was carried to its logical conclusion: how the 'character' became a weapon in the moralist's armoury.

In humorous and ironical 'characters', a lightness of touch, a feeling for linguistic nuances, and the confidence that the reader will recognize caprice and irony without prompting are all necessary. In Germany—and the responsibility must be divided between a relatively unsophisticated reading public and the somewhat guileless authors—these things were in short supply during the period in which the moral weeklies flourished. For one thing, the German writers cannot achieve the genuinely fantastical strain occasionally encountered in the English journals. In one of Addison's *Tatler* papers, for instance (No. 153), different human types are characterized through musical instruments, the blusterer as a drum, the modest and reflective person as a lute, the 'forward, importunate wit' as a violin.

As for irony, the most sustained attempt in the moral weeklies is, as far as I know, to be found in *Der Hamburger* of 1748. Here the fictitious editor gives 'characters' of himself and his father, purporting to illustrate the solid, respectable values of North German mercantile life. The good old days, when a man made money, screwed up the interest rate to what his clients could stand, and generally acted on the principle that charity begins (and ends) at home, have yielded to a restless and innovatory age, in which culture, learning, and foreign travel are lauded and even young ladies are taught all sorts of useless accomplishments. Whether the author could have kept up this irony can never be known, since the paper was discontinued by order of the censors after only two issues.[33] But one may doubt it. Other attempts in the ironic vein show a heavy-handed approach, as if the writer were afraid of being misunderstood. The following 'character' of a miserly Self-made Man (*Der Freydenker*, 1741–3, No. 35) does not, at first sight, lack confidence:

> At length he learnt from one of his comrades the innocent and legitimate art of taking advantage of the customers' inattentiveness or haste when he paid in or took out money. . . . [When choosing a wife,] he was far too sensible to entertain any feelings other than the desire to enrich himself.

But the 'Swiftian' ending, while maintaining the ironic stance, devalues it. The author protests too much: 'I would seriously urge all my readers of both sexes to take Herr Chrysofil and his wife henceforth as models. Their characters are entirely amiable.'

Cruder yet is the satirical self-portrait in verse of a Dandy in *Für Litteratur und Herz* (1775, No. 33):

> I lack understanding: a small fault. To make up for it, my fashionable mien is a golden hook which ensures me many a good catch. . . . To be of use: that is foolery. . . . I live only for myself. What do I care for duty and the state?

The creaking mechanism, intended to ensure that the reader will approve of what the Dandy rejects, would have been regarded as unnecessary by the English character-writers, whose pieces in similar vein allow the subject to take it for granted that he or she is an ornament and benefit to society; the reader can be trusted to see where the truth lies.[34]

The ablest of the German satirists to write 'characters' was G. W. Rabener, whose 'Todtenliste von Nikolaus Klimen . . .' was first published in the monthly *Belustigungen des Verstandes und des Witzes*, in February 1743. Klimen is a sexton in Bergen who has made a list of all those who died in his parish during his term of office and has appended a description of each. The outer wrapping is thus the merest excuse for a series of twenty-one 'characters', explicitly-labelled by Rabener as such. Here is part of the Coward:

> He wished to die for his fatherland and for this reason never left Bergen. He took part in many sieges and battles during his military service, but never away from home. Whenever he received orders to go on active service, he had a severe attack of asthma and—instead of despatching himself—sent a certificate from the town physician stating that he was in poor health and would hardly be cured before the campaign was over. But he was not idle for all that: every day he drank the health of the general in command and all his other comrades in the field. . . . On his deathbed he took particular comfort in the fact that he had never stained his hands with blood.[35]

Verse-characters were not uncommon. Although Hagedorn wittily adapted Horace to the German scene and some of Gellert's *Fabeln und Erzählungen* hint at a Horatian influence,[36] the chief impetus seems to have come from Pope. Löwen's depiction of an idle Society Beauty shows the link clearly enough, despite a certain naïvety on the part of the German poet:

> Die Sonne stand schon hoch, der Zeiger wieß auf Achte,
> Als Sylvia vom Schlaf nun nach und nach erwachte.
> Sie reibt die Augen aus, sie gähnt der Sonne zu,

Und endlich reißt sie sich halb ungern aus der Ruh.
Die Lippen rühren sich, da sie Gebethe heuchelt,
Bald ihren Schooßhund küßt, und ihre Katzen schmeichelt,
Ein silbern Glöckgen tönt, der Coffee dampft herein,
Hochjähnend schlurfet sie zwölf volle Tassen ein.[37]

('The sun was already high and the hands of the clock pointed to eight as Sylvia gradually woke from her sleep. She rubs her eyes, she yawns at the sun and finally drags herself almost unwillingly from her rest. Her lips move as she feigns prayer; now she kisses her lapdog, now fawns upon her cat. A little silver bell rings out and the steaming coffee is brought in. Yawning widely, she sips twelve full cups.' One may note that staying in bed after eight o'clock seems to have been regarded as the height of self-indulgence in Germany.)

To take another example of character-writing influenced by Pope: the descriptions of a Dandy and a grasping and self-righteous Magistrate in Haller's poem 'Der Mann nach der Welt' of 1733[38] are certainly not naïve, but have a flavour very different from Pope's ironical tone by reason of their direct and unsmiling moralizing. For instance, Haller interrupts his account of the Dandy's craze for gambling in order to reflect earnestly on the mad logic which demands that 'debts of honour' must be paid while more deserving creditors go hungry (lines 71–6). The poem ends with a lament for the fatherland: what is to become of Switzerland if such types abound?

Dandies, the Vulgar Rich, Society Beauties, Hypocrites, Cowards, even unjust Magistrates—all are safe and conventional types. The only really fiery and daring verse-character known to me is Ewald von Kleist's 'Ein Gemälde' (A Portrait),[39] which seems directly to anticipate the political radicalism of the *Sturm und Drang*:

He was an enemy of virtue and a hater of men. When his pride commanded it, human blood flowed like water. He was self-seeking and loved flattery, robbed unpunished and never kept his word. He had diverse and ingenious ways of adapting himself to the age and would ally himself to ten in order to oppress one. Religion and solemn oaths were toys to him. He always pursued the immediate goal by labyrinthine paths. He whored and hunted . . . Ah, painter, pause for a moment, I understand you. That means: he was a King.

In fact, the range of types in German character-writing is narrower than in England. There is nothing corresponding to that horde of representatives from the different trades which we encounter in the English writers, and the 'characters' of professional men are, on the whole, the expected ones (Clergyman, Doctor, Teacher, Lawyer, etc.). For the rest, apart from a few types which inhabit a no man's land between moral and social satire (Antiquaries, Bluestockings, Pedants), the majority fully justify the contemporary label of 'moral characters': the Atheist, the Hypocrite, the Angry Man, the Glutton, the Idler, the Virtuous Woman, and so forth.

The ideal of personality, where not entirely classless (as in the Good Christian), is often embodied in the 'character' of a Merchant, especially in the North German periodicals. His scrupulous business methods are often described with a wealth of detail. However, at the same time he is devoted to the interests of his native city, a good family man and a devout Christian. (Thomas Mann's description of the earlier generations of the Buddenbrook family, in which there is a similar fusion of piety, legitimate pursuit of wealth, public duty, and family solidarity, has a long tradition behind it.)[40]

An English reader, coming to these 'moral characters' fresh from a perusal of, say, Addison or Johnson, might well ask himself why so many of the German pieces were so obviously second-rate. One reason, already mentioned, has to do with the state of the language itself. E. A. Blackall, in his authoritative study, *The Emergence of German as a Literary Language, 1700–1775*, shows that there was a widespread feeling in eighteenth-century Germany that the language was in a bad way and was inadequate for both literary and philosophical purposes. Indeed, when one reads early eighteenth-century prose, one often has the impression that the writer is struggling with his medium. The reasons why German lagged behind English and French as a sensitive, precise, and urbane means of communication are complex: the lack of one single capital city which could have acted as a unifying cultural influence, the break in the literary (and hence the linguistic) tradition brought about by the Thirty Years' War, the scholars' preference for Latin, the aristocrats' liking for French, and so on. No two people will exactly agree about the reasons, but the fact of German backwardness in this field is indisputable.

The gulf separating Germany and England can be measured if one examines the early attempts to translate the *Spectator*. Here is Mattheson's rendering, in 1713, of a passage by Steele:

Spectator, No. 33:	*Der Vernünfftler*, No. 37:
That no Woman can be Handsome by the Force of Features alone, any more than she can be Witty only by the Help of Speech.	Daß kein Frauenzimmer schön seyn kan/durch die Krafft der äusserlichen Gestalt allein/eben so wenig/als man verständig seyn kan/allein durch Hülffe der Sprache.
That Pride destroys all Symmetry and Grace, and Affectation is a more terrible Enemy to fine Faces than the Small-Pox.	Daß Stoltz und Hoffart alle *Symmetrie* und Anmuth vernichtet/und daß die *Affectation* den schönen Gesichtern ein weit grösserer und furchtbarer Feind ist/als die Kinder Pocken.

Mattheson expands unnecessarily ('terrible' becomes *groß und furchtbar*), he renders 'features' clumsily by *äusserliche Gestalt*, and distorts 'witty' into *verständig*. He also finds himself compelled to fall back on foreign loan-words for 'symmetry' and 'affectation', thereby destroying the homogeneity and flow of Steele's prose.

The complete translation, dating from a quarter of a century later, is not very much better. Indeed, there are passages where the translator is clearly struggling. This extract is from the 'character of Ignotus (*Spectator*, No. 75):

Humanity and good Nature, fortified by the Sense of Virtue, has the same Effect upon him, as the Neglect of all Goodness has upon many others. Being firmly Established in all Matters of Importance, that certain Inattention which makes Mens Actions look easie, appears in him with greater Beauty.	Leutseligkeit und ein gut Gemüthe, welches durch die Empfindung der Tugend bekräftigt worden, haben eben die Wirkung bey ihm, welche die Hindansetzung alles dessen, was gut ist, bey andern hat. Weil er in allen wichtigen Sachen fest gesetzt ist: So erscheint auch diejenige Unachtsamkeit, welche macht, daß die Verrichtungen leicht aussehen, bey ihm mit einer größern Schönheit.

Blackall argues that such essays in translation helped to refine the language of the *moralische Wochenschriften*, but I believe he is too charitable: examination of those periodicals published between the

1720s and the 1750s shows altogether too much that is laboured and unsupple.

Attempts to resist foreign influences and to eradicate flowery rhetoric put writers very much on the defensive. In their rationalistic and reformist zeal, they stressed above all the need to avoid stylistic excesses and pitfalls; the colourless results of this essentially negative attitude have already been demonstrated. Blackall traces in detail the gradual development of German into a more sensitive and expressive medium—but this came too late to affect the mainstream of character-writing in the moral weeklies.

The German Enlightenment, whose influence was strong in those towns which produced the leading moral weeklies, encouraged and propagated an extraordinarily serious set of values: moderation, orderliness, reason, private morality, civic virtue and responsibility, and so on. These criteria, admirable as they are as ideals of behaviour, could not but encourage a type of writing which was worthy but unexciting. To this must be added the fact that the ruling aesthetic principles of the *Aufklärung*—its distrust of the imagination where not held in check by common sense and verisimilitude, its liking for formal and stylistic rules and norms, its pronounced dislike of anything eccentric—encouraged a rather plodding, middle-of-the-road style.

A more specific reason for the flatness of so many German 'characters' seems to be the traditional German liking for abstraction, which we have seen illustrated in the contrast between the 'characters' of Critias and Addison's Political Upholsterer. I cannot adequately explain this fondness (at least, not in the pre-Kantian era), but no student of German would deny its existence. It is the only reason that I can suggest for the Germans' failure to emulate the concreteness of their predecessors and avowed models in the field of character-writing.

One last factor probably has to do with the author's notion of his reading public. If the moralizing is overt and ubiquitous, if the satire is accompanied by nudges in the reader's ribs to make sure that he has taken the point, the inescapable conclusion is that the author has little confidence in his readers. And if the reader's power to perceive nuances is not constantly stretched, he will continue to place constraints on the author. Therefore the symbiotic process, whereby author and reader support and nourish each other, fails to flourish. This is almost certainly a reason for the paucity of good satirical 'characters' in the period under discussion.

It is at first tempting to seek a partial reason in Germany's lack of democracy and political freedom, a lack which might have encouraged a timid conformity. But the differences have little to do with relative degrees of political or social outspokenness. The writers of the moral weeklies do no more and no less than their English counterparts when they criticize abuses within the system without throwing the system itself into question. There are plenty of blunt 'characters' of snobbish or rakish aristocrats, plenty of clear hints that the good merchant is better than the bad nobleman. Did Addison, Steele, and the rest go any further? Although the Germans looked often enough towards England as a land of greater freedom, political conditions do not seem to have contributed to the differences between German and English character-writing. The chief reason remains the lack of confidence bound up with the shortcomings of the language at that time.

The number of 'characters' in the moral weeklies begins to fall off after the middle of the century. In the 1720s, *Der Patriot* had printed over a hundred 'characters' in its three volumes. Although no other periodical rivals that total, it is very unusual to find a moral weekly between the 1720s and the 1760s that does not contain some 'characters', often a score or so. Yet many periodicals of the 1770s and 1780s have few or none.[41] The probable reasons will be discussed when the general decline of character-writing is examined in chapter 11. Meanwhile, however, we must turn our attention to Austria, where, even if the 'character' in the strict sense never became really popular, a related type of character-sketch flourished throughout the nineteenth century and well into the twentieth.

5

Character-Writing in Vienna: the *Wiener Skizzen*

The moral weeklies came late to Vienna, with the result that character-writing began to be practised there in the decades when it was already beginning to fall off in Germany. The chief models for the Austrian periodicals are the *Spectator* and the German *moralische Wochenschriften*, from which all the familiar forms and devices were taken over. These (to the Viennese) alien influences meant that the Austrian weeklies never really caught on and achieved popularity in Vienna,[1] a city whose culture traditionally had a strong local flavour. The 'characters' have names like Cleont, Arist, or Damon, in the manner which had been fashionable since La Bruyère, and for the most part there is little that is specifically Viennese about them. Here is an extract from C. G. Klemm's *Die Welt* of 1762–3:

> It is true that *Vadius* is learned: he understands Latin and Greek so well that he could converse with native Greeks and Romans. But it is a pity that he cannot talk to Germans.[2] He has extensive knowledge and knows the nature of many things from the most profound observation. Nobody challenges his great understanding, if one excepts only an insight into the minds of other people. All his gestures, all his works and looks prove how contented he is with himself; that is the reason why other people are not contented with him. What good is it to him if his understanding is so highly developed when his manners are so unpolished and wild? (No. 15)

That 'character' could have appeared in any German moral weekly and could have applied to educated circles in any sizeable German town of the eighteenth century. In only two authors, Joseph Richter and Joseph Schreyvogel, do we find 'characters' with genuine local colouring.

The very title chosen by Richter for the paper which he published in 1785–6—*Der Wienerische Zuschauer* ('The Viennese Spectator')—implies an attempt to give this type of periódical a local flavour. The mixture of satirical reflections, essays, 'characters', letters to the editor, and so on is much as in Richter's English and German predecessors, but the stress is on Viennese life. Titles such as 'Ein paar Wienerkaraktere' suggest very clearly the transplanting to Vienna of a genre more commonly associated with England, France, and Germany. Richter's types—the impoverished but vain Nobleman, the Miser, the Grumbler, the Pedant—are obviously not confined to Vienna and have, in fact, their counterparts in the English and German papers of the *Spectator* type, but they are firmly set in Vienna by dint of references to particular churches or pleasure-gardens in that city, to Nußdorf as a place for excursions, and so forth.

Schreyvogel's *Sonntagsblatt* (from 1807 onwards) is written in open and admiring imitation of the English and German periodicals. It follows them in adopting that well-tried fiction of an editorial panel, consisting of a shrewd but good-natured observer of men and manners (here Thomas West) and a club or association of his friends and collaborators, each with a well-defined personality. The *Sonntagsblatt* is the last major attempt in the German language to continue in the vein of the English periodicals of nearly a century before. While some of Schreyvogel's 'characters' (the Society Beauty, the Flatterer) could be transferred to Germany without anyone's being the wiser, others have obviously Viennese characteristics. The Hypochondriac (No. 7) is advised by his doctor to go to the play regularly as part of his cure, and the theatre described is quite explicitly that of early nineteenth-century Vienna. In the following extract a Viennese type (the incorrigible Wit) is portrayed with a characteristic air of tolerant satire for Viennese readers:

> I would not be surprised—should a new Noah's Flood or the Day of Judgement come upon us—to see Vienna's wits sink beneath the waves with a pun on their lips or, laughing, squabble for their bones in the churchyards. A Viennese who makes wit his profession usually has no other business or hardly bothers his head concerning what his office or position requires of him . . . (vol. i, part 1, p. 226)

At the same time as these belated attempts were being made to establish periodicals on the English and German model in Vienna, the ground was being prepared for an indigenous literary form, the so-called 'Viennese Sketch' (*Wiener Skizze*). This was the name given to a prose article or essay, usually quite short, describing some aspect of the life of the city. Local pride and local colour were prominent. The individual sketches were often first published singly and later gathered together into collections. These, mostly smallish books of a hundred or a hundred and fifty pages, appeared in large numbers from the late eighteenth century to the 1920s.

The occasional 'local' items in the Viennese moral weeklies cannot have been entirely without influence, but there were more important and immediate reasons for the sudden growth of the Viennese Sketch. In 1781, Joseph II, in his reformist zeal, ordered the relaxation of censorship in Vienna. This led, among other things, to a flood of pamphlets (Austrian writers talk of the *Broschürenflut*) relating to all imaginable aspects of life in the city, from the Emperor himself to the typical Viennese hairdresser, from educational and theological matters to controversies about burial grounds and the water supply. Anton F. Geißau, writing in 1782, lists over eight hundred items in the first two years of this period. Although his accuracy in minor details has been impugned, there is no reason to doubt the impression of frenzied scribbling which he conveys. These pamphlets, many of which had catchpenny titles, seem to have been read widely and to have lain about in the coffee houses, like magazines in a hairdresser's today.[3]

Many pamphlets were devoted to particular Viennese types. Geißau lists items dealing with lawyers, bakers, doctors, merchants, dandies, various sorts of officials, dressmakers, tailors, waiters, innkeepers, freethinkers, priests, housekeepers, chambermaids, and many others. The pamphlets therefore prepared the ground, no doubt often in a rather crude way, for the later collections of Viennese Sketches. The depiction of local types in the Sketches will have owed at least as much to these mostly ephemeral publications as to the more 'respectable' character-writing in the Viennese moral weeklies. And in the case of Joseph Richter, who both contributed to the *Broschürenflut* and produced his own Viennese equivalent to the *Spectator*, the two lines of development merge.

A more serious and systematic way of describing a great city in all its aspects was probably suggested by L. S. Mercier's famous *Tableau de Paris*, first published in 1781.[4] This is a huge work of nearly seven hundred short chapters, dealing with the various districts of Paris, its institutions, customs, familiar scenes, festive occasions, and, of course, its people. As Mercier says in his

Preface, the book is not a topographical or architectural guide, but an attempt to give the spirit and character of Paris, everything that makes it at once great, ridiculous, and scandalous. There can be little doubt that some of the earlier collections of Viennese Sketches were indebted to Mercier. Johann Pezzl's *Skizze von Wien*, first published in 1786–90,[5] is a case in point, setting out to offer the reader a general 'physiognomy' of the city. Another factor—that of affronted local pride—enters in here. Vienna's reputation had suffered at the hands of German travellers, who had published their impressions of the snobbery, complacency, religious credulity and bigotry, libertinage and epicureanism which were allegedly rife there.[6] Pezzl makes it clear in his Introduction that his work was written in answer to such attacks, as an attempt to set the record straight. At the same time, other writers adopted a more critical tone. In his *Schwachheiten der Wiener* of 1784, a fascinating critique of the foibles of Viennese society, Johann Rautenstrauch deals with religious observances, censorship, theatre, domestic life, sexual mores, eating habits, even the craze for lapdogs. Joseph Richter's *Briefe eines Eipeldauers an seinen Herrn Vetter in Kakran, über d'Wienstadt*, which appeared from 1785 onwards and proved popular enough to be continued first by Gewey and then by Bäuerle, also criticizes the Viennese, this time more obliquely and tolerantly. A visitor from the country reports in his letters home on the sights of the big city. These miniatures of Vienna and its people are thus given an additional twist through being described by a naïve observer who is not always aware of the implications of what he is saying.

Soon after the turn of the century, the practice of gathering together a number of sketches of Viennese life into a single volume was well established. *Wien und die Wiener* (1844), with its 450 pages, is the most substantial collection, containing over fifty items by a dozen or so contributors, the most famous of whom is Adalbert Stifter. The *Vorrede* may serve as point of departure, for it contains a statement of intent which would apply to virtually all such collections of sketches: the reader will not be offered facts and statistics, but a kaleidoscope of impressions (*ernste und heitere Bilder, wie in einem Kaleidoskop*). Such images are not uncommon: Castelli and Bergler, for instance, will talk of a 'peepshow'. What we find is a mixture of pieces dealing with characteristic Viennese scenes and occasions and descriptions of types or classes of people. Taking the collections of Viennese Sketches as a whole, we find that character-portrayal veers between depictions of imaginary persons (whose link with the 'character' will form the main topic of this chapter) and accounts of actual people: either figures celebrated in the political or cultural life of the city or noted eccentrics of the streets and inns. If one wants to know what life was like in Vienna in any decade from the 1820s onwards, there is much to be learnt from the Viennese Sketches. It may be that the 'peepshow' reveals what statistics gloss over or merely hint at.

When one looks at the authors, Stifter's is the only illustrious name which is to be found. A few others—among them, Castelli, Chiavacci, and Schlögl—still enjoy a degree of local fame; the rest are forgotten, although a forgotten writer is not necessarily a bad one. However, the level is certainly very uneven. At its best, the writing has sharp observation and wit, but it can easily degenerate into facetiousness, complacency, or sentimentality. Some of these works are little more than a patchwork of mildly entertaining anecdotes. Yet even a weak collection will somewhere throw a glimmer of light on some aspect of the Viennese scene.

The immediate forerunners of the Viennese Sketch had included 'characters' still unmistakably in the eighteenth-century tradition. Rautenstrauch (1784) describes the *demi-mondaine*, the Lady of Fashion, and a mixed bag of Tricksters and Parasites. Richter, in *Der Wienerische Zuschauer*, attempts to transplant the eighteenth-century 'character' to Vienna. And, of course, the link between character-portrayal in the *Sonntagsblatt* and the eighteenth-century 'character' is obvious throughout. The description of types in the early collections of Viennese Sketches is still quite close to this tradition. Castelli exemplifies this. His 'characters', although placed fair and square in their Viennese setting, are variants on types beloved of the character-writers of preceding centuries: the fashionable Doctor, the Self-important Man, the Swindler, and so on. The local element is not stressed to a point where the figure would be hardly imaginable outside Vienna, nor is there extensive use of dialect as in some later Viennese Sketches. Consider the following extract from 'Mein Freund Spitz' in the *Wiener Lebensbilder*:

If he eats at an inn, he finds fault with everything, calls for the landlord and quarrels with him, sets all the waiters in commotion and always wants to eat whatever is not on that day's menu. . . . He never walks, he runs. If you try to stop him, he never has time to talk to you, he has twenty appointments for that day. . . . If he is travelling to Krems [only about forty miles from Vienna], he publishes a leavetaking for all his friends in the newspapers; if he falls ill, he is convinced that the shares will fall on the Stock Exchange. (i. 140 f.)

This is exactly the manner in which writers in the eighteenth-century periodicals would describe the Self-important Man or the Busy Man; the reference to Krems fixes the 'character' in its locality no more and no less than the allusion to the Half-moon Tavern in the following piece by Dr Johnson establishes Jack Whirler as a Londoner:

When you call at his house, his clerk tells you, that Mr. *Whirler* has just stept out, but will be at home exactly at two; you wait at a coffee-house till two, and then find that he has been at home, and is gone out again, but left word that he should be at the *Half-moon* tavern at seven, where he hopes to meet you. . . . At eight in comes Mr. *Whirler* to tell you, that he is glad to see you, and only begs leave to run a few minutes to a gentleman that lives near the *Exchange*. . . . [Jack] calls often on his friends to tell them, that he will come again tomorrow; on the morrow he comes again, to tell them how an unexpected summons hurries him away. . . . *Jack Whirler* always dines at full speed . . . (*Idler*, No. 19)

Groß-Hoffinger too, in the 1840s, seems still to be quite close to the eighteenth-century style of character-writing (see *Wien wie es ist*, 1847). But, as the nineteenth century wears on, the influence of the eighteenth century, as transmitted by writers such as Castelli and Groß-Hoffinger, becomes very indirect indeed. It is probably more sensible to regard the description of local types in the Viennese Sketches as a Viennese equivalent to character-writing, rather than as a conscious late development of the tradition. Certainly the links are close enough and the best examples interesting enough to make it worth while examining these character-sketches in a little detail. In any such discussion, the combination of general and local features, already touched on, must obviously be of central importance.

Were these sketches written for local consumption? In some cases, the author's determined attempt to reproduce Viennese dialect on the printed page suggests that they were. Here is Chiavacci's 'weiblicher Demosthenes', the proprietress of a vegetable stall who is, at the same time, an amateur politician and a passionate commentator on the local news:

Närrisch sans Alle word'n! Erstens wolln's a Stadtbahn bau'n, aber net auf der Erd', wia sa si für a solide Bahn g'hör'n thät. In der Luft, über unsere Köpf' soll's geh'n. . . . Dös wird schön werd'n, wann d'Wäg'n auf die Leut abifall'n, wia dö Erdäpfeln aus an' Sack, der a Loch hat. I geh' mit mein' Standl liaba am Leopoldi-Berg, bevor i die Angst aussteh!'[7]

On the other hand, Rudolf Steiner's collection of 1926, *Schwankende Gestalten*, contains a glossary, suggesting that the author hoped for readers outside Vienna but realized that they would need some assistance. Most writers use dialect sparingly, no doubt with an eye to sales beyond their national frontiers. Groß-Hoffinger, Bergler, Chiavacci (who is not always so uncompromising as in the extract quoted above), and Pötzl all published collections of Viennese Sketches in Germany. Commonly, the author uses standard German for his narrative and employs dialect only when reproducing alleged conversations. The local nature of the Viennese Sketch helps to determine the tone of the 'characters'. The Viennese are usually depicted as witty and resourceful, fundamentally good, but with their share of quirks and shortcomings. There is none of that mordant wit which we find in some 'characters' of earlier periods.

The atmosphere may be one of comparatively detached irony:

This young woman comes from one of the 'best families', where high culture rages like an epidemic. Her two younger sisters go to the girls' secondary school, she herself rides a bicycle, has—despite her youth—already reduced three stout pianos to permanent ruin and has also given other evidence of her perfect modern education (Bergler, *Wiener Art und Unart*, 1896, pp. 22 f.)

—or it may be more obviously affectionate, as in Eduard Pötzl's treatment of the Diner-out, intimidated by waiters:

'Would you care for an hors-d'œuvre?'

The diner is not really used to hors-d'œuvres, he normally eats only one course in the evening. But when such an elegant young man proposes that one should take an hors-d'œuvre, it must be the normal thing in this restaurant. All right, then!

'Perhaps a fish mayonnaise . . .' The diner nods. He would also have said yes to pickled cockchafers, merely to satisfy the waiter. (*Klein-Wiener*, 1890, p. 197)

In Rudolf Steiner's fourfold 'character' of the tram-conductor, each variation illustrating one of the four temperaments, the tone is one of broad humour and the whole is obviously written *con amore*. Here are the choleric and sanguine conductors, reacting to a passenger with an over-large parcel:

(*a*) Was is mit dem Packl da? Mir san ja ka Transportg'sellschaft! Hintri in'n Beiwag'n, wann er Ihna mit fahr'n laßt! Aber Herr, reg'n S' Ihna net auf, des Packl is z'groß, i brich ma net weg'n Ihna meine Füaß, und a andrer aa net! Ja, beschwer'n S' Ihna, vielleicht hängt die Direktion für Ihna an Strafwag'n [Streifwagen, Lastwagen] an! . . . 's nächste Mal kumman S' halt mit an Schubladkast'n!

(*b*) Geht das Packerl net untern Sitz eine? Aber ja, nur a bißl antauch'n, es muaß einegeh'n—no von mir aus, wann's dem Herrn da recht is, i sitz ja net da, i kann ma aa daher nix tuan!

Translation
(*a*) What's that parcel doing there? We're not a removal firm! Put it behind in the trailer, if they'll take you! Don't get hot under the collar; the parcel's too big and I'm not going to break my legs falling over it, not me or anyone else! Yes, you do that, you go and complain: perhaps the management will put a special luggage-car on just for you. Next time, bring a whole chest of drawers!

(*b*) Won't that little parcel go under the seat? Surely—just a bit of a shove and it'll go all right. Oh well, I don't mind, if it's all right by the gentleman there—I'm not sitting there, it can't hurt me.

Steiner is drawing on a long Viennese tradition of treating the humours playfully, as a framework for comic invention. Nestroy's *Haus der Temperamente* of 1837 is the most famous example, and it is interesting to note that a contemporary review of this play was written in four parts, the style of each corresponding to one of the humours.[8]

'Local' and 'parochial' tend to be loaded terms. If we occasionally find the tone in which these sketches are written too indulgent or cosy, we must reflect that a Viennese writer will almost inevitably see the failings of his fellow Viennese more tolerantly than an outsider. Gottfried Keller, Theodor Storm, and other regional writers of the nineteenth century have not, after all, escaped similar criticism for their portrayal of local types. A nearer parallel might be the descriptions of London and suburban folk in the shilling character-books of the mid nineteenth century (see chapter 6). But, as we shall see presently, some writers of Viennese Sketches describe poverty and hard work realistically and in detail at a time when such things were hardly mentioned, except in sentimental or otherwise falsified terms, in most forms of polite literature.

To return to the question of the balance struck between the local and the universally valid: one can find examples ranging from Castelli's figures, in which the contemporary and local colouring is only lightly sketched, right through to 'characters' with the strongest possible contemporary and local emphasis (Chiavacci's 'weiblicher Demosthenes' would be an example). Steiner ironically describes a local type (the tram-conductor) within a psychological framework previously held to be the key to a universal understanding of human behaviour (the theory of the humours). Before we leave this matter of the local versus the universal, let us briefly examine a type very common in European literature since the seventeenth century: Don Juan, who originated in Spain and made his way to northern Europe by way of Italy. As a flamboyantly wicked figure, he quickly captured the imagination of authors and public: hundreds of plays, novels, and poems were devoted to his exploits; thousands of pages of essays, articles, and treatises attempted to analyse his character. Originally an aristocrat, he reappeared in humbler social spheres or even became completely *déclassé*, transported into the thinner air of philosophical or psychoanalytical speculation. The popularization of Don Juan soon led to 'local' Don Juans in plays and novels. Why should Seville or the never-never-land of Italian *opera buffa* have a monopoly of this fascinating character? And so we encounter him in Wiesbaden, Hamburg, Venice, London, and in many other places.[9] Two writers of Viennese Sketches present the 'character' of a Viennese Don Juan: Bergler's 'Don Juan im Caféhaus' (*Wiener Guckkastenbilder*, 1888) and Ulreich's 'Lully, der Herzensbrecher' (*Wiener Art*, 1925). This type does not wear a cloak and sword, but carries a cane with a gilt knob and sports a silk handkerchief prominently displayed. He is not an aristocrat, but a *petit bourgeois* of rather uncertain means. Far from dispensing purses of gold and laying on lavish banquets, he is often hard up at the end of the month. He haunts not the balconies and courtyards of Seville, but Vienna's shops and cafés and the gardens of its suburbs. His victims do not extend over half Europe and the whole range of society from noblewoman to fisher-girl, but are found among the shopgirls of Vienna. And, at the end, he is not dragged away, defiant, to Hell by the terrible Stone Guest, but is locked up with the goats to muse on the sorry outcome of his latest escapade.

The question of the social spread in character-writing has already been touched on. A greater proportion of the 'characters' in the Viennese Sketches is drawn from the lower ranks of society than anywhere else in the history of character-writing. If we look at the 'characters' in Richter's *Wienerischer Zuschauer*, we find them about equally divided between the minor aristocracy and the bourgeoisie. Castelli too, in the early days of the Viennese Sketch, is still mainly concerned with these groups. However, by the mid 1840s, in *Wien und die Wiener*, most of the 'characters' are drawn from the lower classes, and the Viennese Sketch continues thereafter to pay considerable attention to the humbler members of society. We find 'characters' of the Chambermaid, the Beggar, the Rag-and-bone Woman, the Bill-sticker, the Pedlar, the itinerant Musician, the Washerwoman, the Tailor, the Woodcutter, the Pot-boy, and others.

The reservation which has to be made regarding virtually all 'characters' of working-class figures applies here too: there is no real psychological revelation. For this, we have to wait for Henry Mayhew's extraordinarily successful attempts to persuade the poor of London to speak for themselves (see chapter 7(iii)). The authors of the Viennese Sketches simply describe the lower orders in terms of their appearance and their work, as if this were a full definition. Given the gulf between the classes in nineteenth-century society, and the absence of a Viennese Mayhew, one could hardly expect anything different. Even in *Wien und die Wiener*, the only 'character' which goes beyond external description of working activities is that of the Chambermaid (pp. 10–15), significantly the only working-class figure among those described with whom the prosperous would come into contact in more than a fleeting and superficial way. This is a fairly sympathetic account, although by no means sentimental. The Chambermaid has native wit, intelligence, and good humour, although she is also vain. Her addictions are romantic love-affairs, sentimental novels, plays, and coffee. Thus far, the picture is fairly conventional. But the anonymous writer ends on a compassionate note, with a thought of the danger of destitution in old age. And at least he avoids the stereotyped dark-eyed, scheming minx of the comedy stage. However, apart from this isolated example, Steiner's tram-conductors are the only working-class 'characters' known to me within the tradition of the Viennese Sketch where a balance is achieved between working life and psychological make-up—and they are a comic *tour de force* rather than a serious investigation.

Compassion in the depiction of those who have next to nothing (the Rag-and-bone Woman in *Wien und die Wiener*), an attempt at objectivity in the treatment of the Chambermaid, the utmost joviality in the description of the tram-conductors: these differences of tone raise the question of the intention behind these Viennese 'characters'. As we have seen, 'characters' could be written out of a variety of motives. Theophrastus's exact intentions are obscure and are likely to remain so, but from 1600 onwards the situation is tolerably clear. Although Hall and Thomas Fuller wrote in the hope of edifying and improving their readers, most seventeenth-century writers—at least until the 'character' became virtually restricted to the realms of political and religious polemic— wrote to entertain and to dazzle through wit. The seventeenth-century character-books contain their idealized 'characters', but one seldom has the impression that the author is primarily out to reveal a moral pattern in human behaviour. Only in the eighteenth century did the didactic intention become dominant in character-writing, with the aim of educating the reader into becoming a right-minded, reasonable, balanced person and a good member of society.

In the Viennese Sketch character-portrayal is no longer concerned with high-minded criteria; the aim is by now above all to entertain by depicting the city and its people vividly. Julius Löwy, in the Preface to the first part of his *Geschichten aus der Wienerstadt* (1889), states his intention of showing the ordinary people in their domestic and social life (*diese Wiener in ihrem kleinen häuslichen und geselligen Leben zu schildern*). The desire is to evoke scenes and types to which the reader will react in affectionate recognition (the key words and phrases in Löwy's preface are *gemüthlich*, *herzlich*, *anheimelnde Erinnerungen*, and the like). An air of gentle sentimentality and kindly humour is common. It is also noticeable how character-portrayal is regarded as one of a number of means by which a picture of Vienna could be built up. These writers tend to ask not only 'What sort of man is this?' but also 'How does he fit into and contribute to the life of our city?' This trend is particularly prominent in *Wien und die Wiener*. Something similar can be seen in Pötzl's 'character' of a Godfather (*Jung-Wien*, 1885, pp. 29 ff.);

the author is much more interested in the relationship between godfather and godson and the social ritual surrounding it than in a character-sketch pure and simple. Löwy too is concerned with a portrait of the city rather than a psychological anatomy of its inhabitants (op. cit., *Vorrede*). One can think of a few examples among the English character-writers where the aim seems to have been to build up a picture of the types and scenes that make up a particular city (for example, Lupton's *London and the Country*), but more commonly, if there was a plan at all, a moral, social, or psychological microcosm was aimed at. The creation of a 'portrait' of a city through a combination of scenes, stories, imaginary but typical figures ('characters'), and actual persons seems to be peculiar to the Viennese Sketches.

The foibles of the Viennese are not usually treated in a tone of moral disapproval; instead, they are greeted with amused resignation. This is the way in which Castelli depicts the fashionable, rather treacly Ladies' Doctor, and how Barach describes the Ingratiating Man.[10] The note of resignation is particularly clear in Michael Klapp's 'character' of the scheming and self-seeking Politician, Herr von Aufdringlich (Mr Pushful). Klapp describes his stratagems and his soft tongue, his manipulation of political meetings and electoral machinery. One can picture the shrug of the shoulders as the author adds: 'What is more natural than that Mr Pushful will succeed in life?' (*Wiener Bilder*, 1868, p. 161). As examples of the Viennese Sketch at its most harmless, one could instance Galliny's Society Lady who is a compulsive attender of public lectures (*Wiener Studien*, 1869, pp. 85 ff.) and Steiner's 'Wiener Fußgeher', the casual pedestrian lost in thought and unconsciously inviting disaster with every step he takes (op. cit., pp. 73 ff.). More serious is Groß-Hoffinger's picture of the Viennese Janitor, who bullies the tenants and plays the tyrant over those who fall behind with the rent (*Wien wie es ist*, 1847, ii. 8 f.). From this example we begin to see that character-portrayal in the Viennese Sketches, when at all serious, is concerned with social injustice. The poorer classes described in *Wien und die Wiener* are, on the whole, treated with compassion, and are intended to arouse compassion. Bergler, in his *Wiener Guckkastenbilder* (1888), fully recognizes the suffering, squalor, and vice coexisting with the elegance and jollity in Vienna and treats the seamier side with a notable lack of sentimentality and pathos.[11] Fierce social indignation is apparent throughout Stüber-Gunther's 'Der Piccolo' (*Das Durchhaus*, 1905, pp. 31 ff.), which depicts the miserable and exhausting life of a potboy in an inn.

But serious or tragic 'characters' are the exceptions. It is not without significance that *Das Durchhaus* also contains the 'character' of Herr Neubauer, the man who cannot say 'no'. This is written throughout in a tone of indulgent humour and lightheartedness:

> And so for next Sunday he has provisionally undertaken the following: early in the day a journey to Semmering, at two in the afternoon a wine-excursion to Klosterneuburg, at three a meeting in Vienna and at four a visit in Weidlingau. Assuming that no more invitations arrive—which Herr Neubauer would undoubtedly accept—how can these four things be made compatible? They can't, of course. Does Herr von Neubauer know that? Yes, since he is not weak-minded. Will he then have to break three of his commitments? At least . . . (pp. 121 f.)

The writers of Viennese Sketches did not, in the main, want to play on their readers' heart-strings or send them rushing to man the barricades. The overwhelming impression is of a form of writing designed not to change the world or improve the reader, but to entertain. These sketches are yet another manifestation of the love-affair between the Viennese and their city. Indeed, it is possible to see the Viennese Sketches as one of the means by which the 'Viennese myth' has been perpetuated—the presentation of Vienna as *the* city and its inhabitants as possessed of unique charm, vitality, wit, resourcefulness, and the capacity to enjoy life. Although villains are not lacking (snobs, bureaucrats, all manner of petty tyrants) and although there is poverty and hardship, self-congratulation and celebration dominate.

6

The Nineteenth and Twentieth Centuries

(i) The Nineteenth Century

Although, as we have have seen, there was a falling-off in character-writing towards the end of the eighteenth century, the genre persisted, at least in England, throughout the nineteenth. The nomenclature changed, with 'character' gradually yielding to 'sketch',[1] but the continuity is manifest.

The *Spectator* was often reprinted and Addison was widely admired: many papers in the eighteenth-century mould still appeared in the early decades of the new century, often with titles that openly recall their forebears:

The Saunterer (1803)	*The Rambler, The Idler*
The Trifler (1822–3)	*The Trifler* (1788)
The English Spy (1825–6)	*The Intelligencer* (1729)
The London Spy (1831–2)	*The Peeper* (1796)

These nineteenth-century journals contain 'characters' which closely resemble eighteenth-century models. The following passage, from the *Miniature* (1805), reads like a watered-down extract from the *Spectator*:

> Does any body wish to flatter Trebius? Let him only say that the Duke of——, or my Lord——has enquired after him; his eyes will instantly sparkle with pleasure and self importance. . . . Instead of esteeming his companions in proportion to their intrinsick worth . . . he considers only the costliness of their entertainments, the elegance of their equipage, the grandeur of their titles, or the length of their purses. (p. 148)

The tones of Dr Johnson are echoed in a 'character' (of 'the grand Etonian') from the mid 1820s: 'Proud without property, and sarcastic without being witty, ill temper he mistakes for superior carriage, and haughtiness for dignity' (*English Spy*, i. 38). Johnson had written of Squire Bluster: 'he has birth without alliance, and influence without dignity. His neighbours scorn him as a brute; his dependents dread him as an oppressor' (*Rambler*, No. 142).

This old-fashioned air[2] is often matched by a nostalgic sympathy for the 'good old days'. George Brewer, in the Preface to his *Hours of Leisure* (1806), praises no writer more recent than Addison, Johnson, and Goldsmith. Brewer's Wise Man, Gerradius, is 'one of the old school', always ready to uphold traditional virtues against tawdry new fashions (pp. 218 f.). Oddly enough, an early nineteenth-century reworking of Earle seems less out of date than the new 'characters' then being written. The anonymous author of *A Gallery of Portraits* (1813) sees in the *Microcosmography* a combination of perennial human traits and changing fashions. Comparison of his version with the original shows that he has both omitted details which would no longer make much sense to his readers and also taken some trouble in devising genuine nineteenth-century equivalents to its motifs. For instance, Earle's 'meer dull Physician', who blinds his patients with 'hard names' and burdens them with expensive cures whether they are sick or not, has turned into the fashionable doctor of the nineteenth century, with his imposing façade and obsequious bedside manner.[3]

What is more surprising is to find Thomas Hood reviving the old witty style in this picture of the Greenwich Pensioner:

> Is a sort of stranded marine animal, that the receding tide of life has left high and dry on the shore. He pines for his element like a Sea Bear, and misses his briny washings and wettings. What the Ocean could not do, the land does, for it makes him sick; he cannot digest properly unless his body is rolled and tumbled about like a barrel-churn. . . . Walk he cannot, the ground being so still and steady that he is puzzled to keep his legs, and ride he will not, for he disdains a craft whose rudder is forward and not astern. . . . [He] would give all the singing birds of Creation for a Boatswain's whistle . . . (*Comic Annual*, 1830, pp. 63f.)

It would not, however, be fair to imply that all early nineteenth-century character-writing is backward-looking. C. M. Westmacott's Commercial Man is an accurately observed and witty sketch of a contemporary type in traditional character-form:

> Who can speak of the increasing prosperity, or calculate upon the falling interests of a town, as well as your flying man of business? The moment he enters a new place he expects the landlord to be ready, cap in hand, to

welcome him; he . . . orders boots to bring in his travelling bags or his driving box, and bids the waiter to send the chambermaid to show him his bedroom. . . . [He] directs boots to be ready to make the circuit of the town with him after dinner, carrying his pattern-books, perhaps half a hundred weight of Birmingham wares, brass articles, or patterns of coffin furniture; and having thus succeeded in putting the whole house into confusion, only to let them know that the *Brummagem* gentleman has arrived . . . he places himself down at a side table, to answer to his principals for being some days later on his march than they had concluded . . . (*English Spy*, 1825–6, ii. 289 f.)

The major essayists of the nineteenth century, Hazlitt, Lamb, and Leigh Hunt,[4] wrote 'characters', but not a great number. Hazlitt's essays seem to reflect the importance of the genre at that time with fair exactitude. His sequence of three pieces 'On the Clerical Character' contains both reflections and a short 'character'. The two different but complementary methods of discussing human personality are present as in the eighteenth-century periodical essays, but the proportions are very different (barely one page of 'character' out of a total of seventeen pages). The 'character' seems to be no longer regarded as a major means of commenting on human types. Elsewhere, Hazlitt talks of people collectively or changes from the collective to the individual, from 'them' to 'him', in the course of a paragraph.[5] Yet he could write an extended formal 'character' if he wanted to; his Cockney ('On Londoners and Country People') is one such. In this case Hazlitt chooses an imaginary representative of his category of men and sticks to him: 'The true Cockney has never . . . He despises the country. . . . A real Cockney is . . .'. The following extract felicitously combines terse details in the manner of Theophrastus with the balanced and elegant sentence-construction of the eighteenth-century character-writers:

He notices the people going to court or to a city-feast, and is quite satisfied with the show. He takes the wall of a Lord, and fancies himself as good as he. . . . He despises the country, because he is ignorant of it, and the town, because he is familiar with it. He is as well acquainted with St. Paul's as if he had built it, and talks of Westminster Abbey and Poets' Corner with great indifference. The King, the House of Lords and Commons are his very good friends.[6]

Charles Lamb, too, wrote only a few 'characters', but those few are good. The Poor Relation is the most striking, combining features which again directly recall Theophrastus with stylistic elements reminiscent now of the seventeenth century, now of the eighteenth. Lamb begins with a clutch of metaphors in the seventeenth-century manner:

> [The Poor Relation is] a preposterous shadow, lengthening in the noon-tide of our prosperity . . . a drain on your purse,—a more intolerable dun on your pride,—a drawback upon success,—a rebuke to your rising,—a stain in your blood,—a blot on your 'scutcheon,—a rent in your garment,—a death's head at your banquet . . .

But he presently falls into the traditional Theophrastan method of listing typical actions, while casting his sentences in the balanced, antithetical form of the eighteenth century. As often with the 'characters' in the coffee-house periodicals, the two halves of the sentence mirror the contrast between pretence (here, false modesty) and reality: 'He declareth against fish, the turbot being small—yet suffereth himself to be importuned into a slice . . .'.[7]

At the same time as the 'character' was being pushed into a subordinate place in serious essay-writing, it found favour among the purveyors of light entertainment. From 1837 until about 1850 there was a remarkable proliferation of 'specialized' character-books (*Young Ladies*, *Young Gentlemen*, *Snobs*, *Bores*, *Stuck-up People*, *Humbugs*, etc.). These works usually sold for a shilling, contained no more than a hundred or so pages, and were modest in format. They were nearly always illustrated, often very ably; the artists included Cruikshank, H. G. Hine, A. Henning, H. K. Browne, and, later, W. S. Gilbert. Among the authors were Dickens (*Young Gentlemen* and *Young Couples*, both 1838), Thackeray (*The Book of Snobs*, 1846–7). Albert Smith, A. B. Reach, and various other writers associated with *Punch* and similar periodicals. The actual word 'character' figures in only two of the titles, *Corporation Characters* (1855) and *London Characters* (1870); 'sketch' is more common. Other writers fancy themselves as 'social zoologists' and offer 'natural histories' of their chosen species.[8] Some of these collections are genuine little character-books from beginning to end, while others include only a few 'characters', together with essays and anecdotes.

These works have the obvious and expected limitations: they seldom leave the world of the middle classes[9] and they do not delve very deep. Some suffer from facetiousness, the disease endemic to

Victorian light humour. But within these limitations they are amusing, acute, and often up to the minute. Such figures as 'the Young Lady who sings' (a notorious minor pest of the day) or 'the Gent' (as opposed to the Gentleman) have the authentic flavour of mid nineteenth-century England.

Some of these little books are collections of items which had originally appeared in *Punch*;[10] in fact, the early years of that paper contain many 'characters', often in cycles over a period of months (Snobs, Model Characters, Academical Portraits, Nooks and Corners of Character, etc.). Most are written in tones of fairly harmless mockery. But it is sometimes forgotten that *Punch* had, at first, a strong radical flavour, and this radicalism is reflected in at least a minority of the 'characters'. The hectoring Beadle, the Sempstress, the Model Maid-of-all-Work, the Model Governess, the Model Magistrate, the Model Labourer—all these express varying degrees of social protest.[11] Here is the conclusion of Horace Mayhew's Model Labourer:

> He struggles on, existing rather than living, infinitely worse fed than the beasts he gets up for the Exhibitions—much less cared about than the soil he cultivates, toiling, without hope, spring, summer, autumn, and winter, his wages never higher—frequently less—and perhaps after thirty years' unceasing labour, if he has been all that time with the same landlord, he gets the munificent reward of six-and-two-pence, accompanied, it is true, with a warm eulogium on his virtues by the President (a real Lord) for having brought up ten children and several pigs upon five shillings a-week. This is the MODEL LABOURER, whose end of life is honourably fulfilled if he is able, after a whole life's sowing for another, to reap a coffin for himself to be buried in! (*Punch*, xiv, 1848, p. 259)

The radical seriousness of some of these 'characters' is rivalled only by the collection *Heads of the People* of 1840–1 (see below, p. 175).

Dickens's *Sketches by Boz* will be discussed later, with reference to his novels (below, p. 237). Like Dickens, Thackeray wrote 'characters' before he wrote novels—or, to be more accurate, before he wrote any of the novels on which his fame rests. In *The Book of Snobs*,[12] he devotes a chapter or short run of chapters to the various spheres or breeding-grounds of snobbery—the military life, the London clubs, the universities, etc. Anecdotes and reflections are combined with short 'characters'. Here is an extract from the biting account of Captain Bull, the English Snob abroad:

Yonder comes Captain Bull. . . . Abroad, he has been everywhere; he . . . has seen every palace and picture-gallery from Madrid to Stockholm; speaks an abominable little jargon of half-a-dozen languages—and knows nothing—nothing. Bull hunts tufts on the Continent, and is a sort of amateur courier. . . . We have said Bull knows nothing: he knows the birth, arms, and pedigree of all the peerage . . . he knows all the Continental stories of English scandal. . . . If he can't catch a lord he will hook on to a baronet, or else the old wretch will catch hold of some beardless young stripling of fashion, and show him 'life'. . . . If he has every one of the vices of the most boisterous youth, at least he is comforted by having no conscience . . . (chapter 21)

Side by side with such traditional 'characters' in *The Book of Snobs*, we find episodes which reveal the evolving novelist. There is the long account of Mr Snob's visit to Mangelwurzelshire (chapters 24–31) and the story of the downfall, through snobbery, of the honest Sackville (chapters 42–4). The work, like the *Sketches by Boz*, may thus be regarded as part of the novelist's apprenticeship. Edward Bulwer Lytton (1803–73) is another of the English novelists of the nineteenth century to have written 'characters'. *England and the English* (1833) contains sketches of various Politicians, Dandies, and Writers, of a Respectable Man, a Practical Man, and a good, enlightened Country Gentleman. It is clear from one of his chapter-headings, 'Supplementary Characters' (iv. 10), that the author was aware of his position in a tradition of character-writing.

'Characters' crop up in other, less expected, places throughout the nineteenth century: in sermons, tracts, travel journals, musical criticism, even works on angling.[13] In view of our (perfectly justified) modern notions of the German inn as immaculately hygienic and of the servants there as only one remove from hospital nurses in their sterilized purity, it may afford a piquant contrast to hear Henry Mayhew on the Serving-Maid in the Germany of the 1860s:

The German serving-maid . . . is the most dirty and slatternly trollop in appearance that could be found in any beggar's hole in London; an Irish basket-woman is elegant and pleasant-looking in comparison with her. . . . [She] never thinks it necessary to wash herself on a week-day, and goes about with the dirt on her face almost as thick as the mould on the rind of an ancient cheese . . . and when she *does* scour her face . . . on a Sunday, she still leaves such a water-mark about her neck that, as with some old post in the river, you can tell by the dirt clinging to the base of it exactly how far the water has been in the habit of reaching for ages.[14]

To set off against that insalubrious portrait, here is part of the sanctimonious 'Character of a good and faithful Servant' from a tract published in 1809:

> The good servant rises early. She is quick and diligent at her work; and does it so willingly, and cheerfully, and handily, that it seems a pleasure to her, rather than a task.
>
> She is strictly honest; so that she might safely be trusted with gold untold. . . . She always speaks the truth . . .
>
> She always looks clean and tidy; even when . . . she is doing dirty work. She is never seen going about the house, with holes in her stockings, or slipshod shoes, or a tattered gown, or blowzy hair, or dirty hands . . . (*A Friendly Gift For Servants* . . ., 1809, pp. 7 and 11)

Yet, despite these examples, the 'character' as a medium for serious comment clearly loses ground in the course of the nineteenth century. The reasons for this had little to do with general notions of human personality, but were more matter-of-fact: the paucity of examples in the works of the major essayists and the huge popularity of the novel and the short story. The growing association of the 'character' with various types of light humour may have played at part too. Meanwhile, in the depiction of the humbler classes, the typical but imaginary representative ('character') yields to accounts of actual people. That is to say, the 'portrait'—previously reserved for well-known members of the middle and upper classes—descended the ranks with a vengeance. The ways in which Henry Mayhew's *London Labour and the London Poor* (first published in 1851)—where actual poor people were described and allowed to speak for themselves—came to pose a threat to working-class 'characters' will be demonstrated later (below, pp. 176 ff.). More or less at the same time, other sociological works dispensed with the description of individual persons (whether actual or imaginary) and built up their pictures of contemporary life through a combination of general observations and statistical data. John Hogg's *London as it is* (1837) is an early example; some of Mayhew's contributions to the *Morning Post* follow the same method.

There are, however, two major writers who made significant contributions to character-writing in the second half of the century: George Eliot and Anthony Trollope. Unlike Dickens and Thackeray, George Eliot wrote her 'characters' (in *The Impressions of Theophrastus Such*) late in her career, in 1879, so that they cannot be regarded as 'practice' for the characterization in her novels. In the first chapter ('Looking Inward'), Theophrastus Such establishes his credentials as an observer of human nature, thus allying himself with the Spectators, Observers, Spies, and Censors of the eighteenth-century periodicals as one who holds himself apart from active life, content to watch, record, comment, and occasionally exhort. Since there are also references to Theophrastus and La Bruyère,[15] it is clear that this work is intended as some sort of variant on, or continuation of, character-writing. But it is emphatically not a simple sequence of 'characters' or a succession of short essays with illustrative 'characters' in the style of the *Spectator*. Nor does it resemble La Bruyère's book in its form.

One piece certainly suggests an expansion of the form developed by the eighteenth-century essayists. This is the chapter entitled 'Only Temper' (chapter 6), in which George Eliot (or Theophrastus Such) passes from general reflections on bad temper to mention a type of person in whom good qualities and irascibility are at odds. This leads directly to the 'character' of Touchwood. He is introduced, as were scores of eighteenth-century 'characters', by a formula that makes it clear he is intended as representative of a genus: 'Touchwood is that kind of good fellow . . .' (p. 66). Compare 'Sombrius is one of these Sons of Sorrow' (*Spectator*, No. 494). A short extract will show the close affinity with traditional methods of character-writing, especially those current in the eighteenth century: 'An invitation or any sign of expectation throws him into an attitude of refusal. Ask his concurrence in a benevolent measure: he will not decline to give it—; but he complies resentfully' (pp. 66f.).

Elsewhere, however, we see George Eliot moving away from anything resembling traditional forms of character-writing. For instance, chapter 3 ('How we encourage Research') is really a short story about a scholarly dilettante who tangles with the experts and is humiliated. Chapter 5 ('A too deferential Man') has the narrative leisureliness of an episode in a novel rather than the concision of the 'character'. In other cases, the psychological analysis is much more extended and detailed than in any traditional example. It seems clear that *Theophrastus Such* is not so much an attempt to resuscitate character-writing as an unwitting demonstration of what happens to the 'character' in the hands of the novelist.

Trollope included many 'characters' in the occasional pieces that he published in the *Pall Mall Gazette* between the mid 1860s and

1880. These were republished in book form under the titles *Clergymen of the Church of England* (1865–6), *Hunting Sketches*, *Travelling Sketches* (both 1866), and *London Tradesmen* (1880). In these works, descriptions of typical figures are combined with general reflections and anecdotes in a way somewhat reminiscent of *The Book of Snobs*, although the form is more diffuse. However, the line joining Trollope to the older character-writers is still clear, especially in *Travelling Sketches* and *London Tradesmen*. Here he is on 'The unprotected Female Tourist':

> She is not rich, and travels generally with economy; but she is rarely brought to a shift for money, and her economies conceal themselves gracefully and successfully. She learns the value of every franc, of every thaler, of every zwansiger as she progresses. . . . She never pays through the nose in order that people indifferent to her may think her great or generous, though she always pays sufficient to escape unsatisfactory noises. . . . Her dress is quiet and yet attractive. . . . She can decline all overtures of acquaintanceship without giving offence, and she can glide into intimacies without any apparent effort. She can speak French with fluency and with much more than average accuracy, and probably knows something of German and Italian. . . . She is acquainted with and can explain all galleries, cathedrals, and palaces. . . . She understands politics, and has her opinion about the Emperor, the King of Prussia, and the Pope. (*Travelling Sketches*, chapter 3)

In general, however, a glance at that section of the Bibliography devoted to the nineteenth century tells its own story: there are over fifty items in the first half of the century, barely a score in the second. Even so, the continuity in English character-writing is remarkable in its contrast with the virtual lack of 'characters' in nineteenth-century France and Germany.

In Germany, the moral weekly gradually lost favour from the 1770s onwards. 'Improving' essays spiced with illustrative 'characters' had almost disappeared by the end of the century. In the periodicals of the early nineteenth century, one encounters poems, stories, plays, informative essays on all manner of topics, reviews, retellings of folk-tales, and items on local and national history—almost everything except 'characters'. *Der Leipziger Zuschauer* (1811–12) contains a few, but is very much an exception. (I have glanced through some three dozen runs of periodicals of various types published in German-speaking countries between

1800 and 1850 and have found no other 'characters' whatever.) The growing popularity of the novella must have been a major factor. Apart from the examples in *Der Leipziger Zuschauer*, I have found only one other German 'character' dating from the early nineteeenth century: Brentano's rather testy description of the Philistine ('Schilderung eines Musterphilisters') in his satirical treatise *Der Philister vor, in und nach der Geschichte*, first published in 1811.

In nineteenth-century France, the situation is similar; here there seem to be only two important collections, by Gustave Le Vavasseur (1856) and Gaston de Varennes (1882).[16] Le Vavasseur's *Caractères et portraits rustiques* is a series of longish verse-characters which combine to give a somewhat idealized picture of French rural life. The combination of form and subject-matter is unexpected, in that French character-writers had always concentrated heavily on urban life, but the work is otherwise unremarkable: stodgy and faintly sentimental. Gaston de Varennes' *Types et caractères* consists of twenty-seven prose chapters, devoted to various types and classes, mainly Parisian. Despite the title, there are not many passages which bear much formal resemblance to the 'character' as practised in France in its heyday; the informal mixture of character-portrayal, reflections on the state of society, scenes, anecdotes, and passages of quasi-dramatic dialogue brings the book nearer to the collections of urban 'sketches' such as were popular in Vienna at the time. However, Varennes' title, like Le Vavasseur's, suggests clearly enough that he saw his work as belonging to the tradition of character-writing.

As I have tried to show, the tone of nineteenth-century English character-writing ranges from the facetious, through sanctimonious moralizing, to a fierce note of social indignation. If I have devoted space to lesser writers, it is because many of their 'characters' are well worth rescuing from oblivion, as some of my chosen extracts will, I hope, have demonstrated. Nor can any sense of the unbroken tradition be conveyed if only a few obvious landmarks (such as *The Book of Snobs*) are mentioned. Most people know, at least vaguely, about the seventeenth-century 'characters'; many are aware of the line which joins Addison and Steele to Johnson. But, of the seventy or so writers who composed 'characters' during the nineteenth century, only a dozen at most are still household names.

(ii) The Twentieth Century

Two related but distinct strands run through character-writing in this century: the first is the continued tendency of the 'character' to move into the realm of light humour, the second a use of pastiche. One of the best twentieth-century equivalents to the comic character-books of the Victorian era is Malcolm Bradbury's *Phogey* of 1960. The 'Phogey' is a man who wishes that he could put the clock back and hence clings to the institutions and notions that encourage the illusion that things do not change. One part of the book (pp. 51–84) consists of thirty-nine short 'characters' treating various aspects of phogeydom. As a collection of character-sketches, all illustrating what the author clearly feels to be a fundamental English disease, it resembles Thackeray's *Book of Snobs.*[1]

Pastiche in character-writing has a long history,[2] but had never before been a prominent part of the tradition. In the twentieth century, Mayhew and Chaucer have been the authors most favoured. G. H. Vallins, in his Chaucer-parodies which appeared in *Punch* from the mid 1940s on,[3] takes figures from the period of wartime austerity to the temporary euphoria of the Festival of Britain in 1951 and describes them as though in the Prologue to a new *Canterbury Tales*. His chosen types include the Munition Worker, the Postwoman, the Sanitary Inspector, and the Butcher (in the days of rationing and meat coupons). The subjects are topical: so much so that some would require explanatory notes today. Paradoxically, this precise setting in a modern era is enhanced by the style, for pastiche always draws attention to the gulf between the age in which such a style was appropriate and the era of the pasticheur.

Vallins shows great skill in introducing deliberate anachronisms or modern slang into a Chaucerian style:

> There nas no art that nas to him unknowe
> Of passing on the bukke, soth to seye;
> Of rede tape he coude the nexte weye,
> And ther-withal he festned al his gere:
> A lettre nolde he answere for a yere,
> But 'In god tyme' or 'Wayt a-whil' he cryde,
> And fyled hem in a hepe him bisyde . . .

and in translating modern gadgetry into the historical idiom:

A smale gaget hat she by hir side
Ther-with she ponched billets for the ride
Of everichoon, accordaunt to his wille.

But sometimes, as in most good parody, a serious note can be detected. Of the Schoolmistress, busy with milk, attendance registers, and school dinners:

And yet she seyde hir lerning stod for naughte:
So bisy was she that she seldon taughte.[4]

Mayhew's *London Labour and the London Poor* prompted Alex Atkinson and Ronald Searle to collaborate in *The Big City or the New Mayhew* (1962). Seventeen of the twenty-four chapters include 'characters', all written in a skilful imitation of the original and aptly illustrated by Searle. The collection shows, as well as any single work could, how the art of the draughtsman can unite with the techniques of character-writing. (I say 'character-writing' advisedly, for—unlike Mayhew's figures—Atkinson's are typical but imaginary persons.) The intention of the book, as Atkinson tells us in his Introductory Note, was 'to imagine how Mayhew and his collaborators might have carried out their survey in the big city of our own day'.

In one or two instances, Atkinson and Searle have given close modern equivalents to Mayhew's types:

Two of Mayhew's Street Children

(*a*) He had heard that the earth went round the sun, but from what he'd noticed, shouldn't have thought it. He didn't think that the sun went round the earth, it seemed to go more sideways . . .

(*b*) Yes, he had heer'd of God who made the world. . . . Didn't know when the world was made, or how anyone could do it. It must have taken a long time. It was afore his time, 'or yourn either, sir.' Knew there was a book called the Bible; didn't know what it was about. . . . Didn't dislike foreigners, for he never saw none. What was they? . . .

The New Mayhew: the first of 'Two Street Boys'

He told me that he thought the name of the Prime Minister at present was Winston, but wasn't too sure, and what did it matter? . . . So far as he knew he had never been in a church; thought 'Jesus and all like that' was probably 'all right for old women and that'. . . . [He] had read much of the Bible at school, including, as he assured me with a sly look, 'the dirty bits and all.' He could name three continents: England, the Middle East and Australia, although he was not certain of the last named.

Was never in a church; had heer'd
they worshipped God there; didn't
know how it was done . . .[5]

In as much as one can compare fact with invention (or teachers' gossip?), the comparison must be depressing. For Atkinson's Street Boy attended school until, at fifteen, he was expelled for violence: he had learnt little, remembered still less, and cared not a jot about his ignorance. But of Mayhew's two Street Children, only the second, who had never been to school at all, thought he could get on quite well without education; the first boy was a product of the old Ragged Schools and at least knew more of Queen Victoria and Lord Nelson than his twentieth-century successor knew (or cared) about the Prime Minister. Moreover, the nineteenth-century boy 'would like to read more, if he had time' (p. 473). Other 'characters' in *The Big City* who seem expressly designed as modern equivalents to figures described by Mayhew include the Encyclopaedia Seller and the Sellers of Ice-Cream, Nuts, etc., descendants of Mayhew's street vendors and casual traders. Many, however, belong to our day: the Film Extra, the immigrant Railway Worker, the Television Man, the Rock Star.

There is much that is genuinely funny about the book. The humour is reinforced by irony, in that this modern Mayhew more than once misconstrues what he sees and hears or is gulled by the hard-luck stories told to him. But the overriding impression is one of gloom. The mass of people seem depressed or mindless, like the teenager who 'bore an expression of fathomless vacuity dreadful to behold' (p. 64). Where Mayhew's subjects were often near-destitute but retained some defiance or pride—or at least a wily resourcefulness— Atkinson's are for the most part merely cynical. The highest aim is quick money or a job with an expense account.

To note that many twentieth-century 'characters' belong to the realm of light humour or are cast in the form of pastiche is not to belittle them, merely to indicate that the 'character' has become a literary form of minor importance, associated with the past and, perhaps, no longer thought fit for the serious portrayal of human nature.

We have so far considered Mayhew as the subject of parody, but some twentieth-century writers have followed his methods with serious intentions, thereby unconsciously assisting in the further decline of the 'character': they include Jack London in *The People of the Abyss* (1903) and H. V. Morton in *Our Fellow Men* (1936). The first book describes the poor of London's East End and records their words; the second does the same for a cross-section of Britain's working community—not the desperately poor, but those for whom £2. 10*s*. a week represented scraping along and £5 would have meant affluence. There seems no doubt that the preference is by now for this type of social reportage and that the construction of imaginary 'characters' appears artificial.[6] The only twentieth-century successor to the 'characters' of servants and other members of the working classes as encountered in nineteenth-century periodicals and compendia is, as far as I know, N. M. Marris's Maid of all work in *Living London*, 1902–3.[7] For the rest, it has clearly long been felt that the realities of people's lives can be best communicated either through their own words or in the form of generalized surveys backed up by graphs and statistics.[8]

For all that, 'characters' continue to be written, and not only for purposes of amusement. Or, more exactly: pieces are written which are 'characters' in all but name. Two questions arise: firstly, did the author know anything of the tradition of character-writing? and, secondly, if he did not, could he write a 'character' without intending to?

A tentative answer to the first question is that most educated people in England, at least until fairly recently, would probably have known vaguely what a 'character' was. The *Spectator* was commonly used as a school-text until about the 1940s, while the *Sketches by Boz* and *The Book of Snobs* have always retained their popularity. Some people still read Theophrastus and La Bruyère. There are cases where the link between the twentieth-century 'character' and the tradition can be shown without any difficulty. P. A. Ditchfield, whose *Country Folk* (1923) contains 'characters' of the Squire and the Doctor, quotes from Overbury (pp. 221 f.); G. W. E. Russell, whose *Social Silhouettes* will be discussed presently, will certainly have known his Addison; Harold Nicolson precedes his 'character' of a Bore with a reference to Theophrastus's piece about the same type (*Good Behaviour*, 1955, pp. 279 f.).

It is not merely that a bore is long-winded; he is also touchy. He knows that he is a bore, yet he persists. Unfortunately, he detests the company of other bores, can recognise them immediately, and will avoid them as the plague. He enjoys reminiscences, coincidences and stories about imaginary circumstances and encounters. Wisecracks are a speciality of bores and I have met men in American club-cars who will tell stories as long as the freight-trains that trundle across the prairies through the night. The bore is irrelevant in that he will forget the point or concentration of his narrative to wander down by-paths and into hidden coppices. He indulges also in unnecessary precision, wishing to fix names and dates that have little bearing on his discourse. 'It must', he will inform one at dictation speed, 'have been in October '53—no it can't have been then because we were in Copenhagen—it may have been early in November—anyhow it doesn't matter, and to cut a long story short . . .'

But it is easy to find other authors who have written 'characters' without any apparent awareness of the fact. At one point in John Baynes's examination of army morale, based on the conduct of the Second Scottish Rifles at Neuve Chapelle in 1915 (*Morale*, 1967), he describes the ideal officer, announcing his intention thus: 'I will try to describe the ideal officer as he would have appeared to one of his contemporaries in 1914 . . .' (p. 123). Baynes uses the term 'word portrait', but what follows would have been perfectly recognizable to any eighteenth-century essayist as the 'character' of an Army Officer.[9]

In fact, if you construct a picture of an imaginary representative of a class of people (in order to amuse, edify, illustrate a point, or whatever), if you stick to 'he' or 'she' and operate with a combination of inner character-traits, gesture, appearance, typical actions, and words—if you do all this, you have written a 'character', whatever you decide to call it and regardless of whether you happen to know about the tradition of character-writing. The very fact that there are no established formal criteria makes this possible; after all Theophrastus was not setting out to create a distinct literary genre, but to delineate forms of human behaviour—and his imitators took over from him only the most general framework and modified it at will.

There remain two important twentieth-century character-books, very different from each other in all respects, which deserve to be discussed in some detail. G. W. E. Russell's *Social Silhouettes* (1906) contains forty-five chapters, each devoted to a human type. The form is more diffuse than in older character-books: often a chapter will combine reflections on the chosen type, a 'character', and illustrations from history or from literature, especially the English novel (to which Russell is rather too prone to ascribe objective documentary status). Although the only reference to anything in the tradition of character-writing is, as far as I can discover, a fleeting mention of Thackeray's *Snobs* (p. 16), Gwendolen Murphy is surely right to see Russell as 'a true follower of Theophrastus'[10]—and of the eighteenth-century character-writers in England, one could add. A few examples will demonstrate this.

Addison, Steele, and their imitators had been fond of describing character by means of a typical day in the subject's life. And sure enough, the device occurs in *Social Silhouettes*, in the account of Tommy Tupman, the Buck (pp. 307–11). Country Squires, 'improving' Landowners, and rich Parvenus had always been characterized in large part through exact descriptions of the homes they had bought or created for themselves. Russell's picture of a tasteless Plutocrat is closely related to these eighteenth-century predecessors in the precision of its details and its awareness that in such cases the surroundings mirror the man. However, one seldom encounters such a degree of frank distaste in the coffee-house 'characters':

> If he buys an old house, he commits the most shameless atrocities in the way of reconstruction and decoration. He stuffs the gallery of an Elizabethan manor with furniture of the French Empire, or repairs the breaches of an Edwardian ruin with Italian marble. . . . The house is very hot, and smells overwhelmingly of exotic flowers. From the drawing-room you can step into a winter-garden full of sham rockwork and tin ivy. From the walls of the dining-room Gainsboroughs and Hoppners bought at fabulous prices from decayed gentility, look down with astonished eyes upon their new surroundings. (pp. 226 f.)

Similarly, the Invalid (chapter xxxi) is a descendant of all the Hypochondriacs and Valetudinarians of the eighteenth century.

Social Silhouettes is the last large-scale serious work in English which could, without stretching the term unduly, be described as a character-book. It is a swansong not only in that sense; it also seems to record a dying era, in which the writer could still talk of education exclusively in terms of public schools and Oxbridge, in which the motor car seemed to be something invented for the use of the loathsome Plutocrat, in which the Squire was still a petty despot, lording it over the vicar, distrusting the notion of education for the workers and trying to enforce conservatism in politics by a combination of persuasion, bludgeoning, and discreet blackmail.[11]

The only other major contribution which the twentieth century has to offer to the tradition of character-writing could hardly differ more startlingly from *Social Silhouettes*: it is Elias Canetti's *Der Ohrenzeuge. Fünfzig Charaktere* of 1974. For most of his English admirers, Canetti is chiefly known as the author of *Die Blendung* (*Auto da fé*). What happens when a writer, justly famous for his creation of obsessed eccentrics, turns to the Theophrastan 'character'?[12] Canetti presents a straight succession of 'characters', each occupying about two pages of print. They are not placed in any logical sequence; the order could be changed without affecting the nature or point of the book. So far, the general arrangement is similar to that of Theophrastus's own work and to most character-books of seventeenth-century England. But here the resemblance stops.

When, in a traditional 'character', an impression of grotesqueness or eccentricity is created, it is nearly always by one or more of the following means: an impossible multiplication of examples (as in La Bruyère's Menalcas); comical exaggeration of a trait which, in itself, is perfectly familiar and realistic (as when Hall's Miser returns home and wants to know who has 'rioted among his leeks'); or transformation of an intrinsically realistic feature into a grotesque metaphor (as when Sprigge's Hypocrite says grace 'before a breakfast of widows' houses'). All of these are certainly to be found in Canetti, but he goes much further.

An anonymous reviewer in the *Neue Zürcher Zeitung* of 31 August 1974 talks of Canetti's surrealistic exaggeration (*surrealistische Überhöhung*) and contrasts the matter-of-fact instances of miserliness in Theophrastus's picture of the Stingy Man (above, p. 4) with Canetti's treatment of the Have-and-Hold (*Die Habundgut*):

She feeds her money, so that it doesn't perish. She never eats a morsel without giving some to her money. . . . Often she lays [the notes] side by side on the table, like a numerous, well-behaved family and gives them names. Then she counts them, to make sure that they are all there and, when they have been good and eaten their supper, she puts them to bed.[13]

The more familiar the type, the weirder the effect. Canetti's Loser (*Der Verlierer*) is our old friend the Absent-minded Man. But he loses things on an impossible scale. Why have his goods not run out long since? Perhaps fully laden vans come to his back door and unload while he goes off to lose things (p. 51). Similarly, the Dragger-out (*Verschlepper*) is an incorrigible procrastinator who hides all the letters that arrive for him, so that he is in no danger of having to answer them:

He knows why he is afraid of visitors who tread on his carpets: under the carpets are thousands of unopened letters. The mattresses are so heavy with letters that he could not lift them. In the attic he hardly has an empty case. (p. 79)

Some might argue that Canetti, by moving so far in the direction of the eccentric, has passed beyond the limits of what has traditionally been understood by a 'character'. But his pieces, however fantastical they may at first sight appear, usually turn out to be surrealistic equivalents to, or variants on, familiar types; this is what justifies his title. Where the traditional 'character' had shown one isolated trait starkly illuminated, many of Canetti's resemble grotesque masks—yet masks which, if stripped away, turn out to have been exaggerations of the truth rather than disguises. Thus the hero-worshipper becomes the Hero-tweaker (*Heroszupfer*), who creeps up to statues of eminent men in order to make physical contact with them and feel some of their greatness flowing into him.

What is the picture of mankind that emerges? Two of Canetti's reviewers have argued that his 'characters' are parasitic: they need others to practise or vent their obsessions on. The Tear-warmer (*Tränenwärmer*) satisfies himself vicariously with the emotional experiences of others; *der Schadenfrische*[14] feeds off their misfortunes. But the book cannot be reduced to a formula: other types, far from exploiting their fellows, feel threatened or hounded by them. All one can safely say is that the various obsessions are examined not in isolation but in their social context. That is not, of course, new. What is new is Canetti's attitude to his 'characters'. In the older character-books, types were praised or blamed according to whether they conformed with, or deviated from, a social or moral norm accepted by authors and readers. But here there is no praise or blame because there is no discernible norm; we all seem to be on board the same Ship of Fools and it is up to each of us to pick out his or her obsession, vanity, or folly.

7

The 'Character' and Society

(i) the Good Man, the Country Gentleman, the Merchant, and the Professions

'Characters' are, by their nature, full of exact behavioural details. For instance, we can read how the Village Schoolmaster kept body and soul together, how the Ballad-maker had his new piece hot from the printers almost before the malefactor had stopped twitching at the end of the rope, and how the seventeenth-century Shoplifter went about her trade.[1] Although such things are intrinsically fascinating to anyone at all interested in how people behaved in past ages, no one could reasonably hope to piece together a jigsaw puzzle of any given society from them; there are obviously many better sources of factual information. The chief importance of the 'character' as social evidence lies elsewhere, in helping us to perceive how the various types were regarded by their fellows and, above all, in reflecting changing views of a particular social or moral type. Since many figures recur in 'character' after 'character', detailed comparison is possible and such changes often emerge quite clearly.

Since, as I have said, the character-writers seldom aimed at offering the reader a systematic microcosm of society—and certainly never wrote with the intention of bequeathing such a vision to posterity—one can obviously not expect to find all types treated with the same frequency. In fact, some, especially certain social and professional types as opposed to moral ones, appear with tantalizing *in*frequency. The student of the 'character' has to make the most of what there is. If the figures treated in this chapter seem to make up a rather arbitrary group, this is because I have confined myself to those examples where a clearly perceptible change in attitude is expressed or hinted at and where the number of 'characters' is sufficient, and spread over a sufficiently long period, to illustrate that change adequately. The usual precautions, necessary when one examines literary texts for evidence of non-literary matters, apply here, of course. Almost any given work can be seen at once as the expression of the writer's views, his response to literary fashions, and his attempt to satisfy real or imagined expectations on the part of his readers. In the case of the 'character', the vogue was such that some copying became inevitable, while for most of the seventeenth century a witty manner was considered *de rigueur.*[2]

The 'character' must clearly be seen as complementing evidence contained in other sources; if studied in isolation, it will lack validity as an indicator of social and moral values. However, I have tried, in the investigation that follows, to make clear which parts of the evidence come from 'characters' and which from elsewhere. Since most character-writers have, at some time or another, tried to portray their ideal of personality and since conceptions of that ideal have changed over the centuries, the Good Man provides a suitable starting-point.

The Good Man, the Wise Man, the Happy Man

These three are inseparable, for—in theory at least—goodness, wisdom, and happiness necessarily coexist in the one person. From the Renaissance on, classical Greek and Roman ideals of goodness and wisdom gradually became fused with Christian notions. The classical sources which influenced men's conception of what constitutes the good life and how happiness is to be achieved without sacrificing virtue have been recorded by Maren-Sofie Røstwig.[3] The ideal is always that of a man who has made himself independent of worldly cares and bustle and who has mastered his passions. He is usually represented as having retired to an idyllic rural spot, although there are exceptions to this, cases where the withdrawal is an inner one and independent of place.[4] The commonest direct sources, as far as English literature in the sixteenth and seventeenth centuries is concerned, were Horace and Martial.[5] Horace delights in his farm (not too big but adequate for his needs), lives quietly and contentedly with a small circle of congenial friends, and looks back without regret on the scurry, the jealousy and backbiting, the gossip-mongering and time-wasting of city life (*Satires*, ii. 6). For Horace, the Happy Man is indifferent to riches and public applause, is free from greed and avarice, and obeys the laws because he loves virtue, not out of fear of punishment or desire for a good name

(*Epistles*, i. 16). By contrast Martial seems hedonistic, and it was Horace, with his greater insistence on the life of virtue and his hints of Stoicism, who was by far the more influential in England.

At the same time, a more direct Stoic influence came to Elizabethan England from Seneca. The type of the Wise Man, who lives a frugal and simple life far from court, accepts calmly whatever fate offers, and regards virtue as his highest possession and only inviolable good, is prominent in the *Moral Essays* and *Moral Epistles*. The ideal is present in the tragedies too, here perhaps acquiring even greater force by virtue of the fact that the lives of great men are invariably shown to be full of gruesome violence and appalling misfortunes. To endure stoically or to dream of a life of simple husbandry would seem to be the only palliatives. There are certainly passages in the tragedies which recall the Horatian idyll (such as *Thyestes*, 391–403 and 446–70). Since Seneca was well known in England from the mid sixteenth century, and since his tragedies influenced Elizabethan and Jacobean drama, it is no surprise to find constant echoes of Stoic doctrines in our literature at that time. The sections devoted to Wisdom or the Wise Man in the commonplace books always stressed constancy, indifference to wealth and all external gifts, the power to scorn the vagaries of fortune, and so forth. Seneca and, less frequently, other Stoic sources were quoted.[6] This English Stoicism usually appears in a more or less Christianized form, often fused with the related ideal of the Godly Man,[7] and it is this synthesis which strongly influenced more than one character-writer.

In the imitations of Horace, the form varies from the intensely personal note of the famous Satire ('This is what I prayed for . . .') to the more generalized expression of the second Epode ('Happy is he . . .'). Wherever the picture of happiness and moral self-sufficiency is presented in verse, especially in the first person, Horace's influence is likely to be at work. (Røstwig has unearthed hundreds of these imitations and variations.) Senecan or more generally Stoic elements are commoner in the prose 'characters'. From Hall onwards, the character-books tend to include at least one picture of the Good, Happy, or Wise Man, quite distinct from more specific 'characters' of the Good Prince, Good Magistrate, Worthy Physician, and so forth. But there is much overlapping between the 'character' proper and imitations of the Latin poets, so that rigid distinctions are sometimes difficult.

If we turn to early seventeenth-century character-writing, the nearest thing to a restatement of the Horatian ideal in this new form comes in Simion Grahame's *Anatomie of Humours* (1609). Most of this somewhat misanthropic work is given over to moral denunciation and exhortation, but Grahame also gives the 'character' of a Happy Man, partly in verse, partly in prose. Contentment comes from turning one's back on the 'imperfection of Court . . . a world of fascheries, [and] . . . uncertain toyes', in favour of the secure and peaceful rural life. Surprisingly— since Grahame spent his last years in repentance as a monk—there is no mention of religious faith or piety.

Hall's Happy Man is 'stoical' rather than 'Horatian'. He 'knows the world, and cares not for it', is indifferent to misfortune, master of his will, and free from desires. He 'can so frame his thoughts to his estate, that when he hath least he cannot want'. The Stoic element is clear in this paradox which will recur time and again in later versions of the ideal:

> He is a Paradox to the common opinion of the World, for he values none of those toyes, which the world highly prizes. (Saltonstall, Happy Man)
>
> having nothing, yet hath all . . . (Wotton)
>
> Poore are thy riches, rich my Povertie . . . (Phineas Fletcher)[8]

However, to return to Hall, it is a Christianized Stoicism: 'He walks cheerfully in the way that God hath chalked. . . . His soul is every day dilated to receive that God in whom he is . . .'.

A similar fusion of Christianity and Stoicism can be seen in Saltonstall's Happy Man, who

> is one that cares not for wealth, honor, or riches; and therein resembles his maker that he hath a sufficiency of all things within himselfe. . . . He knowes that the happiness of this life, consists in vertue, which next to God is his Summum bonum, and chiefe good. His minde is like the Halcyon smoothnesse of the Sea, which is not troubled with the least winde of passion, but rests in a quiet calmnesse. Fortune may aflict him, and change his estate, yet he is alwayes the same. . . . Hee esteemes wickednesse to be the greatest misery. . . . He sees the changes of the times, and while worldly accidents turne round about him, he stands like the center immoveable.

There is, notoriously, a cold and heartless element in Stoicism, with its insistence that a man preserve virtuous calm untroubled by his own sufferings—or by those of others. Seneca cites with approval the case of a philosopher whose estate was plundered and whose daughters were raped. When asked what he had lost, he replied, 'Nothing: I have all that is mine with me' (*Nihil, omnia mea mecum sunt—Moral Essays*, v. 6). Even Epictetus's comparatively noble Happy Man seems somewhat self-centred, rather too concerned with the preservation of calm and inner virtue (*Encheiridion*, 48). This element will often figure in later portrayals. Nahum Tate's hermit (in his poem 'The Prospect') watches a proud ship wrecked by a tempest, but it does not occur to him to try to rescue any survivors—he merely retires to his cell in order to meditate on the 'uncertain State' of worldly pomp.[9] Hall and Saltonstall, however, are free from such a blemish, for both insist on compassion and philanthropy as part of their ideal of rectitude.

> He hath hands enow for himself and others: which are ever stretched forth, for beneficence, not for need. (Hall)

> He himself is alwaies doing good. . . . If riches happen to him, hee makes them goods, by good using. (Saltonstall)[10]

Røstwig suggests that, during the Civil War and the Commonwealth, the mood of Stoic withdrawal was strengthened by a sense of instability and the feeling that peace and happiness were to be found only in rural retreats.[11] There is obviously some truth in this. William Habington, Herrick, and Cowley, who equate happiness with the quiet and secluded life, all suffered from the broils and tensions of the age. But such correspondences should not be taken too far. Wotton's chequered and at times hazardous career belongs to the reign of King James, while many of the hymns to the simple life are probably no more than literary exercises, unrelated to the lives of their authors. To imitate Horace or to compose rhetorical tributes to the man who scorns greatness and endures fate's worst offerings stoically was part of a writer's trade and training. (For a verse-character that appears no more than a five-finger exercise, one could cite Thomas Flatman's 'Happy Man' in his *Poems and Songs*, London, 1674.)

With the Restoration, the Horatian ideal sheds its note of resignation and becomes more epicurean: retirement has become 'charming' and 'ravishing'.[12] Soon, however, greater sobriety and respectability were to return.[13] The early eighteenth century shows an interesting synthesis of previous trends. Moderate enjoyment of life is permitted, but not self-indulgent hedonism. Christian virtues are to be practised, of course, but not to the extent of abnegation of the world. Nor does rural retreat mean that life has to be frugal. The ideal is a pleasant house in a beautiful setting, with neat gardens, hunting, fish-ponds and a good cellar, together with enough money to cover one's needs and a little over. The appropriate annual income is often exactly specified in Horatian imitations and verse 'characters' of the early eighteenth century: no paradoxical identification of poverty with true riches here![14] However, the retired life must involve practical philanthropy and useful and improving studies (*Guardian*, Nos. 130 and 175). The Happy Man is indifferent to the applause and the trivial concerns of the fashionable world, but is in no way given over to Stoic quietism.

The attitude towards Stoicism in the early eighteenth century is complex. As might be expected, we find certain criticisms: the Stoics are condemned for rejecting not only self-pity but pity for others and are seen as carrying their regard for virtue to ridiculous extremes (*Spectator*, Nos. 347 and 243). But Steele sees the ability to bear suffering in silence and the refusal to bore other people with one's ailments and grievances as part of civilized life; a touch of Stoicism is a necessary part of good manners (*Spectator*, Nos. 143 and 312). The Stoics would no doubt have been very surprised to find their attitudes worked into a moderate, practical, gregarious, and optimistic philosophy for living.

A few early eighteenth-century 'characters' of the Happy Man continue to stress the notion of religious contemplation,[15] while other writers produce their by now mechanical and artificial variations on the Horatian theme.[16] But, for the rest, the ideal has been invaded by that strain of practicality that runs through so much eighteenth-century thought. The Good/Happy Man is now more often than not an enlightened and busy landowner or a just and civically minded merchant. Addison's picture of Sir Andrew Freeport (*Spectator*, No. 549) may be taken as a paradigm. Deciding that he has made enough money in trade, Sir Andrew resolves to retire into the country and there develop a model estate: 'Setting my poor Neighbours to Work, and giving them a comfortable Subsistence out of their own Industry'. The lands will be developed in a way that combines beauty, profit, and benefit to the tenants. Sir Andrew plans to endow almshouses and to compose his thoughts to the next world. But he is no ascetic hermit; his old friends will always be welcome and will be handsomely, though not ostentatiously, entertained. Thus the ideal of the Good, Wise and Happy Man merges with the figures of the Country Gentleman and the Merchant. Before we turn to these, however, the situation in Germany must be considered.

In eighteenth-century Germany, there is a clear distinction between conventional praise of the Happy Man in an Arcadian setting and less artificial notions of goodness, wisdom, and contentment achievable within society. The first of these types is encountered in the poetry of the early and mid century, the second pre-eminently in the form of 'characters' in the periodicals.

Many poets[17] sang of shepherds or hermits who lived contentedly in their huts and regarded the luxurious and factitious life of city and court with pity or scorn. There is, of course, a strong element of literary fashion at work here in an age when French, Italian, and classical models were eagerly imitated. (In Germany, the influence of Anacreon was at least as strong as that of Horace.) But social and political conditions must have played a part too: the rigidly hierarchical and snobbish courts, the backbiting and self-importance of those who served the rulers, the frustrations experienced by a gifted man without powerful connections, the French affectations in dress and manners—all must have helped to drive the poets back into that nostalgic dream of grassy banks, purling brooks, gentle zephyrs, and simple meals of herbs that taste better than the most refined delicacies served on silver dishes. Reinforced by the ideas of Rousseau, the Arcadian vision is still strong in the revolutionary plays of the 1770s, in which more than one aristocrat dreams of renouncing his heritage and living out his days far from civilization.[18]

The moral weeklies, however, are concerned with an ideal design for social living rather than with any romantic isolationism. 'Character' after 'character' of the Wise or Happy Man (often called *der Weltweise*, with the implication that wisdom needs no hermit's cell, but is compatible with enlightened worldliness) describes the type not only as tolerant, contented, unwavering in mood despite changes in fortune, but also as sociable and altruistic. He is erudite, but not in a purely academic or theoretical way; learning must have practical applicability. Even a knowledge of the past is principally useful in helping to shape the future (*Das Reich der Natur und der Sitten* 1757–62, No. 273). The Wise Man is often represented as teacher or mentor. The religion which informs his actions is usually that familiar Enlightenment combination of Protestantism and Rationalism: belief in a benevolent God, who is pleased if a man reveres nature, respects his fellows, and practises virtue. For the true sage, to follow the voice of the heart under the guidance of reason is to act religiously: *Der Stimme seines Herzens unter Anleitung seiner Vernunft folgen, nennt er religiös handeln.*[19] (For all the rejection of dogma as such, that sentence reverberates with unspoken teleological assumptions!)

The ideal of humane wisdom is sometimes linked with Freemasonry. Indeed, in one Masonic weekly, the figures of the Wise Man and the Freemason merge into a single 'character' (*Der Freymäurer*, 1738, No. 1). The same periodical carries a dedication to Socrates, as a Freemason (*An den alten Freymäurer Socrates*). This is not as surprising as might at first appear, since Freemasonry was at the time passing through a highly idealistic phase and regarded itself as the custodian of tolerance, reasonableness, humane education, and universal brotherhood,[20] while Socrates was often held up in the eighteenth century as the ideal Man of Reason and a great teacher, uncompromisingly dedicated to the truth. He was often used as a stick with which to beat phrase-makers, pedants, and canting Christians (*Maulchristen*), whose actions belied their high-sounding words.[21]

The Country Gentleman and the Merchant

As we have seen, the eighteenth-century ideal of practical goodness came increasingly to be personified in the figures of the enlightened Landowner, the Merchant, or the Merchant-turned-Landowner (see above, pp. 71 ff). Since these were types whose qualities were felt to be inseparable from their social function, we find an acute awareness among the character-writers of the potential for good and ill emanating from the manor and the counting-house. Hence, side by side with the ideal 'characters', are warnings of what happens when the Merchant lapses from probity and the Squire forgets his responsibilities to tenants and community.

All the unfavourable 'characters' depict the Squire as hard-riding and hard-drinking, ignorant and uncouth. Often—too often, perhaps—the perspective is that of the townsman, over-ready to patronize. From this viewpoint, the Squire is seen as out of his element as soon as he ventures beyond the nearest market town

(Overbury, 'Country Gentleman'). With his rustic manners, he is ill at ease in polite society and bores people with endless talk of horses and hounds.[22] A 'character' in the *Mirror* (No. 104) makes the point that country life, if unbroken by visits to town, coarsens a man and renders him parochial. More radical criticisms of the bad Squire show him as a grasping and repressive landlord, treating his tenants like vassals, riding down their fences and crops while hunting, and concerned (as Justice of the Peace) mainly with harsh application of the laws against poaching.[23]

In contrast to all this, the good Landowner is shown as just, patriotic, and public-spirited. As magistrate, he dispenses true justice and, as the focal point of his little community, exercises a conciliatory and harmonious influence. He is a 'father to his tenants' (*Tatler*, No. 169), does good by stealth, provides employment and, where necessary, charity. He is expert in estate management and land improvement (the most detailed account within the realm of character-writing of the practical running of an estate is to be found in the picture of Sir Harry Lizard: *The Guardian*, No. 6). Although the type of the ideal Landowner figures in seventeenth-century character-writing (for instance, in Fuller's 'True Gentleman' of 1642), most examples date from the eighteenth.[24]

'Characters' of the Merchant are at least as numerous as those of the Country Squire and are somewhat wider in their implications. They often give the impression of having been written with greater first-hand knowledge, which is unsurprising, given the urban bias of the English coffee-house papers and the pronounced bourgeois nature of the German moral weeklies.

Throughout the Middle Ages and well into the sixteenth century, the Merchant came in for some rough treatment, especially in the literature of the Estates. He was accused of pandering to men's desires for unnecessary luxuries, of breaking his word and failing to honour his commitments, of pursuing a way of life either vulgarly ostentatious or miserly, of using his surplus wealth in various forms of sharp speculation and usury.[25] More favourable views gradually gained ground during the Elizabethan period; the expansion of trade and the more prominent part played by the wealthy merchant in public life enhanced his reputation, and was directly reflected in literature. One need only think of the hero of Thomas Deloney's novel *Jack of Newburie* (1597): zestful, honest, bountiful, and patriotic. 'I woulde I had moe such subjects,' says the King.[26]

In the seventeenth century, the character-writers take up the theme, representing the Merchant as wholly fair in all his dealings, a benefactor both to his own country and to the lands to which he exports, a man generous and civil in his conduct. Breton stresses his role in furthering those voyages of discovery and commercial exploitation which had so captured public attention since Drake and Hawkins: the Worthy Merchant is 'the heire of adventure . . . a discoverer of countries, and a finder out of commodities'. (That is not mere rhetoric; the early merchants were often voyagers, ranging far in the interests of their business.) Flecknoe, writing in 1653, sees foreign trade as offering the only real opportunities in 'these miserable dead times'.[27] The terms in which the character-writers praised the Merchant were wholly in tune with the merchants' own view of themselves. Thomas Mun (1571–1641) was a rich and successful merchant and, from 1615 onwards, a director of the newly established East India Company. In his *England's Treasure by Foraign Trade*,[28] he describes the merchant as the '*Steward of the Kingdom's Stock*', in whose '*Noble profession*' private gain and public good coincide.

The general hymn of praise has its occasional discords, of course. Breton adds by way of contrast the 'character' of an Unworthy Merchant, in which he resuscitates most of the charges made in earlier centuries, while Fuller, in the course of a laudatory 'character' of the Good Merchant 'who makes England bear wine, and oil, and spices', feels it necessary to add a warning against importing 'foreign needless toys'.[29]

A late seventeenth-century pamphlet, *The Character of an Honest Loyal Merchant* (1686), carries praise to fulsome lengths: the Merchant creates prosperity, he helps to advance exploration, knowledge, medicine, and the cause of religion, is concerned about the good name of his country, and abhors all dishonesty. ('Merchant', in this as in other 'characters' of the seventeenth and eighteenth centuries, means a trader of some substance and influence. Here the author is at pains to distinguish him from 'ordinary *Shopkeepers* and *Retailers*'—p. 6.) This idealized picture hardly hints at the notion that the Merchant's chief aim is to make money; wealth seems to flow towards him as a natural result of his virtue and his patriotic endeavours. And this author is emphatically not one of those who think that trade narrows a man's horizons: 'I scarce know any other Profession which leadeth into so much Knowledge, either of the *Great World* . . . or of the little World. . . . In the understanding of which *two things* seem to consist (if I mistake not) the main part of what we call *civil Knowledge, Wisdom*, or Policy' (p. 9).

Eighteenth-century writers continue in a similar strain. Addison, in his paper on the Royal Exchange (*Spectator*, No. 69), muses on the distribution of foodstuffs, fabrics, and minerals over the globe. What a poor country England would be if dependent only on her native resources! Merchants are the most useful members of the community: as well as increasing prosperity and employment, they 'knit Mankind together in a mutual Intercourse of good Offices [and] distribute the Gifts of Nature'. Addison gives his argument a teleological colouring: 'Nature seems to have taken a particular Care to disseminate her Blessings among the different Regions of the World, with an Eye to this mutual Intercourse and Traffick among Mankind, that the Natives of the several Parts of the Globe might have a kind of Dependance upon one another.' The Merchant thus serves nature's purpose by uniting nations through commerce. E. F. Heckscher[30] has shown that this notion of 'the religious sanctity of international trade' was widespread in various European countries from the mid sixteenth-century on. Addison's formulation is typical of the eighteenth century only in its terminology ('Nature', where the sixteenth-century writers had said 'God') and in its cosmopolitanism: Mr Spectator walks in the Exchange and feels himself to be a 'Citizen of the World'. However, Addison is more willing to admit the existence of a profit motive than the anonymous writer of 1686: merchants 'thrive in their own private Fortunes, and at the same time promote the Publick Stock'. Steele, too, sees the merchant as benefactor to all classes of society, provided that he does not import luxuries or goods which can just as well be manufactured here.[31] Yet this qualification would not have found general agreement. Many seventeenth- and eighteenth-century writers on trade defended luxury goods and a sumptuous style of living on the grounds that they furthered commerce and promoted employment: see Heckscher, ii. 289–91.

Defoe's little inset 'character' of a Merchant in *Roxana* (1724)[32] stresses not only his wealth but also the fact that it is self-renewing: a 'spring', where an estate is a 'pond'. Defoe follows the author of the *Honest Loyal Merchant* in arguing that a 'true-bred Merchant' is not only richer and grander in his way of life than many a landed gentleman, but often outdoes him 'in knowledge, in manners, in judgement of things'. This was true. Foreign trade, especially through the East India Company, brought great wealth, social standing, and political power to many merchants, whereupon they or their sons bought themselves country estates as a means to yet greater prestige and influence—or simply to retire to.[33] Motives must have varied, but the lure was strong. Thomas Mun's son, when publishing his father's proud testimony to the Merchant, styles himself with equal pride 'John Mun of Bearsted in the County of Kent, Esquire'. It may well be that these merchant-landowners helped to refine the squirearchy, bringing in wider experience and more urbane manners. Gentlemanly scorn of 'trade', although it was to play a part in English social life for at least another century and a half, can thus be seen as a fossilized piece of snobbery, if not as downright self-deception. In an interesting *Spectator* paper (No. 174), Sir Roger scoffs at trade and duly receives his come-uppance at the hands of Sir Andrew Freeport. If country gentlemen do not match the Merchant's economic and organizational skills, they will find themselves bought up by 'such new Masters as have been more exact in their Accompts than themselves; and certainly he deserves the Estate a great deal better who has got it by his Industry, than he who has lost it by his Negligence'. Social historians have shown that the process here referred to began in the sixteenth century.[34]

The ideal seems to bring the Merchant and the Squire closer together. The Merchant turns himself into an efficient, civilized, and philanthropic landowner (as in the case of Sir Andrew); the Squire must manage his estate according to strict 'Oeconomy', like a well-run business.

In Germany, the advance of the mercantile bourgeoisie in the early eighteenth century brought huge esteem to the merchant. But eighteenth-century Germany was dominated by the courts and was more rigidly hierarchical than English society. Although the merchant owed part of his livelihood to the demand for luxuries in courts and state capitals, the rising bourgeoisie to which be belonged rejected the values associated with courtly life.[35] Nor did the German merchant show any signs of wishing to ape the country gentry; as we shall see, he viewed his own way of life as at least equal in value to that of the rural *Junker*. Many of the eighteenth-century periodicals, especially those published in Hamburg, contain 'characters' of the Merchant, which promulgate the ideal in confident and assertive terms.

Der Patriot (1724–6, No. 31) contains an account (half 'character', half short story) of a good Merchant, Cerontes, together with his 'testament' to a young nephew, setting out the maxims by which the merchant should conduct himself. If one comes to this piece fresh from the English 'characters', one is struck by the very strong religious element. Cerontes trusts in God and his own efforts (*Cerontes . . . verließ sich, nächst* GOTT, *auf sich selber*—i. 294) and advises his nephew to undertake nothing without both divine and human counsel. But this piety is very much a matter of profit and loss, with God cast as the Great Accountant. 'Do not oppress, do not deny the workers their proper reward. For if this is witheld unjustly, God's punishment will be drawn down on you. If you give of your superfluity to the needy, you in turn will share in God's bounty' (p. 302). Several of the eighteenth-century 'characters' of the Merchant stress that he must combine success in business with true religion.[36] The teleological note, already heard in the *Spectator*, is sounded in Germany too: by redistributing the bounty of the earth over many countries, the Merchant fulfils the Creator's intentions (*Der Bewunderer*, 1742, No. 13).

As shown in the last quotation, morality tends to be pragmatic. J. P. Miller writes of the 'Just Merchant': 'He maintains his honour and good name and that of his master. . . . For with a merchant almost everything depends on credit. . . . He redoubles his industry daily; this is the best way to get on.'[37] The unspoken assumption is that virtue is rewarded in the most tangible way in this best of all possible worlds. For all that, the moral code is occasionally somewhat elastic; Cerontes sees nothing wrong in pushing up prices to exploit shortages (p. 301).

When the writers of these 'characters' leave religion and morality aside, their tone is, if possible, even more thoroughly utilitarian. Cerontes sees learning in a merchant as a means to an end, a source of prosperity (p. 298). J. P. Miller's 'Just Merchant', too, masters only those branches of knowledge necessary to business success. True, Eitelfeind (*Der Freymäurer*, 1738, No. 8) is an expert in, and collector of, old books, coins, and paintings—something of an Antiquarian, in fact. But Eitelfeind inherited wealth and has only needed to add to it, whereas most of the other Merchants in the moral weeklies are represented as having built up their businesses from modest beginnings. The admiration for the self-made man explains what might otherwise appear a rather philistine attitude.

English 'characters' of the Merchant, all written out of a strong sense of nationhood and mostly reflecting a spirit of imperialist and business expansion, had constantly stressed the patriotic value of the Merchant, his contribution to the nation's well-being. Occasionally in the German 'characters' a similar point is made; the Merchant's self-enrichment is shown to further the prosperity of the state as a whole, or his public-spiritedness is emphasized.[38] But this aspect is much less prominent than among the English writers: understandably so at a time when Germany was divided into numerous independent states and hardly had a sense of nationhood at all. When a writer in the moral weeklies talks of the state (*der Staat*), he means a particular state within the Empire, and when Brockes and his companions in Hamburg decided to call their periodical *Der Patriot*, they were thinking of local patriotism.

I have said that the mercantile ideal is always linked with a middle-class way of life and middle-class values. The Merchant enjoys a solid, comfortable, but unostentatious existence, constantly demonstrating Mr Micawber's axiom that to live within one's income means happiness: 'In his [Eitelfeind's] household, everything is plentiful without being extravagant and his conduct is always in keeping with middle-class ways.'[39] The very name Eitelfeind ('enemy of vanity') says much; it is constantly emphasized that the Merchant should avoid the company of spendthrifts, dandies, and those who ape their 'betters'.[40] J. M. von Loen argues that the prosperous merchant classes are at least equal to the landed aristocracy, while Kotzebue maintains that, to be a successful merchant, one needs as great and as varied qualities as to be a ruler or a general.[41]

This is markedly different from the situation in England, both in fact and in fiction. While Thomas Mun's son proudly designates himself 'Esquire' and Sir Andrew Freeport makes his fortune and retires to a country estate, their German counterparts remain within their station and fortify their self-esteem with the feeling that no class of society has any right to feel superior to them. They have an intense dislike of the haughty aristocrat who looks down not only on the bourgeoisie but even on men only recently ennobled for their deserts (this is expressed in the 'character' of the arrogant nobleman, Herr von Adelshausen, in *Der Patriot*, No. 75). It may be added that the German word *bürgerlich* had (and has) positive overtones which make it impossible to render it adequately in English by either 'middle-class' or 'bourgeois'. More than in England, the ideal of goodness came to be personified in the Good Merchant, operating within his middle-class milieu.[42]

As the Merchant was admired, so various types of speculator were vilified: in England, mainly usurers, 'projectors', and the founders and promoters of bubble companies (the most disastrous of these, the South Sea Company, was only one of many). Where the merchant contributed towards England's greatness, the projectors seemed to threaten it by nourishing hopes of quick profit and by undermining confidence and stability.[43] It is well known that unscrupulous projects, aimed at extracting money from a gullible public, followed in the wake of the South Sea Bubble, but the Projector was a familiar and despised figure decades before. Heckscher (ii. 126 f.) mentions some of the more fanciful ambitions of the projectors from the time of Charles I onwards. The most famous attack on this type is contained in Defoe's *Essay upon Projects* (1697). In it Defoe denounces the raising of capital to develop 'fine Discoveries, new Inventions, Engines and I know not what' (p. 11). His 'character' of the 'meer Projector' depicts a contemptible charlatan who passes off 'some Bauble or other' as a great invention, takes out a patent, floats shares, and persuades 'honest coxcombs' to part with their money (pp. 33 f.). The more absurd side of the Projector, with his extravagant and ridiculous plans (which seldom get off the drawing-board), is often mocked in the eighteenth-century periodicals and even recurs in one early nineteenth-century character-book, although Dr Johnson had long since pointed out that not all the Projectors' notions were as ridiculous as they might appear at first sight.[44] In more serious vein, F. G. Tomlins draws the 'character' of a Capitalist, gravely dressed and outwardly respectable, yet willing to further peace *or* war, freedom *or* tyranny in the sole interest of gain. The Financier, totally amoral in his pursuit of wealth, is set off against the Merchant in Germany too.[45]

The distinction, implicit or explicit, is always between trade or manufacture on the one hand and usury, the manipulation of currency, and the more or less fraudulent raising of capital on the other. The Speculator, Capitalist, or Projector is reviled in straightforwardly moralistic terms, just as the Merchant had been reviled centuries before in the Estate Books. Since merchants had always doubled as money-lenders, often advancing money to governments and monarchs, had performed many functions now more commonly associated with bankers, and had provided 'speculative' money to finance the expeditions of the privateers and many other often dubious ventures,[46] the contrast between the 'good' Merchant and the 'bad' Speculator was somewhat over-simplified. That it was also out of date is illustrated by attitudes towards usury. Character-writers attack the Usurer for the 'unnatural act of generation' (Overbury, 'A Devilish Usurer') and see him as 'a kind of cancer' (Breton), or mad with the sin of greed (Thomas Adams, *Mystical Bedlam*, 1615). For Saltonstall, he is 'one that makes haste to be rich, and therefore cannot be innocent' ('An Usurer'). Such censure implies the familiar distinction between a 'proper' way of making money, through trade, and the 'unnatural' breeding of money out of money. But merchants were money-lenders too, and mercantilist writers throughout the seventeenth century increasingly come to defend usury pragmatically as an economic necessity (Heckscher, ii. 286–9). Here is a case where the 'character' mirrors not society but obsolescent prejudices—and persistent prejudices too, one may add. A verse-character in *Punch* (xxix, 1855, p. 257) contrasts the good old type of merchant, who bought and sold, with the bad new type, who speculates with other people's money.

Other Professions

With the exception of the Merchant, trades and professions are represented rather patchily in the character-books. Lawyers are fairly common and here—as might be expected—hostile 'characters' greatly outnumber favourable ones. Even the descriptions of good Lawyers always contain references to the notorious malpractices of those who dishonour the profession: 'Though he knows all . . . the nice *Snapperado's* [i.e. acquisitive tricks] of *Practice*, yet he never *uses* them, unless in a *Defensive way* to *Countermine* the plots of *Knavery*.'[47]

The satirical 'characters' stress the same few points again and again: the Lawyer is greedy for profit, will plead any cause for a fee, prefers rich clients, and keeps dying suits going until the litigant's money has run out.[48] Occasionally, the Lawyer is represented as corrupt, bribing witnesses and jurymen, but in general the feeling is that he can satisfy his 'Crawling Desire' for riches (Ned Ward) by exploiting the law rather than by contravening it. His use of jargon figures most prominently in drama, of course, where he can actually be heard baffling his clients with gobbledegook, but it is mentioned in most of the 'characters' too. Butler writes: 'He overruns *Latin* and *French* with greater Barbarism, than the *Goths* did *Italy* and *France*, and makes as mad confusion of Language by mixing both with English. Nor does he use *English* much better, for he clogs it so with Words, that the Sense becomes as thick as Puddle' (p. 112).

The point about legal cant hints at what I take to be the central motive behind these 'characters'; they are the layman's revenge on the professional man. In this respect, satires on the Lawyer are similar to those directed against the Doctor throughout the ages; both have us at their mercy as soon as we need them. But where the Lawyer merely ruins a man, the Doctor kills him, having first studied his disease in the 'pispot-Almanack', confused him with 'fustian words', and, of course, emptied his purse.[49]

'Characters' of Solicitors—who formerly existed on the disreputable fringe of the legal profession—are uniformly hostile. Attacks on bad Lawyers and Doctors imply the possibility of good ones, but the 'characters' of Solicitors seem to suggest that the occupation itself is bad. The reason for this is historical. The solicitor had no official standing within the legal system in the seventeenth century and was correspondingly held in low repute. It seems that many took up the occupation without much in the way of legal qualifications.[50] The character-writers always represent the Solicitor as a man ignorant of the law who will nevertheless take on any suit for a trivial fee. He is respected only by those too ignorant to know better and conducts his business in an alehouse.[51] The reference to the alehouse is significant; the man who bargains with his clients in a taproom bears the same relationship to a 'respectable' lawyer with his clerk and his chambers in the Temple as a quack doctor does to a qualified practitioner, or a pedlar to a merchant. However, by the middle of the nineteenth century, Leman Rede (*Heads of the People*, 1840–1, ii. 177 ff.) makes it clear from his 'characters' of various types of Solicitor that the profession has, in general, become a respectable one and that 'the *genus* pettifogger, alias sharp-practitioner, has fallen somewhat into decay' (p. 180). Rede attributes this development to the increased importance of trial by jury.

In a comparative study like the present one, it is always informative to come across a marked imbalance. The Private Tutor is such a case; he hardly figures in English character-writing at all, but is among the favourite subjects of the German authors. In eighteenth-century Germany, with the rising prosperity of the middle classes, the habit of employing a tutor (*Hofmeister*, *Informator*) to educate children at home spread from the nobility to the rich bourgeoisie. One reason was the poor quality of many schools, another was no doubt the snobbish desire to be in the fashion and demonstrate one's affluence.[52] Many young men were forced to become tutors to finance their studies, as stopgaps between university and a first pastoral post or other regular employment, or to keep the wolf from the door until they established themselves as writers. A number of famous men would appear in any catalogue of *Hofmeister* in the mid and late eighteenth century: Fichte, Gellert, Gleim, Hamann, Hegel, Hölderlin, Kant, J. M. R. Lenz, Winckelmann, and others.

This was a buyer's market[53] and prospective employers often made near-impossible demands in terms of high qualifications for low pay, as was pointed out by the satirists.[54] Although we know of some men (Gellert, Hamann, C. F. D. Schubart) who spent fairly contented periods as tutors, others (Lenz, Jung-Stilling, Kant) were markedly less happy, and there is abundant evidence to suggest that many tutors were made to feel awkward and inferior, were treated as servants and expected to perform all manner of menial tasks. Adolf von Knigge writes in 1788:

> It grieves me intensely to see the tutor in many a noble household sitting humble and mute at his gracious employer's table, not daring to mingle in any conversation or place himself on a level of equality with anyone present, where even the children under his charge are given precedence over him by parents, strangers and servants—over him who, if he fulfils his function properly, should be regarded as the most important benefactor of the family[55]

Time and again it is pointed out that such attitudes on the part of parents and others must inevitably destroy any respect that the pupils might have for their tutor.

These conditions meant that—apart from the small minority of exceptionally gifted young men temporarily forced into tutorship—the majority of the *Hofmeister* left a good deal to be desired. The writers in the moral weeklies and the satirists have given us a number of 'characters' of them, and there are, in addition, inset 'characters' in many eighteenth-century novels and stories. The tutors are usually represented as harsh disciplinarians and pedants, wheedling sycophants and pliant Jacks-of-all-trades, ignorant idlers or libertines.[56] Where there is an ideal *Hofmeister*, he is shown as learned, virtuous, modest, free from snobbery or pretence, filled with Christian compassion, and possessed of natural good manners. It is occasionally stressed that a tutor is all the better for having seen something of the world before taking up his duties.[57] But the unfavourable 'characters' are more common and suggest that the employer usually got no more than he was willing to pay for. Although Lenz makes the point that better schools would render the whole system superfluous (*Hofmeister*, ii. 1), the solutions more often proposed are less radical: if parents were more responsible and better informed about educational matters and if they were prepared to treat the tutor with respect and create better conditions of employment, the general quality of tutors would improve.[58] There was clearly some justification for this view, as far as it went; the good and wise tutor, whose 'character' is given by J. P. Miller, is not an impossible ideal as such—it is simply difficult to imagine such a person taking on, and staying in, the position with things as they were.

Occasionally in England we hear of the plight of the private tutor: for instance, Hall notes how he is treated like a menial and there are a few laments in the eighteenth-century periodicals about his low standing.[59] But this is only a fraction of what was written on the subject in Germany and the quantitative difference alone reflects educational differences between the two countries. In England it was normal for parents of means to send their children to public schools (in the English sense, not the German), so that the private tutor was never of more than marginal social or educational importance.

(ii) **Old Men, Drunkards, and Others**

Old Men and Children

Of the Ages of Man, it is the Child and the Old Man who have attracted character-writers, if only because extreme youth and age are most easily and naturally regarded as self-contained states; in the intervening years of active adulthood, an individual comes to reveal himself in a social, moral, or professional role and is depicted accordingly.

The historical change of attitude regarding children is well known and has been entertainingly charted by Philippe Ariès, among others.[1] The medieval world seems to have had no awareness that childhood had its particular problems and characteristics; the child was seen as a sort of miniature and immature adult or as a symbol. Only gradually, from late in the sixteenth century onwards, did there grow a realization that the child 'counts' and has a personality quite distinct from that of an adult. Two seventeenth-century 'characters' illustrate the old and the new attitudes. For Earle, the Child is no more than an emblem of innocent happiness and purity: the whole 'character' is, unusually for Earle, little more than a string of figures illustrating this one notion (the Child is 'nature's fresh picture newly drawn in oil', his soul is 'a white paper unscribbled with observations of the world', his games are 'but the emblems and mocking of man's business', and so on).[2] Earle has not attempted to *describe* the Child as he describes his adult figures. But thirty years later, Flecknoe treats his 'School-Boy' with as much exactitude and respectful observation as any other type:

> . . . he has nothing so ready, as his *Hat* at his fingers ends; which he twirls about in mighty agony; when he is out and knows not what to say, and if you question him, he looks another way, as if he sought an Answer in the Seeling, or the Floore. . . . [He] recites his lesson in, as fast as a *Horse* running away with his Rider, and as loud as all the company were deaf . . . (No. 38 in the 1658 edition)

It is not simply that there is a difference of age between Earle's Child and Flecknoe's Schoolboy: there is a fundamental difference in approach too.

The subsequent development of attitudes towards children is too well known to be worth repeating here. The 'characters' of children offer a few amusing postscripts, from the impossibly sentimentalized picture of childhood in a mid eighteenth-century German periodical[3] to the mock outrage of A. B. Reach, nearly a century later, when faced with extremes of parental pride and indulgence. Thus, says Reach, the spoilt child tyrannizes adults and avenges itself on them for 'that one little eccentricity—the Massacre of the Innocents'.[4] But, in general, the character-writers do not more than dot the i's and cross the t's of what is already more than adequately documented. It is a different case with the Old Man.

When one first encounters the seventeenth-century 'characters' of the Old Man,[5] one is surprised by their acid tone. He is not merely shown as physically feeble, forgetful, and given to recounting tedious stories of his youth, but as mean, peevish, greedy, and obstinate. Although in his second childhood, he affects gravity and learning and clings to a life which has little more to offer him. Young men he regards with impatience and envy. As if all this were not enough, he is often represented as untidy, dirty, greasy, and malodorous, with 'putrified breath' (Overbury). Earle, it is true, gives the 'character' of a Good Old Man: a wise and respected teacher of youth, one who, having learnt the vanity of the world, calmly awaits death—but this is an exception. Seventeenth-century French treatments of the Old Man, in 'character' and in comedy, are also hostile in the main.[6]

Such enmity has a very long history. A sketch of the Old Man is one of the models given by Aristotle in his *Rhetoric* (ii. 13) as an indication of how to depict human types. Here he is described as disillusioned and malicious, pessimistic and distrustful, petty and selfish. He clings to life and lives among his memories. Horace gives a similar picture and many writers from classical times to the Renaissance were to follow him.[7] Henry Peacham's treatise on rhetoric, the *Garden of Eloquence* (1593), repeats most of Aristotle's points and adds details of physical decrepitude (see above, p. 8). Henry Crosse, in the *Schoole of Pollicie* (1605), concentrates on a single point, the tedious bragging over youthful exploits (S2^{v}). It seems clear that Hamlet is reading—or pretending to read—some such account when he repeats to Polonius what the 'satirical rogue' of a writer has to say of old men.[8] Occasionally it is the Old Man's fear—of robbery, poverty, hardship, sickness, death—which is stressed.[9]

There were thus plenty of literary models and precedents for the seventeenth-century character-writers. But there were, too, rival and kindlier stereotypes: that of the wise old man who still retained some of his youthful vigour and clarity, or that of the shrewd and revered counsellor.[10] Passages enjoining youth to treat the aged with respect are at least as common as scornful accounts of drooling greybeards. As we have seen, Earle gives an idealized picture—and the *Microcosmography* was one of the most read of all character-books. Moreover, if we turn to that popular source of material for early seventeenth-century writers, the commonplace book, and examine the sections on old age there, we find a mixture of sympathetic and hostile items: fairly evenly balanced in Meres (1598), but with the good traits predominating in Bodenham (1597).

Seventeenth-century authors were therefore presented with two contrasting pictures of the Old Man: as sage or as dotard. If the great majority of character-writers followed the second model, it was not for lack of an alternative. It is tempting to seek sociological reasons for the animus. Did the old men hold on to their property too jealously or otherwise stand in the way of youth? Brillon's Old Man, it is true, threatens to leave his estate now to this person, now to that, and finally dies intestate, but I can think of no similar motif in any other seventeenth-century 'character'. As has already been shown, the recurrent traits have nothing to do with fortunes, heirs, wills, or anything of that sort. The 'characters' say that old men were envious of the young, but not that they hindered them by exploiting financial power or, indeed, power of any other kind. The reason for the preponderance of astringent pictures may, I think, be bound up with the cultivation of 'wit' in character-writing. It is, quite simply, easier to write wittily at someone's expense than in his praise. (The links between the witty manner and the hostile strain in character-writing are discussed further in chapter 8.)

What of the eighteenth century? The periodical *Le Misantrope*, published in The Hague in 1712–13, contains a short satirical 'character' of an Old Man:

> Old Cléante has a banal way of arguing which he thinks can defeat any more reasonable opinions put forward in opposition to his vain prattle which only grows worse with age. 'Don't you know, young man', he will say, 'that you are supposed to keep silent when I speak; you are a mere brat and I am a good seventy years old.'
>
> Much good may it do you, Cléante; you are envied neither for your wit nor for your age. Do you think that long life and experience are synonyms? (No. 9: i. 70 f.)

Apart from this, I know of only two really hostile eighteenth-century 'characters' of the Old Man, both of ageing lechers,[11] a subspecies which has always been fair game for the satirist. For the rest, criticism has become milder and usually concentrates on the tendency to recount boring reminiscences.[12]

Locke had written forcibly about the decay of memory among the aged (*Essay concerning Human Understanding*, Book ii. chapter 10, paragraph 5) and Swift had pursued the point *ad absurdum* when describing the unhappy state of the Struldbrugs (*Gulliver's Travels*, Part 3, chapter 10), but the character-writers do not pay much heed to this particular infirmity, and certainly the Old Man's malice, envy, and repellent physical attributes are no longer mentioned in eighteenth-century 'characters'. Furthermore, two of the periodicals which publish hostile pictures redress the balance with accounts of the wise and good Old Man (*Tatler*, No. 45 and *Lounger*, No. 57). In the German periodicals of the mid century, we can already see that tendency to sentimentalize old age which became prominent in England only in the early nineteenth century. In *Das Reich der Natur und der Sitten* (1757–62) we find the picture of a cheerful and active old age spent in retirement on a country estate. This old man reveres God and looks forward to death without misgiving. His grandchildren learn wisdom from his lips. Thus he passes his last days peacefully, without regrets or remorse.[13]

The tone for nineteenth-century treatments of old age is set by Leigh Hunt's 'character' of the Old Gentleman, published in the *Indicator* for 1820. He is an early riser, still active and healthy, clean and neat. His pleasures are harmless, his tastes and habits old-fashioned—but described so that they seem touching rather than ridiculous.[14] This softer mood prepares us for Dickens, whose pictures of benevolent old gentlemen are too familiar to need any detailed discussion here. True, Dickens occasionally permits himself some kindly teasing, for instance, at the expense of the old men in the village where Little Nell and her grandfather come to rest (*The Old Curiosity Shop*, Book i, chapters 52 and 54), but it is all done very gently. What we emphatically do not encounter in Dickens is mockery of the old as such, any suggestion that senility in itself is comical. Bad old men in Dickens are just that: old men who happen to be bad in some specific way (usually miserly or tyrannical). There is never any suggestion that there exist faults and failings that automatically go with old age.

Therefore, if one examines the evidence offered by 'characters' in conjunction with that in plays and novels, one can see a transition from a predominantly hostile attitude to sentimental veneration. The change is not easy to account for. It may, as I have tentatively suggested, have had something to do with stylistic fashions in character-writing, or it may be related in more general terms to changing moods. Talk of the *Zeitgeist* is generally distrusted, but it is probably true to say that seventeenth-century England was more satirical, heartless, and debunking in its general temper than the eighteenth. With the age of Enlightenment came an increasingly sober and judicious attitude towards people and problems, together with a growing desire to be 'fair'. And it is a truism that very many people in the nineteenth century had a tendency towards sentimentality and tried to ignore embarrassing or unpleasant facts in the hope that they would go away. One thing seems reasonably certain: such things as the proportion of old men in society or their influence for good or ill in the control of money or property did not change dramatically around the end of the seventeenth century, any more than old men suddenly became less garrulous and untidy in 1700 or notably more endearing in 1820. What we have is a change in recorded subjective attitudes apparently unattended by any corresponding change in objective circumstances.

Only when we come to the present century do we find subjective and objective aspects coinciding. Technology is now changing the world with such rapidity that it is no longer easy to see in old people a valuable reservoir of traditional wisdom. At the same time, medicine has increased life-expectancy and, with it, the proportion of old to young in society to a degree where neither sentiment nor satire seems particularly appropriate. Where age is discussed nowadays, it tends to be presented as a 'problem'.[15]

The marked contrast between seventeenth- and eighteenth-century views on the old has its parallel in a change of attitude towards the Drunkard, the Whore and, in a slightly different way, towards the Coward.

The Drunkard and the Whore

The Drunkard, however unpleasant in the flesh, had always been popular as an object of satire or moralizing. He figures in treatises on rhetoric,[16] commonplace books, and moral allegories,[17] and is included in most seventeenth-century character-books. He is shown as physically disgusting, loud-mouthed, quarrelsome, and boastful; he turns night into day, reels home at dawn, squanders his money, ruins his health, and blabs out secrets. He is often either compared to a beast or said to be worse than a beast. The tone of these 'characters' can range from pure wit, with the author obviously enjoying himself in the depiction of noisy carousals or in the invention of elaborate conceits,[18] to a more sombre note.[19] A 'character' may start out as apparently no more than a play of wit, yet end seriously, as if to imply that the tippling must soon come to an end: 'there is death in the Pot' (L. G., 1661). All these seventeenth-century 'characters' regard the Drunkard as a fit subject only for condemnation, mockery, or the display of wit; if there is compassion, it is for his neglected and starving family: 'Hee . . . leaves his owne family so dry, that they are either parch't with famine, or burnt with thirst.'[20]

When one moves on to the eighteenth century, one point of difference is immediately apparent. 'No man is born a drinker,' says Chesterfield (*The World*, No. 92). Seventeenth-century writers had simply described the disgusting habits of the Drunkard; their eighteenth-century successors began to ask how men fall into the habit of drink. A series of short 'characters' in the *Connoisseur* suggests various causes: disillusionment, the inability to stand firm and say 'no' when in a company of drinkers, and so on (No. 92).

In the same issue of the *Connoisseur*, a point is made that had never figured in seventeenth-century 'characters' of this type: 'Poor Heartly was blest with every noble qualification of the head and heart, and bade fair for the love and admiration of the whole world. . . . [But now] he is miserable, when sober; and when drunk, stupified and muddled.' The same motif of the waste of human promise figures very prominently in the German 'characters' of the Drunkard in the moral weeklies. *Der Freydenker* (1743, No. 71) gives the 'character' of Herr von Dürstenbach, an aristocrat and a man of qualities: polite, obliging, generous, warm-hearted, and honest. Unfortunately, he manifests these traits only as long as he is sober, which is seldom far into the day. His tenants (adds the anonymous author, with the only touch of humour in an otherwise grave piece) make a habit of waiting on him at daybreak if they have affairs of moment to discuss. The contrast between Dürstenbach drunk and Dürstenbach sober is made much of: 'He appears no longer kindhearted, but simple-minded and childish. . . . If he had less wit by nature, he would perhaps be less disgusting when he is drunk.' Another German 'character' of the Drunkard which stresses this notion of lost potential is that by J. F. Reupsch.[21] Implicit here is one of the basic tenets of the eighteenth-century

Enlightenment. Since all men are capable of reason and thus of playing a useful part in the life of the community, drinking—since it robs a man of his powers of reasoning—is a tragic waste. So the writer in *Der Freydenker* notes the occasional rays of commonsense (*die wenig überbliebenen Stralen seiner gesunden Vernunft*) which can still penetrate the alcoholic fumes in the mind of Herr von Dürstenbach. He ends, not with a scornful 'Foh! He stinks!', but sadly: 'I think that this description which I have given of him will suffice to afford the reader some insight into the pitiable condition of this good nobleman.'

The more sympathetic and regretful attitude, which we have seen emerging in the eighteenth century, continues in the nineteenth, in Lamb's 'Confessions of a Drunkard', in many a novel, even in some of the tracts.

The treatment of the Whore is oddly similar to that of the Drunkard. Seventeenth-century descriptions are usually savage, often including references to venereal disease. These provide a parallel to the disgusting physical attributes noted in the 'characters' of the Drunkard, but with the added point that the whore infects others. Thomas Jordan epitomizes the common attitude:

> A pittiful example to the *wise*;
> But those whom she abus'd in *life* will *laugh*
> Her final fall, and *curse* an *epitaph*.[22]

However, from the early eighteenth century on, more compassionate voices are heard. In 1703, John Tutchin recorded interviews with whores committed to Bridewell and, while feeling nothing but contempt for the more shameless sort, pities one girl whom he sees as more or less forced into prostitution when turned away by her protector immediately before his 'Marriage with a Fortune' (*Observator*, No. 94). Steele, too, describes the plight of country girls come to London and tricked into prostitution by bawds (*Spectator*, No. 266). He complains of the 'rigider' kind of woman who places the prostitute beyond the pale of compassion. Forty years later, Dr Johnson tells of a girl seduced and presently abandoned by her wealthy protector. Again, heartless attitudes are criticized: 'If those who pass their days in plenty and security, could visit . . . the dismal receptacles to which the prostitute retires from her nocturnal excursions . . . it would not be easy for any degree of abhorrence to harden them against compassion.'[23]

The prostitute's ambiguous and insecure position is stated most forcefully by the eponymous heroine of Defoe's *Roxana*. It is true that Defoe makes no bones about her mercenary disposition and her desire for a life of luxury, true also that she is brought low at the end and dies, penitent, in a debtors' prison.[24] But Defoe's attitude is far from simple condemnation. The following passage is a little inset 'character' in all but name:

> The whore skulks about in lodgings, is visited in the dark, disowned upon all occasions before God and man; is maintained, indeed, for a time, but is certainly condemned to be abandoned at last. . . . If once the man comes to repentance, or makes but one step towards a reformation, he begins with her, leaves her . . . abhors her, and sees her no more . . . the more sincere and unfeigned his repentance is . . . the more his aversion to her increases, and he curses her from the bottom of his soul . . . (ed. cit., p. 115)

In these eighteenth-century treatments, society's attitudes come in for as much criticism as does the whore herself:

> What is the reason WHORES are so in vogue?
> Why, faith, to gain a true one, ask each ROGUE.[25]

Steele suspects the sincerity of those 'over-offended Ladies' who are 'too warmly provoked at other Peoples personal Sins' (*Spectator*, No. 266), while Defoe, Tutchin, and others hint at the illogicality of the male position—for the moral reformation which begins by turning away the kept woman drives her into ever more promiscuous and squalid paths. But Defoe goes much further. Throughout his novel there runs an intermittent discussion of the relative positions of wife and mistress. In a remarkable passage, Roxana is allowed to point out the financial and legal disadvantages of the wife's status. Her wealth is no longer her own; she is a slave who must follow 'the monarch, her husband' even into penury (pp. 125, 129–31). Roxana's notions do not seem to be far removed from today's debates about the tax advantages of unmarried cohabitation as opposed to marriage.

With the Drunkard and the Whore, it is the attitudes that change, not the type. In the case of the Coward, both objective changes of circumstance and subjective changes of attitude are mirrored in the 'characters'.

The Coward

Theophrastus's 'character' of this type is largely taken up with a battle-scene, where the Coward avoids the action first by pretending to lose his sword, then by looking after a wounded man until the fighting is over. The choice of such a setting was natural enough in a society where every able-bodied citizen was expected to bear arms in case of an emergency. But, when we come to seventeenth-century England, where there was a sharper distinction between civilian and military life, the Coward splits into two halves, so to speak. The craven soldier becomes an independent type, merging with that traditional figure of comedy, the *Miles Gloriosus*. From the Renaissance on, Plautus's Pyrogopolynices (*Miles Gloriosus*) and Terence's Thraso (*Eunuchus*) spawned a long succession of chicken-hearted braggarts,[26] and these have their counterparts in the character-books: in Overbury's 'Coward in Command', Jordan's 'plundering Coward' of 1641, later in the anonymous 'Coward in Commission' (*Characterism*, *c.* 1750) and Rabener's 'peaceful soldier', who always manages to produce a medical certificate when there is any threat of active service (*Todtenliste*, pp. 58 f.). Some touches in Rabener's sketch suggest that he was aiming at a modern version of thc *Miles Gloriosus* in character-form.

Most 'characters' of the Coward, however, ignore the martial context and concentrate on civilian life. Earle's Coward is of this sort, as is Breton's: '. . . if a dogge barke, he will not come neere the house. If hee be rich he is afraide of theeves and if he be poore he will be slave to a begger' (p. 13). Fear of a naked sword still figures in these 'characters', but one suspects that this is now the blade sported by the Roaring Boy in London's streets and taverns rather than the bloodstained weapon of the battlefield.[27]

When the Coward was treated at all seriously, there was moral condemnation, strongest among the preachers, who were concerned with showing how excessive fear, because it sacrificed principle to safety, was incompatible with true goodness (see, for example, Thomas Adams's 'Fearful Man' in *The Soul's Sickness*, 1616). Flecknoe, too, examines the dishonourable implications of an undue regard for self-preservation in his 'character' of a 'Profess'd Coward' (p. 20 in the 1673 edition). Adams's point is reiterated by Jeremy Collier in 1709,[28] but in general the eighteenth century was to show a more tolerant and understanding attitude towards fear. How did this come about?

It is obvious that there have always been two possible reactions to the Coward. There was the brisk, no-nonsense approach: 'As we do not drive feare from timerous horses by keeping them in the stable, but by leading them by the force of bitte and spurre into those places, which they feare: so also a fearfull and timerous minde is to be forced, that at length it may put off this vaine feare' (Meres, 192ʳ–193ᵛ). By contrast, there was the awareness that cowardice is a seemingly ineradicable condition, a product of the imagination. Montaigne argues that fear itself is the thing most to be feared, since it paralyses men and makes them incapable of reasoned action ('De la Peur'), and the view that imagination makes cowards is nowhere more tersely expressed than in the words which Shakespeare puts into Caesar's mouth: 'Cowards die many times before their deaths' (*Julius Caesar*, II. ii). Seventeenth-century character-writing, concerned with imperfect types as deviations from an ideal of behaviour, had been content to mock or condemn; only in the eighteenth century did the notion of cowardice as born of an over-active imagination come to predominate and, with that notion, a more indulgent attitude towards the Coward.

Fear is in all of us: 'unavoidable by rational beings, who know that many evils may probably, and some must certainly befall them,' says Boswell.[29] The 'may' and the 'must' provide the key. If reason loses its hold on the mind, it is fatally easy to become obsessed with what might conceivably happen. If there are no real and immediate dangers, we will invent them. This is the case with Dr Johnson's Will Marvel, for whom quite minor hardships and discomforts of travel seem like fearsome dangers stoically endured (*Idler*, No. 49). 'Character' after 'character' in the eighteenth century, in England and Germany alike, shows how it is the imagination that persuades the Coward that every bend in the road could cause the carriage to overturn, that any apparently harmless wayfarer could turn out to be a highwayman, that a tiger might break out of a menagerie, or that the most harmless pleasure-cruise could end in shipwreck and disaster—the list of possible catastrophes is endless.[30] The anonymous author of the *Schilderungen der heutigen Sitten* (1763) speaks quite explicitly of the Coward's judgement and imagination possessed and incapacitated by fear (*seine von der Furcht voreingenommene Beurtheilungs- und Einbildungs-Kraft*).[31]

Fears could be aggravated by reading. Popular medical treatises were, then as now, a fertile source of anxiety; the neurotic philosopher whose 'character' is given in No. 4 of *Geschmack und Sitten* (1752) has worked out that man is subject to at least 2,500 ailments. Since he has a wife and five children, the family has 17,500 chances of falling ill. It is in the nature of things that some of the obsessions which were meant to seem comically exaggerated or groundless at the time of writing fill the modern reader not with mirth but with a wry sense of unease. For instance, there is the prophetic young man who, as early as 1754, had made the discovery 'that the profusion of man consumes faster than the earth produces. Vast fleets, and enormous buildings, have wasted almost all our oak; and the firs of Norway are beginning to fail. What shall we do, he says, when the coal, salt, iron, and lead mines are exhausted?' (*The World*, No. 99)

Thus the switch of attention from the Coward-in-battle to the Coward in an ordinary social context was followed by the realization that fear has little to do with actual danger. All the eighteenth-century Cowards live quietly and in security, as landed gentry or as members of the prosperous bourgeoisie. They have literally nothing to fear but their fear; that is, their imagination. It may be that there is a link here with the intensely introspective strain in eighteenth-century life; the age that saw the *Night Thoughts*, the intense psychological diagnosis of the epistolary novel, the soul-searching of the Pietists, the melancholy cults of friendship, and all the other manifestations of 'sensibility' was well qualified to see the dangers of the imagination. It is perhaps no coincidence that this interpretation of the Coward reaches its climax in a work by Jean Paul Richter, a man in turn elated and alarmed by the intensity and scope of his imagination.

Des Feldpredigers Schmelzle Reise nach Flätz (1807), although of novella length, was described by Jean Paul in his Preface as a 'portrait in the French sense of the word, a character-sketch'. That is, he saw *Schmelzle* as something akin to the protracted 'character' of a Coward. (The failure to distinguish between 'portrait' and 'character' is typical of the lax terminology in Germany, where *Porträt*, *Charakter*, and *Gemälde* were used more or less synonymously throughout the eighteenth century.) Schmelzle is a field-chaplain, journeying to the state capital in order to defend himself against charges of cowardice in the field, and the work takes the form of his travel-journal. Although Schmelzle himself is convinced that his disposition is exactly mirrored in his Christian name (Attila!), almost every word he writes shows him to be an arrant coward. His imagination is wholly concentrated on possible mishaps and disasters. A man can be attacked and robbed, struck by lightning, or felled by a meteor. He can have a child fathered on him by a false oath or be convicted of a crime that he did not commit. To eat a hare from which the shot has not been extracted before cooking may result in poisoning. And who can tell whether a dog encountered in the street has rabies?

Schmelzle's reading confirms and aggravates his fears: he reads of deaths from apparently trivial ailments (Tycho de Brahe is said to have died from retention of urine); popular scientific works of the day gave statistics concerning meteorites and listed precautions to be taken against lightning; one writer even expressed the fear that scientists might one day perform an experiment that would destroy all life on our planet.

It is worth returning to Boswell for a moment: many evils *may* befall a man and some *must*. Schmelzle's fears are ingenious and far-fetched, but never wholly fanciful. All the things that he is afraid of could theoretically happen, and all the alarming passages in his reading refer to actual books of the day.[32] There is a parallel here with the 'character' of Herr Kurl (*Geschmack und Sitten*):

> For instance, there can be a plague, famine can come about, or the enemy can invade our country, the house can be damaged by storm or fire, I can break my leg when I go out. Nothing is more likely—a slate falling from the roof can injure me—or I can suffer some other misfortune—one can be attacked by a thousand diseases . . . (pp. 27 f.)

Nothing could be more significant than the eightfold repetition of 'can' in that passage. Where most men temper their apprehensions with the thought that 'it may never happen', Schmelzle and Kurl are afraid all the time, and of everything. They have the imagination to see possible danger without the common sense to cut it down to size. It is this new interpretation of the Coward in the eighteenth century that has such important consequences in terms of moral evaluation. If he is the victim of an uncontrollable imagination which he can hardly combat in the way that a miser or a glutton can combat his greed, he can no longer be seen as particularly culpable. He is made fun of, to be true, but no longer condemned as in the seventeenth century.

But the attitude did not long survive. A superficial reason might be sought, in England at least, in the combination of patriotism and the public-school ethos, but it may be that more primitive forces were also involved. The tolerant view held by a small minority may have been incapable of surviving for long, since it offended against deep-seated notions that bravery is good in itself and that to show and to yield to fear is shameful.

The Antiquary and the Virtuoso

In the strictest sense of the word, the Antiquary was 'a man studious of antiquity, a collector of ancient things' (Dr Johnson's *Dictionary*). The passion for collecting was not, of course, as limited as that definition might suggest, but commonly extended to minerals, fossils, and insects, as well as all sorts of rarities and curiosities. Through much of the seventeenth century and intermittently thereafter, the term 'Virtuoso' was used more of less as a synonym for 'Antiquary, although, with the foundation of the Royal Society in 1662 and the fame—or notoriety—of some of the early experiments pursued there, 'Virtuoso' came to be applied more specifically to the scientific dilettante. Since the researcher is often a collector too, it is not surprising that the two terms, Antiquary and Virtuoso, overlap a good deal. All one can say is that a man whose overriding interest was the collection and study of ancient and curious objects was usually called an Antiquary, while the man who was primarily concerned with scientific experiments was dubbed Virtuoso.

The first 'character' of the Antiquary occurs in the *Microcosmography.*[33] He admires ancient monuments, half-effaced inscriptions, ruins, and old coins. He likes manuscripts better than printed books ('a novelty of this latter age') and would give all his books for 'six lines of Tully in his own hand'. His passion for all things old is seen as not only eccentric and misguided, but as unnatural. 'He . . . hath that unnatural disease to be enamoured of old age and wrinkles.' Many character-writers were to repeat these charges. The Antiquary emerges as the seventeenth- and eighteenth-century equivalent of the relic-hunter. Indeed, Houghton[34] goes so far as to describe the fascination with secular curiosities as a sublimation of the medieval worship of Christian relics. The character-writers would certainly have agreed, for they depict the Antiquary as priding himself on possessing a humming-bird which an American princess wore in her ear, a tobacco-pipe which once belonged to Raleigh, or a stone from the tower in which Richard the Lionheart was held prisoner.[35] If we turn from the 'characters' to the real world, we find close parallels. While in Florence, John Evelyn had been shown St. John's Gospel, written in the Saint's own hand, 'as they would make one believe'; in Rome he had seen St. Thomas's doubting finger and some of the pieces of silver paid to Judas, 'if one had faith to believe it'. But when, in Rome, he viewed the cabinet of Signor Angeloni, which contained, among other things, 'one great nayle of [Corinthian brasse] found in the ruines of Nero's golden house', he entered no such reservation in his diary.[36] The suspension of disbelief exhibited by the Catholic faithful when confronted by sacred relics is simply transferred to secular objects.

Many 'characters' of the Antiquary refer scornfully to his interest in curiosities from the realm of natural history. Since he values objects mainly for their rarity, a deformed monstrosity means more to him than a perfect specimen.[37] His adored possessions are constantly derided by the satirists as 'trifles'.[38] It is common to find him charged with ignoring current affairs for ancient history or with knowing less about mankind than about spiders and maggots; the fact that he is a passionate collector and student of insects is invariably regarded as hilarious. Occasionally the old charge about the collector's gullibility is revived or he is condemned for his extravagance,[39] but the main points of attack are that he dotes on everything old and useless, that he neglects important things for trivialities, and that he is driven on by idle curiosity.[40]

The first of these charges, made so trenchantly by Earle and repeated in almost every 'character' thereafter, seems to rest on the implicit belief that new things are better than old. In Wycherley's *Gentleman Dancing-Master* (1672), Mrs Flirt is bargaining about the terms on which she will consent to be maintained as a kept woman: 'Then you must take the Lease of my House, and furnish it as becomes one of my Quality; for don't you think we'll take up with your old Queen *Elizabeth* Furniture, as your Wives do' (Act V). Lest the taste of a 'Common Woman of the Town' be considered unreliable evidence, let us turn to a most *un*common woman, Jane Austen. Presented with old-fashioned jewels, her characters immediately think to exchange them or to have the stones new-set.[41] Yet Jane Austen was certainly no uncritical modernist and innovator, as is shown by her treatment of Henry Crawford in *Mansfield Park*. In literature, the notion that the new supplants the old persisted well into the eighteenth century. In music, a similar view—involving something akin to evolutionary assumptions—addled reactions to old music and old instruments until well into the twentieth.

In view of the reverence felt for classical antiquity since the Renaissance, one might expect to find an exception made in favour of those Antiquaries who specialized in collecting Greek and Roman artefacts. It is true that—apart from the occasional quip at the man who has more pieces bearing Caesar's head than current coin of the realm—this type of collecting was obviously felt to be a respectable exception. I know of only two cases where there is anything more than a passing criticism—and there is a particular reason in each. William Law criticizes the collector and connoisseur of classical remains because *any* obsession with 'worldly trifles' hinders true religiosity, while Richard Graves ridicules an Antiquary whose concern with the Roman past is so obsessive that he tries to force present-day life into that mould: 'He would never suffer his little boy to wear a hat, because the Romans, belike, went bare-headed . . . He would have the body of his eldest son, who died, burnt to ashes, because the Romans did so; but his wife would not consent to it.'[42] One further exception was made: the Antiquary who collected on a really grand scale was exempt from mockery.[43] But the actions of the very rich have always tended to be regarded as self-justifying.

Where the English 'characters' of the Antiquary are content to condemn his activities as trivial, German treatments of the type (usually called *der Naturaliensammler*) are more discriminating. Thus H. J. Lasius sets off the idle and boastful curiosity of 'Antiquarius' against a genuine passion for knowledge. When Lasius insists that true learning must involve an awareness of the workings of cause and effect, he is implicitly condemning the mere amassing of, and gaping at, isolated curiosities. A genuine understanding of material phenomena, he adds, leads us to an understanding, however fragmentary and halting, of God.[44] A decade later we find an anonymous author defending the collector of minerals, fossils, natural history specimens, and so on against the popular prejudice that he is engaged in childish, idle, and useless pastimes. A study is not useless merely because there is no immediate and obvious material gain; if pursued seriously, it adds to our understanding of nature.[45] The spirit of the Enlightenment has come to the rescue of the maligned Antiquary.

The discussion of what is 'useful' and what 'useless' in the activities of the collector leads us directly to the Virtuoso. As already mentioned, that term came to be applied to men of science during the early years of the Royal Society. The Society's *Philosophical Transactions,* which appeared from 1665 onwards, recorded the experiments, projects, and speculation of its members. Some items provoked a good deal of mockery, and the *Transactions* certainly make strange reading. One finds details of experiments in agriculture, horticulture, perspective, medicine, navigation, astronomy, and all manner of other subjects, together with designs of the most humane practicality (for example, attempts to help the deaf and dumb or to improve faulty vision). Mixed up with all these, however, are trivialities and rank curiosities: accounts of a serpent with a head at each end of its body (No. 43), of a merman sighted in Virginia (No. 126), of how rain engenders maggots in Jamaica (No. 27). The misfortune of the Society was that the mirth provoked by such fantastic travellers' tales led to ridicule of its activities in general. Moreover, early and primitive experiments in vitally important fields did often sound comic when described in the *Transactions.* Blood transfusion provides a good example: one experiment records how blood was passed from a young dog into the veins of an old and near-decrepit one, which 'two hours after, did leap and frisk' (No. 26). This is taken up by Butler, whose Virtuoso proposes to make old dogs young. Similarly, Butler and others satirized Boyle's experiments on the physical properties of air. Ned Ward explicitly identifies his 'Virtuoso' as a member of the Royal Society (*London Spy*, No. 1), while Steele regarded the activities of the Society as a mockery of 'Natural Philosophy' (*Tatler*, No. 236) and Addison represents a Virtuoso as losing his wits as a result of being made a member (*Tatler*, No. 221). Shadwell joins in the attack in his comedy *The Virtuoso* of 1676, where Sir Nicholas Gimcrack spends a fortune on a microscope, with which he investigates bugs and other insignificant creatures, and has a dozen experiments in train (not all as absurd as Shadwell thought). He prides himself on knowing more about spiders than about mankind and indignantly denies that his experiments have any practical usefulness whatsoever.

The point about usefulness is made more than once by the character-writers. The *Essay in Defence of the Female Sex* (1696) is quite explicit, indeed hortatory: the Virtuoso should concern himself with useful knowledge, should promote luxury, increase trade, and enrich himself and others. If he studies plants, he should concentrate on those which have 'vertue in Medicine' (p. 98). Richard Graham (*Angliae Speculum Morale,* 1670) had taken a more balanced view, distinguishing between true researchers and mere hangers-on and dilettanti. He prized obviously useful knowledge (the grinding of lenses, theories of diet), but also investigations into insect life because these too opened up one more page in nature's book (here he anticipates the German character-writers of the following century). Graham even saw that the early and primitive experiments in blood transfusion were potentially of great practical importance, even if their exact application could not be foreseen (pp.41-2). But such judiciousness was uncommon.[46] Most writers were quite confident of their ability to distinguish between 'useful' and 'futile' research. Swift (*Gulliver's Travels,* III, chapters 2 and 5) manages to have it both ways, satirizing both the philosophers of Laputa for their dislike of 'vulgar and mechanick' skills and the Academicians of Lagado for their crazy, would-be utilitarian projects (such as extracting sunbeams from cucumbers).

The 'characters' of Antiquaries and Virtuosi may be exaggerated for comic effect, but they are not wild caricatures. Evelyn, visiting a certain Signor Rugini in Venice, was fascinated by a collection of petrified objects: 'wallnuts, eggs in which the yealk rattl'd . . . an whole hedgehog'.[47] These are neither more nor less bizarre than the rat's testicles, the fur cap which once belonged to the Czar, the collections of Easter eggs, aborted butterflies, and all the other oddities listed in the 'characters' and satires. As far as the quest for relics is concerned, what is there to choose between Evelyn's nail from Nero's house and Ned Ward's nail from the Ark?[48] We can thus concentrate our attention on the value-judgements expressed in, or implied by, the 'characters' and satires, without having to aim off unduly for malicious or extravagant exaggeration. (Even Swift's surrealism is only apparent.[49])

As for the charge that the Antiquary and the Virtuoso pursued 'useless' learning, some scientists and collectors disarmingly admitted as much themselves. As long ago as 1605, Bacon had vindicated a quest for learning entered on out of 'natural curiosity and inquisitive appetite', intended to entertain the mind with 'variety and delight'. Evelyn, too, recommended study as 'pleasant recreation', a sweet way to pass the time. In more lofty tones, Fontenelle defended apparently 'useless' mathematical studies because they lend precision to our habits of thought and give us intense pleasure by feeding our intellectual curiosity.[50] Fontenelle's arguments will have gained some currency in England from having served as preface to various editions of, and selections from, the *Transactions* of the Royal Society. But the layman could hardly be expected to share such views; he wanted to see immediate and obvious practical possibilities.

The experiments mentioned or satirized in character and comedy are, as we have seen, perfectly recognizable as actual experiments conducted by scientists and virtuosi of the day. In *The Virtuoso,* for example, Shadwell mocks investigations carried out with the aid of the microscope and, like Butler in his 'character', makes merry at the expense of early attempts at blood tranfusion. One could hardly choose *less* ridiculous examples from the Society's activities. But it was easy to mock, less easy to see the serious potential of apparently outlandish experiments. Today, with our more sophisticated understanding of the interrelationship of pure and applied science, we can see the fallacies underlying these satires of the Virtuoso. Similarly, we are bound to regard the scorn poured on the Antiquary as misguided, if only because we no longer have much confidence in the superiority of new things over old. If the Antiquary was slightly ridiculous, so were his critics.

'Characters', therefore, can tell us a good deal about how various human types were regarded in different ages. Sometimes, of course, they merely confirm what we already know about popular prejudices. The many 'characters' of Bluestockings illustrate this point clearly;[51] as do depictions of the Pietist, the Puritan, and the Freethinker (as seen by the orthodox) or the Jesuit (through the eyes of English Protestantism).[52] The situation is much more interesting if we have the other side of the case presented by a sympathizer, either through a 'character'[53] or in some other form (for instance, the numerous diaries, confessions, and laudatory biographies written by Puritans and Pietists). We then have a clash of subjective views, with at least a chance of deciding where, between the two extremes, the truth lies.

A major value of the subjective evidence offered by the 'character' is that it complements and fleshes out the more sober and factual testimony provided by other sources. Or, in the case of the Antiquary and the Virtuoso, the 'characters' (reinforced by satire and comedy) offer us abundant evidence of how such men were regarded by their contemporaries, while the transactions of various learned societies, letters, diaries, catalogues, and so forth show us in equal detail what the Antiquary and the Virtuoso actually did and how they regarded themselves. The treatment of these types in the 'characters' is ribald, but the questions raised are serious ones.

The character-writers certainly help us to see how social attitudes changed. Although generalizations regarding the prevailing temper of this or that historical era are hazardous, one surely should not ignore the evidence in cases where virtually every seventeenth-century 'character' of a particular type is hostile and virtually every eighteenth-century treatment sympathetic. Even if the eighteenth-century 'characters' inform us only of the values expressed in, and encouraged by, the periodical literature of the Enlightenment, their testimony is valuable, since the humane moral and social education attempted by the *Spectator* and its many imitators, in England, Germany, and Switzerland alike, is so obviously an important part of the culture of the time.

Finally, if I may speak personally, to read 'characters' from different countries and different centuries has been a voyage of discovery through the society of past ages. It is doubtful whether anybody, in whatever discipline, could study these little works without either learning something fresh or being prompted to ask new questions or reassess previously held certainties.

One omission will doubtless have been noted: no mention has been made of the hewers of wood and drawers of water. It is to these that we must now turn our attention.

(iii) **The Poorer Classes**

'If you look for the working classes in fiction, and especially English fiction,' says George Orwell in his essay on Dickens, 'all you find is a hole.' Orwell overstates his case, but has a point. However, the statement does not apply to character-writing, where working-class types form an interesting minority. A minority, it must be stressed, for most trades, if they figure at all, crop up only once or twice; the only really popular categories of workers are those who came into fairly frequent personal contact with the middle and upper classes: the servants who waited on them, the tailors who clothed them, and the gaolers who incarcerated them when, not infrequently, they were imprisoned for debt. But there are more Squires than Ostlers among the 'characters', more Society Belles than Dressmakers, more Dandies than any six trades put together. Only one character-book known to me (*Micrologia* by 'R.M.', 1629) has the representatives of the trades in a majority.

The chief reason why the working classes are in a minority compared with those of higher station and generalized moral 'characters' is, in all probability, simple ignorance. 'Persons . . . in a higher or middle rank of life know little or nothing of the characters of those below them.'[1] The gulf between class and class sometimes appeared so wide as to suggest a different species:

> One sees certain wild animals, male and female, spread over the countryside, black with grime, livid and burnt by the sun, bound to the earth which they dig and turn over with unconquerable stubbornness; they have something resembling an articulate voice and when they rise to their feet they show a human face; they are, in fact, human beings . . . (La Bruyère, xi. 128)

That celebrated passage is matched by a remark of Orwell's, in the essay already cited, to the effect that the common man of nineteenth-century England must have seemed like a different kind of animal from the gentleman. One certainly feels that clichés about 'two nations' are pallid understatements when one compares La Bruyère's sun-blackened peasants with his epicures, dandies, or social climbers, or when one reads, in one Victorian character-book, that 'in most of the domiciles of her Majesty's subjects there is a nursery'.[2]

Some character-books ignore the working classes altogether. Breton's is an interesting example, for *The Good and the Badde* appears to be intended as a microcosm of society according to the Estates. Breton begins with the King, the Queen, the Prince, the Privy Counsellor, etc., but proceeds only as far as the professions before abandoning the scheme. There are no representatives of the trades or crafts, so that the work resembles an Estates Book with the bottom tier missing. (Breton gives the 'character' of a Poor Man, but he is not a working man.) Character-writing in eighteenth-century periodical literature is concerned with the encouragement of reason and virtue among people of adequate, or more than adequate, prosperity and hardly features the working classes, mentioning the poor mainly as giving the affluent an opportunity to exercise charity, or as a burden on the rates.[3] While, as we shall see, some nineteenth-century character-writers portray working-class figures with realism and compassion, others confine themselves to the 'respectable' and prosperous middle ranks of society. The humorous character-books of the mid-century are full of young ladies who sketch and may be prevailed on to render a song or two, dandified young gentlemen, and pampered children.[4] The trend towards social selectivity is continued in G. W. E. Russell's *Social Silhouettes* of 1906, where we encounter the Clubman, the Diner-out, the Philanthropist, the Buck, the Hypochondriac, and so on. Russell's Schoolboy is a public schoolboy, his Schoolmaster a public schoolmaster, his Soldier an officer.

So much for the broad distribution of working-class 'characters'. What of the treatment? Occasionally, in early works, we encounter a composite portrayal of 'the Common People' or 'the Lab'ring Poor', as if the writer could not be bothered, or did not deem it possible, to pick out and describe a typical representative;[5] sometimes, too, seventeenth-century 'characters' of rustic types fall into the fashionable Arcadian vein (Overbury's Milkmaid, Stephens's Honest Shepherd). But many (perhaps most) seventeenth-century 'characters' drawn from the working classes are not so much descriptions of the type as opportunities for the writer to exercise his wit. We have already seen this in the cases of Overbury and Earle (above, pp. 29 and 35); an other example is afforded by Francis Osborne's Cook, from his *Miscellany* of 1659. The subject is likened to a priest preparing a sacrifice, then his kitchen is equated with Hell (a conceit already made much of by Earle), and finally his trade is compared to heraldry, 'varying no less in *Sawces*, then they do in *Colours*, *Bendes*, *Fesses* and *Metalls*' (p. 196). We learn very little about the Cook himself. Other 'characters' of tradesmen which are no more than witty exercises occur in R. M.'s *Micrologia* (Rope-Maker, Smith), and the tendency continues into the nineteenth century with the Coachman from W. F. Deacon's *Innkeeper's Album* of 1823, with nineteenth-century facetiousness replacing seventeenth-century wit.

It is necessary to make a distinction here. There are cases where the wit coexists with genuinely observed, realistic touches or illumines an aspect of the particular trade under discussion. Henry

Parrot, for instance, writes of the Tapster: 'Nothing affrights him like the Brewers Clarke whose comming with his Tallies prove more terrible then is a Sergeant to a younger brother.'[6] Such realistic details usually relate to the subject's perks, minor dishonesties, or professional and mercenary preoccupations: the Cobbler prefers foul weather to fair, the Ostler's highest aim is to become an inn-keeper, the Waterman considers London Bridge a 'terrible eye-sore' (because the arches were so narrow).[7] These and similar motifs are quite different from empty 'trade' puns: '[The Gardener] is never rich, yet he is ever raking together' (Saltonstall, No. 29); or cases where the type merely serves the author as a moral emblem: '[The Waterman is] the embleame of deceite, for he rowes one way and looks another' (Saltonstall, No. 15); or, again, conceits which point away from the subject of the 'character' to a different type altogether: '[The Serving-man is] a creature, which though he be not drunk, yet is not his owne man' (Overbury, p. 69).

Saltonstall's *Picturae Loquentes* of 1635 contains an odd mixture of both approaches, sometimes within a single 'character'. For instance, the Mower (No. 35) 'walkes like the Embleme of Tyme, with a Sith upon his backe, and when he cuts the grasse, hee shewes the brevity of man's life'. But presently Saltonstall adds: 'Hee is never vext but when he breakes his Sithe, against a molehill, for hee takes it unkindly that his ill fortune should put him to such charges, as to buy a new one. When he has don his labour, hees paid by the acre, or day, according to former agreement, and the sight of money makes him forget his wearisomenesse.'

Apart from occasional references to mercenary considerations in the minds of working-class people, their 'characters' tend to be written 'from the outside'. The actual work of the Tapster or Waiter may be described, but there is no attempt to get inside his skin, to ask what it is like to be at the beck and call of customers or what effect this has on a man's moods. The Model Waiter, as depicted by Horace Mayhew (*Model Men,* 1848, pp. 16–20) is shown as the diners see him; his private life—or lack of it—is dismissed in an opening paragraph of two sentences. There is one significant exception to this trend, in the 'characters' of the Governess, for here we have an exploited worker who is, more often than not, a distressed member of the writer's own class. He cannot hold himself aloof as from a different species of animal, but must think uneasily, 'There, but for the grace of God, goes my sister, or daughter.'[8]

Usually the character-writer describes the working classes—if he describes them at all, as opposed to exercising his wit at their expense—from the perspective of the consumer, customer, or employer. The Baker gives short weight, the Tapster short measure, the Carpenter charges for more wood than the job requires, and so forth. Similarly, *A Trip through the Town* (1735) gives the 'characters' of a number of Maidservants seen through the eyes of the mistress, who has run through half a score of them in three months and wonders 'whether any body was ever so handled with Servants as I have been'.[9] Although the attitude is slightly different and the types dealt with somewhat higher up the social ladder, the angle from which Anthony Trollope's *London Tradesmen* (1880) is written is no different. These pieces were first published in the *Pall Mall Gazette,* so Trollope can safely assume that his readers will share his position *vis-à-vis* the retail tradesman. The difference between *London Tradesmen* and most earlier accounts of the working or trading classes is that the author has made it his business to find out a good deal more about his chosen subjects. Hence he can afford gentle mockery at the expense of 'the ordinary inhabitant of the West End whose business lies in the law courts, or in office, or in Parliament, or they who have no business at all, [who] think that kidneys and fresh fish, salad and green peas are rained upon them from heaven, at a certain price per pound or per quart' (p. 56). (Note, however, that revealing definition of the 'ordinary inhabitant' of the West End; we are not too far from Reach's view that most houses contain a nursery or Russell's unspoken assumption that anybody who is anybody will have been to a public school.) Trollope's greater knowledge makes him more objective and tolerant. Thus he defends the Chemist against charges of profiteering, referring to the training required for the job and the responsibility involved in it. He draws a sly parallel between the chemist and the barrister: 'Ascending into higher regions, may we not say that the same thing takes place even with the barrister's work? Sir John and Sir Henry, having got to the top of their tree, may charge nearly what they please' (p. 16). Trollope even maintains that the professional Horse-dealer is less likely to swindle a customer than is a wealthy man who sells off a horse, for which he has no further use, to an acquaintance—if only because the horse-dealer must preserve his reputation or starve (pp. 40–2). However, despite his realism and tolerance, he is still drawing from the outside and hence is still capable of the occasional resounding false generalization: 'It is the object of all retail tradesmen to retire quickly from a business which is monotonous, for the most part uninteresting, and wearisome' (p. 53). This external approach to the working classes exactly reflects the authors' relationship to them; the working man seemed to define himself in terms of the activity by which he earned his bread. It was different with the 'characters' of professional men. Here too, of course, the main stress was on professional behaviour, but the author had the knowledge and the insight to venture occasionally into the realm of the values, motives, and moral urges which determined or influenced that behaviour. This is especially noticeable in the favourable 'characters': thus the good Lawyer and the good Magistrate are shown as being in love with the principle of justice. When we move to a yet higher social level, the difference becomes more marked. The Country Gentleman is a case in point. The philanthropic motives behind his estate management, his likes and dislikes, and his social life are all described in the awareness that only the sum of these things makes up the man.

The first instance of real compassion for the deprived classes occurs, as far as I know, in La Bruyère's description of the peasants, part of which has already been quoted. The account concludes: 'They spare other men the trouble of sowing, ploughing and harvesting in order to live, and therefore they deserve not to go short of that bread which they sowed.' The first example in England appears to be Ned Ward's *Wooden World* of 1707. This has already been mentioned as a minor curiosity among character-books, a sort of maritime Book of Estates. In it, Ward depicts a harsh and unfair world, with the officers toadying to the captain and exploiting the common seaman. The fourteenth and last chapter is an extended 'character' of a Sailor, who is represented as a deserving but ill-rewarded man, who receives 'all the Knocks, and none of the Moneys' (p. 96), who is condemned to a hard, coarse, and frugal life and is swindled out of his just rations. He is rough and ignorant—how could he be otherwise?—and yet is 'of more intrinsick Value to the Nation, than the most fluttering Beau in it' (p. 99).

The nineteenth-century character-book which shows most compassion for the poorer classes is *Heads of the People* (1840–1). In the Preface to Volume I, the aim is described as being 'to preserve the impress of the present age; to record its virtues, its follies, its moral contradictions, and its crying wrongs' (p. iii). There are many 'characters' which express social protest, such as the Dress-maker, the Factory Child, the Governess, the Poor Curate, and the Pauper. Of these, Douglas Jerrold's account of the Factory Child and that of the English Pauper by Thornton Leigh Hunt (son of Leigh Hunt) are the most outspoken and radical. The 'Factory Child' is written throughout in a flood of moral indignation: 'if ever angels weep, it must be when . . . they cast their regards upon the factory infants—hapless little ones; children without childhood; poor, diminutive Adams of nine years old, earning their Corn-law loaf in the sweat of their baby faces' (i. 188).

Here, more than in any other piece of character-writing, with the sole exception of the *Wooden World*, the relationship of haves to have-nots is made explicit. The piece on the Factory Child opens with an exchange between a doctor and a factory inspector, showing how such children were medically examined and certified as old enough to begin work in the factory; the Pauper (the 'involuntary stoic') dimly sees the 'comfortable gentlemen' in the magistrate's court as 'the remote, Olympian arbitrators of his destiny, God's viceregents upon earth . . . seldom seen, never understood, always powerful' (i. 352). F. G. Tomlins' Capitalist manipulates currency and, as a direct result, traders are ruined and factory workers laid off (ii. 212). There is no systematic attempt to show the ramifications of the class and economic structure of society—how could there be, for this is a collection of 'characters', not an economic treatise and is, moreover, a compilation to which thirty writers contributed—but there is at least some attempt to see 'John Bull's numerous family' as a family and to show how different classes of society depend on each other. And, in the case of the Factory Child, we find the genre pressed into the service of a real crusading zeal for social reform: 'And is there no remedy for this? Are the triumphs of man's intellect, as manifested in his subjugation and direction of the elements, only to benefit the few to the harder bondage of the many?' (i. 190 f.)

Further isolated examples of 'characters' written out of a mood of social compassion are not hard to find in the nineteenth century. At the same time that *Punch* and other humorous papers were making merry over the 'servant problem' and moralizing tracts were solemnly assuring servants that unremitting work was a privilege and a religious duty, we find 'characters' which stress the hardships of service: the dismal life of an overburdened Maid-of-all-work in a London lodging-house or the strains placed on the Lady's Maid by the unreasonable demands and half-conscious cruelty of her employer.[10] The most surprising treatment of servants comes in the periodical *Fun* which, in 1868, gave short 'characters' of different kinds of lodging-house servants,[11] jocularly describing them as if they were, indeed, specimens of a different, non-human order of existence:

> Like [the donkey, the lodging-house domestic] is small, strong and enduring, but stubborn, and at times refractory. The workhouses ... send out the article young, as a sort of raw material. What becomes of it in a finished state it is impossible to say, as no instance has ever been met with of an aged slavey; a fact which has induced some naturalists to suppose it is the *larva,* or grub, which after passing through the *pupa* stage as a general servant, emerges at last as the *imago,* or housemaid.

The sub-species which the author goes on to describe include the Musical Slavey (*S. vociferans*), the Timid Slavey (*S. trepidula*), and the Contemptuous Slavey (*S. superba*). Yet the piece ends, incongruously, on a compassionate note:

> [The Slavey] rarely knows what 'a Sunday out' means. All that she sees of the world is its boots as it passes the area railings. Her knowledge of the works of nature is confined to a study of the habits of black beetles and the growth of blue mould. Her days are days of ill-requited and unrecognised toil.[12]

In the mid nineteenth century, there appeared an account of the working classes in England which put into the shade even the most sympathetic attempts to portray them in character-form. Henry Mayhew is usually remembered today for his *London Labour and the London Poor*, first published in 1851, but the results of his survey into the working life of the metropolis had begun to appear in the *Morning Chronicle* two years earlier.[13] He claimed that *London Labour and the London Poor* was 'the first attempt to publish the history of the people, from the lips of the people themselves' (Preface). Although there had been various piecemeal undertakings, mostly interviews with criminals, prostitutes, and the like, Mayhew was certainly the first to embark on such a venture systematically and on the grand scale, bringing in all categories of the poor.

What he does, both in letters to the *Morning Chronicle* and in *London Labour*, is to combine the accounts which working people gave of themselves with his own observations, sociological and historical reflections, and statistical tables. Since he took care to interview typical representatives of the various groups, the impression given must have been not unlike that of a series of 'characters' in the first person, bearing in mind that character-writing still flourished in England around 1850. But it must be stressed that these are not 'characters'; they are real people talking about their lives.[14] Mayhew's object, he said, was to 'collect facts, and to register opinions' (*MC* 123), and he took elaborate precautions to ensure that the data he recorded were accurate and reliable (cf. *MC* 127, 138, 220). It is the feeling of authenticity that was, and is, overwhelming.[15]

The maker of penny toys: Trade is very bad at present. . . . As all my goods go to the poor . . . I can tell what's up with working and poor people by the state of my trade—a curious test, isn't it? (*MC* 340)

The street-arab: He had heard that the earth went round the sun, but from what he'd noticed, shouldn't have thought it. He didn't think that the sun went round the earth, it seemed to go more sideways. (*LLLP* i. 473)

The occasional figure of speech or flight of fancy is no longer playfully imposed on the subject by an outsider, but seems to be wrung out of bitter experience:

The crippled bird-seller: I liked the birds and do still. I used to think at first that they was like me; they was prisoners, and I was a cripple. (*LLLP* ii. 67)

Many of the details would hardly seem credible if they were not communicated with Mayhew's calm authority and authorial integrity. One instance is the treatment visited on a missionary who provoked the suspicion of the inmates in a common lodging-house: 'The women then tore the poor gentleman's nether garments in a way I must not describe. The men carried him into the yard, filled his mouth with flour of mustard and then put him in a water-butt' (*LLLP* i. 249). Another is the beggars' social club, with fines for swearing (*LLLP* i. 417).

Yet the horror was never far away: the dread of illness, bad weather, and the workhouse, the lice-ridden, overcrowded lodging-houses, the barely endurable hours and semi-starvation diet in the sweatshops. Mayhew's data were gathered in a period of depression; workers in trade after trade recalled better pay and conditions twenty or thirty years previously. But even allowing for this factor, the impact of his reports is stronger than anything in the working-class 'characters'. Jerrold's description of factory girls as 'children without childhood' or the comment (in *Fun*) that 'all [the Slavey] sees of the world is its boots as it passes the area railings' hardly match the simple force of Mayhew's silk-weaver: 'Weavers were all a-getting poorer, and masters all a-getting country houses' (*MC* 129).

An element which had never received much stress in the 'characters' of working-class types, written as they were from the consumer's point of view, was the craftsman's pride in his work:

> *A skilled toy-maker*: A man who hadn't those qualities [readiness and ingenuity] would have as good a chance of succeeding in my trade, as a man who wrote badly and spelt worse would have in yours, sir. We are all working men, sir—you'll not be offended by my saying that. (*MC* 347)
>
> *A carpenter*: I consider mine skilled labour, no doubt of it. To put together . . . the roof of a mansion so that it cannot warp or shrink . . . must be skilled labour, or I don't know what is. (*MC* 413)

Mayhew, in fact, recorded things that no character-writer would dare to put on paper. Ned Ward had lamented the harsh conditions endured by the Sailor, but had limited himself to noting the disparity between this shabby treatment and the man's deserts. But the Bosun of an emigrant ship tells Mayhew: 'If a war was to break out with America, there's thousands of us would go over to the other country. We're worse than the black slaves; they are taken care of, and we are not' (*MC* 363). Examples of this attitude among seafaring folk could be multiplied.

It seems clear that Mayhew's work rendered character-writing redundant over a whole area of English life. His patient research, his exact knowledge, and his readiness to let people speak for themselves meant that the working man emerged as a human being, not merely as the performer of a paid function. Compared with Mayhew's records, the employer's-eye-view of most working-class 'characters' seems blinkered, and the social protest registered in *Heads of the People*—although deeply felt and well-meaning—reads like sentimental rhetoric.[16]

8

Two Points Regarding Style

(i) The Witty Manner

Without wit, man would be nothing. (Lichtenberg)

For works may have more wit than does 'em good. (Pope)

For the modern reader of seventeenth-century 'characters', the witty manner will certainly be one of the chief delights and, as certainly, an occasional source of exasperation. Echoes of this witty manner persist in the eighteenth century,[1] but already there is influential opposition. Addison is severe, condemning 'hard metaphors' which obscure the writer's thought and likening the proliferation of puns in Jacobean England to the spread of weeds.[2] Henry Gally, writing in 1725, specifically criticizes the Overbury collection on the grounds of affectation and extravagance and insists that character-writing should remain true to nature and express 'much in a little compass'.[3] Those words seem to imply a conflict between matter and art, to which we shall return.

The Overbury definition of a 'character' talks of 'wit's descant on any plaine song' and thus hints at the most common method: the composition of elaborate variations on a simple theme. It is easy to see how similes, metaphors, puns, and fanciful allusions could, by the application of this technique, become a verbal equivalent to the runs and embellishments in contemporary 'music of division'. Since this was an age in which manuals on rhetoric formally codified the ways of elaborating on simple themes and ideas, in which commonplace books obligingly arranged the raw material for such elaboration under alphabetical headings, in which puns and all kind of conceits were lovingly cultivated and writers wore their learning ostentatiously,[4] it is no wonder that there was little attempt at straightforward description in terms of actions, physical appearance, and speech. Theophrastus's original method has been drastically modified, for good or ill, by the pursuit of 'wit'.

Whether for good or ill is the question we must try to answer, as objectively as possible.

There is a danger of adopting an anachronistic stance. Here are extracts from two 'characters':

> The unseasonable man is the kind who comes up to you when you have no time to spare and asks your advice. He sings a serenade to his sweetheart when she has influenza. . . . If he is going to give evidence he turns up when judgement has just been pronounced. When he is a guest at a wedding he makes derogatory remarks about the female sex. (Theophrastus)

> [The Miser] loves Wealth as an Eunuch does Women, whom he has no Possibility of enjoying, or one that is bewitched with an Impotency, or taken with the Falling-Sickness. His greedy Appetite to Riches is but a Kind of Dog-Hunger, that never digests what it devours; but still the greedier and more eager it crams itself becomes more meager. He finds that Ink and Parchment preserves Money better than an iron Chest and Parsimony, like the Memories of Men that lye dead and buried when they are committed to Brass and Marble, but revive and flourish when they are trusted to authentic Writings, and encrease by being used. (Samuel Butler)

We probably prefer Theophrastus, but most seventeenth-century writers were busily pursuing the second method. Boyce thinks that witty elaboration was to some extent a response to the 'threat of exhausted material'.[5] If we look at 'characters' of the Whore or the Drunkard, where the same few points are made over and over again and only the style can provide real variety, this theory seems tenable—but the same witty manner obtains in 'characters' of types which were treated only once or twice: the Ostler, the Lutanist, the Fencer, the Herald, and the Trumpeter. The wit was considered necessary to character-writing, and was practised and admired for its own sake. This is confirmed by Geffray Mynshul's *Essayes and Characters of a Prison and Prisoners* (1617), for Mynshul writes his essay 'Of Prisoners' in a comparatively plain style, but slips into a punning, metaphorical, and allusive manner as soon as he embarks on his 'character' of the Prisoner. The wit, it seems, is put on as a consequence of the author's having chosen to write in a particular form. Half a century later, Ralph Johnson will reiterate the importance of wit in his rules for character-writing (above, p. 36). Although all types of verbal embellishment are encountered in seventeenth-century character-writing, it is the metaphor that dominates and it is the subservience to metaphor on which we shall concentrate.

We have already heard Richard Brathwaite chiding his contemporaries for producing 'squibs and crackers'; Flecknoe, too, believes that a 'character' should be 'all *matter*, and to the *matter*', with 'nothing of *superfluity*, nothing of *circumlocution*'.[6] Witty or would-be-witty metaphors that tell us nothing of the type under discussion are common in the 'trade characters', where the author's direct knowledge of his subject is minimal. For R. M., the Rope Maker is 'the Spider that spins from about his owne bowels his three-fold Web, which may afterward intrap some silly Flies of misfortune'.[7] This clearly offends against Flecknoe's 'to the matter'; it seems reasonable to distinguish between such examples and witty formulations that actually say something about the subject of the 'character'. Both sorts are illustrated by Henry Parrot in his Fiddler. The statement 'He never draws in anger but for profit' succinctly contrasts the peaceable (or timorous) musician with, say, the Roaring Boy. Yet Parrot also writes: 'If any man chance to breake his Instrument, hee bringeth straight his action of the Case being his Fidle case is without action' (*Cures for the Itch*, 1626, No. 6).

The distinction between 'matter' and 'superfluity' can again be seen if we compare the various accounts of the subject's birth or genealogy with which satirical 'characters' often begin. These can be mere invective: for Lenton, the Bawd was 'engendred of divers most filthy excrements'.[8] In 'characters' of tradesmen, we are often given no more than a rather mechanical conceit bound up with the trade. We may even encounter an allegorical pedigree which cuts across the portrayal of the subject as a human being: Lenton's Parasite is 'engendred by Pride, hatcht up by Arrogance and perpetually fostred by fooles' (Lenton, No. 5). By contrast, there is Brathwaite's telling comment on the Shrew, whose 'father was a common Barretter, and her mothers sole note . . . eccoed, *New Wainflete Oysters*'.[9]

In some authors, the wit is like a rampant weed. Samuel Austin, in his 'character' of the Antiquarian, manages to be both tasteless and near-incomprehensible at once:

> That ceremonious *Soul* which idolatrously worship't the *Gentlewomans* thredbare *Garment*, might have quietly kist her *Rear*, which questionless was the *senior* of the two, wip'd his *Mouth* with her *Petticoated Antiquity*, and so had escap'd without a *dry'd jeer* and like a good *Husband* have saved his prodigal Breath to cool his *pottage*.[10]

How different is Sprigge, whose witty particularizations bring an abstract idea to life, as in his lively variation on Matthew 23 : 14: '[The Hypocrite] esteemes it an admirable decorum to sprinkle bad actions with holy-water, to say a long grace before a breakfast of widows houses' (p. 45).

Few 'characters' are downright incoherent. The most common drawback—or, to be rigorously objective, the most common result—of employing a witty style throughout the 'character' is that a little can be made to go a very long way. In his verse-character of a Whore, Thomas Jordan picks on the idea of a foul essence hidden beneath a fair exterior and clothes it in ten different metaphors. Or R. M. writes of the Tobacconist (i.e. fanatically keen smoker): 'The Recorder, Flute, Hoboise or any other Pipe the best Musician can invent, doth yeeld him no such content as doth the Tobacco-pipe; or can afford him like Musicke to please his Nostrils; were it the Oaten Reed of that Rurall Shepheard which so sweetly warbled on the Plaines of *Arcadie*.'[11] It may be ungrateful to carp at a passage which is at least mildy entertaining, but the fact remains that R. M. has taken fifty words to say, 'He loves his pipe'. Think what Theophrastus, La Bruyère, or Addison can say in fifty words! Value judgements aside, there is no doubt that the author's attitude to the 'character'—and, with it, the reader's response—has radically changed. Even Richard Brathwaite, who complained about 'squibs and crackers', wrote in a style that was by no means unadorned. His fairly restrained wit will illustrate my point at least as well as an extravagant passage from a more mannered writer:

> [A Jayler] is a surly hoast, who entertaines his guests with harsh language, and hard usage. Hee will neither allow them what is sufficient for them, nor give them liberty to seeke an other inne. Hee is the physician, and they are his patients; to whom hee prescribes such a strict diet, that if they would, they cannot surfet. . . . His ornaments are fetters, boults, and mannacles. These are his bracelets, yingles, and caparisons: thus must his enthralled crickets live ever in an iron cage. Yet according to a proportionable weight in starling, hee will abate a proportionable weight in iron. (*Whimzies*)

Every one of Brathwaite's readers will have known that jail was no bed of roses and that fetters could be lightened by bribery, so that no unfamiliar facts are being conveyed in this passage. On one level, an element of play is in operation; the reader supplies his knowledge in order to join in a game of guessing or recognition. If the 'character' goes any further or deeper, it is by virtue of provoking the reader to reflections through its imagery and conceits: Are these the prisoner's accoutrements and ornaments? Is this the only use for money in that sad place?

Of course, wit was not regarded in any functional or utilitarian way in the seventeenth century, rather as a means of expanding the boundaries of one's subject, of allowing the fancy to play freely with associations and of uncovering relationships between disparate things and ideas. Similes, metaphors, and analogies became part of a fascinating voyage of discovery through the world of human knowledge and experience. Often the modern reader suspects that the ostensible subject of a passage was merely the springboard for a series of imaginative leaps into apparently unrelated regions and that these peripheral matters were more important to the author than his 'real' theme.

This means that there was bound to be occasional tension between the pursuit of wit and the cultivation of the Theophrastan 'character', in which everything should visibly relate to, and illustrate, the central theme. This tension can be seen in some of the extracts already quoted in this chapter. Thus, having noted that ink and parchment preserve money better than the Miser's cashbox, Butler passes on to the posthumous reputations of great men and the respective merits of monuments and written records: a weightier point, although quite irrelevant to the subject of the 'character'. Similarly we may suspect that, for R. M., the rope dangling from the gallows or binding the malefactor is more important than the Rope Maker, and that the nostalgic reference to Arcady is more than a trill or ornament on the subject of pipe-smoking.

There is evidence that some, at least, of the seventeenth-century character-writers saw the dangers of an unrestrained witty manner partly in terms of how digression might threaten unity. The 'Overbury' definition, if taken *au pied de la lettre*, must imply that the descant should at all times be perceptibly related to, and derived from, the plain song; even Ralph Johnson, with his repeated demands for 'wit and pleasantness', clearly thinks that the allegories, allusions, and other devices should always express the nature of the subject and not lead away from it. Brathwaite and Flecknoe, too, obviously feel that a degree of self-discipline is required if matter is not to be submerged beneath art.

The anonymous author who, in 1678, wrote four 'characters' under the pseudonym of 'poor Robin' seems to have been aware of a clash between the urge to be witty and the desire to communicate facts. In his 'character' of an 'unconscionable Pawnbroker', he begins with a scurry of abusive metaphors and extravagant fancies, as was common in his day. The Pawnbroker is '*Pluto's* Factor, old *Nick's* Warehouse-keeper, an *English Jew*'; his shop is like the gates of Hell (ever open); he plays the pimp by lodging men's and women's clothes together in the same bed of lavender, and so on.[12] This is all good fun, but the author also has a serious purpose: he wants to inform us about the extortionate rates of interest levied. This he does in a perfectly plain style, going into close arithmetical detail in as businesslike a manner as any modern 'investigative' journalist or broadcaster. There are, quite simply, two styles within the one 'character', each performing its separate function.

When one talks of the witty manner in seventeenth-century character-writing, it is the proliferation of metaphors, allusions, and conceits that generally comes to mind, the apparent unwillingness to make an unadorned descriptive or analytical statement. Yet there is one writer who seldom uses an obscure allusion or far-fetched metaphor, but whose 'characters' are among the most mannered in the century. This is Nicholas Breton. Breton's style—in his character-writing at least—is distinguished by a positive mania for sentences which fall into either two or four balancing sections. Here is an example of his passion for the binary construction:

> [A Reprobate] betrayes the trust of the simple and sucks out the blood of the innocent. His breath is the fume of blasphemy, and his tongue the fire-brand of hell. His desires are the destruction of the vertuous and his delights are the traps to damnation. Hee bathes in the bloud of murther and sups up the broth of iniquity. (p. 14)

As an instance of Breton's 'quadrumania' (Boyce), one might take this from his Atheist:

> He is in nature a dogge, in wit an asse, in passion a Bedlam, and in action a divell. He makes sinne a jest, grace an humour, truth a fable, and peace a cowardice. His horse is his pride, his sword is his Castle, his apparell his riches and his punke his paradise. Hee makes robbery his purchase, lechery his solace, mirth his exercise, and drunkennesse his glory. (p. 10)

Breton's summings-up are nearly always fourfold: the Usurer is 'a servant of drosse, a slave to misery, an agent for hell, and a divell in the world'.[13] It is impossible to escape the feeling that the matter is being forcibly accommodated to the manner.

This practice seems most artificial in the case of profoundly serious themes. One is not, I think, guilty of an anachronism in feeling that there is a disharmony between style and subject-matter in the 'character' of the Atheist. Breton certainly imposes limits upon himself through his obsessive sentence-constructions; a writer unencumbered by such formalism will allow the length and structure of each sentence to be determined by what is said at any moment. Flecknoe writes of the Talkative Lady:

> . . . all the wonder is, whilest she speaks onely *Thrums*, how she makes so many different ends hold together (the composition of a Taylors Cushion, all of shreds, being nothing to the wonder of it) but for that she cares not; all her care being onely for some to hear her talk (whom she must hire shortly, none certainly else would undergo the noice and vexation) mean time an engine with so constant a motion as her tongue would be far better than any murmuring Fountain, or purling Brook to make one sleep, and she wants onely the faculty of talking in her sleep herself, to make the perpetuall motion with her tongue. (No. 9 in the 1658 edition)

The rambling sentence becomes an emblem for the *perpetuum mobile* of her tongue. By contrast, Flecknoe employs a simple construction to point a straightforward antithesis between his Excellent Companion and a Buffoon: 'He differs from the *Buffoon*, as an excellent *Comedy* do's from the *Farse*, being pure wit, tother but foolery' (1658, No. 3). The opening of the Flatterer is different again; the sentence branches and sprouts out in all directions, as Flecknoe expands and elaborates on his original simple proposition:

> He is a mid sort of Animal betwixt *man* and *beast*; with the manners of *beast*, under the resemblance of a *man*: nay he is a compound of all base wilde *beasts* together, a *Dog* in fawning, an *Ape* in imitating, a *Fox* in faining and dissembling, and an *Asse* in suffering and bearing every thing. (1658, No. 65).

If there is such a thing as wit in sentence-construction, these extracts from Flecknoe illustrate it. Breton seldom, if ever, exhibits this sort of freedom; it would offend against 'balance'. His rhythmic obsessions can be counter-productive, for the reader may well pay less heed to what is being said than to how it is being said.

Moreover, if more than a few of Breton's 'characters' are read at one time, they begin to have a singsong, hypnotic effect.

Braithwaite, Flecknoe, and, later, Addison and Gally can thus be seen as justified in a number of quite specific respects: the witty manner did sometimes obscure the point or provide the writer with a means of padding out a few sparse thoughts. But blanket denunciations are unfair to authors like Earle, Lenton, or Flecknoe himself, all of whom usually showed themselves capable of disciplining their exuberance. Even the Overbury collection contains more 'characters' which are successful in this respect than some critics concede.

Flecknoe, whose inventiveness in sentence-construction has just been shown, was a master of imagery too. The examples that follow all provoke thought, give us the pleasure of the unexpected, and say much in a few words:

> [The Fantastique Lady's] head is just like a Mill, or Squirrels cage, and her minde the Squirrel that turns and whirls it round. (1658, No. 7)
>
> Not to be Souldier, he was made *Coronel* at first, and to scape fighting, h'as remained so ever since; whence he's a *superlative* without a *positive*. (ibid., No. 37)
>
> *Of one that Zanys the good Companion*: his discourse is rather like fruit tane up rotten from the ground, than freshly gathered from the Tree. (ibid., No. 4)

More unexpectedly, a witty metaphor can create a touch of genuine poetry. Stephens's Fiddler 'can send his little spirit of musick upon a ladder of Lute-strings, into your private chamber' (No. 27).

Saltonstall's *Picturae Loquentes* of 1631 illustrate both the virtues and the hazards of the witty manner. On the one hand, he can be merely coarse—'[A Widow] is like a cold Pye thrust downe to the lower end of the Table, that has had too many fingers in't'—or he can indulge in an empty sort of ingenuity that reads as if it had been patched together out of a commonplace book: '[The Usurer's] case for Heaven is very dangerous, because he sins still with security. . . . His Clearke is the *Vulcan*, that forges the Bonds and Shackels which he imposes on other men. . . . Like theeves he undoes men by binding them.' By contrast, his Townsman in Oxford is a witty reaction to an exactly observed phenomenon:

> [A Townesman in Oxford] is one that hath long liv'd by the well of knowledge, but never sipt at it, for he loves no water in his wine, though it

come from Hellicon. . . .[His words have] such a punctuall stiffe pronunciation, as though they were starcht into his mouth, and durst not come out faster for feare of ruffling.[14]

Most of the examples given above have been humorous or satirical. That the playfulness of wit is also compatible with a serious purpose is a commonplace. What part, then, does the witty manner play in those 'characters' which express compassion for the subject or indignation over his or her lot, or in those where the author externalizes his own predicament and laments over it?[15]

We may begin with two 'characters' of a Prison, both written by men who had seen it from the inside. Geffray Mynshul's piece consists of thirteen short paragraphs, each beginning 'A Prison is' or 'It is', duly followed by a metaphor. Thus the arrangement stresses that this is an exercise in wit—a wit, however, of despair:

A Prison is a grave to bury men alive . . .

It is a Microcosmus, a little world of woe . . .

It is a little common-wealth, although little wealth be common there; it is a desart where desert lyes hood-winckt . . .

This is very different from Dekker's 'character' on the same subject, which was printed in the 1616 edition of the Overbury collection. Dekker's sustained metaphor of the prison as a ship sounds no more than ingenious:

. . . the masters side is the upper deck. They in the common jayle lye under hatches, and helpe to ballast it. Intricate cases are the tacklings, executions the anchors, capiasses the cables, chancery-bils the huge sayles, a long terme the mast, law the helme, a judge the pylot . . . (ed. cit., p. 156)

Where Mynshul's wit makes the suffering more vivid, Dekker's buries it under conceits.

An author who successfully and engagingly demonstrates the possibility of a compassionate and somewhat sorrowful wit is William Sprigge, whose 'character' of 'A Foole or Naturall' was given above (p. 41). But the dilemma illustrated by the two 'characters' of a Prison is a perennial one. The borderline between wit that jokes bravely or stoically at misfortune and wit that appears to turn misfortune into a joke is a narrow one. And, while one may joke at one's own misfortune, it is altogether different to jest at someone else's, as when Ned Ward makes merry over the punishment inflicted on the Foot Soldier: 'He is a man of undaunted courage; dreading no enemy so much as he does the wooden horse, which makes him hate to be mounted, and rather chooses to be a foot soldier.'[16] Here the wit actually disorients the reader: is Ward's point the soldier's courage, or is the motif of courage merely intended to lead up to the punning reference to the infamous wooden horse?

In a later work, *The Wooden World* (1707), Ward seems more aware of when a witty manner is appropriate and how far it can be taken. Parts suggest that he is still in thrall to the pursuit of wit. Much of his opening chapter on the Ship of War is taken up with a string of metaphors: serious ('the Mighty Guardian of our Island'), playful ('the great Wooden Horse of Nature'), or emblematic ('the illustrious Emblem of vain Man').[17] Some of the 'characters' are simply nautical equivalents to types familiar from older character-books and are described in very similar terms. The Sea-Lieutenant is none other than the Coward in Command: 'Speak to him . . . he . . . answers you in Fire and Smoak through his Nostrils: in this kind of *Billingsgate* Clashing, he is a much greater master than at the Clashing of Weapons.' With the Ship's Carpenter, Sea-Cook, and so on, many conceits and puns are lifted bodily from the corresponding trades in Earle, Overbury, and others.

Thus far, then, Ward seems happy to cultivate the witty manner. Yet he also wishes to describe the 'Wooden World' more seriously, as one in which the common sailor is bullied and cheated by those set in authority over him. Is this aim compatible with the pursuit of wit? The notorious matter of corporal punishment at sea suggests itself as a test case. Here, Ward's touch is uncertain: in places he makes light of the matter through witty conceits, while elsewhere he refers simply and directly to the brutality and sadism at work.[18]

But ultimately, the impression made by *The Wooden World* depends on the impact of Ward's last chapter, his 'character' of the Sailor. This is not without its patronizing note: 'His first Labour in a Morning is to hawl ope his Eye-lids, for it costs him many a Rub with his Paws, before he can make his Top-lights to shine clearly' (p. 89). Nor does it lack the rather mechanical seafaring punning that inevitably runs through this book: for instance, whoring while on shore leave is described in terms of 'a Brush with some Vessel of Iniquity or other' (p. 93). However, the hard life is portrayed realistically and the seaman is more than once referred to as a 'poor Slave'.

It is noteworthy that, when he wishes to convey a sense of pity and concern, Ward radically tones down his wit. His opening makes an interesting contrast to the first couple of sentences of the 'Overbury' Sailor:

Ward	*'Overbury'*
A Sailor is a sharp Blade indeed, if kept whetted with good Diet; but bad Usage makes him as dull and useless as an old Razor. (p. 89)	*A Saylor* is a pitcht peece of reason calckt and tackled, and onely studied to dispute with tempests. He is a part of his owne provision, for he lives ever pickled. (p. 75)

And at the end, when Ward's emotions have obviously become involved, he virtually dispenses with figurative language:

In fine, take this same plain blunt Sea-Animal, by and large, in his Tar Jacket, and wide-kneed Trowzers, and you'll find him of more intrinsick Value to the Nation, than the most fluttering Beau in it. . . . Our Ships of War are indisputably the best in the World, and so might the Sailors be too . . . (pp. 98 f.)

We may contrast the unconcerned punning of the early (Overbury) 'character', according to which the Sailor is 'naturally ambitious, for he is ever climing', while his wisdom is 'the coldest part about him, for it ever points to the North' (p. 75).

Two authors, therefore, abruptly reject the witty manner, after seeming for a time perfectly content with it. 'Poor Robin' changes his style in the interests of factual precision, Ned Ward in order to make clear his compassion.

The issues that have just been discussed are hardly new; nor, I imagine, are the conclusions surprising. 'Matter' versus 'art' is an old chestnut in literary criticism. But I do not think that any apology is needed for having examined the 'character' from this point of view. For several decades during the seventeenth century, the assumption was that, if you wrote a 'character', you had to include some wit. Ralph Johnson advised: 'Express their natures . . . by witty Allegories. . . . [Always strive] for wit and pleasantness. . . . Conclude with some witty and neat passage.' As a result, the seventeenth-century 'character' seems to illustrate with particular vividness the pros and cons of a highly embellished style. It shows, at least as well as any other literary genre, how wit can sharply illumine a point or merely decorate it, how a metaphor can provoke reflection and deepen our perception of the matter in hand or irritatingly lead us down bypaths. The witty manner could make its essential contribution to the concentration which is, or should be, part of character-writing, or it could provide a means of writing a clever paragraph about practically nothing. It could give the impression of having arisen spontaneously from a genuine perceptual flash or it could seem as stale as last week's bun—or last year's commonplace book.

Few people today still condemn elaborate figures of speech outright as 'weeds'. It may even be that students of literature are more likely to move to an opposite extreme, ending up more tolerant than some men of the seventeenth century were of their own contemporaries. Clearly, we must strive towards a sympathetic understanding of how and within what limits the seventeenth century celebrated and practised the witty style and with what results—and it does no harm to recall that strictures on elaborate wit were made not only by Addison and Gally, but also by Brathwaite and Flecknoe. It is emphatically not anachronistic to make a critical distinction between the writer who mechanically puts in tired comparisons with 'the boatman who rows backwards' and the 'whited sepulchre' and, for instance, Stephens's Fiddler, with his ladder of lute-strings. There is another point: the 'characters' of a Prison by Mynshul and Dekker were both written out of first-hand experiences and are both couched in a highly metaphorical style. But the impressions made by the two pieces are so different that we are left uncertain as to the exact moods and motives of the writers. If we come to feel that we cannot always be confident that we have re-entered the imaginative world of the seventeenth-century writer and cracked his stylistic code, that too is a gain.

(ii) **Must the 'Characters' of Ideal Types be Dull?**

An admirable moral character is like a beautiful painting. Once seen, it delights us and provokes our admiration. (*Das Reich der Natur und der Sitten*, No. 113)

Frail and wicked men are always more interesting. (Boyce)

Most people would probably agree with the second of those statements. It has long been a truism of literary criticism that the libertine, the rogue, the rebellious sinner, and the eccentric have a greater hold over our imagination—and often over our sympathy—than the virtuous. Milton, Richardson, Goethe, Dickens, Thackeray, and many others have been criticized for making their villains and eccentrics more interesting than their heroes. Historians of the Theophrastan 'character' have said similar things: the good and moderate man is 'tepid and unadventurous', the 'characters' of virtues sin by dullness, the ideal sketches in Law's *Serious Call* are comparative failures. Boyce has pointed out that few authors sought a balance between good and bad 'characters', apparently feeling that the genre was 'best adapted to giving satiric pleasure'.[1] If virtue *is* intrinsically more difficult to make interesting, the character-writer would seem to have a uniquely onerous task. For the novelist and, to a lesser extent, the dramatist can seek to maintain our interest in the hero by involving him in all manner of encounters and adventures; or can arouse our sympathy for the heroine through the vicissitudes that she undergoes. But the character-writer can only hint at such things; he must define and illustrate goodness in a few pages, or he has failed. There seems to be a variety of reasons, some technical, some psychological, why ideal types are more difficult to write about than the foolish and the unregenerate.

One reason is that 'characters' of good types tend towards abstraction: 'The main qualities of a worthy man are to be found in his soul and consist of a constant love of truth and justice and an unceasing desire to do as much good as possible'. (*Der Mensch*, 1751–6, No. 319) In *Der Sammler* (1736, No. 20), the Good Man is described as proceeding on his charitable path, undismayed if his actions go unnoticed ([*er*] *fähret fort mit Wohlthun, wenn gleich die Unwissenden solches nicht bemercken*). Now character-books, sermons, and periodical essays contain many a picture of the opposite type, the Hypocrite, who gives alms to beggars only if the street is full of passers-by, who subscribes only to those charities where the donors' names are made public, who worships in the most frequented churches, sighs in ecstasy when at prayer, ostentatiously leaves devotional books lying about in his room, and so on.[2] The writers have no problem in avoiding dullness when describing the parade of *apparent* goodness. But how can doing good by stealth be made vivid within the confines of the 'character'?

This brings us to a related problem concerning the depiction of the ideal. P. J. Korshin explains the greater appeal of Hall's 'Vices' over his 'Virtues' by pointing out that 'there is a compelling variety about evil'.[3] If we extend the remark to include folly and eccentricity, its relevance to character-writing in general becomes evident. When Hall has said that the Valiant Man 'talks little, and brags less', he has said everything that needs to be said on that topic; when Gellert[4] has informed us that Damis is content with simple dishes, he too has exhausted his subject. By contrast, the flamboyant exaggerations of the Braggart, the Glutton's greasy chops, or the Epicure's spiced French dishes offer endless opportunities. One could even go further and argue that virtue itself had become a somewhat unexciting ideal by the early seventeenth century. Dramatic heroism and extravagant self-denial (previously celebrated in the lives of saints, martyrs, and ascetics) had on the whole yielded to a more sober conception, influenced by Humanist and neo-Stoic notions. The Good Man shunned all extremes, he reduced his vulnerability by a simple and unostentatious mode of life, he fulfilled his station in society without fuss. It appeared that all fascinatingly flamboyant behaviour was now confined to the realm of vice and folly. In the eighteenth century, the tendency to turn virtue into something 'reasonable', 'moderate', and hence rather colourless went still further. For the writer, it must indeed have seemed that the devil had all the best tunes.

These difficulties—the danger of excessive abstraction and the problem of introducing variety and zest into the sketch of an ideal person—can be overcome by technical means, as we shall see presently. But the writer also faces a psychological resistance on the part of the reader. We tend to reject types who are impossibly good. Thomas Ford's 'character' of the Honest Subject is, for this reason, self-defeating, for it no longer seems like the depiction of a plausible human being at all: 'if he see undeserving men preferred before him, he rather pitties than envies them, as counting it more noble to have deserved preferment than to have it'.[5]

This danger of provoking resistance on the part of the reader is obviously intensified by the (implicit) terms of reference of the 'character', which require that an Ideal Wife be nothing but chaste, modest, dutiful, affectionate, and domesticated and a Good Christian nothing but pious, humble, God-fearing, and of immaculate moral rectitude. Although Fielding condemned both perfectly good and utterly depraved characters as equally unnatural (*Tom Jones*, x. 1), it seems that, for no apparent logical reason, we can swallow this 'nothing but' element in foolish or vicious types far more easily than with ideal figures. Character-writers, where they have perceived the problem, have most commonly circumvented it by one of two devices, either by characterizing an ideal figure in terms of what he or she is not, or by introducing some little imperfection which makes the subject appear more human.

As examples of the first technique, here is Henry Peacham on the 'religious honest man':

> He back-biteth and traduceth none, meddleth not with matters and affaires of state; well knowing (like those builders of the towre of BABEL) that a rash affection of things too high, bringeth discord and confusion . . .

and here Humphrey Browne on the Good Woman:

> Her lips are never guilty of a wanton smile; not one lascivious glance doth dart from her eye; her cariage is sober, free from all toyish gestures . . .[6]

Examples of this descriptive method could be multiplied indefinitely. Richard Brathwaite describes the Honest Lawyer almost exclusively in terms of what he is not and what he does not do:

> His tongue's no time-observer, made to please,
> His fist is shut from taking double fees.
> He will not forge a lye, nor wrest the sence,
> Of law or right, for any faire pretence.
> He will not backe his Clyent, or maintaine
> An unjust suit, to reape a private gaine.
> (*A Strappado for the Divell*, 1615, ed. cit., p. 61)

The enlivening of 'characters' through this technique of negation is common in sermons. Isaac Barrow on the Upright Man:

> As he doth not affect any poor base ends, so he will not defile his fair intentions by sordid means of compassing them; such as are illusive simulations and subdolous artifices, treacherous collusions, slie insinuations and sycophantick detractions, versatile whifflings and dodgings, flattering colloquings and glozings, servile crouchings and fawnings, and the like.[7]

The high-spirited *enumeratio* introduced by 'such as are' has the unmistakable ring of the sergeant-major's 'Wake up at the back!'

The above examples showed a simple opposition of good and bad, but there is also a large group of 'characters' where the ideal is represented as a golden mean between two equally objectionable or unwise extremes:

[The Good Husband] neither deceives himselfe with a foolish confidence, nor drawes a disadvantage to himselfe, by being distrustfull . . .

[A Gentleman] will mingle pleasure with profit, but will make recreation his servant, not his master.

without boasting brave:
Well bred, without the trifling Forms of State;
Learn'd, but no Pedant . . .[8]

Of the two approaches, the second seems the more telling; it demands active co-operation from the reader, who must supply the missing middle term himself, and it leads, at its best, to a stylistic concentration and an antithetical sentence-construction which exactly mirrors the subject-matter. Stephens writes of the Good Lawyer: 'He cannot be so confident as to persist in error: nor so ignorant as to erre by weaknes. . . . His modesty was never below his courage in a good cause, nor his courage inclining to impudence.' By contrast, Brathwaite's Honest Lawyer seems like sleight of hand: smuggling in the good through negation of the bad.

The other way of making an ideal type more interesting, by introducing a flaw, often has the effect of 'redeeming' what might otherwise be a stiff and unsympathetic paragon. The point is amusingly illustrated by Mynshul in his 'noble understanding Prisoner'. Much of the piece is taken up with a succession of conventional metaphors expressing nobility of soul and stoical acceptance of suffering. It is therefore with some relief that we read: 'In briefe he can (with Judgement) know when to beat a saucy Jaylor, and when to have him fawn and make a shillings-worth of legs.'[9] The flaw may be a good quality taken a little too far:

This old friend of mine . . . is called *Wilhelm Ernst*, a man of strict virtue, godfearing and of proven honesty. He is what in my youth would have been called a truly honest fellow . . . an energetic defender of the customs of our fathers and a sworn enemy of the corrupt morals of this age. I must admit that he carries his zeal too far . . . is too moody and irritable over the changes that he has seen and condemns them with too much bitterness and spleen . . . (*Der Greis*, 1772–6, No. 6)

Without the last sentence, Ernst would undoubtedly have seemed smug. It should be stressed that such 'humanizing' flaws should visibly and logically proceed from the ruling, good quality that forms the subject of the 'character'.

Can 'characters' of ideal types be enlivened by stylistic embellishment? Can wit descant as happily on the subject of virtue as on vice or folly? Metaphors are certainly not wanting in the 'characters' of ideal types, but they tend to be unenterprising. For Thomas Ford, the Good King is the sun, the head of the body politic, the pilot to the ship of state, and a mortal god.[10] The effect can be that of a totally conventional rhetorical exercise:

> The Sun shall sooner change his course, and finde new paths to drive his chariot in: the Loadstone shall leave his faith unto the North, sooner than shee [the Good Woman] will leave hers to her husband . . .

or of a mechanical process of allegorical personification:

> The Cardinal Vertues are [the Religious Prince's] Domestick Servants, and the Graces are his Maids of Honour: His best Harbingers are fervent Prayers, his Cup-bearer is Temperance . . .[11]

Particularly among the German writers, the abstraction which often seems inseparable from a discussion of ideal virtue is compounded by a liking for abstract figures: the Wise Man is 'serene like the eye of innocence' (*Für Litteratur und Herz*, 1775, No. 36). This type of abstract simile, used to express notions of piety and moral nobility, is very persistent in Germany, reaching from the early Pietists, through Klopstock and the sentimental poets of the 1770s and 1780s, to the early works of Jean Paul Richter.

Unfortunately, however, the converse—the attempt to give abstract qualities visible and concrete form through metaphor—can easily sound strained, as in Humphrey Browne's Good Woman: 'She is Vertues morall Looking-glasse, and desires to excell in vertue, not in vesture. The Vestall fire of chastity continually burnes on the hallowed Altar of her heart.' The play on sounds, near to aural punning, hardly helps to create an atmosphere of moral earnestness. At times, the impression is not merely one of strain, but of near-desperation, as in these two passages, both from the 1660s. The first is a frenzied elaboration on Matthew 10 : 16:

> [The Wise Man] partakes of the Serpents Wisdome, and Doves innocency, the Serpent amongst the *Egyptian* Priests, was an emblem of Wisdome,

which doth extricate and winde it self out of the maze of troubles and dangers, and it insinuates it self into rocks, and winds it self out again. In like manner doth a wise man winde himself out of the Labrynths of trouble, and winde himself out of the Rocks of Error, and there finds the Pearl of Truth . . .

The second takes fifty-three words to say that piety can resist temptation:

[A Pious Man] is the only *Ulysses* that can passe by the *Syrens* of the Earth, and not be taken by them: the Strumpet World, spreads forth her Dangling Tresses to insnare him, warbles her most Ravishing Layes to Court him to her Embraces; but he like *Samson* snaps his bonds in sunder . . .[12]

Nearly a century later, an anonymous writer in *Das Reich der Natur und der Sitten* (1757–62) was to argue that a witty manner is simply not compatible with a serious moral purpose. The 'character', if it is to achieve its moral effect on the reader, must be written in an unforced and natural style 'and therefore cannot consist of glittering words and far-fetched expressions, over-ingenious antitheses and contradictions, let alone puns' (No. 96). This statement is obviously too uncompromising to be taken without reservations. We have seen, for instance, metaphors, puns, and conceits effectively used in the depiction of undeserved misfortune. What does seem difficult to achieve is the right tone for 'characters' of ideal qualities; those just cited, the Wise Man and the Pious Man, do indeed seem 'far-fetched' and 'over-ingenious' in their word-play. It is difficult to resist the impression that Samuel Person and P. B. were using a witty manner as a synthetic means of padding out simple and obvious propositions, exactly as we have seen the authors of satirical 'characters' doing.

Another kind of 'synthetic' writing to be encountered in depictions of the ideal is an emotive pathos which owes much to pulpit rhetoric. An example is the 'character' of Cordillas, the Virtuous Man, from *Der Tugendfreund* (1755–6): 'The oppressed who, with their hot tears, sought refuge with him and implored him with trembling lips to help them, found a faithful protector in him' (volume i, No. 2). The pitfalls, then, are many, and it cannot be denied that one quickly wearies of 'characters' of Noble Judges, True Christians, and the like. Yet such 'characters' can be successful, as passages from Earle and Hall demonstrate.

Although Earle necessarily dwells on the expected qualities of his 'Stayed Man'—constancy, calm, and so forth—it is not an unthinking stereotype. The subject is defined with the utmost care and exactitude, in such a way that the reader almost witnesses and shares the author's thought-processes:

> A stayed man . . . is one that has taken order with himself, and sets a rule to those lawlessnesses within him: whose life is distinct and in method, and his actions, as it were, cast up before. . . . He affects nothing so wholly, that he must be a miserable man when he loses it; but fore-thinks what will come hereafter, and spares fortune his thanks and curses. One that loves his credit, not this word reputation; yet can save both without a duel.

Conventional references to the course of the sun, the loadstone, the fixed star, and so on are, I would guess, rejected as too obvious by Earle, whose figures of speech, sparingly used, are original and telling: 'One whose tongue is strung up like a clock till the time, and then strikes, and says much when he talks little.' Where another writer would pad out his picture with long accounts of what the subject is not, Earle achieves a perfect combination of light and shade to enhance our appreciation of the ideal. Since seventeenth-century definitions of the 'character' insist that it say much in a little space, it should be added that Earle makes his contrasts with intense economy:

> One whose 'if I can' is more than another's assurance; and his doubtful tale before some men's protestations. . . . Whose entertainments to greater men are respectful, not complimentary; and to his friends plain, not rude. A good husband, father, master; that is, without doting, pampering, familiarity.

A similar exact and careful balance can be found in the 'character' of the Grave Divine, again expressed through an antithetical sentence-structure: 'The ministry is his choice, not refuge, and yet the pulpit not his itch, but fear. . . . His discourse is substance, not all rhetoric. . . . He cuts [errors] with arguments, not cudgels them with barren invectives.' Earle is not afraid of abstraction, but also has refreshing and homely touches. The 'Stayed Man', again, is 'One whom no ill hunting sends home discontented, and makes him swear at his dogs and family. One not hasty to pursue the new fashion, nor yet affectedly true to his old round breeches, but gravely handsome.' The most delectable combination of the lofty and the down-to-earth comes in the 'character' of the Grave Divine, who is 'no base grater of his tithes, and will not wrangle for the odd egg. . . . He is a main pillar of our church, though not yet dean or canon, and his life our religion's best apology.'

Hall, like Earle, can achieve a great concentration of expression: 'if there were no heaven, yet [the Honest Man] would be virtuous'. Again like Earle, he knows the value of the simple, homely touch:

[The Good Magistrate] is the faithful Deputy of his Maker; whose obedience is the rule, whereby he ruleth. His breast is the ocean, whereinto all the cares of private men empty themselves. . . . His doors, his ears are ever open to suitors; and not who comes first speeds well, but whose cause is best. *His nights, his meals are short and interrupted* . . . (my italics)

Although the general tenor of Hall's 'characters' of Virtues offers few surprises, there is just enough of the unexpected to provoke thought, as in the following, with its paradox that pity can sometimes turn into a vice:

On the bench, [the Good Magistrate] is another from himself at home: now all private respects of blood, alliance, amity are forgotten; and, if his own son come under trial, he knows him not. Pity, which in all others is wont to be the best praise of humanity and the fruit of Christian love, is by him thrown over the bar for corruption.[13]

I am not one of those who regard Hall's 'Virtues' as inferior in terms of interest and variety to his 'Vices'. If lesser writers seldom manage to bring their 'characters' of ideal types to life, this is due to a failure of insight or of technical skill. The task is not easy, for the reasons suggested in this chapter, but it is certainly not impossible.

9

The 'Character' and the Play

Methods of Characterization

Sooner or later, the student of the Theophrastan 'character' will ask himself the question: how far did this tradition of character-portrayal affect plays and novels? After all, 'characters' were produced in their thousands during a century and a half in which comedy was explicitly concerned with the delineation of types. During the eighteenth century, moreover, the novel gradually moved out of its somewhat exotic adolescence towards more realistic attempts to portray contemporary society and the types to be encountered there. Many critics have noted links,[1] but comments, where not limited to the influences at work on one particular play or novel, have usually been very general; no one, to my knowledge, has attempted a detailed assessment of how the 'character' influenced novels and plays in the two centuries of its greatest popularity. Perhaps the undertaking is too vast. However the following pages will, I hope, provide at least some hints of an answer. We will begin with drama—specifically with comedy, for it is here rather than in tragedy that the links and affinities are to be found.

It is easy enough to show the dramatic potential of much character-writing and to find passages that resemble miniature scenarios. Here is part of Saltonstall's Jealous Man:

> Hee dares not invite his friend to his house, for feare hee should salute his wife, which hee esteemes as a Prologue to an ensuing comedye. At table hee observes upon whom his wife scatters most favorable lookes (for hee feares there may bee a dialogue of eyes as well as tongues:) whom shee oftenest drinks to, whom shee comes to, and then his suspition comments upon every action. Hee's witty in inventing trialls of his wives chastity, and hee pretendeth verie often journeyes into the Countrey, thereby to make her more secure in his absence, but returnes againe unexpectedly.[2]

Similarly, comedies and character-books alike are full of quacks, coquettes, ignorant doctors, misers, hypochondriacs, and so forth.

But how do we tell whether the figure in the play owes anything to the corresponding 'character(s)', rather than to any one of half a dozen possible sources? For it has always been part of the very stuff of drama that one person should describe himself to the audience or, while in conversation with a second person, should characterize a third.

The comedies of Plautus and Terence offer examples of figures characterized in advance, sometimes in a speech which also gives the argument of the play. Alternatively a person in the play—usually the Parasite—may describe himself directly to the audience. Plautus and Terence were, of course, widely known, translated, adapted, and imitated from the Renaissance on.[3] Where we find a comic servant describing his master, either directly to the audience, to a third person or (by way of reproach) to the master himself, we may suspect the influence, direct or through the *commedia dell'arte*, of the slave from Roman comedy.

The *commedia dell'arte*, with its far-reaching influence in Western Europe, poses a special problem in this discussion, if only because we have to make our deductions about techniques of characterization from the evidence of surviving scenarios, eked out by isolated scenes recorded in full and by contemporary accounts of how the actors proceeded. However it seems clear that the audience recognized the characters as familiar types; a figure like Pantalone retained his basic personality from play to play despite changing situations. Given his name, costume, and mask, people knew what to expect of him and did not need a detailed verbal description.[4] Yet there were situations where, we may assume, some kind of set description of character did take place: the servant gave an account of his existing master or recommended himself to a new one, the Doctor or the Braggart boasted of his own prowess, Harlequin appeared in disguise and characterized himself in his new role.[5] The *commedia* influenced English, French, and Viennese comedy in various ways and cannot be ignored when the delineation of character is being considered.

Independently of all this, we can see a strain of character-exposition gradually emerging from the moral allegories to influence English comedy from the second half of the sixteenth century on. Whereas the figures in Ulpian Fulwel's *Like will to Like* (1568) and Robert Wilson's *Three Lordes and Three Ladies of London* (1590) are still typical allegorical personifications, the four sons of the wicked bailiff in the anonymous *A Knacke to knowe a Knave* (1594)—for all that they still stand for reprehensible qualities—emerge as real people as they describe themselves to the audience. The difference is clear if Wilson's 'Dissimulation' is compared to Perin, the flattering and scheming courtier from *A Knacke to knowe a Knave*:

Dissimulation: . . . after my scaping away at the Sessions where I shifted as thou knowest in three sundry shapes, one of a Frier, and they can dissemble: another like a woman, and they doo little else: the third as a Saint and a Devill, and so is a woman. I was banished out of London . . .

That Protean figure closely resembles Langland's 'Coveytise'. Contrast Perin:

I use my wits to flatter with the king.
If any in private conference name the king,
I straight informe his grace they envie him:
Did Sinon live, with all his subtiltie:
He could not tell a flattering tale more cunninglie:
Some tyme I move the King to be effeminate,
And spend his tyme with some coy Curtizan:
Thus with the King I curry favour still . . .[6]

In addition, Roman satire, the literature of the Estates, exemplary sketches contained in rhetorical treatises, and other sources must have given hints to the dramatists.

The position of Ben Jonson in this context is difficult to define exactly. E. C. Baldwin roundly describes him as 'the first to recognise the kinship . . . between the "character" and the drama'.[7] To begin with, there are the character-sketches in the lists of *dramatis personae*, the most famous being those in *Every Man out of his Humour* (1600). Although there is no reason to doubt that a man of Jonson's erudition had read Theophrastus, there is not much of the Theophrastan 'character' about these sketches; they seem rather to be indebted to Roman satire and to the native satirical tradition. In any case, such prefatory sketches have nothing to do with the possible invasion of the play proper by Theophrastan character-writing; their function is to establish the various personalities in advance of the dramatic action.[8] The character-sketches which come in *Cynthia's Revels* (1601) have been more confidently labelled Theophrastan and have been included more than once in anthologies of the 'character'. Even Boyce, always laudably cautious, concedes that the *Characters* of Theophrastus must have been one of a number of literary precedents here. Meanwhile, to illustrate a different line of development, Mosca's description of himself as a parasite (*Volpone*, 1607, III. i) clearly goes back to similar instances of self-characterization in Roman comedy, for all that Jonson's picture is richer in detail and more flamboyant in style. There are, then, quite detailed descriptions of character in Jonson's works of the first decade, and he obviously saw a place within the comedy for such set-pieces. But his closest kinship with Theophrastan character-writing is of a later date, when the Theophrastan vogue was firmly established in England.

There are, of course, many other examples of set characterization in English drama in the first decade of the seventeenth century.[9] However they tend to waver between description and sententious reflection (as in Chapman), or to change perspective constantly between individual and type, singular and plural (as in Dekker). There seems little doubt that, once the 'character' had established itself in England, it provided the dramatists with a much-needed model for a more unified and sustained description of personality, in which the link between the individual and the generic, always important in character-comedy, could be made clear. Before we consider this question of general indebtedness, we may observe the most direct kind of influence possible: cases where the dramatists have openly borrowed from specific, identifiable 'characters'.

Plays Drawing on Identifiable 'Characters'

The first example appears to be Shakerley Marmion's comedy *The Antiquary*, dating from the 1630s and published posthumously in 1641. Anyone familiar with the corresponding 'character' in Earle's *Microcosmography* will immediately recognize Marmion's source. Both Earle's Antiquary and Marmion's Veterano admire the patina on ancient monuments, both despise printed books and all modern 'novelties'. Each collects old coins and manuscripts and, for each, the highest prize of all would be a work by some classical author 'in his own hand'. Occasionally Marmion simply quotes Earle:

Earle	*Marmion*
. . . [he] reads only those characters, where time hath eaten out the letters . . . [and prizes a manuscript] especially if . . . the dust make a parenthesis between every syllable.	. . . time has eaten out the letters, and the dust makes a parenthesis betwixt every syllable.[10]

This, then, is an unambiguous case where the figure in the play has been based on a 'character' from one of the well-known collections of the day. To translate the 'character' into dramatic terms, Marmion had to do little more than turn Earle's third-person description into dialogue, so that we actually hear the Antiquary airing his prejudices and boasting about his rarities. Marmion makes one addition to Earle, however; when quizzed as to the usefulness, if any, of his treasures, Veterano replies: 'Did not the Signiory build a state-chamber for antiquities? . . . they are the registers, the chronicles, of the age they were made in, and speak the truth of history better than a hundred of your printed commentaries' (p. 449). Unfortunately this serious point is neither pursued nor refuted, merely submerged beneath mockery.[11]

In June 1767, Lessing saw a performance, in German translation, of J. F. Regnard's comedy *Le Distrait* (1697), and commented that it cannot have cost the author much effort, since he had found his main character already sketched out in detail by La Bruyère.[12] If one compares Léandre in the play with La Bruyère's celebrated 'character' of Menalcas (xi. 7), this view is confirmed. Like Menalcas, Léandre sends a servant for his gloves when he is, in fact, wearing them, forgets to whom he is speaking and what he is talking about, says 'yes' when he means 'no', addresses a woman as 'sir' and his manservant as 'miss', and so on. There is a variation on La Bruyère's anecdote of how Menalcas wanders into a strange house, believing it to be his own. Regnard's climax is imitated from La Bruyère too: like Menalcas, Léandre, on his wedding-day, manages to forget that he has just got married![13]

George Coleman the elder, in the 'advertisement' to his play *The Jealous Wife* (1761), acknowledges various debts, including that to 'the character of the Jealous Wife, in one of the latter papers of the Connoisseur'. He is presumably being playful, for the 'character' in question (*Connoisseur*, No. 127, 1 July 1756) is contained in a paper he had written himself in collaboration with B. Thornton. Mrs Oakly in the play resembles the (unnamed) wife in the *Connoisseur* in most particulars: she keeps close watch on her husband and opposes his going out. She becomes ill on the rare occasions he manages to leave the house, reads his mail, falls into a passion if he has dealings, however innocuous, with other women, and is deeply suspicious of the bad influence that 'irresponsible' bachelors might have on him. In both works, moreover, it is made plain that the jealousy proceeds from love.[14]

Such examples show clearly enough how character-writing might furnish the dramatist with raw material. But none of these three dramatists borrows the character-writers' actual descriptive techniques, preferring to translate static description of character into dramatic portrayal. This may involve nothing more than straight transcription into dialogue, but it can mean a considerable expansion. In the 'character' of the Jealous Wife, the husband simply recounts that his wife fell into a fit when he went to the tavern one evening. In the play, however, we actually see Mrs Oakly working herself into hysterics to keep her husband at home (Act I). In the *Connoisseur*, we read that the wife looks on bachelors with deep distrust, whereas the play has a sustained scene (in Act IV) in which Mrs Oakly accuses her brother-in-law of being the enemy of all married bliss and fidelity: 'You have no feelings of humanity, no sense of domestick happiness, no idea of tenderness or attachment to any woman.' Hereupon the brother-in-law is goaded into a counter-attack in the course of which he accuses Mrs Oakly of killing her husband with kindness. A brief detail in the 'character' has been expanded into a dramatic confrontation.

A quite different evocation of the 'character' occurs in Collin d'Harleville's comedy *L'Inconstant* of 1786. The Inconstant Man is Florimond. Although he has traits which link him with Don Juan, his changeable nature goes far beyond this: he gives up the army because of the sameness of military life, is first enraptured then bored by Paris in the course of a few hours, dismisses his servant because he cannot bear the same face about him for a month on end, and so on. He defends himself in these terms: 'Are you going to fall out with me over a little inconstancy? Then you would have to do the same with the whole human race. Rightly speaking, every man is inconstant, a little more or a little less, and I know why; it is because the human mind holds fast to so few things' (I. x). Seen thus, Florimond's disposition is an extreme form of something present in all men; the affinity between the comedy of humours and the views of human personality underlying the Theophrastan 'character' is evident. D'Harleville acknowledges this in a graceful and witty way. At one point, bored because there is nobody to talk to Florimond picks up a book at random—and finds himself reading his own character in La Bruyère: 'A changeable man is not one person but several; he multiplies himself as often as he has new tastes and different manners; he is at every minute that which he was not before, and soon he will be what he has never been. He is his own successor' (La Bruyère, xi. 6). The point of this episode I take to be twofold: within the play, it shows ironically that Florimond's attempt to escape from himself through books simply confronts him with a mirror-image of himself. At the same time, d'Harleville is acknowledging that his Inconstant Man is already present in La Bruyère—in essence if not in detail.

General Influences: England

In the four instances just discussed, the dramatist is telling us—or, at least, not bothering to conceal from us—that he is indebted to a particular 'character'. There is a second, larger group of works where the link, although not so specific, is nevertheless clear. These are usually plays in which a figure is described in some detail immediately before his first appearance on the stage. The description is often ushered in by some such exchange as:

Slander. I hear Mr Lovegold is come to town.
Simple (who has never heard of speaking names). I know him not. What manner of man is he?
Slander. Why, sir, he is one of that sort of men who . . .

I am not, of course, saying that all such set-pieces are indebted to character-writing. However, in many cases, what we have is to all intents and purposes a little formal 'character' inserted into the dialogue.

The criteria must be rigorous if anything more than a vague similarity is to be established. I have therefore confined myself to cases where the resemblance is so strong that, with the removal of a 'mark you, sir' or two, the piece could be taken out of its dramatic context and inserted into a character-book or periodical essay of the day without anyone's being the wiser. That criterion presupposes others: the description must be primarily one of character, not of dramatic situation, it must reveal the type hidden within the individual, it must (unlike the passages from Chapman and Dekker referred to above) have the unified form and presentation of the Theophrastan 'character', and, finally, it must be reasonably detailed, not merely a label or the brief mention of a single habit or quirk.[15]

A good starting-point is Ben Jonson's *Bartholomew Fair*, first performed in 1614 although not printed until 1631. In general, the humours of the various figures are revealed through their antics at the fair, but there is a short 'character' of Zeal-of-the-land Busy by Quarlous:

> A notable hypocriticall vermine it is; I know him. One that stands upon his face, more then his faith, at all times; Ever in seditious motion, and reproving for vaine-glory: of a most *lunatique* conscience, and splene, and affects the violence of *Singularity* in all he do's: (He has undone a Grocer here, in Newgate-market, that broke with him, trusted him with Currans, as errant a Zeale as he, that's by the way:) by his profession, hee will ever be i' the state of Innocence, though; and child-hood; derides all *Antiquity*; defies all other *Learning*, then *Inspiration*; and what discretion soever, yeeres should afford him, it is all prevented in his *Originall ignorance*; ha' not to doe with him: for hee is a fellow of a most arrogant, and invincible dulnesse, I assure you . . .[16]

But for the 'I know him' and 'I assure you' and the absence of physical details—superfluous in a play—that passage could take its place in a contemporary character-book. Why, one might ask, does Jonson give a 'character' here and nowhere else in *Bartholomew Fair*? Perhaps it was for the sheer fun of it, and for the pleasure of scoring off that old enemy of the players and dramatists, the Puritan.

In *The Magnetic Lady* (1632), Jonson goes further: Compasse's description of Parson Palate is still nearer to the formal 'character'. It is introduced by 'I can gi' you his Character' and ends by ironically placing Palate in a category:

> Hee, is the Prelate of the Parish, here;
> And governes all the Dames; appoints the cheere;
> Writes downe the bils of fare; pricks all the Guests;
> Makes all the matches and the marriage feasts
> Within the ward; drawes all the parish wils;
> Designes the Legacies; and strokes the Gills
> Of the chiefe Mourners; And (who ever lacks)

Of all the kindred, hee hath first his blacks.
Thus holds hee weddings up, and burials,
As his maine tithing; with the Gossips stals,
Their pewes; He's top still, at the publique messe;
Comforts the widow, and the fatherlesse,
In funerall sack! Sits 'bove the Alderman!
For of the Ward-mote *Quest*, he better can,
The mysterie, then the Levitick Law:
That peece of Clark-ship doth his Vestry awe.
Hee is as he conceives himselfe, a fine
Well furnish'd, and apparaled Divine (ed. cit. vi. 516 ff.)

The interesting thing is that Palate, unlike Zeal-of-the-land Busy, is a comparatively minor figure. He is seen flattering Lady Loadstone (I. iv) and shows himself ready to be Diaphonous's creature if there is promise of gain, but that is about the sum of it. Not only is this a fairly extended 'character'; it points beyond Palate's role in the play by showing him as a force in his parish. Unlike those cases where a 'character' features only qualities which will presently be manifested in the dramatic action, Jonson here uses the situation as an excuse to insert a satirical 'character' which, from a strictly dramatic point of view, is something of a luxury. (Murphy criticizes him for reverting to an 'undramatic' mode of characterization,[17] but this stricture is a trifle austere.)

Jonson does not borrow actual motifs from the character-writers, but comparison of the two passages quoted with the extracts given from early seventeenth-century character-writing in the opening chapter can leave one in no doubt of his methodological affinity with them. (Indeed, as already mentioned, he has been included in anthologies of the 'character'.) A somewhat similar case to his Parson Palate can be found in James Shirley's treatment of Sir Nicholas Treedle in *The Witty Fair One* (1628):

Clare. Didst ever see him?
Aimwell. No; but I've heard his character.
Manly. Prithee let's have it.

Boyce is certainly right to single out what follows as an authentic example of characterization fathered by the neo-Theophrastan vogue.[18] Both the matter and the witty manner support his view:

They say he's one, was wise before he was a man, for then his folly was excusable; but since he came to be of age, which had been a question till his death, had not the law given him his father's lands, he is grown wicked enough to be a landlord: he does pray but once a year, and that's for fair weather in harvest; his inward senses are sound, for none comes from him; he speaks words, but no matter, and therefore is in election to be of the peace and quorum, which his tenants think him fit for, and his tutor's judgement allows, whom he maintains to make him legs and speeches. He feeds well himself, but, in obedience to government, he allows his servants fasting days; he loves law, because it killed his father, whom the parson overthrew in a case of tithes; and, in memory, wears nothing suitable, for his apparel is a cento, or the ruins of ten fashions. He does not much care for Heaven, for he's doubtful of any such place; only hell he's sure of, for the devil sticks to his conscience: therefore, he does purpose, when he dies, to turn his sins into alms-houses, that posterity may praise him for his bountiful ordination of hot pottage; but he's here already: you may read the rest as he comes towards you.[19]

Although there is no wholesale theft, as there will be in the case of Marmion's *Antiquary* a few years later, the affinity with the 'character' is beyond doubt:

Shirley	*The character-writers*
. . . he [prays] for fair weather in harvest . . .	exactly similar motifs in various 'characters' of rustic types.
. . . feeds well himself . . . allows his servants fasting days . . .	'. . . his servants have not their living, but their dying from him, and that's of hunger' (Webster's Usurer in the Overbury collection).
. . . turn his sins into alms-houses . . . hot pottage . . .	the sort of formulation which the character-writers loved. 'With the superfluity of his usury, he builds a hospital . . . so, while he makes many beggars, he keeps some' (Hall's Hypocrite).
. . . you may read the rest as he comes towards you.	a stage equivalent to the closing formulas of the character-writers ('Enough of him' . . . 'But we leave him', etc.). And note Shirley's 'read', as if the living figure in the play had originated on the printed page.

As with Jonson's description of Palate, this speech takes us far beyond the subject's actual function within the play, for Treedle's dramatic role is the simple and abject one of the suitor who is cozened out of his intended bride. As often, there is an expansive feeling and an element of luxury in the interpolated 'character'. To apply notions of strict dramatic relevance to a type of comedy more interested in quirks of character than in stringently economical construction of plot would be anachronistic. A play was elastic enough to permit a little social satire for its own sake—and the character-books of the day provided models and hints.

Shadwell, in *A True Widow* (1679), goes a stage further in integrating the 'character' into the dramatic dialogue. Here, Bellamour and Stanmore discuss first Maggot, then Selfish. As one speaker pauses, the other steps in. The substance is that of a pair of short 'characters' (of a would-be Wit and a vain Coxcomb), but the element of witty competition between the two speakers gives a greater degree of dramatic liveliness than would have been the case if one had talked and the other listened:

Bellamour. [He] never was known to speak, but 'I did,' or 'I said' was at the beginning or end of it.
Stanmore. He is as lean as a skeleton, and yet sets up for shape: he changed his tailor twice, because his shoulder-bones stick out.
Bellamour. He thinks all women in love with him . . . (I. i)

There is a similar instance in Dryden's *Marriage à la Mode* (1673), where Rhodophil confides to his friend Palamede that he desires to take a mistress and gives her 'character'. Palamede's promptings and interpolations ('Yet hitherto, methinks, you are no very unhappy man' . . . 'I confess, she had need be handsome, with these qualities') keep us aware that this *is* a conversation; one danger of inserting a 'character' into the dramatic dialogue[20] is that it stands out from its context like the set-piece it is, as in the following example from Farquhar's *The Constant Couple* (1699):

He's [Sir Harry Wildair] a Gentleman of most happy Circumstances, born to a plentiful Estate, has had a genteel and easy Education, free from the rigidness of Teachers, and Pedantry of Schools. His florid Constitution being never ruffled by misfortune, nor stinted in its Pleasures, has rendered him entertaining to others, and easy to himself—Turning all Passion into Gaiety of Humour, by which he chuses rather to rejoice his Friends, than be hated by any . . . (I. i)

That is an odd anticipation of the stately rhythms of the more formal type of 'character' in early eighteenth-century periodicals. Vizard here speaks like a printed book.

One consequence of giving a person's 'character' immediately before his first appearance on the stage is illustrated—unwittingly and without irony, I take it—by Henry Higden, in his *Wary Widdow* of 1693:

Scaredevil. I will prepare you with a hint of his Character. This Knight is . . . [etc., etc.]. But you will ken him upon the first view . . .[21]

The person thus described is unlikely to offer us many surprises when he steps on to the stage.[22] But that very limitation can have advantages within the context of character-comedy. The victim, by demonstrating the truth of what has just been said about him, raises a laugh against himself. Since the inset 'character' is itself entertaining in most cases, it contributes in a twofold way to the comedy, as we see in Colley Cibber's *Love's Last Shift: or, the Fool in Fashion* (1696). The 'fool' is Sir Novelty Fashion, who is first discussed in his quality of a Dandy and then confirms this 'character' with great exactitude:

The 'character'	*The dramatic confirmation*
A thing that affects mightily to ridicule himself, only to give others a kind of necessity of praising him . . .	'Why, does your ladyship really think me tolerable? . . . the devil take me, in my mind, I am a very ugly fellow.'
I can't say he's a slave to any new fashion, for he pretends to be master of it, and is ever reviving some old, or advancing some new piece of foppery . . .	'The cravat-string, the garter, the sword-knot, the centurine, bardash, the steinkirk, the large button, the long sleeve . . . were all created, cry'd down, or revived by me . . .'
He's so fond of a public reputation, that he is more extravagant in his attempts to gain it, than the fool that fir'd *Diana's* temple to immortalize his name.	He walks out of a *good* play before the first act is over, to hint at important business and make plain his contempt for what the rest find diverting.[23]

All the above examples have been from the work of competent dramatists. Only very rarely do we get the impression that a writer introduces a 'character' into his play because he lacks the skill to make his figures reveal themselves through words and deeds. Edward

Moore, in *The Foundling* (1748), makes such an impression—but Moore was, as he tells us in his Prologue, 'unpractis'd in the Drama's artful page'. The general level of comedy-writing in England throughout the seventeenth and eighteenth centuries was very high; if writer after writer adopted the 'character' to his dramatic ends, it cannot have been because it seemed an easy path to instant characterization but because it was thought to be effective and entertaining. The purpose served by these and similar 'characters' is basically a simple one: they tell us in advance what to expect of Sir This or Mr That. The 'character' can, however, be made to serve a variety of subtler dramatic purposes. But before we examine some instances, we must glance at the situation in the German-speaking countries.[24]

General Influences: Germany

Since, as we have seen, the vogue of character-writing spread to Germany only in the early eighteenth century, and since character-comedy was out of favour there by 1800, any enquiry must concentrate on the eighteenth century. A brief account of the general nature of German comedy in that era may therefore be helpful.

In the 1730s, J. C. Gottsched attacked the popular stage of the day, with its extemporization, clowning, coarse jokes, and knockabout.[25] He had some reason to complain. Even late seventeenth-century school dramas had shown some debts to this tradition. As more extreme examples of the type, one might mention the stage plays and puppet pieces devoted to Dr Faust or Don Juan, in which the clown played as important a role as the hero, or the out-and-out farcical adaptations of Molière which were played between 1680 and the 1720s.[26] The best-known comedies in the period immediately before Gottsched's attack were those of Christian Reuter and 'Picander' (C. F. Henrici), which represent at least a toning-down of the farce and vulgarity rampant in the popular extempore pieces. But this was not enough for Gottsched, whose own exemplary collection of plays (*Deutsche Schaubühne*, 1740–5) reveals a liking for 'regular' French comedy, together with a pronounced distaste for anything related to the popular, improvisatory stage.

Gottsched's influence was considerable. Given the practical examples contained in his *Deutsche Schaubühne*, together with contemporary admiration for French literature in general, it is not surprising to find that large numbers of French comedies were translated for the German stage.[27] As German writers found their confidence, original German comedies were written. In these, the didactic element is always strong; the conviction that a folly exposed was a folly shunned was dear to the heart of every man of the German Enlightenment. These plays often end not only with the cure of the foolish character but with his explicit acknowledgement that argument and good example have converted him. Figures on the stage are made mouthpieces for the authors' views on moral education.

In the 1740s and 1750s, satirical character-comedies were joined by a more sentimental type of drama, the French *comédie larmoyante*. It was popularized in Germany, where it was usually called *das rührende Lustspiel*, by Gellert. In these plays, comic characters and incidents are subordinate, and the interest is usually centred on the fortunes of a pair of deserving young lovers. However, in Germany at least, the boundaries between *comédie larmoyante* and character-comedy are not as clear as writers on the history of comedy sometimes make out, for most *rührende Lustspiele* contain at least one vain or foolish person, while character-comedies include good as well as ridiculous figures.[28]

This, then, was the situation in the middle decades of the eighteenth century. The values extolled in the comedies were closely similar to those of the moral weeklies: reason, virtue, moderation, unostentatious and unaffected sociability, a good upbringing, learning without pedantry, and so on. These affinities often result in a sort of mutual backslapping. In the comedies, the reading of the *Spectator* or any of its imitators immediately labels a character as good and sensible, while, conversely, the moral weeklies frequently express their support for the reformed theatre, together with disapproval of Hans Wurst and his *confrères*. There is, too, a similarity between the theories underlying character-writing in the periodicals and those propounded for the writing of comedy. The 'character' concentrates on one quality incorporated in a representative figure. Theories of comedy likewise insist that the figures be types. The proud man must be all pride, the miser all miserliness (cf. Gottsched, *Kritische Dichtkunst*, I. v, §24). Nevertheless, the writer must stop short of caricature. For Gottsched, Molière offends against this rule in *L'Avare*; Breitinger criticizes La Bruyère for having created the 'unnatural' figure of Menalcas.[29] The dramatist and the character-writer walked the same tightrope.

Given these common aims and values, it is not surprising that the 'characters' in the German periodicals influenced characterization in the comedy, particularly as comedies from the popular tradition, which might have offered alternative models for set-piece description of character, were rejected by the dramatists of the German Enlightenment.

J. F. von Cronegk wrote *Der Mißtrauische* (*The Distrustful Man*) while still a student, and it was published in 1760, two years after his untimely death at the age of twenty-six. It is a serious comedy centred around Timant, a distrustful young man who lacks all self-confidence. At the beginning of the play, his father returns from his travels and questions the servant, Philipp, about his son. As an expository device, this would appear to derive from Roman comedy, but the description that follows is similar to those in the moral weeklies. General formulations ('he is his own worst enemy . . . he is over-cautious') are followed by clusters of examples and short anecdotes:

He often stops speaking to wonder whether perhaps something compromising could not be read into his words. When two people are talking in the street, he thinks they are talking of him. If someone greets him in a friendly way, he thinks he is being made fun of or is about to be cheated. If someone acts indifferently, he thinks it's an attempt to pick a quarrel. Recently he was in the playhouse; when the audience laughed at Harlequin, he thought they were laughing at him and went out in anger.[30]

Stylistically, the passage shows clear affinities with character-writing. The behavioural details—all manifestations of one ruling characteristic—are given in a series of parallel constructions, as they are in Theophrastus: 'If he has done you a favour. . . . If a passer-by asks him. . . . When he is elected. . . . If he passes you in the street. . . . When he entertains friends. . . . When he goes visiting' (Arrogance). Within each sentence, the relationship of subordinate clause to main clause mirrors the relationship between the outside world and Timant's tormented inner world. That sort of sentence-construction had often figured in character-writing to stress the disparity or maladjustment between the norm and the deviant quality being described. A comparison between Timant and Addison's Sombrius, much admired throughout the eighteenth century and much imitated in the German weeklies, makes the resemblance clear:

Timant

Wenn zwo Personen . . . so glaubet er . . .
Wenn man ihm . . . so glaubet er . . .
Thut man gleichgültig, so glaubet er . . .

Sombrius

Tell him . . . he lifts up his hands . . .
Describe . . . he shakes his head . . .
Show him . . . he blesses himself . . .[31]

Cronegk's little dramatic 'character' is ably done. But, as we have noted in the case of Edward Moore, the 'character' could offer an easy way out for the third-rate dramatist. In Gottlieb Fuchs' *Die Klägliche* (1747), Frau Ditrich—a whining, superstitious, over-anxious woman—is described at the outset of the play by her servant (I. i), a common enough situation. However, the recipient of these confidences is Frau Ditrich's own daughter, who lives in the same house. There is no attempt to motivate this piece of character-exposition; the impression is that an unskilful dramatist is clutching gratefully at a ready-made device.

Gellert's position is a little uncertain. We have seen plenty of cases where direct description of character and its indirect revelation through words and deeds complement each other happily; we have seen a couple of instances where direct description is used as the easy solution. But Gellert is seemingly not able to make up his mind about how he ought to proceed. In 1745 he published *Die Betschwester*, the study of a pious hypocrite. Wolfgang Martens has pointed out links with the many 'characters' of this type of woman in eighteenth-century periodicals,[32] but this is not primarily a question of borrowed motifs, such as we saw in the cases of Marmion, Regnard, or Coleman; what we have here is the presentation of the *Betschwester* in a series of descriptions which closely resemble types of 'character'. Gellert begins with a plausible piece of character-exposition: Ferdinand has been endeavouring to see the *Betschwester*, Frau Richard, only to be told repeatedly that she is at her prayers. 'But she surely does not pray incessantly?' he asks in frustration. Lorchen, the resident companion, explains:

No, she alternates. When she doesn't wish to pray, she sings. And when she no longer has any desire to sing, she prays. And when she wishes neither to pray nor to sing, then she talks of praying and singing (I. i).

The exchange quite naturally develops into a picture of Frau Richard as Lorchen explains things to Ferdinand, the visitor. But suddenly Ferdinand makes a strange request: 'Give me a little character of her'. No member of Gellert's audience will have missed the significance of that form of words (*Machen Sie mir doch einen kleinen Charakter von ihr*). He has not asked merely for her character to be described; he has demanded that the description be put into the specific form of the Theophrastan or 'moral' character-sketch, as widely practised in the journals of the day. Lorchen duly obliges:

> No one who is accustomed to look for virtue in the features and on the lips can possibly deny Frau Richard her reputation. Everything about her is pious: her features, her language, her gait, her dress . . . (I. i)

That rather formal and sententious description is indistinguishable from the style of character-writing in the German weeklies. Presently we find Ferdinand requesting a picture of a typical day in Frau Richard's life: 'Tell me what she does all day'. His two requests to Lorchen therefore correspond to two basic methods of character-writing in the eighteenth century: the straight depiction, and the account of a typical day in the subject's life. And again Lorchen complies:

> She gets up at about eight. And as soon as she puts her feet into her slippers, she begins to sing. Singing, she combs her pug; singing, she looks after the cat. Singing, she feeds the canary. . . . And as soon as it strikes nine, she stops singing, even if it is in the middle of a verse. She runs as quickly as she can, so as to be sitting at her prayers before it has finished striking. . . . From nine till ten she reads three morning prayers . . .[33]

Gellert's procedure is curious here; it is as if he did not trust himself to establish Frau Richard's character by purely dramatic means and resorted instead to this essentially literary device. Lorchen talks for all the world as if she were reading out passages from a moral weekly. Yet immediately after this, Frau Richard herself appears and we see for ourselves what sort of person she is. Gellert certainly did not lack the basic skills necessary for the 'indirect' exposition of character. Perhaps the author of the *Moralische Charaktere* simply enjoyed the direct description of personality.

The 'Character' and the Viennese Stage

The theatre in Vienna has always occupied a special position within the drama of German-speaking countries, largely due, no doubt, to that city's geographical situation and the resultant mingling of cultures. In the early eighteenth century, a rich mixture of influences had helped to create a robust popular drama. Elements from opera and ballet, from the *commedia dell'arte* and the plays—at once sensational and farcical—given by itinerant troupes of German actors, somewhat vulgarized adaptations of French comedy: all these were fused with local ingredients to produce a unique blend. There was much extemporization and knockabout and the clown played a central part with his coarse witticisms, puns, misunderstandings, acrobatic tricks, disguises, and impersonations. The celebrated Viennese comic actors of the day enjoyed huge popularity.

From the 1740s on, there were attempts to introduce into Vienna (or perhaps 'force on the Viennese theatre-goers' might be more accurate) a more decorous type of play of the sort championed at the time in Germany by Gottsched. Sides were taken, pamphlets and articles abounded.[34] The purists, chief among whom were J. H. Engelschall, T. P. Gebler, and Joseph von Sonnenfels,[35] took it as axiomatic that the theatre should be an instrument of moral improvement. This clearly could not be achieved as long as popular plays were full of vulgarity and indecency, or while extemporization remained widespread. Therefore cleaning up the stage inevitably meant putting an end to improvised clowning. Extemporized theatre was in all seriousness represented as a threat to public morality. The extraordinarily high-minded attitude of the theatrical purists is not unique; what can still surprise the outsider is the way in which the Emperor, the nobility, and the state were drawn into the argument. Engelschall, Gebler, and Sonnenfels all demand official action: if the state is responsible for public morals, the state must further types of drama which improve morality and discourage—or ban—any that threaten it. The reformers admired Gottsched, but regarded him as too much of a theorist. What they wanted was to see his ideals realized by practical men of the theatre.[36]

Sonnenfels, in particular, had great influence.[37] However the reformers did not have it all their own way. J. B. Pelzel, in his comedy *Die Schauspieler* of 1769, makes one of the actors lament the fact that farces get the biggest audiences, while serious plays are performed to half-empty houses (I. iii). C. G. Klemm, a one-time follower of Sonnenfels turned rebel, mocks the reformers' dictatorial and austere attitude towards 'good taste' in his satirical comedy *Der auf dem Parnaß versetzte grüne Hut* (1767):

Lysimon. What is good taste then?

Hannswurst. What I say it is. Nothing entertaining, but long moral disquisitions.[38]

Philip Hafner, the most effective of Sonnenfels' opponents, makes clear that a middle position is the solution for him: he attacks the purism of Gottsched's disciples, but also mocks excessive reliance on extempore clowning.[39] The solution to the Hans Wurst problem is not to banish him, but to make him respectable. And so the comedies of Klemm, Hafner, and other like-minded men take over the clown figure but write out his part fully, leaving no opportunity for coarseness or uncontrollable antics.[40] Hafner and his associates thus attempt to get the best of both worlds. The 'regular' pieces in the German manner were all too often worthy but lifeless, while the out-and-out popular plays possessed vitality, but were fantastic and vulgar. In the long run, the fusion between these two strains was undoubtedly a healthy development, for it helped to preserve a living theatrical tradition which was genuinely popular and local, but which did not alienate serious theatre-lovers.

Where characterization is concerned, the union of serious and popular elements in eighteenth-century comedy makes for complications. A set piece of characterization may be indebted to any one of several strands. In Vienna as elsewhere, the popular plays may include a scene in which the servant describes his master's shortcomings, at the same time giving the argument of the play.[41] Or Hans Wurst may satirically describe himself as a typical member of whatever profession he happens to be impersonating at the moment. With a more sedate piece of character-description in the type of Viennese comedy which has banished or tamed Hans Wurst, we may be faced with a debt to the 'regular' German comedy, or to some French play[42]—or to the 'character'. Care is needed.

The playwrights most likely to adapt the techniques of character-writing to the needs of the drama were either the champions of the reformed theatre, such as J. C. Bock, Joseph von Petrasch, and Paul Weidmann, or of a type of comedy in which the clown and other popular elements had been made 'respectable', such as Klemm.

Paul Weidmann's comedy *Der Stolze* (1774) deals with a proud nobleman surrounded by a group of toadies and parasites who, however, abandon him when he appears to have lost his position and riches. One of these hangers-on, an 'Occasional Poet', characterizes himself at some length on his first appearance:

I am familiar with all branches of learning, but I am particularly inexhaustible in well-wishing. I receive the new-born babe into the world with my song; I serenade infants in the cradle; I lead the young man to the altar and sing the bride her nuptial song. My muse creeps into the most secret lying-in chambers. Again I join the fray. I weep at the tombs of the dead. No festivity takes place which I do not attend, placing my humble wit at people's disposal. The rest of the time I devote to weekly journalism. I praise and blame according to how I am paid. (I. i)

That reads like a satirical 'character' transcribed into the first person. The result is, perhaps, an uncertainty of tone. Is the Poet, Lorbeerfeind, preening himself, or is he the puppet of a moralistic author? His 'inexhaustibility in well-wishing' seems like a malicious comment from outside and the final sentence sounds too much like a hostile definition of the venal writer for it to belong in a passage of *self*-characterization.

Rabener's 'Todtenliste' (see above, p. 95) contains the satirical 'character' of a Commemorative Poet which is worth quoting by way of comparison:

Gustav Trolle always took a lively interest in the happiness and misfortune of his fellow-citizens. His enemies, in mockery, named him 'the congratulator'. No name-day or birthday passed without his presenting signs of his respect in printed form. Untiringly he commanded that the houses of his patrons and friends should be bathed in joy and bliss. . . . At every death, he dipped his quill in bitterness and wormwood. . . . He kept the Muses in constant employment. . . . No bridegroom or bride had a name so far-fetched that he could not twist and turn it until he drew from it a reference to the cradle. . . . He was neither selfish nor miserly; for half-a-crown he would empty his heart . . .

Rabener's 'character' was first published in the *Belustigungen des Verstandes und des Witzes* in 1743.[43] Since that was one of the best-known moral weeklies, there is a possibility of direct influence, but even if there is none the affinity is clear. If Weidmann's piece were put into the third person, the two passages would be interchangeable.

A case where the 'character' has been worked rather more skilfully into the dramatic texture can be found in Joseph von Petrasch's comedy *Der Lächerliche Erforscher* (1765). The central figure is a man who constantly searches for hidden motives in the conduct of his fellows (hence *Erforscher*). He is closely linked with Cronegk's Distrustful Man (*Der Mißtrauische*); this would, indeed, be a better title for Petrasch's play. Here, Philander (*der Erforscher*) is described at length by his servant Heinrich. He is expressly shown as belonging to a category of rich malcontents (*diese vornehme*

Leute haben alles: und sind doch misvergnügt) and his ruling characteristic, like that of Cronegk's Timant, is communicated through a list of typical actions, exactly as in the Theophrastan 'character':

When two people are talking together, he pricks up his ears like a hare and asks what they said about him. Even in unfamiliar places where no one knows him, he eavesdrops on everything and thinks that people are talking about him . . . Whenever I come home, I must tell him what I have seen or heard from other people. But who can always think of something? Then he says I am in league with his enemies—although he has none (I. iv)

Turn each 'I' into 'his servant', and the passage would slip into, and illustrate, a periodical essay on 'Distrust'. At the same time, however, Petrasch does not lose sight of the immediate dramatic situation, for the servant interrupts his catalogue of Philander's shortcomings with laments about his own position: '[I] don't know what will finally become of me. How often am I not on the point of leaving him!' Thus any impression that the action is being halted for the purpose of a static and undigested piece of character-portrayal is minimized. This 'dramatization' of the interpolated 'character' resembles that in Shadwell's *True Widow* and Dryden's *Marriage à la Mode*.[44]

Beyond the Exposition of Character

Virtually all the above examples, from Jonson to Cronegk, have been fairly straightforward in their aim and effect; the 'character' has been employed within the play to reveal a ruling temperament more quickly than could be done by less direct, purely dramatic means. However, the inset 'character' could have more diverse and subtle functions.

One of the most interesting examples—quite apart from the surprise of meeting a formal 'character' in a tragedy—occurs in the trial scene of Webster's *White Devil*. Cardinal Monticelso lets fall the word 'whore'.

Vittoria. Ha! whore! what's that?
Monticelso. Shall I expound whore to you? sure I shall;
I'll give their perfect character. They are first,
Sweetmeats which rot the eater . . .

There follow twenty lines of heated metaphorical description, whereat Vittoria comments: 'This character scapes me' (III. ii). The 'character', then, is labelled and recognized as such by both accuser and accused—and would also have been recognized by contemporary audiences. The plural number, highly unusual in character-writing,[45] seems appropriate here, reinforcing the impression that Monticelso is trying to place Vittoria in a company of whores and that she rejects this categorization. It should be stressed that Monticelso's 'character' is a general indictment, couched in a series of bitter metaphors; the detailed evidence comes later and is presented more soberly and circumstantially. The 'character' is the opening rhetoric before the prosecuting counsel gets down to brass tacks; with its metaphors of ruin, disease, hellfire, and falsehood, it is intended to produce a feeling of horror at Vittoria's corruption in the listening ambassadors and thus to make her trial politically acceptable (see the opening of III. i). It is significant that the French Ambassador's comment ('she hath liv'd ill') comes immediately after the 'character' and before any proofs are given whatever.

Where a 'character' is used in a play for simple purposes of character-exposition, the author is saying in effect: this is what X is; he is both individual and type. But some of the most intriguing examples of the 'character' in drama are descriptions of a type as yet unrelated—or not yet definitely related—to any figure in the play. The action then reveals, or allows us to decide, whether the individual in question fits into the category. Farquhar's comedy *Sir Harry Wildair* (1701) is a sequel to *The Constant Couple*: Standard is married to Lurewell and meets his sailor-brother, Captain Fireball, newly returned from sea. Fireball's reaction to the marriage is one of horror:

> Shall I tell you the Character I have heard of a fine Lady? A fine Lady can laugh at the Death of her Husband, and cry for the loss of a Lap Dog. A fine Lady is angry without a Cause, and pleas'd without a Reason. A fine Lady has the Vapours all the Morning, and the Chollick all the Afternoon. The Pride of a fine Lady is above the merit of an understanding Head; yet her Vanity will stoop to the Adoration of a Peruke. And in fine, A fine Lady goes to church for fashion's sake, and to the Basset-Table with Devotion; and her passion for Gaming exceeds her vanity of being thought Vertuous, or the desire of acting the contrary (I. i)

The element of play here, and the uncomplicated desire to entertain should not be overlooked, but, in addition, the 'character' fulfils a definite dramatic function by creating suspense: will Lurewell turn out like the fine Lady of the 'character' or will she live up to her protestations? As in *The White Devil*, the question is posed: does the individual fit the definition? This dramatic use of the 'character' springs from one of its basic features: its combination of the individual and the generic.

A 'character' is frequently employed in comedy to suggest an ideal to be striven for or a part to be played. In Shakerley Marmion's *Holland's Leaguer* (1632), the sub-plot deals with the adventures and mishaps of two dupes, Trimalchio and Capritio. Miscellanio, the tutor, undertakes to turn Capritio into a 'perfect cavaliero':

> he shall wear
> His clothes as well, and smell as rank as they,
> And court his mistress, and talk idly . . .

and so on, for another eighteen lines (II. v). Change the 'shall wear . . . shall smell . . . shall court' into 'wears . . . smells . . . courts', and we would have a satirical verse-character of the Town Gallant. But, dramatically speaking, the passage has an ironic function, for it stresses the abject contrast between these brave prospects and Capritio's eventual fate—to be gulled and robbed in a whorehouse and married off by a trick to a serving-wench.

A similar device occurs in Richard Brome's *City Wit*, where Linsey-Wolsey is exhorted to play the courtier in order to ingratiate himself with a supposed rich widow (actually a man in disguise):

> *Linsey-Wolsey*. Your Courtier, Sir, I pray.
> *Toby*. Ile tell you in a briefe character was taught me. Speake nothing that you mean, performe nothing that you promise, pay nothing that you owe, flatter all above you, scorne all beneath you, deprave all in private, praise all in publike; keepe no truth in your mouth, no faith in your heart; no health in your bones, no friendship in your mind, no modesty in your eyes, no Religion in your conscience; but especially no Money in your Purse.
> *Linsey-Wolsey*. O that Article spoyles all.
> *Toby*. If you do, take heed of spending it on any thing but Panders, Puncks, and Fidlers; for that were most unfashionable.[46]

As with Farquhar's 'fine Lady', the 'character' both fulfils a role within the play (here, a profoundly ironical one) and gives the dramatist scope for his satirical zest. The link with character-writing is unashamedly conceded: 'Ile tell you in a briefe character was taught me'.

Another common form of dramatic irony is, of course, the unconscious self-revelation which comes about when a blinkered person airs his prejudices. The Theophrastan 'character' can play its part here too. Lessing's early comedy *Der junge Gelehrte* (1747) deals with the vain and arrogant would-be scholar, Damis. When his father informs him that a marriage has been arranged, he replies scornfully with what his notion of a woman is:

> . . . vain, arrogant, talkative, quarrelsome and childish throughout her whole life. A woman hardly knows that she has a soul that she ought to consider infinitely more than her body. To dress herself, undress and dress herself differently; to sit in front of the mirror and admire her own charms; to devise artful expressions; to laze at the window with inquisitive eyes; to read silly novels or at best take up her needlework to pass the time; these are her occupations, that is her life.[47]

This is the 'character' of a vain and empty-headed Beauty, as if put together from a reading of contemporary satires and moral weeklies; it is Lessing's way of intimating that Damis's views of the opposite sex are not merely arrogant, but are—like all his views—gathered from books.

We have seen how Jonson and Shirley introduced into their 'characters' of Parson Palate and Sir Nicholas Treedle details which could not be enacted before us, if only because they would take us into realms far removed in space or time from the domain of the play. By thus extending the reach of a play, the inset 'character' can also radically enlarge its implications. This occurs in a bitterly anti-clerical comedy published in 1743: *Die Geistlichen auf dem Lande*. The author, J. C. Krüger, is mainly concerned with the rural clergy, whose two representatives, Muffel and Tempelstolz, are shown as ignorant, hypocritical, gluttonous, and lecherous. But Krüger does not wish us to assume that all is well in the towns, so he directs the conversation to the subject of the urban clergy. In reply to Muffel's questioning. Tempelstolz draws an envious picture of yet richer pickings there. He does this through two quite extended character-sketches (I. viii). The first begins: '[Hieronymus] has grown fat in his calling. . . . He has been there almost thirty years. In the first three years, he worked up all his sermons word for word; in the following years he merely learnt them by heart.' When Muffel asks about Hieronymus's learning, the answer is that he has other fish to fry. What follows is an exact parallel to the day-in-the-life type of character-sketch in the eighteenth-century periodicals: 'He can spend his time better and more peacefully [than at study], getting up at nine o'clock, drinking tea till ten, dressing by eleven, eating by two and resting till three.' Tempelstolz goes on to relate how Hieronymus makes visits, cultivates his richest parishioners in order to sponge off them, and fancies himself as a ladykiller. The moral weeklies offer many a 'character'[48] of the clergyman who 'preaches water and drinks wine', to borrow Heine's phrase, but none so bitter as in this play of Krüger's. It may be noted that the 'day-in-the-life' convention underlines Hieronymus's idleness, since this form of character-writing was virtually reserved for the depiction of social parasites in the moral weeklies. Tempelstolz's second example, that of Tartüffe, concentrates on the unctuous and hypocritical way in which a fashionable clergyman wheedles money out of his parishioners. So the dramatist has employed these two inset 'characters' in order to double the range of his satire. (Neither Hieronymus nor Tartüffe actually appears on stage at any point.)

'Characters' employed within plays obviously share the limitations of the Theophrastan 'character' in general: they are not suitable for depicting very complex personalities, or for detailed development. But since seventeenth and eighteenth-century comedy is largely concerned with two-dimensional types who are, moreover, fully developed at the time of their first appearance on the stage, these limitations are unimportant. There are, perhaps, cases where the 'character' would be inappropriate or unsatisfactory for technical reasons rather than psychological ones (plays which revolve around the unmasking of an impostor or which reveal character through a man's professional jargon). Such cases apart, however, there are very many instances where an inset 'character' can place a figure fair and square before us, fulfil some additional dramatic function, and amuse us into the bargain.

As long ago as 1812, Friedrich Schlegel had pointed out that merely to dramatize a Theophrastan 'character' did not in itself produce a work of art (*Die Charaktere von La Bruyère oder Theophrast in dramatischer Einkleidung sind . . . noch keine Poesie*: *Geschichte der alten und neuen Literatur*, xiv). However, dramatically interesting and effective results can certainly be achieved when a skilful dramatist borrows the techniques and devices of the character-writers and works them into his play, while never losing sight of the fact that it *is* a play, and not merely popular psychology spoken out loud on the stage. But the employment of 'characters' in drama declined with the sort of comedy which had encouraged it. As more three-dimensional figures drove typecast characters into minor roles, a more oblique and gradual exposition came to be favoured. 'I'll tell you his character' no longer seemed appropriate or adequate.

10

The 'Character' and the Novel

(i) **England**

The modern reader has become accustomed to view the novel as a literary form in which characters and events are inextricably linked, in which personalities gradually reveal themselves through speech and action. Yet the great majority of novels before, say, Richardson, Marivaux, and Gellert were, as Pat Rogers has expressed it, 'series of adventures . . . connected by the fact that they happen[ed] to the same person'.[1] Often, characters did not 'emerge', but were described by the novelist in some detail when they first appeared on the scene. Exotic or Arcadian tales of adventure, featuring improbably handsome and virtuous kings and princesses, may have disappeared by about the mid-seventeenth century in France and England (much later in Germany), but the formal characteristics just mentioned did not vanish; they passed over into the picaresque novels. These are full of minor figures whose only causal link with the plot is that they happen to share a stage-coach or a dining-table with the hero. The Theophrastan 'character', popular in England when the picaresque fashion was beginning to catch on, was bound to influence the portrayal of such figures, especially where the author wished to set them up as typical of a social class or moral category.

The first instances known to me of 'characters' within the novel occur in Richard Head's *The English Rogue* (1650) and Thomas May's *Life of a Satyrical Puppy, called Nim* (1657). Head's novel, first published in 1650 and added to in subsequent editions, is an early attempt to import the *picaro* into England. It tells the history of the 'rogue' and gives a picture of the English underworld and *demi-monde* at the same time. The employment of 'characters' is impudent in its simplicity and directness, for Head and his collaborator Francis Kirkman (who seems to have written the second part) simply filch passages from Overbury, Mynshul, and others in order to flesh out their satirical picture of English life.[2]

In Thomas May's novel, Nim is an impoverished gentleman's son who comes to London and turns satirist. At one point he addresses the reader thus: 'I intend to pick out from the whole rable a *Whore*: and prefer her in a *Character* to thy immaginary view . . .' There follows a long formal 'character' in which the Whore's gaudy clothes are contrasted with her diseased body and foul breath.[3] The material is in no way original—similar motifs can be found in all seventeenth-century 'characters' of Whores—but at least May, unlike Head, has written the 'character' himself. The only slender justification for including this set-piece is, I suppose, that Nim is here exercising his art as a satirist.

These two examples show one rather crude way in which 'characters' could be employed within the novel: to provide an element of social satire without in any way relating to the action. The next stage was to introduce actual protagonists in the form of 'characters'. Many later novelists, working in the picaresque vein, did this as an easy short cut to characterization.[4] The following example, from Francis Coventry's *History of Pompey the Little*, recalls the style of character-writing in the coffee-house periodicals:

Theodosia was largely possessed of all those good Qualities, which render Women agreeable without Beauty: She was affable and easy in her Behaviour; well-bred without Falshood; chearful without Levity; polite and obliging to her Friends, civil and generous to her Domestics. Nature had given her a good Temper, and Education had made it an agreeable one. She had lived much in the World, without growing vain or insolent; improved her Understanding by Books, without any Affectation of Wit or Science, and loved public Places, without being a Slave to Pleasure.[5] (ii. 3)

In the eighteenth century, character-writers began to show increased interest in the development of personality, a factor which must have deepened the novelists' interest in the genre. With very few exceptions,[6] seventeenth-century authors had portrayed their subjects as fully-fledged personalities. But Addison and his successors are no longer always content to do this. One of Frazer Tytler's contributions to the *Mirror* (No. 17, 23 March 1779) takes the form of a letter from a grocer's wife, telling how a shrewd and businesslike tradesman was gradually transformed into a besotted collector of antiques and curios. The process began when a curious coin was given to him in mistake for a shilling. This led him to become fascinated with old coins. Later, from being a rather gullible numismatist, he became a fanatical collector of all sorts of oddities, from stuffed crocodiles to tarantulas.

As an example in more serious vein, one could turn to a 'character' in the *Friend* (1755, No. 4): that of Marcia, a girl whose religion is 'a jumbled medley . . . of God and superstition'; here again the anonymous author is not content with depicting Marcia as she is, but is concerned with showing the process of becoming. Similarly, in the *Trifler* (1788, No. 18), we learn by what combination of cirumstances a gifted girl develops into an obsessed and embittered bluestocking. In these cases, the borderline between 'character' and short story has obviously become much less clearly marked than previously. For instance, is Tytler's work the 'character' of an Antiquary, or a short story about a sensible man led into ruinous folly? Is the account of Marcia the 'character' of a confused and superstitious believer, or a story about the malign effects of the wrong kind of upbringing? It hardly seems to matter what one calls such borderline cases, although it is worth pointing out that the contributions to the *Friend* and the *Trifler* are both labelled 'characters'. What is significant is that the challenge to older, static notions of personality brings with it a movement away from the 'character' pure and simple. What a man is becomes increasingly bound up with the question of how he became what he is.[7]

Where earlier character-writers had tended to give a string of typical actions which in sum made up the type that they wished to describe, their eighteenth-century successors frequently developed one single episode or anecdote in such a way that it came to epitomize the whole personality. For instance, Johnson[8] conveys the 'character' of a *nouveau riche* through a visit paid to him by an old friend from humbler days, who is kept waiting, entertained in a back room, given the second-best china, and generally made to feel that he is not a person of quality or consequence.[9] The anecdote *is* the 'character'. A further development, to be seen in at least some of the eighteenth-century papers, occurs when a character, once invented and introduced to the readers, takes on a life of his own and reappears in later issues, with different associates and in different settings. The most famous example is Sir Roger de Coverley, who is seen at home and in town, in church and on the hunting-field, in his relations with friends and servants. Many people have noted that the de Coverley papers, if taken as a group resemble chapters or episodes from a novel. (Indeed, Sir Roger, in his mixture of good-heartedness, practical wisdom, and quirkishness, is much more like a rounded figure in a novel than any 'character'.) Macaulay, in fact, describes Addison as the 'forerunner of the great English novelists'.[10]

Thus an increasing interest in the development of personality and a tendency to pick on one sustained and particularly revealing episode combined to bring the 'character' much nearer to the short story and the novel than ever before (or, if one prefers, the 'character' strayed into a kind of no man's land between 'character' proper and narrative fiction, while still retaining its original label). As the novelists of the eighteenth century increasingly came to draw their material from contemporary life, it became natural and inevitable that they should find hints in the 'characters' scattered about the periodicals from the *Tatler* and *Spectator* onwards. Yet the variety of ways in which eighteenth-century 'characters' aspired to the condition of prose fiction makes the task of defining possible influences a complex one. Questions such as whether Addison is the father of the English novel seem to me unanswerable except in very general terms. I have therefore set myself a more modest but more tangible task: to examine the novel for specific techniques borrowed from character-writing, to seek types of set description in which the individual and the generic are combined as in the 'character', so that a figure is established as a personality operating and having his being within the world of the novel, while at the same time standing for a type and being recognized as such by the reader.

All our major novelists, from Defoe to Trollope, will have been acquainted with character-writing and many of them wrote 'characters' themselves: Dickens and Thackeray at the beginning of their careers, George Eliot at the end of hers, Trollope intermittently from the 1860s to 1880. Thackeray and Dickens are the only two whose 'characters' can be shown to have provided actual material for their novels,[11] and even here the links are slight. By far the more important question is the one just mentioned: whether techniques of character-writing passed over into the novel. 'Characters' are most likely to occur where the author wishes to introduce and label a figure quickly. This will often be a minor figure who will play a brief part and then disappear from view, but can be a more important character, provided that he is not so complex or unpredictable as to deviate radically from the pattern of behaviour implied by the initial description.

For convenience—although at some risk of appearing schematic—I will cite a few examples, together with the labels that such figures would have been given by the character-writers.

Swift,	*Gulliver's Travels* (1726, iv. 6)	The Chief Minister	Minister of State
Fielding,	*Joseph Andrews* (1742, chapter 57)	Beau Didapper	Beau, 'Pretty Fellow'
Smollett,	*Sir Launcelot Greaves* (1760, chapter 14)	Squire Sycamore	the foppish Dupe
Jane Austen,	*Persuasion* (1815–16, chapter 1)	Sir Walter Eliot	the Vain Man
	Sanditon (1817, chapter 3)	Lady Denham	the mean and bossy Great Lady
	ibid. (chapter 8)	Sir Edward	the affected Ladykiller
Bulwer Lytton,	*Eugene Aram* (1831, i. 4)	Sir Lionel Garrett	Enthusiast
	ibid. (ii. 2)	Lord xxx	enlightened Nobleman
	ibid. (ii. 6)	Sir Peter Hales	mean and selfish Country Gentleman[12]
	Ernest Maltravers (1837, iv. 5)	unnamed banker	Hypocrite
	ibid. (vii. 4)	Lord Saxingham	Worldly Man
Thackeray,	*Vanity Fair* (1847–8, chapter 11)	The Revd Bute Crawley	Sporting Parson
	The Newcomes (1854–5, chapter 11)	Mr Bagshot	the first-floor Lodger
	ibid. (chapter 17)	Dick Tinto	the Art Student
Trollope,	*The Warden* (1855, chapter 15)	Dr Pessimist Anticant	Pamphleteer
	ibid.	Mr Popular Sentiment	polemical Novelist

	Barchester Towers (1857, chapter 4)	Mr Slope	the fawning and ambitious Chaplain
	ibid. (chapter 9)	Dr Stanhope	Worldy Cleric
	Dr Thorne (1858, chapter 32)	The Revd Caleb Oriel	High-Church Rector
Geroge Eliot,	'Amos Barton', in *Scenes of Clerical Life* (1858, chapter 6)	the 'Clerical Meeting'	various types of Clergyman

It is striking how often such figures are explicitly set up as types:

Mr Thomas Heartfree . . . was of that sort of man whom . . .

Every neighbourhood should have a great lady.—The great lady of Sanditon was Lady Denham . . .

Sir Lionel Garrett was a character very common in England, and in describing him, I describe the whole species . . .

He was one of those earnest and high-wrought enthusiasts . . .

He was a very *remarkable*, yet not . . . a very *uncommon* character—this banker![13]

Compare:

Lydia is a finished coquette, which is a sect among women . . . (*Tatler*, No. 126)

Sombrius is one of these Sons of Sorrow . . . (*Spectator*, No. 494)

. . . cousin Tom, who is one of those country squires that set up for plain honest gentlemen . . . (*Guardian*, No. 162).

The 'characters' within the novels are often ushered in by little introductory formulas, only a shade less explicit than those used earlier by Head or May:

As [a Coquette] is a particular kind of folly, I will endeavour to describe it (*Joseph Andrews*, chapter 38)

. . . some further particulars of her history and her character served to lighten the tediousness of a long hill, or a heavy bit of road (*Sanditon*, chapter 3)

And, as we bring our characters forward, I will ask leave, as a man and a brother, not only to introduce them, but occasionally to step down from the platform and talk about them (*Vanity Fair*, chapter 8).

Such are the novelist's equivalents to the comedy-writer's 'I'll give you his character' or 'I'll tell it to you in a Character'. Trollope even resorts to old-fashioned speaking names with the most unsophisticated directness (Dr Pessimist Anticant, Mr Popular Sentiment), labelling their possessors in advance as two-dimensional figures. (In fact, his treatment of these two men contrasts signally with the careful and judicious delineation of character elsewhere in *The Warden*.)

As with inset 'characters' in comedies, there is often an impression of innocent self-indulgence. An example is Mr Wilson's account of Sapphira, with whom he had been infatuated as a young man (*Joseph Andrews*, chapter 38):

'. . . She was indeed a coquette *achevée*.'
'Pray sir,' says Adams, 'what is a coquette?'—

and thereupon Wilson gives her 'character':

Were all creatures to be ranked in the order of creation according to their usefulness, I know few animals that would not take place of a coquette; nor indeed hath this creature more pretence to anything beyond instinct; for, though sometimes we might imagine it was animated by the passion of vanity, yet far the greater part of its actions fall beneath even that low motive. . . . Indeed its characteristic is affectation, and this led and governed by whim only. . . . Its life is one constant lie . . .

Having given the generic definition, Wilson relates Sapphira to it: 'And indeed this was the case of my Sapphira . . .'. But Fielding's readers, more worldly than Parson Adams, will have known perfectly well what a coquette was; the value of the passage lies in its trenchant style, not in its strict necessity within the economy of the story (Adams's guilelessness and naïvety have been demonstrated many times already).

Bulwer Lytton's portrayal of Mr Dyebright in *Paul Clifford* (1830) is a similar case. It is clearly related to character-writing and could easily serve as illustration to a rather jaundiced essay on 'Justice and the Law':

Mr Dyebright was a lawyer of great eminence; he had been a Whig all his life, but had latterly become remarkable for his insincerity and subservience to the wishes of the higher powers. His talents were peculiar and effective. If he had little eloquence he had much power; and his legal knowledge was sound and extensive. Many of his brethren excelled him in display; but no one, like him, possessed the secret of addressing a jury. Winningly familiar; seemingly candid to a degree that scarcely did justice to his cause, as if he were in an agony lest he should persuade you to lean a hair-breadth more on his side of the case than justice would allow; apparently all made up of good, homely, virtuous feeling, a disinterested regard for truth, a blunt yet tender honesty, seasoned with a few amiable fireside prejudices, which always come home to the hearts of your fathers of families and thorough-bred Britons; versed in all the niceties of language, and the magic of names; if he were defending crime, carefully calling it misfortune; if attacking misfortune, constantly calling it crime; Mr Dyebright was exactly the man born to pervert justice, to tickle jurors, to cozen truth with a friendly smile, and to obtain a vast reputation as an excellent advocate. (chapter 35)

But Mr Dyebright appears only once in the novel, as prosecutor at Paul Clifford's trial (the result of which is a foregone conclusion anyway). If Dyebright is described in such detail, it must be out of the author's desire to give the satirical 'character' of a devious Advocate; the plot in no way requires such a degree of insight into his general character and conduct.[14]

It will be seen that the inset 'characters' in the novel have much in common with those in seventeenth- and eighteenth-century comedies. They are often formally introduced, it is usually made clear that the subject is both individual and type, and the character-sketch frequently gives the impression that it is there as much for its own sake as to further the plot. Moreover, as in plays, the subject, once described, tends to act out the description. This is demonstrated in Trollope's *The Prime Minister*:

The Mongrober estates were not supposed to be large, nor was the Mongrober influence at this time extensive. But this nobleman was seen about a good deal in society when the dinners given were supposed to be worth eating. He was a fat, silent, red-faced, elderly gentleman, who said very little, and who when he did speak seemed always to be in an ill-humour. He would now and then make ill-natured remarks about his friends' wines, as suggesting '68 when a man would boast of his '48 claret; and when costly dainties were supplied for his use, would remark that such and such a dish was very well at some other time of the year. So that ladies attentive to their tables and hosts proud of their cellars would almost shake in their shoes before Lord M. And it may also be said that Lord M. never gave any chance of retaliation by return dinners. There lived not a man or woman who had dined with Lord M. (chapter 9)

Immediately after this, we hear Lord Mongrober being loudly rude about the wine provided by his host.[15]

Such advance characterization does not diminish our interest in the figure concerned, but certainly alters it. In the case of Lord Mongrober, we await with some amusement the confirmation of the 'character'; in other instances, our interest moves from 'What manner of man will this turn out to be?' to 'How will he fare?'— or 'Will he achieve his ambitions?'—or 'How will he affect the hero's fortunes?' It is wrong to assume that a person becomes less interesting once his 'character' has been given.

Sometimes the 'character' may have a more complex and subtle function within the novel. The first example known to me occurs in Defoe's *The Fortunate Mistress; or, a History of the Life . . . of the Lady Roxana*, first published in 1724, a work which, among other things, boldly examines the relative positions of wife and mistress. Roxana (who ought to know what she is talking about, having been both) examines the pros and cons. The wife enjoys respectability but is financially dependent on her husband to the point of slavery; the mistress has apparent freedom but lives an ambiguous and furtive life. Her situation is described by Roxana in a little formal 'character' of a Whore (see above, p. 158); by 'whore', a kept woman is meant, not a casual prostitute. Similarly, the 'character' of a Merchant in the same novel (above, pp. 142 f.) has some thematic relevance, for the merchant himself is arguing that he and his like are in many ways superior to noblemen—and arguing it to Roxana, the one-time mistress of a prince. It is part of his courtship, extending to Roxana her only chance of respectable affluence.

A similar 'organic' use of the 'character' occurs in Fielding's *Jonathan Wild* (1743). The novel depends to a large part on the sustained ironic pretence that the scoundrel Wild is a great man, while the honest and trusting Heartfree is a 'silly' or 'low' fellow. The contrast is encapsulated in a pair of 'characters', expressly described as such in the chapter-headings (ii. 1 and iv. 15). Since one 'character' introduces us to Heartfree and the other sums up Wild after his inglorious death, and since the contrast between 'great' and 'silly' permeates the novel and gives it wider meaning, we have here a true example of the 'character' used to serve a structural purpose.[16]

Although anything resembling a 'character' in Jane Austen is rare, James Sutherland[17] has seen the influence of the character-writers at one point in *Sense and Sensibility*. Elinor, Marianne, and Edward are arguing about the picturesque:

'I suspect,' said Elinor, 'that to avoid one kind of affectation, Edward here falls into another. Because he believes many people pretend to more admiration of the beauties of nature than they really feel, and is disgusted with such pretensions, he affects greater indifference and less discrimination in viewing them himself than he possesses. He is fastidious and will have an affectation of his own.' (chapter 18)

That, says Sutherland, reads like a 'character of a plain honest fellow': one could add that most of Edward's following speech, if put into the third person, would continue the 'character': 'He does not like crooked, twisted, blasted trees. He admires them much more if they are tall, straight and flourishing . . .' Sutherland goes on to remind us that this is part of a conversation which throws light on all three speakers. Thus we appear to have an example of how the 'character' can be assimilated into the novel and made to serve its purpose. If this is so, it is a more enterprising application of 'Theophrastan' techniques than one usually encounters.

The question remains whether the 'character' has any place in the delineation of central figures whose gradual development—usually towards maturity and some form of self-realization—is the novelist's central concern. From the intrinsic nature of the 'character', it would seem not. But it can serve a limited purpose here too, as Thackeray shows us. Arthur Pendennis is too complex and contradictory to be contained in the form of a 'character', yet his creator finds it convenient to sum him up at one stage in his career in this way. This is when he cuts a figure as the University Buck, living hopelessly beyond his means:

His manner was frank, brave, and perhaps a little impertinent, as becomes a high-spirited youth. He was perfectly generous and free-handed with his money, which seemed pretty plentiful. He loved joviality, and had a good voice for a song. . . . Pen rode well to hounds, appeared in pink, as became a young buck, and not particularly extravagant in equestrian or any other amusement, yet managed to run up a fine bill at Nile's, the livery stable-keeper, and in a number of other quarters . . . (chapter 18)

In *The Newcomes* (1854–5), Thackeray again exploits the possibility of using a set 'character' to describe one stage in a person's career or one facet of his personality, presenting Barnes Newcome to us as a heartless, go-getting man of business (chapter 8) and the Revd Charles Honeycomb as a fashionable and worldly cleric (chapter 11). Employed thus, the inset 'character' is not an introduction to a new figure, but a means of filling out or summing up to date a personality already encountered (for we have seen the objectionable Barnes lording it at his club and have met Charles Honeycomb at a *soirée*). Nor does the 'character' exhaust the subject: there is more to be learnt about Barnes's malice, treachery, and cowardice; more to be learnt too about the extravagance that will briefly land Charles Honeycomb in a debtors' prison. The justification for the employment of the 'character' is that the subject is, for that moment and in that capacity, seen as typical. Barnes is the young man of business, no better and no worse than many another, while Honeycomb is explicitly labelled as a type ('such a personage as the Incumbent of Lady Whittlesea's Chapel, Mayfair').[18]

The Epistolary Novel

The demonstration of links between the Theophrastan 'character' and character-portrayal in the epistolary novel presents a difficulty all of its own. When the 'straight' novelist holds up his narrative in order to give a set character-sketch, he is clearly stepping in to give the reader information which he feels—rightly or wrongly—cannot be as forcefully or rapidly conveyed through narrative. And he operates differently. With 'X entered the room . . .', there is nothing interposed between the events and the reader. The moment we read, 'X was the type of man who . . .', we are aware that material is being directly presented to us by the novelist. But what the letter-writer offers in the epistolary novel is single and indivisible. Whether it is a case of 'Mr X led me into the garden . . .' or 'You ask me what manner of man Mr X is. Well, then . . .', it is all part of the one person's experience as communicated to his or her correspondent. It is neither necessary nor possible for the novelist to intervene, except as 'editor'.

The case of Richardson is instructive. It has often been argued that he was indebted to the character-writers in the eighteenth-century periodicals. Clarissa Harlowe's icy account of Mr Tourville seems at first glance not unlike the 'character' of a Coxcomb or vain Society Gentleman from one of the coffee-house papers: 'In his person and manner, [he is] more of what I call the coxcomb than any of his companions. He dresses richly . . .'[19] Yet one cannot say that Richardson has inserted a 'character' into the texture of his novel quite as we have seen Fielding or Coventry or Trollope doing. Clarissa naturally wishes to describe these unpleasant new acquaintances to her friend in as telling a way as possible. The elegance, shrewdness, and exactitude of her comments may well suggest to us that the *Spectator* has figured among her favourite reading and this, in turn, may support the notion that Richardson drew on, or was guided by memories of, the portrayal of human types in such periodicals, but the situation is in no way comparable to that in a 'straight' novel where the author stops telling the story in order to do something quite different. Clarissa's account of Mr Tourville and similar sketches[20] seem to arise quite naturally out of the situation and experiences of the correspondent and his or her desire to communicate them. One can say that the style occasionally resembles that of the 'characters' in the *Spectator* or other papers, but that is all.

In Smollett's *The Expedition of Humphry Clinker* (1771) there are set descriptions which more closely resemble inset 'characters': for example, the sketches of Jack Holder, the *nouveau riche* spendthrift, and of Quin, the epicure.

> Jack Holder, who was intended for a parson, has succeeded to an estate of two thousand a year, by the death of his elder brother. He is now at the Bath, driving about in a phaeton-and-four, with French horns. He has treated with turtle and claret at all the taverns in Bath and Bristol, till his guests are gorged with good cheer; he has bought a dozen suits of fine clothes, by the advice of the master of the ceremonies, under whose tuition he has entered himself; he has lost some hundreds at billiards to sharpers, and taken one of the nymphs of Avon Street into keeping . . .[21]

Jack Holder and similar figures play little or no part in the story, except to contribute their mite to the satirical microcosm of English society which is given—zestfully, if unsystematically—in all these latter-day picaresque novels and comic travel journals. The description, which could have been slotted into an issue of, say, the *Rambler* without more ado, is different from that of Mr Tourville, who is shown as part of Clarissa's experience and hence a more essential part of the texture of the novel:

> He dances finely, Mr Lovelace says . . . and singing is one of his principal excellences. They prevailed upon him to sing . . . and, to do him justice, his songs in both [Italian and French] were decent. . . . To me he appeared to have a great deal of affectation. (v. 455 f.)

In this respect, the situation in *Clarissa* seems to me thoroughly convincing, despite the strictures of some critics about more general improbabilities in the work.[22] By contrast, some set 'characters' in the epistolary novel produce a hopelessly artificial effect. In Susannah Minifie's *The Count de Poland* (1780), Lord Castledown writes to a friend, setting off the happy state of married life against the lonelier existence of the bachelor:

> I shall hold up to your view the picture of a *bachelor*, and oppose it to the portrait of a married man. . . . A *bachelor* is a sort of whimsical being, which nature never intended to create. . . . No tender impressions enliven his waking hours. . . . If he ever speaks the language of sensibility, he speaks it on the excellence of some favourite dish. . . . A coffee-house is his *sanctum sanctorum* . . . here he lounges out half his days—at home he sits down to his *unsocial* meals, and when his *palate* is pleased, he has no other passion to gratify. Such is a bachelor . . .
>
> Now for the *married man*. The felicity of a married man never stands still; it flows perpetual, and strengthens its passage. . . . By an union with the *gentlest*, most *polished*, most *beautiful* part of the creation, his *mind* is harmonized, his *manners* softened, his *soul* animated. . . . The house of a married man is his *paradise*; he never leaves it without regret, never returns to it but with gladness . . . (iv. 128 ff.)

Castledown is not making his point in a natural way; he is inventing a pair of contrasting 'characters', as if he were penning a contribution to a literary magazine rather than a letter to a friend. The situation is much more forced than in *Humphry Clinker*, where the inset 'characters' at least harmonize with the style and personalities of the letter-writers. Since one reason for the popularity of the epistolary novel was that the reader felt that he was 'eavesdropping' on an actual exchange of letters, the effect of verisimilitude must have been threatened by such an over-literary device. To put it crudely, the author of an epistolary novel cannot get away with an inset 'character' half as easily as he could in a 'straight' novel.

Dickens

Our starting-point with Dickens must clearly be the *Sketches by Boz* (1836). Although the author was to look back on these pieces as the hasty and imperfect productions of an inexperienced writer, we might today prefer to see them as trial runs, part of the novelist's training. But what of the specific question of character-portrayal?

As examples of true 'characters', one could mention the Old Lady (which must be ranked with Leigh Hunt's Old Gentleman as an example of the most affectionate and gentle style of nineteenth-century character-writing), the Clerk and the Misanthrope ('Thoughts about People'), the Parlour Orator, the Schoolmaster, and the Beadle. But there are also pieces which show Dickens moving away from the type towards the eccentric, the 'card'. In a sketch like 'The Last Cab-driver', 'character' in the Theophrastan sense yields to 'character' in the colloquial one.

When one remembers that *Pickwick Papers* is, chronologically, very near to the *Sketches by Boz*, and that Mr Pickwick and his companions travel round the country observing 'character and manners', one might expect to find many short character-sketches of figures briefly encountered by the Pickwickians on their quest. That we do not testifies to the speed with which Dickens found his feet as a novelist in the creation of character, if not yet in plot-construction. Even where two-dimensional types, such as the medical student or the ignorant and splenetic magistrate, appear, they are not described in the manner of the Theophrastan 'character', but are demonstrated in action and conversation. The difference in technique between Dickens and the character-writers is most clearly shown in two episodes: the visit to Bath and Mr Pickwick's sojourn in prison.

The coffee-house periodicals had often given groups or little cycles of 'characters': people to be encountered in fashionable watering-places, inns, and the like. Dickens certainly offers the reader a highly entertaining depiction of the various types at Bath: the foppish Angelo Cyrus Bantam, Lord Mutanhed, the servants who entertain Sam at the 'swarry', and so on. But they are not presented in the form of 'characters'; they reveal themselves to Mr Pickwick and Sam through their behaviour. The way in which novelist and character-writer could treat similar material but, technically, could go their different ways is even more clearly demonstrated if one compares Mr Pickwick's experiences in the Fleet with Mynshul's *Essayes and Characters of a Prison* (1618). The unfortunate prisoner, the scrounger, the venal turnkey—all these have more or less near relatives in Mynshul's book on prison life. But the presentation is different: Mynshul's avowed aim is to describe typical persons to be encountered in a prison, while Dickens asks the questions, 'How did Mr Pickwick and Sam fare in prison? How did the people there affect Pickwick's views and how did he alter their lives?'

In the *Sketches by Boz*, we can (with a little hindsight, perhaps) already see Dickens the novelist impatient to take over from Dickens the writer of set character-pieces. 'The Misplaced Attachment of Mr John Dounce', included by Dickens among the 'Characters', certainly starts with a 'character' of what the author calls a 'steady old boy', but quickly expands into a story as Dounce becomes ruinously infatuated with a young woman, with the consequence that the settled routine of his life is destroyed. This process of narrative expansion is simply taken further in *Pickwick Papers*.

Two other things can be said of the characterization in *Pickwick Papers*, which will apply increasingly to Dickens's later works. Firstly, Dickens already displays his interest in the development of character (here, the effect of wider experience on the naïve Mr Pickwick and that of suffering and disinterested kindness on Mr Jingle). Secondly, the movement away from 'character' in the Theophrastan sense towards 'character' in the colloquial sense, already noted in the *Sketches*, is much more marked (witness Mr Jingle, the Fat Boy, and the elder Mr Weller).

These trends are continued in Dickens's later novels. Even in the case of figures dominated by one ruling humour—figures, that is, whose link with the 'character' is strong—Dickens seldom makes use of a set descriptive piece, preferring to let them demonstrate what kind of people they are. In *Oliver Twist*, this applies to Mr Fang and Mr Grimwig, who, as types, resemble the arbitrary and ignorant Magistrate and the Choleric Man of the character-writers.[23] Even more striking is the case of Mr Bumble. Dickens himself had already written the 'character' of a Beadle in the *Sketches by Boz* and takes up some features from it: the pomposity, the pride in the awe-inspiring cocked hat, the feeling that the Beadle in his majesty *is* the parish. But no traces of character-writing remain. Dickens's debt to his own early work is confined to thematic details, raw material.

There are, however, a number of figures whom Dickens introduces by means of short 'characters', for instance in *Our Mutual Friend*. The initial description of the Revd Frank Milvey (i. 9) could easily be included in a periodical essay as the 'character' of a poor Clergyman, that of Fledgeby (ii. 5) as the 'character' of a Miser and Usurer. A more celebrated example is the description of Mr

Podsnap, with his pretentiousness, humbug, blinkered patriotism, and refusal to look unpleasant facts in the face (i. 11). This virtually establishes Mr Podsnap once and for all; what follows, however brilliant and entertaining it may be, does little more than elaborate and illustrate what we already know. Similarly, from *The Mystery of Edwin Drood*, one could instance Mr Sapsea and Mr Honeythunder (the stupid and conceited man and the pugnacious and self-righteous do-gooder respectively). Like Bulwer Lytton, Dickens classifies his figures in an almost Theophrastan way, describing Sapsea as 'the *type* of self-sufficient stupidity and conceit' (my italics) and referring to Honeythunder sometimes by name, sometimes as 'the philanthropist'.[24] Since *Edwin Drood* is unfinished, one can do no more than surmise, but it is unlikely that either of these figures would have come to display any important features not already hinted at in the introductory descriptions. These character-sketches from *Our Mutual Friend* and *Edwin Drood* thus offer fairly exact parallels to the many instances in comedy where a character is first described and then acts out the description.

But Dickens's interest in character-development usually takes him far beyond the limits of any possible 'character'. One can see the process unfolding in the treatment of Mrs Varden in *Barnaby Rudge*. She is introduced to us quite explicitly as one of a category: 'Mrs Varden was a lady of what is commonly called an uncertain temper . . .' (i. 7); and there follows a 'character' of her as a specimen of this type. But where the 'character', explicitly or tacitly, normally assumes that personality, once established, is fixed, Dickens even at this stage hints at a possible reform: 'divers wise men and matrons . . . even went so far as to assert, that a tumble-down some half-dozen rounds in the world's ladder . . . would be the making of her'. That is prophetic: in the end, Mrs Varden will be chastened and reformed by experience.

The other way in which Dickens moves away from the traditional notion of the 'character' is, as already hinted, in his liking for the eccentric. The most revealing demonstration of this is his treatment of Mr Squeers. We know that Squeers was intended to represent the typical proprietor of the worst sort of Yorkshire School; he is, as Dickens tells us in his Preface, 'the representative of a class, and not of an individual'. But Dickens's celebrated fondness for the grotesque detail runs away with him. In the Theophrastan 'character', the generic must be manifest in the particular, and each detail, however exaggerated, should be typical of the whole class, susceptible of indefinite multiplication. We should be able to imagine *all* Antiquaries collecting tarnished old coins, *all* Misers living off mouldy crusts, *all* Dandies rising at eleven and spending a couple of hours in front of the mirror. But imagine a 'character'—any 'character'—beginning: 'He had but one eye, and the popular prejudice runs in favour of two.' It could even be argued that the same element of grotesquerie runs through the whole section on Dotheboys Hall, and detracts from its force as a social *exposé*.

Dickens seems to me to offer the most fascinating and revealing illustration of how a highly imaginative novelist stands in relation to the 'character'. He wrote 'characters' before he ever attempted a novel, but, as he found his feet as a novelist, he became more adept at revealing personality through appearance, actions and words, and conspicuously more interested in showing how character develops. Moreover, his penchant for the grotesque helped to distance his creations still further from the traditional 'character'.

Conclusion

The Theophrastan 'character', given its wide popularity, was bound to influence the novel and, having found its way there, was bound to be edged into a subordinate position. Novelist after novelist illustrates this. For instance, Defoe's contributions to *Applebee's Journal* include many 'characters', but there are very few in his novels, apart from those noted in *Roxana.* There are possibly special and personal reasons in his case; he seems to have been temperamentally less interested in the analysis of character than in maintaining a ceaseless flow of absorbing events. Moll Flanders, for instance, is married, widowed, remarried, and sees her second husband ruined all within five pages. Indeed one critic has described the book as 'only a string of diverting incidents'.[25] Often, too, Defoe preferred to base his characters on famous (or notorious) persons of the day rather than invent representative figures.

Fielding is explicit. Since he himself averred that he described not individuals but 'species',[26] one might expect to find him drawing heavily on the techniques of character-writing in his novels. Yet this is not so; he regards description as less effective than the manifestation of personality through words and actions. At one point in *Tom Jones*, having briefly defined the chief differences between Tom and Blifil, he adds: 'An incident which happened about this time will set the character of these two lads more firmly before the discerning reader than is in the power of the longest dissertation' (iii. 2). In introducing Sophia to the reader, he goes further; to dwell on her inner characteristics would be 'a kind of tacit affront to our reader's understanding, and may also rob him of that pleasure which he will receive in forming his own judgement of her character' (iv. 2). This is surely the main technical argument against the widespread employment of the 'character' in the novel and Fielding is, as far as I know, the first novelist to have pointed it out.[27] That Smollett takes the same view is suggested by an episode in *The Adventures of Roderick Random* (1748). A chapter-heading promises us 'the character of my fellow-traveller'. Yet Smollett does not mean that he proposes to describe the man concerned, rather to tell how his character revealed itself to Random. (The fellow-traveller is the young Capuchin, Balthazar, who shows more liking for a roll in the hay with the innkeeper's daughter than for prayers.)[28] The obvious advantage of this technique is that a man's character and his actions are shown to be an indivisible whole and to manifest themselves simultaneously. A danger of the set 'character' within the novel is that, simply by giving the 'dissertation' before the 'incidents', it sets up an artificial distinction between what a person is and what he does. Coventry, whose mock-picaresque novel *Pompey the Little* has already been cited, makes this division in almost comically naïve terms: 'And now that we have drawn the Characters of so many People, let us look a little into their Actions; for Characters alone afford a very barren Entertainment to the Reader' (ii. 7). Coventry can get away with this, but only because he is operating on a burlesque level.

Jane Austen's case is complex. She can certainly sum up a human being in an icily objective miniature,[29] but seldom does so. One reason is her interest in character-development. The most striking example of this must surely be in *Emma*, where virtually the whole novel revolves around the heroine's passage from over-hasty judgements and romantic fallacies to a realization of her past folly and the fact that she has consistently got all her matchmaking and manipulating wrong. 'Character is not cut in marble,' George Eliot will say; 'it is something living and changing.'[30]

Jane Austen also has a fondness for delayed character-exposition and innocent mystifying. Willoughby in *Sense and Sensibility* is first shown to us from his superficially attractive side, and his unpleasant traits emerge only gradually. But even then Jane Austen is not content merely to 'unmask the villain': we hear Willoughby's own explanation of his conduct, which has the effect of slightly ameliorating it in Elinor's eyes (and in the reader's). It is not simply that Willoughby is more complicated than any stereotyped picture of 'the Libertine';[31] Jane Austen has no intention of showing or telling us what he is like at the outset (the character-writer, on the other hand, has no secrets from the reader). She is interested in the contrast between apparent and real worth and in the emergence of the truth. A more straightforward example would be that of the General in *Northanger Abbey*: imposing at first sight, he gradually reveals himself as tyrannical and inhumane.

But there is a yet stronger reason why Jane Austen steers clear of the techniques of the character-writers, which is that her figures are too strongly individual and complex to be summed up in that way. Even Edward, whom we have seen cast as a 'plain honest fellow', illustrates this, for the passage quoted from his debate with Marianne and Elinor shows only one part of his personality. It has to be complemented by what he says and does (often too by what he fails to say and do), and by authorial comment. Marianne too is complex. She is made fun of for her 'sensibility', of course, but becomes a near-tragic figure after her abandonment by Willoughby. Here we have an example of Jane Austen's desire for truth to life. In the conventional world of literary characterization—and certainly within the conventions of the Theophrastan 'character'—you can be tragically sick with love, or comically devoted to dead leaves and gnarled trees, but you cannot be both. Jane Austen, however, realizes that you can indeed be both: one reason why she condemned trivial novels for being alien to real life, and probably one motive behind her notorious attack on the *Spectator* in *Northanger Abbey* (chapter 5), where she talks of 'unnatural characters'. To what can this refer? To be true, the *Spectator* offers its readers Eastern potentates, pirates, and negro slaves enacting a *Liebestod* in the Leeward Islands, but such interludes are too few and far between to justify a contention that the periodical is full of unnatural characters. The really extravagant caricatures of indigenous types are likewise rare. I think it much more likely that Jane Austen's criticism is directed against the artificial restrictions placed on character-delineation by the notion of the Theophrastan 'character'.

This theory seems to gain support from a passage in *Mansfield Park* where generalizations about whole classes of people (meat and drink to the character-writers) are condemned: 'Where any one body of educated men . . . are condemned indiscriminately, there must be a deficiency of information, or . . . of something else' (chapter 11). Therefore the techniques made familiar and popularized by the periodicals of the eighteenth century could be of only limited usefulness to Jane Austen, interested as she was in the complexities of human nature, the development of character, and the constant possibility of being misled by or about a person. As we have seen, similar considerations must have been in the minds of Dickens, Thackeray, and others, reinforced in Dickens's case by his liking for the eccentricities of human nature.

R. C. Jebb, musing on the relationship between the Theophrastan 'character' and characterization in the novel, makes the expected contrast between typology and individualization and then adds a further point: 'Again, these subtler characteristics are not seen so much in particular actions as in the relations of one action to another. . . . A novelist is able to develop tolerably complete theories of character because he takes a long series of connected actions.'[32] This development is evident where the novelist has taken a type familiar from the character-writers and made a major figure out of him, as with Scott's *The Antiquary* (1816).

Like Earle's Antiquary, Scott's Jonathan Oldbuck prizes 'rust and the antiquity which it indicates'; like the collector described by Johnson in the *Rambler* (No. 177), he is immensely proud of a rare edition of an old ballad; and, like virtually all the Antiquaries depicted by the character-writers, he easily persuades himself that a half-legible inscription testifies to great age. The thematic parallels are close, but Scott is able to expand these motifs into a long description of Jonathan's 'den' and a whole episode concerning his misreading of an inscription (chapters 3 and 4). Similarly, where Earle briefly notes that the Antiquary discourses endlessly on his collections and dresses out of fashion, Scott elaborates on Jonathan's old-fashioned way of life and gives us samples of his long and erudite speeches.

Scott can amplify the character-writer's single sentence into a chapter if he chooses. More important, however, is the psychological diversification which the novelist can allow himself. The character-writers had been content to portray the Antiquary as ludicrous, but Jonathan Oldbuck is an interesting mixture of sense and folly, the eccentric and the worthy. His passion for everything ancient is not merely ridiculous: 'To trace the connection of nations by their usages and the similarity of the implements which they employ, has long been my favourite study' (chapter 30). Also, despite the little matter of a misread inscription, he is not unduly credulous, commenting on *Ossian*: 'Did you absolutely believe that stuff of Macpherson's to be really ancient, you simple boy?' (chapter 30). No character-writer would ever have shown his Antiquary doubting the authenticity of anything that seemed intriguingly and romantically old. It may be added that, where the 'characters' of the Antiquaries nearly always show them throwing good money away on junk, Jonathan is a shrewd bargainer (chapter 3). More seriously, he is good-hearted, determined in his efforts to right wrongs, and a loyal friend. In these matters, to return to Jebb's point, the novelist exploits the possibility of retailing 'long series of connected actions'.

Thus, although the thematic links with the 'characters' are very close, Scott expands and elaborates in three ways: he is able to give much greater detail,[33] he translates description into action, and he gives us a fascinating mixture of good and bad in exchange for the monochrome productions of the character-writers. Mr Neefit in Trollope's *Ralph the Heir* (1871) offers another, somewhat similar example, all the more interesting since the comparison is with Trollope's own depiction of the Tailor in his *London Tradesmen*. Neefit is very rich, whereas his counterpart in *London Tradesmen* shows in his features 'those lines of little but still anxious thought which come from the daily making of money in small parcels'. Although the Tailor in *London Tradesmen* has his professional pride, he is quite different from Neefit, who moves from living above his working premises to a villa in Hendon and has an almost fanatical degree of vicarious ambition on behalf of his daughter.[34] That is to say, many of the traits which make Neefit what he is could not possibly be given as characteristics of a typical member of his profession.

The implicit restrictions of the Theophrastan 'character' clash with the novelist's desire to show the *un*characteristic elements which single a man out from his fellows. Only where the novelist is content—for whatever reason—with a type, is the influence of character-writing likely to be strong. In addition, the psychological and technical limitations of the 'character' show up more clearly within the novel than anywhere else, for the two-dimensional figures thus portrayed always coexist with richer and more complex personalities in the same work. Such contrasts are not present in the character-book, where all the figures are two-dimensional, or in the periodical essay, where the 'character' is usually brought in to illustrate one specific point, or even in comedy, where nearly all the roles exemplify one ruling humour.

Novelists who resort to the devices of character-writing as an easy short cut are few; most seem to know instinctively where a 'character' would be appropriate and where more oblique methods are called for. Fielding and a few others appear to think that the oblique method is intrinsically superior, but most novelists were guided by pragmatic considerations. Trollope writes: 'As this lady's character will, it is hoped, show itself in the following pages, we need not now describe it more closely' (*Dr Thorne*, chapter 1).

The foregoing account has concentrated on the English novel. Since the situation in Germany was different, it must be discussed separately.[35]

(ii) **Germany**

In Germany, the novel was held in low repute for much of the eighteenth century and was frequently attacked in the moral weeklies as trivial, remote from reality, and a threat to morals.[1] The character-writers seldom failed to mention that the Idler, the Dandy, or the vain Society Belle was addicted to novel-reading. Three main types of novel were particularly popular in the first half of the eighteenth century: courtly tales of adventure (mostly still written in a stilted pseudo-Baroque style), trumpery and often vulgar picaresque novels, and feeble imitations of *Robinson Crusoe*.[2] The picaresque novels touched real life here and there, but were hardly 'improving'; the courtly novels were full of lofty sentiments, but had as little to do with life in eighteenth-century Hamburg or Leipzig as had the imitations of Defoe. When attempts began to be made, from about the middle of the century onwards, to make the novel both more 'respectable' and truer to contemporary realities, writers turned to the moral weeklies rather than seeking their models among the earlier German novels.[3] Some of the 'reforming' novelists contributed to one or more of these weeklies, played with the idea of editing one, or published 'moral characters'.[4] In addition to such manifest links, one can safely say that no educated person in eighteenth-century Germany was unacquainted with at least some of the moral weeklies (excluding the remoter parts of Catholic Southern Germany, not notable for the production of novels in this period anyway).

To read German novels published between about 1750 and 1790 is to become aware of a general affinity between the novelists and the essayists which goes far beyond anything to be observed in England, for all the veneration in which the *Spectator* was held there. The novels and the moral weeklies uphold the same complex of moral, philosophical, and social values; they show the same insistence on a respectable and solid middle-class (often mercantile) way of life, on sociable, moderate, tolerant, and philanthropic values, on a broadly optimistic view of the world and an undogmatic religious faith.

If we turn from this general affinity to the specific matter of characterization, we find, not surprisingly, close links. The character-writers offered sketches of exactly those types with which the 'reformed' novel was to occupy itself, often describing them with fair precision in terms of appearance, speech, and behaviour. As in England, the fact that many of these 'characters' edged towards the short story—or at least the protracted anecdote—must have helped to attract the novelists.[5] It may be added that, even if a serious novelist of the 1750s or 1760s had been inclined to turn to the popular novels of earlier decades, he would have found few useful hints regarding characterization. The authors of the picaresque novels and desert-island stories were unconcerned with subtleties of personality; it was what happened to the hero that was important. The courtly novels of adventure usually began with a set description of the hero and/or heroine, but in absurdly glowing terms and in what by now must have seemed almost a parody of a defunct Baroque style:

> From her sixteenth year she was venerated by many admirers and the court and the whole town spoke of no one else, for she was prized as a true paragon of perfect beauty. . . . Her hair was of a chestnut colour and long enough to cover her feet. Her eyes were large and of a heavenly blue. . . . Her fair cheeks were the most perfect mixture of milk and blood. Her little mouth put the most regal purple to shame and her regular teeth seemed to rival the finest *Oriental* pearls. . . . Her skill and art made her natural beauty

yet more admirable. She spoke French so pleasingly and with such purity as if she had been born in Paris. . . . She played the lute with such perfection that the hearers were enchanted. . . . Her intelligence far exceeded her years . . .[6]

The best starting-point for our investigation is J. M. von Loen's novel *Der redliche Mann am Hof* (1760), for no other single work of fiction stands so obviously at the watershed between old and new. The 'honest man', Count Rivera, is summoned to court by the King of Aquitania and reluctantly leaves his peaceful life in the country. The novel traces his faithful service to the king and his influence in raising the court out of its previous disorder and corruption. Rivera loves the Countess Monteras, but sees a rival suitor in the king and so feels in duty bound to step back. However, the king finally marries the princess of a neighbouring kingdom, leaving Rivera free to marry his countess. The work is complicated by numerous intrigues, adventures, sub-plots, and interpolated exemplary 'biographies'.

In his Preface (*Vorbericht*), Loen gives pocket-sized descriptions of the main protagonists, exactly as English comedy writers had done in their lists of *dramatis personae*. These are supplemented in the novel proper by longer introductory 'characters', and only then do we see the figures in action. The treatment of Rivera exactly illustrates this rather naïve approach:

Count Rivera shows a young man of high birth how he must restrain himself and limit his desires as his fortunes rise. He can perhaps serve as an example of innocence and honesty in a corrupt world. People do not believe any more that virtue . . . has its place at court. . . . The behaviour of Count Rivera nevertheless shows us that virtue is at home everywhere. (*Vorbericht*)

The courtly novel—which had usually credited the high-born heroes and heroines with spotless virtue as a matter of course—has been invaded by the values of the moral weeklies, which locate their ideal of virtue in bourgeois urban life or on the model country estate. Loen feels it necessary to argue that virtue is indeed possible at court.

The second stage in Rivera's characterization is a longer description in the opening chapter of the novel. The sycophantic tone in which the heroes of the older courtly novels had been depicted is combined with the somewhat homely ethics of the moral weeklies.

Substitute 'business' or 'estate management' for 'state affairs', and the passage could take its place in an issue of *Der Patriot*. (Loen had already published the *Moralische Schildereyen*, in which the links with periodical character-writing are perfectly clear.) Here is part of Rivera's 'character':

Nature had given him all the great qualities which make a man excel. He was well-formed, of something more than average height and altogether handsome. His eyes shone with as much grace as earnestness. Whoever saw him was moved by him; no one could be indifferent to him. One had to share his pleasure when he was content and feel unease when one saw him suffer. . . . He was thoroughly learned, not only in state affairs, but also in practical philosophy and the arts. His intelligence was receptive to all things and he possessed as much wit as insight and reflection. At the same time, he had the best of hearts and his impulses were that much purer and more virtuous in that they were governed by a hidden fear of God.

Hereafter, Rivera's conduct can cause us no surprises. It seems clear that, for the author of the *Moralische Schildereyen*, characterization is based on the notion of a 'moral character' from which all actions logically proceed. Rivera will be set in motion, his qualities will be put to the test by circumstances—but Loen has nothing up his sleeve.

Der redliche Mann am Hof is a half-way house between the old-style courtly novel, which it resembles in plot and structure, and the moral weeklies, whose values it clearly espouses. As the German novel broke free of its exotic and adventurous past, the influence of periodical character-writing on techniques of characterization became, if possible, more marked. Even major figures in the novel might be introduced through set 'characters' if they were comparatively straightforward personalities.[7] However, as in England, such set-pieces were much more widely used as a means of introducing minor figures. The practice was common enough to become the object of mockery, as when G. C. E. Westphal introduces his character-book with a tongue-in-cheek apology for his old-fashioned manner of presentation:

I am not modern; I have presented these sketches neither in the form of a journey nor a novel. It would not perhaps have cost me much sweat to do so. I would have had my Spectator depart from Berlin, or Stettin or wherever; two miles from town, he would perhaps have had the misfortune to break a wheel, which would have forced him to spend the night with the vicar of XXX—and who will fail to see a splendid opportunity for characterization here? And so it would go on and everywhere—on the sofa, at the border, in the castle—I could have written a little chapter on manners and morals . . .[8]

Here is a representative selection of novels which feature interpolated 'characters':

W. E. Neugebauer,	*Der teutsche Don Quixhotte* (1753)	Court Poet (iii. 2)
Anon.,	*Der Leipziger Avanturieur* (1756)	dandified Student (i. 240)
Friedrich Nicolai,	*Das Leben und die Meinungen des Herrn Sebaldus Nothanker* (1773-6)	time-serving Clergyman (vi. 2) Antiquarian (vi. 1) mercenary Printer (vii. 7)
C. M. Wieland,	*Die Geschichte der Abderiten* (1774–81)	see below
	Bonifaz Schleichers Jugendgeschichte (1776)	stern and pedantic Tutor (*Vermischte Schriften*, 1838–40, xxvii. 168 f.)
Müller von Itzehoe,	*Siegfried von Lindenburg* (1779)	poetic Dilettante (ii. 215) female Miser (iv. 175 f.)
C. F. Bretzner,	*Das Leben eines Lüderlichen* (1787–8)	Clergyman turned Tutor (i. 35–7)
F. C. Laukhard,	*Franz Wolfstein* (1799)	various types of Schoolmaster (i. 57 ff.)

Wieland's *Geschichte der Abderiten* is worth singling out as an amusing example. The setting is Abdera in Thrace, where the citizens, according to tradition, were ignorant, stupid, and prejudiced. Wieland exploits this legend in order to make a thinly veiled attack on eighteenth-century German attitudes, together with the institutional absurdities of provincial life. The folly of the 'Abderites' is set off against the wisdom of the philosopher and man of science, Democritus (or, the man of the Enlightenment). The rather loose satirical form gives Wieland an excuse for all manner of thumbnail sketches, some of which closely resemble little 'characters'.[9] For all the zest and elegance, the method is essentially that derided by Westphal. The historical setting, which gives unmistakably German figures classical names, heightens rather than obscures the links with contemporary character-writing, since the authors of the moral weeklies also give many of their 'characters' antique-sounding titles. The satirical twist-that the reader has to 'translate' certain details from the Greek—has its parallel in La Bruyère. In Wieland, Agathyrsus, the worldly and sceptical cleric, makes fun of the sacred frogs of the goddess Latona (i.e. miracles or sacred relics), while La Bruyère's Hypochondriac visits Aesculapius at Epidaurus (i.e. any fashionable Parisian doctor).[10]

The foregoing examples have shown a link between the comic novel and satirical character-writing. For more serious instances, one might turn to Christiane Sophie Ludwig's *Erzählungen von guten, und für gute Seelen* (1799–1800). Despite the late date, the work is in all respects closely in harmony with the moral weeklies. The first story in the collection, 'Lage von Austädt', concerns the moral education of two girls. The educator, Frau Weinard, is first described in terms that exactly resemble the 'characters' of the ideal Wife or Mother in the weeklies:

> To her husband, Frau Weinard was the most faithful and noble companion on life's journey; she caused him such sweet joy that earthly life became heaven for him. Her morals were pure, her heart noble and she understood the great art of gaining the love of every good soul. She was feared by the vicious but prized by those who resembled her in virtue. She had no enemies; only Envy occasionally rose up against her. And even Envy had to concede unwillingly that she was a model woman. To her children she did not only bring the simple mother-love which is the common gift of nature, but—what is more—she was their educator and understood how to guide each movement of their souls towards a noble goal, so that they found pleasure in goodness . . . (i. 3 f.)

She takes her *protégées* into the countryside and talks sententiously of nature, God, virtue, and the blessings of doing one's duty. Even the structure of this story resembles—or is an expansion of—those periodical essays in which the 'character' of an ideal type is followed by a set of 'maxims' (see above, p. 144). Another story in the collection, 'Das eitle Mädchen', tells of Julie, a proud beauty, who is gradually cured of her vanity as she comes to realize that physical charms fade and only inner worth is indestructible. Again, the authoress presents her heroine to the reader in the form of a 'character' (i. 43 f.). For a similar 'character' of a girl made vain through flattery, one could cite the account of Wandala, in the

Discourse der Mahlern (i. 9). Ludwig, within the more generous dimensions of a long short story, can go on to show how vanity is gradually conquered, but there is nevertheless a close resemblance between her somewhat nagging description of Julie and character-writing in the weeklies.[11]

As in England, the novelist often expands his introductory character-sketches beyond what strict economy and relevance require. Müller von Itzehoe, in his comic novel *Siegfried von Lindenburg*, gives us the 'character' of the heroine's first husband. Yet he not only has no part to play in the novel, but is already dead when we first hear of him. The most that could possibly be said is that his rascally nature serves as foil to the hero's transparent honesty:

> . . . a scoundrel who had no sense of her worth, an animal phlegmatic to the point of laziness and unfeelingness, a creature without a soul—unless the most rustic unmannerliness constituted his soul—, a monster who devoted his mornings to brandy, his afternoons to wine, his evenings to gambling and who passed his nights in houses of ill-repute—and consequently spent his whole life in the most worthless idleness. (ii. 326 in the 1784 edition)

The presence of 'characters' in the moral weeklies must surely have encouraged this sort of writing. Having mentioned a type, the novelist feels that he might as well spend a paragraph describing him; having touched on the notion of lazy boorishness, Müller follows this up with the account of a typical day's activities—the form taken by scores of 'characters'. Similarly, in A. F. F. von Knigge's *Die Reise nach Braunschweig* (1792), we find a long account of Schottenius, an enlightened clergyman (*ein aufgeklärter Geistlicher*—chapter 1). The novel tells the adventures of a group of friends who have decided to travel to Brunswick to see a balloon ascent, but although the opening chapter introduces us to the whole company, Knigge gives us a 'character' of Schottenius only. Why? It cannot be because he is more important than his companions as far as the action of the novel is concerned, for he has no effect upon it. It seems that Knigge simply wanted to present the 'character' of a particular type of clergyman not uncommon in eighteenth-century Germany: the man who managed to combine his beliefs with a degree of 'enlightenment', who rejected much of the dogma of Christianity without prejudice to its ethical content, who tried to proclaim what Lessing called 'the religion of Jesus Christ' (*die*

Religion Christi) and, at the same time, champion reason and keep abreast of intellectual and scientific developments. This may seem a serious tone in which to discuss a figure in a comic novel, but it is justified, for Schottenius is treated with a greater degree of respect that are his companions, who are constantly made to look ridiculous. In a novel where people are locked in privies, mistake other men's beds for their own, fall into moats, and generally behave idiotically, he has only the gentlest and kindliest sort of fun poked at him. His pride in his fifty-seven sermons, and the fact that he loses one of them in mildly ludicrous circumstances, is the sum of it.

No doubt because many German novelists of the eighteenth century were decidedly minor talents, while other and better writers, such as Gellert, Loen, and Nicolai, cultivated the novel only as a sideline, one often—certainly more often than in England—gains the impression that the inset 'character' was used as a ready-made route to characterization. It should not be forgotten that the novel had only gradually and with difficulty adapted itself to the task of depicting real people in the real world (witness Loen). The moral weeklies were far ahead in this field, so that it is not surprising that the novelists turned to them. We may take Joseph Richter's *Herr Kaspar* (1787) as a simple, even crude example. Here the author employs set introductory 'characters' quite openly, proclaiming, for instance: 'My readers will be introduced to [a type of] merchant who will continue to exist as long as there are merchants' (summary of contents to chapter 28). When we turn to the chapter in question, it is clear enough where Richter had learnt his trade; what we have is a 'character' in all but name: 'He was nothing but a merchant. . . . He had never experienced the joys of youth. . . . His only pleasures were carrying out business deals and counting his money . . . He did everything by the clock . . .' (pp. 181 f.)

The use of the 'character' as a short cut is, naturally enough, marked in strongly episodic novels, where figures appear only fleetingly. F. X. Huber's *Herr Schlendrian* (1787) is a parody on the law, couched in just such an episodic form. It is set in an unnamed land, where—the age of reason having dawned—the old lawbooks are thrown out and a new, less obscure legal system is introduced. Herr Schlendrian is the judge in the town of Tropos and the book concerns his administration of the new laws. The 'novel' thus consists of a long succession of cases and trials. What could be easier than to introduce new figures as they appear by means of short 'characters'? The techniques of description were ready to hand in the moral weeklies and little thought or effort was needed. Here is Herr Liebreich—or, should we say, 'the Generous Man'?

> This young man, of about twenty-five years of age, was known in the whole region as a very good-natured, friendly and philanthropic man. His neighbours loved him because of his peaceable and tolerant character; the poor blessed him for his lavish deeds of charity. . . . Herr Liebreich, kindly as he was towards those in real need and helpful to the very limit of his powers when he saw virtue suffering, was severe towards the dissolute . . . (chapter 3)

We have seen that figures thus characterized in advance seldom do much beyond confirming what has been said of them. The only important difference between England and Germany in this respect is that German novelists seem to feel a need to justify themselves theoretically. Merck, after giving a long 'character' of the hero as prologue to one of his stories, exculpates himself: 'Why should I not be permitted to give an exposition of the character, around whom all the events revolve, or whose individuality gave to a great part of those events the particular turn which justifies one in calling them remarkable?' In more jocose vein, C. F. Sintenis, in exact contrast to Fielding, excuses himself on the grounds that few readers want to take the trouble of abstracting character from events: 'Nor is it necessary to withhold these characters from the reader for a long time or even give him the trouble of extracting the characters out of the book for himself as he reads.' Those readers who do not want to know everything in advance are advised to skip the prefatory chapter.[12]

But, as in England, 'characters' within the novel can go beyond simple advance labelling. In the anonymous *Faust der zweyte* (1782–3), we find the 'character' of a Whore (*Charakter einer Buhlerin*), given with the specific function of showing that Louise, with whom the hero is infatuated, belongs to this category of beings. The inset 'character' thus fulfils the same function as similar set-pieces in Webster's *White Devil* or Farquhar's *Sir Harry Wildair*; it tests the individual against a generic definition:

> A Whore is the most contemptible creature in nature. . . . No person works against the common purpose as she does. Everyone should contribute to the perfection of the whole, but she tries to despoil all who cross her path; she

attracts them, ruins them and leaves gnawing remorse behind in many hearts and embitters whole lives . . .

The sententious and somewhat abstract tone, together with the reference to the welfare of society, links this passage very clearly to the 'moral characters' which were written in Germany between the 1720s and the 1780s.[13]

In the above instance, the 'character' is presented to the reader directly by the novelist; in one of J. J. Engel's novels, *Herr Lorenz Stark* (1795–6), it is a figure in the novel who employs 'characters' for his own didactic purposes. Stark, a rich merchant, has a son whom he regards as a wastrel and whose association with a widow, Frau Lyk, he deplores, since he views her as extravagant and frivolous. At the end of the novel, however, the tension between father and son is eased, as old Stark comes to realize that his son is not (or is no longer) what he had feared and that Frau Lyk's reputation had suffered unjustly as a result of the character and behaviour of her late husband. The form in which Stark airs his prejudices is through 'characters'. At one point, the old man taxes his son with a picture of the Merchant as he should be, and follows this with his image of the young man as a spendthrift:

[Your friend Eberhard] is an orderly, industrious, well-behaved man, as if born to be a merchant. Full of enterprise, but never lacking in deliberation; so respectable and simple in his appearance, no friend of satin or embroidered trimmings and—what particularly endears him to me—not a gambler. . . . If he plays, it's not at cards, but with his children . . . (chapter 2)

Every day I feel more annoyed at having [a son who] squanders one ducat after another—sometimes a dozen at a time—on his finery, his pleasures, at l'hombre and whist; who only yesterday played far into the night and who, if he had to do a generous deed, would probably not have a single coin at his command. A man who remains unmarried because he cannot find anyone rich enough; yet he always has money to squander on travelling by coach, riding, playing the cavalier and dressing up in satin and embroidered stuffs. (ibid.)

The effect is exactly like that of a pair of contrasting 'characters' from a paper on the virtues of the merchant's life and the dangers of abandoning it for a fashionable and extravagant existence. Later, we find old Stark at his character-drawing again, treating Frau Lyk—towards whom he is still hostile—to a picture of the ideal *Hausfrau* (chapter 21). One could easily imagine the speaker, with his robust praise of everything traditional and truly 'German', as the editor of, say, the Hamburg *Patriot* or *Der alte Deutsche*. (He is, indeed, once described as *altdeutsch*: p. 321).

The use of the 'character' in this novel seems to me subtle and ironic. Old Stark's conservatism is not presented to us by the author as misguided (on the contrary, Engel will have expected most of his readers to share the attitude); Stark is wrong because his strictures are misdirected. The 'characters' both celebrate the shared values of the author and his readers and ironically reveal Stark's short-sightedness.

In the above two instances, the 'character' is being exploited for its combination of the individual and the generic. The author of *Faust der zweyte* is saying, in effect: this is the picture of any Whore; let us see whether Louise fits the definition. Engel allows Stark to hold up his ideals of mercantilism and womanhood in the belief that his son and his prospective daughter-in-law need badgering or shaming into conformity.[14]

By far the most enterprising use of the 'character' within the novel occurs in an early work by Jean Paul Friedrich Richter. He admired La Bruyère, claimed to have learnt English mainly in order to read 'the excellent *Spectator*', and was acquainted with at least one of the collections of 'moral characters' which abounded at the time. He knew the German satirists, including Rabener, well, and—being an omnivorous reader—will undoubtedly have read more than one of the moral weeklies. There are, in fact, one or two 'characters', written in a contorted witty style, in his earliest collection of satires, *Grönländische Prozesse* (1783).[15]

In his first novel, *Die unsichtbare Loge* (1792), Jean Paul makes the 'character' serve a definite structural function. It has long been a commonplace of criticism that the action of this strange, unfinished work has little to do with its true themes. On the one hand, it is full of the conventional trappings of the silliest popular fiction of the day: masks and disguises, hidden identities, stolen children, a castle filled with eerie symbols of mortality in the best Gothic style, a quasi-Masonic secret society, and so on. However, the essential inner theme of the work is concerned with the opposition of transcendental to earthly values. The main characters are divided into two camps, those who despise the world and those, in court and counting-house, who are enslaved to it. To give some sort of transparency to an otherwise obscure texture, Jean Paul has expressed this contrast through two sustained 'characters'. The first carries the heading 'Of Noble Beings' (*Von hohen Menschen*) and describes a wholly unworldly ideal of virtue:

> By a 'noble man' I do not mean the straightforward, honest, steadfast man . . . nor do I mean the delicate and fastidious soul . . . nor the man of honour whose word is a rock . . . nor, finally, the coldly virtuous man who is guided by principle or the man of sentiment . . . nor even the merely *great* man of genius. . . . I mean the sort of man who, in addition to possessing all these qualities to a greater or lesser degree, has something else which is very rare on earth: the elevation above earthly things, an awareness of the triviality of all earthly activity and the disparity between our hearts and our location, a glance which ranges above the confusing tangled growths and the nauseating enticements of the ground which we tread, a wish for death and an eye that reaches above the clouds . . .[16]

The opposing camp is represented by the courtiers and the mercenary bourgeoisie, and the second of Jean Paul's 'characters' is a picture of the miserly, unscrupulous, and grasping merchant Röper, with the heading 'the imperfect character' (*der unvollkommene Charakter*). Each of these passages interrupts, and stands out from, the action and, by its title, suggests a generic slot into which specific persons are to be fitted. In the case of the *hohe Menschen*, Jean Paul is explicit, obviously feeling that individual differences between the various figures concerned might obscure their fundamental similarity: 'There are certain people whom I call noble or feast-day beings and, in my story, they are represented by Ottomar, Gustav, the Genius [the hero's educator], the Doctor and no one else.' The second 'character' draws our attention to a money-grubbing attitude which threatens, or at least contrasts radically with, the values of the *hohe Menschen*. (The courtiers are left to expose their own failings.) The two passages thus take up the traditional notion of a contrasting pair of 'characters' (the ideal, and a deviation from it) and develop this to suit the purposes of the novel. The *petit genre* serves to hold together a large-scale work and hints at a conceptual unity which might not otherwise have been apparent in a maze of fantastic and mysterious happenings. The dichotomy of noble and squalid is heightened by a stylistic contrast; whereas the *hohe Menschen* are discussed, as we have seen, in ecstatic and rather abstract terms, Röper is described satirically, with lavish use of concrete details and brilliantly grotesque imagery. Here, of course, Jean Paul's stylistic virtuosity allows him a dimension denied to most of his predecessors in the field of German character-writing:

> The Imperfect Character alloyed his thrift with a measure of deceit. He misrepresented goods which he received in perfect condition and wrote that they were faulty . . . and that he could only accept them at half price. And so, skilfully and at long range, he picked the merchant's pocket of a third of the price. Wares, barrels, and sacks, which were only making a brief stay in his house before travelling further, yielded him a transit-fee through a little hole which he made in them, in order to take out a small quantity, the lack of which, if noticed, could be blamed on the carrier. He set up a numismatic infirmary for poor, invalid gold pieces which had suffered amputation. And to other suspect coins, he restored their honest name and forced his clerks to accept them as legitimized and rehabilitated. (p. 142)

The Decline of the 'Character' in the German Novel

The 'character', having played a larger part in German novels of the eighteenth century than in English ones, disappeared abruptly. One reason is that character-writing itself fell out of favour with the culture of the *Aufklärung* that had given rise to it. German novelists a generation or two after Jean Paul (who was born in 1763) hardly knew of the 'character', or, if they did, rejected it as a manifestation of what now seemed an obsolescent set of values and attitudes. Furthermore, the German language had developed so quickly in the course of the eighteenth century that most of the 'characters' in the moral weeklies now seemed stylistically crude. It is impossible to imagine cultivated Germans in the early years of the nineteenth century reading *Der Patriot* or *Der Biedermann* as their English contemporaries still read and admired the *Spectator*.

Another contributory factor was the development and popularity of the novella, which, from the early nineteenth century on, ceased to be regarded as no more than an entertaining short story and acquired dignity, literary recognition, and a body of aesthetic theory of its own. It was seen as a form which restricted itself necessarily to one central event or problem, aiming at strict formal unity, concentration, and psychological depth. As a consequence of its deliberate self-limitation, it often focused on one central character (the German word for this sort of story is *Charakternovelle*). What happened, to over-simplify slightly, is that the 'character' became absorbed into the *Charakternovelle*; it evolved and integrated itself to the point of self-immolation.

The process had begun well before the vogue of the novella proper. By the 1770s there were many short stories of which it is difficult to say whether they are greatly extended 'characters', generously illustrated by anecdotes, or stories which depend on and revolve around one central figure. However one chooses to define them, they represent a combination of character-portrayal and story-telling that was obviously already in competition with the 'character' pure and simple.[17] In addition, such tales were usually less didactic than the 'moral characters' of the early and mid century, more concerned with entertainment than improvement. (The nagging tone of many of the moral weeklies was undoubtedly one reason why they went out of favour.)

The most striking example of the way in which 'character' turns into *Charakternovelle* comes in one of the later works of Jean Paul, *Des Feldpredigers Schmelzle Reise nach Flätz* (1807), which, as we have seen, the author himself regarded as an expanded 'character'.[18] From the Romantic era throughout the nineteenth century, there was a steady stream of *Charakternovellen*, suggesting that this medium-length narrative form had taken over from the 'character' as a means of portraying human types. Only in Vienna, in the collections of 'Viennese Sketches', did anything resembling the 'character' persist. More or less concurrently with this shift away from the set character-sketch towards the revelation of character through narrative came a marked reaction against typology in favour of the individualistic and the eccentric.

The 'moral characters' of the weeklies had depended on an agreed norm, an accepted notion of what was a proper way of life; if you were not broadly in sympathy with the reasonable, moderate, bourgeois-mercantile culture out of which, say, the Hamburg *Patriot* had emerged, you would not admire the ideal 'characters' or scorn the satirical ones. But from the 1770s on, increasing numbers of German writers embraced individualistic and subjective attitudes which placed them outside the consensus—as rebels, as men of feeling who found conventional modes of existence stifling, as artists who wanted to make their own rules. There is a whole cluster of novels which, by exploring the minutest details of what is regarded as a unique psychological constitution, are in absolute opposition to the typological assumptions underlying character-writing. Goethe's *Leiden des jungen Werthers* (1774) is the most famous: others are F. H. Jacobi's *Eduard Allwills Papiere* (1776),

F. T. Hase's *Auszug aus Eduard Blondheims geheimem Tagebuch* (1777), and K. P. Moritz's *Anton Reiser* (1785–90).

At approximately the same time as these and similar novels attempted to probe the uniqueness of a human personality, many humorous and satirical writers were showing an increasing preference for the grotesque in human nature. It is probably true to say that there is a traditional penchant for the grotesque among the Germans—shown in their visual arts as well as in their literature—and that this had merely been temporarily checked and pushed into the background by the moderate and normative views of the Enlightenment. If we turn to one of the minor figures in Bretzner's *Leben eines Lüderlichen*, we find an interesting move from typicality back towards eccentricity. Bretzner's account of Dr Bartolus, who kills more patients than he cures and impresses the naïve through his jargon and his collection of anatomical specimens, sounds at the outset like no more than the 'character' of a Charlatan (*ein elender Charlatan und Empirikus*)—but Bretzner goes on to inform us that Bartolus finds a profitable sideline in passing off human remains to the pious as sacred relics. The 'character' in the technical, Theophrastan sense is quite destroyed by this bizarre addition which could not, by any stretch of the imagination, be offered as a trait of the typical Quack.[19]

To return to Jean Paul's comic novels, it is clear that Schmelzle's successors have moved much further away from the 'character' in the direction of the out-and-out eccentric. The eponymous hero of *Dr Katzenbergers Badereise* (1807) is a doctor for whom scientific objectivity is everything, and who constantly rejects all sentiment, romanticism, and aesthetic values. Defined thus, his obsession might seem to belong to that order of ruling qualities which have always attracted character-writers and, in fact, many details of his behaviour could fit into the 'character' of a certain kind of obsessed Physician: he spoils his companions' appetite through his 'disgusting' conversation and scorn of polite social taboos, he prefers comedy to tragedy because laughter is healthy, he collects monsters and abortions out of scientific curiosity, and so on. However, Jean Paul takes the characterization of Katzenberger to extremes of exaggeration and intensification quite different from those which operate in a 'character', where each detail—however exaggerated or even grotesque—must nevertheless reinforce our impression that the person represented could stand for a category of human beings.

A comparison of Katzenberger with two eighteenth-century 'characters' (of a Misogynist and a Pedant) will make the difference clear. The Misogynist insists on having his meals brought out to the coach if he suspects that there are women at the inn; the Pedant divides up his day into exactly calculated periods of study, one for metaphysics, one for the natural sciences, and so forth. These two figures we accept as types, even if seen through the distorting mirror of satire, but it is difficult to regard Katzenberger as anything other than a monster himself when his love of monsters leads him to confess to his daughter:

> I will not conceal the fact from you, Theoda—since it happened out of a pure love of science—that I did not take too many pains during your dear mother's pregnancy to spare her the sight of dancing-bears, apes, horrible apparitions and the treasures of my collection [of monsters and abortions], since the worst that could have happened would be that she could have enriched my collection with a monstrous birth. But unfortunately (I almost said), but praise be to God, she presented me with you . . .[20]

The movement away from the typical towards the grotesque goes, if possible, even further in the Romantic period in Germany, notably in the works of E. T. A. Hoffmann, some of whose figures border on the insane. Still later, Paul Heyse comments that the novella is well suited to deal with cases of extreme individualism or quirkishness,[21] and in fact such writers as Stifter, Keller, Storm, Raabe, and Heyse himself—although never going as far as those wayward masters, Jean Paul and Hoffmann—show a liking for the eccentric. The heroes of their *Novellen* certainly differ markedly from the recognizably typical figures created by the character-writers of the eighteenth century.

The direct presentation of character through set description was, in any case, going out of fashion by the mid nineteenth century, regardless of whether 'types' or 'individuals' were being dealt with. The writers of the novella show a strong preference for indirect characterization, letting the reader deduce personality through observable details. The implicit reasoning is presumably that this manner of presentation is truer to life and technically more subtle; the desire to raise the status of the novella and show it to be capable of the highest technical and formal refinements is no doubt a factor here. Theoretical support for indirect characterization was to come, later, from Friedrich Spielhagen.[22]

The main reasons why the 'character' disappeared so abruptly from the German literary scene in general and from the novel in particular[23] have seemed worth pursuing in a little detail. They are complex and have no exact parallels in England. To begin with, the English 'character' was never exclusively associated with, or dependent on, any single period or literary trend and was thus not as vulnerable as the German 'character' of the eighteenth century, which proved unable to survive the abandonment of *Aufklärung* habits of thought and literary fashions. Nor is there any parallel in England to the rise of the *Charakternovelle* and its assimilation and modification of material that had previously been treated in character-form. Nor were English novelists—less given to theorizing about their craft than their German *confrères*—much inclined to look down on direct characterization as such. In Germany, we find an almost total lack of character-writing from about 1800 on, accompanied by a conviction that oblique methods of characterization in narrative fiction were somehow 'better' than direct ones; in England, on the contrary, there was a lively and unbroken tradition of character-writing, together with a comparatively unreflective and pragmatic approach which at least did not close the door on the set character-sketch if the subject and the circumstances seemed right.

11
Conclusion

There are three 'characters of a character': the first in the 1616 edition of the Overbury collection, one by Flecknoe (1658), and one by Samuel Person (1664). In addition, Ralph Johnson in 1665 gave rules for the composition of 'characters' and Henry Gally prefaced his translation of Theophrastus in 1725 with an 'Essay on Characteristick-Writings', the longest and most reflective of these five attempts at definition.[1] Let us try to take the sum of them.

According to Gally, each 'character' deals with one dominant humour or 'Master-Passion' and must be selective. As a consequence, it paints in black and white: 'it or extols to *Heaven*, or depresses unto *Hell*; having no mid' place for Purgatory left' (Flecknoe). Gally adds a warning: 'Nature must not be distorted, to excite either Ridicule or Admiration' (p. 73). Only Samuel Person makes the explicit point that the 'character' combines the individual and the generic, and he does so in a rather mannered figure of speech: the 'character' has not only the '*Signatura rerum* but also *Personarum* stamped upon it'. However the combination is implicit in Ralph Johnson's use of phrases like 'sort of people . . . sort of men' and was probably regarded as self-evident by Flecknoe and the contributor to 'Overbury'. Gally is the only writer to make the important point that each feature mentioned must proceed from the essential unity of the personality described and help to express it (p. 30). Flecknoe and Person see the 'character' as combining entertainment and instruction; Person, in one of his most striking phrases, talks of a 'stigmatizing Iron to those that are bad'. The Overbury definition omits this point as, more surprisingly, does Gally. But he doubtless takes it as read; after all, he entitles his translation *The Moral Characters of Theophrastus* and concludes his essay with praise of the 'characters' in the *Tatler* and the *Spectator*, pieces which certainly set out both to amuse and to instruct.

Strict formal criteria are lacking in these definitions and are probably impossible to lay down for such a flexible genre. It is generally agreed that terseness is necessary:

. . . an imprese, or short embleme; in little comprehending much. (Overbury)

. . . all *matter*, and to the *matter*, and has nothing of *superfluity*. (Flecknoe)

. . . a great deal in a little room. (Person)

Much must be contain'd in a little Compass. (Gally, p. 43)

'Overbury' and Ralph Johnson insist on a witty style of writing, but Gally, from the more 'polished' vantage-point of 1725, sees undisciplined wit as a danger.

Gally, alone among the theorists of the 'character', would accept the presence of subsidiary qualities, provided that these do not obscure the ruling humour (p. 34). The redeeming feature mentioned at the end of Addison's Sombrius would be an instance of this, as also, in a different way, those sorrowful eighteenth-century 'characters' of the Drunkard which combine a description of his beastly conduct with a lament over wasted potential. However character-writers usually seem to have felt instinctively that too complex a mixture would destroy the genre. If La Bruyère had suddenly interrupted his catalogue of Menalcas's feats of absent-mindedness to tell us how that notable scatterbrain nevertheless had a freakish ability to remember dates, the 'character' would have been undermined.

Thus the only serious disagreement concerns style and reflects a change of taste between the seventeenth and eighteenth centuries. For the rest, a number of obvious and essential points are made in these definitions, although they are by no means exhaustive. I propose to expand on some of the points and add a few of my own.

Coleridge, discussing characterization in general, has this to say:

The ideal consists in the happy balance of the generic and the individual. The former makes the character representative and symbolical, therefore instructive. . . . The latter gives it living interest; for nothing lives or is real, but as definite and individual. (*Biographia Literaria*, chapter 23)

The point deserves closer attention, for it is at the very heart of the 'character'. The novelist may introduce us to Mr Pickwick, Emma Woodhouse, or Werther quite non-committally, leaving us to decide whether and in what ways his or her figures are typical of sections of humanity. But as soon as the character-writer embarks on his sketch of the Miser or a Proud Man, he is implicitly laying claim to some sort of 'balance of the generic and the individual', although, as we shall see, this may take a variety of forms which can hardly have been in Coleridge's mind when he wrote the passage.

The dual nature of the 'character' seems in some degree to have influenced its composition, if we may believe Thackeray: 'As Phidias took the pick of a score of beauties before he completed a Venus, so have we to examine, perhaps, a thousand Snobs, before one is expressed upon paper' (*The Book of Snobs*, chapter 8). That is, no doubt, in part a satirical reference to the monstrous army of snobs in English social life, but it also shows how Coleridge's point applies to the actual business of character-writing. In more serious vein, La Bruyère claimed to have copied from nature, not by portraying this or that individual, but by constructing human mosaics: 'I took one trait from here and another from there, and out of these various traits . . . I have made convincing portraits.' Similarly, Gottsched maintains that he went around noting details of the appearance and behaviour of numerous people before writing his 'character' of a *galant homme*.[2]

Such statements go hand in hand with the frequent assertion that no individual portraits are intended and that any search for keys would be misguided. The most amusing expression of this idea occurs in the Preface to *The Guardian's Instruction* (1688), where the author, Stephen Penton, describes the 'character' in terms of Platonic Ideas: 'no single Person alive is aimed at . . . in the angry [i.e. hostile] Characters. . . . I set up one of Plato's Idea's, and sometimes shoot Bitter Words, but this hurts none; there is no Bloud drawn from Universals.' But the dividing-line between the portrait of a 'single Person' and the generalized 'character' is not as easy to draw as that confident passage suggests. We have seen how the 'character' and the portrait virtually merge in seventeenth-century France; nor is it always easy to make sharp distinctions in England and Germany.[3] With all deference to Penton, I do not believe it possible that a writer can sit down to invent a typical Coward, Lawyer, or Bluestocking without in some way drawing on living specimens. Provided that it is not merely cobbled together from conventional topoi, a 'character' may combine features from a number of actual individuals (as La Bruyère, Gottsched, and Thackeray claim), or the character-writer may encounter an individual, see him as in some way typical, and portray him so that his typicality becomes apparent. In this no man's land between two closely related *petits genres*, it is the effect of the final product, rather than the process of composition (in most cases undiscoverable) that is paramount.

Where the impression given is overwhelmingly that of a type, one can say that the piece is a 'character', even if the author had a single living model in his mind when he started out; the potential portrait has been made to serve its turn as illustration of the generic. It is agreed that Steele's Good Judge (*Tatler*, No. 14) is based on Sir John Holt, Lord Chief Justice under William III. However, the qualities stressed by Steele are all general ones which would be shared by all good magistrates: hatred of vice, legal erudition, impartiality, the ability to see through hypocrisy, and so on. That is to say, the method and effect are those of character-writing, not of portraiture. The character-writer, broadly speaking, chooses traits which would be shared by all members of his chosen category; the portraitist, if objective, will put in what he sees, regardless of whether it reveals truths about human nature in general or the quirks of an individual. The contrast is well illustrated on the one hand by Chesterfield's portrait of Alexander Pope, full of 'the contrarieties and inconsistencies of human nature',[4] and, on the other, by Steele's thoroughly generalized Good Judge. Another example of a portrait which has edged so far in the direction of typology that it virtually becomes a 'character' is Richard Savage's poem 'The Gentleman', dating from about 1726:

A decent mien, an elegance of dress,
Words which, at ease, each winning grace express;
A life where love, by wisdom polish'd, shines,
Where wisdom's self again by love refines;
Where we to chance for friendship never trust,
Nor ever dread from sudden whim disgust;
The social manners and the heart humane,
A nature ever great, and never vain . . .

Although the poem is addressed to John Joliffe, there is nothing in it to suggest anything more than a friendly dedication until the very last line: 'These graces all are thine, and thou art he'.[5]

The situation is quite different with Steele's portrait of Sir Christopher Wren as 'Nestor' (*Tatler*, No. 52), which certainly illustrates the subject of the paper (modesty) but is in no way the 'character' of a typical Modest Man, rather the portrait of a very remarkable man who also happened to be self-effacing. The traits and incidents cited would easily be decoded by any reader: 'Soon after . . . Athens was . . . burned to the ground. This gave Nestor the greatest occasion that ever builder had to render his name immortal . . . for all the new city rose according to his disposition.'[6]

Just as the validity of the 'character' can be threatened from one quarter if it is too obviously based on a known person, so too it can lose its typicality if pushed to psychological or behavioural extremes. You can have the 'character' of a Pious Man or a Reverend Divine, but hardly that of a saintly Mystic; there are many 'characters' of Puritans, but none of raging Ascetics. For the same reason Vauvenargues' 'characters' of unbridled iniquity are much less successful than the various sketches of Libertines, Slanderers, and so forth who represent possible degrees of wickedness. The 'character' may 'extol to Heaven or depress unto Hell', but Gally's warning against unnatural distortion remains valid. Undue quirkishness may endanger the wider validity of a 'character' too. Leigh Hunt makes the point explicitly: 'We speak of the Waiter properly and generally so called,—the representative of the whole, real, official race,— and not of the humorist or other eccentric genius occasionally to be found in it.' Selection and exaggeration are inseparable from character-writing, but should always be directed towards the creation of a type. The author of *The Laughing Philosopher* (1777) concludes his 'character' of a Male Coquette: 'Such is *Beau Bell*; yet though he is singular in the lengths to which he has carried this character, yet he is by no means so in the adoption of it' (No. 16). The category is not an uncommon one, but Beau Bell shows its characteristics raised to the *n*th degree. Some eighteenth-century readers objected to La Bruyère's Menalcas on the score of implausibility, but we today would probably accept this type of exaggeration as a fanciful demonstration of what happens when a quality, present to some degree in all of us, dominates and runs riot. Canetti, in my opinion, shows the boundary beyond which it is impossible to proceed without annihilating the 'character'.

Boyce (*The Polemic Character*, p. 46) talks of the 'portrait-character', meaning that an actual person might be made to stand for a class or party, or that a 'character' might be given recognizable traits from a living or recently dead individual. However, it is possible to examine the total effect made by each piece, noting its form, style, and imagery as well as the type of motifs included, and see the scales tilting in one direction or the other. To take a familiar example, Pope's Chloe is wittily and convincingly individualized: she can 'mark the figures on an Indian chest' while in her lover's embrace and ponder on how much chintz exceeds mohair while others pour out their woes to her. Those are the sort of details which, for Coleridge, gives a depiction 'living interest'. At the same time, the author manages to suggest that Chloe has a generic identity and is hence part of each reader's experience: 'would you too be wise?/Then never break your heart when Chloe dies.' There is an implied 'multiplication' too in La Bruyère's casual pretence that the subject of the 'character' is a common acquaintance of author and reader. In both cases it is assumed that, even if we do not know that Chloe or that Europyle, we will know one of his or her species. Other character-writers make the same point more directly, referring to the chosen representatives of the various types with such formulas as '. . . the sort of man who . . .' or '. . . one of these false friends . . .'.

But such formulas, although they may strengthen the effect, cannot in themselves achieve it. The central criterion, if the individual subject of the 'character' is to be recognized as having generic significance, is that each detail should be capable of being applied to all representatives of the type under discussion. Each action recounted in the 'character' of a Coward should be of the very nature of cowardice; every word put into the mouth of the Bore should mark him as the quintessence of boredom. Any student of the Theophrastan 'character' will have his favourite examples; the following extract from Earle's Shark (i.e. Scrounger) is as good as any:

> He offers you a pottle of sack out of joy to see you, and in requital of his courtesy you can do no less than pay for it. . . . His borrowings are like subsidies, each man a shilling or two, as he can well dispend; which they lend him, not with a hope to be repaid, but that he will come no more. . . . He is proud of any employment, though it be but to carry commendations, which he will be sure to deliver at eleven of the clock [i.e. at dinner-time].

The characteristics may be seen through the distorting-mirror of exaggeration or they may be expressed through fantastic images or allusions, but they should all contribute to the impression that we are faced with the chosen representative of a category of humankind. Since virtually every extract quoted in the course of this study bears on and illustrates this point, it is not necessary to pursue it further. Let us instead turn to some less obvious aspects of the theme: the part played by figurative language in seventeenth-century character-writing, the ways in which the subject of a 'character' could be placed in a general moral framework or related to society as a whole, the possibilities of exploiting the form of the 'character' (or, later, the absorption of the 'character' into the essay) to point to the coexistence of individual and generic. Some of these things are common to all literary forms in which human types are portrayed; others are peculiar to the 'character'. Some achieve their effect by radiating out from the personal, others by first stating a general proposition and then focusing on an individual by way of illustration. Imagery will be discussed first.

Although many witty writers of the seventeenth century used images 'centrifugally', to fly off without notice into realms which had nothing to do with the ostensible subject of the 'character', other authors seem to have realized that figures of speech could serve to reveal the generic or the generally valid within the particular. The following examples are taken from a wide variety of sources:

Mopsus, the social climber, is like a dog; if you drive it from the king's chair, it will clamber up into the preacher's pulpit. (La Bruyère)

The Farmer Tenant is 'the very drudge or doghorse of the world'. (Lenton)

The double beneficed Parson is a shepherd who wears the fleece without feeding the flock. (Lenton)

The Prison is like Hell or Purgatory. (Edmund Gayton, 1655)

The Whore is a Siren. (frequent)

The Usurer is 'cousen to good Monsieur Midas'. (K. W., 1661)

The Excellent Actor is a 'delightful Proteus'. (Flecknoe)

The Drunkard is a beast. (*passim*)

The Usurer is a fox clad in a lambskin. (Lenton, 1631)

The Good King is like the sun. (Thomas Ford, 1647)

The Quack Doctor is an 'epidemical disease'. (pamphlet of 1676)

The Countryman lets himself lie fallow and untilled. (Earle)

The Envious Man is a thorn-hedge, covered with nettles. (Hall)

In each case the image leads us away from the immediate empirical reality of the individual subject into a different sphere, one which invites speculation of a broader kind: What turns a man into an animal? In what ways is Lenton's Parson, exactly placed in a particular historical context, fitly to be described in the timeless image of the shepherd and his flock? What links between the cultivation of land and the 'cultivation' of personality are implied in the extracts from Hall and Earle? One remarkable metaphor of Hall's, both grim and paradoxical, manages in a few words to relate the individual life simultaneously to the past and the future: '[The Unthrift] is the living tomb of his fore-fathers, of his posterity: and, when he hath swallowed both, is more empty than before he devoured them.' The figures of speech radiate out from the individual case, but their implications are not exhausted by it. All the images just mentioned have generalizing force: timeless, legendary, relating to natural forces or phenomena, belonging to that world of fable where animals ape human behaviour or men seem to turn into animals—or even occasionally going back to an allegorical realm which helps to set the person in a perennial moral framework (see above, pp. 90 and 195).

Of course, such nudges in the direction of the generic last only until the next concrete behavioural detail brings us back to the particular person. Thus, although we may not be fully aware of it at all times, the reading of a 'character' has us constantly veering between the opposite poles of the individual and the generic. So it is that Earle places us in a timeless and generalized situation through the opening to his Younger Brother: 'His elder brother was the Esau, that came out first and left him like Jacob at his heels.' But we are soon firmly back in the author's age:

> If his annuity stretch so far, he is sent to the university, and with great heart-burning takes upon him the ministry. . . . His last refuge is the Low-countries . . . where he lives a poor gentleman of a company, and dies without a shirt. He loves not his country for this unnatural custom [i.e. the right of primogeniture], and would have long since revolted to the Spaniard, but for Kent only [where the practice of equal division of property among male children still survived].

Saltonstall concludes his 'character' of the Happy Man with three images. He is like the still centre, unaffected by 'worldly accidents' around him; virtue is his mistress; his life is a voyage in which religion is his compass and Heaven his destination. Strictly speaking, no doubt, the first and last of those figures are mutually incompatible, a result of piling up similes and metaphors regardless of whether the cumulative effect also possesses logic and unity.

(This, I take it, is what Harold Osborne means when he says that a collection of points about a type need not in itself make a satisfactory 'character'.[7]) But here our concern is with the particular and the general, and there seems little doubt that Saltonstall is deliberately placing his Happy Man in a wider context by relating his life and disposition firstly to external happenings, then to general moral principles, and lastly to immortality. This orientation of the single 'character' within a moral pattern figures in the next piece too. When Saltonstall notes that the Arrant Knave thinks that 'none tell truth but children and Idiots', the contrast with the preceding 'character' is manifest. The Knave tells his lies to overreach others, but will eventually be paid in shame and beggary; the Happy Man practises virtue disinterestedly and is happy as a consequence, almost by accident. Saltonstall ensures that we make the link between the two 'characters' by using exactly similar formulations:

The Happy Man	*The Arrant Knave*
. . . vertue . . . is the Mistris which hee serves, and hee thinkes himselfe happy in her favor.	. . . vice is his Mistresse, whom he serves till she pay him his wages in shame and Beggery.

Even the 'character' of the True Lover, in the main composed of the expected sighs, complaints, frenzies, and tender epistles, contains one remark which seems to relate to the wider moral pattern: he loves his mistress 'not for her beauty, but for her inward vertue'. That is not far from the terms in which virtue and inner sufficiency are discussed in the Happy Man: 'He knowes that the happiness of this life, consists in vertue. . . . He esteemes not the empty mirth of this world, but delights in the inward joy of his owne conscience.' The Lover worships his mistress because of her virtue; the Happy Man serves virtue as a lover serves his mistress.

If we turn to the Jealous Man, we find that the comic scenario (above, p. 199) is preceded by a serious attempt to explain his humour: 'His passion proceeds from the superfluity of his love, or from the consciousnesse of some deficiency or inability in himselfe.' That is a psychological rather than a moral diagnosis, but the links with the 'characters' just mentioned cannot be overlooked. For the jealous 'superfluity' of love contrasts with the True Lover's trust in his mistress, as does the 'consciousness of deficiency or inability' with the Happy Man's calm self-sufficiency. Saltonstall is not systematic (for instance, his professional and trade 'characters' stand outside this implied moral pattern) and certainly not schematic in the way of the older allegories or the Books of Estates. The wider references and parallels just noted seem to proceed naturally from his ruling moral attitude, a sort of Christianized Stoicism not uncommon in his day. The effect is certainly to relate at least an important minority of his 'characters' to a general ethical viewpoint.

The Overbury collection, with its wealth of local and contemporary detail and its witty conceits, might at first sight seem heavily weighted towards the particular. The Elder Brother

> speakes no language, but smels of dogs or hawks. . . . He summoneth the old servants, and tels what strange acts he will doe when he raignes. . . . His insinuation is the inviting of men to his house; and he thinks it a great modesty to comprehend his cheere under a peece of mutton and a rabbet . . .

But the same 'character' concludes with an annihilating moral judgement which forces us to view the subject from an altogether more distant and exacting perspective: he is 'good for nothing, except to make a stallion to maintaine the race'. The account of the Melancholy Man begins and ends with just such a wider view. He is

> a strayer from the drove: one that nature made sociable, because shee made him man, and a crazed disposition hath altered . . .
>
> Lastly, he is a man onely in shew, but comes short of the better part; a whole reasonable soule, which is mans chiefe preeminence, and soul marke from creatures sensible.

It seems that the basic form of the 'character' directly encouraged a combination of general and particular, disposed as follows:

opening: definition of ruling quality or social role; could include or imply moral judgement.

middle part: list of actions or details of appearance, conceits demonstrating the ruling quality, etc. Likely to involve many local and contemporary references.

ending: leave-taking; often a moral summing-up or other broadening of perspective.

(This would apply only to the more serious 'characters' or those from which serious implications could be drawn; we should not expect to find anything so earnest in the 'characters' of Watermen, Cooks, or any other types who simply provided the writer with an opportunity of practising his wit.)

Earle exploits the formal possibilities of the 'character' very effectively. The opening of his Discontented Man gives not only a definition of the quality but a terse moral judgement which, at the same time, manages to imply that the humour brings its own retribution: he is 'one that is faln out with the world, and will be revenged on himself'. The close of a 'character' is, for obvious reasons, more likely to embody some sort of judgement. The ending of the 'meer formal man' is if possible even more devastating and bleak than that of Overbury's Elder Brother: 'He hath staid in the world to fill a number; and when he is gone, there wants one, and there's an end.' A slightly different function is performed by the laconic ending to 'the world's wise man': 'His conclusion is commonly one of these two, either a great man, or hanged.' Here we are invited to muse not only on the general implications of the human characteristics just discussed, but also in what guises and disguises they are to be encountered. Elsewhere, details of the most homely nature rub elbows with exalted evaluations of a man's moral worth and standing (see above, p. 198). Here our perception of the dual nature of the 'character' is probably at its strongest: the clergyman who 'is no base grater of his tithes and will not wrangle for the odd egg' is described almost in the same breath as 'a main pillar of our church', whose life is the 'best apology' for religion.

The appeal is not always to an abstract moral order; reference is often made to the welfare of the state or of society. Despite the moral and religious orientation of most of his 'characters', such references are not uncommon in Hall. He can veer between totally conventional formulas (the Good Magistrate is 'the father of his Country') to more imaginative flights:

> [A Flatterer is] the moth of liberal men's coats; the ear-wig of the mighty; the bane of courts . . .
>
> [The Ambitious Man] is in the common body, as a mole in the earth, ever unquietly casting . . .

Breton is much given to such remarks; the following, reaching out as it does from the individual to the city, to society and finally to the ruler, is a case where his 'quadrumania' is totally justified: 'A Worthy Merchant is the pillar of a city, the enricher of a Country, the furnisher of a court and the worthy servant of a King.'

In eighteenth-century 'characters' the tendency to relate the role or behaviour of the individual to the common weal ran strong.

Coquettes, says Steele, are 'a sect among women [which] makes the greatest havoc and disorder in society' (*Tatler*, No. 126). The German moral weeklies, with their ever-present and solemn moralizing, often interrupt the listing of character-traits and actions to appeal to the reader directly: 'How much, or how little, does this benefit society?' Such 'characters' not only set up the chosen individual as one of a host of similar individuals, as all 'characters' do or should do; they also relate that individual (and, through him, the genus to which he belongs) to his fellow-men in general. His function, his usefulness (if any), his power to do good or evil within society broaden the implications of the individual picture. This is obviously a different sort of balance between the individual and the generic from that which Coleridge had in mind, but it is certainly one which is very important within the tradition of the Theophrastan 'character'.

Such 'generalization' of the single person forming the subject of a 'character' can be achieved in other ways: by relating his disposition to one of the humours (see below) or by assigning him his place in the Estates. Much more radical than anything yet mentioned in this context are the implications of this extract from Peter Shaw's Courtier: 'Among all the Creatures, there is none stranger than Man; and among all Men, there is none so strange as a Courtier' (*Reflector*, 1750, chapter 12). Shaw's 'character' makes much of the paradoxes of the Courtier's existence: he is miserly in amassing money yet a spendthrift; he is both proud and sycophantic; he voluntarily enchains himself to court life yet complains about his enslavement, and so on. By placing him at the centre of a series of concentric circles (the Courtier, all men, all creatures), the author invites us to reflect on these paradoxes in universal terms, as aspects of an existence stranger than that of the most outlandish animal or insect.

The greatest possible contrast between the particular and the general occurs where the subject of the 'character' is seen *sub specie aeternitatis*, as when La Bruyère annihilates the 'characters' in his chapter on Fashion by his concluding meditations on time and eternity (above, p. 55) or when L. G. scornfully consigns his subjects to the next world even as he mocks their antics in this. Of the Drunkard: 'there is no tippling in Hell'; of the Ignorant Old Man: 'like a Crab-fish, he is crawling towards his long home'.

The foregoing discussion has been mainly concerned with what is done *within* the 'character' to achieve a fusion of the individual and the generally valid. There are also, of course, countless examples where the 'character' is enclosed within an essay, as in the English, German, and Swiss periodicals of the eighteenth century: here the prefatory remarks evoke a general quality or category and the ensuing 'character(s)' provide a representative illustration, often contrasting with the rather abstract preamble by virtue of specific details and a more vivid tone. This was shown in Johnson's paper on peevishness (above, p. 68).

first part: Peevishness . . . is a species of depravity . . .

second part: Her tea is never of the right sort; the figures on the *China* give her disgust . . .

To borrow Coleridge's terms again: Johnson's musings on the topic of peevishness help to make the 'character' of Tetrica representative and instructive while the examples he gives of her fretful complaints lend her 'living interest'. An issue of the *Idler*, devoted—appropriately—to idleness, provides a further illustration. The preamble talks of idleness as

> an expedient, by which life may be passed unprofitably away without the tediousness of many vacant hours. The art is, to fill the day with petty business, to have always something in hand which may raise curiosity, but not solicitude, and keep the mind in a state of action, but not of labour. (No. 31)

Johnson then passes to the 'character' of Sober, who practises this 'art' by dabbling in one trade or hobby after another, playing at being amateur carpenter, shoemaker, potter, chemist, and so on. He produces useless essences and spirits from his home-furnace, 'sits and counts the drops as they come from his retort, and forgets, that, whilst a drop is falling, a moment flies away'. The 'character' and the framework in which it is enclosed complement each other in such a way that Sober is seen not only as one of the genus of 'busy Idlers', but as illustration of the wider proposition that life is to be used, not frittered away in time-killing activities.

Let us return for a last time to Coleridge. It will have become clear that the 'character' combines the individual and the generic in more ways than one. Firstly and most obviously, the subject must always be perceptible as individual *and* type. In addition, he may be shown as both rooted in his contemporary reality and timeless; he may be linked through his individual personality and actions to an impersonal world of moral absolutes or a collective realm represented by the society or state in which he lives. The writer may give us a close-up of his most minute characteristics and then retreat to place him within the context of the whole of living creation (Shaw) or even of eternity (La Bruyère). The generic quality makes a figure 'representative and symbolical, therefore instructive', says Coleridge. It is worth lingering for a moment on that 'instructive'. 'Characters' are not instructive only when they serve as moral lessons or warnings; they may offer us a microcosm of our own or another society, open the prosperous reader's eyes to the realities of life in humbler stations, or simply expand our imaginative horizons by giving us vicarious experience of an existence—whether moral, professional, or social—remote from our own. The 'character' may provoke us to reflect on what alters and what remains constant in human nature and behaviour. In the case of the most earnest writers (Hall, La Bruyère, William Law) we may be inspired to view all human vanity, ambition, and folly *sub specie aeternitatis*. In all cases, the coexistence of general and particular within the 'character' will help to determine our reaction to it and what we derive from it. There can be no doubt that this dual nature of the 'character' was one of the chief things that made it attractive to writers over the centuries; no doubt, either, that this is what drew so many novelists and dramatists to incorporate 'characters' into their works precisely at those points where they wished to draw attention to a combination of individual and generic within the figures thus portrayed.

It will be clear by now that a 'character' can be made up of any or all of the following: dress and appearance, actions, habits of speech, possessions, opinions. These may be expressed through, or augmented by, witty figures and analogies or by more serious comments from the author, including passages of moral diagnosis.

Physical indicators, although important, do not play such a dominant part as might have been expected. The reasons are not altogether easy to surmise. The fact that Theophrastus himself pays little heed to his subjects' appearance, that Hall is, broadly speaking, more interested in the state of a man's soul than his body, and that the 'Overbury' collection moves increasingly in the direction of witty arabesques must have helped to set the pattern. A few early 'characters', such as those in Thomas Adams's *The Soul's Sickness* (1616)[8] draw on the theory of humours, according to which each temperament had its characteristic physical signs. But it is likely that, as soon as the 'character' became the property of the wits, such straightforward and rather academic equations between temperament and mood on the one hand and physical appearance on the other would have had too much of the schoolroom about them. There is a hint of impatience in this reference to the Melancholy Man's outward appearance: 'Hee carries a cloud in his face, never faire weather: his outside is framed to his inside . . .'[9] The writer obviously feels that his readers can fill in the details for themselves and hurries on to his next point. Where the 'witty' character-writers dwell on physical appearance, it is precisely as a springboard for the display of wit; contemporary lore concerning the correspondence between the inner and the outer man is more or less assumed to be part of the shared background of author and reader, so that the latter is expected to admire the novel manner in which familiar material is presented. The point is illustrated if we compare Thomas Adams's penny-plain description of the Usurer with K. W.'s tuppence-coloured version:

Adams (1616): A usurer is known by his very looks often. . . . He hath a lean cheek, a meagre body, as if he were fed at the devil's allowance. . . . His whole carcase [is] a mere anatomy.

K. W. (1661): His rinckled jaws, like an old cows neck, hang chathernwise [i.e. like entrails], lank and loose; his whining and pelting posture have distracted his chops beyond their bounds, and his skin to a greater and more large extention, so that now it superabounds in vacuits, and like his grand sires double ruff hangs in pleats and folds . . .[10]

It is more common to find outward signs used as a conventional means of identification, like the crook in the hand of the porcelain shepherdess. The practice becomes widespread in the seventeenth century, where a man's position, profession, character, or religious persuasion was often quite clearly indicated by dress and other external features. Physical appearance is most likely to dominate in those cases where the writer emphasizes sartorial fripperies in order to show that there is nothing behind the foppish exterior:

'An Idle Gallant is one that was born and shaped for his clothes. . . . He is a kind of walking mercer's shop . . . (Earle)

A modern Beaux . . . is a pretty neat, phantastical Outside of a Man . . . (*The Comical Pilgrim*, 1722, p. 8)

One seventeenth-century author makes a serious moralizing distinction between essence and appearance: 'servants ought to imitate the vertues of their Masters and not the fashion of their Cloaths' (L. G., 1661, No. 6: A debaucht Courtier). Similarly, an anonymous author in *Der Patriot*, after giving the expected details regarding the ornate tobacco-box and diamond studs, adds: 'all his virtues consist in external finery, while he is dissolute within' (No. 111).

The way in which details of dress and appearance could either serve as indicators to character or point to a gulf between appearance and inner reality is strikingly shown by the following extracts from seventeenth-century 'characters':

You may know him by his diminitive *band*, that looks like the *Forlorne-hope* of his Shirt crawling out at his Collar . . . his *purity* consists onely in his dress. (*The Character of a Quaker*, London, 1671, pp. 1 f.: that last quip may have been taken from Earle's 'she precise hypocrite'.)

> [A Puritan is one]
> That at his Belt a buffe clad Bible beares,
> stampt with the true *Genevah* Characters . . .
> Whose Haire, and Ruffes, dare not his Eares exceed:
> that on high Saints dayes weares his working Weed . . .
> That Crosses each doth hate, save on his pence,
> and loaths the publicke Rope of Penitence . . .
> (*A Dialogue* . . ., London, 1640)

When Theophrastus's Arrogant Man goes visiting, he sends a servant on ahead to announce his coming; Sombrius crosses himself at the sight of a 'gay Equipage'; Johnson's Squire Bluster drives a day-labourer from his cottage for picking a few blackberries (*Rambler*, No. 142). The advantages of conveying character by recounting typical actions have been perceived by most character-writers, except those quite obsessed by 'wit' or driven into reflective abstraction by their moralizing intentions. Some of the finest 'characters', from Theophrastus to the age of Johnson, are straightforward catalogues of revealing actions. Theophrastus's Man of Petty Ambition is ostentatious in dress, makes himself prominent on public occasions, is attended by a black slave (which seems to have conferred distinction on a citizen of Athens in those days), keeps a monkey, gives costly presents, sacrifices under conditions of maximum publicity, and so on. The 'character' consists of about two dozen manifestations of this ruling quality, simply retailed one after the other without comment or linking passages. Addison's 'character' of Sombrius differs only in its greater terseness, containing no more than a dozen behavioural examples. The 'characters' make their point through the precision of their details and the cumulative effect produced by them, through the impression of unity underlying the variety, through the authors' objectivity, and, in Addison's case, the elegance and rhythmic balance of the style. The method is effective and, with certain types, is virtually the only one possible. (It is difficult to see, for instance, how the Superstitious Man could be described successfully other than through a list of his obsessions and taboos.) There are dangers; a mere list can become boring. *Die Zellischen vernünftigen Tadler* (1742) contains the 'character' of Lappalius, a Busybody and Knowall (No. 4), entirely built round two points: his ability to spy out things and his pertinacity in asking questions. The first point is illustrated by twenty closely similar items, the second by twenty-seven! Since we quickly realize Lappalius's ruling humour, and since the author cannot remotely approach either the forcefulness and variety of Theophrastus or Addison's urbane refinement, the reader is bound to tire.

One obvious way of avoiding the 'catalogue' effect is to concentrate on a few more extended incidents or even to base the 'character' on a single anecdote. Again Theophrastus provides a model, this time in his 'character' of the Coward, who is seen on board ship and on (or, rather, off) the battlefield. His terror of shipwreck and of fighting tells us all that we need to know, and Theophrastus has, at the same time, made himself space to develop his chosen motifs more fully than usual. Many were to adopt this method. An example from Vauvenargues is worth quoting, for it shows very clearly the advantages which may be gained:

> Thyestes was born simple and naïve. He loves pure virtue, but does not take another's virtue as his model. . . . When some moral law does not accord with his feelings, he sets it aside and thinks no more of it. If at night he meets one of those women who lie in wait for young men, Thyestes lets her talk to him and walks for a while at her side. When she complains of the necessity which destroys all virtue . . . he replies that poverty is not after all a vice if one can live without harming anyone. And, after having exhorted her to lead a better life and finding himself without money because of his youth, he gives her his old-fashioned watch, which was a present from his mother. His friends make fun of him and ridicule him for his misplaced generosity, but he replies: 'My friends, you are laughing at too slight a

thing. I pity these poor women who are obliged to follow such a trade in order to live. The world is full of misery which grips one's heart; if one only did good to those who merit it, one would have hardly any opportunities.' (ed. cit., pp. 166 f.)

The sustained anecdote expresses Thyestes' nature better than a series of actions, briefly recounted, could do. We see his tendency to mild sermonizing, but also his charity. The touching gift of the watch shows a profound warm-heartedness, while his response to his friends' mockery reveals a tolerant morality which makes no distinction between deserving and undeserving supplicants. (It also shows an unexpected sharpness, as the last sentence demonstrates.) The effect of expansion is, paradoxically, one of economy.

Next in importance to actions comes speech. Again, certain types positively demand to be characterized by this method:

The Slanderer: To hear him talk on another occasion: Amyntas is really an obliging and upright man; I know this side of him. If he's not the wittiest of men, well, honesty is more important than wit. And if, as they say, he is not equal to his office, that is not the fault of his heart.

The Man of Sensibility: He visits the temple, where others go to church; he has Aurora's teardrops on his shoes, wanders in the darkling groves, flees the clamour of the towns. . . . When he sees you after an absence, his heart surges out to you . . . for it is three summers since his eyes rested on you and in that time you roamed on distant shores.

The Bore: He remarks how far inferior men of the present day are to the ancients; how reasonable wheat is now in the shops; how full of foreigners Athens is getting. He observes that since the Dionysia it has been good sailing weather; and that if only Zeus would send more rain it would be better for the farmers . . .[11]

Sustained speech is not always necessary; Lord Froth betrays his arrant snobbery through subtle gradations in his ways of greeting acquaintances:

'My lord such a one,' says he, 'your most humble servant. Sir Richard, your humble servant. Your servant, Mr Ironside. Mr Ducker, how do you do? Ha! Frank, are you there?' (*Guardian*, No. 137)

Reading habits and possessions have from time to time been considered useful indicators by the character-writers. In the eighteenth century, as already mentioned, the habit of reading popular novels always stamped a person as frivolous, while a liking for the *Spectator* vouched for good sense. Leigh Hunt's 'character' of the

Maid-Servant (1820) contains a list of her books and other possessions which shows how telling this aid to characterization can be:

Here stands . . . the box—containing among other things, her clothes, two or three song books, consisting of nineteen for the penny; sundry Tragedies at a half penny the sheet; the *Whole Nature of Dreams Laid Open*, together with the *Fortune-teller* and the *Account of the Ghost of Mrs. Veal*; the *Story of the Beautiful Zoa* 'who was cast away on a desert island, showing how,' etc; some half-crowns in a purse, including pieces of country-money; a silver penny wrapped up in cotton by itself; a crooked sixpence, given to her before she came to town, and the giver of which has either forgotten or been forgotten by her, she is not sure which;—two little enamel boxes, with looking-glass in the lids, one of them a fairing, the other 'a Trifle from Margate'; and lastly, various letters, square and ragged, and directed in all sorts of spellings . . .

The third-person 'character', as created by Theophrastus and taken up by Hall and most of his immediate successors, came to be supplemented by variants in the first person. These, common in the eighteenth-century periodicals, usually took the form of a fictitious letter to the editor or an extract from the subject's diary. Since such 'characters' almost invariably deal with some sort of Idler (of drawing-room, boudoir, college set, club, or coffee house), the form has the advantage that it allows for unconscious self-revelation. The 'character' becomes a sustained exercise in irony, in which 'editor' and reader see through, and side against, the letter-writer or diarist. One of Addison's 'characters' in this form, by juxtaposing trivia against great events in the wider world, neatly pinpoints the diarist's paltry existence:

TUESDAY . . . *Ten, Eleven, Twelve*. Took a Walk to *Islington*.
One. Took a Pot of Mother *Cob's* Mild.
Between two and three. Returned, dined on a Knuckle of Veal and Bacon. *Mem*. Sprouts wanting.
Three. Nap as usual.
From Four to Six. Coffee-house. Read the News. A Dish of Twist. Grand Vizier strangled. (*Spectator*, No. 317: see also above, p. 70).

Formal oddities include a 'character' in the form of a mock-anthropological report and one in the guise of a recipe: 'Proper Ingredients to make a Modern Beaux'.[12] The 'character' can even take the form of a kind of riddle. The most ingenious example known to me is an early nineteenth-century sketch, ostensibly of an Aristocrat:

—Elated with the dignity of his situation, and proud of the possession of power, he assumed the reins of an oligarchical government, and, from the seat of magistracy, he viewed with a malignant glance, his populous but circumscribed empire. Transported with the extent of his authority, he sways the sceptre with autocratic dignity; and displays in his pride-flushed countenance the frownings of a forbidding mien. . . . [From his subjects] he exacts the most abject and servile subjection; the least offence incurs his severe and lasting displeasure;—his menials are punished with deprivation of office, his superior vassals with fine and imprisonment, with banishment temporal and eternal . . .

But the title is misleading and the piece turns out to have been an extended metaphor, whose subject is revealed only in the last sentence: 'Thus lives unbeloved and dies unlamented a—resident OXFORD FELLOW!!!'[13]

As we have seen, almost all definitions of the 'character' insist on brevity. The average length is, in fact, no more than a page or two and it is remarkable what Theophrastus, Earle, or Addison can pack into that brief compass. But one cannot legislate for precise length as if the 'character' were a sonnet. All that one can say is that a 'character' must be long enough to build up a satisfying picture of the chosen type but should not be swollen out to a point where it sacrifices its essential tightness and unity, whether through digressions and reflections, unduly self-indulgent anecdotage, or a too-detailed exploration of character-development. The practice, common in eighteenth-century periodical essays, of including six, eight, or even ten mini-characters in a single issue obviously threatens the 'character' from one direction; the reader is offered little more than a series of definitions which he must fill out as best he may from his own experience.[14] The opposite extreme is well illustrated by J. B.'s piece on the Assembly-Man, first published in 1662.[15] This is long-winded and rambling, occupying twenty-two quarto pages in the original printing. It is puffed out by all manner of witty figures, digressions, and learned references. Towards the end, the author seems to realize his fault, and says: 'But I forget, a Character should be brief.'

The question of how far a 'character' may hint at development without turning into something nearer a short story is again not readily answerable. Earle, as in everything, is commendably terse.

Of the Discontented Man: 'The root of his disease is a self-humouring pride, and an accustomed tenderness not to be crossed in his fancy; and the occasion commonly of one of these three, a hard father, a peevish wench, or his ambition thwarted.' The 'character' of Wandala in the *Discourse der Mahlern* (i. 9), with its slightly longer demonstration of how a young girl is perverted into vanity, is still well within the confines of the 'character'. However, most readers would probably agree that George Eliot's account of Merman (*Theophrastus Such*, chapter 3) is on the far side of the boundary line separating 'character' from short story.

A more difficult formal problem is this: must the 'character' be written in the singular number? The answer would, at first sight, seem to be obvious, for the 'character' has, from the outset, sought to present a species through a chosen individual member. When Robert Burton talks of fearful men and unconcernedly switches from plural to singular, the impression is not that of a 'character', rather of a disquisition on a class of men with occasional touches of individuation:

> *They* cannot endure to see any terrible object. . . . *They* complaine of toyes & feare without a cause. . . *They* are commonly distrustful. . . . If two talke together, discourse, whisper, jest, or tell a tale in general, *he* thinks presently they mean *him*. . . . Or if they talk with *him* . . .[16]

Yet Ralph Johnson's definition talks of a description 'of the nature and qualities of some person, or sort of people', leaving the issue open, and there are pieces, labelled by their authors as 'characters' and presumably accepted by contemporary readers as such, which are in the plural throughout or which veer between singular and plural.[17] One may recall that dramatic moment in Webster's *White Devil*: 'Shall I expound Whore to you? sure I shall; I'll give their perfect character'. Webster at least has no excessively formalistic notions. The more one examines this instance, the more wavering the dividing-line between 'he/she' and 'they' becomes. For Monticelso is to expound the word or concept 'whore', which, after all, must stand for a class of woman. Since every use of the word must comply with an accepted content of meaning, to talk to 'them' or to choose a typical representative and talk of 'her' amounts virtually to the same thing. Earle, it may be noted, is fond of switching to the plural number towards the end of a 'character', as if to underline the fact that the single person so far described stands for a class: '[A profane man] is one seems to dare God in all his actions, but indeed would out-dare the opinion of him, which would else turn him desperate; for atheism is the refuge of such sinners, whose repentance would be only to hang themselves.'[18] However, it is a different matter when the author of a paper on jealousy in *Der Weltbürger* (1741) talks now of 'jealousy', now of the 'jealous man', now of the 'jealous man or woman' (No. 27). This constant switching of perspective certainly destroys the 'character', but it would be introducing a note of formal purism foreign to the seventeenth century to cavil at the other examples just mentioned. The vast majority of 'characters' are consistent in sticking to a representative individual, and this probably expresses the essence of character-writing better than any other method: that is all one can usefully say on the subject.

The 'Character' and Theories of Personality

It is tempting to relate character-writing to the theories of personality current at different times, to see the 'character' flourishing together with the notion that temperament was determined by a conjunction of 'humours', and declining as more empirical theories gained ground. Such links are present, but can easily be exaggerated.

The 'character' first came to popularity in England at a time when the theory of humours was still accepted. The theory saw human nature as compounded of four elements, analogous to those which were thought to make up the physical universe:

> . . . there be iiii. Elements, Fyer, Ayre, Earth & Water, which of al things made, are the original beginnings. Next are the Qualities, that is to say, the myxture of Hoat, Cold, Moyst and Dry: of whom, proccede the differences of Complexions. Last of all, the foure Humours, whose force and Nature, ye seede comprehendeth and conteyneth wythin it: unto whom . . . the chiefe cause next under God, of the fourmyng and creation of al ye parts is truly to be attributed.[19]

A perfectly balanced temperament was very rare; commonly, there was an unequal mixture which allowed one humour to dominate:

> This notion of temperament is nothing other than a mixture of the four elemental qualities. Since these are not found exactly balanced in one and the same person, we describe the temperament by the name of that quality which dominates and surpasses the others in power.[20]

The theory of humours, although it certainly must have encouraged a view of human temperament as something fixed, is not as deterministic as is sometimes supposed. The combination of humours, as it was physiologically determined, could be altered or corrected by diet or by a person's way of life (*The Soul's Sickness* is full of references to this). On a more exalted level, the ruling humour was subject to the soul and could be modified or conquered by free will.[21] So it was recognized that a man could yield to and nourish his ruling humour or resist and modify it. If the character-writers continually imply that personality does not change, it is because they choose to represent it in this way, not because current psychological theory forces them to. There would seem to be a variety of reasons for this fact.

With the exception of explicitly 'moral characters' (such as Hall's), where the possibility of moral progress and reform is taken for granted, the great majority of seventeenth-century 'characters' are sketches of social, professional, or working-class types. The motives in writing these pieces were various—to give a microcosm of society, to expose abuses, to mock folly, to try one's hand at a popular literary exercise, to display one's wit— but it is noteworthy that none of these motives necessarily involves the writer in an attempt to show development or the possibility of change. Nor, when we read these 'characters', do we get any strong impression that general theories of personality can have played much part in their conception, except in the case of someone like Adams, who constantly refers to the theory of humours.

Locke's ideas became familiar to educated men in the eighteenth century and led to an increasing awareness of the importance of external influences on the development of character.[22] Yet the new idea of personality does not form an absolute antithesis to older notions based on the humours. For the latter theory, as we have seen, admitted the possibility that a man's ruling humour could be modified, while Locke certainly did not see the whole of personality as empirically determined, but admitted an innate element, a 'native propensity' or 'peculiar physiognomy of the mind' (*Thoughts concerning Education*, § 101 f.). What has changed is the stress. The older conviction—that the pre-ordained element is the more important—is well put by Montaigne: 'The natural leanings are aided and fortified through the force of social institutions, but they hardly change. . . . One does not extirpate these original qualities; one overlays them, one conceals them.'[23] The whole of Locke's *Thoughts concerning Education*, to take a single, familiar example, is motivated by the conviction that you can do a good deal more than that. It should therefore come as no surprise that eighteenth-century writers (who knew their Locke or, at least, would have been indirectly acquainted with his theories)[24] wrote 'characters' in which the notions of development, the education of personality, the flowering of good qualities under humane guidance and the compounding of folly through foolish example were more prominent than ever before. The German author J. F. Reupsch gives an interesting illustration of this, for he has two 'characters' clearly linked to the 'Choleric Man' of past ages: a Quarreller and an Angry or Quick-tempered Man (*Der Jachzornige*).[25] The first of these simply describes the Quarreller as if it were his 'humour' to see insults everywhere and to fall out with his neighbours. However the second explains how an over-indulgent upbringing has made the Quick-tempered Man what he is (i. 242 f.). What past ages would have seen as a physiological condition is here interpreted as caused by environmental factors.

Yet hosts of 'static' character-sketches continued to be written throughout the eighteenth century, differing from seventeenth-century 'characters' in style and detail but not in their implied view of personality. That is to say, authors (who, no doubt, knew better from a strictly philosophical point of view) happily went on in the old manner if a 'character' was required to illustrate a particular social or moral point or quirk of personality.[26] The form of the Theophrastan 'character', with its 'he is . . . he does . . . he says', its small scale, and the limited illustrative function which it came to serve in the eighteenth-century essay all helped to ensure that the treatment of character-development remained sketchy. Examples such as that of the grocer turned Virtuoso or the clever girl who develops into a sour Bluestocking remain exceptions.[27]

The gulf between theory and practice, between what men appear to believe about the formation of human personality and what they imply through their writing of 'characters', can be seen in a variety of ways. La Bruyère, in one of his reflections, denies the very possibility of discovering and defining character, since men are so full of contradictions (xi. 147). Had he acted on that belief, he would not have written the 'characters' of the Hypochondriac, the Epicure, the Parasite, and the rest. Pope sometimes talks of a ruling passion, but his famous definition of man as 'the glory, jest and riddle of the world', with its stress on mysterious dualism and irreconcilable contradictions, is clearly incompatible with the views implicit in character-writing.[28]

Thus any notion that the writing of 'characters' was bound to a particular theory of personality and must necessarily decline when that theory became outdated is over-simplified. Writers seized on the 'character' as a convenient form in which to portray human types without, in most cases, bothering much about general philosophical or psychological implications. Indeed, one can take this point of the separation of theory from practice further. It is easy to criticize the simplified and two-dimensional 'character' as heedless of, or unfair towards, the psychological complexity of real life. But in doing so we forget that we are all guilty of simplification and compartmentalization. We are theoretically convinced that all human beings are unique, but only really act on that belief within a fairly small circle of intimate acquaintances. The rest of humanity tends to be grouped into categories. Such a practice is obviously noxious when it nourishes social, racial, or religious prejudice,[29] but it is, in some of its forms, arguably unavoidable in the involved network of casual relationships that makes up much of our daily life. We do not see a complex and unique individual, who happens to be carrying a sackful of letters, approach our door; we say, 'Here comes the postman'. Any feelings of guilt can quickly be assuaged if we reflect that each of us is on the receiving end too. We have four or five stereotypes of the Waiter or the Taxi-Driver, but we may be confident that they have their stereotyped notions of the Diner-Out and the Fare. It is impossible to go through life perceiving every person with whom we have superficial contact as 'the glory, jest and riddle of the world'.

If life is too short for such an exercise, so too, as a literary genre, is the 'character'. The character-writer cannot, as the novelist can, give us a picture of the complexities of human nature, except perhaps implicitly, through the sum of his 'characters'. Each of them, taken singly, has limitations very similar to those shown by the figures in the comedy of humours: limitations which theatre audiences take in their stride. It would be a very austere person who complained of the comedy he had just seen that the quack or miser was too one-sided and obsessed to be true to life. The same acceptance of a psychological convention must apply when we read a 'character'. Comedies and 'characters' both represent the Lawyer as willing to plead any cause for a sufficient fee and expect the audience or readers to disapprove. To defend the lawyer's apparent amorality by reference to the delicate balance of the legal and moral considerations involved would, no doubt, be truer to life and fairer, but it would spell death to the Theophrastan 'character' and would turn the comedy into a Shavian problem play. Quite simply, we accept conventions in certain kinds of literature, well knowing that these involve a simplification of human nature and motives.

If I seem to have laboured this point, it is because I have discovered that many people find difficulty in approaching the 'character' because of its psychological limitations and its apparent divorce, certainly from the early eighteenth century onwards, from what was (and is) theoretically believed about human personality. The difficulty seems to be greater than in the case of comedy, probably because the 'character' is less familiar today, perhaps also because it offers its simplified views of mankind in a less diluted form than the novel or drama. Yet over the centuries, 'characters' have been written, read, and enjoyed in their thousands, despite their obvious and avowed limitations.

The Popularity of the 'Character'

The enduring affection and respect commanded by Theophrastus gives one clue as to the reasons for the popularity of the 'character'. None of his thirty types has disappeared from the social scene, but virtually all the details of dress and behaviour by which they manifest themselves are different: the way in which the 'character' makes us aware of the constantly changing forms assumed by perennial human characteristics is undoubtedly a major reason for its appeal. Many authors of 'characters' themselves point to this combination of the perennial and the contemporary: Brillon promises us *Le Théophraste Moderne*, G. C. E. Westphal calls his *Portraits* 'a fragment of a history of German morals and manners in the eighteenth century' (*Fragment einer teutschen Sittengeschichte des achtzehnten Jahrhunderts*).

If we look at character-writing from the early seventeenth century onwards, with its proliferation of types, we seem to be presented with a microcosm of society, even if a very unsystematic one. Here, of course, our pleasure is different from that of the contemporary reader. He will have enjoyed the pleasures of recognition, which are probably often underestimated when we consider the attraction of certain sorts of art; that is, he will have delighted in the witty presentation of things which were, in the main, familiar to him. We, on the other hand, find our historical curiosity satisfied, both as to the physical details of life in past centuries and the way in which social attitudes have changed.

Yet it would not be true—or not wholly true—to suggest that the popularity of the 'character' depends on serious and high-minded historical or psychological curiosity. There is another and more vulgar type of curiosity which also motivates us: 'characters' provide a sort of high-class gossip about typical specimens of our fellow-men. (This is particularly marked in the satirical 'characters' contained in the eighteenth-century periodicals.) Moreover, the best 'characters' are, stylistically speaking, small-scale masterpieces, as I hope some of the extracts cited in this book may have shown. The laconic piling-up of exactly observed details in Theophrastus, the witty precision of Earle and the more ribald comedy of some of his immediate successors, the eloquence and patent moral sincerity of Hall or Adams, the surgical objectivity of La Bruyère, the urbane and controlled style of Addison, Steele, and Johnson (where elegance of manner is often combined with broad humour in the choice of behavioural particulars), even the innocent humour of the shilling character-books of the nineteenth century: all these constitute sufficient reason for popularity.

The Decline

The decline in the fortunes of the Theophrastan 'character' started in the second half of the eighteenth century and was much more rapid in France and Germany than in England. In Germany, as we have seen, the 'character' was associated with the Enlightenment and fell from favour with it, while, as a technical means of describing personality, it gradually merged into the short story and the *Charackternovelle* as a tributary loses itself in a river.[30] In France, the 'character' could not survive the decline of the fashionable and exclusive society in which it had first prospered. Its demise was certainly hastened by the fact that, unlike the English 'character', it had never become a vehicle for the portrayal of the various professions and trades. The traditionally wide social spread of character-writing in England from the early seventeenth century onwards meant that nineteenth-century character-writers could turn out their sketches of the Waiter, the Innkeeper, the Coachman, and the Solicitor with the utmost naturalness. I do not believe that this would have occurred to their French, contemporaries, for whom the 'character' belonged to a socially limited and, by now, vanished world.

However, more general reasons for the decline of the 'character' must be sought. The main single factor was undoubtedly the growing interest in the puzzling complexity of human nature and the tendency to see personality as the product of a long and gradual process of development. This was not, as I have tried to show, a simple matter of literary practice following psychological and philosophical theories, rather the result of empirical observation, at most encouraged and accelerated by contemporary speculation.

'What . . . so diversified as man? What so little to be judged by his fellow?' asks Fanny Burney (*Camilla*, x. 14). If one took that literally, one would logically have to regard the 'character' as played out. (Flecknoe, it will be recalled, had said that the character-writer consigns his subjects to Heaven or Hell.) A century after Flecknoe, J. J. Ebert attacks the sweeping moral judgements of the character-writers, for whom a libertine is nothing but a libertine and a virtuous woman all virtue. He does this by imagining two 'characters'. The first, Dorant, visits brothels and showers gifts on loose women. The conventional moralist would cry 'Libertine' (*Erzwollüstling*) and leave it at that. But Ebert goes on to relate how Dorant had abandoned a courtesan on learning of her humble origin. He is not only a libertine, but a snob. Ebert's second example is that of Celimene, an apparently virtuous and modest paragon who, on closer examination, turns out to be vain and selfish in a number of less conspicuous ways.[31] In each case the type has, by taking on greater complexity, become markedly less suitable for treatment in character-form. The criticism seems the more telling as the examples are so obviously drawn from the realm of contemporary character-writing in the moral weeklies.

Such moral caution in the face of human complexity, coupled with steadily growing interest in character-development, inevitably favoured the novel at the expense of the 'character'. The gradual exile of this *petit genre* to the realm of light humour and its restriction to minor roles within the novel were the necessary and logical results. The other factor in the decline of the 'character', especially in the depiction of the poorer classes, was, as we have seen, the rise of two contrasting but complementary methods of social reportage: the habit of encouraging people to speak for themselves and recording their words verbatim, and the social survey, supported by statistics and graphs.

All these factors have combined to make the 'character' virtually extinct. Another Canetti may come along and surprise us, but, until and unless that happens, I find it difficult to disagree with Boyce, who sees little likelihood of a revival (*The Character to 1642*, p. 156). A revival of interest in existing 'characters' is another matter; I hope that this book may contribute a little to bring that about.

APPENDIX 1

Physiognomy and the 'Character'

Physiognomy originated in ancient Greece, and the science (or would-be science) was kept alive in treatises on medicine, ethics, and rhetoric. With the Renaissance came a new surge of interest in the subject. Physiognomy was often linked with the doctrine of the humours, each of which was thought to influence a man's appearance in a characteristic way.[1] One of many examples of how treatises on psychology, based on the humours, drew on physiognomical indicators is Cureau de la Chambre's *L'Art de Connoistre les Hommes* (Amsterdam, 1660, ii. 4).

Arguments for and against physiognomy continued intermittently through the centuries. Addison is cautious: 'It is an irreparable Injustice we are guilty of towards one another, when we are prejudiced by the Looks and Features of those whom we do not know.'[2] Interest in physiognomy—not only in German-speaking countries—was fuelled by J. C. Lavater's *Physiognomische Fragmente zur Beförderung der Menschenkenntniß und Menschenliebe* of 1775–8, in which the author pictured both heads and individual features and drew dogmatic conclusions as to what they signified in terms of personality. Lavater's exaggerated claims on behalf of his 'science' caused a protracted controversy, with many writers simply rejecting his theories or making fun of them.[3] The most detailed and balanced criticism came from Lichtenberg, who had started off as one of the faithful but had drifted into scepticism.

Physiognomy can never be developed into an exact science, says Lichtenberg (here anticipating Schopenhauer). While conceding that there is some correspondence between a man's features and his inner nature, he is deeply suspicious of Lavater's attempts to produce a series of schematic equations. He prefers an undogmatic and empirical approach and believes that the mobility and expressiveness of a man's face tell us much more than does the shape of his nose or forehead.[4] And so to the *reductio ad absurdum*: 'If physiognomy develops as Lavater expects [i.e. into an exact and generally accepted scientific theory and method], children will be hanged before they have committed the deeds which merit the gallows. . . . A physiognomical auto-da-fé' (ed. cit. i. 532). One further criticism of Lavater bears directly on the application of physiognomy to character-writing. Matthias Claudius, in his review in 1778 of the *Physiognomische Fragmente*, made the point that any reader who looks at one of Lavater's illustrations without first reading the text is very unlikely to guess what sort of temperament is being illustrated.[5]

We come to the question of how physiognomy links up with character-writing. Authors of some early 'characters' give physical details which might hint at knowledge of physiognomical theories, but the threads are so tangled (physiognomy? the theory of the humours? physical characteristics as part of the technique of *descriptio* in rhetorical treatises?) that it is hard to say anything definite.[6] For an explicit invasion of character-writing by the ideas of the physiognomists, we have to wait until the eighteenth century. The first example known to me is in the moral weekly *Die Zigeunerin* of 1765–6 (a decade before Lavater).[7] The anonymous author talks confidently of the possibility of deducing character from external appearances, and bolsters up his argument with teleology—can one imagine that a wise Creator would have placed the soul of a dove in the body of a hawk? (No. 1) In a later paper, he exactly anticipates Lavater's theories and methods, describing in detail what aspects of temperament can be postulated from this or that type of forehead or eyes and claiming that a man's face is 'nature's secret writing', in which she reveals his inner faculties (Nos. 8 and 10). The author then works this idea out in detail through the 'character' of the ideally wise and virtuous Teliander, examining eyes, brow, nose, mouth, posture, and gait in turn and finding in them an exact mirror of the soul: 'His incomparable form tells us without need of words that a noble spirit inhabits this fair body' (No. 10). All this is pure Lavater *avant la lettre*, with the sole exception that there are no pictorial illustrations to support the argument. However, these are present in all subsequent essays in 'physiognomical' character-writing.

One such is the anonymous *Kunst, die Männer und Frauen aus ihren Gesichtszügen zu erkennen. Ein physiognomisches Taschenbuch nach Lavaters Grundsätzen.*[8] The Preface makes the claim, familiar by now, that physiognomy is a science, even capable of thwarting the ignoble attempts of the devious and hypocritical to conceal their true natures. The first part of the book is devoted to a list of separate features and an analysis of what they can reveal; the second and longer section gives thirty-six coloured engravings representing different human types, each with its paragraph of explanation:

> This square forehead testifies to a good memory and much sound commonsense. But its vertical slant indicates a certain unyielding character, which can easily degenerate into obstinacy. The somewhat protuberant lower lip and the flat chin are signs of a peaceable and upright good-heartedness . . . (p. 55)

Die Kunst, die Männer und Frauen . . . zu erkennen can justly be regarded as a physiognomical character-book, confident to the point of dogmatism. I may add, having often put it to the test, that it bears out Claudius's criticism: no one to whom the book was shown came anywhere near to deducing the characters from the pictures.

With interest in character-writing riding high at the same time that physiognomy was enjoying a vogue, it was inevitable that someone should conceive the idea of providing Theophrastus himself with 'scientific' illustrations; this was done by Francis Howell, in *The Characters of Theophrastus; translated from the Greek, and illustrated by Physiognomical Sketches* (1824). Howell thinks that Theophrastus's 'characters' are 'materials for a comprehensive, and a scientific Natural History of Man' and hopes that the illustrations supplied will bring about a better understanding of 'the correspondence between external forms and the qualities of mind' (Preface, pp. xiv and xix). Each 'character', then, is accompanied by its physiognomical sketch, and Howell has augmented his edition with copious notes which comment on the parallels between text and pictures. These parallels are somewhat more plausible than those in *Die Kunst, die Männer und Frauen . . . zu erkennen*.

Hereafter, character-writing and physiognomy seem to have parted company. Although interest in physiognomy continued uninterrupted well into this century, the 'science' was never again evoked by the character-writers. (Caricatures with mock-physiognomical captions or verses were frequent in the comic English periodicals of the nineteenth century,[9] but are too trivial to add anything either to character-writing or to physiognomy.)

APPENDIX 2
Original Versions of Passages Quoted in Translation

(References are to the page and the commencing line-number.)

47(epigraph) Livre admirable que celui *De La Bruyère*! Caractères inimitables qu'on s'eforça pourtant d'imiter!

48[12] . . . des Peintures sans couleur, où la Nature de chaque Passion est exprimée par les marques qui luy sont propres . . .

48[27] Il n'attend pas que le feu luy ait préparé ses viandes; il les prend toutes cruës, & quelquefois encore sanglantes & pleines de vie . . .

51[18] Je connais *Mopse* d'une visite qu'il m'a rendue sans me connaître; il prie des gens qu'il ne connaît point de le mener chez d'autres dont il n'est pas connu; il écrit à des femmes qu'il connaît de vue. Il s'insinue dans un cercle de personnes respectables, et qui ne savent quel il est, et là, sans attendre qu'on l'interroge, ni sans sentir qu'il interrompt, il parle, et souvent, et ridiculement. Il entre une autre fois dans une assemblée, se place où il se trouve, sans nulle attention aux autres, ni à soi-même; on l'ôte d'une place destinée à un ministre, il s'assied à celle du duc et pair; il est là précisément celui dont la multitude rit, et qui seul est grave et ne rit point. Chassez un chien du fauteuil du Roi, il grimpe à la chaire du prédicateur . . .

51[40] Est-ce en lui zèle du prochain? est-ce habitude? est-ce une excessive opinion de soi-même?

52[2] . . . la mort seule lui ôtera avec la vie cette soif d'empire et d'ascendant sur les esprits. . . . Il écoute, il veille sur tout ce qui peux servir de pâture à son esprit d'intrigue . . .

52[14] *Irène* se transporte à grands frais en Épidaure, voit Esculape dans son temple, et le consulte sur tous ses maux. . . . Elle lui demande pourquoi elle devient pesante, et quel remède; l'oracle répond qu'elle doit se lever avant midi, et quelquefois se servir de ses jambes pour marcher. Elle lui déclare que le vin lui est nuisible: l'oracle lui dit de boire de l'eau . . .

52[20] . . . le monde est plein d'Euthyphrons . . . on ne tarit point sur les Pamphiles . . .

52[34] Je nomme *Europyle*, et vous dites . . . Je vais, *Clitiphon*, à votre porte . . .

53[21] . . . il croit naïvement que ce qu'il en a [intelligence] est tout ce que les hommes en sauraient avoir . . .

53[23] Un Pamphile en un mot veut être grand, il croit l'être; il ne l'est pas, il est d'après un grand.

53[28] *Narcisse* se lève le matin pour se coucher le soir . . .

53[29] Toutes ses vues, toutes ses maximes, tous les raffinements de sa politique tendent à une seule fin, qui est de n'être point trompé, et de tromper les autres.

55[3] Si la vie est misérable, elle est pénible à supporter; si elle est heureuse, il est horrible de la perdre. L'un revient à l'autre.

55[15] . . . tous les temps ne sont qu'un instant, comparés à la durée de Dieu, qui est éternelle: tous les espaces du monde entier ne sont qu'un point, qu'un léger atome, comparés à son immensité.

55[26] Les jours, les mois, les années s'enfoncent et se perdent sans retour dans l'abîme des temps; le temps même sera détruit: ce n'est qu'un point dans les espaces immenses de l'éternité, et il sera effacé. Il y a de légères et frivoles circonstances du temps qui ne sont point stables, qui passent, et que j'appelle des modes, la grandeur, la faveur, les richesses, la puissance, l'autorité, l'indépendance, le plaisir, les joies, la superfluité. Que deviendront ces modes quand le temps même aura disparu? La vertu seule, si peu à la mode, va au delà des temps.

56[29] Laissons le dehors pour venir à la recherche du dedans de Myrille.

58[6] S'il se trouve chez le duc Eugène lorsque celui-ci se débotte, Thersite fait un mouvement pour lui présenter ses souliers; mais comme il s'aperçoit qu'il y a autour de lui beaucoup de monde, il laisse prendre les souliers à un valet, et rougit en se relevant.

58[15] De retour chez soi, on lui dit que cet homme a fort attendu et s'en est enfin allé; il répond qu'il n'y a pas grand mal, et commande qu'on le fasse souper.

58[24] S'il a de l'argent à donner à un homme . . . qui est . . . pauvre et de petite condition, la seule crainte de Varus, c'est de donner à ce misérable d'une manière qui lui fasse sentir son état; il l'embrasse, il lui serre les mains, il s'excuse, en quelque manière, de son propre bienfait . . .

59[22] Toutefois, qu'on ne pense pas que Clazomène eût voulu changer sa misère pour la prospérité des hommes faibles: la fortune peut se jouer de la sagesse des gens courageux; mais il ne lui appartient pas de faire fléchir leur courage.

60[1] Varus hait le faste inutile, et la profusion sans dessein; il est vêtu simplement, il marche à pied; il aime l'ordre dans ses affaires, et fait des retraites à la campagne, afin de moins dépenser.

60[16] Il ne connaît ni l'amour, ni la crainte, ni la bonne foi, ni la compassion; il méprise l'honneur autant que la vertu . . . le crime lui plaît par lui-même; il est scélérat sans dessein . . .

82[16] Abermal ein moralisches Wochenblatt!—Es giebt derselben bald soviel, daß man einen Berg damit auftührmen, oder den Rheyn zudämmen könnte!

83[5] Da muß man nicht arbeiten den Hoof-Pracht zu erhalten, da muß man keinen Sold zur Leibwacht herschiessen, da sind keine von des Königs Grimm anlauffende Todes-Botten, da sind keine güldene Fessel-tragende Schmeichler, welche dem gemeinen Volck eiserne anlegen, da . . . bleibet [jeder] ein Herr seiner Besitzung.

86[14] Bey dem größten Theile der Menschen ist die Freundschaft nichts anderes als ein bloßer Zeitvertreib. Sie suchen sich dadurch nur von dem Misvergnügen zu befreyen, welches ihnen die Einsamkeit verursachen würde: Und ein beständiger Wechsel in ihrer Freundschaft, macht sie wiederum von dem ekelhaften Verdrusse los, welchen ihnen eine dauerhafte Freundschaft erwecken würde.

Ein solcher Freund ist Hermippus.

87[8] Aller Wolstand ist ihm eine Thorheit. Er lachet über die so genannte artige Aufführung. Alle Zierlichkeit und Höflichkeit sind ihm läppische Possen.

88[13] Herr Faulthier . . . hat nicht Lust etwas zu hören. Er fragt beständig, was? weil er sich niemals zu der geringsten Aufmerksamkeit angestrenget. Die Worte scheinen in seiner Seele nicht einmal so viel Eindruck zu haben, als ein vorbeyfliegender Vogel in einen Spiegel. Es giebt sehr träge Seelen; aber Herr Faulthier ist eine nichtsthuende.

88[23] *Critias* ist allein mit der Verbesserung seines Verstandes beschäftigt. Er widmet alle seine Sorgen dieser Pflicht. Er bemüht sich, seinen Geist täglich mehr zu schärfen. Allein über diese Sorgen vergißt er die Sorgen für sein Haus. Er denkt immer nur an Wahrheiten, und denkt darüber nicht an seine Frau und seine Kinder. Er freut sich, wenn er eine Wahrheit deutlicher eingesehen hat, und die Thränen seiner Frau, die die Unordnungen in seinem Vermögen sieht, bekümmern ihn nicht. Sein Vermögen geräth von Tage zu Tage in noch größre Unordnungen.

89[5] Der Abergläubige dienet einem Gott, dem er menschliche Fehler andichtet. . . . Um seine strenge Gottheit zu versöhnen und eingebildete und abwesende Übel abzuwenden, erduldet er grosse und gegenwärtige Übel. . . . Ein Traum, ein falscher Trit über seine Thürschwelle, ein Hase, der ihm vor dem Thor quer über den Weg läuft, eine Krähe, sind für ihn wichtig genug, um ihn zu bewegen, eine Reise aufzuschieben, welche ihm seine eigene Vortheile und die vernünftigsten Freunde angerathen haben. Er wird vor Furcht plötzlich krank, wenn er auf seinem Dache eine Eule erblickt . . .

89[30] Argus . . . trincket, er isset, er schläffet, er stehet wieder auf, er thut alle Tage weiß Leinen an, spielet im l'Ombre, gehet zur Opera: allein was hilfft dieß alles dem gemeinen Wesen? Was nützet es einem Armen . . . ? Was haben Wittwen und Waisen davon . . . ?

89[36] *Chrysophilo* . . . speiset . . . schlecht, wohnet schlecht, kleidet sich schlecht, und hat sehr schlechte Aufwartung. Ich weiß nicht, wer sein Erbe seyn wird. Denn er hat weder Kinder, noch Brüder, noch Schwestern, noch andere Anverwandten. Wem zu Liebe kürtzet er sich denn dasjenige ab, was doch die Wolanständigkeit und Nothdurft erfordern?

90[22] Eckele Schmeichler und rauschende Schwärmer machen den größten Theil seiner Gesellschaften aus. Ihre Vergnügungen fangen sich [*sic*] mit einem leeren Geschwätze an . . . geschmacklose Einfälle eines schwindelnden Witzes . . .

90[26] Dem geselligen Lautus geht der schäckernde Leichtsinn und der hirnlose Spott oder die Verläumdung zur Seite, die Arglist führt die Gesellschaft . . .

90[39] Was ich an meisten an diesem sonst glückseligen Thoren beklage, ist dieses, daß er nicht nur das Irrdische, sondern auch den Himmel und die Seeligkeit mit blossem Hoffen zu erlangen, und dazu keine weitere Bemühung vonnöthen zu haben vermeynet, als die äusserliche Bekäntnis zur seeligmachenden Kirche.

91[34] Gieng er aus, so war er zu weltförmig; blieb er zu Hauß, so störte er sie in ihrer Andacht. Bat er gute Freunde zu sich, so waren es Weltkinder, die nur sündliche Gespräche führten.

92[7] Sein Körper ist nicht groß, und seine Glieder haben nichts von der Gelenksamkeit, die man an einem geschickten Tänzer bewundert. Sein Wesen ist steif, und seine Maniern haben etwas gezwungenes, wann er artig thun will. Er hat schwarze, tief im Kopf liegende kleine Augen. Sein Gesicht ist mager, und seine Farbe gelblich braun. . . . Wann er lacht, so scheinet er ein wenig albern, ja selbst seine Freundlichkeit hat nichts anmuthiges . . .

93[3] *Damon* sorgt für nichts, als wie er seine Wünsche und Leidenschaften befriedigen will. Er liebt eigentlich nichts, als was seinen Sinnen schmeichelt. . . . Billiget Ihr Herz diese Handlungen und Neigungen? . . . Damon treibt seine Sinnlichkeit so hoch, daß er seine Gesundheit schwächt und sich unleidliche Schmerzen verursachet. Wird er Ihnen nicht noch verächtlicher?

93[12] Denken Sie sich nunmehr einen Menschen von entgegengesetztem Charakter. *Semnon* genießt die sinnlichen Ergetzungen mit einer gewissen Einschränkung, damit er gesund bleibe. Wir billigen ihn mehr, als den Damon. . . . Er wendet seine Reichthümer zu Schmuck und Bequemlichkeiten an, weil sich seine Freunde daran vergnügen und ihm danken—Semnon gefällt schon mehr. . . . Er verbessert seinen Geschmack und seine Einsicht so sehr, daß er Andre dadurch vergnügen kann; und es ist seine Absicht, sie zu vergnügen. Wir fühlen schon mehr Wohlgefallen an ihm.

94[31] Endlich lernete er von einem seiner Kammeraten die unschuldige und erlaubte Kunst, sich im auszahlen und einnehmen der Zerstreuung oder der Übereilung derjenigen zu seinem Vortheil zu bedienen, mit welchen er zu thun hatte. . . . Er war viel zu vernünftig, als daß er in seiner Sele anderen Empfindungen als bloß der Begierde Schätze zu sammeln Platz geben sollte.

94[36] Alle meine Leser und Leserinnen aber will ich hier ernstlich ermahnet haben, den Herrn Chrysofil und seine Gemalinn sich hinführo zum Muster dienen zu lassen. Ihr Charakter ist überaus liebenswürdig.

95[3] Mir fehlt Verstand—o ein geringer Mangel,
Davor ist mein BON AIR—auch eine goldne Angel
Die manches fischt . . .
O nützlich seyn—das sind nur Narrens Possen . . .
Ich lebe mir—
Was frag ich Pflicht und Staat nach dir!

95[21] Er wünschte für sein Vaterland zu sterben, und kam deswegen niemals aus Bergen. Er hat Zeit seiner Kriegsdienste vielen Belagerungen und Schlachten beygewohnt, aber nur von Haus aus. Etlichemal geschah es, daß er mit ins Feld rücken sollte; so bald er aber Ordre bekam, so überfiel ihn eine starke Engbrüstigkeit, und er überschickte an seiner Stelle ein Attestat vom Stadtphysikus, daß er im Leibe nicht richtig wäre, und von dieser Krankheit vermuthlich nicht eher, als nach geendigtem Feldzuge, geheilt werden dürfte. Deswegen aber war er zu Hause nicht müßig; denn er trank alle Tage die Gesundheit des commandirenden Generals und seiner übrigen Kameraden, die im Felde stunden. . . . Es gereichte ihm auch auf dem Todbette zu sonderbarem Troste, daß er seine Hände niemals mit Blute befleckt hatte.

96[32] Er war ein Tugendfeind, er war ein Menschenhasser;
Wenn ihn sein Stolz befiel, floß Menschenblut, wie Wasser;
Er war voll Eigennutz, und liebte Schmeicheley;
Raubt' ungestraft, und blieb nie seinen Worten treu;
War vielfach, und gelehrt, sich in die Zeit zu schicken;
Verband mit zehnen sich, um Einen zu erdrücken;
Religion und Eid war ihm ein Puppenspiel;
Durch Labyrinthe gieng er stets zum nahen Ziel;
Hurt', und verfolgte Wild;—O Maler, halt ein wenig!
Halt! ich versteh dich schon, das heißt: Er war ein König!

101[14] Es ist wahr *Vadius* ist gelehrt: er versteht das Latein und das Griechische so gut, daß er mit gebohrnen Griechen und Römern umgehen könnte. Aber es ist Schade, daß er nicht mit den Deutschen sprechen kann. Er besitzt weitläuftige Wissenschaften, er kennt die Natur so vieler Dinge aus den tiefsinnigsten Betrachtungen. Niemand macht ihm seinen großen Verstand streitig, die Einsicht ausgenommen, den Verstand anderer Menschen einzusehen. In allen seinen Geberden, in allen seinen Werken und Minen liegt ein Beweis, wie zufrieden er mit sich selbst ist, und das ist die Ursache, warum andre nicht mit ihm zufrieden sind. Was hilft es ihm, daß sein Verstand so ausgearbeitet ist, da seine Sitten so rauh und wild sind?

102[29] . . . es soll mich nicht wundern,—wenn etwa eine neue Sündfluth oder das jüngste Gericht über uns ausbricht,—die witzigen Köpfe Wiens mit einem Wortspiel im Munde in die Wellen versinken, oder auf den Kirchhöfen sich lachend um ihre Gebeine zanken zu sehen. Ein Wiener, der Profession von dem Witze macht, treibt gewöhnlich kein anderes Geschäft, oder kümmert sich wenig um das, welches sein Amt oder Stand ihm auflegt.

105[37] Speis't er in einem Gasthause, so findet er Alles schlecht, läßt den Wirth kommen und zankt mit ihm, setzt alle Aufwärter in Bewegung, und will immer gerade das essen, was heute nicht vorhanden ist. . . . Er *geht* nie, immer *läuft* er. Wollt ihr ihn aufhalten? er hat keine Zeit euch Rede zu stehen! er hat zwanzig Bestellungen für diesen Tag. . . . Wenn er nach Krems reisen muß, so läßt er ein Lebewohl an alle seine Freunde in die Zeitungen einrücken, und wenn er krank wird, so ist er überzeugt, die Papiere müßten auf der Börse fallen.

107[21] Die junge Frau stammt aus einer der 'besten Familien', wo die höhere Bildung förmlich epidemisch grassirt. Ihre zwei jüngeren Schwestern besuchen das Mädchengymnasium; sie selber fährt Bicycle, hat trotz ihrer Jugend bereits drei robuste Claviere in den dauernden Invaliditätszustand versetzt und auch sonstige Proben einer vollkommen modernen Bildung abgelegt.

107[29] —'Eine Vorspeise gefällig?'

Der Gast ist wahrhaftig nicht bei Vorspeisen aufgewachsen, er pflegt gewöhnlich nur Eine Schüssel zum Nachtmahl zu nehmen. Aber wenn Einem so ein eleganter Jüngling eine Vorspeise anträgt, so muß es wohl in diesem Gasthause üblich sein, sie zu nehmen. Also ja!

—'Vielleicht eine Mayonnaise vom Fisch . . .' Der Gast nickt. Er hätte auch zu marinirten Maikäfern Ja gesagt, nur um den Absichten des Speisenkellners gerecht zu werden.

112[23] Was ist natürlicher, als daß Herr von Aufdringlich reussirt?

113[9] Für den nächsten Sonntag hat er also vorläufig diese Verpflichtungen übernommen: Zeitig früh eine Reise auf den Semmering, nachmittags zwei Uhr eine Heurigenfahrt nach Klosterneuburg, um drei eine Vereinssitzung in Wien und um vier einen Besuch in Weidlingau. Vorausgesetzt, daß nun keine Einladung mehr kommt, die Herr Neubauer zweifellos auch noch akzeptieren würde—wie lassen sich jene vier Dinge vereinigen? Natürlich gar nicht. Weiß das der Herr von Neubauer? Ja, weil er nicht schwachköpfig ist. Wird er also drei seiner Zusagen brechen? Mindestens . . .

130[27] Sie gibt ihrem Geld zu essen, damit es nicht eingeht. Keinen Bissen tut sie, ohne daß für ihr Geld auch etwas abfällt. Manchmal legt sie sie [die Noten] einzeln nebeneinander auf den Tisch, wie eine zahlreiche, sittsame Familie und gibt ihnen Namen. Dann zählt sie nach, ob sie auch alle da sind, und wenn sie brav gegessen haben, legt sie sie schlafen.

131[1] Er weiß, warum er Scheu vor Besuchern hat, die ihm auf die Teppiche treten: unter den Teppichen liegen Tausende von ungeöffneten Briefen. Die Matratzen sind von Briefen so schwer, daß er sie nicht zu heben vermöchte. Auf dem Dachboden hat er kaum noch einen leeren Koffer . . .

144[13] Drücke nicht die bedrückten, und entziehe den Arbeitern den billigen Lohn nicht. Denn durch dessen ungerechte Entziehung wird GOTTES Straffe auf einen gezogen. An deinem Uberflusse laß die Nothleidenden Theil nehmen, so wirst du wieder Theil an den Göttlichen Verheissungen haben.

144[23] Er bewahret sowol seine als seiner Herrschaft *Ehre*. . . . Denn bey einem Kaufmanne kömt fast alles auf den Kredit an. . . . Er verdoppelt täglich seinen Fleis: dieß ist der beste Weg, weiter zu kommen.

145[21] In seiner Haushaltung geht es reichlich, aber nicht verschwendrisch zu, und seine Aufführung bleibt allezeit bürgerlich.

149[27] Es kann mir durch die Seele gehn, wenn ich den Hofmeister in manchem adeligen Hause demüthig und stumm an der Tafel seiner gnädigen Herrschaft sitzen sehe, wo er es nicht wagt, sich in irgend ein Gespräch zu mischen, sich auf irgend eine Weise der übrigen Gesellschaft gleichzustellen, wenn sogar den ihm untergebenen Kindern von Eltern, Fremden und Bedienten der Rang vor ihm gegeben wird, vor ihm, der wenn er seinen Platz ganz erfüllt, als der wichtigste Wohlthäter der Familie angesehn werden sollte.

153[28] Le vieux Cléante a un raisonnement banal, dont il croit mettre en déroute tout ce qu'on peut opposer de plus raisonable à son vain babil, qui ne fait que crôitre avec son âge; savez-vous, jeune homme, dira-t-il, que c'est à vous taire quand je parle; vous n'êtes qu'un *morveux*, et j'ai soixante et dix ans bien comptez.

Grand bien vous fasse, Mr. Cléante; on ne vous envie ni votre esprit ni votre âge. Croïez-vous que vivre long-tems et avoir de l'expérience, sont des expressions sinonimes?

156[35] Er scheinet . . . nicht mehr gutherzig, sondern einfälltig und kindisch. . . . Wäre er von Natur weniger witzig; so würde er vielleicht minder abgeschmackt seyn wenn er betrunken ist.

157[8] Ich meyne, daß die Züge, welche ich von ihm entworfen habe, schon zureichend sind den bedaurenswürdigen Zustand dieses guten Edelmannes einzusehen.

162[20] Es kan z.E. die Pest kommen, Hungersnoth entstehen, oder der Feind kan ins Land kommen, das Wetter kan ins Hauß schlagen, es kan Feuersnoth entstehen, ich kan mirs Bein zerbrechen, wenn ich ausgehe. Es ist nichts leichter als daß—es kan mich ein Ziegel vom Dache beschädigen—oder ich kan sonst ein Unglück haben—man kan in tausend Krankheiten verfallen.

170[14] L'on voit certains animaux farouches, des mâles et des femelles, répandus par la campagne, noirs, livides et tout brûles du soleil, attachés à la terre qu'ils fouillent et qu'ils remuent avec une opiniâtreté invincible; ils ont comme une voix articulée, et quand ils se lèvent sur leurs pieds, ils montrent une face humaine, et en effet ils sont des hommes.

190(epigraph) Es ist mit einem vortreflichen Caracter in der Moral beschaffen, wie mit einem schönen Gemählde. Wer es nur ansiehet, wird entzückt und bewundert es.

191[24] Die Haupteigenschaften eines würdigen Menschen sind in seiner Seele zu suchen, und bestehen in einer beständigen Liebe der Wahrheit und Gerechtigkeit, und in einer ununterbrochenen Begierde, alles Gute zu thun, was nur möglich ist.

194[32] Dieser alte Freund . . . heißt *Wilhelm Ernst*, ein Mann von einer strengen Tugend und von einer bewährten Redlichkeit und Gottesfurcht. Er ist das, was man in meiner Jugend einen rechten *Biedermann* nannte . . . ein eifriger Vertheidiger der Sitten unserer Väter, und ein geschworner Feind der verderbten Sitten dieses Zeitalters. Ich muß gestehen, daß er seinen Eifer zu weit treibt . . . und zu mürrisch und verdrüßlich über die Veränderung ist, die er erlebt hat, und sie mit zu vieler Bitterkeit und Galle bestraft.

196[16] . . . und [darf] folglich nicht aus schimmernden Worten und weit hergesuchten Ausdrücken, nicht aus gekünstelten Gegensätzen und Widersprüchen, oder gar aus Wortspielen, bestehen.

196[32] Die Bedrengten, welche mit heissen Thränen zu ihm ihre Zuflucht nahmen, und seine Hülfe mit bebenden Lippen anfleheten, fanden an ihn [*sic*] einen treuen Beschützer.

204[34] M'allez-vous quereller pour un peu d'inconstance?
A tout le genre humain dites-en donc autant.
A le bien prendre, enfin, tout homme est inconstant;
Un peu plus, un peu moins, et j'en sais bien la cause:
C'est que l'esprit humain tient à si peu de chose . . .

205[5] Un homme inégal n'est pas un seul homme, ce sont plusieurs: il se multiplie autant de fois qu'il a de nouveaux goûts et de manières différentes; il est à chaque moment ce qu'il n'était point, et il va être bientôt ce qu'il n'a jamais été: il se succède à lui-même.

213[16] Er hält oft mitten im Reden inne, um nachzudenken, ob man nicht aus seinen Worten etwan eine gefährliche Folge ziehen könnte. Wenn zwo Personen auf der Straße miteinander reden, so glaubet er, sie reden von ihm. Wenn man ihm freundlich begegnet, so glaubet er, man habe ihn zum Besten, oder man wolle ihn betriegen. Thut man gleichgültig, so glaubet er, man suche Händel an ihm. Neulich war er in der Comödie; und da man über den Arlekin lachte, so glaubte er, man lache über ihn, und gieng voll Zorn hinaus.

214[32] Nein! Sie wechselt ab. Wenn sie nicht beten will; so singt sie. Und wenn sie nicht mehr Lust zum Singen hat; so betet sie. Und wenn sie weder beten, noch singen will; so redet sie doch vom Beten und Singen.

215[6] Wer die Tugend in den Mienen und auf den Lippen zu suchen gewohnt ist, der kann der Frau Richardinn ihren Ruhm unmöglich absprechen. Alles ist fromm an ihr; ihre Mienen, ihre Sprache, ihr Gang, ihre Kleidung!

215[17] Gegen acht Uhr steht sie auf. Und so bald sie den Fuß in den Pantoffel setzt; so fängt sie auch an, zu singen. Singend nun kämmt sie zuerst den Mops. Singend versorget sie ihre Katze. Singend füttert sie den Canarienvogel. . . . Und so bald es neune schlägt; so hört sie auf zu singen, wenn es auch mitten in dem Gesätze eines Liedes wäre. . . . So bald es also neune schlägt, so läuft sie, was sie kann, damit sie, ehe es ganz ausschlägt, schon an ihrem Gebettische sitzt. . . . Von neun bis zehn Uhr liest sie erst drey Morgenseegen.

216[38] *Lysimon.* Was ist denn der gute Geschmack?
Hannswurst. Was ich davor angebe. Nichts lustiges, aber lange moralische Abhandlungen . . .

217[38] Ich bin zwar in allen Gattungen der Gelehrsamkeit bewandert; aber besonders in Wünschen bin ich unerschöpflich. Ich empfange mit meinem Gesange die Neugebohrnen; ich besinge die Säuglinge in der Wiege, ich führe den Jüngling zum Altar, und singe der Braut das Hochzeitlied. Meine Muse schleicht sich in die geheimsten Wochenstuben. Ich schlage das Treffen nochmal. Ich weine beym Grabmal der Verstorbenen. Es wird keine Feyerlichkeit begangen, wo ich nicht in das Gewehr trette, und meinen unterthänigen Witz anbiete, die übrige Zeit verwende ich auf Wochenblätter. Ich lobe und tadle, wie man mich bezahlt.

218[16] *Gustav Trolle* . . . nahm jederzeit an dem Glücke und Unglücke seiner Mitbürger vielen Antheil. . . . Seine Feinde nennten [*sic*] ihn nur spottweise den Gratulanten. Kein Namens- oder Geburtstage ward begangen, an welchem er nicht gedruckte Merckmaale seiner Ehrfurcht überreichte. Unaufhörlich ließ er die Häuser seiner Gönner, und Freunde mit Freude und Wonne überschatten. . . . Bey jedem Todesfalle tauchte er seinen Kiel in bittere Salsen und herben Wermuth ein. . . . Die Musen unterhielt er in beständiger Bewegung. . . . Der Name des Bräutigams oder der Braut mochte noch so verwirrt klingen, so wußte er ihn doch so lange herum zu zerren, bis er in demselben einen Gedanken fand, der sich zur Wiege schickte. . . . Er war weder eigennützig noch geizig, und für 16 Ggr. schüttete er sein ganzes Herze aus.

219[4] Wenn zwey mit einander sprechen, spitzt er die Ohren, wie ein Haas, und fragt: was man von ihm gesprochen habe? So gar an fremden Orten, da ihn niemand kennet, horchet er an allen Wänden, und glaubt man rede von ihm. . . . So oft ich nach Haus komme, soll ich erzählen, was ich gesehen, oder von andern gehöret habe. Allein wer weiß immer etwas zu sagen? Da heist es alsdenn: ich hielte es mit seinen Feinden, deren er doch keine hat.

222[6] Jedes Frauenzimmer ist eitel, hoffärtig, geschwätzig, zänkisch und zeitlebens kindisch, es mag so alt werden, als es will. Jedes Frauenzimmer weiß kaum, daß es eine Seele hat, um die es unendlich mehr besorgt sein sollte als um den Körper. Sich ankleiden, auskleiden und wieder anders ankleiden; vor dem Spiegel sitzen, seinen eignen Reiz bewundern; auf ausgekünstelte Mienen sinnen; mit neugierigen Augen müßig an dem Fenster liegen: unsinnige Romane lesen und aufs höchste zum Zeitvertreibe die Nadel zur Hand nehmen: das sind seine Beschäftigungen; das ist sein Leben . . .

222[32] . . . der Mann ist in seinem Amte recht fett geworden. . . . Nun ist er beynahe 30 Jahr im Amte. In den 3 ersten Jahren hat er alle seine Predigten von Wort zu Wort studiret, in den folgenden Jahren aber nur besser auswendig gelernt . . .

222[39] Er kan seine Zeit besser und geruhiger hinbringen. Wann er um 9 Uhr aufgestanden ist, bis 10 Uhr Thee getruncken, bis 11 Uhr sich angezogen, bis 2 Uhr gespeiset und bis 3 Uhr Mittagsruhe gehalten hat . . .

247[34] [Sie] wurde von ihren [*sic*] 16ten Jahre an von vielen Liebhabern verehret, und es ward, sowohl bey Hofe, als in der Stadt von niemand mehr als von ihr geredet, und dieses aus der Ursache, weil man sie vor ein rechtes Ebenbild vollenkommener Schönheit schätzte. . . . Die Haare hatten eine Castanien Farbe, und konten mit ihrer Lange die Füsse bedecken. Die Augen waren groß und Himmelblau. . . . Die holden

Wangen waren mit Milch und Blut aufs sauberste vermischet. Der kleine Mund beschämte den hochsten Purpur, und die fest aneinander stehende Zähne schienen den reinesten *Oriental*ischen Perlen den Vorzug streitig zu machen. . . . Die Geschicklichkeit und Kunst hatten diese natürliche Schätzbarkeiten noch schatzbarer gemacht. Sie sprach so nett und rein Frantzösisch, als wenn sie in Paris gebohren. . . . Sie spielte eine Laute in solcher *Perfection*, die den Zuhörer entzuckte. . . . Ihre Klugheit übertraff bey weiten [*sic*] ihr Alter.

248[24] Der Graf von Rivera zeiget einer jungen Standesperson, wie sie, bey den Erhebungen ihres Glückes, sich mässigen und ihre Begierden einschränken soll. Er kann in einer so verdorbenen Welt vielleicht zum Muster der Unschuld und der Redlichkeit dienen. Man glaubet nicht mehr, daß sich die Tugend . . . an Hof schicke. . . . Die Aufführung des Grafens von Rivera zeiget uns nichts desto weniger, daß sie allethalben zu Hause sey . . .

249[6] Die Natur hatte ihm alle große Eigenschaften gegeben, welche einen Menschen über andere erheben. Er war von einer überaus angenehmen Bildung, von einer etwas mehr als mittelmäßigen Länge, und durchaus schön gewachsen. Aus seinen Augen blitzte so viel Anmut als Ernst. Wer ihn sahe, der fand sich von ihm gerühret; er konnte einem nicht wohl gleichgültig seyn. Man mußte mit ihm die Annehmlichkeiten theilen, wenn er vergnügt war, und man empfand nicht minder eine gewisse Unruhe, wenn man ihn leiden sahe. . . . Er war nicht allein in den Wissenschaften des Staats, sondern auch in der Weltweisheit und schönen Künsten gründlich gelehret. Sein Verstand war zu allem aufgelegt, er besaß so viel Witz, als Einsicht und Überlegung: er hatte dabey das beste Herz, und dessen Neigungen waren um so viel reiner und tugendhafter, weil sie durch eine verborgene Gottesfurcht regieret wurden.

249[35] Ich bin nicht neu, ich habe diese Gemählde weder in eine Reise noch in einen Roman eingekleidet. Es würde mir vielleicht nicht viel Schweiß gekostet haben es zu thun: ich hätte meinen Zuschauer nur dürfen aus Berlin, oder Stettin, oder wo es sonst beliebte, ausfahren lassen; zwey Meilen von der Stadt hätte er etwan das Unglück gehabt ein Rad zu zerbrechen, dies hätte ihn genöthigt beym Pfarrer zu ** ein Nachtquartier zu suchen—und wer sieht nicht hier gleich eine herrliche Gelegenheit zu charakterisiren? dann ging' es weiter, und überall, auf dem Sofa, an der Barriere und auf dem Schlosse, hätte sich ein Kapittelchen über Zucht und Sitten abhandeln lassen.

251[19] Frau Weinard war [ihrem Gatten] die treueste, edelste Gefährtin auf der Lebensreise, sie schenkte ihm so süße Freuden, daß die Erde ihm zum Himmel ward. Ihre Sitten waren rein, ihr Herz edel, sie verstand die große Kunst, sich die Liebe jeder guten Seele zu erwerben: von den Lasterhaften wurde sie gefürchtet, und von denen, welche ihr an Tugend ähnlich waren, werth geachtet. Sie hatte keine Feinde, nur wurde gegen sie der Neid zuweilen rege, und doch mußte sie auch dieser, obgleich mit Unmuth, ein Muster edler Frauen nennen. Ihren Kindern war sie nicht nur solch eine Mutter, welcher die Natur die Mutterliebe als eine rohe Gabe mitgetheilet hatte, sondern was mehr als dieses ist, sie war Erzieherin, und wußte jede Regung ihrer Seelen so zu leiten, daß sie sie immer nur zum edeln Endzweck, nur dahin lenkte, daß sie Gefallen an dem Guten fanden . . .

252[14] . . . einen Buben, der für ihren Werth keinen Sinn hatte, ein träges, bis zur äußersten Faulheit und Fühllosigkeit phlegmatisches Thier, ein Geschöpf ohne Seele,—wofern nicht die bäurischste Ungezogenheit seine Seele war,—ein Ungeheuer, das den Morgen beym Branntwein, den Nachmittag beym Wein, den Abend beym Spiel, und die Nacht in schändlichen Häusern, folglich sein ganzes Leben in der nichtswürdigsten Unthätigkeit zubrachte . . .

253[28] [Er] war . . . nichts als ein Kaufmann. . . . Er hatte nie die Freuden der Jugend genossen. . . . Seine einzige Wollust war, Geschäfte machen, und Geld zählen. . . . Uebrigens gieng bey ihm alles nach der Uhr.

254[6] Dieser iunge Mann, ongefer fünf und zwanzig Jahre alt, ward in der ganzen Gegend umher als ein ser gütiger, menschenfreundlicher, woltätiger Mann bekannt. Seine Nachbarn liebten ihn seines friedlichen, verträglichen Karakters wegen, und die Armen segneten ihn für seine reiche Woltaten. . . . Herr Liebreich, so gütig er gegen wahre Bedürftige sich bezeugte, und die leidende Tugend, so viel es seine Kräfte zuliesen, unterstüzte; so streng war er gegen Ausschweiflinge . . .

254[17] Warum sollte es nicht erlaubt seyn, hier die Exposition des Charakters vorzutragen, um den sich alle Ereignisse winden, oder dessen Individualität einen großen Theil dieser Ereignisse diejenige Wendung gab, warum man sie eigentlich merkwürdig nennen könnte?

254[24] Es ist auch nicht nöthig, daß man den Lesern die Karaktere derselben lange vorenthalte, oder, daß sie gar die Mühe auf sich nehmen sollten, dieselben erst während des Lesens ausm Buche selbst zu abstrahiren.

254[37] Eine Buhlerin ist . . . das verachtungswürdigste Geschöpf aus der ganzen Natur. . . . Sie ist gerade die dem allgemeinen Zweck entgegen arbeitendste Person. Anstatt daß alles zur Vollkommenheit des Ganzen beyträgt, so sucht sie alle die ihr in den Wurf kommen, unvollkommen zu machen, sie reitzt und stürzt und läßt nagende Reue in so vielen Herzen zurück, die hernach ihr ganzes Leben verbittert . . .

255[21] Ein ordentlicher, arbeitsamer, gesitteter Mann, wie geboren zum Kaufmann. Voll Muts, etwas zu unternehmen, aber nie ohne Bedacht; in seinem Äußerlichen so anständig, so einfach: von Samt und Stickereien kein Freund, und was ich an ihm ganz vorzüglich schätze—kein Spieler. . . . Wenn er ja einmal spielt, so ist es nicht in der Karte, sondern mit seinen Kindern.

255[27] . . . es wird mir von Tage zu Tage immer ärgerlicher, daß ich [einen Sohn habe,] der für seinen Putz, sein Vergnügen, der in L'Hombre und Whist ein Dukätchen nach dem andern, oft auch wohl dutzendweise, vertändelt; der nur noch gestern wieder bis in die sinkende Nacht gespielt hat, und der, wenn er eine großmüthige Handlung thun sollte, vielleicht keines Thalers Herr wäre;—einen Menschen, der ewig ledig bleibt, weil keine Partie ihm reich genug ist, und der doch immer übrig hat, zu fahren, zu reiten, den Kavalier zu machen, Samt und Stickereien zu tragen.

257[5] Unter einem hohen Menschen mein' ich nicht den geraden ehrlichen festen Mann . . . noch mein' ich die feine Seele . . . noch den Mann von Ehre, dessen Wort ein Fels ist . . . und endlich weder den kalten von Grundsätzen gelenkten Tugendhaften, noch den Gefühlvollen . . . auch den bloßen *großen* Menschen mein' ich nicht . . .

Sondern den mein' ich, der zum größern oder geringern Grade aller dieser Vorzüge noch etwas setzt, was die Erde so selten hat—die Erhebung über die Erde, das Gefühl der Geringfügigkeit alles irdischen Thuns und der Unförmlichkeit zwischen unserem Herzen und unserem Orte, das über das verwirrende Gebüsch und den ekelhaften Köder unsers Fußbodens aufgerichtete Angesicht, den Wunsch des Todes und den Blick über die Wolken.

257[25] Gewisse Menschen nenn' ich *hohe* oder Festtagmenschen, und in meiner Geschichte gehören Ottomar, Gustav, der Genius, der Doktor darunter, weiter niemand.

258[3] Diese Sparsamkeit legierte der unvollkommne Charakter noch mit einigem Betrug. Er interpolierte die Güter, die er gut bekam, und schrieb zurück, er habe sie schlecht bekommen . . . und er könnte sie nur um den halben Preis gebrauchen. Ein Drittel des Preises spielt' er so dem Kaufmann geschickt genug aus der entfernten Tasche. Waren, Fässer, Säcke, die in seinem Hause nur ein Absteig-Quartier hatten und weiter reisen mußten, gaben ihm den Transito-Zoll durch ein kleines Loch heraus, das er in sie hineinmachte, um das Wenige daraus sich zu entrichten, was dem Fuhrmann aufgebürdet werden konnte, wenns fehlte.—Er legte ein Münzkabinet oder Hospital für arme invalide amputierte Goldstücke an. Andern verrufenen Münzen gab er den ehrlichen Namen, den sie verloren, wieder und zwang seine Faktore, sie als legitimiert und rehabilitiert anzunehmen.

261[11] . . . ich will dirs nicht verstecken, Theoda—da die Sache aus reiner Wissenschaftliebe geschah . . . daß ich an deiner seel. Mutter während ihrer guten Hoffnung eben nicht sehr darauf dachte, aufrechte Tanzbären, Affen oder kleine Schrecken und meine Kabinets Preziosen fern von ihr zu halten, weil sie doch im schlimmsten Falle blos mit einem monströsen Ehesegen mein Kabinet um ein Stück bereichert hätte; aber *leider*, hätt' ich beinah' gesagt, aber gottlob sie bescheerte mir dich . . .

279[31] Thyeste est né simple et naïf: il aime la pure vertu, mais il ne prend pas pour modèle la vertu d'un autre . . . Lorsqu'il y a quelque loi de la morale qui ne s'accorde pas avec son sentiment, il la laisse à part et n'y pense point. S'il rencontre, la nuit, une de ces femmes qui épient les jeunes gens, Thyeste souffre qu'elle l'entretienne et marche quelque temps à côté d'elle; et, comme elle se plaint de la nécessité qui détruit toutes les vertus . . . il lui dit qu'après tout, la pauvreté n'est point un vice, quand on sait vivre sans nuire à personne; et, après l'avoir exhortée à une vie meilleure, ne se trouvant point d'argent parce qu'il est jeune, il lui donne sa montre qui n'est plus à la mode, et qui est un présent de sa mère; ses camarades se moquent de lui, et tournent en ridicule sa générosité ainsi placée; mais il leur répond : «Mes amis, vous riez de trop peu de chose. Je plains ces pauvres femmes d'être obligées de faire un tel métier pour vivre. Le monde est rempli de misères qui serrent le cœur; si on ne faisait de bien qu'à ceux qui le méritent, on n'en trouverait guère d'occasions.»

280[15] Ja, hören wir ihn einandermal reden, Amynt ist wirklich ein dienstfertiger, aufrichtiger Mann; von dieser Seite kenne ich ihn. Wenn er nicht der witzigste Mann ist, so ist Rechtschaffenheit doch immer mehr, als Witz; und wenn er seinem Amte, wie man sagt, nicht gewachsen ist, so ist das doch nicht der Fehler seines Herzens.

280[19] Er geht in den Tempel, wenn andere in die Kirche gehen, hat Aurorens Zähren auf den Schuhen, wandelt in der Nacht des Hains, entflieht der Städte Geräusch. . . . Wenn er dich wieder sieht, so wallt sein Herz dir entgegen . . . denn drey Sommer sind es, da sein Auge dich nicht sahe und du wandeltest an fremden Ufern.

284[35] Ce temperament n'est autre chose qu'un meslange des quatre qualitez premieres: lesquelles ne se trouvans en un mesme subject toutes en mesme quantité, poidz & mesure, l'on qualifie le temperament du nom de celle qui domine & surpasse les autres en force.

285[38] Les inclinations naturelles s'aident et fortifient par institution; mais elles ne se changes guiere. . . . On n'extirpe pas ces qualitez originelles, on les couvre, on les cache.

292[29] Wenn die Physiognomik das wird, was Lavater von ihr erwartet, so wird man die Kinder aufhängen, ehe sie Taten getan haben, die den Galgen verdienen. . . . Ein physiognomisches Auto da Fe.

293[22] Seine unverbesserliche Gestalt saget uns stillschweigend, daß ein fürtrefflicher Geist diesen schönen Cörper bewohne.

293[36] Diese viereckige Stirne verspricht ein großes Gedächtniß und viel gesunden Menschenverstand; allein die senkrechte Wölbung derselben bezeichnet eine gewisse Unbiegsamkeit des Charakters, die leicht in Halsstarrigkeit ausartet. Die etwas hervortretende Unterlippe und das flache Kinn sind Zeichen ruhiger und aufrichtiger Gutherzigkeit.

Notes

CHAPTER 1 (i)

1. Carl Hoffman, 'Das Zweckproblem von Theophrasts Charakteren', Diss. (Breslau), 1920, takes this view.
2. G. S. Gordon, 'Theophrastus and his Imitators', in *English Literature and the Classics*, Oxford, 1912, p. 50; R. C. Jebb in his edition of the *Characters*, p. 17 in the revised edition of J. E. Sandys, 1909.
3. Benjamin Boyce, *The Theophrastan Character in England to 1642*, new impression, London, 1967, p. 11.
4. R. G. Ussher (ed.), *The Characters of Theophrastus*, London, 1960, Introduction, pp. 5 f. and 11. For Vellacott, see his translation of Theophrastus for the Penquin Classics, Introduction, p. 9. Quotations are from this edition.
5. Ussher, p. 3.
6. Other possible forerunners are suggested by Ussher, p. 27, and by various other critics and editors. But nothing has been put forward that would seriously detract from Theophrastus's originality.
7. *The Classical Heritage and its Beneficiaries*, CUP, 1950, p. 38.
8. Boyce, p. 23; Ussher, p. 10.
9. *Institutio Oratoria*, 1, ix, 3 and 6, ii, 17.
10. Boyce's translation: op. cit., p. 22.
11. J. J. Murphy, *Rhetoric in the Middle Ages*, University of California Press, 1974, p. 18.
12. See Boyce, p. 29 and Ussher, p. 10n. For Casaubon, see pp. 89 f. in the 1617 edition.
13. Page 187 in the edition by G. H. Mair, OUP, 1909.
14. See Foster Watson, *The English Grammar Schools to 1660*, CUP, 1908, p. 440.
15. The notion that the description of actual persons could and should be arranged according to a set scheme runs parallel with these depictions of imaginary types. Cicero laid down eleven headings: name, manner of life, fortune, passions, habit of speech, etc. (*De inventione*, i. 24) The pattern recurs, with variations, in many later writers and is still current in mid sixteenth-century England. But such formalized schemes did not play a great part in the development of the 'character' proper.
16. John Bodenham and Nicholas Ling, *Politeuphuia* (1597); Francis Meres, *Palladis Tamia* (1598).
17. Bodenham, fo. xxxv[v].
18. In his Introduction to the Scholars' Facsimile edition of Meres's *Palladis*, p. iii.
19. See chapter 7(i). For a more hedonistic version of the happy life, see Martial, *Epigrams*, x. 47. A detailed account of the notion of the Happy Man from classical times to the mid eighteenth century is given by Røstvig: see General Bibliography.
20. See Boyce, op. cit., p. 56. J. F. Goodridge, in the Introduction to his edition of *Piers the Ploughman* in Penguin Classics, has an interesting section on the allegorical *dramatis personae* (pp. 15–17).
21. Skelton, *Complete Poems*, ed. Henderson, London and Toronto, 1931, pp. 50 f.
22. Quoted from the English translation by Barnabe Googe, edited by R. Tuve (Scholars' Facsimiles, New York, 1947, p. 21).
23. *Works*, edited by R. B. McKerrow (reprint: Oxford, 1958), i. 169.

24. Wye Saltonstall, *Picturae Loquentes*, 1631: Luthren Reprints, No. 1, Oxford, 1946, p. 36.
25. Thomas Tymme, *A Plaine Discoverie of ten English Lepers* (1592), presents a similar case, as does a later work: *The Isle of Man* . . . , London, 1627, by R[ichard] B[ernard]. No value-judgement is intended, of course.
26. H. Morley, *Character Writings of the Seventeenth Century*, London, 1891, p. 17; Ussher, in his Introduction to Theophrastus, p. 30; Boyce, op. cit., p. 61.
27. Boyce, pp. 35 f.; H. R. Patch, 'Characters in Medieval Literature' in *Modern Language Notes*, xl (1925), p. 3; Morley, p. 17.
28. The Virtuous Wife (Proverbs 31) provided the basis for many a 'character' of the Good Wife or the Ideal Woman.
29. See Ruth Mohl, *The Three Estates in Medieval and Renaissance Literature,* New York, 1933 (reprint, 1962). For primary sources consulted, see Bibliography, section v.
30. Rich lifts some of his conceits (e.g. on the Drunkard) bodily out of the commonplace books. As a contrast in method, Brant's chapter 26 ('Von unnutzem Wunschen') is in no way the picture of one representative fool, but a shapeless mass of moralizing reflection and learned allusions.
31. Boyce (op. cit., pp. 229 f.) speculates on the sources from which Breton might have derived his notion of the Book of Estates, but, given the plenitude of models, the question is not important. Thomas Fuller (1642) also uses the framework offered by the literature of Estates to give a general plan to his moral character-book.
32. Cf. Mohl, op. cit., pp. 6 f.
33. Op. cit., pp. 69 and 75.
34. Thomas Lodge, *The Complete Works* (Hunterian Club), first published 1875–87: reprint, 1966, iv. 13, 23.
35. Edition: *EETS*, edited by Furnivall, London, 1876, pp. 39, 66, and 87. For the fish Polipus, see Meres, fo. 319[v]. The motif of the carrion crow is applied to the Flatterer in many commonplace books.

CHAPTER 1 (ii)

1. The Penitent and the Happy Man are the later additions. See Bibliography for details.
2. Joseph Hall, *Works*, 12 volumes, Oxford, 1837–9, vi. 88 f. All quotations are from this edition.
3. What follows is largely based on the 'characters' of the Wise Man and the Happy Man.
4. G. Müller-Schwefe, 'Joseph Hall's *Characters of Vertues and Vices*', in *Texas Studies in Literature and Language*, xiv (1972), p. 245.
5. See Bibliography, section vii.
6. See Walker, *English Essay*, p. 46; Boyce, op. cit., pp. 143 f. Examples could be multiplied. See also chapter 8(i).
7. Page 169 in Overbury's *Miscellaneous Works*, London, 1890. All quotations are from this edition. I am also indebted to W. J. Paylor's Introduction and Notes to his edition, Oxford, 1936.
8. Boyce singles out this 'character' for censure, as consisting of witty 'embroidery' (p. 143).
9. There are many editions of Earle. I quote from that in the Temple Classics, London, 1899.

10. Page 85. The plural forms here may seem puzzling, in view of the accepted notion of a 'character' as the depiction of an imaginary but typical individual. For a discussion of this point, see below, chapter 11.
11. For an example from Hall, who was the first to practise this device, see above, p. 23.

CHAPTER 1 (iii)

1. See Boyce, op. cit., pp. 177 f.
2. William Fennor, *The Counter's Commonwealth* . . . , 1617, reprinted in *The Elizabethan Underworld*, edited by A.V. Judges, London, 1930, p. 434.
3. The 'characters' of a Tavern and of a Town-Gallant (both anonymous and both appearing in London in 1675) are from Earle. Considerable parts of the *Character of a Turbulent, Pragmatical Jesuit* (London, 1678) are copied out of Overbury. Examples could be multiplied.
4. Brathwaite, *Whimzies*, edited by Halliwell, London, 1859, pp. viii and xi.
5. *An Anatomical Lecture of Man* . . . , London, 1664, pp. 39–41.
6. For an example in which the witty manner occasionally leads to total incomprehensibility, see Samuel Austin, *Naps upon Parnassus*, 1658.
7. Saltonstall, *Picturae Loquentes*, 1631, No. 31. See also chapter 8 (i).
8. Lenton, *Characterismi* . . . , 1631, No. 15.
9. See G. R. Owst, *Literature and Pulpit in Medieval England*, CUP, 1933, pp. 87 and 278 f.
10. Adams, *Works* (3 volumes), Edinburgh, 1861-2, i. 283.
11. A similar example occurs in the fourth of Robert Sanderson's *35 Sermons*, 7th edition, London, 1681: see pp. 187 ff. See also Bibliography, section xv.
12. In *Characters and Elegies*, London, 1646, No. 6.
13. In *A Dialogue*, London, 1640 and John Geree's *Character of an Old English Puritane*, London, 1646.
14. *The Polemic Character 1640–61*, University of Nebraska Press, 1955.
15. *The Character of a Quaker*, London, 1671, pp. 1, 4, and 6.

CHAPTER 2

1. *Le Théophraste Moderne, ou nouveaux Caracteres sur les Mœurs*, The Hague, 1700, p. 23.
2. *Caracteres de Vertus et de Vices* . . . , Paris, 1610. Further editions in 1619 and 1634.
3. See Pierre Richard, *La Bruyère et ses 'Caractères'*, Paris, 1965, p. 49.
4. See, for instance, the Fearful Man: op. cit., p. 90.
5. Other psychological and moral treatises of the seventeenth century, for instance Gomberville's *La Doctrine des Mœurs* of 1681, have been cited from time to time by critics over-eager to discover 'predecessors' of La Bruyère.
6. For the *Peintures Morales*, I have used the second edition (1645) for volume i and the first (1643) for volume ii. See too H. Chévot, *Étude sur la Vie et les Œuvres du P. le Moyne*, Paris, 1887.
7. Victor Cousin (*La Société française au xviie siècle* . . . , Paris, 1858) gives a key to *Cyrus*, dating from 1657: see Appendix to volume i. See too 'Claude Aragonnès' (Marguerite Teillard-Chambon), *Madeleine de Scudéry, Reine du Tendre*, Paris, 1934, chapter vi and Georges Mondrédieu, *Madeleine de Scudéry et son salon*, Paris, 1946, chapters ii (especially p. 48) and v.
8. Edition used is that by E. de Barthélemy, Paris, 1860.

9. Only one piece in the *Galerie* is quite unambiguously of an imaginary person (Nestor: ed. cit., pp. 497-500).
10. See, for example, the opening of the anonymous portrait of the Countess de la Marck, p. 134.
11. *Les Précieuses ridicules*, scene 9; Segrais, 'Avant-propos'.
12. See La Rochefoucauld, *Œuvres Complètes*, Paris, 1964, pp. 7-9.
13. For a use of the word *portrait* to signify an *un*flattering description, see Abbé Bellegarde, *Les Reflexions sur la Ridicule* . . . , Paris, 1696, p. 141. For satires on the idealized portrait in the early seventeenth-century novel, see Charles Sorel, *Francion* (1623) and Scarron, *Roman Comique* (1651). See too Antoine Bodeau, Sieur de Somaise, *Le Dictionnaire des Précieuses*, 1659, part ii, for a parody of the *salon* portraits.
14. For a summary of this process, see Jean Stewart's Introduction to her edition in the Penguin Classics (pp. 12 f.). Modern printings of La Bruyère are based on the ninth edition of 1696, which contained the same material as the eighth, but with some revision and correction.
15. For speculation as to the exact stage at which La Bruyère decided to do this and the considerations that led him to it, see Gustave Michaut, *La Bruyère*, Paris, 1936, chapter iv.
16. See his Preface to his speech on being admitted as member of the French Academy, 15 June 1693. For a discussion of the keys, see P. Morillot, *La Bruyère*, Paris, 1904, pp. 124-9 and A. Stegmann, *Les Caractères de La Bruyère*, Paris, 1972, pp. 19-22. Keys appeared in English translations from 1699 on.
17. See ii. 32 and xii. 56.
18. Stegmann, op. cit., p. 22.
19. See i. 17, 56, and 57.
20. La Bruyère, iv. 32 and viii. 39; La Rochfoucauld, ed. cit., pp. 412 and 407. See too Odette de Mourgues, *Two French Moralists*, CUP, 1978, p. 98.
21. See, for example, ii. 38 and 40; viii. 10 and 19; x. 29.
22. See ix. 51; xi. 81 and 133; xvi. 31.
23. For a brief discussion of this point, see de Mourgues, op. cit., pp. 96-8.
24. *Memoires pour l'Histoire des Sciences et des beaux Arts*, Trevoux, March–April 1701, pp. 76 f. G. Servois, in his edition of La Bruyère (Paris, 1922, iv. 85 ff.), lists over forty items by 1701.
25. In one case, the title makes the combination quite explicit: *Suite des Caracteres de Theophraste et des Pensées de Mr. Pascal*, Paris, 1697. Further editions in 1710 and 1720: commonly attributed to P. J. Brillon. Some imitations of La Bruyère contain no 'characters' at all and are hence not considered here.
26. See, for example: Mme de Pringy, *Les Differens Caracteres des Femmes du Siecle*, Lyons, 1695 (second edition, Paris, 1699); Mme de Puisieux, *Les Caracteres*, first published in 1747.
27. Where this is not the case, Brillon tends to say so: see pp. 38 and 51.
28. The Abbé Bellegard's *Reflections sur la Ridicule* is equally didactic, although the 'characters' are somewhat more vividly written.
29. Edition used: *Œuvres*, edited by Pierre Varillon, Paris, 1929, i. 142-244. For a tribute from Voltaire, who encouraged Vauvenargues as a writer, see Voltaire to Marmontel, 30/4/1749, in *Œuvres Complètes*, Paris, 1877-85, xxxvii. 15.
30. Theophrastus, 'The Toady or Flatterer'; Vauvenargues, ed. cit., p. 151. See too 'Midas ou le Sot qui est glorieux', pp. 220 f.
31. For a biography, see May Wallas, *Luc de Clapiers, Marquis de Vauvenargues*, CUP, 1928, pp. 3-150. See especially pp. 68-70.
32. Pages 148 f. 195 f., and 207-10. See too Wallas, pp. 24 and 103.
33. For Thyeste, see pp. 166 f.; for Titus, pp. 181 f.

34. In the eighteenth century, character-writing spread to the journals published in France and Holland in imitation of *The Spectator*. In general, it is true to say that these 'characters' are formally indebted to Addison, stylistically to La Bruyère. A selection of titles is given in the Bibliography, section viii.
35. Even the mention of Theophrastus's name does not guarantee much. Although Marivaux styled himself 'the modern Theophrastus', his pieces in the *Mercure* (1717–20) and other journals show few links with character-writing. Similarly, in Brillon's *Théophraste Moderne* (1700), 'characters' are greatly outweighed by reflections.
36. See David Nichol Smith's anthology, *Characters from the Histories and Memoirs of the Seventeenth Century*, Oxford, 1918.
37. For the 'character', of course, chiefly Theophrastus. For the portrait: Thucydides, Plutarch, Livy, Tacitus, and others. For a discussion of this, see Nichol Smith's Introduction, xix ff.
38. See Vauvenargues' Preface to his *Essai*, ed. cit., p. 146.
39. Cf. La Bruyère, v. 82 and Vauvenargues, ed. cit., pp. 216 f.

CHAPTER 3

1. There were reprints of Earle in 1733 and 1740. For the plagiarism, see James Puckle, *The Club* (1711), which contains many borrowings from Hall and Earle. The anonymous *Wit's Cabinet* (London, *c.* 1700) reprints Breton's Drunkard without acknowledgement.
2. See the 'characters' of the Cuckold (1700), the Monster (1703), the Sneaker (1705), and the Addresser (1710). Details in Bibliography.
3. *The Wooden World dissected* (1707) and *The Modern World Disrob'd* (1708). Ward's periodical *The London Spy* (1698–1700) is somewhat different; it contains a mixture of reflections, anecdotes, descriptive passages, and 'characters' which makes it in some degree an anticipation of the more famous journals of later decades. But the style of character-writing is still a watered-down form of the late seventeenth-century witty manner.
4. For example, the 'characters' of a Beau (pp. 51–7) and a Country Squire (pp. 58–60) are taken from *An Essay in Defence of the Female Sex* (1696). For 'characters' borrowed from La Bruyère, compare Boyer, pp. 47 and 74, with La Bruyère, iii. 8 and vi. 60.
5. *The Spectator*, No. 77. See too *The Tatler* (1709), No. 9; *The Censor* (1717), No. 49; *The Mirror* (1779), No. 31; and *The Looker-on* (1793), No. 55.
6. *The Adventurer* (1753), No. 49.
7. There were translations of Theophrastus by Eustace Budgell in 1699 (reprinted 1714) and by Gally. For tributes to the Greek, see *The Guardian* (1713), No. 168; *The Lover* (1714), No. 39; *The Mirror* (1779), No. 31; and *The Observer* (1785), No. 107. Theophrastus is placed second to La Bruyère by Warton in *The Adventurer* (1754), No. 133 and by Goldsmith in his review of Butler's *Characters* (Goldsmith, *Collected Works*, edited by A. Friedman, OUP, 1966, i. 209).
8. For more on the benefits derived from enclosing the 'character' in an essay-framework, see p. 275.
9. For the strictures on 'false wit', etc., see *The Spectator*, Nos. 35, 58–63, and 285. For Gally, see his essay on 'Characteristick Writings', which precedes his translation of Theophrastus, London, 1725, p. 89.
10. For similar examples of the straightforward use of a single 'character' within the essay, see *The Guardian* (1713), No. 161 and *The Rambler* (1751), No. 103. Examples could, of course, be multiplied.
11. *The Rambler*, No. 74. See too *The Idler* (1758–60), No. 19.

12. *The World* (1754), No. 95. For other examples of the contrasting pair of 'characters', see *The Tatler*, Nos. 4 and 42; *The Spectator*, No. 33; *The Censor*, No. 17; *The Free-Thinker* (1718–19), No. 14; *The Intelligencer* (1729), No. 7; and *The Adventurer*, No. 16.
13. See *The Adventurer*, No. 129 and *The Idler*, Nos. 78 and 83.
14. See too the diaries of a well-to-do Idler (*The Spectator*, No. 317) and of a Society Lady (ibid., No. 323). The idea of conveying character by describing a typical day in the subject's life had entered character-writing in the seventeenth century: see, for instance, the *Character of a Town-Gallant* (1680). But the form was not to become popular until the eighteenth century.
15. *Lives of the English Poets*, edited by G. B. Hill, OUP, 1905, ii. 92 f.
16. *The Intelligencer*, No. 7 and *The Rambler*, No. 142.
17. See too *The Connoisseur* (1755), No. 76 and *The Lounger* (1786), No. 88.
18. One must exclude the polemical 'characters' of the mid and late seventeenth century, which were inspired by *dis*agreement.
19. For the 'character' of a militant Feminist, see G. A. Stevens, *A Lecture on Heads*, 1765 (pp. 33 f. in the 1812 edition).
20. For a 'character' of the Devotee, see *The Spectator*, No. 354.
21. See too *The Spectator*, Nos. 15 and 302.
22. *The Visions of Sir Heister Ryley*, London, n.d. [1710], No. 21.
23. For a treatise containing illustrative 'characters' in the manner of the day, see David Fordyce, *Dialogues concerning Education*, 1745.
24. Swift, *The Prose Works*, edited by W. E. H. Lecky, London, 1898, iv. 145.
25. For a more sustained single 'character' used to present one part of the preacher's argument, see John Wesley's 'The Almost Christian' of 1741, in *Sermons upon several Occasions*, 1st series, London, 1944, pp. 11 ff.
26. For further examples of character described through abstract moral qualities in the sermon, see Joseph Roper's *Character of the Liberal Man* (1734) and Samuel Walker's Careless Sinner in *The Christian* . . . , London, 1756, pp. 108 f.
27. Robert South, *Sermons*, 11 volumes, London, 1715–44, v. 511 and vi. 100.
28. William Law, *Works*, 9 volumes, Brockenhurst, 1892–3, iii. 138 f.
29. William Law, *A Serious Call* . . . , in *Works*, ed. cit. iv. 109.
30. By contrast, John Wesley's famous 'character' of a Methodist (see the *Works of J. W.*, 1872, photorepr. Michigan, n.d. xi. 366 ff.) is written in an abstract vein throughout.
31. *A Serious Call* . . . , in *Works*, ed. cit. iv. 109.
32. Examples are *The Character of a Covetous Citizen* . . . , London, 1702; Sir Charles Sedley, 'The Happy Pair', in *The Miscellaneous Works*, London, 1702, pp. 153 ff.
33. Pope's 'characters' have been studied in detail by Benjamin Boyce: *The Character-Sketches in Pope's Poems*, Durham, NC, 1962.
34. See Horace, *Satires*, i. 9. Pope is tormented by a host of bores and dullards, Horace by only one, but the basic similarities are clear.
35. *Epistle to Sir Richard Temple, Lord Cobham* (1733), iii. 1–5. See too Boyce, *Character-Sketches in Pope's Poems*, chapter vi.
36. See Pope, *Works*, edited by Elwin and Courthope, London, 1881, iii. 93.
37. *Moral Essays*, Epistle ii, 157–80: *Works*, ed. cit. iii. 107 f.
38. See 'The Man of Pleasure', first published in the *Scarborough Miscellany*, 1732. I have used the second edition, 1734.
39. See volume ii (1732), p. 1074; xxx (1760), 536; xxxiv (1764), 492.
40. There are still a fair number of 'characters', some of them very good, in *The Mirror* (1779–80) and *The Lounger* (1785–7), but few in, for instance, *The Observer* (1785) and *The Ranger* (1794–5).

CHAPTER 4

1. No. 3. The author is probably J. J. Spreng, clergyman and Professor of German in Basle.
2. *Der Zuschauer, Aus dem Englischen übersetzt*, 9 parts, Leipzig, 1739–51. The translators included J. C. Gottsched.
3. Volume i, No. 1. See too T. Vetter, *Der Spectator als Quelle der 'Discurse der Maler'*, Frauenfeld, 1887.
4. For a reference to the 'immortal Addison', see *Meine Einsamkeiten*, 1771–2, No. 1; for a reference to Steele as 'our ancestor', see *Der Hypochonder*, 1767, No. 1; J. G. Altmann, in the *Bernisches Freytags-Blätlein* (1722–4) and elsewhere, consistently names Steele when talking of *The Spectator.*
5. In this chapter, 'German' is used as shorthand for 'written in German', except where specific distinctions are made between German and Swiss papers.
6. For the best general account of the values expressed in the moral weeklies, see Wolfgang Martens, *Die Botschaft der Tugend*, Stuttgart, 1968.
7. Volume i, No. 2; vol. ii, No. 2.
8. Ian Watt (*The Rise of the Novel*, London, 1974, p. 52) notes that the English periodicals were 'for the middle-class way of life but . . . not exactly of it'. As far as the German weeklies are concerned, Pamela Curry adds a necessary caution: for 'middle-class' one should read 'upper middle-class' (see 'Moral Weeklies and the Reading Public in Germany, 1711–1750', in *Oxford German Studies*, iii (1968), 69–86).
9. Examples are *Der alte Deutsche* (1730), *Der Bewunderer* and *Der Weltbürger* (both 1742), the short-lived *Der Hamburger* (1748), Rabener's *Hofmeister* (1751–3), *Der Freund* (1754–5) and, in Switzerland, *Das Sintemal* (1759).
10. See, for instance, *Der Freymäurer*, 1738, No. 13; *Der Druide*, 1748–50, Nos. 44 and 100; *Der Mensch*, 1751–6, No. 415. Gottsched, who edited *Die vernünftigen Tadlerinnen* (1726) and *Der Biedermann* (1727–9), praises Theophrastus and La Bruyère in his *Kritische Dichtkunst* (1730): see Part 2, i. 7, §11.
11. For a passage which clearly resembles Theophrastus in method, see below, p. 89. But this is a rare example.
12. For the forms 'der Caractere' and 'der caractére', see the *Discourse der Mahlern* and *Der Patriot* (1724–6). O. A. Müller ('La Bruyère in Deutschland', Diss., Heidelberg, 1923) somewhat exaggerates the French writer's influence. The only full-length imitation of La Bruyère's work is, as far as I know, the anonymous *Schilderungen der heutigen Sitten* of 1763, containing 14 chapters which combine reflections and 'characters' exactly as La Bruyère had done. But this came much too late to be a formative influence on the character-writing in the moral weeklies. For an individual 'character' which clearly shows La Bruyére's influence, see the Society Beauty in No. 22 of F. J. Riedel's *Einsiedler* (1774). 'Characters' in J. G. Lindner's *Daphne* (1750), Lamprecht's *Weltbürger* (1742), and Naumann's *Vernünftler* (1754) are also indebted to La Bruyère in some particulars.
13. Hall was translated into German as early as 1652: *Pentagone Histoirique . . . : Diesem sind angefüget H. Joseph Halls Kennzeichen der Tugenden und Laster gedolmetscht Durch ein Mitglied der hochlöblichen Fruchtbringenden Gesellschafft*, Frankfurt-on-Main, 1652. 'Characters' from the *Microcosmography* are translated in *Der Eidsgenoß* (1749) and *Sintemal* (1759). But I know of no way in which Hall or Earle influenced German or Swiss character-writing.
14. *Der Freydenker*, 1741–3, No. 30. See too *Der Druide*, Nos. 11, 20, and 43. Examples could be multiplied.
15. See too *Der Unsichtbare*, 1770, No. 9 and the 'characters' of two Landowners in Gellert's *Moralische Charaktere*, chapter 1: in *Sämmtliche Schriften*, 10 volumes, Leipzig, 1769–74, reprinted Hildesheim, 1968, vii. 613–18.

16. See too *Der Freund*, 1754–5, Nos. 11, 23, and 35; *Der Mann*, 1756–8, Nos. 13 and 37; *Die Unsichtbare*, 1770, Nos. 20 and 21; *Der Greis*, 1772–6, No. 43.
17. For the fictitious letter, see *Die vernünftigen Tadlerinnen*, No. 42; for the self-portrait, see *Für Litteratur und Herz*, 1775, No. 33. For the diary-form, see *Der Pilgrim*, 1743–4, No. 97 and *Der Redliche*, 1751, part ii, No. 6, among others.
18. See, for example, *Das Reich der Natur und der Sitten*, No. 263. 'Separatistus' (*Der Brachmann*, No. 25) is Sombrius under a new name.
19. Op. cit., p. 39.
20. For a bitter parody of a Gallicized German, see *Der Eidsgenoß*, No. 18; for an example of stilted German 'corrected' and rewritten in a plain style, see *Der Weltbürger*, 1742, No. 43.
21. *Der Schutzgeist*, 1746–7, No. 6. For other examples of an abstract style, see *Das Reich der Natur und der Sitten*, 1757–62, No. 30 and *Der Freygeist*, 1745, No. 7.
22. See *Der Brachmann*, No. 1, for the claim that the moral weekly complements what is said from the pulpit.
23. For a 'synthetic' composition, in which trait has been added to trait in order to make a didactic point, see the 'character' of Polysophus (*Die Freunde*, 1753, No. 3). For cases in which the 'character' has become submerged under moralizing reflections, see *Die Macht der Vorurtheile*, 1765–9, vol. i, Nos. 4 and 12.
24. *Der Patriot*, No. 58. Such regulations exist in the English periodicals, but they are neither so common nor so fussily hortatory.
25. This is very marked in *Der Weltbürger* and *Der Patriot in Bayern* (1769).
26. In Loen's *Kleine Schriften*, Frankfurt and Leipzig, vol. i (1750).
27. See Martens, op. cit., p. 126.
28. Gellert, ed. cit., vols. vi and vii. First published in 1770.
29. 11th *Vorlesung*, ed. cit. vi. 266.
30. Ed. cit. vi. 251 f. and 254.
31. For a selection from these imitations, see Bibliography, section xi.
32. *Portraits*, 1779–81, Preface to volume ii.
33. There is a note to this effect on the copy in the City Archive in Hamburg. For more on ironic techniques in the moral weeklies, see Martens, op. cit., pp. 66–9. Censorship of these journals does not seem to have been very widespread, but where it did operate, it seems to have been directed against the sharper forms of satire, especially where it was known or suspected that the satire was aimed at particular individuals (see Martens, pp. 139–41). For a brief but amusing account of censorship in Switzerland, see C. L. Lang, *Die Zeitschriften der deutschen Schweiz . . .* , Leipzig, 1939, pp. 5 f.
34. An exception would be Addison's *The Spectator* paper (No. 323), where Clarinda, after giving an extract from her diary, is led to wonder whether she is not wasting her life. But the didactic point is made much more lightly than in the German paper.
35. Quoted from Rabener's *Sämmtliche Schriften*, Leipzig, 1777, ii. 58. For an exactly similar conceit used to bind together a group of 'characters', see *Der Glückselige*, No. 338.
36. For Hagedorn, see 'Der Schwätzer, nach dem Horaz' (*Satires*, i. 9), in *Poetische Werke*, Hamburg, 1764, i. 61–7. For Gellert, see 'Der baronisirte Bürger', ed. cit. i. 99 f.
37. J. F. Löwen, *Poetische Werke*, Hamburg and Leipzig, 1760, pp. 318 f. See too the verse-character of a Hypocrite in *Der Eidsgenoß*, 1749, No. 9.
38. Reprinted in *Deutsche National-Litteratur*, xli, part ii, 76–80. For clear echoes of the *Essay on Man*, see Haller's 'Gedanken über Vernunft, Aberglauben und Unglauben' of 1729.

39. In *Sämtliche Werke*, 3rd edition, Berlin, 1771, p. 112.
40. The idealized 'character' of an Enlightened Nobleman is occasionally given, as if to imply that not all German aristocrats were tyrants, snobs, boors, or courtly sycophants. But middle-class resentment was the commonest motive force behind the treatment of the aristocracy.
41. *Der Casselsche Zuschauer* of 1772, although written in open imitation of *The Spectator*, contains only two 'characters'.

CHAPTER 5

1. The principal Viennese moral weeklies are given in the Bibliography, section xiii (a). Martens points out that the most influential editors and contributors were, by origin, German, not Austrian (*Die Botschaft der Tugend*, p. 164).
2. 'German' (*die Deutschen*) here includes Austrians.
3. There is more on these pamphlets in L. Bodi, 'Enlightened Despotism and the Literature of the Enlightenment', *German Life and Letters*, n.s. xxii. 1968–9, pp. 324–33 and L. H. Bailey, 'The Image of Vienna in the *Wiener Skizze* and related short prose forms, 1780–1914', Diss. (Cambridge), 1976, especially pp. 19 f. and 39 ff. See too Kurt Strasser, *Die Wiener Presse in der Josephinischen Zeit*, Vienna, 1962, pp. 82 f. For details on Geißau, see Bibliography, section i. Anybody with the patience to hunt out surviving examples of these works could add a fascinating footnote to the social history of Vienna in the 1780s.
4. I have used the 8-volume edition, Amsterdam, 1782–3.
5. I have used the edition by G. Gugitz and A. Schlosser, Graz, 1923.
6. See, for the most notorious instance, Friedrich Nicolai, *Beschreibung einer Reise durch Deutschland und die Schweiz im Jahre 1781*, 12 volumes, Berlin and Stettin, 1783–96, especially iii. 189–92 and v. 3–7, 49, 109, 115–17, 200–19, and 253.
7. *Aus dem Kleinleben*, 1884, i. 97. Untranslatable.
8. For Steiner, see *Schwankende Gestalten*, 1926, pp. 35 f. For the review, see W. E. Yates's edition of *Das Haus der Temperamente* in the *Historisch-kritische Ausgabe* of Nestroy's plays, xiii (1981), 210–14.
9. P. F. Trautmann, *Don Juan in Wiesbaden*, Berlin, 1856; Ludwig Engel, *Der Don Juan vom Jungfernstieg*, Leipzig, 1922; E. Kratzmann, 'Don Juan in Venedig', in *Regina Sebaldi*, Vienna, 1939; J. E. Flecker, *Don Juan*, London, 1925.
10. Castelli, *Wiener Lebensbilder*, 1828 (i. 75–8 in the 2nd edition, Vienna, 1835); Barach, *Wiener Bilderbogen*, 1869, iii. 38 f.
11. See, for instance, pp. 81 ff.

CHAPTER 6 (i)

1. Hazlitt, 'Oliver Oldstyle' (1824), Charles Knight (1844), and a few others still use 'character', many writers simply label their pieces according to the type described ('The Waiter', etc.), while 'Sketch' is in wide use before the end of the 1830s. 'Portrait' is also used from time to time to designate an unambiguous 'character', e.g., by 'Sir Frederick Foppling' (1811) and the anonymous rewriter of Earle (1813).
2. See too the anonymous *Sketches from Clerical Life*, London, 1850, chapters 3 and 5. For a 'character' from the mid century which is still exactly in the style of the eighteenth century, see Catherine Gore, *Sketches of English Character*, 1846, i. 55 (Sir John Sensitive).
3. For mere uncritical plundering of Earle, see 'Oliver Oldstyle', *Every-Day Characters . . .*, 1824, pp. 18 f. (the Antiquary).
4. Hunt's Old Gentleman, the Coachman, the Maidservant, and the Old Lady appeared in *The Indicator* during 1820; the Waiter was first published in 1835 and reprinted in *The Seer* (1840).

5. See, respectively, 'On Disagreeable People' and the account of 'literary footmen' in the essay 'On Footmen'.
6. Hazlitt, *Complete Works*, Centenary Edition by P. P. Howe, London, 1933, xii. 67.
7. From the essay 'Poor Relations' in *Last Essays of Elia*, 1833. The *Last Essays* also contain the 'characters' of the Convalescent and Dr Monoculus (in 'Amicus Redivivus').
8. See *The Natural History of the Gent* and *The Natural History of 'Bores'* (both 1847). The term 'social zoology' is used by Albert Smith, *The Natural History of the Ballet Girl*, 1847, p. 8.
9. Smith's *Ballet Girl*, which concludes with a protracted and sympathetic 'character', is an exception.
10. Thackeray's *Book of Snobs* is the celebrated example.
11. See *Punch*, ii (1842), 147; vi (1844), 220; xiv (1848), 32, 51, 176, and 259. There are 'characters' too in the *Comic Almanach* for 1847–8 and in *Fun* (1868). After about 1860, one encounters very few 'characters' in *Punch*. The Governess, Maid-of-all-Work, Magistrate, and Labourer are by Horace Mayhew and were reprinted in 1848 in *Model Men* and *Model Women*.
12. First published in *Punch* in the form of individual papers during 1846 and 1847. Thackeray had already contributed to the collection *Heads of the People* (1840–1) and there is a 'character' in the *Paris Sketch Book* of 1840.
13. For the sermon, see Sydney Smith, *Sermons*, 2nd edition, London, 1801, ii. 129 ff., 147 ff. and 186 ff.; for treatises, see the 'Character of a good and faithful servant' in *A Friendly Gift for Servants* . . . , York, 1806, pp. 7–17 and John Henry Newman's Gentleman, first published in his *Idea of a University*, 1852; for the 'character' of a German Serving-Maid, see Henry Mayhew's *German Life and Manners* of 1864; G. B. Shaw wrote five short 'characters' of various types of music teacher in 1889 (see Bibliography); William Scrope gives three 'characters' of Anglers in the preamble to *Days and Nights of Salmon Fishing in the Tweed* (1843).
14. *German Life and Manners*, i. 362 f. The inclusion of 'characters' in travel-books was by no means new: see James Howell, *Instructions for Forreine Travell*, 1642; E. B., *A Trip to North Wales*, 1701; Anon., *The Comical Pilgrim; or, Travels of a Cynick Philosopher*, 1722.
15. Pages 18 and 94 in the edition published in Edinburgh, n.d. (1879).
16. G. Servois' Bibliography (La Bruyère, *Œuvres*, Paris, 1922, iv. 101 f.) mentions four additional works from the nineteenth century which may well contain 'characters' but which I have not been able to consult. But it is in any case a sparse crop when compared with nineteenth-century England.

CHAPTER 6 (ii)

1. Professor Bradbury informs me that he was well aware of the Theophrastan tradition and the *Book of Snobs* when he wrote this book. For other examples of 'characters' in light humour, see Bibliography under Jennings (1963), Raeburn (1975), and Hewison (1978).
2. For Chaucer-parodies, see *The Tincker of Turvey* (1630) and C. G. Fagan's 'Chaucer in Oxenforde' (1883); for 'characters' in the style of Spenser, see Mark Arkenside (1737) and Cornelius Arnold (1755).
3. Collected in *Sincere Flattery* (1954) and *After a Manner* (1956).
4. The Civil Servant, the Conductress, and the Schoolmistress: *After a Manner*, p. 18; *Sincere Flattery*, pp. 25 and 33.
5. *London Labour* . . . , i, part 1 (1851), pp. 473 f.; *The Big City*, pp. 31 f.

6. Whether Morton took the 'characters' in *Heads of the People* to be portraits of actual persons is impossible to determine. What is certain is that his updated variant of that work is no longer a character-book.
7. Edited by George R. Sims. For the 'character', see ii. 352 f.
8. See, for instance, Geoffrey Gorer's *Exploring English Character* (1955), with its 154 pages of statistical tables. Gorer did, however, give himself a holiday from statistics and collaborate with Ronald Searle in a little character-book entitled *Modern Types* (1955).
9. See too Francis Hope's typical but imaginary graduates in 'Are Arts Graduates Employable?', in the *New Statesman*, 22/3/1968. For other examples of what I take to be 'unconscious' character-writing, see Bibliography under Chandler (1940), Carrington (1965) and Cooper (1967).
10. *A Cabinet of Characters*, p. 418.
11. For a discussion of the class limitations of this book, see below, p. 171.
12. Canetti acknowledged a debt to Theophrastus and, less expectedly, to Gogol's *Dead Souls*. See *Die Provinz des Menschen*, Munich, 1973, p. 283 and *Die Weltwoche*, 26/6/1974, p. 33.
13. *Der Ohrenzeuge. Fünfzig Charaktere*, Munich, 1974, p. 25. The contrast between the title and the style in which the 'character' is written is typical of this collection. The titles are fanciful compound-words (Canetti's own coinings); the style of the 'characters' themselves is simple, at least as far as vocabulary and sentence-construction go.
14. Untranslatable: a variant on 'schaden*froh*' (malicious).

CHAPTER 7 (i)

1. For the Schoolmaster, see above, p. 40; for the Ballad-maker, see Parrot, 1626, No. 1; for the Shoplifter, *A Warning for Housekeepers*, London, 1676, pp. 6 f.
2. See also C. N. Greenough: 'The "Character" as a source of information for the historian', in *Collected Studies*, Harvard, 1940, pp. 123 ff.
3. *The Happy Man*, 2 volumes, Oslo, 1954–8.
4. For the 'inner' retreat, see, for instance, Sir Henry Wotton's famous poem, 'The Character of a Happy Life'. For the more orthodox view that contentment is to be achieved in rural surroundings, see Herrick, 'A Country Life'.
5. For Horace, see *Epode* ii; *Epistles*, i. 16; *Satires*, ii. 6. For Martial, *Epigrams*, x. 47.
6. F. L. Lucas, *Seneca and Elizabethan Tragedy*, CUP, 1922, p. 129. See too J. W. Cunliffe, *The Influence of Seneca on Elizabethan Tragedy*, 1893, reprinted 1965, also the essays by G. K. Hunter and G. M. Ross in *Seneca*, edited by C. D. N. Costa, London, 1974 and Røstwig, op. cit. i. 84 f. For Seneca in the commonplace book, see Meres, 118^{v}.
7. For an extract from Francis Thynne's 'Godly Man' of 1600, see above, p. 19.
8. Wotton, 'The Character of a Happy Life', line 24; 'Against a rich man despising povertie', in Giles and Phineas Fletcher, *Poetical Works*, 2 volumes, edited by F. S. Boas, CUP, 1908–9, ii. 236.
9. *Poems written on several Occasions*, 2nd edition, London, 1684, p. 27. There is a similar motif in Aaron Hill's poem on the 'Happy Man', in *Works*, London, 1753, iii. 163 f.
10. Breton's Holy Man and Good Man are more direct expressions of a Christian ideal, the Good Man being set off against the Atheist.
11. Røstwig, i. 54 and 132 ff. Trevor-Roper also notes that a philosophy of Christianized Stoicism appeals to insecure and distraught ages: see *Princes and Artists*, London, 1976, p. 32.

12. See Røstwig, i. 314 f. Wycherley's praise of 'wise selfishness' in 'A song, in praise of Solitude' illustrates this point.
13. Cf. Røstwig, i. 397 f.
14. John Pomfret, 'The Choice' (1699), in A. Chalmers, *English Poets*, London, 1810, viii. 307 f. See too the *London Magazine*, iv (1735), 502 f.; vii (1738), 301 f.; xi (1742), 506.
15. See, for instance, Thomas Parnell, 'The Happy Man', in Chalmers *English Poets*, ix. 402 f.
16. Mary Chudleigh, 'The Happy Man', in *Poems on Several Occasions*, London, 1703, pp. 35 f.; Anon., 'The Happy Man', in *A New Miscellany of Original Poems*, London, 1720, pp. 62 f.; Anon., 'The Country Gentleman', in the *London Magazine*, ix (1740), 42 f.
17. Gleim, Hagedorn, E. C. von Kleist, J. P. Uz, and many others.
18. For example, Julius von Tarent, the eponymous hero of Leisewitz's tragedy. The contrast between this dream of escape and the horrid realities of courtly life is pungently expressed in Schiller's early tragedy, *Kabale und Liebe*.
19. 'Character' of a True Wise Man, in *Schilderungen vortreflicher Menschen*, 1782, p. 314.
20. For a famous statement of Masonic ideals in eighteenth-century Germany, see Lessing, *Ernst und Falk, Gespräche für Freymäurer*, 1778.
21. See Gottsched, 'Sokrates, ein unüberwindlicher Weltweiser' (1749), in *Ausgewählte Werke*, Berlin, 1976, ix. 2, pp. 474 ff. There are also tributes to Socrates in *Der Chamäleon* (1759), Nos. 10 and 12 and in J. J. Engel, *Der Philosoph für die Welt* (1775–7), No. 37. See too B. Böhm, *Sokrates im 18. Jahrhundert*, Leipzig, 1929.
22. Flecknoe (1658), No. 57; Butler, Bumpkin or Country Squire; *Essay in Defence of the Female Sex* (1696).
23. *Essay* (1696); Defoe, *Applebee's Journal* for 7/3/1724; *Schilderungen vortreflicher Menschen*, p. 207.
24. The most famous is, of course, Sir Roger de Coverley in *The Spectator* (see especially Nos. 2, 106, 107, 112, and 116), although Sir Roger is more like a figure in a novel than a 'character'. In addition to the examples cited from *The Tatler* and *The Guardian*, one might mention *The Spectator*, No. 622 and Bulwer Lytton's 'great country Gentleman', in *England and the English*, 1833, Book ii, chapter 1. In *The Spectator* (No. 583), Addison reflects on estate management.
25. See William Caxton, *The Game and Playe of the Chesse* (1474); Chaucer, *Prologue*, 270–83; Robert Crowley, *One and Thyrtye Epigrammes* (1550), edited by J. M. Cooper in *EETS*, e.s. xv (1872), pp. 41 f.; Erasmus, *Encomium Moriae* (1509), p. 82 in the University of Michigan 1958 reprint of John Wilson's translation of 1668; Edward Hake, *Newes out of Powles Churchyarde* (1567), Satire 4; *De Diversis Ordinibus Hominum* (c. 1200), lines 185–8, in *Latin Poems commonly attributed to Walter Mapes*, edited by Thomas Wright, London, 1841, p. 234.
26. Thomas Deloney, *Novels*, edited by M. E. Lawlis, Indiana UP, 1961, p. 40. For other instances of the praise lavished on the merchant in the sixteenth century, see L. B. Wright, *Middle-class Culture in Elizabethan England*, University of North Carolina Press, 1935, chapter 2.
27. Breton, p. 9; Flecknoe, 'Character of an English Merchant', in *Miscellania*, 1653, pp. 132 f.
28. *c.*1630. Published posthumously by his son in 1664. Edition used is that by W. J. Ashley, New York and London, 1895. See especially pp. 2, 4, and 119. See too Roger Coke, *A Discourse of Trade . . .*, London, 1670, B2^{v} and C. Davenant, *An Essay upon Ways and Means of Supplying the War*, 3rd edition, 1701 p. 57.
29. Breton, pp. 9 f.; Fuller, ed. cit., p. 103. Butler has a hostile 'character' of a Merchant.

30. *Mercantilism*, translated by M. Shapiro, 2 volumes, London, 1935, ii. 278–81.
31. *The Guardian*, No. 170. See too *The Spectator*, Nos. 174 and 248.
32. In *Works* (Bohn's British Classics) iv. London, 1855, 148 f.
33. See Dorothy Marshall, *English People in the Eighteenth Century*, 1956, especially pp. 8 f. and 75; also T. S. Ashton, *An Economic History of England: The Eighteenth Century*, London, 1955, pp. 20–3 and 34.
34. See R. H. Tawney, 'The Rise of the Gentry, 1558–1640', in *Economic History Review*, xi (1941), 1–60 and Christopher Hill, *Reformation to Industrial Revolution*, London, 1967, pp. 16 and 45.
35. See R. Vierhaus, *Deutschland im Zeitalter des Absolutismus*, Göttingen, 1978, especially pp. 36 f. and 114 f.
36. See, for example, *Der Mensch* (1751–6), No. 385.
37. 'Karakter eines rechtschaffenen Kaufmanns', in *Historischmoralische Schilderungen*, 1779–81, iii. 626 f. See too *Der Freymäurer* (1738), No. 7.
38. *Schilderungen der heutigen Sitten . . .* , 1763, p. 201; *Der Bürger* (1732–3), No. 4; *Der Freymäurer*, No. 8.
39. *Der Freymäurer*, No. 8 (p. 63).
40. See, for instance, *Der Patriot*, i. 293.
41. J. M. von Loen, *Der Adel*, 1752, pp. 134–7; A. von Kotzebue, *Vom Adel*, 1793, p. 197.
42. See *Der alte Deutsche* (1730), No. 30; *Der Bewunderer* (1742), 'Vorrede'; *Der redliche Hamburger* (1767), *passim*.
43. For a contrast between the speculative fever of the early eighteenth century and the solid and respected way of life among merchants, see W. Sombart, *The Quintessence of Capitalism*, translated by M. Epstein, London, 1915, pp. 88–92 and 153–60.
44. See *The Spectator*, No. 31; *The Guardian*, No. 107; *The World*, No. 55; also 'Oliver Oldstyle', *Every-Day Characters . . .* , 1824, pp. 22–5. For Dr Johnson, see *The Adventurer*, No. 99.
45. *Heads of the People*, 1840–1, ii. 208 ff.; *Schilderungen der heutigen Sitten*, pp. 17 and 201.
46. See Christopher Hill, op. cit., pp. 37 and 57; D. C. Coleman, 'Sir John Banks, Financier . . . ', in *Essays in the Economic and Social History of Tudor and Stuart England*, edited by F. J. Fisher, CUP, 1961, pp. 204–30; T. S. Ashton, op. cit., pp. 180 f. Also K. R. Andrews, *Elizabethan Privateering . . .* , CUP, 1964, chapter 6.
47. H. C., *The Character of an Honest Lawyer*, 1676. For other 'characters' of the Good Lawyer, see Brathwaite, *Strappado*, 1615; Dudley, Lord North, 1645 and *Der Patriot*, No. 9. Only in Germany, where the lawyers were highly respected professional men, do we find a balance between good and bad Lawyers in the 'characters'.
48. Overbury, 1614; Taylor, 1630; Humphrey Browne, 1642; 'Florilegus', 1653; K. W., 1661; Butler; Ned Ward, *The London Spy*, No. 8 and *The Modern World*, p. 148; *Characterism*, 1750; 'Oliver Oldstyle', 1824; Rabener, *Todtenliste*, 1743.
49. Sprigge, *Philosophical Essayes*, 1657, p. 40; Breton, *The Good and the Badde*, p. 9. See too Earle's 'meer dull physician', Flecknoe's Physician (1658), *Pecuniae Obediunt Omnia*, 1696, pp. 28 f. and the *Gentleman's Magazine*, li (1781), p. 188. There are differences of manner and detail throughout the centuries, of course. For the transformation of Earle's Physician into a smooth and fashionable nineteenth-century doctor, see above, p. 115.
50. See Harry Kirk, *Portrait of a Profession. A History of the Solicitor's Profession . . .* , London, 1976, especially pp. 14 f.
51. *Two Essays of Love and Marriage*, 1657, pp. 120 ff.; Anon., *The Character of a Soliciter*, London, 1675; *The Pettifoggers* (verse-satire in the style of Butler), 1723.
52. See W. Meier, 'Der Hofmeister in der deutschen Literatur des 18. Jahrhunderts', Diss. (Zurich), 1938, especially pp. 13–15. Cf. Goethe: 'Distrust of

teaching in the schools increased from day to day. People looked for private tutors.' For the original German, see *Dichtung und Wahrheit*, Book 4: xv. 108 in the *Festausgabe*, Leipzig, 1926.

53. Cf. W. H. Bruford, *Germany in the Eighteenth Century*, p. 248.

54. See *Der Einsiedler* (1740), pp. 289 ff.; Rabener, *Sämmtliche Schriften*, 1777, iii. 19 f.; also Meier, op. cit., p. 26.

55. *Über den Umgang mit Menschen*, 1788, Part 2, chapter x, § 5; p. 232 in the Reclam edition, Leipzig, n.d. See too *Der Gesellige* (1748–50), No. 221; Jung-Stilling's *Lebensgeschichte* (pp. 160–2 in the 1968 edition) and J. M. R. Lenz's comedy *Der Hofmeister* (1774).

56. Disciplinarian: C. F. Weiße, *Der Kinderfreund* (1775–9), No. 65.

Pedant: F. W. Zachariae, *Das Schnupftuch*, 1754, canto i and the inset 'characters' in the novels *Bonifaz Schleicher* by Wieland (1776—in *Vermischte Schriften*, xxvii. 168 f.) and *Das Leben eines Lüderlichen* by C. F. Bretzner, 1787–8, i. 35–7.

Sycophant: *Der Mensch* (1751), No. 150 and M. Claudius, *Der Wandsbecker Bothe*, 1774, No. 141.

'Renommist': *Bonifaz Schleicher*, ed. cit. 165 f. and J. G. Büsch, *Vermischte Abhandlungen*, 1777, pp. 132–7.

57. Büsch, op. cit., pp. 148 f.; J. P. Miller, *Historischmoralische Schilderungen*, 1779–81, i. 422 f.

58. Gellert, *Moralische Vorlesungen*, xxii; Büsch, 183 ff. See too Karoline von Wobeser's novel *Elisa* (1795): pp. 211–13 in the 6th edition, 1816.

59. Hall, *Satires*, ii. 6 (in *Works*, xii. 185 f.); *The Guardian*, No. 94; *The Mirror*, No. 88. The attitudes recorded in *The Mirror* are closely similar to those noted in Germany by Knigge.

CHAPTER 7 (ii)

1. *Centuries of Childhood*, translated by R. Baldick, London, 1962.

2. The Child is the opening piece in *Microcosmography*, but Earle does not persist with the Ages of Man.

3. *Das Reich der Natur und der Sitten* (1757 ff.), No. 293.

4. *The Natural History of Bores*, 1847, p. 55.

5. Overbury, 1614; Henry Parrot, 1626; Saltonstall, 1631; L. G., 1661; Panton, 1671. See too Dryden, 'Upon the Death of Lord Hastings' (1649), lines 81–4.

6. There is an unsympathetic description as early as 1622 (Refugé). La Bruyère (xi. 115 ff. and 124) is clinical, Brillon (1696, pp. 191 ff.) heartless. For the Old Man in comedy, see Rotrou, *La Sœur* (1645), ii. 2 and Quinault, *La Mère Coquette* (1664).

7. See Horace, *De Arte Poetica*, lines 169–74 and M. J. Herrick, *Comic Theory in the Sixteenth Century*, University of Illinois Press, Urbana, 1964, pp. 154–9.

8. *Hamlet*, II. ii. See too Sonnet xvii, lines 9–10;

9. See, for instance, S. C. Chew, *The Pilgrimage of Life*, Yale University Press, 1962, Plate 115. Robert Burton, in *The Anatomy of Melancholy*, is severe on the old.

10. See E. R. Curtius, *Europäische Literatur und lateinisches Mittelalter*, Berne, 1948, pp. 106–9; also the *Iliad*, iii. 105 ff.

11. Cornelius Arnold, *The Mirror* . . . , 1755, p. 17; George Alexander Stevens, *A Lecture on Heads*, 1765, pp. 49 f.

12. See *The Tatler*, No. 132 and *The Observer*, No. 109. For an ageing man-about-town, see *The Lounger*, No. 26.

13. No. 299. See too *Mannigfaltigkeiten* (1769–72), No. 90.

14. For very good-natured teasing on the subject of forgetfulness in the old, see S. L. Blanchard, *Sketches from Life*, 1846, iii. 142–4.

15. The setting-up of towns and colonies for the aged in America is a sign of the times.
16. For example, that of Rutilius Lupus: see above, p. 7.
17. For early seventeenth-century treatments, see Crosse (1605) and Rich (1606). Briefly in Rowlands, *Looke to it . . .* (1604), here still in the Dance of Death tradition.
18. Stephens, 1615; Parrot, 1626; Brathwaite, 1631; Butler.
19. Earle; Jordon, 1641.
20. Lenton. There is already a similar point in Crosse. See too Breton, 1616; Watts, 1641; Younge, 1655, and L. G. Other seventeenth-century 'characters' of the Drunkard in Taylor, 1630; *Two Essays*, 1657; P. K., 1684 and *Country Gentleman*, 1699. Young (1617), *Looking-Glasse* (1652), and *Wit's Cabinet* (1700) all plagiarize Breton. A few eighteenth-century 'characters' continue in this scornful vein: *The True-Born Englishman* (1700); *The Spectator*, No. 569; *Der Patriot*, No. 58.
21. *Schilderungen*, ii. 136.
22. *Poeticall Varieties*, London, 1637, p. 25. Jordan returned to the subject in 1641. For other 'characters' of the Whore, see Overbury, Taylor, Lenton, Fuller, L. G., and the anonymous *Character of a Town Misse* (1675). For a scornful eighteenth-century treatment, see *Characterism*, 1750.
23. *The Rambler*, No. 171. See too the account in Boswell (entry for June 1784) of how Johnson found a prostitute lying in the street and had her cared for at his own expense.
24. Her decline and death are related in the 1745 continuation, which may or may not be by Defoe.
25. *The Whore: a Poem . . .* , London, 1782, p. 14 (It is a satirical poem, not a 'character'.) See too Charles Horne, *Serious Thoughts on the Miseries of Prostitution*, London, 1783.
26. See D. C. Boughner, *The Braggart in Renaissance Comedy*, University of Minnesota Press, 1954 and H. Graf, 'Der Miles Gloriosus im englischen Drama bis zur Zeit des Bürgerkrieges', Diss. (Rostock), 1891.
27. Butler's Coward consists largely of a string of martial images, but it is impossible to say—given the author's obsessively figurative style—whether he wishes us to imagine his coward as actually being on the battlefield or is merely expressing the essence of cowardice through the metaphors of battle.
28. *Essays upon Several Moral Subjects*. See volume iv, 224 f. in the 6th edition, London, 1722–5.
29. 1777: in the *Hypochondriack Papers*, i. 114.
30. See *The Rambler*, No. 34; *Der Biedermann* (1728), No. 74; G. C. E. Westphal, *Portraits*, 1779–81, i. 184 ff.
31. Page 169. See too J. F. Reupsch, *Schilderungen*, 1759–60, ii. 98 ff. and Gellert, *Moralische Vorlesungen* (*Sämtliche Schriften*, 1770, vii. 415).
32. See the Notes to my edition of *Schmelzle* in the Clarendon German Series, Oxford, 1966.
33. For a brief satire on the Antiquary's gullibility as a collector, see *Skialethia*, 1598: above, p. 11.
34. W. E. Houghton, 'The English Virtuoso in the seventeenth century', in *Journal of the History of Ideas*, iii (1942), p. 192.
35. *The Rambler*, No. 82; *Sonntagsblatt* (1807), No. 16. See too *The Ranger* (1794), No. 18. Ned Ward and Edward Young show the Antiquary as collector of both religious and secular relics: see *The London Spy*, No. 1 and *The Love of Fame*, iv. 119–22.
36. Evelyn, *Diary and Correspondence*, edited by W. Bray, new edition, London, 1906, i. 106, 207, and 194. Houghton also draws attention to these instances.

37. La Bruyère, xiii. 2; Elisabeth Bonhote, *The Rambles of Mr Frankly*, Dublin, 1773, i. 24.
38. See Butler's Virtuoso; *The Tatler*, No. 216; Pope's *Dunciad*, iv. 397–438; *The Rambler*, No. 177.
39. See Smollett, *Count Fathom*, 1753, chapter 32 and *Der Sachsen-Spiegel* (1728), No. 3. For a satire on gullible Antiquaries whose erudition leads them to misconstrue a simple inscription, see *The Town and Country Magazine*, iii (1771), 595–7. This motif will reappear in Scott's *Antiquary* (chapter 4) and in *Pickwick*.
40. For treatments of the Antiquary and Virtuoso other than those here mentioned, see John Constable, *The Conversation of Gentlemen*, 1738, p. 169; P. J. Brillon, *Le Théophraste Moderne . . .*, The Hague, 1700, pp. 396 f.; Smollett, *Peregrine Pickle*, 1751, chapter 103. For a caricature of the scholar and antiquary Dr John Woodward, see Dr Fossile in the comedy *Three Hours after Marriage* (1717), by Gay, Pope, and Arbuthnot.
41. See *Sense and Sensibility*, chapter 33 and *Emma*, chapter 54. See too the General's attitude towards his Staffordshire china, *Northanger Abbey*, chapter 22.
42. Law, *Practical Treatise*, 1726: see above, p. 77. For Graves, see *The Spiritual Quixote*, 1773, chapter 6.
43. For an account of some more-than-princely collections, see V. de Swarte, *Les Financiers amateurs d'art aux xvie, xviie et xviiie siècles*, Paris, 1890.
44. *Satyrische Abbildungen*, 1746, pp. 96–8 and 107–9.
45. 'Von der Samlung der Naturalien', in *Das Reich der Natur und der Sitten*, No. 5 (1757). A similar point is made in *Die Zigeunerin* (1765), No. 10.
46. There is also mockery of the Virtuoso in Swift (*Gulliver*, book 3) and in C. F. Weiße's comedy *Die unerwartete Zusammenkunft oder der Naturaliensammler*, 1764.
47. Ed. cit. i. 257.
48. For Evelyn, see above, p. 167; for Ward, see *The London Spy*, No. 1. It should be added that the treatment of Woodward in *Three Hours after Marriage* is much less than fair, as will be seen by anyone who cares to glance through the 287(!) pages of the *Catalogue of the Library, Antiquities, &c. of the late learned Dr Woodward . . .*, London, 1728.
49. See Marjorie Nicolson and Nora M. Mohler, 'The Scientific Background of Swift's *Voyage to Laputa*' in *Annals of Science*, ii (1937), 299–334.
50. For Bacon, see *The Advancement of Learning*, book 1, in *Works*, edited by Spedding, Ellis, and Heath, London, iii (1857), p. 294. For Evelyn, see the letter to Maddox of 10/1/1657: ed. cit. iii. 225. For Fontenelle: *Œuvres*, Amsterdam, 1764, v. 1–14.
51. For two among many, see Ned Ward, *The Modern World*, 1708, pp. 10 f. and *Das Reich der Natur und der Sitten*, No. 85.
52. For the Pietist, see *Mocquerien*, 1754, pp. 251 ff. and Reupsch, op. cit. i. 129 f. For the Puritan: Overbury and Addison (*The Spectator*, No. 494). For a hostile 'character' of the Freethinker (*Freigeist*), see *Der Gesellige*, No. 184. For the Jesuit, see Overbury, Taylor's *Water Cormorant* of 1630, and the anonymous *Jesuits Character* of 1642.
53. See, for instance, the verse-character of a Puritan which concludes *A Dialogue*, London, 1640.

CHAPTER 7 (iii)

1. Hazlitt, 'On the Knowledge of Character', in *Complete Works*, viii. 307. See too Thackeray (*Pendennis*, chapter 62) on the Major's ignorance of his valet: 'so pitiless [is] the distinction between class and class'.

2. A. B. Reach, *The Natural History of Bores*, 1847, p. 46.
3. See *The Guardian*, No. 79; *The Rambler*, No. 166; *The Looker-on*, No. 41, and Dorothy Marshall, *The English Poor in the Eighteenth Century*. For the comparative lack of interest in the working classes shown by eighteenth-century German writers, see Martens, *Die Botschaft der Tugend*, pp. 383 f.
4. See, for instance, 'Quiz', *Sketches of Young Ladies*, 1837; 'Quiz junior', *Characteristic Sketches of Young Gentlemen*, 1838; Albert Smith, *The Physiology of Evening Parties*, 1846.
5. See Humphrey Browne, *A Map of the Microcosme*, 1642, No. 9 and Defoe, *The True-Born Englishman*, 1700, pp. 27 f. Fuller (1642) has a generalized 'character' of the Handicraftsman.
6. *Cures for the Itch*, 1626, No. 2.
7. R. M., *Micrologia*, No. 8; Overbury, ed. cit., pp. 71 and 136.
8. See *Heads of the People*, i. 209 ff.; Albert Smith, *The Natural History of 'Stuck-up' People*, 1847, pp. 32 ff.; Horace Mayhew, *Model Women*, 1848, pp. 35–8.
9. In *Tricks of the Town . . .*, edited by R. Straus, London, 1927, p. 133.
10. See George R. Sims (editor), *Living London*, 1902–3, ii. 352 f. and Catherine Gore, *Sketches of English Character*, 1846, i. 180 f.
11. *Fun*, n.s. vii (1868), p. 101.
12. See too Horace Mayhew, *Model Men*, 1848, pp. 24–6 and *Model Women*, 1848, pp. 35–8 and 81 f. For a discussion of lower-class types in the sketches of Viennese life (*Wiener Skizzen*), see above, chapter 5.
13. Selections from the *Morning Chronicle* have been edited by E. P. Thompson and Eileen Yeo in Pelican Classics, Penguin Books, 1973 (here referred to as 'P'). The first edition of *London Labour and the London Poor* (1851) contained 3 volumes in 2. There was a 2nd edition in 1861 in 3 volumes, with a fourth added in 1862 ('Those that will not work'). I have used the 1st edition for all material except that contained in the 1862 supplement. All volumes referred to as 'LLLP'.
14. For a 'character' by Mayhew, see above, p. 119.
15. There were a few attacks on Mayhew's reliability, smacking rather of vested interests than of objective regard for the truth. For an account of these, see Thompson's Introduction to the Pelican selection, pp. 42–4. I find Mayhew's accounts of London prostitutes less than convincing in many particulars.
16. The treatment of beggars and swindlers from the Middle Ages up to Mayhew's day would make an interesting study, but—since character-writing did not make a significant contribution—I have left these types out of account here.

CHAPTER 8 (i)

1. See *The Entertainer* (1717–18), No. 6; also L. Theobald, *The Censor* (1717); *The Comical Pilgrim* (1722), especially pp. 8–10; Peter Shaw, *The Reflector* (1750), pp. 219–25 and *Characterism, or, the Modern Age Display'd*, c.1750.
2. *The Spectator*, Nos. 35, 39, and 61. See too No. 285.
3. *The Moral Characters of Theophrastus. To which is prefix'd a Critical Essay on Characteristick-Writings*, London, 1725, pp. 37–43, 73, and 89. See too above, p. 66.
4. For more on the commonplace books, see above, chapter 1, also Thomas Ford's Hypocritical Convert in *The Times Anatomiz'd* (1647), No. 4. For a textbook example of rhetoric in character-writing, consider the following extract from Thomas Tuke, *The Christian's Looking-Glasse* (1615): '[The Proud Man] useth his equals as inferiors, his inferiors as servants, his servants as beasts: he thunders, lightens, crackes, threatens'. Puns on the subject's name or title (Jesuit, Justice of the Peace, Puritan, etc.) were common.

5. *The Character to 1642*, p. 180.
6. See No. 47 in the 1658 edition. For contemporary criticisms of Cleveland's undisciplined wit, see Boyce, *The Polemical Character*, p. 34.
7. *Micrologia* (1629), No. 4. Other examples in chapter 1.
8. *Characterismi* (1632), No. 10.
9. *Essaies upon the five senses* (1620), p. 134. ('Barretter' = 'barrator'.)
10. *Naps upon Parnassus* (1659), n.p. K. W. (1661) shows something of the same incoherence of wit.
11. For Jordan, see *Pictures of Passions* (1641), E3[v]; for R. M., see *Micrologia* (1629), No. 6.
12. Reprinted in the *Harleian Miscellany*, x (1745), 141 f. The author, according to Murphy, is William Winstanley.
13. Page 271. For a contrast between Breton's closing formulas and the wide variety of different endings devised by Earle, see above, pp. 34–35.
14. Nos, 4, 13, and 12 (ed. cit., pp. 22, 37 f., and 36).
15. The role played by the witty manner in 'characters' of ideal types will be discussed in the second part of this chapter.
16. 'The Character of a Foot Soldier', in *The London Spy*, No. 8 (ed. cit., p. 155). The Wooden Horse was an instrument not unlike the rack and was used for the punishment of soldiers.
17. Ed. cit., pp. 11 f.
18. Compare ed. cit., pp. 73 and 74.

CHAPTER 8 (ii)

1. G. S. Gordon, 'Theophrastus and his Imitators', in *English Literature and the Classics*, 1912, pp. 54 and 86; Richard Aldington, *A Book of Characters*, 1924, Introduction, p. 5; P. Malekin, 'The Character-Sketches in the Serious Call', in *Studia Neophilologica*, xxxviii (1966), p. 317; Boyce, *The Character to 1642*, p. 186.
2. See La Bruyère, xiii. 24; *The Spectator*, No. 354; J. F. Reupsch, *Schilderungen* (1759–60), ii. 112 f.; J. J. Ebert, *Tapeten* (1771 ff.), No. 46.
3. P. J. Korshin, 'The Development of Abstracted Typology in England, 1650–1820', in *Literary Uses of Typology*, edited by Earl Miner, Princeton University Press, 1977, p. 172.
4. *Moralische Vorlesungen*, No. 18: ed. cit. vii. 422.
5. *The Times Anatomiz'd* (1647), No. 3. Nearly all the idealized 'characters' of young women in the eighteenth-century periodicals share this fault, as do many of the (neo-Stoic) Wise Men. For a revoltingly self-satisfied 'character' (in the first person) of the Ideal Father, see C. F. Weiße, *Der Kinderfreund* (1775-9), No. 1. See too *Schilderungen vortreflicher Menschen*, 1782, *passim*.
6. Peacham, *The Truth of our Times*, 1638; pp. 146 f. in R. R. Cawley's edition (Facsimile Text Society, No. 55, 1942). For Browne, see *A Map of the Microcosme* (1642), No. 15.
7. Sermon v ('Upright walking sure walking'), in *Works*, 3 volumes, London, 1700, i. 59.
8. Stephens, *Essayes and Characters* (1615), p. 139; Dudley, Lord North, *A Forest of Varieties*, London, 1645, p. 90; J. D., 'The Character of a Friend', in *Oxford and Cambridge Miscellany Poems*, edited by Elijah Fenton, n.d. (*c.*1708), p. 244.
9. *Essayes and Characters of a Prison and Prisoners*, ed. cit., p. 44.
10. Ford, *The Times Anatomiz'd*, No. 1; see too Anon., *Characterism, or, the Modern Age Display'd*, *c.*1750, p. 99 (on the Bountiful Lady).

11. Browne, op. cit., No. 15; L. G., *Essayes and Characters* (1661), p. 10. For a 'character', virtually the whole of which is a sustained exercise in rhetoric, see the Good Man in John Ford, *A Line of Life* (1620), pp. 97–100.
12. Samuel Person, *An Anatomical Lecture of Man . . .* , 1664, p. 13; P. B., *Juvenilia Sacra . . .* , 1664, pp. 37 f.
13. Other 'characters' of ideal types which, in my view, succeed, include Overbury's Wise Man, Earle's Good Old Man, Saltonstall's Happy Man, Lenton's Constant Man, and Flecknoe's Excellent Actor.

CHAPTER 9

1. See W. L. Cross, *The Development of the English Novel*, New York, 1912, pp. 24 f.; R. Boxberger, *Die Charakterzeichnung bei Dickens*, Havelberg, 1882; J. Schönert, *Roman und Satire im 18. Jahrhundert*, Stuttgart, 1969, p. 115; Hugo Beyer, *Die moralische Erzählung in Deutschland*, Frankfurt-on-Main, 1941, p. 18; Eugen Wolff, *J. E. Schlegel*, Berlin, 1889, pp. 124–6; F. Heitmüller, *Hamburgische Dramatiker zur Zeit Gottscheds*, Dresden and Leipzig, 1891, p. 66. Examples could be multiplied.
2. *Picturae Loquentes*, ed. cit., p. 43. This trend is already apparent in Theophrastus (see, for instance, his Coward). See too Brathwaite's Wine-Soaker (*Whimsies*, 1631) and J. J. Ebert's Jealous Husband (*Tapeten*, 1771 ff., No. 49).
3. See Karl von Reinhardstoettner, *Bearbeitungen plautinischer Lustspiele*, Leipzig, 1886; E. W. Robbins, *Dramatic Characterisation in Printed Commentaries on Terence, 1473–1600*, University of Illinois Press, 1951; R. W. Bond, *Early Plays from the Italian*, OUP, 1911, especially pp. 91 and 111.
4. Cf. Allardyce Nicoll, *The World of Harlequin*, CUP, 1963, pp. 21 f. Something similar seems already to have existed in Terentian comedy: see Robbins, op. cit., pp. 65 f.
5. See P. L. Duchartre, *The Italian Comedy*, translated by R. T. Weaver, London, 1929, especially pp. 50 ff. There are scenarios also in: J. des Boulmiers, *Histoire anecdotique et raisonnée du théâtre italien . . .* , 7 volumes, Paris, 1770 and K. M. Lea, *Italian Popular Comedy*, OUP, 1934, ii. 555 ff. E. Gherardi, *Le Théâtre Italien . . .* , Amsterdam, 1695, gives many extracts from pieces played by the Italian comedians in Paris.
6. Both quoted from *Old English Drama. Students' Facsimile Edition*: No. 119 (1912), D1^{r} and No. 60 (1911), B3^{v} respectively.
7. 'The "Character" in Restoration Comedy', in *PMLA* xxx (1915), pp. 67 f.
8. Such advance notices are common in the plays of d'Urfey and Shadwell. Something similar reappears in the theatre of George Bernard Shaw, where brief character-sketches are sometimes included in the stage-directions, especially where a character is seen as typical of a class or profession.
9. See, for instance, Chapman's *All Fools* (I. ii) and Dekker's *Honest Whore* (II. i).
10. Edition used: *Dodsley's Old Plays*, revised by Hazlitt and reprinted London, 1975: xiii. 475.
11. The Antiquary is made fun of in d'Urfey's comedy *Madame Fickle* of 1676, but it is not possible to say whether the author drew directly on Earle or picked up motifs from Marmion's play. Marmion's 'character' of a Parasite (*Holland's Leaguer*, 1632, I. i) shows some similarity to Overbury's Flatterer.
12. Lessing, *Hamburgische Dramaturgie*, No. 28.
13. This is not the only case in which Regnard borrows from La Bruyère: see A. Calame, *Regnard, sa vie et son œuvre*, Paris, 1960, p. 374. But it is certainly the most striking.
14. Another clear-cut example of direct copying is Arthur Murphy's Afterpiece *The Upholsterer* (1758), where the central figure is based on Addison's Political

Upholsterer (*Tatler*, No. 155). According to Dr Johnson, Goldsmith owned that he had borrowed the character of Croaker in his comedy *The Good Natured Man* c.1766) from Suspirius in *The Rambler* (No. 59). But the similarities are not as marked as in the foregoing pieces.

15. For a passage which concentrates on dramatic exposition rather than character, see William Haughton, *English-men for my Money*, 1616 (Pisaro's account of himself). P. V. Kreider (*Comic Character Conventions as revealed in the comedies of George Chapman*, 1935) gives many examples of brief labelling. For a description entirely concentrated on one quirkish habit, see Chapman, *A Humorous Day's Mirth*, Act II, lines 23–51.

16. *Works*, edited by C. H. Herford and Percy Simpson, Oxford, 1925 ff., vi. 27.

17. *A Cabinet of Characters*, p. 72. Another 'character' to include material outside the scope of the dramatic action is that of Sir Amorous La-Foole (*The Silent Woman*, 1609, I. iii).

18. *The Character to 1642*, p. 309.

19. Act II. xi: pp. 31 f. in the edition by Edmund Gosse (Mermaid Series, London, 1888).

20. For other straightforward examples of 'characters' employed in comedies, see Cibber, *The Refusal*, 1721, Act I (Sir Gilbert Wrangle as South-Sea Director) and the anonymous *The Humours of Oxford, a comedy*, London, 1730, p. 23 (a College Fellow). See too Boyce, *The Character to 1642*, p. 309.

21. *The Wary Widdow*, London, 1693, p. 3. For a similar case, see Bubble on Alderman Fumble in d'Urfey's *Fond Husband* of 1676.

22. Even if the 'character' has described actions and places which will not or cannot figure in the play, the dominant *humour* will have been established.

23. *Dramatic Works*, 5 volumes, London, 1777, i. 29, 38, and 45 f. There are other witty examples in George Etherege's *Man of Mode*, 1676 (compare I. i with III. ii) and in Shadwell's *True Widow*, I. i.

24. Character-writing influenced characterization in French comedy during the eighteenth century, as may be seen in works by Destouches, Piron, Saurin, and others: see Bibliography, section xvi(b). But the influence was not as strong as in either England, Germany, or Austria.

25. Gottsched, *Versuch einer kritischen Dichtkunst* (1730); see also *Der Gesellige*, Halle, 1764, No. 54.

26. See A. Ehrhard, *Les Comédies de Molière en Allemagne*, Paris, 1888, pp. 63–73. For the pieces devoted to Faust and Don Juan, see my *Faust in Literature*, OUP, 1975, Bibliography, sections iii–iv and ix–x.

27. English comedies were translated in fair numbers: see J. N. Beam, *Die ersten deutschen Übersetzungen englischer Lustspiele im 18. Jahrhundert*, Hamburg and Leipzig, 1906. But they do not seem to have had much influence on German comedy.

28. Gottsched disapproved of *das rührende Lustspiel* as being an unsatisfactory mixed genre.

29. *Kritische Dichtkunst*, 2. i. xi, §20; *Discourse der Mahlern*, iii. 16.

30. *Der Mißtrauische* has been edited by Sabine Roth in the series *Komedia* (No. 14, Berlin, 1969). The passage quoted is on p. 11.

31. *The Spectator*, No. 494. For German 'characters' which resemble Addison's from the point of view of their style, see above p. 87. For other inset 'characters' in German comedy, see C. F. Mylius, *Die Aerzte* (1745), I. iii and *Der Unerträgliche* (1746), I. i; C. F. Weiße, *Der Projektmacher* (1766), I. i.

32. Those which Gellert might confidently be expected to know would include two each in *The Spectator* (Nos. 46 and 354) and *Der Patriot* (Nos. 58 and 139), together with one in *Der Biedermann* (No. 54). *Die Betschwester* is one of the few comedies

which can be shown to have *inspired* 'characters'. Gellert wrote a verse-character based on his own creation of Frau Richard, while Rabener, in his 'character' of Frau Eigenwille (*Der Hofmeister*, volume i, No. 44), seems to have taken up a few hints from Gellert.

33. Act I, scene i. For a full-scale dramatic 'character' in this day-in-the-life form, incidentally, see Vanbrugh's *Relapse*, II. i.

34. For an article which links the state of the theatre to the question of Vienna's prestige as a capital city, see 'Was haben die Kritiken zur Gründung des gesitteten Theaters beygetragen?' in *Theatralkalender von Wien, für das Jahr 1772 . . .*, Vienna, 1772, pp. 28 f.

35. See, especially, Engelschall, *Zufällige Gedanken über die deutsche Schaubühne in Wien*, Vienna, 1760; Gebler's Preface to his *Theatralische Werke*, Prague and Dresden, 1772–3; Sonnenfels, *Briefe über die wienerische Schaubühne*, Vienna, 1768–9 (reprinted in *Wiener Drucke*, vii, Vienna, 1884).

36. As exponents in Vienna of 'regular' comedy in the Gottschedian sense, one could cite Gebler, Joseph von Petrasch, and Franz Heufeld (*Die Haushaltung nach der Mode*, 1765 and *Doktor Guldenschnitt*, 1781). The Viennese moral weeklies tended to support the reformers' cause. *Der Verbesserer* (1766) is an exception, however, defending Hans Wurst and regarding the reformers as puritanical (see No. 11).

37. For his position, see *Der Mann ohne Vorurtheile*, Vienna, 1765–7, especially i. 193 ff. and ii. 17, 735, 747, and 758–61.

38. Act III, scene vii. See too Klemm's periodical, *Die Welt*, iv (1763), 163 ff.

39. See Hafner's pamphlet, *Der Freund der Wahrheit*, Vienna, 1760 and his one-act comedy, *Die dramatische Unterhaltung unter guten Freunden*, Vienna, n.d.

40. Perhaps the oddest manifestation of this compromise is J. G. Heubel's play *Marianna*, Vienna, 1758: based on Marivaux's novel, it still has a substantial part for Hans Wurst.

41. See Karl von Görner, *Der Hans Wurst-Streit in Wien*, Vienna, 1884, pp. 60 f.

42. Translations and adaptations of French plays were so common on the Viennese stage in the eighteenth century that authors of original plays were in the habit of including some such term as *Originallustspiel* on the title-page.

43. Part iv, 107 f.

44. Klemm shares Petrasch's indebtedness to character-writing and his unwillingness to halt the play while a set description takes place: see *Die seltne Zärtlichkeit*, I. v and *Die Schule der Liebhaber*, II. ii.

45. Webster labels it a 'character' and he ought to know. F. L. Lucas, editing Webster, accepts it as such, as does Boyce, normally very cautious. Stylistically, it is different from the 'characters' attributed to Webster in the Overbury collection, but this is to be expected, given its context and function. For further discussion of 'characters' in the plural number, see chapter 11.

46. Act II scene iii. First printed posthumously but dating from the 1630s, the play also contains a number of short 'characters' which fulfil a more orthodox expository function. For another instance of a 'character' used for the purpose of deceit, see John Wilson, *The Projectors* (1665), II. i.

47. Act I, scene ii. For other 'characters' used to achieve dramatic irony see J. E. Schlegel, *Die stumme Schönheit* (1747), scene xiii and J. C. Bock, *Die Parodie*, I. ix. Similarly, Mr Paris, the Fop in Wycherley's *Gentleman Dancing Master* (1672), dispraises Gerrard, his rival, in a 'character'. But Hippolita, to whom he is speaking, rejects his criteria, as must the audience (see I. i). See too H. Borkenstein, *Der Bookesbeutel* (1742), II. v.

48. See, for example, the *Bernisches Freytags-Blätlein* (1722–4), i. 18 and *Der Brachmann* (1740), No. 15.

CHAPTER 10 (i)

1. *The Augustan Vision*, London, 1974, p. 246.
2. For brief details of the early editions and of the collaboration between Head and Kirkman, together with the provenance of some of the 'characters', see Murphy's *Bibliography*, pp. 143 f.
3. Chapter 11.
4. See Francis Coventry, *History of Pompey the Little, or the Life and Adventures of a Lap-dog* (1751), *passim*; also Richard Graves, *The Spiritual Quixote* (1773) and Edward Kimber, *The Life and Adventures of Joe Thompson* (1783). Details in Bibliography, section 16.
5. For 'characters' of Ideal Women in the periodicals, see *The Tatler*, No. 42 and *The Spectator*, No.302. As if to make fun of his own fondness for character-writing, Coventry ends with a valedictory 'character' of his canine hero, based in part on another satirical animal 'character', that in the anonymous *Essay towards the Character of the late Chimpanzee*, London, 1739. (I am indebted to Professor W. P. Bridgwater for drawing my attention to this work.)
6. For example, K. W., *Confused Characters*, 1661, No. 1; Anon., *The Character of a Town-Gallant*, 1680.
7. See too *The Idler*, No. 95.
8. *The Rambler*, No. 200. See too *The Guardian*, No. 162.
9. For other pieces which seem on the borderline between 'character' and short story, see *The Tatler*, No. 126; *The Intelligencer*, 1729, No. 7; *The Rambler*, No. 12; *The Idler*, Nos. 13, 62, and 64.
10. 'The Life and Writings of Addison', in *Critical and Historical Essays contributed to the Edinburgh Review*, London, New York, and Bombay, 1903, ii. 748 f.
11. In *Vanity Fair*, Thackeray draws on material from *The Book of Snobs*: see L. Ennis, *Thackeray: the sentimental cynic*, Northwestern University Press, 1950, p. 140. Compare too Archer's name-dropping (*Pendennis*, chapter 30) with Wiggle's (*The Book of Snobs*, chapter 40). For Dickens, see below.
12. The veiled 'portraits' in Bulwer Lytton's novels (notably *Pelham*, 1828) are left out of account here. The whole question of the portrait in the *roman-à-clef*, from early Arcadian novels right up to this century, is far too complex to be dealt with in passing and merits a detailed examination of its own.
13. Fielding, *Jonathan Wild*, ii. 1; Jane Austen, *Sanditon*, chapter 3; Bulwer Lytton, *Pelham*, chapter 3, *Eugene Aram*, i. 4 and *Ernest Maltravers*, iv. 5.
14. See too the brief 'characters' of the clergymen who attend the Clerical Meeting in George Eliot's 'Amos Barton', chapter 6 (in *Scenes of Clerical Life*). The only justification for the episode in terms of strict thematic relevance is that the debate (*not*: the characters of the debaters) shows the spread of rumours concerning Amos. Thackeray's 'character' of a Society Lady (*Pendennis*, chapter 44) is the purest luxury.
15. Chapter 10. For similar instances in English comedy, see above, pp. 210 f. Compare P. J. Korshin's statement that the novel-reader, faced with a 'character' within the work, would be able to predict that person's future behaviour ('The Development of Abstracted Typology in England, 1650–1820', in *Literary Uses of Typology*, edited by Earl Miner, Princeton University Press, 1977, p. 161).
16. For a similar device in Jean Paul Richter's novel, *Die unsichtbare Loge*, see below, pp. 256 f. Jean Paul was an admirer of Fielding and may have picked up the hint from him.
17. *English Satire*, CUP, 1958, pp. 117 f. Sutherland invokes the English 'characters' of the seventeenth century; he must, however, mean the eighteenth.
18. See too *Dombey and Son*, where the account of Sir Barnet Skettles as host (i. 24) is like a short 'character' of a Tuft-hunter. But Sir Barnet has already been

typecast as a snob; in this case the 'character' (in the technical sense) shows one additional form taken by the ruling quality. Or see, in *Middlemarch*, the description of Caleb Garth as a hard-working man who understands the working classes and that of Bulstrode as hypocrite (chapters 56 and 61).

19. Letter of 1 May. *Works*, edited by Leslie Stephen, London, 1883, v. 455.

20. For example, Clarissa on Lovelace (vi. 240–2) or Mrs Norton on Mr Brand (viii. 2–4). Miss Howe's thoroughly artificial description of what sort of person Clarissa was before she met Lovelace (included in a letter to Clarissa herself!) is an exception: see vi. 13–15. For the 'character' of a Sporting Parson in an epistolary novel, see William Cole, *The Contradiction*, London, 1796, pp. 180 f.

21. *Works*, edited by L. Moore, revised by J. P. Browne, London, n.d. (1872), vii. 68. For Quin, see p. 80. See too pp. 230 f. (the uncouth Yorkshire Squire) and p. 240 (Mr Pimpernel, the mean and oafish Landowner).

22. See Diana Spearman, *The Novel and Society*, London, 1966: 'The conduct of everyone in the first part of *Clarissa* is highly improbable from start to finish' (p. 183).

23. For other examples, see Mr Gregsbury, MP (*Nicholas Nickleby*) and the unnamed doctor who attends Little Nell (*The Old Curiosity Shop*, i. 46).

24. For the 'characters' of Sapsea and Honeythunder, see *Edwin Drood*, chapters 4 and 6. See too the description of Miss Edwards (*The Old Curiosity Shop*, i. 31); Volumnia Dedlock (*Bleak House*, i. 28); Bradley Headstone and Miss Peecher (*Our Mutual Friend*, ii. 1). There are also a few equivalents in Dickens to the seventeenth and eighteenth-century 'characters' of places (inns, prisons, coffee houses, etc.). These include the commercial room of the Peacock (*Pickwick*, i. 14); Golden Square (*Nickleby*, i. 2) and the Commercial Boarding House (*Chuzzlewit*, i. 8).

25. William Minto, *Daniel Defoe*, London, 1902, p. 141.

26. *Joseph Andrews*, chapter 36. See too Ian Watt, *The Rise of the Novel*, 1957, pp. 271–3.

27. Another way in which Fielding makes us aware of the limitations of the 'character' is that, having given us an initial description, he gradually adds fresh traits as the novel progresses. Parson Adams is presented in what is virtually the 'character' of an unworldly Divine (*Joseph Andrews*, chapter 3), but important characteristics—his absent-mindedness, his innocent vanity—are left to emerge later. Similar examples are to be found in *Tom Jones*.

28. Chapter 42. See too chapter 46.

29. See the descriptions of the Thorpes and of Elinor Tilney (*Northanger Abbey*, chapters 4 and 8) or that of Mr Collins (*Pride and Prejudice*, chapter 15). But such sketches lack the typicality of the 'character'.

30. *Middlemarch*, chapter 72. Maria Edgeworth, in *Belinda* (1801), labels her opening chapter 'characters'. But after a brief description of Belinda, she adds: 'her character, however, was yet to be developed by circumstances'. Ian Watt (op. cit., p. 21) has related the growing interest in character-development to Locke's empirical philosophy. There may be something in this, although it must be remembered that Addison, who accepted Locke's philosophy, wrote many 'static' character-sketches while, on the other hand, there are plenty of novelists of a most *un*philosophical turn of mind who were deeply interested in showing the gradual development of character. (For more on this, see below, chapter 11.)

31. For 'characters' of the Libertine in the expected, hostile vein, see Steele, *The Lover*, 1714, No. 3; Goldsmith's *Citizen of the World*, 1762, letter ix; George Alexander Stevens, *A Lecture on Heads*, 1765 (pp. 5 f. in the 1812 edition). There are many hostile 'characters' of the Rake in the German moral weeklies of the eighteenth century. For a more unexpected approach, see *The Tatler*, No. 27, where Steele portrays the Libertine as a potentially good man gone astray, one to be pitied. This is, as far as I know, a unique example in eighteenth-century character-writing, although compassionate treatments of the Prostitute are not uncommon.

32. See the Introduction to Jebb's edition of Theophrastus: pp. 22 f. in the revised edition by J. E. Sandys, London, 1909.
33. A similar process of expansion can be seen in Smollett's *The Adventures of Peregrine Pickle*, where the hero falls in with a company of virtuosi and exposes a 'genuine antique' as a badly worn English farthing (chapter 103). This and similar examples in Smollett's works seem to suggest that his imagination was set off by a motif in a 'character', but that, as a novelist, he wished to make a longer episode out of it. An interesting example of expansion during the process of writing can be seen in Fanny Burney's *Camilla* (1796). The jottings contain the sketch—a little 'character' in all but name—of Mr Jocoso, some of whose traits are taken up into the depiction of Sir Sedley and Lionel. See E. A. and L. D. Bloom's Introduction to their edition, OUP, 1972, p. xi.
34. See *London Tradesmen*, ed. cit., pp. 4 f.; *Ralph the Heir*, chapters 5 and 6.
35. The influence of the 'character' on the French novel has not, as far as I know, ever been systematically investigated. Any such enquiry would have to begin with Lesage's *Diable Boiteux*, first published in 1707. The plot, if plot it can be called, concerns a young student of Madrid (= Paris), who falls in with a devil who promises him inside knowledge of his fellow-men. The student is taken round the city by his tutelary demon and is shown the folly, immorality, and injustice that hold sway. The plot is thus the merest excuse for wholesale satire and the book is a string of character-sketches, anecdotes, and novellas. The 'characters' are quite obviously inspired by La Bruyère. There seems little doubt that Lesage himself saw this work as a collection of 'characters' held together by a narrative conceit of secondary importance, for the 1707 table of contents consists largely of a list of the characters who will be encountered ('Le nouveau marié', 'Le vieux garçon', etc.). Lesage's later and more famous picaresque novel, *Gil Blas* (1715–34), shows occasional links with La Bruyère's manner of character-writing, but these links are not nearly as strong as some critics maintain, certainly nowhere near as close as in the case of *Le Diable Boiteux*. There must be many other examples of eighteenth-century French novels which borrow techniques or motifs from the character-writers, but I am not sufficiently expert in the field to pursue the theme. It would certainly repay some attention.

CHAPTER 10 (ii)

1. For three such attacks among many, see *Der alte Deutsche* (1730), No. 52; *Der Teutsche Bernerische Spectateur* (1734), No. 4; *Die Zellischen vernünftigen Tadler* (1742), No. 32.
2. For accounts of some of the German essays in the picaresque, see B. Mildebrath, '*Die deutschen "Aventuriers" des achtzehnten Jahrhunderts*', Diss. (Würzburg), 1907 and H. Nimtz, '*Motive des Studentenlebens in der deutschen Literatur . . .*', Diss. (Berlin), 1937, chapter 4. Imitations of *Crusoe* include: Anon., *Der Sächsische Robinson . . .* , Leipzig, 1722; J. G. Schnabel, *Die Insel Felsenburg*, 1731–43; 'Selimen' (J. M. Fleischer), *Der nordische Robinson . . .* , Copenhagen, 1749.
3. There was, however, indebtedness to English novels, notably those of Richardson and Fielding.
4. See Martens, *Die Botschaft der Tugend*, pp. 125 f. and the accounts of Loen and Gellert in chapter 4.
5. Examples are: *Die Discourse der Mahlern*, i.8; *Der Patriot*, Nos. 9, 10, 26 and 67; *Die vernünftigen Tadlerinnen*, No. 19; *Der Sammler* (1736), No. 15; *Der Freydenker* (1741–3), No. 35; *Belustigungen des Verstandes und des Witzes* (1741–5), iv. 114–19.

6. 'Damabellante', *Rares Portrait einer allzugalanten Dame . . .*, n.p., 1725, pp. 3–5. See too the description of Caliste in Thomasius's miniature courtly novel (*Lustige und Ernsthaffte Monats-Gespräche*, part i, Halle, 1688, 639 f.); also 'Meletaon' (J. L. Rost), *Venda, Königin in Polen . . .*, Nuremberg, 1715, pp. 2 f. and 'Beninde', *Die von der Liebe verfolgte . . . Printzeßin Hermoine*, Frankfurt and Leipzig, 1733, pp. 7 f. Examples could be multiplied.

7. As in C. F. Sintenis's 'character' of his hero in *Hallo's glücklicher Abend*, 1786. An example which antedates Loen is Gellert's *Leben der Schwedischen Gräfin von G**** (1748–9), which includes a long 'character' of Herr R**, the heroine's second husband.

8. G. C. E. Westphal, *Portraits*, volume i, Leipzig, 1779, Preface. Westphal describes the hero of his imaginary novel as 'spectator' in order to underline the link with the observers of manners and morals in the periodicals; his word (*Zuschauer*) was the commonest German translation of Addison's 'Spectator'.

9. For instance, Gryllus, the vain and over-productive composer (iii. 2) and two clergymen (iv. 6).

10. Wieland, iv. 6; La Bruyère, xi. 35. Other novels by Wieland, notably *Agathon*, contain portraits, as do Jean Paul's *Titan* and *Die Flegeljahre*. Jean Paul, in particular, is very interesting in this respect, since the one work offers thinly veiled critical pictures of Goethe and Schiller, the other a glowing tribute to Herder. But such cases go beyond the scope of this study.

11. Some further examples of stories and novels which feature 'characters' are mentioned in the Bibliography, section xvi(b).

12. For Merck, see 'Lindor, eine bürgerlich-teutsche Geschichte', in *Der Teutsche Merkur vom Jahr 1781*, Weimar, 1781, iii. 109; for Sintenis, see *Max Wind und Konsorten*, Frankfurt and Leipzig, 1780, p. 14.

13. Volume i, 248 f. For Webster and Farquhar, see chapter 9. For a 'character' which relates the subject to the common weal, see the Idler from *Der Patriot*, above, p. 89.

14. In Susanne B. Knab's short novel in diary-form, *Tagebuch einer jungen Ehefrau* (Stuttgart, 1780), 'characters' are used to give general validity to the individual cases. See especially pp. 31 f. (Young Wife) and 165 f. (Dandy). From the novel in diary-form it is only a short step to the epistolary novel (*Briefroman*). There were many of these in eighteenth-century Germany, mostly influenced to a greater or lesser degree by Richardson. Since the cautions and reservations noted in respect of the English epistolary novel apply here too, I have left the *Briefroman* out of account; in any case, the 'straight' German novel offers plentiful material.

15. For the learning of English, see *Sämtliche Werke, hist.-krit. Ausgabe*, edited by E. Berend, Weimar, 1927 ff., 3. Abteilung, 1. 32; for a reference to Westphal's *Portraits*, ibid., pp. 72 and 440; for La Bruyère, see 3. Abteilung, i. 73, ii. 562 and iv. 277. For the early 'characters', see 1. Abteilung, i. 63 f. and 93–6.

16. Ed. cit., 1. Abteilung, ii. 209 f. 'The merely *great* man of genius' may sound odd in English, but is an attempt to reproduce Jean Paul's distinction between *der große Mensch* (great in deeds or accomplishments) and *der hohe Mensch* (morally elevated).

17. See, for instance, 'Tobias Witt' and 'Joseph Timm' in J. J. Engel's *Philosoph für die Welt* (1775–7), No. 5.

18. For a more detailed examination of how Jean Paul stands in regard to the character-tradition, see my article 'Jean Paul und die Tradition des Theophrastschen "Charakters"', in *Jahrbuch der Jean-Paul-Gesellschaft*, i (1966), 53–77; for more on *Schmelzle* itself, see my Introduction in the Clarendon German Series (1966).

19. Book iii, 4. Another minor figure in the same novel is expressly described as *ein Original* (iii. 18).

20. For the Misogynist, see *Der Freund* (1754-5), i. 23; for the Pedant, see *Die Macht der Vorurtheile* (1765-9), i. 25. For the quotation from *Katzenberger*, see ed. cit., 1. Abteilung, xiii. 117 f.
21. In the Introduction to volume i of his anthology of novellas (*Novellenschatz*), first published in 1870.
22. *Beiträge zur Theorie und Technik des Romans*, 1883, section 3. Many German critics followed Spielhagen in taking this view.
23. There is an amusing 'character' of a *Katzphilister* in E. T. A. Hoffmann's *Kater Murr* (1820, ii. 3). This has the effect of convincing the feline hero of this fantastic novel that he has been just such a Philistine up till now. This near-surrealistic use of a 'character' in the early nineteenth-century German novel remains an isolated curiosity, however.

CHAPTER 11

1. For Johnson and Gally, see above, pp. 36 and 66.
2. For La Bruyère, see the Preface to the Academy Discourse, in *Œuvres*, edited by G. Servois, 3 volumes, Paris, 1865-78, ii. 450. For Gottsched, see *Die vernünftigen Tadlerinnen* (1725-6), No. 10.
3. Terminology is of little help, since English writers applied 'character' more or less indiscriminately to sketches of real and imaginary persons. In Germany, *Charakter, Porträt, Abbildung*, and *Schilderung* are used at random.
4. *The Letters of Philip Dormer Stanhope Earl of Chesterfield with the Characters*, edited by J. Bradshaw, 3 volumes, London, 1926, iii. 1410.
5. The poem is given in Bell's edition of *The Poets of Great Britain*, lxxxix. 124 f. For another portrait, which has virtually become a 'character' due to the author's mode of treatment, see Dr Johnson's Gelidus (*Rambler*, No. 24: based on one Coulson, a mathematician); for a 'character' which contains elements of portraiture, see the anonymous *Character of a Quack-Astrologer* (1673), which borrows traits from John Gadbury. For the links between portrait and 'character' in Pope, see above, pp. 79 f.
6. A similar case, where contemporary readers will certainly have identified the model even if we today require a footnote, is the description of 'Mr Charwell' (=Edward Colston, MP for Bristol) in *The Guardian*, No. 9. For a seventeenth-century example, see 'The Jesuite' in Nathanael Richards, *Poems sacred and satyricall*, London, 1641, pp. 45-53, with its clear biographical references to Henry Garnet.
7. *A Mirror of Charactery*, London, 1933. Introduction, p. xxx.
8. Adams's Usurer is linked to the Melancholy Man. Both Hall and Adams have fairly detailed physical descriptions of the Slothful or Lethargic Man. For a brief discussion of the links between character-writing and physiognomy, see below, Appendix 1.
9. Overbury, ed. cit., p. 74. Exactly imitated by Thomas Ford (1647), in his 'character' of the Discontented Person.
10. Adams, *The Soul's Sickness*, ed. cit. i. 484; K. W. (1661), 'A Covetuous Usurer'.
11. Gellert, *Moralische Charaktere*, ed. cit. vii. 648; G. C. E. Westphal, *Portraits*, 1779-81, i. 75; Theophrastus, No. 3.
12. For the 'anthropological character', see *The Lounger* 1785-7, No. 15; for the recipe, see *The Gentleman's Magazine*, xxiv. 90.
13. *The Literary Lounger*, London, 1826, pp. 143 f. See too the 'character' of a Squire in *The Gentleman's Magazine*, xxvii. 136.
14. Examples in *Der Redliche* (1751), volume i, Nos. 2, 6, 11, 12, and 13 and in *Der Chamäleon* (1759), No. 7.

15. Reprinted in the Harleian Miscellany, v. 93–8. The author was Sir John Birkenhead.
16. *The Anatomy of Melancholy*, part i, section 3, member 1, subsection 2: pp. 330–3 in the edition by F. Dell and P. Jordan-Smith, New York, 1951. My italics.
17. See for instance K. W., 'A Meere Politician' and Edward Panton, *Speculum Juventutis*, 1671, pp. 172 f. (on the Old Man).
18. See too his 'characters' of 'A meer empty wit', 'An Insolent Man', 'A lascivious man', and 'An affected man'.
19. Levinus Lemnius, *De habitu et constitutione corporis* (1561). Here quoted in the translation by Thomas Newton, London, 1576, 86^{r}.
20. Eustache Du Refugé, *Traicté de la Cour*, n.p., n.d. (1615), p. 24.
21. I am indebted to the accounts of the theory of humours and of Elizabethan psychology in general to be found in Edward Dowden, P. Ansell Robin, P. V. Kreider, and L. Babb (see General Bibliography for details).
22. See *Essay concerning Human Understanding*, book ii, 27, §§ 9 f. and 16 and *Some Thoughts concerning Education*, §§ 100–2. The best single work on Locke's influence on English men of letters is K. Maclean, *John Locke and English Literature of the Eighteenth Century*, New York, 1962.
23. *Les Essais*, edited by A. Armaingaud, Paris, 1927, v. 53.
24. Knowledge of Locke's empirical philosophy spread to Germany in the first half of the eighteenth century, both through translations and via the coffee-house periodicals. References to him in the moral weeklies are quite common. For an acknowledgement of the importance of environment on the development of character, see *Der Zerstreuer* (1737), No. 10.
25. *Schilderungen*, Frankfurt and Leipzig, 1759–60, i. 103 ff. and 242 ff.
26. Addison faithfully summarizes Locke's view that personality depends on a flux of consciousness (*The Spectator*, No. 578). This view clearly implies the importance of development and of empirical stimuli. But *The Spectator* is full of 'characters' which present personality as something fixed, dominated by a 'humour'. Only the old terminology has been abandoned. See too Ute Schneider, *Der moralische Charakter . . .*, Stuttgart, 1976, pp. 247 f. on this question.
27. See above, pp. 226 f.
28. For the 'ruling passion', see above, p. 78. For the rival definition, see the *Essay on Man*, ii. 18. Both Vauvenargues and Gellert (in the *Moralische Charaktere*) show somewhat similar contradictions.
29. 'Characters' of national types are nearly always distorted by prejudice: Charles Molloy, *Hollands Ingratitude . . .*, 1666, pp. 44–6; Anon., *Poor Robins Character of a Dutch-man . . .*, 1672; E. B., *A Trip to North Wales . . .*, 1701, pp. 3 f.
30. The 'character' also lost ground to the short story in England in the late eighteenth and early nineteenth centuries. See, for instance, *The Hermit in the Country . . .*, 4 volumes, London, 1820–2. But the process was not as far-reaching as in Germany.
31. J. J. Ebert, *Fidibus*, 6 volumes, Leipzig, 1768–9, vi. 377 ff.

APPENDIX 1

1. See L. Babb, *The Elizabethan Malady. A Study of Melancholia . . .*, Michigan State College Press, 1951, p. 9.
2. *The Spectator*, No. 86. See too Nos. 206 and 518. Henry Mackenzie (*The Man of Feeling*, 1771, chapters 25 and 27) makes fun of physiognomy; Fielding and, later, Dickens seem to entertain ambivalent feelings on the subject.

3. For a rejection, see Lessing's letter to Nicolai of 9/7/1776 and J. G. Hamann, *Schriften*, edited by F. Roth, 8 vols., Berlin, 1821–43, ii. 383 and vi. 112. For mockery, see C. F. Bretzner's comedy *Karl und Sophie, oder die Physiognomisten*, dating from the 1780s (in *Schauspiele*, 4 vols., Leipzig, 1792–1808, vol. 3) and C.F. Bahrdt's comic novel, *Geschichte des Prinzen Yhakanpol . . .*, 1790. For a more temperate critique, see Schopenhauer, *Die Welt als Wille und Vorstellung*, i, §12, in *Sämtliche Werke*, edited by Frauenstädt, 2nd edition, Leipzig, 1891, ii. 67 f.
4. Lichtenberg, *Schriften und Briefe*, 4 volumes, Munich, 1968, i. 414, 460, 472, 493, 507, 556 f., and 600; ii. 560 f. For a more favourable, but still slightly cautious verdict, see H. P. Sturz, 'Erklärung über die Physiognomik', in *Schriften*, new edition, 2 volumes, Leipzig, 1786, ii. 202–16.
5. Claudius, *Werke*, edited by G. Behrmann, Leipzig, n.d. (1908), p. 153.
6. For possible links between character-writing and physiognomical theories via the doctrine of the humours, see above, chapter 11.
7. G. A. Stevens's *A Lecture on Heads* (1765) is not so closely linked with physiognomy as the title might suggest. The book takes the form of a mock-lecture in which the illustrations to the printed text are to be thought of as the lecturer's visual aids. But the 'characters' are perfectly orthodox and in no way physiognomical illustrations of the various heads in the pictures.
8. I possess the third edition, Budapest, 1829. The title-page states that the work is translated from the French, but I have not been able to identify or date the original. At a guess: about 1810–15.
9. See, for instance, the would-be humorous 'Studies from Lavater' in *The Gallery of Comicalities*, ii (1832). A sculptor who believed that he had mastered the secret of creating physiognomically accurate character-busts was Franz Xaver Messerschmidt (1732–83). See Albert Ilg, *F. X. M.s Leben und Werke*, Leipzig and Prague, 1885, especially pp. 50 f. For a contemporary account of Messerschmidt, see Nicolai, *Beschreibung einer Reise durch Deutschland . . .*, Berlin and Stettin, 1785, pp. 405–20.

Bibliography

(i) Bibliographies
(ii) Anthologies
(iii) Theophrastus: Editions and Translations
(iv) Treatises of Rhetoric and the Commonplace Books
(v) The Literature of the Estates
(vi) The Period immediately preceding Hall's *Characters*
(vii) The 'Character' in Seventeenth-Century England
(viii) France
(ix) The 'Character' in Eighteenth-Century England
(x) Germany and Switzerland in the Eighteenth Century
(xi) Loen and his Imitators
(xii) The Nineteenth Century
(xiii) Vienna (*a*) Periodicals in the Tradition of the Moral Weeklies
(*b*) The Viennese Sketch
(xiv) The Twentieth Century
(xv) 'Characters' in Sermons
(xvi) The 'Character' and the Play (*a*) England
(*b*) France
(*c*) German-speaking Countries
(xvii) The Novel (*a*) England
(*b*) Germany
(xviii) Studies on the 'Character'
(xix) General Bibliography

(i) **Bibliographies**

W. Engelmann, *Bibliotheca scriptorum classicorum*, London, 1847 (for Theophrastus, see pp. 248–50).

Anton F. Geißau, *Alphabetisches Verzeichniß derjenigen Brochüren* [*sic*] *und Schriften welche seit der erhaltenen Preßfreyheit herausgekommen sind*, Vienna, 1782.

C. N. Greenough, *A Bibliography of the Theophrastan Character in English* (*Harvard Studies in Comparative Literature*, xviii). Prepared for publication by J. M. French. Harvard University Press, 1947. An invaluable guide to much obscure source-material, but contains many minor inaccuracies.

Alexander Ireland, *A List of the Writings of William Hazlitt and Leigh Hunt*, London, 1868.

C. L. Lang, *Die Zeitschriften der deutschen Schweiz bis zum Ausgang des 18. Jahrhunderts . . .* , Leipzig, 1939.

Gwendolen Murphy, *A Bibliography of English Character-Books, 1608–1700*, London, 1925.

G. Servois, *Œuvres de La Bruyère* (= *Les Grands Écrivains de la France*, Paris, 1922, vol. iv): list of works inspired by La Bruyère on pp. 84–98. Servois had clearly not examined all the items listed and so must be treated with caution.

See also General Bibliography under Kawczynski and Martens.

(ii) **Anthologies**

The Harleian Miscellany: or, a Collection of scarce, curious, and entertaining Pamphlets and Tracts . . . , London, 1774–6 (vols. i–viii) and 1812–13 (vol. ix and Supplement). Contains Lupton's character-book of 1632 and numerous single polemical 'characters' of the late seventeenth century.

J. O. Halliwell, *Books of Characters*, London, 1857.

H. Morley, *Character Writings of the Seventeenth Century*, London, 1891.

Elisabeth Lee, *La Bruyère and Vauvenargues. Selections . . .* , translated by E. L., London, 1903.

Richard Aldington, *A Book of 'Characters'*, London, 1924. Those translated from the French are often abridged without any indication of this from the editor.

Gwendolen Murphy, *A Cabinet of Characters*, London, 1925.

Harold Osborne, *A Mirror of Charactery*, London, 1933.

Heinz Bergner, *English Character-Writing*, Tübingen, 1971.

(iii) **Theophrastus: Editions and Translations. In chronological order**

Isaac Casaubon, *Theophrasti, Characteres ethici . . .* , 1592. Greek text, followed by Latin translation and commentary. I have used the 1617 edition, published in Lyons.

John Healey, *Theophrastus, his Morall Characters.* First published in 1616. Many editions.

La Bruyère, 1687: see below, section (vii).

Eustace Budgell, *The Moral Characters of Theophrastus. Translated from the Greek.* First published in 1699. I have used the 2nd edition, London, 1714.

Henry Gally, *The Moral Characters of Theophrastus . . .* , London, 1725.

Francis Howell, *The Characters of Theophrastus . . . illustrated by Physiognomical Sketches . . .* , London, 1824.

Jebb/Sandys, *The Characters of Theophrastus*, originally edited by R. C. Jebb, 1870; new edition by J. E. Sandys, London, 1909.

J. M. Edmonds, *The Characters*, Loeb Edition, 1929. Greek and English parallel text.

R. G. Ussher, *The Characters of Theophrastus*, London, 1960.

P. Vellacott, *Theophrastus, The Characters. Menander, Plays and Fragments*, edited and translated by Philip Vellacott. Penguin Classics, 1967.

(iv) **Treatises of Rhetoric and the Commonplace Books**

William Baldwin, *A Treatice of Moral Philosophy . . .* augmented by Thomas Paulfreyman . . . , London, 1571. Commonplace book.

J. Bodenham, *Politeuphuia, Wits Common Wealth*, London, 1597. A commonplace book, planned by J. B. and edited by Nicholas Ling.

Cicero, *De Inventione*, Loeb edition, edited by H. M. Hubbell.

—— *De Oratore*, Loeb edition, edited by H. Rackham.

Leonard Cox, *The Arte or Crafte of Rhetorique*, c.1530. Edited by F. I. Carpenter, Chicago, 1899; repr. New York, 1970.

E. Faral, *Les Arts Poétiques du xii*[e] *et du xiii*[e] *siècle*, Paris, 1924. An essay on rhetoric followed by the Latin texts of the treatises.

N. Ling, see Bodenham.

Francis Meres, *Palladis Tamia*, 1598. Edition used: Scholar's Facsimiles . . . , New York, 1938. Introduction by D. C. Allen.

T. Paulfreyman, see Baldwin.

Henry Peacham, *The Garden of Eloquence*, London, 1593.

Quintilian, *Institutionis Oratoriae*, edited by F. H. Colson, CUP, 1924.

Richard Rainolde, *The Foundacion of Rhetorique*, 1563. Edition used: facsimile edition with Introduction by F. R. Johnson, New York, 1945.

Anon., *Rhetorica ad Herennium*, Loeb edition, edited by H. Caplan.

Rutilius Lupus, *De figuris sententiarum et elocutionis*, edited by Edward Brooks, Leiden, 1970.

Richard Sherry, *A Treatise of Schemes and Tropes . . .* , London, 1550.

Richard Taverner, *The Flowers of Sencies, gathered out of sundry wryters by Erasmus in Latine & Englished by R. T.*, London, 1547.

Nicholas Udall, *Apopthegmes . . . first gathered and compiled in Latine by . . . Erasmus . . . And now translated into English by N. U.,* London, 1542.

Thomas Wilson, *The Arte of Rhetorique*, 1553. Edited by G. H. Mair, OUP, 1909.

(v) **The Literature of the Estates**

Anon., *Das Pabstumb mit seinen glydern gemalet und beschriben*, n.p., 1537.

Anon., *Des Teufels Netz*, c.1415. Edited by K. A. Barack, Stuttgart, 1863.

Anon., *Sermones nulli parcentes*, *c.*1220. Edited together with a German translation of *c.*1276, by T. von Karajan in *Zeitschrift für deutsches Alterthum*, ii (1842), pp. 6–92.

William Caxton, *The Game and Playe of the Chesse*, 1474. Edited by W. E. A. Axon, London, 1883. (The chess pieces as symbols of the Estates).

Edward Hake, *Newes out of Powles Churchyarde*, 1567. Edited by C. Edmunds, London, 1872.

William Harrison, *The Description of England*, 1577. Edited by G. Edelen, Cornell University Press, 1968. (See Book ii, chapter 5.)

Lydgate, *The Daunce of Machabee*, in EETS, e.s. cxxiii, London, 1924, pp. 1025–44.

Sir David Lyndsay, *The Dreme*, 1528. In *Minor Poems*, EETS, xi, xix, xxxv, xxxvii, xlvii, pp. 263–302.

Walter Mapes(?), 'De Diversis Ordinibus Hominum', in *Latin Poems commonly attributed to Walter Mapes* edited by T. Wright, London, 1841, pp. 229–36.

See also General Bibliography under Mohl.

(vi) **The Period immediately preceding Hall's Characters**

Thomas Bastard, *Chrestoleros. Seven Bookes of Epigrames* (1598). Edition used: Spenser Society, Manchester, 1888.

Henry Crosse, *The Schoole of Pollicie*, London, 1605. (Originally published in 1603 with the title *Vertues Common-Wealth.*)

Robert Crowley, *Works*, EETS, e.s. xv.

Thomas Dekker, *The non-dramatic Works*, edited by A. Grosart, 5 volumes, London, 1884–6.

John Donne, *The Satires, Epigrams and Verse Letters*, edited by W. Milgate, OUP, 1967.

Everard Guilpin, *Skialethia. Or, A Shadowe of Truth, in certaine Epigrams and Satyres*, London, 1598.

Thomas Lodge, *The Complete Works*, 4 volumes (The Hunterian Club, 1875–87). Reprint: New York and London, 1966.

Thomas Nashe, *Works*, edited by R. B. McKerrow, Reprint, Oxford, 1958. 5 volumes.

Barnaby Rich, *Faultes, Faults, And nothing else but Faultes*, London, 1606.

Samuel Rowlands, *Complete Works*, 4 volumes, 1880. Reprint: New York and London, 1966.

Francis Thynne, *Emblemes and Epigrames*, 1600; EETS, lxiv, 1876.

Thomas Tymme, *A Plaine Discoverie of ten English Lepers*, London, 1592.

(vii) **The 'Character' in Seventeenth-Century England**

Joseph Hall, *Characters of Vertues and Vices*, London, 1608. Contains only 9 'characters' in Part 1, ending with the Good Magistrate.

—— *A Recollection of such Treatises as have bene heretofore severally published* . . . , London, 1615. Characters, pp. 217 ff.; The Penitent and the Happy Man here published for the first time. The complete Characters were then included in *Meditations and Vowes*, London, 1621, in the *Works*, 1625, and in all subsequent editions.

—— *Works*, 12 volumes, Oxford, 1837–9. The *Characters* are in volume 6. All quotations are from this edition. The *Satires* are in volume 12.

Simion Grahame, *The Anatomie of Humours* . . . , 1609. Reprinted Edinburgh, 1830. Contains the rather stereotyped 'character' of a Happy Man, living contentedly in simple retirement.

John Davies, *The Muses Sacrifice, or Divine Meditations* . . . , London, 1612. Contains 2 verse-characters.

Sir Thomas Overbury, *A Wife . . . Whereunto are added many witty Characters* . . . , London, 1614. Contains 21 'characters'. Subsequent editions add to these: there are 82 by 1616 and an 83rd is added in 1622. Full details in Murphy's *Bibliography*.

—— *Miscellaneous Works*, edited by E. F. Rimbault, London, 1890. All quotations are from this edition. I am also indebted to W. J. Paylor's Notes to *The Overburian Characters*, Oxford, 1936.

Richard Brathwaite, *A Strappado for the Divell*, London, 1615. Contains 3 verse-characters.

John Stephens, *Essayes and Characters*, 1615. Reprinted by J. O. Halliwell, *Books of Characters*, London, 1857. I have used this edition.

Thomas Tuke, *The Christian's Looking-Glasse*, London, 1615. Treatise on Christian love; includes the 'character' of a Proud Man.

—— *A Treatise against Painting . . . Whereunto is added the picture of a picture, or, the Character of a Painted Woman*, London, 1616.

Nicholas Breton, *The Good and the Badde*, 1616. In *Works*, 2 volumes, edited by A. B. Grosart, 1879; repr. New York, 1966, volume ii.

William Fennor, *The Counter's Commonwealth*, 1617. Reprinted in *The Elisabethan Underworld*, edited by A.V. Judges, London, 1930, pp. 423 ff. Contains the 'character' of a Prison.

Thomas Young, *Englands Bane* . . . , London, 1617. Contains the 'character' of a Drunkard.

Geffray Mynshul, *Essayes and Characters of a Prison and Prisoners*, 1618. I have used the edition published in London in 1638.

Henry Hutton, *Follie's Anatomie*, 1619. Edition used: *Percy Society Reprints*, London, 1842.

Richard Brathwaite, *Essaies upon the five senses* . . . , London, 1620. Contains the 'character' of a Shrew.

John Ford, *A Line of Life*, London, 1620. Contains the 'character' of a Good Man.

Alexander Garden [Gardyne], *Characters and Essayes*, Aberdeen, 1625. Versification of Breton.

George Wither, *The Schollers Purgatory*, London, n.d. [1625]. Has the 'character' of a Stationer (printer and bookseller).

H. P. [Henry Parrot], *Cures for the Itch* . . . , London, 1626. Contains 13 'characters'.

'Pasquil' [Breton], *Pasquils Mad-cappe* . . . , London, 1626. Verse satire on the theme that 'money makes or marres the man'. Includes a number of short 'characters'. In Grosart's edition, volume i.

John Earle, *Microcosmography*, 1628. I have used the edition by W. H. D. Rouse, London, 1890. I am also indebted to that by A. A. West, CUP, 1920.

R. M., *Micrologia. Characters, or Essayes, of Persons, Trades, and Places* . . . , London, 1629. 16 'characters'.

Anon., *The Tincker of Turvey* . . . , London, 1630. Imitation of Chaucer. Each tale-teller is described 'in a Neate Character'.

John Taylor, *Works*, 3 volumes in l, London, 1630. Contains a number of verse-characters.

Richard Brathwaite, *Whimzies*, 1631. Edition used is that by J. O. Halliwell, London, 1859. 24 'characters', arranged in alphabetical order.

Frances Lenton, *Characterismi* . . . , London, 1631. 41 'characters'.

Wye Saltonstall, *Picturae Loquentes, Or Pictures Drawne forth in Characters.* First published in 1631, with 27 'characters'. The second edition of 1635 has 12 additional 'characters'. I have quoted from C. H. Wilkinson's edition, Oxford, 1946 (*Luthrell Reprints*, No. 1).

Donald Lupton, *London and the Country* . . . , 1632. Reprinted in the *Harleian Miscellany*, ix (1812). I have used this edition. 36 'characters', mostly of places.

Anon., *A strange Metamorphosis of Man, transformed into a Wildernesse. Deciphered in Characters*, London, 1634. 40 'characters', mostly of animals, birds, and insects.

William Habington, *Castara*. The 2nd edition of 1635 contains 3 'characters'; a fourth was added in 1638. Edition used is that by C. A. Elton, Bristol, n.d. [1812].

Thomas Jordan, *Poeticall Varieties* . . . , London, 1637. Contains the verse-character of a Whore, different from that in the 1641 collection.

Henry Peacham, *The Truth of our Times*, 1638. Edition used is that of the Facsimile Text Society, No. 55, New York, 1942, edited by R. R. Cawley. Contains 2 'characters'.

Anon., *A Dialogue* . . . , London, 1640. Contains the verse-character of a Puritan.

Thomas Jordan, *Pictures of Passions, Fancies, and Affections*, London, n.d. [1641]. 19 rhymed 'characters'.

Nathanael Richards, *Poems sacred and satiricall*, London, 1641. 'The Jesuite' (pp. 45–53) is half-way between a portrait of Henry Garnet and a 'character'.

Richard Watts, *The Younge Man's Looking Glasse . . .* , London, 1641. Contains 2 'characters'.

Anon., *The English Irish Souldier*, London, 1642.

Anon., *The Jesuits Character . . .* , London, 1642.

Humphrey Browne, *A Map of the Microcosme, or, A Morall Description of Man*, London, 1642. 17 'characters'.

Thomas Fuller, *The Holy State, and the Profane State*, 1642. 48 'characters', written in the form of a succession of maxims, some followed by illustrative lives. I have used the edition by J. Nichols, London, 1841.

James Howell, *Instructions for Forreine Travell*, 1642. I have used E. Arber's edition, *English Reprints*, London, 1869. Includes 'characters' of a Frenchman and a Spaniard.

Dudley, Lord North, *A Forest of Varieties*, London, 1645. Contains 10 'characters', written *c.*1625.

Anon., *The Picture of an English Antick . . .* , London, n.d. [1646].

John Cleveland, *The Character of a London-Diurnall*, London, 1646.

John Geree, *The Character of an Old English Puritane . . .* , London, 1646.

Sir Francis Wortley, *Characters and Elegies*, London, 1646. 14 'characters'.

Anon., *The Character of an Agitator*, London(?), 1647.

J. B., *The Assembly-Man*, 1647. Reprinted in the *Harleian Miscellany*, v. 93–8.

Thomas Ford, *The Times Anatomiz'd, in severall Characters*, London 1647. 30 'characters'.

Ralph Venning, *Orthodoxe Paradoxes . . .* , London, 1647. See pp. 41 ff. for the 'character' of a Good Christian.

R. Y., *A Touch-Stone to try . . . whether we be Christians . . . Or, The Character of a True Beleever . . .* , London, 1648.

'R. Junius', *The Drunkard's Character*, London, 1638. Reprinted as *The Odious . . . Condition of a Drunkard . . .* , London, 1649, under the pseudonym 'Junius Florilegus'. I have used the later edition.

Anon., *The Routing of the Ranters*, London, 1650.

Anon., *The Character of an honest and worthy Parliament-Man*, n.d. [*c.*1650]. Reprinted in the *Harleian Miscellany*, ii. 336 f.

Sir Henry Wotton, 'The Character of a Happy Life', first published posthumously in *Reliquiae Wottonianae*, London, 1651.

Anon., *A Looking-Glasse for a Drunkard . . .* , London, 1652.

John Donne, *Paradoxes, Problemes, Essayes, Characters . . .* , London, 1652. Posthumous publication, including the 'characters' of a Dunce (reprinted from the 11th edition of the Overbury collection, 1622) and of a Scot, here published for the first time.

George Herbert, *A Priest to the Temple; or, the Country Parson, his Character, and Rule of Holy Life*, written *c.*1632 and first published 1652. Edition used: *Works*, London, 1853, i. 143 ff. Chapters 3, 7, 8, and 9 virtually form an extended 'character' of a Country Parson.

Richard Flecknoe, *Miscellania, or, Poems of all Sorts, with divers other Pieces*, London, 1653. Includes 4 'characters', one of which (the French Lutanist) was taken up in the 1658 collection.

'Junius Florilegus', *Philarguromastix* . . . , London, n.d. [1653]. Moralizing tract on covetousness, including the hostile 'character' of a Lawyer.

John Cleveland, *A Character of a London Diurnal-Maker*, London, 1654.

Edmund Gayton, *Wil. Bagnal's Ghost* . . . , London, 1655. Includes 4 'characters' concerning prison life.

Richard Younge, *The Blemish of Government* . . . , London, 1655. Has the 'character' of a Drunkard.

Anon., *Two Essays of Love and Marriage . . . Together with some Characters and other Passages of Wit*, London, 1657. 13 'characters'.

William Sprigge, *Philosophicall Essayes* . . . , London, 1657. Part iii contains 5 'characters'.

Samuel Austin, *Naps upon Parnassus*, London, 1658. Contains 2 extremely mannered 'characters'.

Samuel Crook, *Divine Characters* . . . , London, 1658. Includes 'characters' of various types of Hypocrite.

Richard Flecknoe, *Enigmaticall Characters* . . . , London, 1658. 69 'characters'.

—— *Characters made at Several Times* . . . London, 1673. 19 are here published for the first time. The way in which successive editions of Flecknoe print old and new 'characters' in various combinations is confusing: see Murphy's *Bibliography* for details.

—— *Heroick Portraits* . . . , London, 1660. An attempt to import the French *portrait* into England.

Francis Osborn, *A Miscellany* . . . , London, 1659. Contains 3 'characters'.

C[lement] E[llis], *The Gentile Sinner, or, England's Brave Gentleman Characterized* . . . , Oxford, 1660. A treatise on manners, incorporating a few rather diffusely written 'characters'.

L. G., *Essayes and Characters*, London, 1661. 18 'characters'.

K. W., *Confused Characters of Conceited Coxcombs*, 1661. Reprinted by Halliwell, London, 1860. I have used this edition. 23 'characters'.

Anon., *The Coffee Scuffle* . . . , London, 1662. Includes the verse-character of a Pedagogue.

George Leyburn, *Holy Characters* . . . , 2 books, Douai, 1662. The hostile descriptions of sinners are nearer to true character-writing than the idealized pictures.

P. B., *Juvenilia Sacra, or, Divine Youthfull Meditations* . . . , London, 1664. Includes 4 'characters' in 2 contrasting pairs.

Samuel Person, *An Anatomical Lecture of Man. Or a Map of the Little World, Delineated in Essayes and Characters*, London, 1664. About a score of pieces can strictly be designated 'characters'.

Richard Brathwaite, *The Captive-Captain* . . . , London, 1665. Contains a group of prison-characters.

Ralph Johnson, *The Scholar's Guide* . . . , London, 1665. Gives a recipe for character-writing.

Charles Molloy, *Holland's Ingratitude* . . . , London, 1666. A political pamphlet, with 'characters' of a Dutchman and a Frenchman appended.

L. P., *The Vertuous Wife*, London, 1667. Concludes with the Virtuous Woman from *Proverbs* 31.

Samuel Butler, 'Characters' written between 1667 and 1669. 121 of these were first published in 1759, another 75 in this century. I quote from the edition by C. W. Daves, Cleveland, Ohio, and London, 1970; I have also consulted that by A. R. Waller, CUP, 1908.

Jeremiah Wells, *Poems upon divers Occasions* . . . , London, 1667. One 'character', of a Scrivener.

Richard Graham, *Angliae Speculum Morale* . . . , London, 1670. Contains 12 'characters'.

Anon., *The Character of a Quaker*, London, 1671.

Edward Panton, *Speculum Juventutis*, London, 1671. Contains a number of 'characters', the most interesting being the hostile picture of an Old Man.

Anon., *Poor Robins Character of a Dutchman* . . . , London, 1672.

Anon., *The Character of a Coffee-House* . . . , London, 1673.

Anon., *The Character of a Papist*, London, 1673.

Anon., *The Character of a Quack-Astrologer* . . . , London, 1673.

Thomas Flatman, *Poems and Songs*, London, 1674. Includes the verse-character of a Happy Man.

Anon., *Ape-Gentle-women, or the Character of an Exchange-wench,* London, 1675.

Anon., *Character of a Fanatick* . . . , London, 1675.

Anon., *Character of an Informer* . . . , London, 1675.

Anon., *The Character of a Soliciter* . . . , London, 1675.

Anon., *The Character of a Tavern* . . . , London, 1675.

Anon., *The Character of a Town-Gallant* . . . , London, 1675.

Anon., *The Character of a Town Misse*, London, 1675.

Thomas Traherne, *Christian Ethicks* . . . , London, 1675. Contains the 'characters' of a Magnanimous Soul and of a Liberal Man.

Anon., *The Character of an Honest Lawyer*, London, 1676.

Anon., *The Character of a Quack-Doctor* . . . , London, 1676.

Anon., *A Warning for Housekeepers* . . . , London, 1676. Describes various types of thieves. The old vagabond-literature influenced by character-writing. See too 'J. W.', 1698.

Anon., *A brief Character of the Low-Countries* . . . , London, 1677. Includes the 'character' of a Dutchman.

Anon., *The Character of a Turbulent, Pragmatical Jesuit* . . . , London, 1678.

Poor Robin [William Winstanley?], *Four for a Penny*, London, 1678. Reprinted in the *Harleian Miscellany*, iv. 141 f. 4 'characters'.

Anon., *The Character of a Compleat Physician* . . . , London, n.d. [*c.* 1680]. The British Museum copy has 'by Dr. Mee' in ink beneath the title.

Anon., *The Character of an English-Man*, London, n.d. [1680].

Anon., *The Character of a Town-Gallant* . . . , London, 1680.

Anon., *The Character of a disbanded Courtier*, 1681. Reprinted in the *Harleian Miscellany*, i. 356 f.

Anon., *The Character of a Jesuit*, London, 1681.

Anon., *The Character of an Unjust Judge,* London, 1681.

Anon., *The Character of a Church-Trimmer*, London, 1683.

Anon., *The Character of a Trimmer*, London, 1683. Different from the previous item.

P. K., *Floskulum Poeticum* . . . , London, 1684. Has 4 'characters' in prose.

Anon., *The Character and Qualifications of an Honest Loyal Merchant*, London, 1686.

Anon., *Twelve Ingenious Characters* . . . , London,, 1686.

Stephen Penton, *The Guardian's Instruction* . . . , London, 1688. A treatise on the education, accomplishments, and behaviour of a gentleman. Contains a few illustrative 'characters'.

Anon., *The Character of a True English Protestant Souldier* . . . , London, 1689.

Anon., 'The Fop', in *The Gentleman's Journal*, iii (London, 1694), 228 f.

Anon., *The Character of the Beaux* . . . , London, 1696. 5 'characters' of different kinds of Beau.

Anon., *Pecuniae Obediunt Omnia* . . . , York, 1696. A long satirical poem on the power of money. It is divided into sections, each devoted to a class, trade, or profession. Somewhere between a character-book and the older type of satire on the shortcomings of the Estates.

Anon., *An Essay in Defence of the Female Sex*, 1696. I have used the 3rd edition, London, 1697. Contains 9 'characters'.

Daniel Defoe, *An Essay upon Projects*, London, 1697. Includes the 'character' of a Projector.

Charles Boyle, 4th Earl of Orerry, *Dr. Bentley's Dissertations . . . Examined*, London, 1698. Contains the 'character' of a Good Critic.

Algernon Sydney, *Discourses concerning Government*, 1698. Edition used: Edinburgh, 1750, 2 volumes. Contains the 'characters' of a Good and a Bad Magistrate (ii. 171 ff.).

J. W., *Youth's Safety . . .*, London, 1698. Gives 'characters' of various types of swindlers.

Ned Ward, *The London Spy*, 1698–1700. I have used K. Fenwick's edition, London, 1955. Contains a number of 'characters', both prose and verse.

Anon., *The Country Gentleman's Vade Mecum . . .*, London, 1699. Gives 'characters' of London rogues and idlers.

(viii) **France**

(Many imitations of La Bruyère concentrate on reflections and aphorisms to the virtual or entire exclusion of 'characters' and have therefore been omitted from this list.)

Joseph Hall, *Caracteres de Vertus et de Vices . . .*, translated by J. L. de Tourval, Paris, 1610. A faithful version by early seventeenth-century standards, but not as stylish as the rendering by Chevreau in 1646 (see below).

Eustache Du Refugé, *Traicté de la Cour*, n.p., n.d. [1615]. 'Character' of the Fearful Man (*Le Craintif*) on p. 90.

Pierre le Moyne, *Les Peintures Morales . . .*, first published 1640–3. I have used the 2nd edition of 1645 for volume i and the 1st edition of 1643 for volume ii.

Urbain Chevreau, *L'Escole du Sage*, 1646. I have used the 'dernière edition augmentée', Paris, 1609 [= 1659].

Regnauld de Segrais, *La Galerie des Portraits . . .*, 1659. I have used the edition by E. de Barthélemy, Paris, 1860.

James Dynocke, *Le Vice ridicule et la Vertu loüée*, Louvain, 1671. 94 'characters', mostly translated from Overbury, Earle, and Flecknoe. Some, for which I could not trace any English originals, may have been written by Dynocke himself.

Jean de La Bruyère, *Les Caractères de Théophraste traduits du grec avec les Caractères ou les Mœurs de ce Siècle*. First published in 1688 and expanded in subsequent editions. Modern printings are based on the 9th edition of 1696. A chronological list of editions and translations consulted follows.

—— *The Characters, or the Manners of the Age . . .*, London, 1699. The translation is preceded by a Key to about 60 of the 'characters'.

—— *Works*, 6th edition, London, 1713. The Index to volume ii gives a Key.

—— *Works*, 2 volumes, London, 1723.

—— *Œuvres*, 3 volumes, edited by G. Servois, Paris, 1865–78.

—— *The 'Characters' . . .*, translated and edited by Henri van Laun, London, 1885.

—— *Œuvres*, edited by G. Servois, 3rd edition, Paris, 1922.

—— *Les Caractères*, edited by R. Pignarre, Paris, 1965. French quotations given in Appendix 2 are from this edition.

—— *Characters*, translated by Jean Stewart, Penguin, 1970.

Mme de Pringy, *Les Differens Caracteres des Femmes du Siecle*, 1694. I have used the 2nd edition of 1699.

Claude Boyer, *Les Caractères des Prédicateurs* . . . , Paris, 1695. Contains verse-characters of various kinds of Preacher.

Abbé Bellegarde, *Les Reflexions sur la Ridicule* . . . , Paris, 1696. Contains numerous short 'characters' woven into the essays. Translated into English, 1706–7. Numbered by some critics among the forerunners of *The Tatler* and *The Spectator*.

P. J. Brillon, *Portraits serieux, galands et critiques*, Paris, 1696.

—— *Suite des Caracteres de Theophraste, et des Pensées de Mr. Pascal*, Paris, 1697.

Urbain Chevreau, *Chevraeana, ou diverses Pensèes* . . . , first published in 1697. I have used the 2-volume edition, Amsterdam, 1700. Paraphrased and versified adaptations of 'characters' by Hall: i. 177–9; i. 354–7; ii. 405–11. For a short prose-character in imitation of Hall, see i. 169 f.

—— *Œuvres meslées* . . . , 1697. I have used the 2-volume edition (numbered through), published in The Hague, 1717. Includes portraits (e.g., on pp. 62–71) and a short paraphrase of Hall's Hypocrite (p. 627).

P. J. Brillon, *Le Théophraste Moderne, ou nouveaux Caracteres sur les Mœurs*, The Hague, 1700.

J. P. de Varennes, *Les Hommes*, 1712. Edition used: Paris, 1727. Closely modelled on La Bruyère, both in its general plan and in the style of character-writing.

Justus van Effen, *Le Misantrope*, 2 volumes, The Hague, 1712–13. Contains 'characters' indebted both to La Bruyère and to *The Spectator*.

Anon., *Les Caracteres du faux et du veritable Amour* . . . , Paris, 1716.

Justus van Effen, *La Bagatelle*, 1718–19. Contained in volumes 3–4 of *Œuvres diverses*, Amsterdam, 1742. 4 brief 'characters' in No. 44. No. 17 of *Le Nouveau Spectateur françois*, in volume 5, also contains 'characters'. First published in 1724.

Marivaux, *Le Cabinet du Philosophe*, 1733–4. No. 5 contains 2 'characters' of Coquettes: see Marivaux, *Journeaux et Œuvres diverses*, edited by F. Deloffre and M. Gilot, Paris, 1969, pp. 371 ff.

Luc de Clapiers, Marquis de Vauvenargues, *Essai sur quelques caractères*, written 1746–7 and published posthumously. Edition used: *Œuvres*, Paris, 1929, i. 143 ff.

Mme de P____ [Puisieux], *Les Caractères*, 1747. I have used the London edition of 1750.

Anon., *Petit Reservoir* . . . , 5 volumes, The Hague, 1750–1. Contains 3 'characters' from the *Rambler* in translation, but no original 'characters'.

Anon., *Le Spectateur françois, pour servir de suite à celui de M. de*

Marivaux, Paris, 1770. Contains tributes to Addison and La Bruyère, but only a few 'characters'.

J. J. Rutlidge, *Le Babillard*, 3 volumes, Paris, 1778. Some 'characters'.

Anon., *Les Numéros*, 4 volumes, Amsterdam, 1783–4. No. 19 gives the 'character' of a Timid Man.

Sénac de Meilhan, *Considérations sur l'Esprit et les Mœurs*, London, 1787. Modelled on La Bruyère.

S. R. N. Chamfort, 'Caracteres et Anecdotes', first published posthumously in volume 4 of the *Œuvres*, Paris, 1795, pp. 211–442; then in *Maximes, Pensées, Caracteres et Anecdotes*, Paris, 1796, pp. 139–284. Modern edition by A. van Bever, Paris, 1924. Only a few 'characters', mostly very short; the 'character' has deteriorated into gossipy anecdotage. (The 'Maximes et Pensées' is a separate work and contains no 'characters'.)

Stéphanie-Félicité, Countess de Genlis, *Le Petit La Bruyère* . . . , 1799. I have used the 2nd edition, Paris, 1801.

Sénac de Meilhan, *Portraits et Caractères* . . . , posthumous publication, Paris, 1813. Not the orthodox distinction. Here *portrait* stands for an explicitly identified sketch of a famous person, while *caractère* is a camouflaged portrait hidden behind a fictitious name.

Gustave Le Vavasseur, *Caractères et portraits rustiques*, first published in 1864; then, augmented, in *Poésies Complètes*, ii (Paris, 1888), 69 ff.

Gaston de Varennes, *Types et Caractères* . . . , Tours, 1882.

(xi) **The 'Character' in Eighteenth-Century England**

Anon., *The Lively Character of a Contented and Discontented Cuckold* . . . , London, 1700.

Anon., *The Character of a Whig*, London, 1700.

Anon., *Wit's Cabinet* . . . , London, n.d. [*c*.1700].

Anon., [Defoe], *The True-Born Englishman. A Satyr*, n.p. [London], 1700.

Thomas Brown, *Amusements serious and comical*, 1700. In *Works*, 4 volumes, 7th edition, London, 1730, vol. 3. Contains a few 'characters', including a vivid picture of an Innkeeper.

Ned Ward, *The Reformer. Exposing the Vices of the Age in several CHARACTERS* . . . , 1700. Edition used: London, 1705.

E. B., *A Trip to North Wales* . . . , London, 1701. Contains a scornful 'character' of the Welsh.

Anon., *The Character of a Covetous Citizen . . . A Poem*, London, 1702.

Anon., [Abel Boyer], *The English Theophrastus, or, the Manners of the Age* . . . , London, 1702. Modern edition by W. E. Britton, *Augustan Reprint Society* (i. 3), Michigan, 1946 (extracts only).

Anon. [Defoe], *Matrimony; or, Good Advice to the Ladies to keep single*, 1702. Edition used: London, 1739.

Anon. [Richard West?], *The True Character of a Church-Man . . . together with the Character of a Low Church-man . . .* , London, 1702.

Sir Charles Sedley, *The Miscellaneous Works*, London, 1702. 'The Happy Pair' contains the verse-character of a miserly Husband.

Anon., *An English Monster: or, the Character of an Occasional Conformist*, London, 1703.

Mary Chudleigh, 'The Happy Man', in *Poems on Several Occasions*, London, 1703, pp. 35 f.

Anon., *The Character of a Sneaker*, 1705. Reprinted in the *Harleian Miscellany*, ii (1744), pp. 337–40.

Thomas Brown, *A Legacy for the Ladies: or, Characters of the Women of the Age*, 1705. In T. B., *Remains*, London, 1720, pp. 145 ff. Twelve 'characters' in six contrasting pairs.

Isaac Watts, 'True Wisdom' and 'True Courage', both dating from 1706, contain short 'characters'. Many editions. I have used that in Bell's *Poets of Great Britain*, lx–lxv.

Ned Ward, *The Wooden World Dissected . . .* , 1707. I have used the edition by G. Callender, London, 1929.

Anon., *Satyrical Reflections on the Vices and Follies of the Age . . .* , 7 parts, London, 1707–8. Part i, 18 f. contains the verse-character of a Sea-Captain.

Matthew Prior, 'The Chameleon', a verse-character, written before 1708. Edition used: *The Literary Works*, edited by H. B. Wright and M. K. Spears, 2 volumes, OUP, 1959, i. 269 f.

'J. D.', 'The Character of a Friend', in *Miscellany Poems*, edited by Elijah Fenton, London, n.d. [*c.*1708], pp. 244 f.

Ned Ward, *The Modern World Disrob'd*, London, 1708.

Jeremy Collier, *Essays upon several Moral Subjects*, first published in its entirety in 1709. I have used the 6th edition, 4 parts, London, 1722–5. Contains some 'characters', including the Noble Man, the Covetous Man, and the Coward.

The Tatler, 1709–11. Edition used: *British Essayists*, i–v. Mostly by Steele. About 40 papers by Addison. Swift also contributed.

Alexander Pope, Various 'characters' and portraits scattered about the works. Written between 1709 and 1735. Edition used: *Works*, 10 volumes, edited by Elwin and Courthope, London, 1871–86.

Anon., *The Character of a Modern Addresser*, London, 1710.

Anon., *A Dream . . . A Poem, containing Characters of the Company now at the Bath . . .* , London, 1710. In fact, these are sycophantic portraits with keys supplied.

C. Povey, *The Visions of Sir Heister Ryley . . .* , London, n.d. [1710]. No. 21 contains the 'character' of a Virtuous Woman.

Anon., *The Character of a True Churchman . . .* , London, 1711.

James Puckle, *The Club . . .* , 1711. Edition used: London, 1834.

The Spectator, 1711–14. Edition used is that by D. F. Bond, 5 volumes, OUP, 1965. Contributors: Addison, Steele, Budgell, and others.

The Guardian, 1713. Edition used: *British Essayists*, xvi–xviii. Contributors: Steele, Addison, Pope, Gay, Budgell, and others.

The Lover, 1714. In *Steele's Periodical Journalism*, edited by R. Blanchard, OUP, 1959.

L. Theobald, *The Censor*, 3 volumes, London, 1717.

The Entertainer, London, 1717–18. Contains echoes of a by now outdated witty manner.

The Free-Thinker, 1718–19. Book-form: 3 volumes, London, 1722–3. Mostly written by Ambrose Philips.

Thomas Gordon, *The Humourist*, first published in 1720. I have used the 4th edition, London, 1741.

Anon. [Defoe?], *The Comical Pilgrim* . . . , 2nd edition, London, 1722. A 'General Satyr' on vice and folly. Contains 4 'characters'.

Applebee's Journal, 1722 ff. Contains 'characters' by Defoe: 27/10/1722, 7/3/1724, 5/12/1724, 6/3/1725, 17/4/1725, 30/10/1725, and 6/11/1725. Reprinted by William Lee in *Daniel Defoe: his Life, and recently discovered Writings*, London, 1869, volume 3.

Anon., *The Pettifoggers* . . . , London, 1723. Verse-satire: includes a number of short 'characters'.

The True Briton, London, 1723–4. A political weekly, containing some 'characters'.

William Law, *A Practical Treatise upon Christian Perfection*, 1726. In *Works*, 9 volumes, edited by G. B. Morgan, Brockenhurst, 1892–3, volume 3.

Richard Savage, 'The Gentleman': verse-character, *c*.1726. Edition used: Bell's *Poets of Great Britain*, lxxxix. 124 f.

William Law, *A Serious Call to a Devout and Holy Life*, 1728. Ed. cit., volume iv.

Edward Young, *Love of Fame* . . . , 1728. In *The Poetical Works*, London, n.d. [1830–6), ii. 54–140. Contains a number of verse-characters in the style of Pope.

The Intelligencer, Dublin, 1729. Contributors include Swift and Thomas Sheridan.

Henry Stonecastle, *The Universal Spectator*, 1731. I have used the 4-volume selection, London, 1747.

The Gentleman's Magazine . . . , London, 1731 ff. Contains many short verse-characters.

The Scarborough Miscellany for the Year 1732, 2nd edition, London, 1734. Contains a 'character' of a Beau, pp. 35–8.

John Earle, *Microcosmography* . . . , London, 1733. Slightly modernized reprint. 78 'characters'.

Grub-street Journal, 22/5/1735: 'character' of a Pretty Fellow.

Anon., *A Trip through the Town . . .*, 1735. Reprinted in *Tricks of the Town . . .*, edited by R. Straus, London, 1927. Gives 'characters' of Servants and Beggars.

William Melmoth, *Of Active and Retired Life . . .*, 1735. In *A Collection of Poems by Several Hands*, London, 1748, i. 185 ff. Has a verse-character of a True Patriot.

Mark Arkenside, 'The Virtuoso', 1737. Verse-character in *Poetical Works*, London, 1884, pp. 286–9.

John Constable, *The Conversation of Gentlemen . . .*, London, 1738. Dialogues on men and manners, containing a number of 'characters'.

Anon., *An Essay towards the Character of the late Chimpanzee*, London, 1739. A take-off of the laudatory portrait.

The Champion, 1739–40. Fielding's contributions to this paper are given in volume xv of his *Collected Works*, edited by W. E. Henley, London, 1903. See pp. 95 f. for the 'character' of a Hypocrite. Otherwise, however, Fielding does not seem interested in the genre.

John Earle, *The World Display'd . . .*, London, 1740. Reprint of 1733 edition under a new title.

O. Sedgewick, *The Universal Masquerade . . .*, London, 1742. Contains 'characters' of two sorts of Critic.

Anon., *An Epistle to the Fair Sex on the subject of Drinking . . .*, London, 1744. Temperance tract, with 'characters' serving as awful warnings.

David Fordyce, *Dialogues concerning Education*, London, 1745. Contains various illustrative 'characters'.

Eliza Haywood, *The Female Spectator*, 4 volumes, London, 1745. Contains a letter giving the 'characters' of three Suitors (ii. 105 ff.) and that of a 'City Lady turned courtier' (iii. 220 f.).

Soame Jenyns, *The Modern Fine Gentleman*, London, 1746. Verse-character.

'Philautus' [Nathaniel Lancaster], *The Pretty Gentleman . . .*, London, 1747.

Anon., *An Earnest Appeal to Passionate People*, London, 1748. Moral tract with illustrative 'characters': the Passionate Man, the Peevish Man, etc.

Anon., *The Retirement. An Ethic Poem . . .*, London, 1748. Contains the 'character' of a Miser.

Anon., *Characterism, or, the Modern Age Display'd*, London, n.d. [*c.*1750]. 30 'characters'. A rare eighteenth-century example of a character-book in seventeenth-century form.

Peter Shaw, *The Reflector . . .*, London, 1750. Moral treatise with exemplary 'characters'.

The Rambler, 1750–2. Mostly written by Dr Johnson. Edition used: *British Essayists*, xix–xxii.

Anon. [Soame Jenyns], *The Modern Fine Lady*, 2nd edition, London, 1751. Verse-character.

The Adventurer, 1752–4. Edition: *British Essayists*, xxiii–xxv. John Hawkesworth wrote about half. Dr Johnson also contributed.

John Hill, *The Inspector*, 2 volumes, London, 1753.

The World, 1753–65. Edition: *British Essayists*, xxvi–xxix. Contributors included Edward Moore, Chesterfield, and Horace Walpole.

The Connoisseur, 1754–6. Edition: *British Essayists*, xxx–xxxii. Written almost entirely by George Coleman the elder and Bonnel Thornton.

The Friend, London, 1755.

Cornelius Arnold, *The Mirror* . . . , n.p. [London], 1755. A pastiche of Spenser. 15 'characters'.

The Idler, 1758–60. Edition, *British Essayists*, xxxiii. Mostly written by Dr Johnson.

J. Langhorne, 'The Happy Villager', *c.*1760. Verse-character. In *Poetical Works*, Cooke's Edition, London, n.d., p. 63.

Oliver Goldsmith, *The Citizen of the World*, 1762. Contains various 'characters'. In volume ii of the *Collected Works* in 5 volumes, edited by A. Friedman, OUP, 1966.

George Alexander Stevens, *A Lecture on Heads*, 1765. I have used the edition published in London in 1812. Combines 'characters' with parody of physiognomical speculation.

Robert Noyes, 'Female Characters' (1770), in *Miscellanies*, Canterbury, n.d. [1785]. Verse-characters in the style of Pope.

Hester Chapone, *Miscellanies in Prose and Verse*, 1775. Edition used: London, 1807. Contains a number of 'characters', probably dating from *c.*1770.

The Laughing Philosopher, Dublin, 1777.

James Boswell, *The Hypochondriack* . . . (essays from the *London Magazine*, 1777–83), edited by Margery Bailey, 2 volumes, Stanford University Press, 1928. 'Character' of a Hypocrite: ii. 40–6.

George Keate, *Sketches from Nature* . . . , 1779. Edition used: London, 1802. 'Sentimental Journey' type of travel journal; contains short 'characters' of various types of readers.

The Mirror, 1779–80. In *British Essayists*, xxxiv–xxxv. Produced in Edinburgh by a group including R. Cullen, McLeod Bannatyne, and G. Ogilvy.

William Creech, 'Character' of an Ideal Wife, dated 1784, in *Fugitive Pieces*, Edinburgh, 1815, pp. 233 ff.

Richard Cumberland, *The Observer*, 1785. In *British Essayists*, xxxviii–xl.

The Lounger, 1785–7. In *British Essayists*, xxxvi–xxxvii. For the contributors, see *The Mirror*, 1779–80.

(John Earle), *Micro-cosmography* . . . , Salisbury and London, 1786. A different edition from those of 1733 and 1740. 74 'characters'.

Variety: a Collection of Essays, London, 1787. Contains 'characters'.

'Timothy Touchstone', *The Trifler*, London, 1788–9. Written by R. Oliphant, J. H. Allen, and others. Has the 'characters' of the Bluestocking and the Country Justice.

James Austen (Jane's brother), 'Character' of an Oxford Beau in *The Loiterer*, 21/2/1789. Reprinted in R. Brimley Johnson, *Jane Austen . . .*, London and Toronto, 1930, pp. 220 f.

'The Rev. Simon Olive-Branch', *The Looker-on*, 1792–4. In *British Essayists*, xli–xliv.

M. Hawke and R. Vincent, *The Ranger*, 2 volumes, Brentford, 1794–5.

The Sylph, London, 1795–6. No. 8 has two short 'characters'.

K. Watkins, *The Peeper*, London, 1796. Nos. 5 and 13 contain 'characters'.

The Flapper, Dublin, 1796–7.

The Philanthrope, London, 1797.

The Quiz, London, 1797–9. By 'a Society of Gentlemen'.

(x) Germany and Switzerland in the Eighteenth Century

Der Vernünfftler. Das ist: Ein teutscher Auszug aus den Engelländischen Moral-Schrifften Des Tatler und Spectator . . ., von Joanne Mattheson, Hamburg, 1721. First published 1713–14.

Die Discourse der Mahlern, Zurich, 1721–3. J. J. Bodmer and J. J. Breitinger.

Bernisches Freytags-Blätlein . . ., 6 parts, Berne, 1722–4. Written by a group headed by J. G. Altmann. Many short 'characters'.

Der Patriot, 3 volumes, Hamburg, 1724–6. I have used the 2nd edition of 1728–9. One of the most important German moral weeklies. Contributors included Heinrich Brockes.

Die vernünftigen Tadlerinnen, 2 volumes, Leipzig, 1725–6. J. C. Gottsched. I have also consulted the 2nd edition of 1738.

Der Biedermann, Leipzig, 1727–9. J. C. Gottsched. Edition used: *Faksimiledruck*, edited by W. Martens, Stuttgart, 1975, 2 volumes in 1. Another very important early moral weekly.

Die Matrone, Hamburg, 1728.

Der Sachsen Spiegel, n.p. [Leipzig], 1728.

Der alte Deutsche, Hamburg, 1730.

Der Bürger, Göttingen, 1732–3.

Der Teutsche Bernerische Spectateur, Berne, 1734. 26 numbers in 1 volume. Edited by J. G. Altmann, this is a continuation of the *Freytags-Blätlein*; in fact, the separate issues still bear that name and only the bound edition has the new title. Only a few 'characters', but the periodical is of great interest as an expression of Swiss civic pride.

Der Sammler, Göttingen, 1736. Many short 'characters'.

Der deutsche Diogenes, Danzig, 1736–7. Contains 13 'characters', all in verse.

Die mühsame Bemerckerin derer menschlichen Handlungen . . ., Danzig, 1737. Many 'characters'.

Der Zerstreuer, Göttingen, 1737. Sequel to *Der Sammler*.

Der Menschenfreund, Hamburg, 1737–9. J. F. Lamprecht.

Der Freymäurer, Leipzig, 1738.

Der Zuschauer. Aus dem Englischen übersetzt, 9 parts, Leipzig, 1739–51. Complete translation of *The Spectator*; translators included J. C. Gottsched.

Der Brachmann, Zurich, 1740. Edited by J. G. Altmann and contains much material taken over from his earlier periodicals. Many 'characters', not all new.

Der Einsiedler, Königsberg, 1740–1.

Der Weltbürger, Berlin, 1741.

Der Freydenker, Danzig, 1741–3.

Belustigungen des Verstandes und des Witzes, 8 volumes in 5, Leipzig, 1741–5. A monthly; G. W. Rabener contributed some 'characters'.

Der Bewunderer, Hamburg, 1742.

Der Weltbürger, Berlin, n.d. [1742]. Edited and largely written by Lamprecht. 52 numbers in 1 volume. Many 'characters'.

Die Zellischen Vernünftigen Tadler, Celle, 1742. Many 'characters', written in a rather wooden style.

Der Kundschafter, eine Sitten-Schrift, n.p., 1743–4. Many short 'characters', mostly rather conventional.

Der Pilgrim, 2 parts, Königsberg, 1743–4.

Der Freygeist, eine Wochenschrift auf das Jahr 1745, Leipzig, 1746. The editor was C. Mylius.

Der Fremde, Copenhagen, 1745–6. Edited by J. E. Schlegel.

Ergetzungen der vernünftigen Seele, Leipzig, 1745–9. Edited by J. H. G. von Justi. A quarterly.

Der freymüthige Erdbürger im Jahr 1746, Wismar, 1746.

H. J. Lasius, *Satyrische Abhandlungen*, Greifswald, 1746. The sixth and last piece has a group of 'characters' illustrating various types of curiosity.

Der Schutzgeist. Ein moralisches und satyrisches Wochenblatt, Hamburg, 1746–7. More moral than satirical.

Neue Beyträge zum Vergnügen des Verstandes und Witzes, 5 volumes, Bremen and Leipzig, 1746–50.

Der Jüngling, 2 volumes, Leipzig, 1747–8.

Der Hamburger, n.p. [Hamburg], 1748. Satirical. Stopped by the censor after only two issues.

Der Gesellige, eine moralische Wochenschrift, 1748–50. I have used the 'new edition', 2 volumes, Halle, 1764.

Der Druide. Eine moralische Wochenschrift, Berlin, 1748–50.

Der Eidsgenoß, eine moralische Wochenschrift, Basle, 1749. Edited by J. J. Spreng. Various contributors connected with the *Baseler deutsche Gesellschaft*. Numerous 'characters', including unacknowledged translations from Earle.

Daphne, 2 volumes, Königsberg, 1750. J. G. Lindner. Unusual, in that the 'characters' show the direct and unmistakable influence of La Bruyère.

Der Neue Eidsgenosse, Eine Moralische Wochenschrift, Basle, 1750. Continuation of *Der Eidsgenoß* of 1749. The 'characters' are more serious in tone.

Der Redliche, eine Wochenschrift, 2 volumes, Nuremberg, 1751.

Der Hofmeister, 3 volumes, Leipzig, 1751–3. Edited and, to a large part, written by G. W. Rabener. Many 'characters', some labelled as such in the list of contents, others scattered about in essays.

Der Mensch, eine moralische Wochenschrift, 12 parts, Halle, 1751–6.

Geschmack und Sitten, Göttingen, 1752–3. Bi-weekly.

Die Freunde, eine Wochenschrift, Göttingen, 1753.

Der Vernünftler, 3 parts, Berlin, 1754. The editor was C. N. Naumann. Many short 'characters'.

C. L. Troschel, *Die Studenten Moral, eine Satyre*, Jena, 1754. Contains 'characters' of various types of Student.

J. F. W. Zachariae, *Scherzhafte Epische Poesien*, Brunswick and Hildesheim, 1754. For verse-characters in the style of Pope (though much inferior), see pp. 5 and 210 f.

Der Freund, 2 volumes, Ansbach, 1754–5. Edited by J. F. von Cronegk and J. P. Uz.

Der Helvetische Patriot, 2 volumes, Basle, 1755–6. 17 substantial monthly numbers. Several 'characters', some labelled *Charakter*, some *Abschilderung*.

Der Redliche, ein Wochenblatt, Eisleben, 1755–6.

Der Tugendfreund, 3 volumes, Berlin, 1755–6. Strongly Lutheran in tone and message. Contains some 'characters.

J. F. Löwen, *Walpurgis Nacht*, 1756. In *Poetische Werke*, Hamburg and Leipzig, 1760. Contains a few verse-characters, including one of a Vain Society Beauty, clearly based on Pope's famous 'character' of Chloe: see pp. 318 f.

Die Frau, eine sittliche Wochenschrift, Leipzig, 1756–7.

Der Mann, eine wöchentliche Sittenschrift, Leipzig, 1756–8.

Niemand. Eine Wochenschrift, Göttingen, 1757.

Das Reich der Natur und der Sitten, eine moralische Wochenschrift, 12 parts, Halle, 1757–62.

Der Chamäleon, eine moralische Wochenschrift, Berlin, 1759.

Die Helvetische Nachlese, Basle, 1759. Not a periodical, but a collection of miscellaneous items gathered together into a volume as appendix to, or overflow from, *Der Helvetische Patriot* of 1755–6. Contains 'characters'.

Der Leipziger Zuschauer. Eine Wochenschrift auf das Jahr 1759, Leipzig, 1759.

Der Sintemal. Eine eidsgenössische Wochenschrift . . . , Basle, 1759. Edited by J. J. Spreng. Many 'characters'.

Der nordische Aufseher, 3 volumes, Copenhagen and Leipzig, 1760–70. Edited and in part written by J. A. Cramer.

Der Apotheker, eine Wochenschrift, Cologne, 1762–3.

Anon. [C. C. Sturm], *Das Frauenzimmer in der Einsamkeit*, 1763. I have used the 'neue Auflage', Halle, 1765. Essays about various aspects of womanhood, with a few interpolated 'characters' borrowed from other sources (the moral weeklies, Pope).

Der Glückselige, eine moralische Wochenschrift, 12 parts, Halle, 1763–8. By S. G. Lange and G. F. Meier, the authors of *Das Reich der Natur und der Sitten*. Numerous short 'characters'.

Die Witzige Tyrolerin, eine Wochenschrift, Nuremberg, 1765. Aims more for entertainment and less for moral improvement than most.

Die Zigeunerin. Eine Wochenschrift, Nuremberg, 1765.

J. H. G. von Justi, *Scherzhafte und satyrische Schriften*, 2 volumes, Berlin and Leipzig, 1765. For 'characters', see i. 136 ff. (Dandy) and ii. 206 ff. (Coquette and too-modest Woman).

F. J. Riedel, *Sieben Satyren*, n.p. [Jena], 1765. Contains a few satirical 'characters'.

Die Macht der Vorurtheile, eine Wochenschrift, 2 volumes, Altdorf, 1765–9.

Der Niederrheinische Zuschauer, 'Rhenopolis', 1766.

Die Biene . . . , Stuttgart, 1767. Extracts from English periodicals in translation.

Der Hypochondrist, eine hollsteinische Wochenschrift, Leipzig and Frankfurt, 1767. It is here that H. W. von Gerstenberg singled out Steele rather than Addison as 'unser Stammvater'.

Die Muse an der Niederelbe, eine Wochenschrift, Hamburg, 1769. In verse. Contains the 'character' of a Happy Man (*Der Vergnügte*).

Der Patriot in Bayern, 2 parts, Munich, 1769.

Mannigfaltigkeiten. Eine gemeinnützige Wochenschrift, Berlin, 1769–73.

Die Niederrheinische Zuschauerin, 'Rhenopolis', 1770. Continuation of *Der Niederrheinische Zuschauer*. No. 1 gives the 'Schilderung eines wahrhaften Weltweisen, mit Anmerkungen vermehrt'—a verse-character in which, rather oddly, the notes take up much more space than the actual 'character'.

Die Unsichtbare, Prague, 1770. J. J. Nunn.

Die Zuschauerin an der Spree, Berlin, 1770. Moves away from the notion of the moral weekly and places more stress on entertainment. 'Characters' in Nos. 2 and 8.

Ewald von Kleist, 'Ein Gemälde', in *Sämtliche Werke*, 3rd edition, Berlin, 1771, p. 112. Verse-character of a tyrannical Ruler.

Meine Einsamkeiten, Prague, 1771-2. F. Kepner.

J. J. Ebert, *Tapeten*, Wittenberg, 1771-6. A satirical weekly. No. 46 contains 6 'characters'.

Der Casselsche Zuschauer, Cassel, 1772. 24 numbers only. For 'characters', see Nos. 10 (Quack) and 12 (would-be Scholar).

Der Greis, Leipzig, 1772-6.

Für Litteratur und Herz. Eine Wochenschrift, Berlin and Leipzig, 1775. G. W. Burmann.

Der Kinderfreund. Ein Wochenblatt, 1775-9. I have used the 2nd edition, Leipzig, 1777-82. C. F. Weiße.

Vermischte Aufsätze zur Beförderung der Litteratur und der Sitten. Eine Wochenschrift, Halle, 1780-1.

J. C. Lavater, *Der Christliche Dichter. Ein Wochenblat*, Zurich, 1782-3. Contains the verse-character of a Good Christian (No. 27).

From the mid-1780s onwards, 'characters' largely vanish from the German and Swiss weeklies.

(xi) **Loen and his Imitators** (*selection only*)

J. M. von Loen, *Moralische Schildereyen* (*Kleine Schriften*, Frankfurt and Leipzig, volume 1, 1750).

C. N. Naumann, *Von dem Erhabenen in den Sitten*, Erfurt, 1751. The character-writing is rather abstract.

J. F. Reupsch, *Schilderungen*, 2 parts, Frankfurt and Leipzig, 1759-60. A naggingly moralizing tone. Lacks economy.

J. J. Dusch, *Moralische Briefe zur Bildung des Herzens*, 2 volumes, Leipzig, 1762-4. Character-delineation greatly subordinated to the author's moralizing intentions.

C. F. Gellert, *Moralische Vorlesungen*, in *Sämtliche Schriften*, Leipzig, volumes vi-vii (1770).

—— *Moralische Charaktere*, in *Sämtliche Schriften*, volume vii.

Johann Peter Miller, *Historischmoralische Schilderungen* . . . , 4 parts. I have used the 3rd/5th edition (the BM copy) of 1770-81, published in Leipzig. The hostile 'characters' are the best.

G. C. E. Westphal, *Portraits*, 2 volumes, Leipzig, 1779-81. Outstanding among the followers of Loen.

Anon., *Schilderungen vortreflicher Menschen*, Berlin and Leipzig, 1782. Long-winded and woodenly didactic.

(xii) The Nineteenth Century

The Burnisher, London, 1801. Contains a few 'characters.

Thomas Love Peacock, 'The Man of Fashion': verse-character dating from 1801. In *Works*, edited by H. F. B. Brett-Smith and C. E. Jones, 10 volumes, London, 1924–34, vii. 162.

The Intruder, a periodical paper, Aberdeen, 1802. A few 'characters.

'Solomon Grildrig'. *The Miniature*, Windsor, 1805. A fortnightly paper, containing a few 'characters' still clearly linked to those in the eighteenth-century periodicals.

George Brewer, *Hours of Leisure . . .* , London, 1806. Contains a few 'characters' written in a rather laboured style.

Hewson Clarke, *The Saunterer, a Periodical Paper in two volumes*, London, 1806. An explicit attempt to continue in the vein of *The Spectator* and *The Rambler*. Contains several 'characters'.

Anon. [S. W. H. Ireland], *Stultifera Navis*, London, 1807. A modern *Ship of Fools*, based on the Barclay translation of Brant. A few pieces qualify as verse-characters.

Anon., *A Friendly Gift for Servants and Apprentices*, York, 1809. A six-penny tract. Chapter 1 gives the 'Character of a good and faithful Servant'.

The Reflector, 2 volumes, London, 1811. Edited by Leigh Hunt, but the 'characters' are not by him.

Clemens Brentano, *Der Philister vor, in und nach der Geschichte*, first published anonymously in 1811. Edition used: *Werke, Meyers Klassiker-Ausgaben*, Leipzig, n.d. iii. 269 ff. For the 'character' of a Philistine, see pp. 298–301.

'Sir Frederick Foppling', *Portraits of Fops . . .* , London, 1811.

Der Leipziger Zuschauer, eine neue Wochenschrift (continued after No. 13 as *Argus*), 6 volumes, Leipzig, 1811–12. Nos. 10, 11, and 13 contain 'characters'; those in No. 13 are translated from the English.

Anon., *A Gallery of Portraits*, painted by an old and celebrated Master, and re-touched by an Irish Artist, Dublin, 1813. Earle up to date.

William Hazlitt, 'Character of John Bull' (1816). In *Complete Works, Centenary Edition*, by P. P. Howe, London, 1933, iv. 97–100.

—— 'On the Clerical Character' (1818), in *Complete Works*, ed. cit. vii. 242 ff.

Anon. [F. Mc. Donogh], *The Hermit in London*; *or, Sketches of English Manners*, 5 volumes, London, 1819–20. Contains a few 'characters'.

Leigh Hunt, *The Indicator*, London, 1820. 'Characters' of the Coachman (30/8/1820); the Maidservant (22/11/1820); the Old Gentleman (29/11/1820).

Washington Irving, *Sketchbook*, 1820. Contains a 'character' of the Stage-coach Man. Many editions.

'Philanthropus', *The Character of a Soldier*, London, 1821. Twopenny pamphlet of 8 pages.

The Trifler, London 1822–3. No. 1 contains the 'character' of a Slanderer.

W. F. Deacon, *The Innkeeper's Album*, London, 1823. A miscellany containing 3 'characters'.

William Hazlitt, 'On Londoners and Country People' of 1823 contains the 'character' of a Cockney: *Complete Works*, ed. cit. xii. 66–9.

Mary Russell Mitford, *Our Village*, London, 1824. Contains 'character' of the 'Talking [i.e. talkative] Lady'.

'Oliver Oldstyle', *Every-Day Characters or the Club Worthies . . .* , London, 1824. A late example of a character-book, which uses the traditional fiction that the figures represented are members of the clubs frequented by the author.

Anon., *Characters, A Sketch: and other Pieces, by a Character*, London, 1825. Contains a long poem entitled 'Characters', which consists of a number of short verse-characters.

'Bernard Blackmantle' [C. M. Westmacott], *The English Spy . . .* , 2 volumes, London, 1825–6. Sketches of English life, including 'characters'. Very ably illustrated by George Cruikshank.

The Literary Lounger, London, 1826. Contains short satirical 'character' of an Oxford Fellow (pp. 143 f.).

The Pocket Magazine, London, 1827. Contains the 'character' of a Contented Man (i. 72–4).

Thomas Hood, *The Comic Annual*, London, 1830. Contains the 'character' of a Greenwich Pensioner (pp. 63 f.).

The London Spy: a weekly Magazine . . . , London, 1831–2. Contributors included William Cobbett, C. M. Westmacott, and Thomas Hood. Nos. 31 and 40 contain 'characters'.

Edward Bulwer Lytton, *England and the English*, 2 volumes, London, 1833. Contains many 'characters'.

Charles Lamb, *The Last Essays of Elia*, London, 1833. Contains 'Poor Relations' (pp. 10–21); 'The Convalescent' (pp. 70–7); 'Amicus Redivivus (pp. 129–37). Dr Monoculus in the last-named essay is arguably too eccentric to qualify as a true 'character'.

Leigh Hunt, *The Seer*, London, 1840. Vol. i. 45–7: 'The Waiter' (first published in Hunt's *London Journal* in 1835: cf. Ireland, p. 160).

The Comic Almanack, 2 Series, London, 1835–53. Contributors included Thackeray, Albert Smith, and the Mayhew brothers; George Cruikshank did some of the illustrations. Contains a number of light-hearted 'characters'.

Charles Dickens, *Sketches by Boz*, 1836. See the sections 'Seven Sketches from our Parish' and 'Characters'.

'Quiz' [Edward Caswell], *Sketches of Young Ladies . . .* , with illustrations by 'Phiz' (George Cruikshank), London, 1837.

'Quiz Junior' [Dickens], *Characteristic Sketches of Young Gentlemen*, London, n.d. [1838].

'Quiz' [Dickens], *Sketches of Young Couples*, 1838. Edition used: *Sketches of Young Couples, Young Ladies, Young Gentlemen*, by Quiz, London, n.d. [1869], pp. 1–79.

W. M. Thackeray, *The Paris Sketch Book*, 1840. In *Works in 13 volumes*, London, 1898–9, vol. 5. Contains the 'character' of Major British, a half-pay army officer (pp. 28 f.).

Heads of the People: or, Portraits of the English. Drawn by Kenny Meadows. With original essays by distinguished writers. 2 volumes, London, 1840–1. A sort of nineteenth-century *Microcosmography*. Contributors included Leigh Hunt and many of the writers later to be associated with *Punch*, notably Thackeray.

Punch, 1841 ff. The early volumes (to the beginning of the 1860s) contain many short 'characters', in both prose and verse. Thackeray's 'Snobs' were first published here in 1846–7.

William Scrope, *Days and Nights of Salmon Fishing in the Tweed*, London, 1843. Gives 3 'characters' of different types of angler as a preamble.

Charles Knight (ed.), *A Volume of Varieties*, London, 1844. Contains the 'Character of an honest and contented Burgess' (pp. 22–4).

S. Laman Blanchard, *Sketches from Life*, 3 volumes, London, 1846. A posthumous collection; Blanchard had died in 1844. Contains a number of 'characters'.

Catherine Gore, *Sketches of English Character*, 2 volumes, London, 1846.

Albert Smith, *The Physiology of Evening Parties*, London, 1846. Chapter 10 includes 'characters' of three types of Young Lady to be encountered at parties.

W. M. Thackeray, *The Book of Snobs*, 1846–7. First published in *Punch*. First edition in book-form: 1848. I have used the edition published by Edward King, London, n.d. [1895].

A. B. Reach, *The Natural History of 'Bores'*, London, 1847.

—— *The Natural History of Humbugs*, London, 1847. Illustrated by A. Henning. One of the weaker humorous character-books of the mid-century.

Albert Smith, *The Natural History of the Ballet Girl*, London, 1847. Illustrated by A. Henning. The final two chapters give a 'character' of the Ballet Girl.

—— *The Natural History of the Gent*, London, 1847. The illustrator appears to have been Henning again.

—— *The Natural History of 'Stuck-up' People*, London, 1847. Contains 'characters' of various kinds of Snob.

W. M. Thackeray, *The Christmas Books*, 1847–9. 'Mrs Perkins's Ball' (1847), 'Our Street' (1848), and 'Dr Birch and his young friends' (1849) all contain 'characters'. The best are Miss Bunion (Poetess), Mr Hicks

(Poet), Mr Ranville of the Foreign Office, 'A Hopeless Case' (backward pupil), and 'A Young Fellow who is pretty sure to succeed'. See *Works*, ed. cit. ix. 15, 16, 20, 82 f. and 90 f.

Horace Mayhew, *Model Men*, London, 1848. First published in *Punch*.

—— *Model Women*, London, 1848. First published in *Punch*.

Albert Smith, *The Idler upon Town*, London, n.d. [1848]. Chapter 6 gives a 'character' of 'the Mooner' (i.e. Idler).

—— *The Natural History of the Flirt*, London, 1848.

—— (ed.) *Gavarni in London: Sketches of Life and Character . . .* , London, 1849. Contains the 'character' of a Barmaid by J. Stirling Coyne (pp. 87–90).

'John Smith' [John Delaware Lewis], *Sketches of Cantabs*, London, 1849.

Anon., *Sketches from Clerical Life*, London, 1850. Contains the 'characters' of 'A Country Gentleman in Orders' (pp. 27–33) and Dr Quiteright (a bigoted Clergyman, pp. 42–5).

Charles Dickens, 'The Begging-Letter Writer', first published in volume i of *Household Words*, 1850, then in *Reprinted Pieces*, 1858.

Douglas Jerrold, *The Writings . . . , Collected Edition*, 8 volumes, London, 1851–4. The 'character' of an old Pauper is given in volume iv. 333–6. 'Sketches of the English' (volume v) is a reprint of 'characters' originally published in *Heads of the People* (1840–1).

Charles Dickens, 'Our Honourable Friend' and 'The Bore'. Both first published in 1852, then in *Reprinted Pieces* (1858).

John Henry Newman, 'character' of a Gentleman in *The Idea of a University*, first published in 1852. Many editions.

S. L. Blanchard, *Corporation Characters . . .* , London, 1855. Posthumous publication: contains 12 'characters', each preceded by a caricature by K. Meadows.

J. E. Ritchie, *The Night Side of London*, 1857. Edition used is that published in London in 1869. Contains the 'character' of a Ballet Girl, pp. 87 f.

E. L. L. Blanchard, *Dinners and Diners at home and abroad*, London, 1860. Contains 3 'characters'.

G. A. Sale (ed.), *Temple Bar, A London Magazine*, London, 1861 ff. Contains a few 'characters', of which the best is that of a 'Quack Literary' (ii. 270 f.).

Henry Mayhew, *German Life and Manners as seen in Saxony at the Present Day*, 2 volumes, London, 1864. Contains the 'character' of a Serving-Girl (i. 362–4).

Anthony Trollope, *Clergymen of the Church of England*, 1865–6. First published in the *Pall Mall Gazette*. Edition used is that by Ruth apRoberts in the *Victorian Library*, Leicester University Press, 1974.

—— *Hunting Sketches*, 3rd edition, London, 1866. First published in the *Pall Mall Gazette*.

—— *Travelling Sketches*, London, 1866. Reprinted from the *Pall Mall Gazette*. Nos. 3, 5, and 6 are true 'characters'.

Edward Bulwer Lytton, *Miscellaneous Prose Works*, 3 volumes, London, 1868. 'Characters' of the 'Superior Man' (in the Pecksniffian sense) and of the Modern Misanthrope (iii. 39 f. and 241 ff.).

Fun, new series, vii, London, 1868. The series of articles 'Life in Lodgings' contains 'characters' of Landladies, Servants, and Lodgers (see pp. 69, 101, 118, and 185).

The Mayhew brothers, *London Characters and the Humorous Side of London Life*, London, 1870. Illustrated by W. S. Gilbert. Numerous short 'characters'.

George Eliot, *Impressions of Theophrastus Such*, Edinburgh and London, n.d. [1879].

'The Silent Member', *Sketches of Parochial Life and Character*, London, 1880. A book dealing with types encountered in local government. Chapters 3, 5, 6, and 9 contain 'characters'. 'The Cantankerous Member' (pp. 22–9) is the best.

Anthony Trollope, *London Tradesmen*, first published in the *Pall Mall Gazette* in 1880. Edition used is that by Michael Sadleir, London, 1928.

C. G. Fagan, 'Chaucer in Oxenforde', in *Oxford Magazine*, 14/2/1883. Edition used: *Echoes from the Oxford Magazine*, Oxford and London, 1890, pp. 31–3. 2 'characters' in a parody of the Chaucerian style.

'Corno di Bassetto' [G. B. Shaw], 5 short 'characters' of types of music teacher, first published in 1889. In *London Music in 1888/89 as heard by Corno di Bassetto*, London, 1950, pp. 271–3.

W. E. Henley, *London Types*, London, 1898, with illustrations by William Nicholson. 13 full-page coloured illustrations, each accompanying a verse-character.

(xiii) **Vienna**

(*a*) *Periodicals in the Tradition of the Moral Weeklies*

(A few of the less important ones, together with those which contain no 'characters', have been omitted.)

Die Welt, 4 volumes, Vienna, 1762–3 (C. G. Klemm).

Der Österreichische Patriot. Eine Wochenschrift, 2 volumes, Vienna, 1764–5.

Der Vertraute, Vienna, 1765 (Joseph von Sonnenfels). Explicitly modelled on *The Spectator*. Edition used: *Gesammelte Schriften*, 10 volumes, Vienna, 1783–7, i. 9–96.

Der Mann ohne Vorurtheile, 3 volumes, Vienna, 1765–7 (also Sonnenfels).

Der Verbesserer, eine Wochenschrift, 2 volumes, Vienna, 1766.

Theresie und Eleonore, 1766–7 (Sonnenfels). I have used the second edition, Frankfurt and Leipzig, 1773.

Der Einsiedler, Vienna, 1774 (F. J. Riedel).
Der Weltmann, Vienna, 1782 (O. H. von Hofenheim).
Der Spion in Wien, Vienna, 1784–9.
Der Wienerische Zuschauer, 6 volumes, Vienna, 1785–6 (Joseph Richter).
Das Sonntagsblatt, 3 volumes, Vienna, 1807–9 (Joseph Schreyvogel).

(*b*) *The Viennese Sketch*

(Some very trivial examples are omitted, also those which have no bearing on the discussion of character-portrayal.)

Peter Altenberg, *Die Auswahl aus meinen Büchern*, Berlin, 1908.
M. Barach: see 'Dr Märzroth' (pseud.).
H. Bergler: see 'Ottokar Tann-Bergler' (pseud.).
I. F. Castelli, *Wiener Lebensbilder*. First published 1828. Edition used: second edition, 2 volumes, Vienna, 1835.
V. Chiavacci, *Bei uns z'Haus. Genrebilder aus dem Wiener Leben*, Vienna, 1889.
—— *Wiener Typen*, Stuttgart, 1894.
—— *Aus dem Kleinleben der Großstadt. Wiener Genrebilder*, Vienna, 1884.
K. Fajkmajer, *Skizzen aus Alt-Wien*, Vienna and Leipzig, n.d. [1913].
A. E. Forschneritsch, *Von unsern Grund! Wiener Skizzen*, Vienna, n.d. [1915].
F. Galliny: see 'Bruno Walden' (pseud.).
F. Gräffer, *Wiener Dosenstücke*, 2 parts, Vienna, 1846.
A. H. Groß-Hoffinger, *Wien wie es ist*, Leipzig, 1847.
R. Kalmar, *Vater Ramsauer. Heitere Wiener Skizzen*, Vienna and Leipzig, 1919.
M. Klapp, *Wiener Bilder und Büsten*, second edition, Troppau, 1868.
—— *Vom grünen Tisch*, Berlin, 1866. Not 'Wiener Skizzen'; deals with German gambling resorts and gives a few 'characters' of the types encountered there.
H. von Levitschnigg, *Wien, wie es war und ist*, Budapest and Vienna, 1860.
J. Löwy, *Geschichten aus der Wienerstadt*, Vienna, 1889.
'Dr Märzroth' [M. Barach], *Wiener Bilderbogen*, 8 volumes, Vienna, 1869.
J. B. Moser, *Das Wiener Volksleben . . .* , 9 volumes, Vienna, 1842–5.
Johann Pezzl, *Skizze von Wien*, 1786–90, edited by G. Gugitz and A. Schlossar, Graz, 1923.
E. Pötzl, *Jung-Wien. Allerhand Wienerische Skizzen*, Berlin and Leipzig, 1885.
—— *Klein-Wiener. Skizzen in Wiener Art und Mundart*, Vienna, 1890.
—— *Stadtmenschen. Ein Wiener Skizzenbuch*, Vienna, 1903.
Friedrich Schlögl, *Gesammelte Schriften*, 3 volumes, Vienna, Budapest, and Leipzig, n.d. [1893–4]. Contains *Wiener Blut* (1873), *Wiener Luft* (1875), and *Wienerisches* (1883).
Rudolf Steiner, *Schwankende Gestalten*, Vienna, 1926.

Adalbert Stifter: see *Wien und die Wiener.*

F. Stüber-Gunther, *Das Durchhaus. Wiener Skizzen*, Vienna, 1905.

—— *Das neue G'wand. Wiener Skizzen und Geschichten*, Vienna, 1907.

'Ottokar Tann-Bergler' [H. Bergler], *Wiener Guckkastenbilder*, Berlin, n.d. [1888].

—— *Wiener Art und Unart*, Vienna, 1896.

A. Ulreich, *Wiener Art aus der Gegenwart*, Vienna, 1925.

'Bruno Walden' [F. Galliny], *Wiener Studien*, Vienna, 1869.

Wien und die Wiener in Bildern aus dem Leben. Contributors include Adalbert Stifter, C. E. and C. F. Langer, A. Ritter von Perger, D. F. Reiberstorffer, L. Scheyrer, and F. Stelzhammer. Budapest, 1844.

Max Winter, *Im unterirdischen Wien* (*Großstadt-Dokumente*, edited by Hans Ostwald, xiii), Berlin and Leipzig, n.d.

(xiv) **The Twentieth Century**

George R. Sims (ed.), *Living London*, 3 volumes, London, 1902–3. See volume i. 357 ff. for various types of London Spongers and Loafers and ii. 352 f. for a Maid-of-all-work.

George W. E. Russell, *Social Silhouettes*, London, 1906.

H. L. Mencken, *Prejudices*, 1919 ff. Edition used: *Selected Prejudices*, 2 volumes, London, 1926–7. The section called 'Types of Men' includes brief sketches, some of which are not unlike very terse 'characters': see the Romantic and the Business Man, i. 121 and 124.

P. H. Ditchfield, *Country Folk . . .*, London, 1923. 'Characters' of the Squire and the Country Doctor (pp. 11 f. and 41 f).

W. Macneile Dixon, *The Englishman*, London, 1931. A series of lectures given in University College, London, in 1929. The 2nd lecture includes the 'character' of an English Gentleman.

Raymond Chandler, 'Character' of a Detective in 'The Simple Art of Murder', *in Pearls are a Nuisance*, Penguin Books, 1950, pp. 198 f. The essay appears to date from 1940.

G. H. Vallins, *Sincere Flattery*, London, 1954. A book of literary parodies, containing 12 'characters' in the manner of Chaucer. They first appeared in *Punch* from the mid-1940s on.

Geoffrey Gorer and Ronald Searle, *Modern Types*, London, 1955.

Harold Nicholson, *Good Behaviour*, London, 1955. The final chapter contains the 'character' of a Bore.

G. H. Vallins, *After a Manner. A Book of Parodies*, London, 1956. Contains further 'characters' in pastiche-form.

Malcolm Bradbury, *Phogey!*, London, 1960.

Alex Atkinson and Ronald Searle, *The Big City, or the New Mayhew*, Penguin Books, 1962. Originally published in *Punch*.

Paul Jennings, *The Jenguin Pennings*, Penguin Books, 1963. Has short 'characters' of various types of Doctors and Party Guests (pp. 148–52 and 183–6).

Elias Canetti, *Aufzeichnungen 1942–48*, Munich, 1965. 'Characters' on pp. 113 f., 142–5, and 178.

Charles Carrington, *Soldier from the Wars Returning*, London, 1965. Contains the 'character' of an Old Soldier (pp. 97 f.).

John Baynes, *Morale. A Study of men and courage*, London, 1967. 'Character' of an Officer, pp. 123–5.

Derek Cooper, *The Bad Food Guide*, London, 1967. Gives pictures of typical restaurants. These descriptions are, in all but name, a survival of the old device of writing 'characters' of places.

Francis Hope, 'Are Arts Graduates Employable?' *New Statesman*, 22/3/1968, pp. 376–9. Gives 'characters' of 3 typical Graduates.

Elias Canetti, *Die Provinz des Menschen. Aufzeichnungen 1942–1972*, Munich, 1973. Contains 'characters' on pp. 283 and 331.

—— *Der Ohrenzeuge. Fünfzig Charaktere*, Munich, 1974. This, as far as I know, is the last genuine character-book to date.

Anna Raeburn, 'Man at Bay', *Sunday Times Magazine*, 2/11/1975, pp. 20/4. 'Characters' of different types of Husband. Illustrated by Arthur Robins.

Edward Stourton and Nick Mostyne, Brief 'characters' of types of Student, *Punch* 12–18 October, 1977, pp. 642 f.

William Hewison, 'Hewison's People': various 'characters' of contemporary types in *Punch* throughout 1978.

'Brathwaite redivivus', 'Four Oxford "Characters"' *Oxford. The Journal of the Oxford Society*, xxxii (May 1980), pp. 42–4. 'Characters' of 2 Dons and 2 Students in a rather weak parody of seventeenth-century character-writing.

(xv) 'Characters' in Sermons

Thomas, Adams, *The White Devil, or the Hypocrite uncased: in a sermon* . . ., London, 1614. See p. 31 for a 'character' of a Hypocrite.

—— *Mystical Bedlam; or, the World of Madmen*, 1615. In *Works*, 3 volumes, Edinburgh, 1861–2, i. 254 ff. A long sermon on the 'madness' of sin and folly, illustrated by many 'characters'.

—— *The Soul's Sickness: a Discourse* . . ., 1616. Ed. cit. i. 471 ff. The various sins are seen as 'diseases' of the soul and are described in 'characters'.

John Rawlinson, *The Unmasking of the Hypocrite. A Sermon* . . ., London, 1616. Includes the 'character' of a Patron.

Robert Sanderson, *Thirty-five Sermons*, 7th edition, London, 1681. Contains depictions of types which show close similarity with late seventeenth-century character-writing. See especially p. 196.

Thomas Heyricke, *The Character of a Rebel* . . ., London, 1685. A sermon containing a political 'character'.

Isaac Barrow, *Works*, 3 volumes, London, 1700. Sermon 5 contains the 'character' of an Upright Man (i. 59 f.).

Anon., *The True Character of a Virtuous Wife; being a wedding Sermon preached on board The English Admiral* . . ., London, 1702. A curiosity: compares the Virtuous Wife to a ship! The style shows clearly the influence of the witty character-writing of the seventeenth century.

Robert South, *Sermons*, 11 volumes, London, 1715–44. 'Characters' of a Puritan (v. 511 f.) and of a Hypocrite (vi. 100 f.).

Jonathan Swift, The sermon 'On Brotherly Love' (1717) contains a pair of contrasting 'characters'. See *The Prose Works*, edited by W. E. H. Lecky, London, 1898, iv. 145 f.

John Tillotson, *Works*, 2 volumes, 3rd edition, London, 1722. Sermon xxxix (i. 413 ff.) contains 3 short 'characters'.

William Butler, *The Character of a good Magistrate, a Sermon* . . ., London, 1729.

Joseph Roper, *The Character of the Liberal Man, set forth in a Sermon* . . . , London, 1734.

John Wesley, 'The Almost Christian', in Sermon ii (1741). In *Sermons upon several Occasions*, 1st series, London, 1944, pp. 11 ff.

—— 'A Methodist', 1739. Included by Wesley in his *Plain Account of Christian Perfection*, which appeared in a number of editions during the author's lifetime. Edition used: *Works of John Wesley*, 1872, photorepr. Michigan, n.d. [1958–9], xi. 371–3.

Samuel Walker, *The Christian. Being a Course of Practical Sermons*, London, 1756. 3 'characters', including that of a Careless Sinner (pp. 108 f.).

Anon., *The Character of a good Ruler* . . ., Ipswich, 1758.

Gottfried Käppel, *Der Edle. Ein kleines moralisch-religiöses Charakter-Gemälde*, Leipzig, 1800. Revised version of a sermon, published in the form of a pamphlet.

Sydney Smith, *Sermons*, 2nd edition, 2 volumes, London, 1801. 'On Vanity' and 'On Men of the World' contain 'characters'.

The above are a selection only. The influence of the 'character' on the sermon would undoubtedly repay closer attention. The situation in France, for instance in the sermons of Bossuet and Bourdaloue, is less clear, in that it is not always easy to say whether we are dealing with a 'character' or a portrait. Hence I have concentrated on England, where the position is usually unambiguous. The situation in Germany, especially in cities like Hamburg and Leipzig, where the influence of the moral weeklies was strong, would also be worth investigating.

(xvi) The 'Character' and the Play

(a) *England*

Anon., *The Humours of Oxford, a comedy*, 2nd edition, London, 1730. 'Character' of a College Fellow, Act II.

Anon., *A Knacke to knowe a Knave*, 1594, in *Old English Drama*, Students' Facsimile Edition, 1911, No. 60.

Richard Brome, *Dramatic Works*, 3 volumes, London, 1873. Photorepr. New York, 1966.

Colley Cibber, *Dramatic Works*, 5 volumes, London, 1777.

George Coleman, the Elder, *The Jealous Wife* (1761), in *Lesser English Comedies of the Eighteenth Century*, OUP, 1927.

William Congreve, *Complete Works*, edited by Montague Summers, London, 1923.

Thomas Dekker, *The Honest Whore, Part the First*, 1604. I have used the Mermaid edition by E. Rhys, London, 1887.

John Dryden, *Marriage à la Mode*, 1673. In the Mermaid Series, edited by G. Saintsbury, volume i.

Thomas d'Urfey, *A Fond Husband* . . ., London, 1678. Contains an advance 'character' of Fumble, the Alderman.

—— *Trick for Trick* . . ., London, 1678. Has brief 'character' of Sir Wilding Frollick, explicitly labelled as such (I. i).

George Etherege, *Dramatic Works*, edited by H. F. B. Brett-Smith, Oxford, 1927.

George Farquhar, *Complete Works*, 2 volumes, London, 1930. Edited by C. Stonehill.

David Garrick, *Lethe*, 1749. A dramatic satire which contains 'characters', in the first person, of a Fine Gentleman (Dandy and Man of Pleasure) and a Fine Lady. In volume i of *The Dramatic Works*, London, 1798.

Henry Higden, *The Wary Widdow*, London, 1693.

Ben Jonson, *Works*, edited by C. H. Herford and Percy Simpson, Oxford, 1925 ff.

Shakerley Marmion, *The Antiquary*, 1630s. Edition used: *A Select Collection of Old English Plays*, originally published by Robert Dodsley, 4th edition, London, 1795, xiii. 411 ff.

—— *Holland's Leaguer*, 1632. In *Dramatic Works*, edited by Maidment and Logan, Edinburgh, 1875, pp. 1–97.

Edward Moore, *The Gamester*, London, 1753.

Arthur Murphy, *The Upholsterer*, 1758. In *Eighteenth Century Drama: Afterpieces*, edited by R. W. Bevis, Oxford Paperbacks, 1970.

Thomas Shadwell, *The Complete Works*, edited by M. Summers, 5 volumes, London, 1927. I have also consulted George Saintsbury's edition in the Mermaid series.

James Shirley, *Works*, edited by Edmund Gosse, London, 1888.

Sir John Vanbrugh, *Works*, edited by A. E. H. Swaen (Mermaid Series), London, 1896.

John Webster, *The White Devil*, 1612. Contained in volume i of F. L. Lucas's edition of the *Complete Works*, London, 1972.

John Wilson, *Dramatic Works*, edited by James Maidment and W. H. Logan, Edinburgh and London, 1874.

R[obert] W[ilson], *The pleasant and statelie Morall, of the three Lordes and three Ladies of London . . ., 1590, in Old English Drama*, Students' Facsimile Edition, No. 119 (1912).

William Wycherley, *The Complete Works*, edited by Montague Summers, London, 1924.

(*b*) *France*

J. G. de Campistron, *Le Jaloux Désabusé*, 1709. In *Œuvres, Nouvelle Édition*, 3 volumes, Paris, 1750, repr. 1972, iii. 99–214.

P. M. Destouches, *Œuvres Dramatiques*, 6 volumes, Paris, 1822: see especially *L'Irrésolu*, 1713, I. i.

Collin d'Harleville, *L'Inconstant*, 1786. In *Répertoire Général du Théâtre françaix*, xlviii.

A. Piron, *La Métromanie, ou le poëte*, 1738. In *Répertoire Général . . .*, xliv. See I. ii.

J. F. Regnard, *Le Distrait*, 1697. *In Répertoire Général . . .*, xxvi.

B. J. Saurin, *L'Anglomane*, 1772. In *Répertoire Général . . .*, xlvi. See scene i.

(*c*) *German-speaking countries*

J. C. Bock, *Die Parodie . . . Ein Lustspiel*, Vienna, 1771.

H. Borkenstein, *Der Bookesbeutel*, 1742. Edition used: *Deutsche Litteraturdenkmale des 18. und 19. Jahrhunderts*, lvi–lvii, Leipzig, 1896, edited by F. F. Heitmüller.

J. F. von Cronegk, *Der Mißtrauische*, 1760: in *Komedia*, No. xiv, Berlin, 1969, edited by Sabine Roth.

Gottlieb Fuchs, *Die Klägliche, ein Lustspiel . . .*, Hamburg, 1747.

C. F. Gellert, *Die Betschwester*, 1745. Many editions; paperback in Reclam.

C. G. Klemm, *Beyträge zum Deutschen Theater*, Vienna, 1767.

J. C. Krüger, *Die Geistlichen auf dem Lande*, Frankfurt and Leipzig, 1743.

G. E. Lessing, *Der junge Gelehrte*, 1747. Many editions, including a paperback (Reclam).

C. Mylius, *Die Aerzte, Lustspiel*, Leipzig, 1745.

—— *Der Unerträgliche*, Leipzig, 1746.

Joseph von Petrasch, *Sämtliche Lustspiele*, 2 volumes, Nuremberg, 1765.

J. E. Schlegel, *Die stumme Schönheit*, 1747. In *Komedia*, No. i, 1962, edited by W. Hecht.

Paul Weidmann, *Der Stolze,* Vienna, 1774.

C. F. Weiße, *Der Mißtrauische gegen sich selbst*, in *Neue Sammlung von Schauspielen, welche auf der k. k. priv. dt. Schaubühne zu Wien aufgeführet werden*, volume x, Vienna, 1767.

—— *Lustspiele*, 3 volumes, Leipzig, 1783.

(xvii) **The Novel**

(a) *England*

Anon., *The Devil upon Crutches in England . . .*, London, 1755. Imitation of Le Sage's *Le Diable Boiteux*. Contains 'characters'.

Jane Austen, *The Novels*, edited by R. W. Chapman, 5 volumes, OUP, 1923. Volume vi (1954), *The Minor Works*.

Hilaire Belloc, The acidly entertaining novels in which he took the lid off our political and business life contain a few satirical 'characters'. See, for instance, the two Doctors in *A Change in the Cabinet*, 1909, chapter 11.

Elisabeth Bonhote, *The Rambles of Mr Frankly*, 2 volumes, Dublin, 1773. Poised between character-book and novel proper.

Edward Bulwer Lytton, *The Disowned*, 1828. Edition used: London, 1895.

—— *Pelham*, 1828. Edition used: London, 1895.

—— *Paul Clifford*, 1830. Edition used: London, 1840.

—— *Eugene Aram, a tale*, 1831. Edition used: London, n.d. [*c.* 1890].

—— *Ernest Maltravers*, 1837. Edition used: London, 1901.

—— *Night and Morning*, 1845. Edition used: London, 1851.

William Cole, *The Contradiction*, London, 1796.

Francis Coventry, *History of Pompey the Little, or the Life and Adventures of a Lap-dog*, 1751. The edition used is that by R. A. Day, OUP, 1974.

Daniel Defoe, *The Fortunate Mistress*; *or, a History of the Life . . . of the Lady Roxana*, 1724. A second part, published in 1745, may or may not be by Defoe. Edition used: *Works* (Bohn's British Classics), volume iv, London, 1855.

Charles Dickens, *Complete Works*, 30 volumes, London, n.d. [1874].

Maria Edgeworth, *Belinda*, 1801. Edition used: *Novels*, 12 volumes, London, 1893, volumes i–ii. Contains the 'character' of a 'buck parson', chapter 23 (ii. 102 f.).

—— *Patronage*, 1814. Gives the 'character' of 'French Clay' (a Frenchified Englishman): ed. cit. viii. 8 f.

Henry Fielding, *Complete Works*, 16 volumes, edited by W. E. Henley, London, 1903.

Richard Graves, *The Spiritual Quixote . . ., a comic romance*, 1773. The edition used is that by C. Tracy, OUP, 1967. There are many short 'characters' as figures appear on the scene for the first time. See, for instance, book iv, chapter 11.

Richard Head, *The English Rogue*, first published in 1665. Many reprints. Modern paperback edition: Four Square Books, 1966 (spelling modernized).

Charles Johnstone, *Chrysal: or, the Adventures of a Guinea*, 2nd edition, 2 volumes, London, 1761. Part ii, chapter 13 gives the 'character' of a good and pious Clergyman.

Edward Kimber, *The Life and Adventures of Joe Thompson*, London, 1783. A milk-and-water exercise in the picaresque manner. Contains a few 'characters', explicitly described as such in the chapter-headings. Examples: Mr Prosody, the Schoolmaster and Mr Diaper, the Linen-draper (chapters 2 and 8).

'A. Marsh', *The Ten Pleasures of Marriage*, 2 parts, 1682–3. I have used the edition by John Harvey, London, 1922. There is a 'character' of an Unmarried Girl on p. 134, but Harvey exaggerates when he claims that this amiable romp is of 'historical and literary interest' in providing a link between seventeenth-century character-writing and the novel.

T[homas] M[ay], *The Life of a Satyrical Puppy, called Nim . . .*, London, 1657.

Susannah Minifie, *The Count de Poland*, 4 volumes, London, 1780.

Thomas Love Peacock, *Works*, edited by H. F. B. Brett-Smith and C. E. Jones, 10 volumes, London, 1924–34.

Samuel Richardson, *The Works*, edited by Leslie Stephen, London, 1883. *Clarissa*: volumes iv–viii.

Sir Walter Scott, *The Antiquary*, 1816. In *The Waverley Novels*, Edinburgh, 1871, volume iii.

Tobias Smollett, *Works*, edited by J. Moore and revised by J. P. Browne, 8 volumes, London, n.d. [1872].

W. M. Thackeray, *Works*, 13 volumes, London, 1898–9.

Anthony Trollope, *The Warden*, 1855. Edition used: London, 1952.

—— *Barchester Towers*, 1857. Edition used: 2 volumes, London, 1953.

—— *Dr Thorne* (*Chronicles of Barsetshire*, volume iii), London, 1879.

—— *The Prime Minister*, 1876. Edition used: 2 volumes, OUP, 1952.

—— *Ralph the Heir*, Chapman and Hall, London, 1876.

(b) *Germany*

Anon., *Der Leipziger Avanturieur*, 2 volumes, Frankfurt and Leipzig, 1756. Contains the 'character' of a Dandy, i. 240 f.

Anon., *Faust der zweyte . . .*, 2 volumes, Stettin, 1782–3. 'Character' of a Coquette, i. 248 f.

C. F. Bretzner, *Das Leben eines Lüderlichen . . .*, 3 parts, Leipzig, 1787–8. 'Character' of a Tutor: i. 35–7.

J. G. Büsch, 'Geschichte des Junkers von Nasbach und seiner Hofmeister', 'Geschichte des Hoch- und Edelgebohrnen Freyherrn von Hochberg und seiner Hofmeister', 'Geschichte der Grafen von Ehrenwert und ihres Hofmeisters Treu', in *Vermischte Abhandlungen*, Hamburg, 1777, pp. 114–212. 'Characters' of different kinds of Tutor.

'Damabellante', *Rares Portrait, Einer allzugalanten Dame, Oder Kurtze und warhaffte Lebens-Geschichte der Gräfinn von Sigarien*, n.p., 1725.

J. J. Engel, *Der Philosoph für die Welt*, 3 parts, 1775–7. I have used the original edition for parts i–ii and a later edition (Berlin, 1800) for part iii. Contains two pieces exactly balanced between the 'character' and the short story: see i. 65–75 and iii. 120–31.

—— *Herr Lorenz Stark. Ein Charaktergemälde*, 1795–6. Edition used: *DNL* 136, edited by F. Bobertag.

Theodor Fontane, *Unterm Birnbaum*, 1885. Many editions, including a paperback (Reclam).

C. F. Gellert, *Leben der schwedischen Gräfin von G——*, first published anonymously in 1748–9. I have used J.-U. Fechner's edition, Reclam, 1968, which follows the 2nd edition of 1750.

E. A. von Göchhausen: see 'Martin Sachs'.

F. T. Hase, *Auszug aus Eduard Blondheims geheimem Tagebuche*, Leipzig, 1777. A work in diary-form and full of elaborate psychological analysis: an example of a type of novel which contributed to the demise of the 'character' in Germany.

Hermann Hesse, *Unterm Rad*, 1903. Innumerable editions. I have used the *Suhrkamp Taschenbuch* (No. 52, 1972). Begins with an account of the hero's father, represented as a typical small-town Philistine.

F. X. Huber, *Herr Schlendrian oder der Richter nach den neuen Gesetzen. Ein komischer Roman*, 2nd edition, 3 volumes, Berlin, 1787. An episodic novel satirizing the law. Many short 'characters'.

F. H. Jacobi, *Eduard Allwills Papiere*, first published in 1776, revised and expanded in 1792. I have used the facsimile edition of the 1st version, edited by Heinz Nicolai, Stuttgart, 1962. An example of the new 'subjective' novel of the 1770s.

J. H. Jung-Stilling, *Lebensgeschichte*, originally published in 6 parts between 1777 and 1817. Edition used: Munich, 1968. Shows the type of introspection that helped to drive the 'character' out of fashion.

Susanne B. Knab, *Tagebuch einer jungen Ehefrau*, Stuttgart, 1780.

A. F. F. von Knigge, *Geschichte des armen Herrn von Mildenburg . . .*, 3 volumes, Frankfurt and Leipzig, 1792. Epistolary novel: contains a tutor's 'characters' of his employers (i. 60 ff.). The passage has unmistakable links with character-writing in the moral weeklies.

—— *Die Reise nach Braunschweig. Komischer Roman*, 1792. In *DNL* 136.

F. C. Laukhard, *Franz Wolfstein, oder Begebenheiten eines dummen*

Teufels, 2 volumes, Leipzig, 1799. Short 'characters' of the masters at the grammar school attended by the hero: i. 57 f.

J. M. von Loen, *Der redliche Mann am Hofe oder die Begebenheiten des Grafen von Rivera*, 1740. Edition used: Ulm, Frankfurt and Leipzig, 1760.

Christiane Sophie Ludwig, *Erzählungen von guten, und für gute Seelen*, 2 parts, Leipzig, 1799–1800.

J. H. Merck, 'Lindor, eine bürgerlich-teutsche Geschichte', in *Der Teutsche Merkur vom Jahr 1781*, Weimar, 1781, iii. 107–23.

K. P. Moritz, *Anton Reiser*, 1785–90. Modern edition in Reclam, with a good Afterword by Wolfgang Martens. After *Werther*, the most striking example of how the late eighteenth-century novel moves away from typology towards intense individualism.

Johann Christian W. Müller, *Fragmente aus dem Leben und Wandel eines Physiogonomisten . . .*, Halle, 1790. Satire on physiognomy, cast in the form of a comic novel. Contains the 'character' of the hero's prospective bride (p. 428).

J. G. Müller von Itzehoe, *Siegfried von Lindenberg*, 1779. I have used the edition published in Leipzig in 1784 (4 parts in 2). The author likes to introduce minor figures in the form of 'characters'.

W. E. Neugebauer, *Der teutsche Don Quixhotte*, 1753. Edition used: *Deutsche Neudrucke, Reihe: Texte des 18. Jahrhunderts*, Stuttgart, 1971. For the 'character' of a Court-Poet, see iii. 2.

Friedrich Nicolai, *Das Leben und die Meinungen des Herrn Magister Sebaldus Nothanker*, 1773–6. Modern edition: *DLE, Aufklärung*, xv (1938), edited by F. Brüggemann. I have also consulted the 3-volume edition of 1775–6.

Jean Paul Friedrich Richter, *Sämtlich Werke. Historisch-kritische Ausgabe*, edited by Eduard Berend, Weimar, 1927 ff.

Joseph Richter, *Herr Kaspar. Ein Roman wider die Hypochondrie*, n.p. [Vienna], 1787. Comic novel in crude imitation of Smollett and Fielding. 'Characters' used to introduce new figures.

'Martin Sachs' [E. A. von Göchhausen], *Meines Vaters Hauschronika*, Erfurt, 1790.

C. F. Sintenis, *Max Wind und Konsorten*, Frankfurt and Leipzig, 1780. The hero's companions are described in advance of the action in short 'characters'.

—— *Hallo's glücklicher Abend*, 2 parts, Frankfurt and Leipzig, 1786. Begins with a 'character' of the hero as an Honest Man (*Biedermann*).

J. C. Wezel, *Lebensgeschichte Tobias Knauts, des Weisen . . .*, 4 volumes, 1773–6. Facsimile edition in *Deutsche Neudrucke, Reihe: Texte des 18. Jahrhunderts*, Stuttgart, 1971. 'Characters' of the hero's parents, i. 1.

—— *Peter Marks. Eine Ehestandsgeschichte*, Leipzig, 1779. Here the 'character' can clearly be seen expanding in the direction of the *Charakternovelle.*

C. M. Wieland, *Vermischte Schriften*, 36 volumes, Leipzig, 1839–40.

(xviii) Studies on the 'Character'

Benjamin Boyce, *The Theophrastan Character in England to 1642.* First published in 1947; new impression, London, 1967.

—— *The Polemic Character 1640–61*, University of Nebraska Press, 1955.

—— *The Character-Sketches in Pope's Poems*, Duke University Press, Durham, N.C., 1962.

Ute Schneider, *Der Moralische Charakter. Ein Mittel aufklärerischer Menschendarstellung in den frühen deutschen Wochenschriften* (*Stuttgarter Arbeiten zur Germanistik*, xix), Stuttgart, 1976. Concentrates on the moral weeklies of the 1720s.

(xix) General Bibliography

Anon., 'In der Tradition Theophrasts und La Bruyères', in *Neue Zürcher Zeitung*, 31/8/1974, p. 73. Review of Canetti, *Der Ohrenzeuge.*

R. Adolph, *The Rise of Modern Prose Style*, Cambridge, Mass. and London, 1968. Interesting on rival attitudes towards what constituted good style in seventeenth-century England, but his remarks on the 'character' are to some extent undermined by his odd notion that the genre 'virtually disappeared' after the Restoration.

B. Aikin-Sneath, *Comedy in Germany in the First Half of the Eighteenth Century*, Oxford, 1936.

F. Arnold, 'Von der Charakter-Beschreibung zur Charakter-Erzählung', Diss. (Würzburg), 1956.

L. Babb, *The Elizabethan Malady. A Study of Melancholia in English Literature from 1580 to 1642*, Michigan State College Press, 1951.

E. C. Baldwin, 'The Relation of the Seventeenth Century Character to the Periodical Essay', in *PMLA* xix (1904), 75–114.

—— 'La Bruyère's Influence upon Addison', in *PMLA* xix (1904), 479–95.

—— 'Marivaux's place in the development of character portrayal', in *PMLA* xxvii (1912), 168–87. Sees Marivaux as providing a link between Addison and Richardson.

D. Barnouw, *Elias Canetti* (*Sammlung Metzler*, 180), Stuttgart, 1979.

M. Beaujean, *Der Trivialroman in der zweiten Hälfte des 18. Jahrhunderts*, Bonn, 1964.

E. D. Becker, *Der deutsche Roman um 1780*, Stuttgart, 1964.

M. W. Black, *Richard Brathwait*, Philadelphia, 1928.

E. Blackall, *The Emergence of German as a Literary Language*, CUP, 1959 (new edition: 1978).

G. Boissière, *Urbain Chevreau (1613–1701)* . . ., Niort, 1909.

R. R. Bolgar, *The Classical Heritage and its Beneficiaries*, CUP, 1954.

F. Bondy, 'Canettis Charaktere', in *Die Weltwoche*, Zurich, 26/6/1974, p. 33.

André le Breton, *Le Roman au 18ᵉ siècle*, 1898, repr. Geneva, 1978.

J. H. Brown, *Elizabethan Schooldays*, Oxford, 1933.

W. H. Bruford, *Germany in the Eighteenth Century*, CUP, 1935.

Douglas Bush, *English Literature in the Earlier Seventeenth Century*, 2nd edition, OUP, 1962.

W. Busse, 'Der Hypochondrist in der deutschen Literatur der Aufklärung', Diss. (Mainz), 1952.

H. Chérot, *Étude sur la Vie et les Œuvres du P. le Moyne*, Paris, 1887.

Leo Cholevius, *Die bedeutendsten deutschen Romane des 17. Jahrhunderts*, 1886, repr. Darmstadt, 1965.

Mechthild Curtius, 'Einkreisung der Wirklichkeit. Die Rolle der extremen Charaktere für Canettis Dichtung', in *Literatur und Kritik*, Salzburg, 1975, pp. 176–82.

Louis van Delft, *La Bruyère moraliste*, Geneva, 1971. 'Du Caractère de Théophraste à La Bruyère', in *Papers on French Seventeenth Century Literature*, vol. viii (1981), No. 15, 2, pp. 165–92.

Peter Dixon, *Rhetoric* (*The Critical Idiom*, xix), London, 1971.

Edward Dowden, 'Elizabethan Psychology', in *Essays Modern and Elizabethan*, London, 1910, pp. 308–33.

H. W. Drescher, *Themen und Formen des periodischen Essays im späten 18. Jahrhundert*, Frankfurt, 1971. Concentrates on the *Mirror* and the *Lounger*.

W. H. Dunham, 'Some forerunners of the "Tatler" and the "Spectator" ', in *Modern Language Notes*, xxxiii (1918), 95–101.

A. Ehrhard, *Les Comédies de Molière en Allemagne*, Paris, 1888.

L. Ennis, *Thackeray: the sentimental cynic*, Northwestern University Press, 1950.

L. Fauler, 'Der Arzt im Spiegel der deutschen Literatur . . .', Diss. (Freiburg), 1941.

O. Fest, *Der Miles Gloriosus in der französischen Komödie*, Erlangen and Leipzig, 1897 (*Münchener Beiträge zur romanischen und englischen Philologie*, xiii).

W. Flemming, 'Die Auffassung des Menschen im 17. Jahrhundert', in *DVjs* vi (1928), 403 ff.

Rudolf Fürst, *Die Vorläufer der modernen Novelle*, Halle, 1897.

H. Gaston Hall, 'Molière, Chevreau's *École du Sage*, and Joseph Hall's *Characters*', in *French Studies*, xxix (1975), 398–410.

R. Genée, *Lehr- und Wanderjahre des deutschen Schauspiels*, Berlin, 1882.

H. Gnau, *Die Zensur unter Joseph II*, Strasburg and Leipzig, 1911.

G. S. Gordon, 'Theophrastus and his Imitators', in *English Literature and the Classics*, Oxford, 1912, pp. 49–86.

K. von Görner, *Der Hans Wurst-Streit in Wien und Joseph von Sonnenfels*, Vienna, 1884.

Walter Graham, *English Literary Periodicals*, 1930. Repr. New York, 1966.

C. N. Greenough, 'The "Character" as a source of information for the historian', in *Collected Studies*, Harvard, 1940, pp. 123 ff.

J. Y. T. Greig, *Thackeray. A Reconsideration*, OUP, 1950. Severe on Thackeray for the 'inconsistency' of his characterization, but a zestful and stimulating book.

G. Gugitz, 'Die Wiener Stubenmädchenlitteratur von 1781 . . .', in *Zeitschrift für Bücherfreunde*, 1902–3, i. 137–50.

W. Haacke, *Handbuch des Feuilletons*, volume ii, Emsdetten, 1952.

A. Haas, 'The Comedies of J. C. Krüger', in *PMLA* xvii (1902), 435 ff.

M. Hadley, *The German Novel in 1790*, Berne and Frankfurt, 1973.

W. Hartung, 'Rabener und die Leipziger moralische Wochenschrift *Der Hofmeister* . . .', in *Euphorion*, xx (1913), 61–76.

G. Hay, *Die Darstellung des Menschenhasses in der deutschen Literatur des 18. und 19. Jahrhunderts*, Frankfurt, 1970.

Carl Heine, *Der Roman in Deutschland von 1774 bis 1778*, Halle, 1892.

W. E. Houghton, 'The English Virtuoso in the Seventeenth Century', in *Journal of the History of Ideas*, iii (1942), New York, 51–73 and 190–218.

R. Jasinski, 'Influences sur La Bruyère', in *Revue d'Histoire de la Philosophie et d'Histoire Générale de la Civilisation*, X (1942), 193–229 and 289–328.

M. Kawczyński, *Studien zur Literaturgeschichte des 18. Jahrhunderts. Moralische Zeitschriften*, Leipzig, 1880.

H. Kindermann, *Theatergeschichte Europas*, volume 5, Salzburg, 1962.

Doris Kirsch, *La Bruyère ou le Style Cruel*, Montreal, 1977.

E. E. Kluge, '*Der Erinnerer*. Eine moralische Wochenschrift (1765–1767)': first published as an article in the *Landbote*, Winterthur, 1937, and contained in a bound volume of Kluge's articles in the Zurich *Zentralbibliothek* [DA 1158(5)].

Richard Kralik, *Geschichte der Stadt Wien und ihrer Kultur*, 2nd edition, Vienna, 1925.

P. V. Kreider, *Elizabethan Comic Character Conventions as revealed in the Comedies of George Chapman*, University of Michigan Press, 1935.

L. E. Kurth, 'W. E. N.—Der Teutsche Don Quichotte . . .' in *Jahrbuch der deutschen Schillergesellschaft*, ix (1965), 106–30.

A. Lanavère, 'A la Manière de la Bruyère: La Suite des Caractères de Théophraste . . . (1700)', in *Xvii*[e] *Siècle*, No. 116 (1977), 66–80.

Kurt Lange, 'Der Student in der deutschen Literatur des 18. Jahrhunderts', Diss. (Breslau), 1930.

Maurice Lange, *La Bruyère*, Paris, 1909.

K. M. Lea, *Italian Popular Comedy. A Study in the Commedia dell'Arte, 1560–1620 . . .*, 2 volumes, OUP, 1934.

Karl Lichtenberg, 'Der Einfluß des Theophrast auf die englischen Character-writers des 17. Jahrhunderts', Diss. (Berlin), 1921.

E. Liepe, 'Der Freigeist in der deutschen Literatur des 18. Jahrhunderts', Diss. (Kiel), 1930.

W. Litz, 'The Loiterer: A Reflection of Jane Austen's early environment', in *Review of English Studies*, n.s. xii (1961), 251 ff. An account of the paper founded and edited in 1789 by Jane's brother, James.

Claude Lloyd, 'Shadwell and the Virtuosi', in *PMLA* xliv (1929), 472–94.

P. Malekin, 'The Character-Sketches in the *Serious Call*', in *Studia Neophilologica*, xxxviii (1966), 314–22.

Jill Mann, *Chaucer and Medieval Estates Literature*, CUP, 1973.

Dorothy Marshall, *The English Poor in the Eighteenth Century*, London, 1926.

—— *English People in the Eighteenth Century*, London, 1956.

Wolfgang Martens, 'Der Hochgeehrte Herr Freymäurer . . .', in *Euphorion*, lvi (1962), 279 ff.

—— *Die Botschaft der Tugend*, Stuttgart, 1968. The best account of the moral weeklies.

Hermann Meyer, *Der Sonderling in der deutschen Dichtung*, Munich, 1963.

G. Michaut, *La Bruyère*, Paris, 1936.

B. Mildebrath, 'Die deutschen "Avanturiers" des 18. Jahrhunderts', Diss. (Würzburg), 1907.

W. F. Mitchell, *English Pulpit Oratory*, London, 1932.

Ruth Mohl, *The Three Estates in Medieval and Renaissance Literature*, 1933, repr. New York, 1962.

P. Morillot, *La Bruyère*, Paris, 1904.

O. A. Müller, 'La Bruyère in Deutschland', Diss. (Heidelberg), 1923.

G. Müller-Schwefe, 'Joseph Hall's CHARACTERS OF VERTUES AND VICES . . .', in *Texas Studies in Literature and Language*, xiv. 2 (1972), 235–51.

J. J. Murphy, *Rhetoric in the Middle Ages*, University of California Press, 1974.

O. Navarre, 'Théophraste et La Bruyère, in *Revue des Études Grecques*, xxvii (1914), 384–440. Somewhat overstates the influence.

H. Nimtz, 'Motive des Studentenlebens in der deutschen Literatur von den Anfängen bis zum Ende des 18. Jahrhunderts', Diss. (Berlin), 1937.

W. Papenheim, *Die Charakterschilderungen im 'Tatler', 'Spectator' und 'Guardian' . . .*, Leipzig, 1930.

A. A. Parker, *Literature and the Delinquent*, Edinburgh, 1967. A study of the picaresque novel.

C. E. Petersen, *The Doctor in French Drama 1700–1775*, Columbia University Press, 1938.

Uwe Pörksen, 'Elias Canetti, *Der Ohrenzeuge*', in *Neue Deutsche Hefte*, xxi (1974), 844–7.

Harald Rehm, 'Die Entstehung des Wiener Volkstheaters am Anfang des 18. Jahrhunderts', Diss. (Munich), 1936.

Karl Reichert, 'Utopie und Satire in J. M. von Loens Roman "Der Redliche Mann am Hofe" (1740)', in *GRM*, n. F. xv (1965), 176–94.

C. von Reinhardstoettner, *Spätere Bearbeitungen plautinischer Lustspiele*, Leipzig, 1886.

Pierre Richard, *La Bruyère et ses 'Caractères'*, Paris, 1965.

P. Ansell Robin, *The Old Physiology in English Literature*, London, 1911.

R. C. Rosbottom, *Marivaux's Novels*, Cranbury, NJ and London, 1974.

Maren-Sofie Røstwig, *The Happy Man* . . ., 2 volumes, Oslo, 1954–8.

The Royal Society, *Philosophical Transactions* . . . , London, 1665 ff.

M. Sadleir, *Bulwer, a Panorama*, London, 1931. Good on the 'keys' to the various novels.

G. Salgãdo, *The Elizabethan Underworld*, London, 1977. See too Valerie Pearl's review in *TLS*, 17/3/1978, p. 326.

E. Showalter, *The Evolution of the French Novel 1641–1782*, Princeton, 1972.

Lotte Simon-Baumann, *Die Darstellung der Charaktere in George Eliots Romanen*, Leipzig, 1929.

David Nichol Smith, *Characters from the Histories and Memoirs of the Seventeenth Century*, Oxford, 1918.

Diana Spearman, *The Novel and Society*, London, 1966.

M. Spiegel, *Der Roman und sein Publikum im frühen 18. Jahrhundert*, Bonn, 1967.

M. H. Spielmann, *The History of 'Punch'*, London, 1895.

F. K. Stanzel, *Typische Formen des Romans*, Göttingen, 1964.

H. A. Stavan, *Sénac de Meilhan (1736–1803)* . . ., Paris, 1968.

A. Stegmann, *Les Caractères de La Bruyère*, Paris, 1972.

H. Steinmetz, *Die Komödie der Aufklärung*, Stuttgart, 1971.

Dorothy Stimson, *Scientists and Amateurs. A History of the Royal Society*, New York, 1948.

H. Dugdale Sykes, 'Was Webster a Contributor to Overbury's *Characters*?', in *Notes and Queries*, 11th series, xi (1915), pp. 313–15, 335–7, 355–7, and 374 f.

M. Tronskaja, *Die deutsche Prosasatire der Aufklärung*, Berlin, 1967.

C. J. Ribton-Turner, *A History of Vagrants and Vagrancy*, London, 1887.

Margaret Turner, 'The Influence of La Bruyère on the "Tatler" and the "Spectator"', in *MLR* xlviii (1953), 10–16.

G. Varcoe, 'The Intrusive Narrator', Diss. (Uppsala), 1972.

T. Vetter, *Der Spectator als Quelle der 'Discurse der Maler'*, Frauenfeld, 1887.

R. Vierhaus, *Deutschland im Zeitalter des Absolutismus*, Göttingen, 1978.

Klaus Völker, 'Canettis Charaktere', in *Frankfurter Rundschau*, 23/11/1974: section 'Zeit und Bild', p. iv.

Hugh Walker, *The English Essay and Essayists*, London, 1923.

May Wallas, *Luc de Clapiers, Marquis de Vauvenargues*, CUP, 1928.

Albert Ward, *Book Production, Fiction and the German Reading Public, 1740–1800,* Oxford, 1974.

Foster Watson, *The English Grammar Schools to 1660*, CUP, 1908.

Ian Watt, *The Rise of the Novel*, London, 1974.

Joan Webber, *The Eloquent I: Style and Self in 17th-century Prose*, University of Wisconsin Press, 1968.

Charles Whibley, *William Makepeace Thackeray*, Edinburgh and London, 1903.

G. Wicke, *Die Struktur des deutschen Lustspiels der Aufklärung*, Bonn, 1965.

G. Williamson, *The Senecan Amble . . .*, London, 1951.

L. B. Wright, *Middle-Class Culture in Elizabethan England,* University of North Carolina Press, 1935.

Index of Types Treated in the Form of 'Characters'

To keep this index within reasonable bounds, I have excluded 'characters' which are mentioned only briefly in passing, together with a number which occur in titles listed in the Bibliography but not dealt with in the text.

Absentminded Man, 65, 130, 203, 212, 267
Actor, 269
Affected Man, 34
Ambitious Man, 8, 273, 278
Angry Man, 286
Antiquary, 11, 33, 163 ff., 181, 202 f., 226 f., 244 f., 329
Army Officer, 58, 128
Arrogant Man, 278
Assembly-man, 282
Astrologer, 336
Atheist, 184 f.
Attorney, 34

Bat, 38
Bawd, 29, 181
Beadle, 239
Beau, *see* Dandy
Beauty, 37, 79 f., 95 f., 268
Bluestocking, 74, 227
Boaster, 8
Boor, 20
Bore, 4, 5, 10, 127 f., 280
Bus Conductress, 125
Busybody, 279
Busy Idler, *see* Self-important Man
Butler, 30
Button-maker, 39

Capitalist, 175
Carrier, 34
Chambermaid, 110
'Character', 25, 29, 263 f.
Chemist, 173
Child, 30 ff., 151 f.
Civil Servant, 124
Clergyman, 31, 33, 40, 206 f., 223, 269, 346
Coachman, 171
Cobbler, 172
Cockney, 116
Commercial Traveller, 115 f.
Conceited Man, 33
Constant Man, *see* Staid Man
Contemplative Man, 30 f.
Contemptuous Man, 19
Cook, 25, 29, 35, 39, 171
Coquette, 274
Country Fellow, 33, 269
Country Gentleman, Country Squire, 27, 72 f., 80 f., 115, 139 ff., 278, 315
Country Lady, 71
Courtier, 25 f., 274, 278
Covetous Man, *see* Miser
Coward, 1, 3, 95, 158 ff., 186, 188, 279
Crab, 39
Critic, 78

Dandy, 10, 37, 56, 95 f., 277, 281, 315
Devotee, 316
Dilettante, 77
Diner-out, 107
Discontented Man, 16, 90, 273, 283
Dissembler, Dissimulator, 20, 27
Distrustful Man, 4
Doctor, 31, 115, 148, 269
Dog, 38
Don, 70, 282
Drunkard, 7, 34, 37, 40, 43, 92, 155 ff., 274, 315
Dunce, 24, 345
Dutchman, 25, 39

Elder Brother, 27, 272
Englishman, 45
Envious Man, 71, 269
Excellent Companion, 185

Factory Child, 175, 178
Faithful Man, 22

Fantastic Lady, 186
Fashionable Lady, 68, 74, 316
Father, 328
Feminist, 316
Fiddler, 35, 181, 186
'Fine Gentleman', 27
Flatterer, 22, 25 f., 32, 185, 273, 329
Flirt, 74
Fool, 41
Fop, 79
Formal Man, 273
Forward Man, 33
Frenchman, 39
Friend, 86

Gaoler, 182
Gardener, 172
Gentleman, 69, 72, 194, 266, 320
Glory-hunter, 26
Gnat, 39
Goat, 38
Godfather, 111 f.
Godly Man, 19
Good Man, 42, 133 ff., 191 f., 329
Good Wife, Good Woman, 25 f., 28, 75, 193, 195, 312, 332, 347
Governess, 172 f.
Grave Divine, 197 f.
Greenwich Pensioner, 115

Happy Man, 21, 23, 59, 133 ff., 270 f.
Hedonist, 67, 93
Honest Man, 194 f., 198
Honest Subject, 192
Horse-courser, Horse-dealer, 29, 173 f.
Host, *see* Innkeeper
Humble Man, 23
Husband, 194
Hypochondriac, 52, 70, 102, 251
Hypocrite, 10, 31, 33 f., 42 f., 76, 91, 182, 191, 208, 214, 290, 318

Idler, 89, 275, 316
Inconstant Man, 21, 204 f.
Inn, 34, 313
Innkeeper, 25, 27
Inns of Court Man, 28
Insolent Man, 31 f.

Janitor, 112
Jealous Man, 199, 271, 284
Jealous Wife, 203 f.
Jesuit, 25, 45, 313, 336
Jilt, *see* Flirt
Judge, 25, 28, 266

King, 96, 195
Knave, 271

Labourer, 118
Lascivious Man, 32
Law-term, 39
Lawyer, 37, 147 f., 193 f.
Lazy Man, 88
Liberal Man, 58, 60, 316
Libertine, 74, 109 f., 290, 333; *see also* 'Fine Gentleman'
Lover, Lovesick Man, 25, 271

Magistrate, 23, 96, 198, 273
Maidservant, 119 f., 173, 176, 178, 281
Malcontent *see* Discontented Man
'Male Coquette', 267
Man of Business, 77
Man of Honour, 73
Man of Pleasure, *see* Hedonist
Man of Sensibility, 280
Melancholy Man, 29, 272, 277
Merchant, 97, 139 ff., 223, 273
Methodist, 316
Milkmaid, 28
Miser, 4, 8, 10, 22 f., 28, 39, 41, 89, 94, 130, 180
Misogynist, 261
Moderate Man, 76
Modest Woman, 68
Mower, 172

Newsmonger, 20
Newspaper, 39
Noble Man, 22

Obliging Man, 70
Old Lady, 238
Old Man, 8, 57, 152 ff., 274
Optimist, 86
Ostler, 25, 27, 172

Parasite, 40, 181
Parson, *see* Clergyman
Pauper, 175
Pawnbroker, 184
Peasant, 170
Pedant, 27, 101, 261
Penitent, 23
Peevish Man, 87
Peevish Woman, 68
Pessimist, 86
Philistine, 123, 336
'Phogey', 124

Physician, *see* Doctor
Pietist, 87
Pious Man, 196
Pleasant Fellow, 73
Plutocrat, 129
Poet, 218
Political Upholsterer, 74, 88, 329 f.
Politician, 86, 106 f., 112
Poor Man, 31, 170
Poor Relation, 116 f.
Potboy, 113
Preacher, *see* Clergyman
Presumptuous Man, 23
Pretender to Learning, 32
Prince, 195
Prison, 25, 36, 187, 238 f.
Prisoner, 180, 194
Private Tutor, 149 f.
Procrastinator, 130 f.
Profane Man, 32, 284
Protestant, 45
Proud Man, 28, 42, 327
Prude, 74
Puritan, 45, 66 f., 76, 206, 278 f., 313

Quaker, 45, 278
Quarrelsome Man, 286

Rake, *see* Libertine
Religious Man, 193
Reprobate, 184
Republican, 85
Rich Man, 227
Rope-maker, 38, 181

Sailor, 29, 174, 188 f.
St Paul's, 39
Savage, 48
Schoolboy, 151
Schoolmaster, 40
Schoolmistress, 125
Scot, 346
Scrounger, 268
Self-important Man, 105 f.
Servant (male), 25, 172; *see also* Maid-servant
Sexton, 25
Shopkeeper, 35
Shrew, 181, 343
Simple Man, 279 f.
Sinner, 316
Slanderer, 280
Slattern, 68
Sluggish Man, 58
Smithfield, 39
Smoker, 182
Snail, 39
Snob, 114, 118 f., 280
Social Climber, 51, 269
Soldier, 188
Solicitor, 148
Squirrel, 38
Staid Man, 30, 197
Stationer (printer and bookseller), 344
Street Boy, 125
Student, 30 f.
Superstitious Man, 5, 21, 89, 279

Tailor, 245
Talkative Lady, 185
Tapster, 172
Tavern, *see* Inn
Tenant Farmer, 41, 269
Too-scrupulous Woman, 68
Tourist, 122
Town Gallant, 313, 316
Townsman in Oxford, 13, 186 f.
Tram-conductor, 107 f.
Traveller, 26
Trumpeter, 35

Unseasonable Man, 180
Unthrifty Man, 270
Upright Man, 193
Usurer, 10, 25, 29, 184 ff., 208, 269, 277

Vain Girl, 251 f.
Vainglorious Man, 22
Valiant Man, 192
Village, 40
Virtuoso, 69 f., 77 f., 166 ff.
Virtuous Man, 196

Waiter, 172, 267
Watchman, 25
Waterman, 172
Welshman, 25, 27, 39
Whore, 29, 37, 157 f., 182, 226, 233, 269
Wicked Man, 60
Widow, 25, 40, 186
Wise Man, 21, 25 f., 92, 115, 133 ff., 195 f., 293
Wit, 34, 102
Working Man, Working Classes, 170 ff.
Worldly-wise Man, 273

Younger Brother, 270
Young Woman, 107

General Index

Page-references have been given to items in the Bibliography where the subdivisions of the Bibliography might otherwise make consultation difficult. In addition, some entries in the Bibliography offer brief comments or details not given in the text or Notes; entries of this kind have also been indexed.

Adams, Thomas, 42 f., 147, 159, 277, 285, 368
Addison, Joseph, 64, 66, 68, 71 ff., 75, 84 f., 87 f., 91, 94, 97, 99 f., 114 f., 123, 127, 129, 137, 142, 166, 179, 182, 186, 190, 213, 226, 228, 264, 278 f., 281 f., 289, 292, 315, 318, 322, 326, 329 f., 333, 335, 337, 351 ff., 359
Adventurer, 65, 70, 315 f., 323, 355
Aldington, R., 328, 340
Allen, Don Cameron, 10
Altmann, J. G., 317, 356 f.
Anacreon, 138
Andrews, K. R., 323
Arbuthnot, John, 326
Ariès, Philippe, 151
Aristotle, 3, 5 ff., 48, 86, 152
Arkenside, M., 320, 354
Arnold, Cornelius, 320, 324, 355
Ashton, T. S., 323
Atkinson, Alex, 125 f.
Aufklärung, 99, 212, 258, 262, 289
Austen, James, 356
Austen, Jane, 164, 229 f., 233, 242 f., 264, 332
Austin, Samuel, 181, 313, 346

'B., E.' (*A Trip to North Wales*), 320, 337, 351
'B., J.' (*The Assembly-Man*), 282, 345
'B., P.' (*Juvenilia Sacra*), 196, 329, 347
Babb, L., 337
Bacon, Francis, 167
Bahrdt, C. F., 338
Bailey, L. H., 319
Baldwin, E. C., 201
Barach, M., 112, 366
Barclay, Alexander, 16
Barrow, Isaac, 193, 369
Barthélemy, E. de, 313
Bäuerle, Adolf, 104
Baynes, John, 128
Beam, J. N., 330
Bellegarde, Abbé, 314, 350
Belloc, Hilaire, 372
Belustigungen des Verstandes und des Witzes, 95, 218, 334, 357
'Beninde', 335
Bergler, H., 104, 107, 109, 112, 366
Bernard, Richard, 312
Bernisches Freytags-Blätlein, 86, 317, 331, 356
Beyer, H., 329
Birkenhead, Sir John, 337
Blackall, E. A., 97 f.
Blanchard, S. L., 324
Bock, J. C., 217, 331
Bodeau, Antoine, Sieur de Somaise, 314
Bodenham, John, 153, 311, 341
Bodi, L., 319
Bodmer, J. J., *see Die Discourse der Mahlern*
Böhm, B., 322
Bolgar, R. R., 6, 9
Bond, R. W., 329
Bonhote, E., 326
Borkenstein, H., 331
Boswell, James, 160, 162, 325, 355
Boughner, D. C., 325
Boulmiers, J. des, 329
Boxberger, R., 329
Boyce, Benjamin, 14 f., 18, 20, 27, 32, 45, 180, 184, 190 f., 202, 207, 267, 291, 311, 312 f., 316, 328, 330 f.
Boyer, Abel, 64, 351
Boyer, Claude, 57, 315, 350
Boyle, Robert, 166
Bradbury, Malcolm, 124, 320
Brant, Sebastian, 16, 312, 361
Braithwaite, Richard, 39, 181 ff., 186, 190, 193 f., 323, 325, 329, 343 f., 347

Breitinger, J. J., *see Die Discourse der Mahlern*
Brentano, Clemens, 123, 361
Breton, Nicholas, 17, 34, 37, 41, 44, 141, 147, 159, 170, 184 ff., 273, 315, 321, 323, 343 f.
Bretzner, C. F., 250, 260, 324 f., 338
Brewer, George, 115
Bridgwater, W. P., 332
Brillon, P. J., 47, 56, 62, 153, 288, 314 f., 324, 350
Brockes, Heinrich, 145, 356
Brome, Richard, 221
Brown, Thomas, 64, 352
Browne, H. K., 117
Browne, Humphrey, 44, 193, 195, 323, 327, 345
Bruford, W. H., 324
Budgell, Eustace, 65, 87, 315, 340, 353
Bulwer Lytton, Edward, 119, 229, 231 f., 322, 332, 365
Burney, Fanny, 290, 334
Burton, Robert, 283, 324
Büsch, J. G., 324
Butler, Samuel, 39, 44, 148, 166, 168, 180, 183, 315, 322 f., 325 f., 347

'C., H.' (*The Character of an Honest Lawyer*), 323
Calame, A., 329
Canetti, Elias, 130, 267, 291, 368
Caractères du faux et du veritable Amour, 57
Carrington, Charles, 321
Casaubon Isaac, 8, 12, 311, 340
Castelli, I. F., 104 ff., 109 f., 112
Caxton, William, 322
Censor, 315 f., 327, 353
censorship, 94, 318
Chambre, Cureau de la, 292
Chandler, Raymond, 321
Chapman, George, 202, 206, 329 f.
Character of a Soliciter, 323
Character of a Town-Gallant, 316, 332
Character of a Town Misse, 325
Characterism (*c.*1750), 159, 323, 327 f., 354
Charakternovelle, 258 f., 262, 289
Chaucer, Geoffrey, 14 f., 124, 322, 365, 367
Chesterfield, Lord, 65, 73, 266, 355
Chévot, H., 313
Chevreau, Urbain, 47, 349 f.
Chew, S. C., 324
Chiavacci, V., 105 ff., 109
Chudleigh, Mary, 322, 352
Cibber, Colley, 210, 330
Cicero, 7 f.
Citizen of the World, 85
Claudius, Matthias, 292 f., 324
Cleveland, John, 39, 328, 345 f.
Coke, Roger, 322
Cole, William, 333
Coleman, D. C., 323
Coleman, George (the elder), 203, 214, 355
Coleridge, S. T., 264 f., 268, 274 ff.
Collier, Jeremy, 159, 352
Comédie larmoyante, 212, 330
Comic Almanach, 320
Comical Pilgrim, 277, 320, 327, 353
Commedia dell'arte, 200, 215
commonplace books, 9 f., 20, 26, 28, 39, 153, 179, 312, 321, 341
Connoisseur, 156, 203 f., 316, 355
Constable, John, 326, 354
Cooper, Derek, 321
Corporation Characters, 117
Country Gentleman's Vade Mecum, 325
Cousin, Victor, 313
Coventry, Francis, 226, 242, 332
Cowley, Abraham, 136
Cronegk, J. F. von, 213 f., 218 f., 358
Cross, W. L., 329
Crosse, Henry, 152, 325, 342
Crowley, Robert, 322
Cruikshank, George, 117, 362
Cunliffe, J. W., 321
Curry, Pamela, 317
Curtius, E. R., 324

'D., J.' (*The Character of a Friend*), 328
'Damabellante', 335
Daphne, 317, 358
Das Reich der Natur und der Sitten, 85 f., 88 f., 138, 154, 190, 196, 318, 324, 326, 358 f.
Das rührende Lustspiel, see *Comédie larmoyante*
Das Sintemal, 317
Das Sonntagsblatt, *see* Schreyvogel
Davenant, C., 322
Deacon, W. F., 171
Defoe, Daniel, 142, 146, 158, 228, 233, 241, 246, 322, 325, 327, 334, 348, 351, 353
Dekker, Thomas, 16, 24, 187, 190, 202, 206, 329, 342

Deloney, Thomas, 140
Der alte Deutsche, 85, 256, 317, 323, 334, 356
Der Bewunderer, 144, 323, 357
Der Biedermann, 86, 90 f., 258, 317, 325, 330, 356
Der Brachmann, 86, 318, 331, 357
Der Bürger, 323, 356
Der Casselsche Zuschauer, 84, 319, 360
Der Chamäleon, 322, 336, 358
Der Druide, 317, 357
Der Eidsgenoß, 82, 318, 358
Der Einsiedler, 317, 324
Der Freund, 317 f., 336, 358
Der Freydenker, 94, 156 f., 317, 334, 357
Der Freygeist, 318, 357
Der Freymäurer, 139, 144, 317, 323, 357
Der Gesellige, 324, 326, 330, 357
Der Glückselige, 318, 359
Der Greis, 194, 318, 360
Der Hamburger, 94, 317, 357
Der Helvetische Patriot, 85, 358 f.
Der Hofmeister, 317, 331, 358
Der Hypochonder, 317
Der Kundschafter, 90, 357
Der Leipziger Avanturieur, 250, 373
Der Leipziger Zuschauer, 83, 122 f., 359
Der Mann, 318, 358
Der Mann ohne Vorurtheile, 331
Der Mensch, 191, 317, 323 f., 358
Der Neue Eidsgenosse, 82, 84, 90, 358
Der Patriot, 86 f., 89 ff., 100, 144 f., 249, 256, 258 f., 278, 317 f., 323, 325, 330, 334 f., 356
Der Patriot in Bayern, 318, 359
Der Pilgrim, 318, 357
Der Redliche, 318, 336, 358
Der redliche Hamburger, 323
Der Sachsen-Spiegel, 326
Der Sammler, 191, 334, 356
Der Schutzgeist, 318, 357
Der Teutsche Bernerische Spectateur, 83, 86, 334, 356
Der Tugendfreund, 196, 358
Der Unsichtbare, 317
Der Verbesserer, 331, 365
Der Vernünfftler (1713–14), 83, 98, 356
Der Vernünftler (1754), 317, 358
Der Weltbürger, 284, 317 f., 357
Der Wienerische Zuschauer, *see* Richter, Joseph
Der Zerstreuer, 337, 357
Dickens, Charles, 117 ff., 127, 154, 191, 228, 237 ff., 244, 264, 326 f., 337, 362 ff.
Die Deutsche Zuschauerin, 83
Die Discourse der Mahlern, 82 f., 212, 252, 283, 317, 330, 334, 356
Die Freunde, 318, 358
Die Macht der Vorurtheile, 318, 336, 359
Die mühsame Bemerckerin, 88, 357
Die Niederrheinische Zuschauerin, 83, 359
Die Unsichtbare, 318
Die vernünftigen Tadlerinnen, 317 f., 334, 356
Die Welt, *see* Klemm
Die Zellischen Vernünftigen Tadler, 279, 334, 357
Die Zigeunerin, 293, 326, 359
Ditchfield, P. A., 127
Don Juan, 109, 204, 211
Donne, John, 24, 342, 345 f.
Dowden, E., 337
Dryden, John, 78, 209, 219, 324
Duchartre, P. L., 329
Dudley, Lord North, 44, 323, 328, 345
Du Refugé, Eustache, 47 f., 324, 337, 349
d'Urfé, Honoré, 48
D'Urfey, Thomas, 329 f., 370
Dynocke, James, 47, 349

Earle, John, 1 f., 24, 30 ff., 35, 37, 40, 47, 53, 93, 115, 151 f., 159, 163 f., 171, 186, 188, 196 ff., 202 f., 244, 268 ff., 273, 277 f., 282 f., 289, 312 f., 315, 317, 319, 323 ff., 328 f., 344, 353 ff., 358
Ebert, J. J., 290, 328 f., 360
Edgeworth, Maria, 333, 372
Effen, Justus van, 349
Ehrhard, A., 330
Eliot, George, 120 f., 228, 230, 242, 283, 332 f.
Engel, J. J., 255 f., 322, 335, 374
Engel, Ludwig, 319
Engelschall, J. H., 216
English Spy, 114
Ennis, L., 332
Entertainer, 327, 353
Epictetus, 136
Erasmus, 16, 322
Essay in Defence of the Female Sex, 166, 315, 322, 348

Essay towards the Character of the late Chimpanzee, 332
estates, 14 ff., 20, 44, 140, 146, 174, 201, 274, 312, 341 f., 348
Etherege, George, 330
Evelyn, John, 163 f., 167

Fagan, C. G., 320
Farquhar, George, 209, 220 f., 254
Faust, 211
Faust der zweyte (novel), 254, 256
Fennor, William, 36, 343
Fielding, Joseph, 192, 229 ff., 233, 241 f., 246, 254, 332, 334, 337, 354
Flatman, Thomas, 136, 347
Flecker, J. E., 319
Flecknoe, Richard, 37 f., 141, 151, 159, 181, 183, 185 f., 190, 263 f., 269, 290, 322 f., 329, 346
Fletcher, Phineas, 135
'Florilegus', 323, 345 f.
Fontenelle, 167 f.
'Foppling, Sir Frederick', 319
Ford, John, 41 f., 329, 344
Ford, Thomas, 44, 192, 195, 269, 327, 336, 345
Fordyce, David, 316
Freemasonry, 139, 256
Free-Thinker, 316
Friend, 227, 355
Fuchs, Gottlieb, 214
Fuller, Thomas, 44, 61, 111, 140 f., 312, 325, 327, 345
Fulwel, Ulpian, 200
Fun, 176, 178, 320, 365
Für Litteratur und Herz, 95, 195, 318, 360

'G., L.' (*Essayes and Characters*), 156, 274, 278, 325, 346
Gadbury, John, 336
Gallery of Comicalities, 338
Gallery of Portraits, 115
Galliny, F., 112, 366
Gally, Henry, 66, 179, 186, 190, 263 f., 267, 315, 340
Garnet, Henry, 336
Garrick, David, 370
Gay, John, 65, 326, 353
Gayton, Edmund, 269, 346
Gebler, T. P., 216, 331
Geißau, A. F., 103
Gellert, C. F., 91 ff., 95, 192, 212, 214 f., 225, 253, 317, 324 f., 331, 334 ff., 360
Genlis, Mme de, 56 f.
Gentleman's Magazine, 323, 336, 353
Geree, John, 313, 345
Geschmack und Sitten, 160, 162, 358
Gewey, F. X. C., 104
Gherardi, E., 329
Gilbert, W. S., 117, 365
Gleim, J. W. L., 322
Goethe, J. W. von, 259, 264, 323 f., 335
Gogol, 321
Goldsmith, Oliver, 65, 85, 115, 315, 330, 333, 355
Gomberville, Marin le Roy, Seigneur de, 313
Goodridge, J. F., 311
Googe, Barnabe, 311
Gordon, G. S., 8, 311, 328
Gore, Catherine, 319, 327
Gorer, Geoffrey, 321
Görner, K. von, 331
Gottsched, J. C., 86, 211, 216 f., 265, 317, 322, 330, 356 f.
Graf, H., 325
Graham, Richard, 167, 347
Grahame, Simeon, 135, 343
Graves, Richard, 165, 332
Greenough, C. N., 321, 339
Groß-Hoffinger, A. H., 106 f., 112
Guardian, 72 f., 137, 140, 230, 280, 315, 323 f., 327, 332, 336, 353
Guilpin, Everard, 11, 342

Habington, William, 136
Hafner, Philip, 217
Hagedorn, F. von, 95, 322
Hake, Edward, 322, 342
Hall, Joseph, 4 f., 6, 18 ff., 26, 30 f., 35, 37 ff., 41 f., 44, 46 ff., 71, 111, 130, 134 ff., 150, 192, 196, 198, 208, 269 f., 273, 276, 281, 285, 289, 336, 343, 349 f.
Haller, A. von, 96
Hamann, J. G., 338
Harleville, Collin d', 204 f.
Harvey, John, 373
Hase, F. T., 260, 374
Haughton, William, 330
Hawkesworth, John, 355
Hazlitt, William, 116, 319, 326, 339, 361 f.
Head, Richard, 225 f.

Heads of the People, 118, 148, 174 f., 178, 323, 327, 363 f.
Healey, John, 35, 340
Heckscher, E. F., 142, 146 f.
Heitmüller, F., 329
Henning, A., 117, 363
Henrici, C. F., 211
Herbert, George, 346
Herder, J. G., 335
Hermit in the Country, 337
Herrick, M. J., 324
Herrick, Robert, 136, 321
Hesse, Hermann, 374
Heubel, J. G., 331
Heufeld, F., 331
Hewison, William, 320
Heyse, Paul, 261
Higden, Henry, 210
Hill, Aaron, 321
Hill, Christopher, 323
Hine, H. G., 117
Hoffmann, E. T. A., 261, 336
Hogg, John, 120
Homer, 324
Hood, Thomas, 115
Hope, Francis, 321
Horace, 10 f., 21, 45, 78, 81, 95, 133 f., 136 ff., 152
Horne, Charles, 325
Houghton, W. E., 163
Howell, Francis, 294, 340
Howell, J., 320, 345
Huber, F. X., 253
Humours, 277, 284 f., 292 f.
Humours of Oxford, 330
Hunt, J. H. Leigh, 116, 154, 238, 267, 280, 339, 361 ff.
Hunt, Leigh Thornton, 175
Hunter, G. K., 321
Hutton, Henry, 11, 343

Idler, 70, 77, 85, 106, 114, 160, 275, 315 f., 332, 355
Intelligencer, 114, 316, 332, 353
Irving, Washington, 361

Jacobi, F. H., 259
Jansenists, 48
Jebb, R. C., 244 f., 311
Jennings, Paul, 320
Jerrold, Douglas, 175, 178
Johnson, Ralph, 36, 39, 180, 183, 189, 263 f., 283
Johnson, Samuel, 65, 68 ff., 71 ff., 75, 77, 85, 91, 97, 106, 114 f., 123, 146, 157, 160, 163, 227, 244, 275, 278, 289, 325, 330, 336, 354 f.
Johnstone, Charles, 373
Jonson, Ben, 201 f., 206 f., 209, 222
Jordan, Thomas, 78, 157, 159, 182, 325, 344 f.
Joseph II, 103
Judges, A.V., 313
Jung-Stilling, J. H., 324, 374
Juvenal, 11

'K., P.' (*Floskulum Poeticum*), 78, 325, 348
Keller, Gottfried, 108, 261
Kimber, E., 332, 373
Kirk, Harry, 323
Kirkman, Francis, 225
Klapp, Michael, 112
Kleist, Ewald von, 96, 322, 360
Klemm, C. G., 101, 216 f., 365, 371
Klopstock, F. G., 195
Knab, S. B., 335
Knacke to knowe a Knave, 201
Knigge, A. F. F. von, 149, 252, 324
Knight, Charles, 319
Korshin, P. J., 192, 328, 332
Kotzebue, A. von, 145, 323
Kratzmann, E., 319
Kreider, P. V., 330, 337
Krüger, J. C., 222 f.
Kunst, die Männer und Frauen aus ihren Gesichtszügen zu erkennen, 293

La Bruyère, Jean de, 47 ff., 60 ff., 64 ff., 77 ff., 85 f., 91, 93, 101, 121, 127, 130, 170, 174, 182, 203, 205, 212, 223, 251, 256, 264 f., 267 ff., 274, 276, 286, 289, 313 ff., 317, 320, 324, 326, 328 f., 334, 349 ff., 358
Lamb, Charles, 116 f., 157, 362
Lamprecht, J. F., 317, 357
Lang, C. L., 318
Langland, William, 12, 14, 18, 201, 311
La Rochefoucauld, 49 f., 54, 64
Lasius, H. J., 165
Laughing Philosopher, 267
Laukhard, F. C., 250
Lavater, J. C., 292 f., 338, 360
Law, William, 76 ff., 91, 165, 191, 276, 353
Lea, K. M., 329

Leisewitz, J. A., 322
Le Misantrope (periodical, 1712–13), 153
Lemnius, Levinus, 337
Le Moyne, Pierre, 48, 349
Lenton, Francis, 40 f., 181, 186, 269, 325, 329, 344
Lenz, J. M. R., 150, 324
Lesage, A. R., 334, 372
Lessing, G. E., 85, 203, 222, 322, 338
Le Vavasseur, G., 123, 351
Leyburn, George, 346
Lichtenberg, G. C., 179, 292
Lindner, J. G., 317, 358
Ling, Nicholas, *see* Bodenham
Literary Lounger, 336
Locke, John, 154, 285 f., 333, 337
Lodge, Thomas, 18, 342
Loen, J. M. von, 91 ff., 145, 248 f., 253, 323, 334 f., 360
London, Jack, 126 f.
London Characters, 117
London Magazine, 322
London Spy, 114, 328
Looker-on, 315, 327, 356
Looking-Glasse for a Drunkard, 37, 325, 345
Lounger, 154, 316, 324, 336
Lover, 315, 333, 353
Lovibond, Edward, 68
Löwen, J. F., 95, 358
Löwy, Julius, 111 f.
Lucas, F. L., 321, 331
Ludwig, C. S., 251 f.
Lupton, Donald, 38 f., 62, 112, 340, 344
Lupus, Rutilius, 7 f., 325

'M., R.' (*Micrologia*), 170 f., 181 ff., 327, 344
Macaulay, Lord, 228
Mackenzie, H., 337
McKerrow, R. B., 311
Maclean, K., 337
Mair, G. H., 311
Malekin, P., 328
Manley, J. M., 14
Mannigfaltigkeiten, 90, 324, 359
Mapes, Walter, 322, 342
Marivaux, 225, 315, 331, 350 f.
Marlowe, Christopher, 13
Marmion, Shakerley, 202 f., 208, 214, 221
Marris, N. M., 127
'Marsh, A.' (*Ten Pleasures of Marriage*), 373
Marshall, Dorothy, 323, 327
Martens, Wolfgang, 82, 214, 317 ff., 327, 334, 356
Martial, 10 f., 133 f., 311
Mattheson, Johann, 83, 98, 356
May, Thomas, 225 f.
Mayhew, Henry, 110, 119 f., 124 ff., 176 ff., 320, 327, 362, 364 f.
Mayhew, Horace, 118, 172, 320, 327, 362, 364 f.
Meier, W., 323 f.
Meilhans, Sénac de, 56, 351
Meine Einsamkeiten, 317, 360
'Meletaon' (J. L. Rost), 335
Mencken, H. L., 367
Mercier, L. S., 103 f.
Merck, J. H., 254
Meres, Francis, 10, 153, 160, 311 f., 321, 341
Messerschmidt, F. X., 338
Michaut, G., 314
Mildebrath, B., 334
Miller, J. P., 144, 150, 324, 360
Miniature, 114
Minifie, Susannah, 237
Minto, W., 333
Mirror, 140, 226, 315 f., 324, 355
Mocquerien, 326
Mohl, Ruth, 312
Mohler, N. M., 326
Molière, 49, 211 f.
Molloy, Charles, 337, 347
Mondrédieu, G., 313
Montaigne, 50, 160, 285
Montpensier, Mlle de, 49
Moore, Edward, 210 f., 214, 355
Morillot, P., 314
Moritz, K. P., 260, 375
Morley, H., 14, 312
Morton, H. V., 127
Mourgues, O. de, 314
Müller, J. C. W., 375
Müller, O. A., 87, 317
Müller-Schwefe, G., 21
Müller von Itzehoe, 250, 252
Mun, John, 143, 145
Mun, Thomas, 141
Murner, Thomas, 16
Murphy, Arthur, 329
Murphy, Gwendolen, 129, 207, 332, 343, 346
Murphy, J. J., 311

Mylius, C. F., 330
Mynshul, Geffray, 180, 187, 190, 194, 225, 238, 343

Nashe, Thomas, 12 ff., 342
Natural History of 'Bores', see A. B. Reach
Natural History of the Ballet Girl, 320
Natural History of the Gent, 320
Naumann, C. N., 317
Nestroy, Johann, 108
Neugebauer, W. E., 250
Newman, J. H., 320, 364
Newton, Thomas, 337
Nicholson, Harold, 127
Nicolai, F., 250, 253, 319, 338
Nicoll, A., 329
Nicolson, M., 326
Nimtz, H., 334

Observator, see Tutchin
Observer, 315 f., 324
'Oldstyle, Oliver', 319, 323, 362
Orwell, George, 169 f.
Osborne, Francis, 171, 346
Osborne, Harold, 271
Overbury, Sir Thomas, 24 ff., 30 f., 35, 37 ff., 47, 66, 127, 140, 147, 152, 159, 171 f., 179, 183, 186 ff., 208, 225, 263 f., 272 f., 276, 312 f., 323 ff., 326 f., 329, 331, 336, 343
Owst, G. R., 313

Palingenius, Marcellus, 12, 18
Panton, Edward, 324, 337, 347
Parnell, Thomas, 322
Parrot, Henry, 171 f., 181, 321, 324 f., 344
Pascal, Blaise, 50
Patch, H. R., 312
Paylor, W. J., 312
Peacham, Henry, 8, 152, 193, 341, 344
Peacock, Thomas Love, 361
Pecuniae Obediunt Omnes, 323, 348
Peeper, 114
Pelzel, J. B., 216
Penton, Stephen, 265, 348
Person, Samuel, 10, 39, 44, 196, 263 f., 329, 347
Petrasch, Joseph von, 217 ff., 331
Pettifoggers, 323, 353
Pezzl, Johann, 104
'Picander', *see* C. F. Henrici
Plautus, 159, 200
Pomfret, J., 322
'Poor Robin', 184, 189, 348
Poor Robins Character of a Dutchman, 337
Pope, Alexander, 64, 78 ff., 95 f., 179, 266, 268, 286 f., 326, 336, 352 f., 355, 358 f.
Portrait, 48 ff., 56, 60 f., 79, 265 ff., 314, 332, 335 f., 346, 352, 354, 369
Pötzl, E., 107, 111
Povey, Charles, 75, 352
Pringy, Mme de, 314, 350
Prior, Matthew, 352
Puckle, James, 315, 352
Puisieux, Mme de, 314, 350
Punch, 117 f., 147, 175, 363 f., 367

Quinault, Philippe, 324
Quintilian, 7
'Quiz', 327
'Quiz junior', *see* Dickens

Raabe, Wilhelm, 261
Rabener, G. W., 95, 159, 218, 256, 317 f., 323 f., 331, 357 f.
Raeburn, Anna, 320
Rambler, 68 f., 70 f., 74 f., 77, 114 f., 236, 244, 278, 315 f., 325 ff., 330, 332, 336, 350, 354, 361
Ranger, 316, 325, 356
Rautenstrauch, Johann, 104 f.
Rawlinson, John, 43, 368
Reach, A. B., 117, 151, 173, 320, 324, 327
Rede, Leman, 148
Reflector, see Shaw, P.
Regnard, J. F., 203, 214, 329
Reinhardstoettner, K. von, 329
Reupsch, J. F., 156, 286, 325 f., 328, 360
Reuter, Christian, 211
Rhetoric, 6 ff., 22 f., 26, 54, 179, 292 f., 327, 329, 341
Rich, Barnaby, 16, 325, 342
Richard, Pierre, 313
Richards, Nathanael, 336, 346
Richardson, Samuel, 191, 225, 235 ff., 334 f.
Richter, Jean Paul Friedrich, 161, 195, 256 ff., 332, 335
Richter, Joseph, 101 ff., 110, 253
Riedel, F. J., 317, 359, 366
Robbins, E. W., 329
Robin, P. A., 337

Rogers, Pat., 225
roman à clef, 49, 332
Roper, Joseph, 316, 369
Ross, G. M., 321
Røstwig, Maren-Sofie, 133 f., 311, 321 f.
Rotrou, Jean de, 324
Rousseau, J. J., 138
Rowlands, Samuel, 16, 325, 342
Royal Society, 163, 166, 168
Russell, G. W. E., 127 ff., 171, 173

Saltonstall, Wye, 13, 38 ff., 59, 135 f., 147, 172, 186, 199, 270 f., 312, 324, 329, 344
Sanderson, Robert, 313, 368
Saunterer, 114
Savage, Richard, 80, 266, 353
Scarborough Miscellany, 316, 353
Scarron, 314
Schilderungen der heutigen Sitten, 160, 317, 323
Schilderungen vortreflicher Menschen, 322, 328, 360
Schiller, Friedrich, 322, 335
Schlegel, Friedrich, 223
Schlegel, J. E., 331, 357
Schlögl, Friedrich, 105
Schneider, Ute, 337
Schönert, J., 329
Schopenhauer, Arthur, 292, 338
Schreyvogel, Joseph, 101 f., 105, 325
Scott, Sir Walter, 244 f., 326
Scrope, W., 320
Scudéry, Madeleine de, 48
Searle, Ronald, 125, 321
Segrais, Regnauld de, 49, 349
Seneca, 8, 134 f.
'Sentimens critiques sur les Caracteres de Mr. de la Bruyère', 56
sermons (featuring 'characters'), 42 ff., 75 f., 193, 316, 320, 368 f.
Servois, G., 314, 320
Shadwell, Thomas, 166, 168, 209, 219, 329 f.
Shakespeare, 152, 160, 324
Shaw, G. B., 320, 329, 365
Shaw, P., 274 f., 327, 354
Shirley, James, 207 f., 222
Sims, G. R., 327
Sintenis, C. F., 254, 355
Skelton, John, 12
Sketches from Clerical Life, 319
Smith, Albert, 117, 327, 362 ff.
Smith, David Nichol, 315
Smith, Sydney, 320, 369
Smollett, Tobias, 229, 236 f., 242, 326, 334
Socrates, 139, 322
Sombart, W., 323
Sonnenfels, Joseph von, 216 f., 365
Sorel, Charles, 314
South, Robert, 76, 369
Spearman, D., 333
Spectator, 64 ff., 69 ff., 73 ff., 82 ff., 85, 87, 91, 93, 98, 101 ff., 114, 121, 127, 137, 142 ff., 157 f., 169, 212, 228, 230, 236, 243, 247, 256, 258, 280 f., 315 f., 318 f., 322 f., 325 f., 327 f., 330, 332, 335, 337, 350, 353, 356 f., 361, 365
Spenser, Edmund, 355
Spielhagen, Friedrich, 261
Spreng, J. J., 317, 358 f.
Sprigge, William, 41, 130, 182, 187, 323, 346
Steele, Richard, 64, 67 ff., 72 ff., 84 f., 91, 98, 100, 123, 129, 137, 142, 157, 166, 266, 274, 289, 333, 353, 359
Stegmann, A., 51, 314
Steiner, Rudolf, 107 ff., 112
Stephens, John, 18, 171, 186, 190, 194, 328, 343
Stevens, G. A., 316, 324, 333, 338, 355
Stewart, Jean, 314, 350
Stifter, Adalbert, 104 f., 261, 367
Stoicism, 45, 55, 59, 134 f., 137, 192, 272
Storm, Theodor, 108, 261
Strange Metamorphosis of Man, 38 f., 344
Strasser, K., 319
Stüber-Gunther, F., 113
Sturm und Drang, 96
Sturz, H. P., 338
Suite des Caracteres de Theophraste et des Pensées de Mr. Pascal, 314
Sutherland, James, 233
Swarte, V. de, 326
Swift, Jonathan, 64, 75 f., 94, 154, 167, 229, 326, 352, 369

Tate, Nahum, 136
Tatler, 64, 66, 68, 72, 74 f., 82 f., 85, 87, 94, 140, 154, 166, 228, 230, 274, 315 f., 324, 330, 332 f., 350, 352, 356
Taverner, Richard, 9
Tawney, R. H., 323

Taylor, John, 323, 325 f., 344
Teillard-Chambon, M., 313
Terence, 159, 200
Thackeray, W. M., 117 ff., 122 f., 124, 127, 129, 191, 228 ff., 234, 244, 265, 320, 326, 332, 362 f.
Theobald, L., *see Censor*
Theophrastus, 3 ff, 12, 14 f., 17, 20 ff., 27 f., 30, 32 f., 35, 38 f., 40, 47 f., 50, 53, 57 f., 61 f., 65, 79, 85 f., 91, 93, 111, 116, 121, 127, 129 f., 158, 179 f., 182, 201 f., 213, 223, 263, 276, 278 f., 281 f., 288 f., 294, 311, 315, 317, 321, 329, 336, 339 ff.
Thomasius C., 335
Thompson, E. P., 327
Thornton, B., 203, 355
Thynne, Francis, 18 f., 321, 342
Tillotson, John, 76, 369
Tincker of Turvey, 15, 320, 344
Tomlins, F. G., 146, 175
Tourval, J. L. de, 47, 349
Town and Country Magazine, 326
Trautmann, P. F., 319
Trevor-Roper, Hugh, 321
Trifler (1788), 114, 227, 356
Trifler (1822–3), 114
Trip through the Town, 173
Trollope, Anthony, 120 ff., 173, 228 ff., 232, 245 f., 364 f.
True-Born Englishman, see Defoe
Tuke, Thomas, 42, 327, 343
Tutchin, John, 157 f.
Tuve, R., 311
Twelve Ingenious Characters, 37
Two Essays of Love and Marriage, 323, 325, 346
Tymme, Thomas, 312, 342
Tytler, Frazer, 226 f.

Udall, Nicolas, 9
Ulreich, A., 109
Ussher, R. G., 3, 14, 311
Uz, J. P., 322, 358

Vallins, G. H., 124 f.
Vanbrugh, Sir John, 331
Varennes, Gaston de, 123, 351
Varennes, J. P. de, 56, 350
Varillon, P., 314
Vauvenargues, Luc de Clapiers, Marquis de, 57 ff., 61, 92, 267, 279, 315, 337, 350
Vellacott, P., 3
Vetter, T., 317
Vierhaus, R., 323
Voltaire, 314

'W., K.' (*Confused Characters*), 269, 277, 323, 328, 332, 337, 346
Walker, Hugh, 312
Walker, Samuel, 316, 369
Wallas, M., 314
Ward, Edward (Ned), 17, 46, 64, 148, 166 f., 174, 178, 187 ff., 323, 325 f., 349, 351 f.
Warning for Housekeepers, 321, 347 f.
Warton, Joseph, 65, 315
Watson, Foster, 311
Watt, Ian, 317, 333
Watts, Isaac, 352
Watts, Richard, 325, 345
Webster, John, 24, 28, 208, 219, 254, 283
Weidmann, Paul, 217 f.
Weiße, C. F., 324, 326, 328, 330, 360
Wells, Jeremiah, 78
Wesley, John, 316, 369
Westmacott, C. M., 115
Westphal, G. C. E., 93, 249, 288, 325, 335 f., 360
Wezel, J. C., 375
Wieland, C. M., 250 f., 324, 335
Wien und die Wiener, 104, 110 ff.
Wilson, John, 331
Wilson, Robert, 200 f.
Wilson, Thomas, 8, 341
Wit's Cabinet, 37, 315, 325
Wobeser, K. von, 324
Wolff, E., 329
Woodward, John, 326
World, 73, 156, 161, 316, 323, 355
Wortley, Francis, 45, 345
Wotton, Sir Henry, 135 f., 321, 345
Wren, Sir Christopher, 266
Wright, L. B., 322
Wycherley, William, 164, 322, 331

Yates, W. E., 319
Yeo, E., 327
Young, Edward, 325, 353
Young, Thomas, 37, 41 f., 325, 343
Younge, Richard, 325, 346

Zachariae, F. W., 324, 358